Charles Matton

Enclosures

Editorial direction:
Sylvie Matton
with the assistance of Yann Matton and Léonard Matton
Editor: Julie Rouart

Translated from the French by David Radzinowicz
Design: Élisabeth Chardin and Jean-François Couvreur
Copyediting: Anne Korkeakivi
Typesetting: Gravemaker+Scott
Proofreading: Helen Woodhall
Color Separation: Les Artisans du Regard, Paris
Printed in Italy

Originally published in French as *Charles Matton, Emboîtements*

English-language edition

87, quai Panhard et Levassor
75647 Paris Cedex 13

editions.flammarion.com

11 12 13 3 2 1

ISBN: 978-2-08-020087-7

Dépôt légal: 06/2011

www.charlesmatton.com

Unless otherwise indicated, the photographs
in this book are works of art by Charles Matton.

Charles Matton

Enclosures

Preface by Paul Virilio
Text by Sylvie Matton

Flammarion

*I don't want
to write my
memoirs.
Words are
useless for
what I wanna say.
To show is the only hope.*

Je n'ai pas envie
d'écrire mes
mémoires
Les mots sont
impuissants pour
c'que j'veux dire.
Montrer seul espoir

A WORK OF CONFISCATION

PAUL VIRILIO

The strange depth of field evinced by the oeuvre of Charles Matton would deserve a philosophy thesis in itself. Indeed, if reduced-scale models are such magical, fascinating objects, it is because the aesthetic question of actual size slips through the fingers of those who venture to convey it directly—be it in painting or sculpture (three dimensionality and its "relief" effects, let it be said, making little difference). For, in fact, each and every representation is an initial reduction in the compass of the objective world, amounting to the presumptuous appropriation of a reality that is forever receding, its true proportions remaining elusive. Every time artists or authors try to equivocate regarding the dimensions of a subject, they are misled and mislead their audience in the bargain.

This truth sums up the whole history of realism and that painstaking activity of mapmaking, which ends up overlaying the very territory it purports to represent.

With Charles Matton, the question is, then, not so much that of the "miniature" as of the (telluric) compression of his environment.

The unprecedented thing about today is what "real" time has become, the skewing of proportion, time, and distance, the sudden loss of the once dependable idea of "actual size," and the temporal compression of a geophysical continuum that, nonetheless, still surrounds us on every side. Hence, our disbelief faced with the extreme precision of Charles Matton's "Boxes": a veritable sequestration of a reality subjected to disproportion, a "sub-realistic" art or, rather, a nanotechnological art that tallies with the most advanced research in the infinitesimal realm of elementary particles.

But in order to adhere as exactly as possible to the restrictive relevance of the moment, Charles calls on a kinematic intelligence of motion and of a cinematography that emphasizes not so much "film as art" as an art that strives to encompass all others through the scopic drive of an aesthetics of disappearance whereby the energy from what is visible in the moving image is no longer content as it used to be with reducing the space in which the scenes it presents take place. It now contracts time as well, the very tempo of the instantaneity of vision itself.

In this sense, kinematic energy supplements the much-vaunted pictorial "chiaroscuro" and eminently tenebrous spatial perspective of film with a perspective on time whose relativity perplexes the viewer with the magical spell created by a screen, of which Charles Matton's famous translucent jewel boxes are but a 3-D interpretation.

The screen "squared" of film becomes a screen "cubed," a "box of tricks" that monopolizes the observer's attention in the way of a viewer hypnotized by a television.

Following the *apparitions*, at the origin of prehistoric cave art, there emerged at the turn of the twentieth century in darkened rooms the kinematic disappearance of the appearances of a world that seems to lie buried in the trans-appearance of an *ultra-thin* screen whose flatness is, ultimately, the acme of abstract art.

In consequence, the once-numerous hordes of "visionaries"—religious and atheist alike—have been brushed aside by a wave of "divisionaries," adept at sampling and mashing. The art of seeing has been ousted by an art "as far as the eye can see," the "scope" of our view of the world gradually contracting into the narrow field permitted by the countless monitors now surrounding us. In this regard, then, let us note the clear parallel between the claustrophobic effect of the confiscation (by video) of the world's grandeur by Google Earth and Charles Matton's art of "boxing up" (enclosure in translucent containers). The microscopic vitrines of the latter offer a perfect symbolic illustration of those, macroscopic, of the universal search-engine screens of the former, whose megalomania is equaled only by the "megaloscopy" of all-encompassing remote monitoring; the "teleobjective" overkill of Internet TV here standing in for an "objective" sightlessness, a blindness to what was once a grounded vision.

In fact, the depth of field of an oeuvre such as Charles Matton's, where the recurrent theme is none other than the outlandishness of a world contemporary with its own end—with its plenitude, in other words—raises a major philosophical question: the choice between "almost everything but right now" and "almost nothing but all of the time." Eternal recurrence of that questioning of the power of the scientific spirit which today is leading to the accelerating ecological poverty of a contracting world to all intents and purposes on a stay of execution.

Confronted by the life-threatening risks harbored by this disproportion or gigantism, for which the Enlightenment cult of progress once proved such a vocal propagandist, Charles Matton's "restrictive principle" becomes a more commonplace precaution.

Seen in the tradition of Voltaire's "Micromégas," Matton's oeuvre is a "reliquary" for a sense of proportion about the things in our lives; an aesthetic downsizing at the precise moment when the long-lens perspective afforded by our means of mass communication is occasioning the disappearance of art. Over-exposed, this "art as far as the eye can see"[1] only survives thanks to the efforts of its dealers.

Monumental or infinitesimal.... Today the only viable choice is between exhibitionism and voyeurism; between the love of art and ad porn by third-rate nobodies, whose notoriety now outshines the fame of yesteryear's geniuses.

1. Paul Virilio, *L'Art à perte de vue* (Paris: Éditions Galilée, 2006).

Though it once clarified the vanishing points of our sense data, the real-space perspective of the Italian Renaissance has now been jettisoned in favor of a real-time outlook—an instantaneousness that depreciates truth and undermines authenticity, favoring the optical illusion of a trans-appearance that fosters amnesia and obliterates actual physical size, in nature and culture alike.

So it is that the depth of field afforded by Charles Matton's Boxes are today of the utmost relevance. For, in them, the sacred arts of iconology are immediately transferred over to ordinary things, into everyday life, into the plethora of domestic utensils that surround us, sparking—and this despite the incoherence of the contemporary period—a controversy, a kind of quarrel over dimensions that is sure to wreak havoc with our relationship to place and the bonds we once maintained in our homes within our eminently fragile private lives.

Charles Matton's work of confiscation, the long gallery of his "reliquaries," resembles a treasury in a cathedral, a crypt in the catacombs of a long-forgotten religion—that of the enormous unnaturalness of unlimited technological progress, whose sole outcome is the extinction of common sense.

30/3/97

1) Finir la boîte (plate) Vélasquez (Canon et pastel.)

2) Pour faire les 7 (?) grandes boîtes, il me faut d'abord, entre 10 ou 15 jours de liberté sur les principaux thèmes : a) des romantiques (voir aussi ESCHER (?)). b) c) Rembrandt, Bacon. b) Nabis, fauve et BONNARD (CANON.) ~~d) La bibliophilie~~. (aquarelles et pastels.) et gravures

— La peinture des boîtes après moulurage et pose de détails, interrupteurs, poignées de porte (pour 2 ou 3 d'entre elles.) sera faite par Isabelle.

— En « Confrontation de Velasquez → { - La touche Vélasquez sur verre. / La reine. (menuiserie à faire.) }

— En « confrontation avec Rembrandt » touche sur verre, dans l'espace et ébauches sculptures Rembrandt s'autoportraiturant.

~~En confrontation~~ (assister à son absence)

— Murs d'un amateur de riens → trace au mur — } Isabelle.

EXISTANT { Tirage trace radiateur. (dominante jaune.)
Tirage trace tableau. (dominante verte.)

À FAIRE { Peinture { dominante bleue. / dominante fuchia-orange. (?) }

- VOIR À RETROUVER TRACE LAVABO LOUVECIENNES.

ACHAT : COPIÉ :
- Plein de découpes d'altuglace 30/40.
- Cristal clair.
- Colle à bois (à l'eau.)
- Pastel (VOIR LISTE.)
- Fil de cuivre ou bien mais rigide.
- CARTON.
- KADAPAC 3 ou 4 feuilles.
- DECAPEX.
- Vitre biseautée poète myope.
- Brou de noix.

Grande édition {
— L'atelier d'un sculpteur de têtes.
— Giacometti → la table.
— César → une table avec des morceaux de sculpture. (utiliser machine ?)
— Art africain (?) Mur d'un
— poète myope.
} Petites boîtes plates (et moyennes) 60/45 environ.

14/3/2003

Confrontation sculpteur de têtes : { chorales dont aimantées. la sculptrice de tête

BOÎTES PROFONDES

Bibliothèque { Le balcon, L'hôtel du lac. Salle de la MEP.

22 liv

Confrontation → acheter ce qui est d'ores et déjà fait (?) sur le livre.

— Direction de pensées : Ce qui m'intéresse dans la peinture descriptive c'est la Poésie, or cette poésie peut exister hors description (Turner.) — Je suis donc moins concerné par la trajectoire : « du récit au gestuel » et je vise à présent à confondre dans la même image poésie et peinture. page.

12 liv

Personal note,
March 30, 1997.
11 ¾ × 8 ¼ in.
(29.7 × 21 cm).

(Selected notes:)
1) Finish the (flat) Velásquez box (Canon and pastel)

2) To do the seven (?) large boxes, I initially need between ten or fifteen days free for the principal themes:
a) the Romantics
b) the Nabis, the Fauves, and Bonnard
c) Rembrandt, Bacon.

- In Confrontation with Velásquez*:*
→ Velásquez brushstroke on glass
→ the queen (woodworking to do)

- In Confrontation with Rembrandt *brushstrokes on glass in the space and models for sculptures of Rembrandt doing his self-portrait.*

- Walls of an amateur of odds and ends (witnessing his absence) → mark on the wall – Isabelle
Printing mark radiator (dominant yellow)
Printing mark table (dominant green)

Facing page:
Self-portrait Painting a Miniaturized Wall, 1985.
Photograph.

Self-portrait Painting Silk for Curtains, 1985.
Photograph.

Investigation into Electricity, 1989.
Pencil and ink on cardboard,
2 ½ × 3 in. (6.5 × 8 cm).

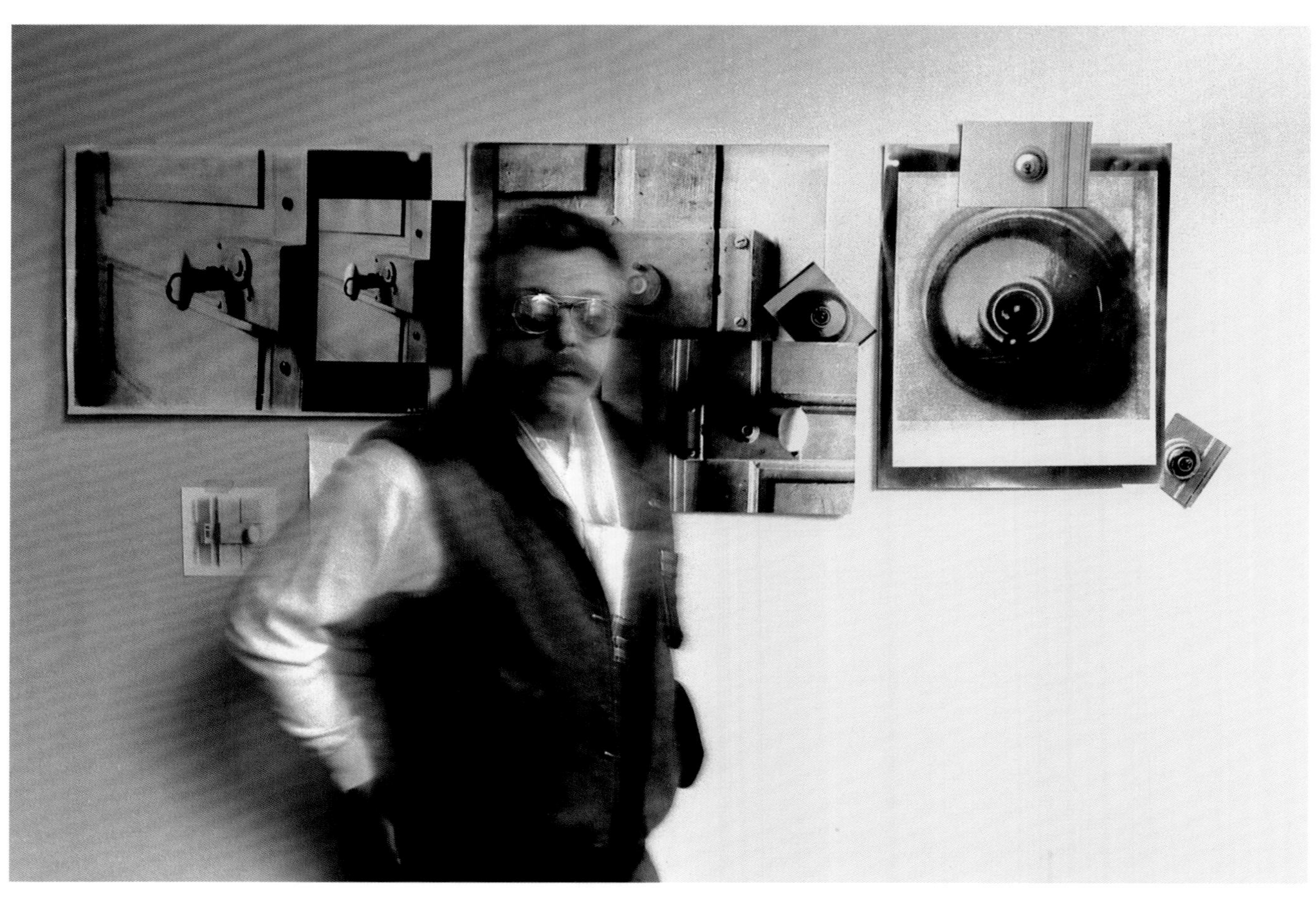

Self-portrait in front of Investigations into Switches *and* Investigations into Door-handles, 1988.
Photograph.

ENCLOSURES

BY **SYLVIE MATTON**

"All I wanted to do was to paint places, some apartments, in a very realistic way. Perhaps the anachronistic thing about realism is the time it takes. When one spends a month on a realistic picture, it's only to be expected that this work makes one think of other ideas, of other images, so many that one could never hope to do them all. They bottleneck, as it were. So, I said to myself: I'm going to construct these places. And I started painting walls exactly as I would paint on a canvas."[1]

Charles Matton created his first miniaturized structures in 1985. He designed, drew, built, sculpted, and painted them, aligning smooth walls in brick or saltpeter, installing cornices, windows, and parquet floors, as well as the fixtures and fittings, and all those everyday details that our sated eyes find it so hard to take in at the human scale: pipes, electric sockets, switches, the smears, the wear and tear.

He painted pieces of silk, turning them into cushions, curtains, or blinds. "I tried to give life to their colors," he said. He sculpted and painted chairs, tables, and easels, his main "concern being that they must be absolutely realistic." He made reduced versions of Persian rugs and electroplated brass or silver objects that he had carefully crafted in paste: light fittings, television sets, a sculptor's pedestal, coolers of Coca-Cola, paint pots and tubes—all to a scale of 1:7. He conditioned or distressed fabrics, which gained a new lease of life as painter's rags, bathrobes, or towels; sprayed with starch, preserved, and fixed, their folds telling of the exact weight of the cloth, every accessory looked more real than the real thing.

Because, since his early pictorial work and subsequently, with the recourse to miniaturization, the artist's goal was to return to a more tangible relationship to appearances, to delve deeper into the stuff of reality and so bear witness to "what seems"—to understand it better and offer it up to beholders, thus "purging their eyes" of the visual habits that blind them. Circumscribed, ensnared—as if in our absence—everything is presented with a lucid objectivity that harbors no illusion as to its limits and paradoxes. The object itself can only emerge from the exactitude of bricks in a wall, from the seepage, from the hairline cracks, from a heap of rubble or plaster—from this protracted painstaking inventory in which the flimsiest storyline is laden with reality, in which the least misstep would jeopardize the illusion of the whole construct.

But the nature of such formal accountability is transformed when things deliver themselves up—reduced, yes, but not slavishly so—to our view. For the re-creations that the artist deployed in his exploration of changes in scale are of a kind no pantograph could hope to realize; ensconced within their three walls, these ostensibly literal, reduced-scale versions of real objects were actually

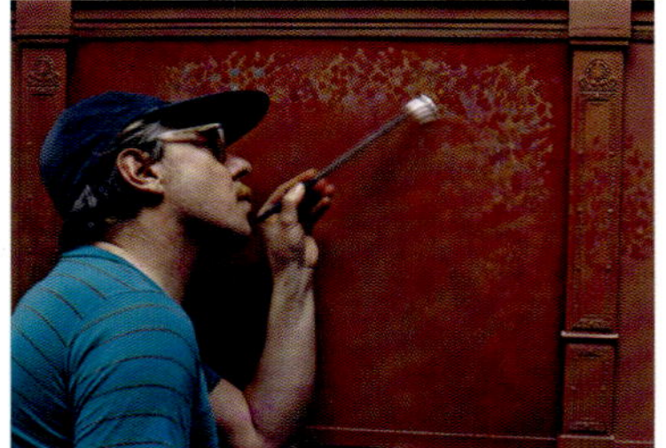

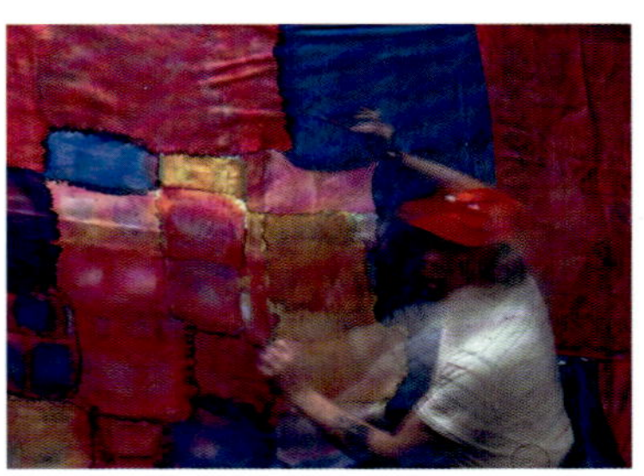

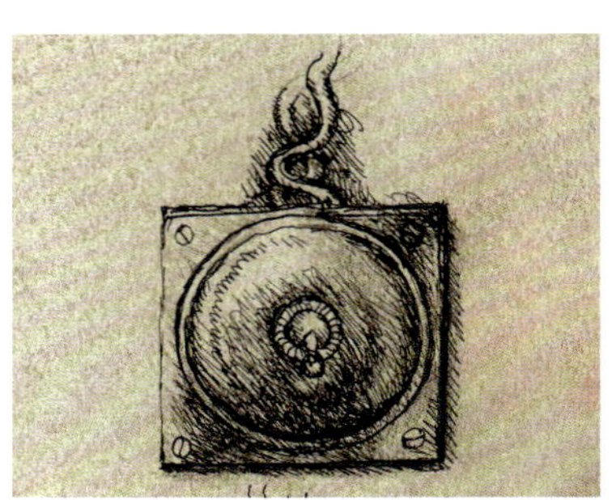

1. Private recording for the long-short film, *Douanes* (by Sylvie Matton), 1989.

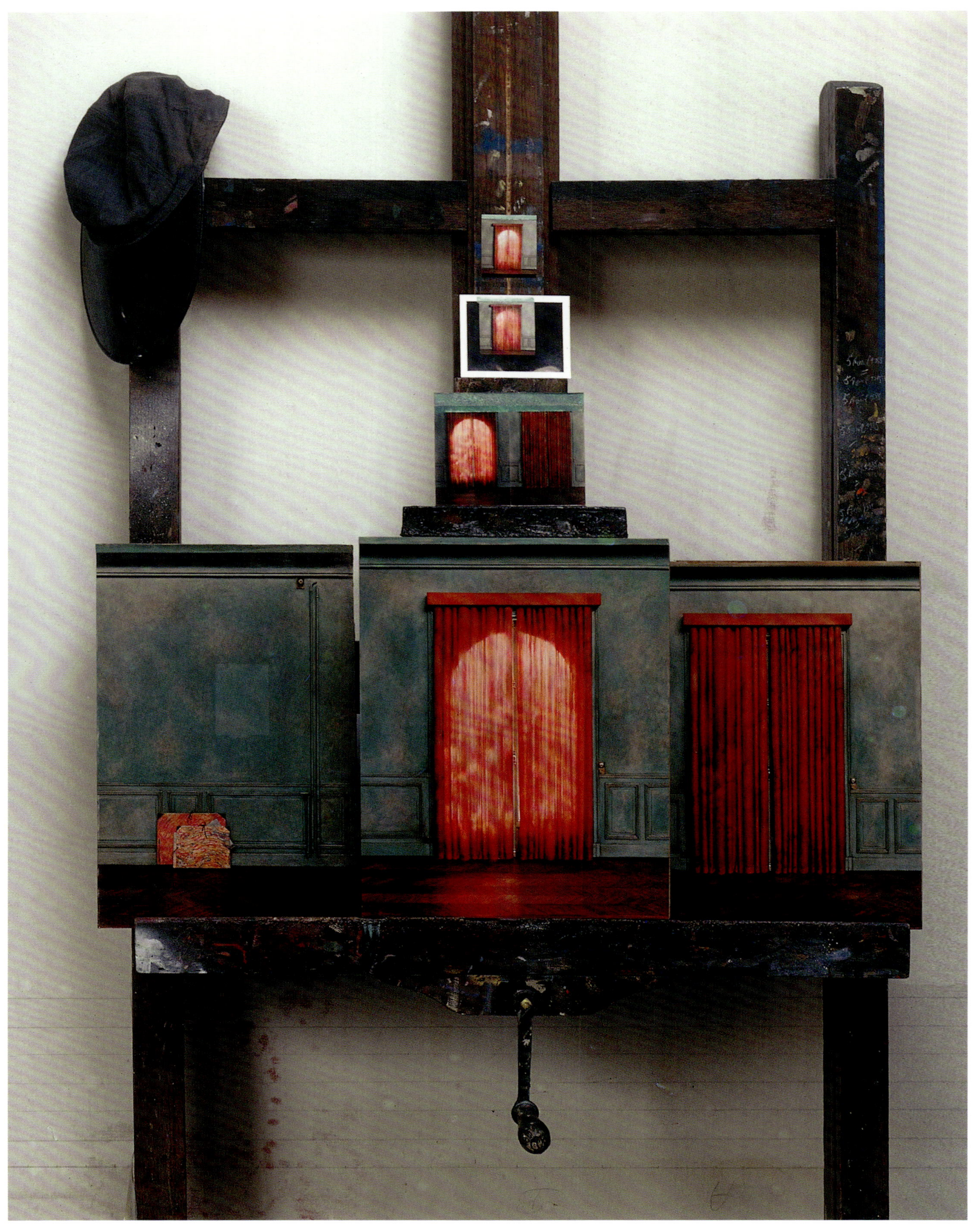

Facing page:
Working Method, 1987.
Photograph.

The Tubular Steel Chair II, 1986.
Photograph.

The Conversation, 1986.
Photograph.

Nicolas's Leg in front of the Miniaturization of a Bow Window, 1987.
Photograph.

The Bow Window Miami, 1991.
Oil on Cibachrome, 37 × 44 ¾ in. (94 × 114 cm).

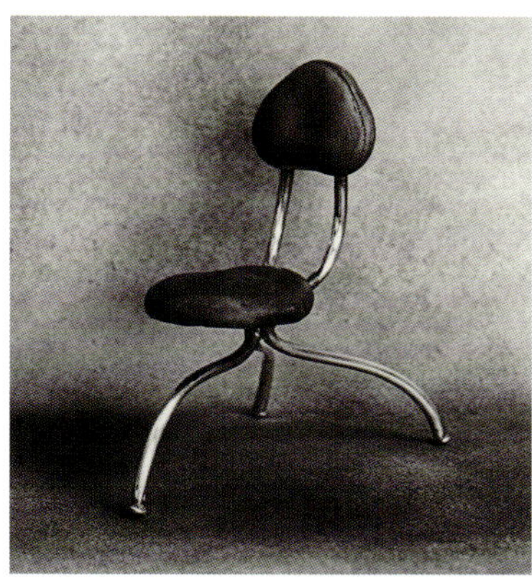

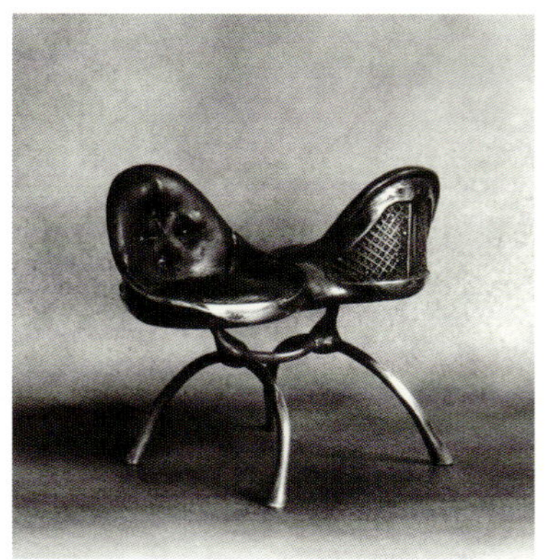

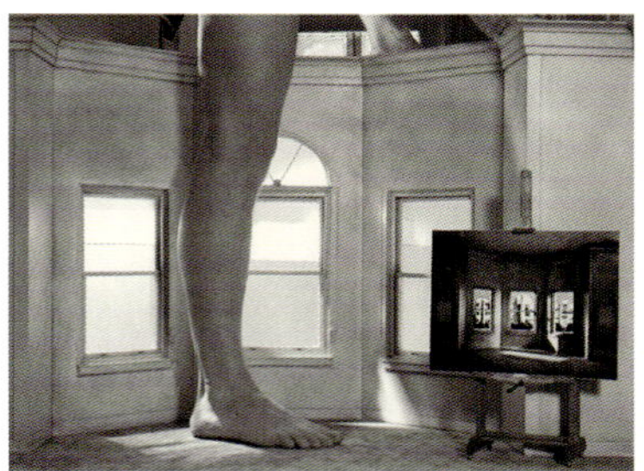

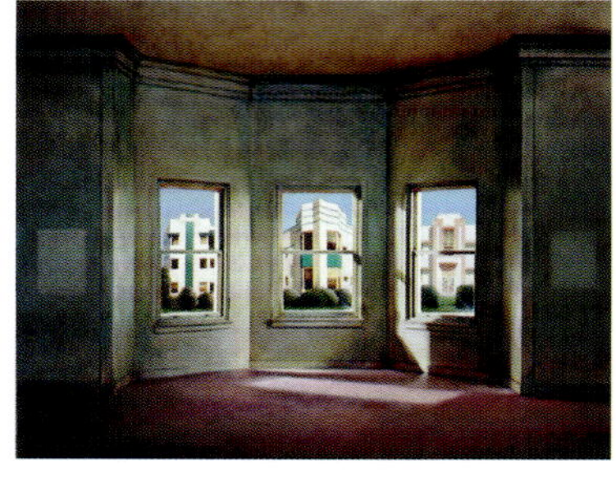

reconfigured, modified, slimmed down—or else, plumped up—and each form and color accentuated. Charles liked to quote Louis-Ferdinand Céline, who on being asked one day for a definition of art replied, "When I plunge my cane into the water it appears broken. So, if I want it to look straight, I have to break it before plunging it into the water." This new element, water, like a prism that filters what appears, isn't it very like a magnifying glass? So that's it. Breaking the cane first, creating disorder—a minor "mental tremor" that short-circuits our visual conformism; that, for Charles Matton, was art.

He hung his own pictures and drawings from various periods onto the walls of the boxes, tailoring them to this new miniature space. Those sculptures, conceived prior to and outside these "studio reconstitutions" and possessing a fully-fledged actual-size existence, appear enormous among the scraps of plaster, beneath the pulleys fixed to the skylight in his studio.

Being empirical, the whole enterprise began with improvisation. Everything had to be invented, made from scratch, experimented on—a vast panoply of materials and all the "mixed media" in the three-dimensional works, not yet dubbed "boxes": the wood, resin, electroplate, glass, Altuglas, plaster, different metals, mirror-glass (reflecting and two-way), cardboard, paper of every grade, paint, photography, electrical supplies.... Like illusions of an outside view made on location, Matton's exterior photographs—of cities, landscapes, or the sky—are placed behind windows or glass canopies. But, like that of a demiurge, all this toil acquired meaning only once lit. So, once the accessories were all arranged, the lighting too might need to be adjusted *ad infinitum*.

In the next stage, Charles took photographs of his reconstitutions from various angles, making large-size prints, over which he would later paint. "My intention," he said, "was to use these as models for photographs whose lighting environment I adjusted until, at the end of the process, they turned into extremely realistic paintings of interiors."

The artist did not consider the prints thus obtained as mere photographs that anyone might take in a similar location, since he had planned all the visual effects—the proportions, the range of forms, colors, and lighting—long beforehand. "Never before had a photographer been so comprehensively responsible for the creation of his models"—that is to say, with respect to every instant of the image taken. Using photography as a binding agent, Matton devised his pictures in the manner of Poussin modeling a landscape or of Degas—all but one of whose innumerable dancers, now cast in bronze, were conceived simply as clay *bozzetti* for a future pastel or painting, substitutes for static models (and more readily at hand than any flesh-and-bone ballerina), arranged in what were often extreme anatomical poses and not so much sculptures as finalities.

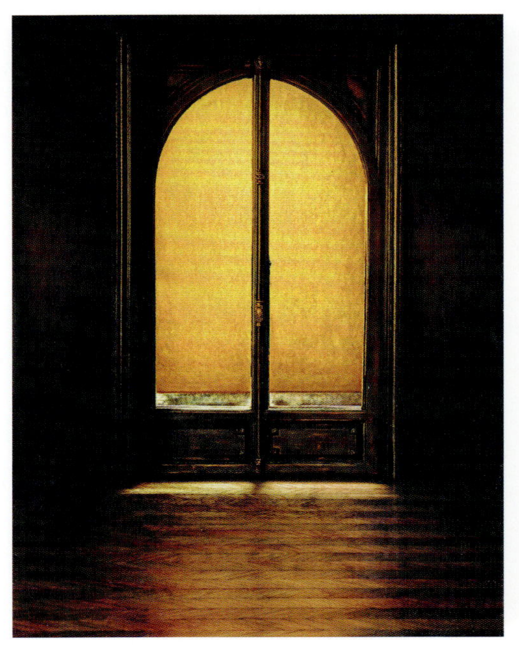
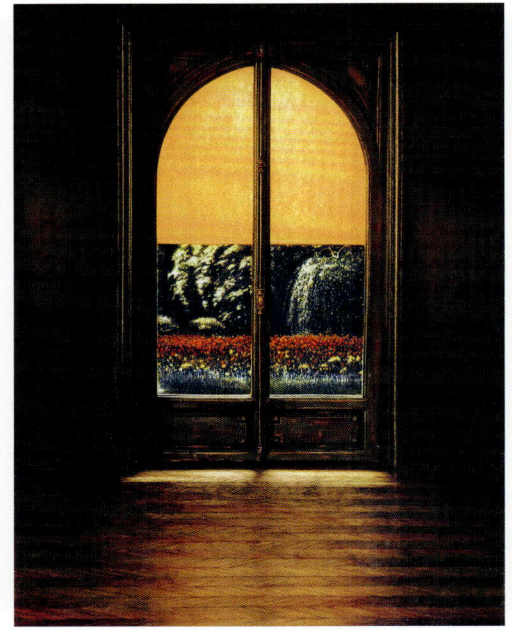
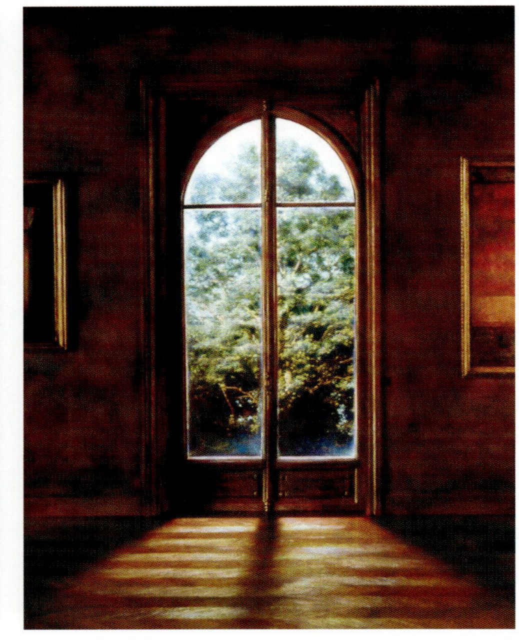
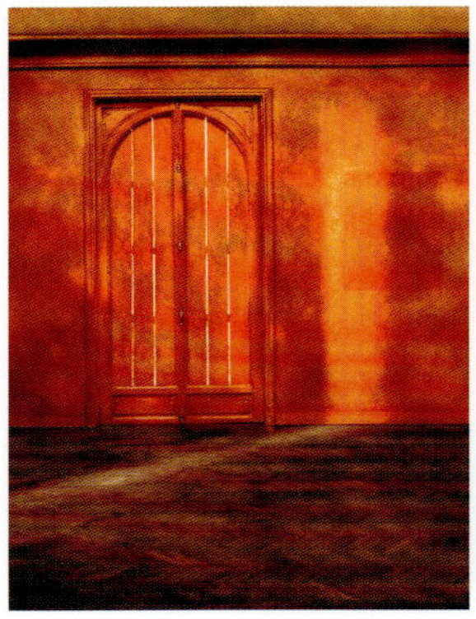
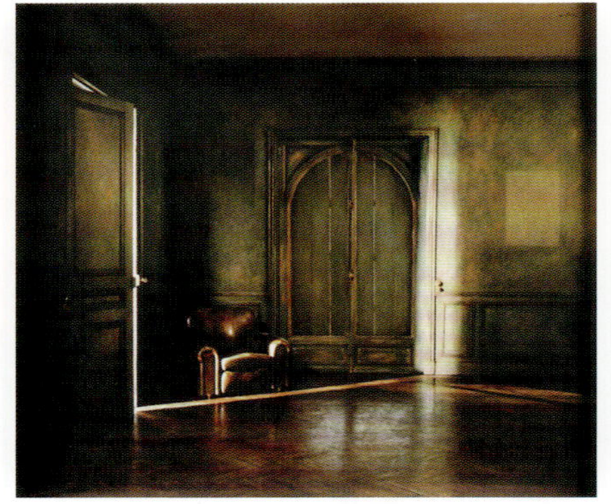
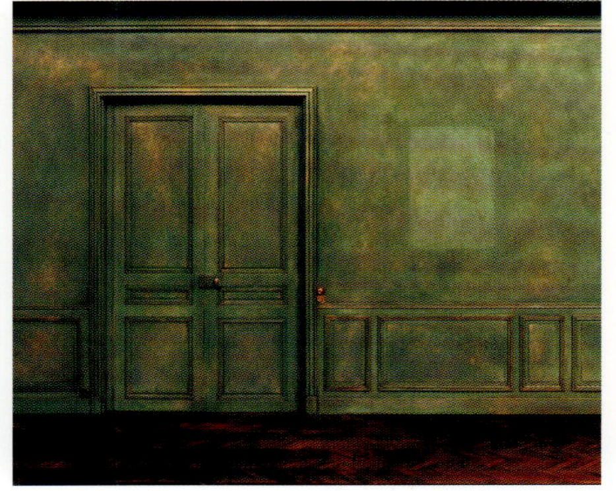

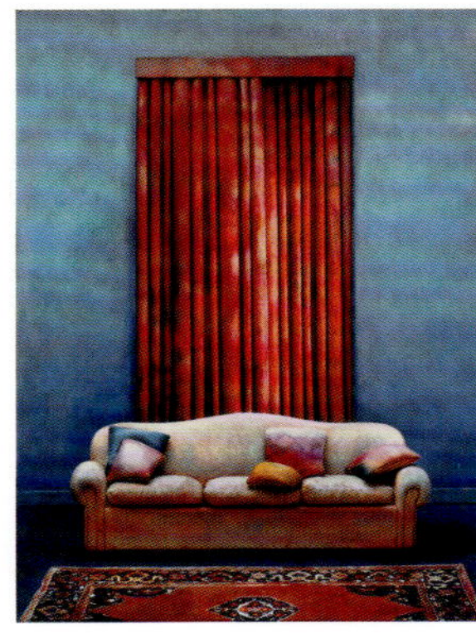
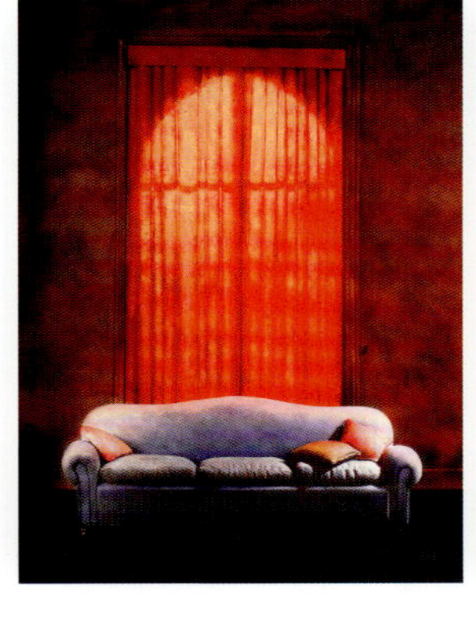
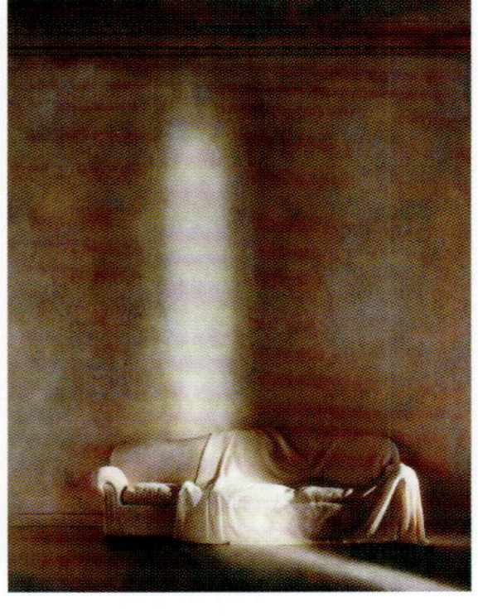
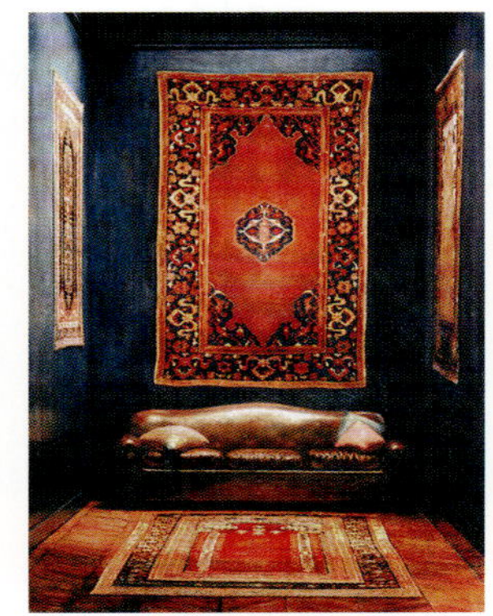
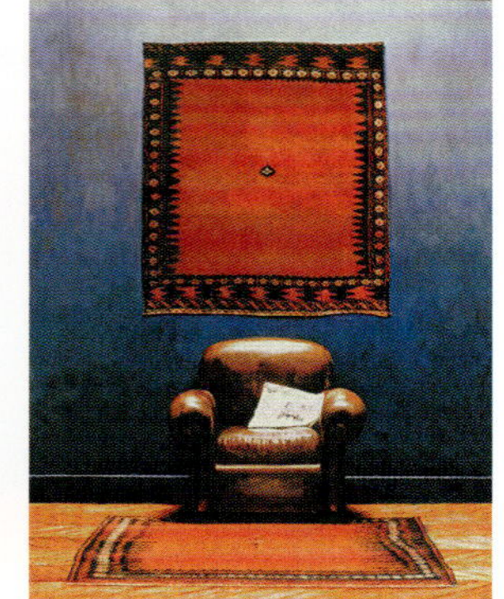

Facing page:
The Lowered Blind II, 1986.
Oil on Cibachrome, 75 ½ × 49 ¼ in.
(192 × 125 cm).

The Yellow Blind, first narrative (noises off of flies and children laughing), 1987.
Oil on Cibachrome, 31 ½ × 24 in.
(80 × 61 cm).

The Drawing Room I, 1987.
Oil on Cibachrome, 31 ½ × 24 in.
(80 × 61 cm).

Uncle Georges's Lounge II, 1987.
Oil on Cibachrome, 31 ½ × 24 in.
(80 × 61 cm).

Lounge on the Promenade des Anglais, Shutters Closed, 1987.
Oil on Cibachrome, 38 ½ × 56 in.
(98 × 142 cm).

The Mark Left on the Wall by a Picture I, 1987.
Oil on Cibachrome, 11 ½ × 15 in.
(29 × 38 cm).

The Corner of the Red Wall, 1987.
Oil on Cibachrome, 58 × 44 ½ in.
(147 × 113 cm).

The Avenue Elisée-Reclus, Drawing Room, 1986.
Oil on Cibachrome, 31 ½ × 24 in.
(80 × 61 cm).

The Lounge with Red Curtains, 1986.
Oil on Cibachrome, 31 ½ × 24 in.
(80 × 61 cm).

The White Sofa II, 1989.
Oil on Cibachrome, 58 ¼ × 44 in.
(148 × 112 cm).

Carpet Gallery II, 1987.
Oil on Cibachrome, 67 ¾ × 48 in.
(172 × 122 cm).

Carpet Gallery III, 1987.
Oil on Cibachrome, 31 ½ × 24 in.
(80 × 61 cm).

As the final stage of these artistic operations, paint was deposited on the half-finished works: "I wanted to be able to state that 'this photograph is not a photograph.' The only thing missing from the paintings in progress was pictorial substance and it is this with which I became concerned in the last phase of my work." The less cluttered the miniature space, the more painterly the final image will appear, in terms of composition, lighting, color, and material. *Carpet Gallery*, *The Lounge on Avenue Elisée-Reclus*, *The Yellow Blind: First Narrative*, *Portfolios, Bow Window*—all the "interiors" that crystallize at the end of this process of initiation, all these manipulations generally coalesce around a mid-shot of a wall seen from the front in a sparsely furnished space.

Such pictures amount to stills in time, to snapshots. The space sometimes rustles in tranquil serenity; other settings seem to reverberate with a drama that must have occurred before we blundered in. The human occupiers are not far away; if their rupture wasn't too violent, perhaps they will be back, unless they've decided to move on, as the marks left on the wall by a picture recently taken down sometimes imply.

As for the various "hangings"—a picture of medium or large size placed on a wall above a chair in a room with parquet flooring or carpet—they afford a pretext for a derisory fiction that lets Matton (together with his deeply-rooted painting impulse) stand to one side. Thus, he is able to depict any subject without misgivings, to make the most improbable appear pictorial: romantic landscapes, a cow or pig, a tubular-steel chair, tent fabric on the Normandy coast.

On the occasion of some umpteenth derivation, these arrangements morphed into homage. The process though is the same: one or two pictures on a wall accompanied by a seat or a light. But, at the moment of designing the piece, in manufacturing the model, in the photograph, and then in the extrapolation into painting, the artist entered into a dialogue with a member of his personal artistic pantheon, such as Ingres, Picasso, Fernand Léger, Jean Fautrier. . . . Every now and again, he also encouraged them to join forces, as in *Two Ways of Seeing Louise*, in which re-readings-cum-appropriations of Picasso and Balthus face one another on the wall. These secretive encounters, these conversation pieces about painting, are also a method for rethinking art history. In this manner, Matton hosted discussions with Picasso, Velásquez, Rembrandt, Beuys, Turner, López García, and Hopper among others, and, in the course of a lengthy interchange curtailed only by death, with a genuine brother-in-arms, Francis Bacon.

"Now that I have taken possession of this parallel miniaturized world," he averred, "I am able to produce images in numbers unthinkable with traditional means." The philosopher Jean Baudrillard, a friend of the artist for twenty-five years and the author of more than one preface to Matton's oeuvre, expressed doubts over

A Morvan Landscape in a Museum, 1988.
Oil on Cibachrome, 46 ½ × 38 ½ in. (118 × 98 cm).

Picture Representing a Parasol Hanging in a Museum, 1987.
Oil on Cibachrome, 49 ½ × 39 ¾ in. (126 × 101 cm).

A Very Fine Picasso Confronted by Two Tubular Steel Chairs, 1987.
Oil on Cibachrome, 24 ½ × 19 ¾ in. (62 × 50 cm).

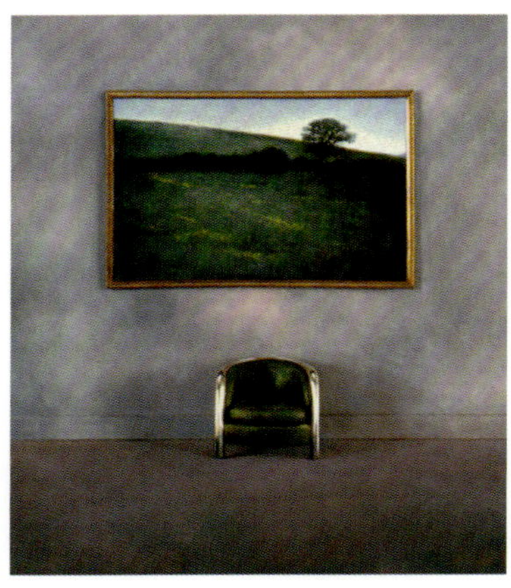

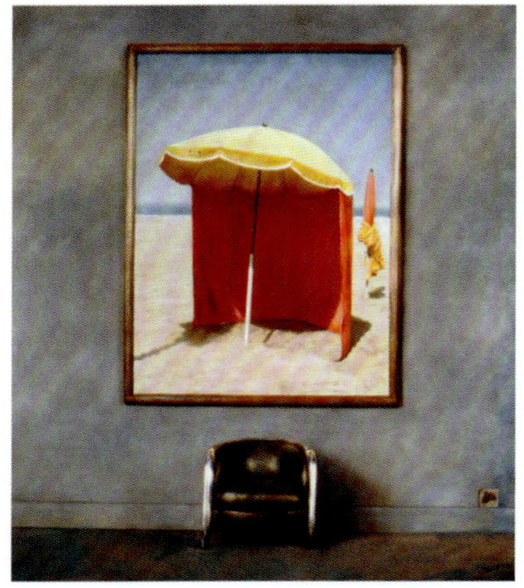

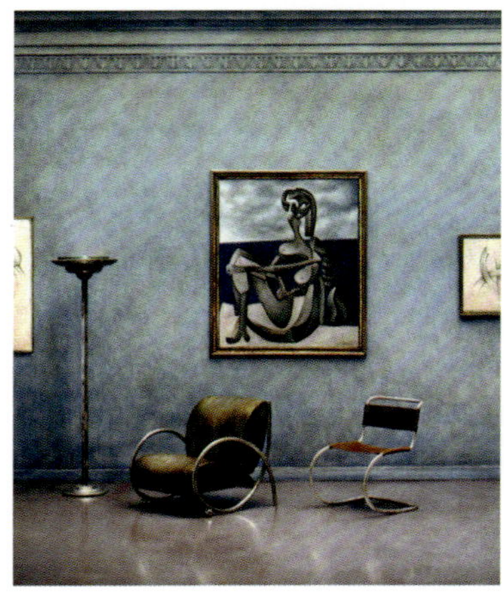

2. Extract from the catalog of the exhibition *Antipodes*, Palais de Tokyo, Paris, May–September 1987.

the long-term productiveness of such an approach. He thought of Matton as a pioneer—as one who, once this empirical exercise had proved the supremacy of the imagination (once the act as well as the result of the creative effort had demonstrated their conceptual perfection), would surely change tack. "Matton's idea," he said, "is that thanks to these matrixes he can generate images in unlimited quantities. But I don't really believe him, because the care and time he lavishes on the process must surely cost him more effort than if he simply painted and had done with it. Moreover, he himself has only come up with a handful of variants, as if to demonstrate its potential, while deep down remaining at the stage of initiation, keeping the secret of the many other forms to himself."[2]

And so it was that, having shown himself master of a scaled-down parallel universe of interiors and accessories, and after crafting some sixty tableaux according to this unprecedented creative method, Charles was to abandon the pictorial objective of the process and take up an intermediate position with the use of 3-D, joyously expanding each anecdote to its limit in countless series of experiments. "At the outset the boxes were just a model, a working tool," he said. "I never thought they'd be exhibited. It was only little by little that the idea dawned on me of treating such reconstitutions as polychrome sculptures, and of showing them."

Very quickly, the boxes seemed to become everything to their creator, who, having tackled the notion of appearance in every medium from the age of twenty, always preferred—to terms such as painter, sculptor, draftsman, photographer, director, etc.—the generic, unassuming, yet mysterious description "manufacturer of images." For Matton, by focusing so close, the analysis of appearances that miniaturization incites allowed the viewer to snatch up more of the reality they obscure.

Serving as a new medium—a link in the chain joining not only painting, drawing, and sculpture, but also painting and film—the boxes were thought of, above all, by their creator as microcosms of art.

Even in his very first paintings of the 1950s, scrutinizing with good humor people and things, Charles Matton was already "encircling" his subjects (human figures, cities, bouquets of flowers, swimmers, newborns), in order to grasp more firmly "what appears," before proceeding to break it down into endless interpretations. Thus, in oscillating between an examination resembling a survey and a less restrictive descriptive painting—as when, in more liberated, more painterly gestures, the pictorial substance becomes a language and the brushwork raw material for sensation and reflection—as he explores every square inch of the gap bridged by these two completely distinct ways of seeing, the artist's aim remained to plumb as deeply as possible into the very heart of things.

Reality is for Matton a fiction to which only art can testify. Reality, the ever-present center of operations, lies concealed behind its outward appearance and simulacrum. Herein lurks one of the mysteries most urgent for the artist to solve: he must instill doubt into what appears, the better to capture both these appearances and the reality they only unwillingly divulge. This is the reality that subsists beyond the compass of our vision, in our absence. This is the reality that makes a woman's voice in his short film of 1966, *The Apple, or the Story of a Story*, say, "The point is to catch things in the act of being—red-handed, one might say. . . ." or the young man in *The Italian of the Roses*, his first full-length feature, in 1972, declare, "Sometimes I turn round so quickly that things aren't the same as before." Or else, when Charles, the nine-year-old played by his own son Léonard in *Light from Dead Stars* in 1994, says, "I'm afraid things might change in the dark."

Art as a palliative to schizophrenia—Matton, indeed, proudly claimed to have cured himself of this disease partly thanks to his boxes and the objects they contain. Iconic in reduction, they are no less so in real life. In both, they bear witness to human existence, often little more than keepsakes no one has the heart to throw out from respect for how they faithfully fulfilled their function, down to some cigarette butts wedged into a pocket. Creation as passion, as obsession, as compulsion, and functioning as therapy.

As a medium, the box serves as a no-man's-land in which the artist can operate unhindered, in which he can reinstate emotion and beauty; it is at once an exact science for adepts and a mirror held up to the real.

The earliest boxes were shown at the Palais de Tokyo in Paris in 1987,[3] together with paintings on Cibachrome and photographs that gave them a human scale. Some are reconstitutions of places imprinted with the memory of a time without regrets, that of the artist's childhood, that lost paradise of discovery and of the quest for emotion—that is, by the comfort of a localized space within time, secure and free from danger. Time suspended, time regained, a time nothing will ever debase—as in the early *Hotel Hall*, with its orphaned suitcases, witnesses to the dying embers of the Riviera's social whirl.

The New York Loft, meanwhile, amalgamates in a single space two locations in that mythical city in which, for a time, Matton made his home. *The Delivery Room* recalls the birth of his first son in the hospital at Pontoise—long ago, when the ethics of childbirth confused the obstetric environment with a place of torture and pain. Other spaces ensconced between three walls and a pane of glass are inch-perfect replicas of existing sites, such as the first and second *Studios*, of Francis Bacon and Alberto Giacometti, or imaginary places, such as *The Attic of Leopold von Sacher-Masoch*. The quiet glow diffusing through certain reconstitutions

3. At the instigation of Robert Delpire, publisher and director of the Centre National de la Photographie from 1982 to 1996.

contrasts with the most utter darkness, that of the chasms of the mind, the abyssal zone. So it is that feelings aroused by man's sharing a fate common to all living things—the reiteration of which in art is often little more than threadbare redundancy—are here finessed beneath the benevolence of compassion, beneath the ecstatic hushed aspic that coats the luminous moment. Or else, stifling the screams, they lie buried under the excrescence of a thick patina.

The next stage is represented by the "illusion" boxes, in particular the *Vampire Studios* boxes, where a fake mirror "reflects" identical elements arranged to either side of beveled Altuglas, on the "mantelpiece" over a fireplace or slipped between the "mirror" and its frame—but anyhow never reflecting the viewer's face. Such, for instance, is the *Mirrored Wardrobe*, with toile de Jouy from a nostalgia-tinged Deauville, or *The Bathroom at Mariefried*, in an Ingmar Bergman-like universe chez the Swedish in-laws, or *Anna Freud's Living Room*, a free interpretation of the study in which Anna Freud worked while in exile in London and where the pain of her family's flight is encapsulated behind frosted glass reflected in a (false) mirror which, as we look on, frames absence. Absence (expectant places) and presence (the human figure) are two recurrent themes in Charles Matton's oeuvre, in every media and in countless variants.

Other decoy boxes, those of the greatest depth, possess a mirror that replicates the space, reflecting half a folding ladder and some double-sided objects and sculptures. Finally come those with two mirrors that, by reflecting one other, extend the volume of the box, creating perspectives rendered still more abyssal by scorch marks left by the sun: such as in *Hotel Halls* , closed for refurbishment and awash with memories of remote flamboyant dandies, or in *The Libraries*, tributes to Proust, Georges Perec, or Borges, remote galleries lined with shelves down which our gaze plunges, captivated. Real or false mirrors, two-way mirrors, others screening a film—even more than a hologram, in this reduced setting they leap into life. As with Velásquez, the mystery is probed without being dispelled.

The artist sets forth the rules governing these looking-glass games in a sequence in his full-length film, *Light from Dead Stars*, in 1994. A young German soldier, member of the unit that has requisitioned the house belonging to the filmmaker's parents, presents the ten-year-old Charles with the keys to the mirror game called *Spiegelspiel*. This perilous game consists in staring at one's image in a mirror until one sinks into its depth and passes through to the "other side," into a similar if unrecognizable "elsewhere" that reveals what is absent, through the mirage of a double that lies in wait in a homely bounded present now as irremediable as the already past.

Inextricably bound up with other techniques that similarly betoken the visible, these boxes—flawless reconstitutions, objects of experiment, artistic microcosms—were to undergo one more metamorphosis. Works such as *The Bedroom of a of Romantic Art Collector* or the various versions of the *Artist Studios* should not be seen as mere workspaces displaying variations on themes in every medium. Here, these miniature spaces—the works of an allegedly fictional sculptor, but in fact pieces by Matton in both traditional and contemporary veins—exemplify their creator's reflections on form. These cover a broad spectrum of the whole history of sculpture—the human figure in all its guises and extravagances, where the flesh dilates, swollen to the point of necrosis, or slims down vertiginously in experimental anamorphous sculptures. As for *The Scrupulous Reconstitution of an Upcoming Exhibition*, shown in 1989 at the Centre Pompidou in an evident declaration of intent, it is a self-contained showcase compensating for a legion of miniature exhibits, as well as the forerunner of the exhibition, *Rétrospective et Citations,* unveiled in 1992 over 21,528 square feet in the Centre d'Art Contemporain in Fréjus.

In the same fashion as other media, the boxes became autonomous links in the mesh of encirclement that characterizes the oeuvre of Charles Matton. As the years passed and the exhibitions continued, the boxes synthesized the artist's investigation of appearances. Enclosures into which the various techniques he mastered interpenetrated, they condense and circumscribe the perspectives of numerous themes in his work.

In this far from exhaustive volume and the far from exhaustive account of his creative output that follows, we see the artist's favorite subjects range between boxes and other media. This is also the case with texts—some already available, others as yet unpublished—jotted down at any moment of the day (or night) as personal memoranda in notebooks, sketchbooks, on a sheet of paper, even on a paper tablecloth or a train ticket—in what is a ceaseless back and forth between that which binds and the bonds formed.

Art as instructions for life: for Charles Matton, art was the most effective activity through which to channel that universal tension that, from bacteria to human, seems to galvanize nature, perpetuating and perfecting life: to capture the appearances, to encompass things, beings in all their reality—significant, even in our absence—so as to restore them to us. Always striving in this active contemplation to put the self to one side, to the point of dissolution even, was Charles' overriding aim—until that very last moment when, welling up with tears, his eyes veiled over forever.

Paris, April 7, 2010

The 3-D viewer designed for this book can be found in a flap at the end of the volume and can be tried out on the two stereoscopic images on this double page.

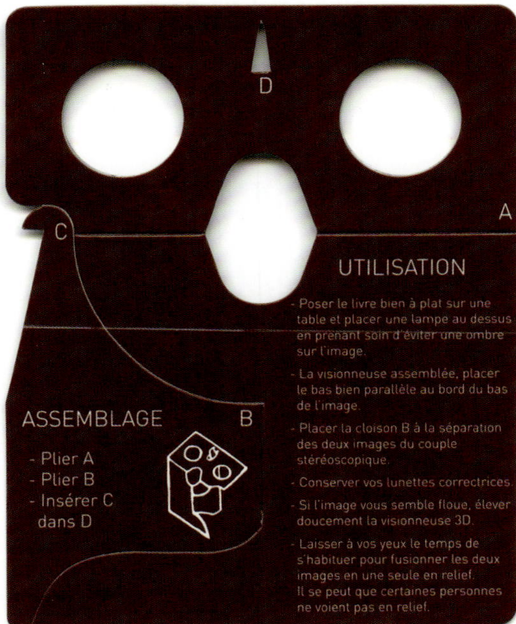

INSTRUCTIONS FOR USE

- Lay the book flat on a table beneath a lamp to prevent shadows from falling on the image.
- Once assembled, place the lower edge of the viewer along the bottom of the image.
- Align partition B with the line between the two stereoscopic images.
- If you wear glasses, keep them on.
- If the image appears blurred, raise the viewer slowly until the image comes into focus.
- Allow time for your eyes to adjust, fusing the two images together into a single 3-D image.
- Some people may find it impossible to see in 3-D.

All stereoscopic photographs in this volume are preceded by the following symbol

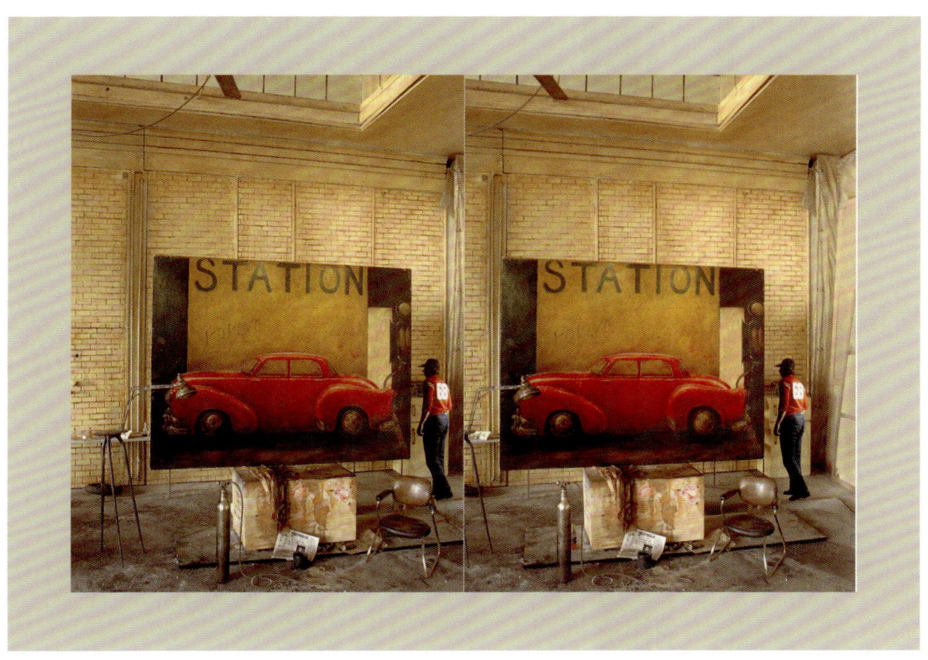

The Large Loft, 26th Street, New York, (detail), 2005.
Installation no. VII, the Buick Eight, and a cutout of Charles Matton.

Stereoscopic viewer for the exhibition *Rétrospective et Citations* in Fréjus, 1992. Felt pen on paper.

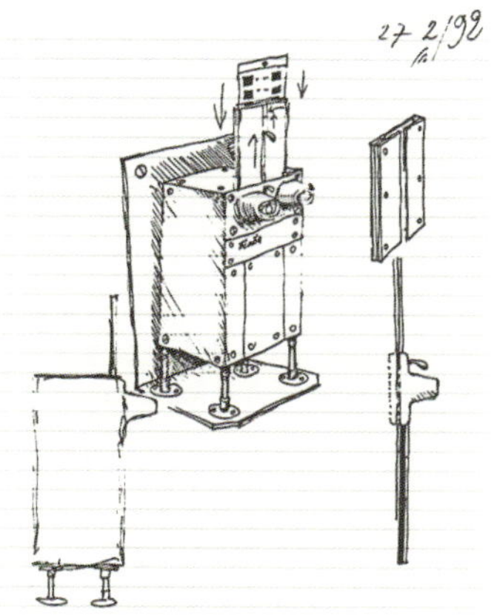

Over about fifteen years, Charles Matton took photographs of his boxes using a stereoscopic process. At exhibitions, displayed in conjunction with the boxes and looked at through viewers specially designed by him, these "relief photographs" accentuated the mise en abyme of the various stages of his creative process. It was Charles's wish that a fold-away viewer be included with a forthcoming volume on his oeuvre. In this way, the added relief afforded by special photographic reproductions of some of the boxes might imprint itself on the mind of the reader, who would go on to recall their 3-D effect when looking at the other illustrations.

S.M.

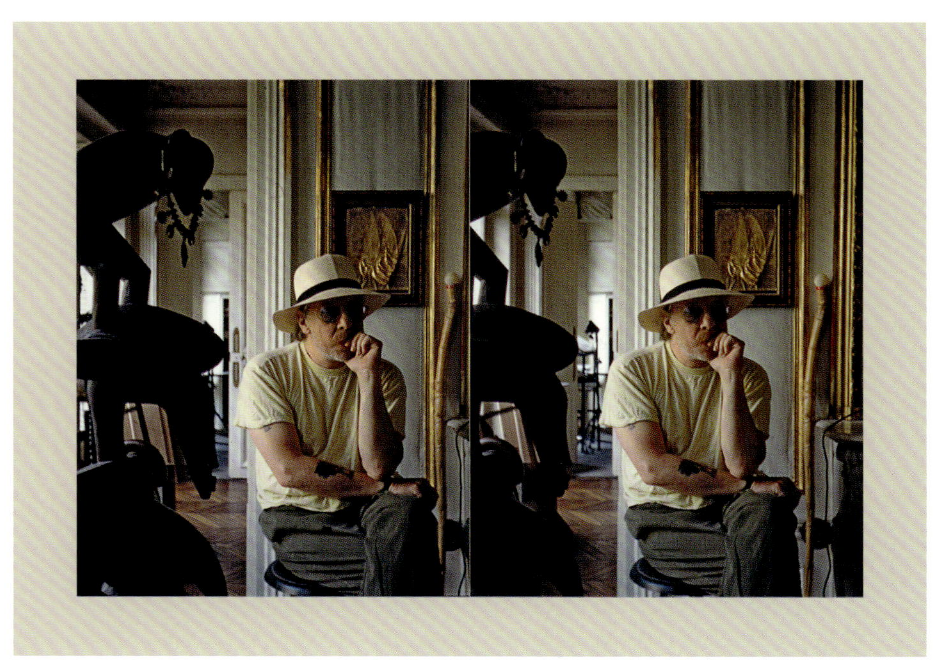

Charles Matton, boulevard Saint-Germain, Paris, 2004.

Representing a space, or a scene, on a reduced scale means moving in more closely, more thoroughly; it's a method of initiation. The illusions created by these reconstitutions of places—the *theatrum simulacrum* set up by Matton with a meticulous craftsmanship that verges on the sublime—and these template images, perhaps because they are embedded in the secret of perception where miniature images travel from eye to brain, are tenacious indeed. One day, coming into a New York loft belonging to a friend of mine, I was more than surprised to have the impression of entering one of Charles Matton's boxes for real. Everything, the lines of each brick, the telephone, the rocking chair, everything was as though prefigured in the model's past existence, yet subtly altered by the change in dimension.

—Jean Baudrillard, from *Antipodes* (Paris: Palais de Tokyo, 1987). Exhibition catalog

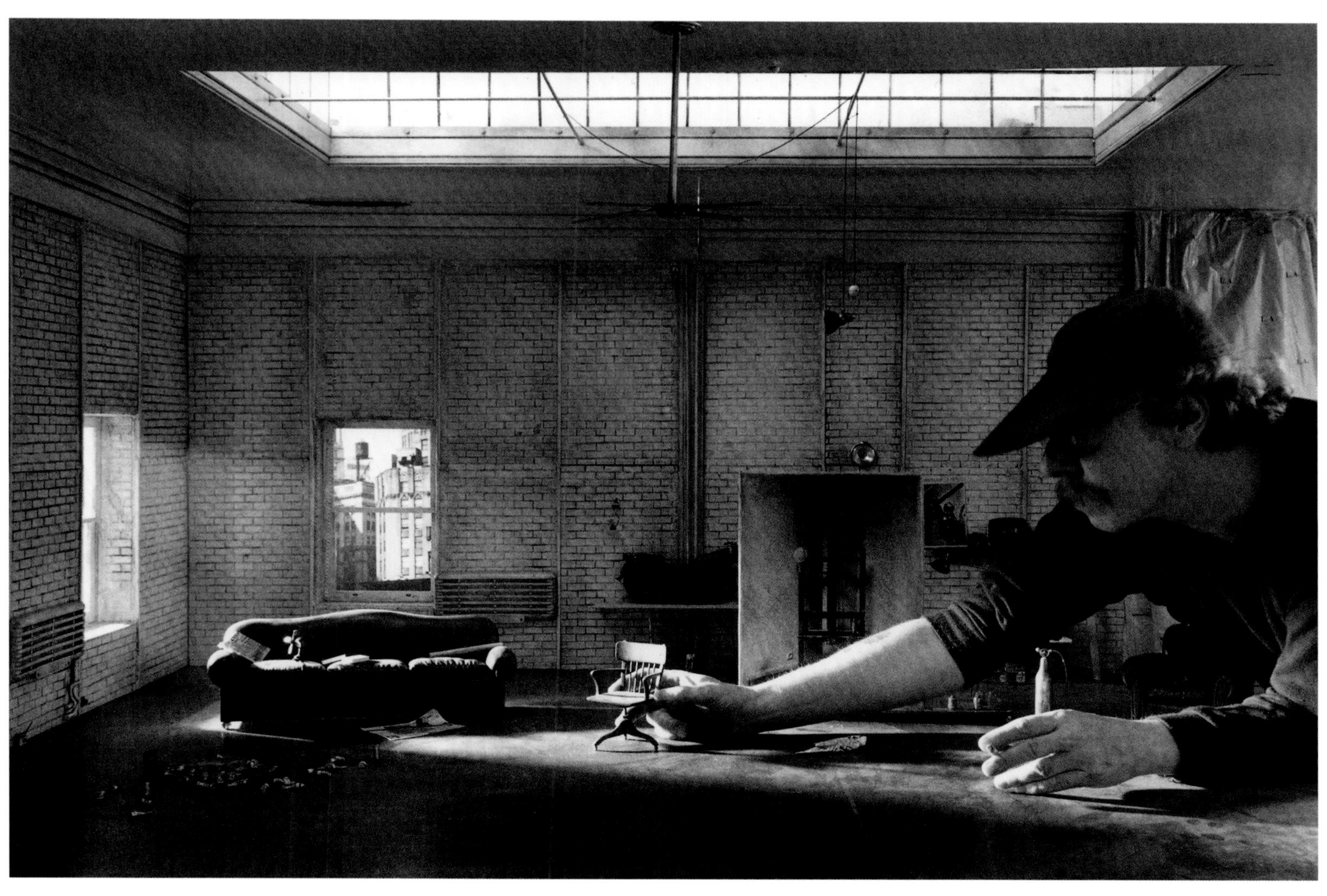

Self-portrait in the Large Loft, 26th Street, New York, 1986.
Photograph.

Rather quickly I felt that the analysis of appearances to which I subjected myself in my miniaturizations was salutary, therapeutic even, for me, in that it was a bulwark against the terrifying sense of the inconsistency of things, of what is there, of what, more exactly, seems to be there.

Personal note, January 1, 2002

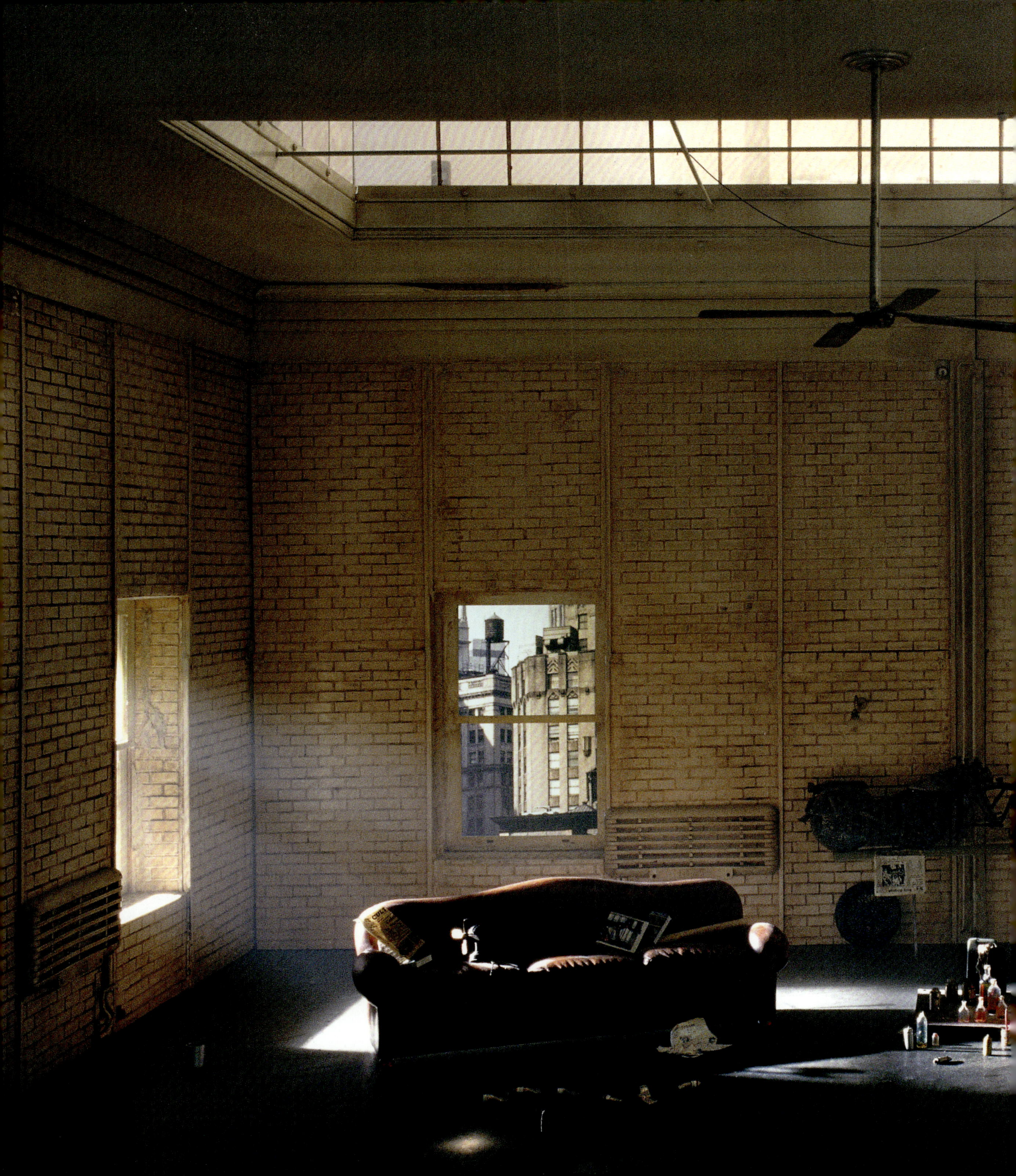

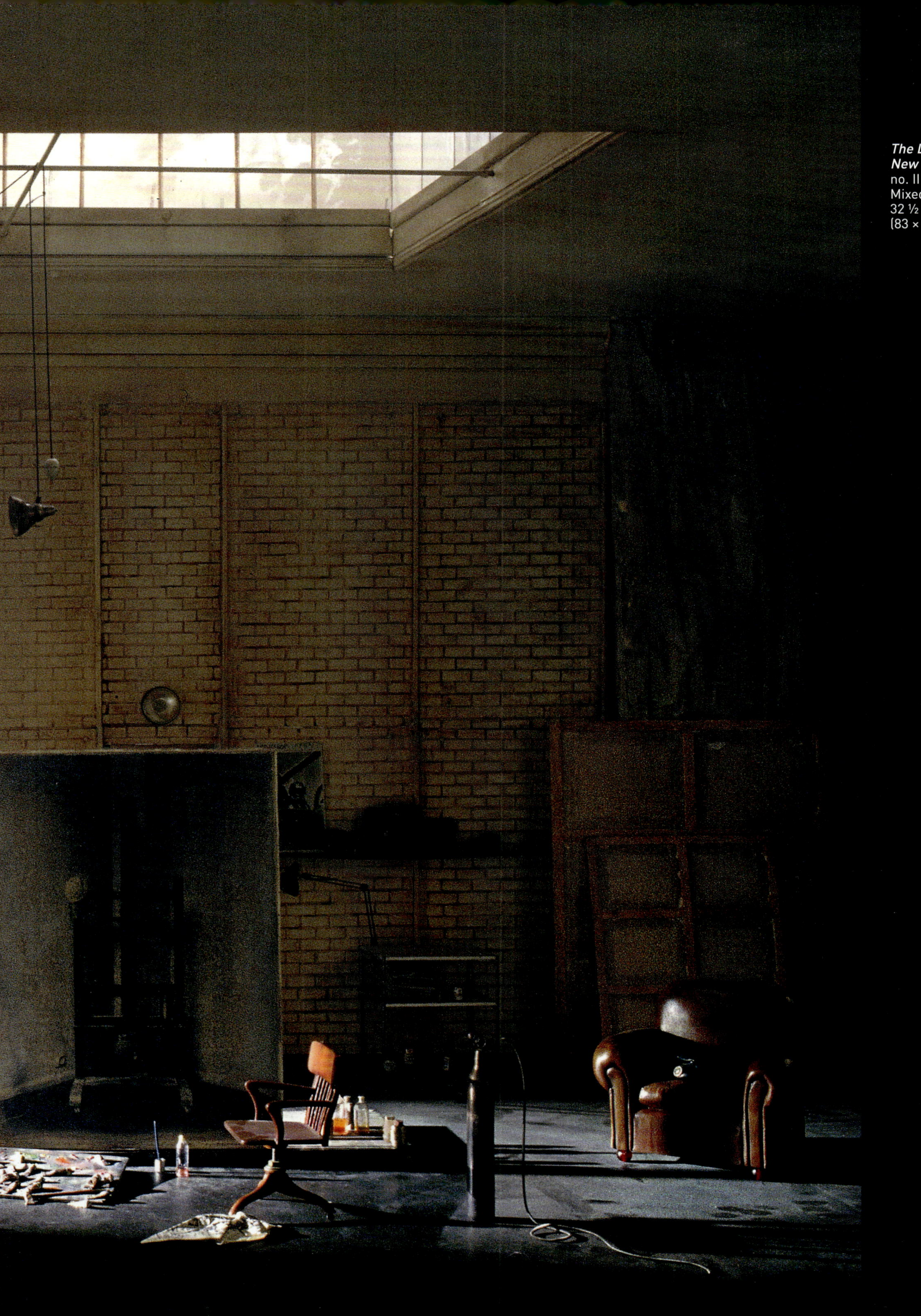

The Large Loft, 26th Street New York, installation no. III, 1986.
Mixed media,
32 ½ × 65 × 34 in.
(83 × 165 × 86 cm).

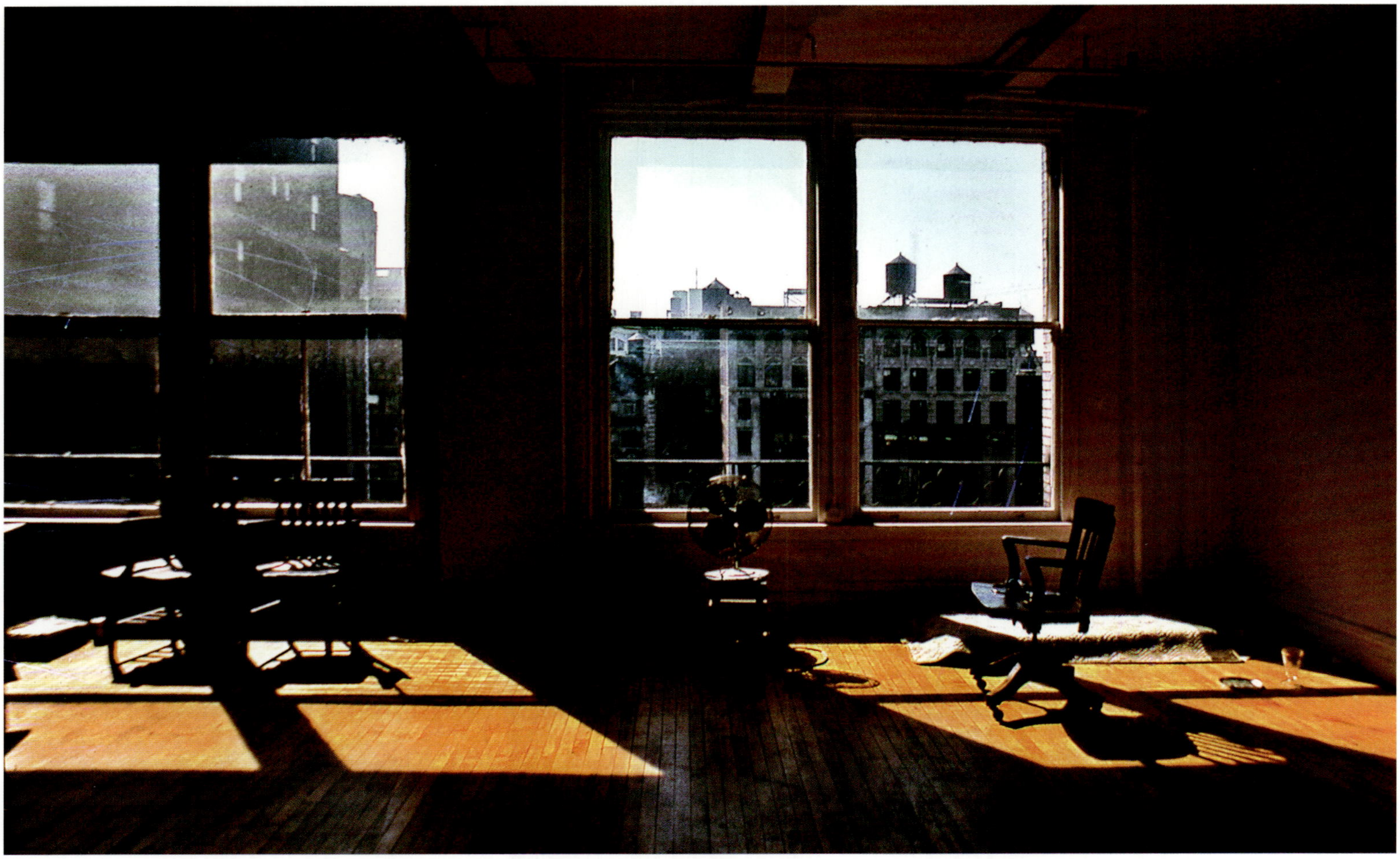

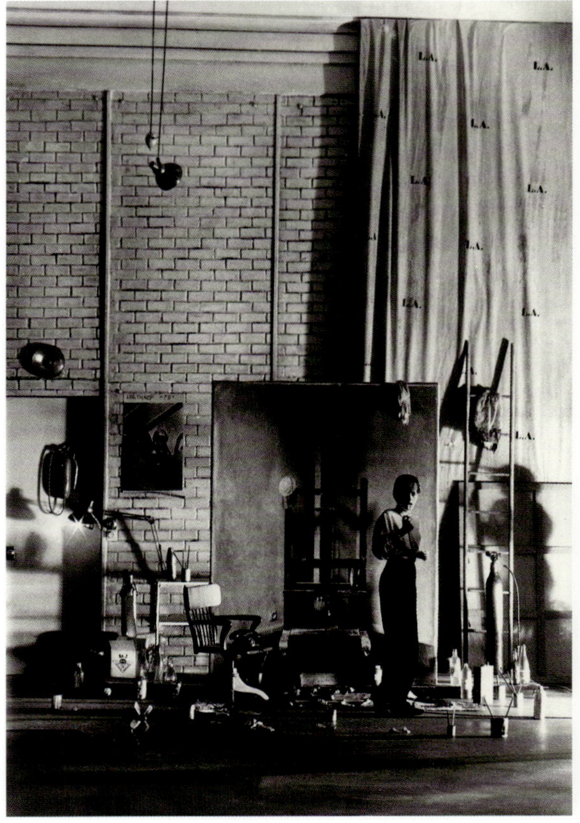

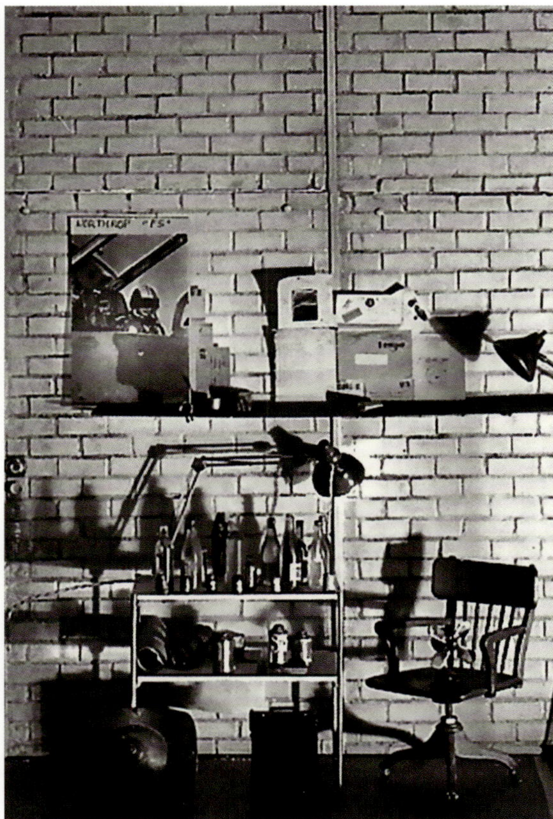

The Loft, 26th Street, Broadway, 1980.
Photograph.

Sylvie passing in front of the homage to Andy Warhol (positioning the cutouts—Sylvie and Charles's shadow in *The Large Loft, 26th Street, New York*), 1987.
Photograph.

The Large Loft, 26th Street, New York, detail, 1987.
Photograph.

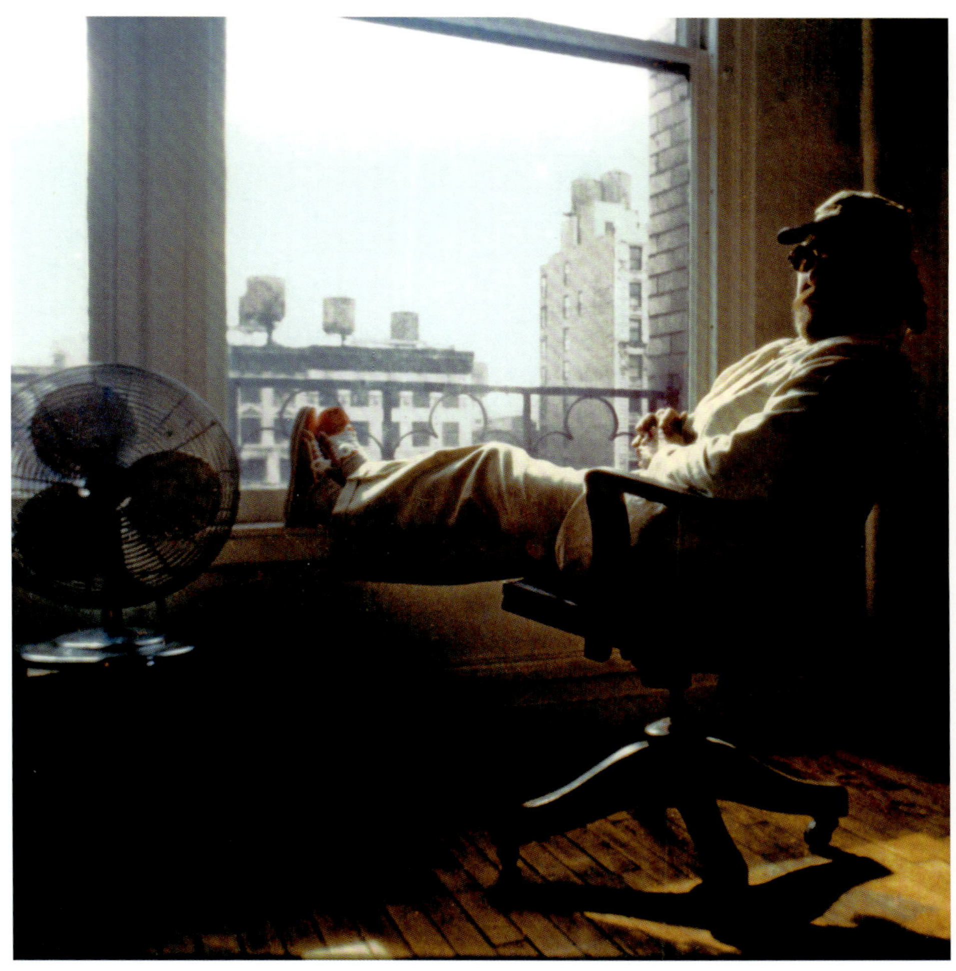

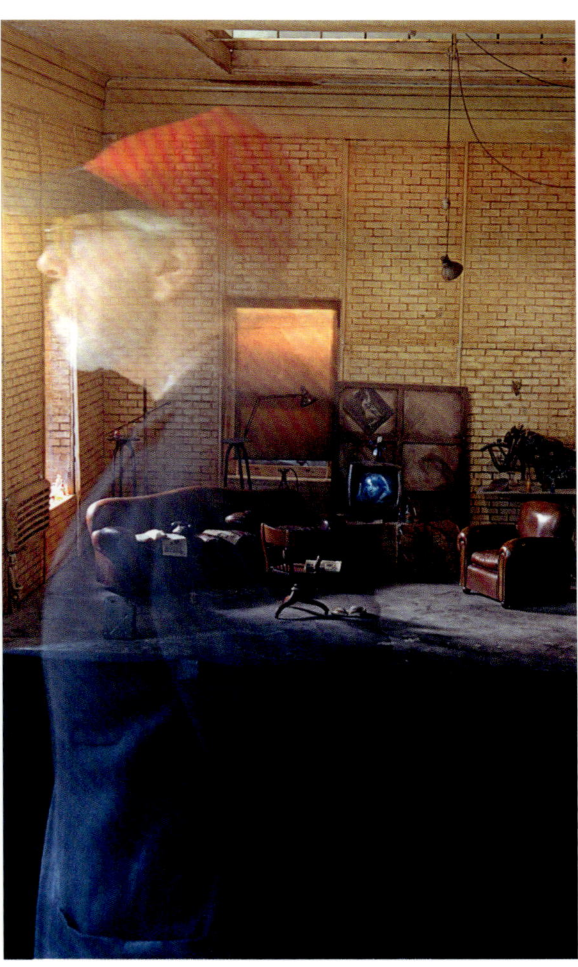

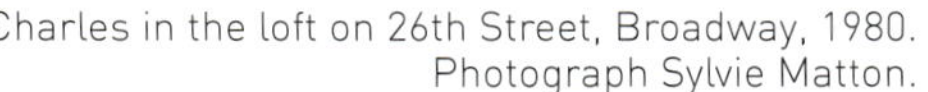

Charles in the loft on 26th Street, Broadway, 1980.
Photograph Sylvie Matton.

Self-portrait in front of the Large Loft, 26th St., New York, 2004. Photograph.

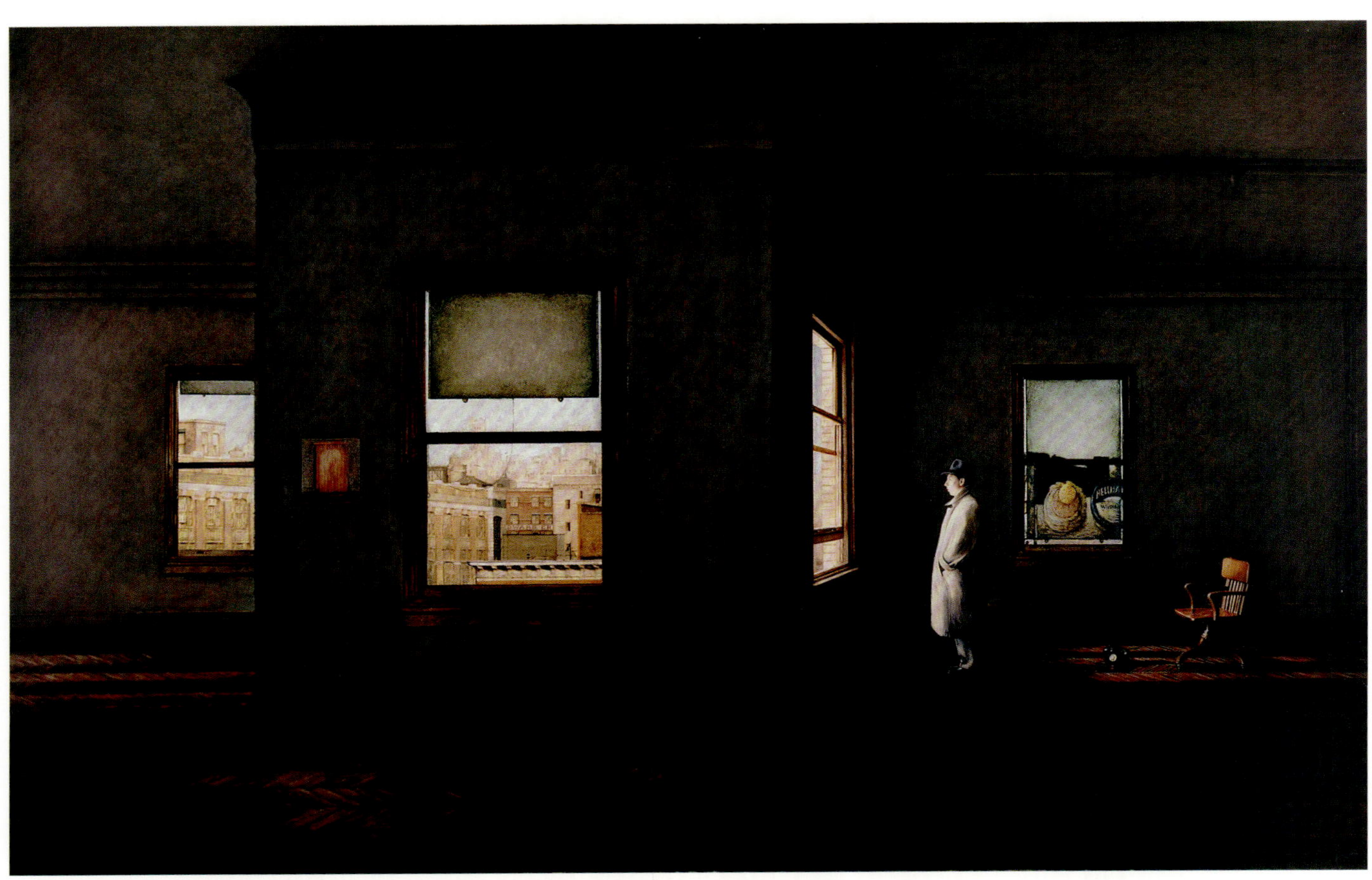

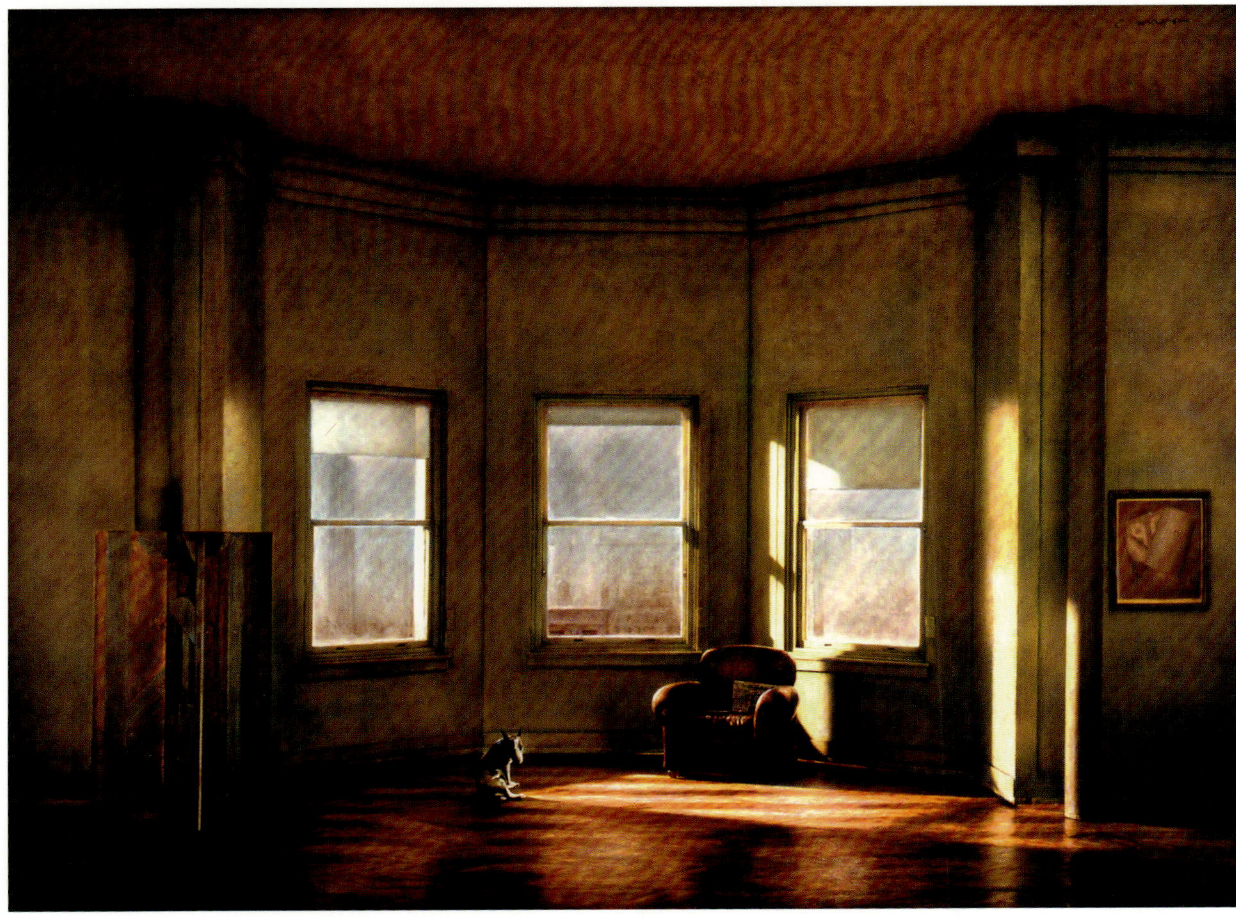

Facing page:
26th Street, Nicolas Blaise,
1987.
Oil on Cibachrome,
28 × 49 ½ in. (71 × 126 cm).

Bow Window N.Y. with Urbain, the Bull-terrier, 1987.
Oil on Cibachrome,
24 × 31½ in. (61 × 80 cm).

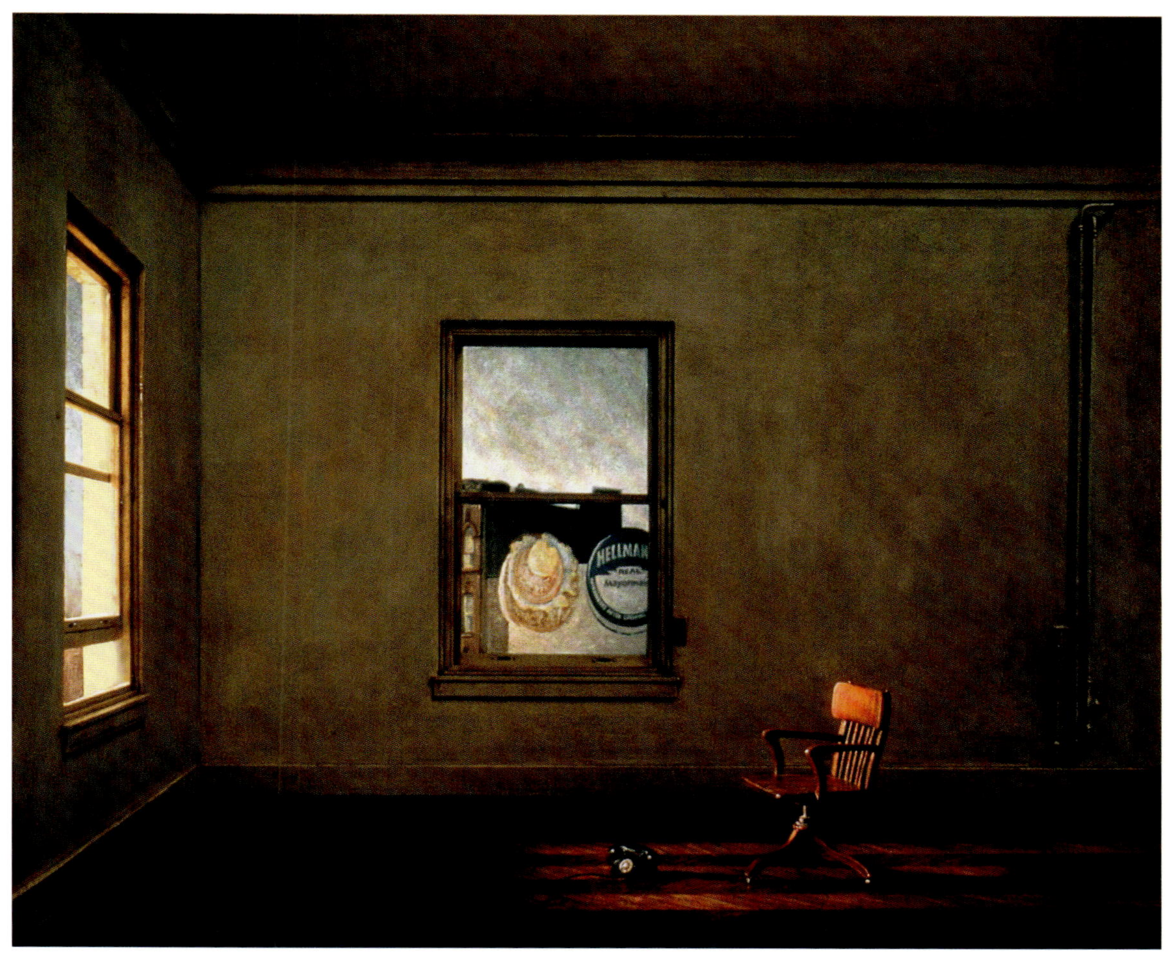

26th Street, 1987.
Oil on Cibachrome, 9 ½ × 13 in.
(24 × 33 cm).

An Interior behind a Window in the Large Loft, 26th Street, New York, 1987.
Photograph.

Windows in vis-à-vis, N.Y., 2001.
Pencil on paper, 11 ¾ × 8 ¼ in.
(29.7 × 21 cm).

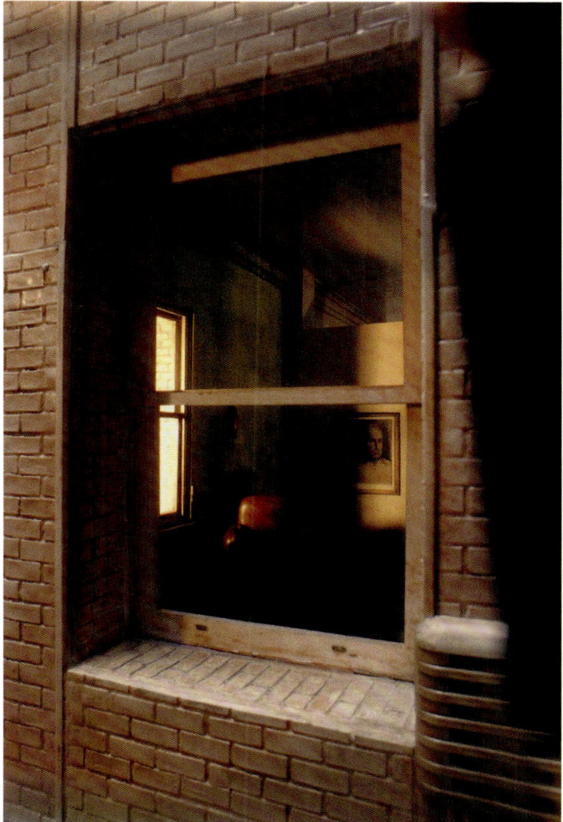

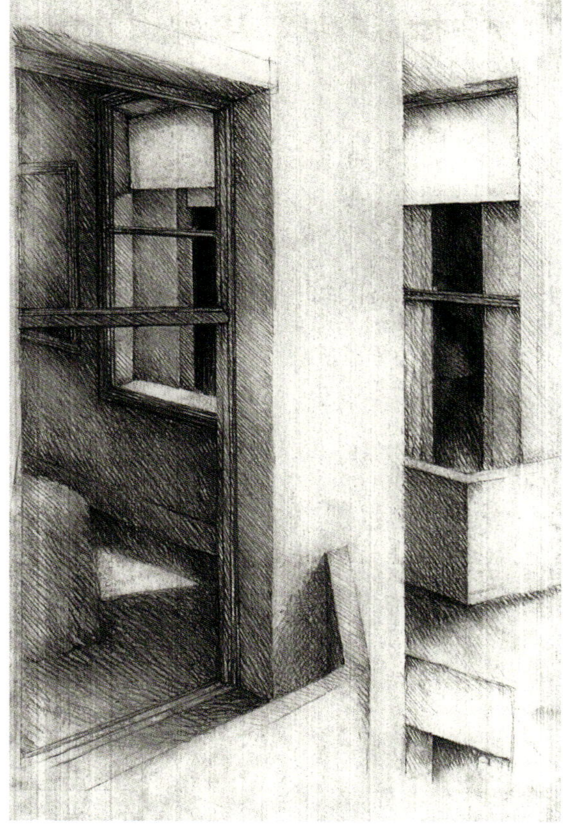

New York 4, 1986.
Sanguine and soft pastel on photostat, 16 ½ × 11¾ in. (42 × 29.7 cm).

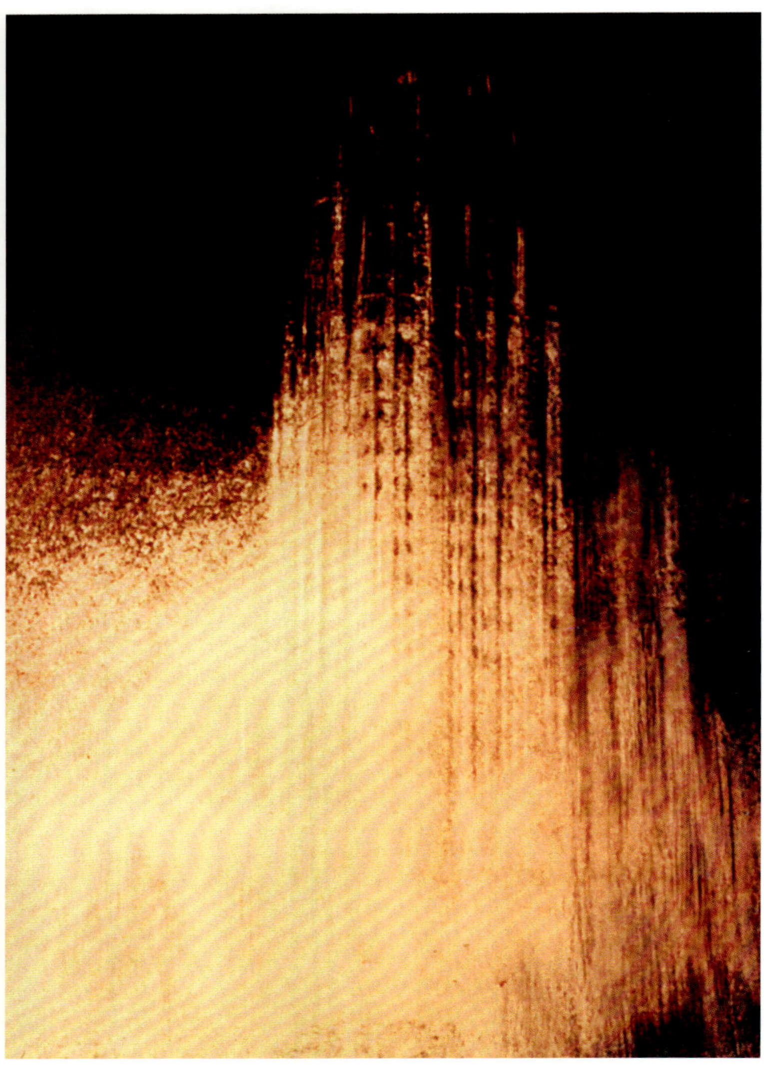

New York 7, 1986.
Soft pastel on photostat, 16 ½ × 11¾ in. (42 × 29.7 cm).

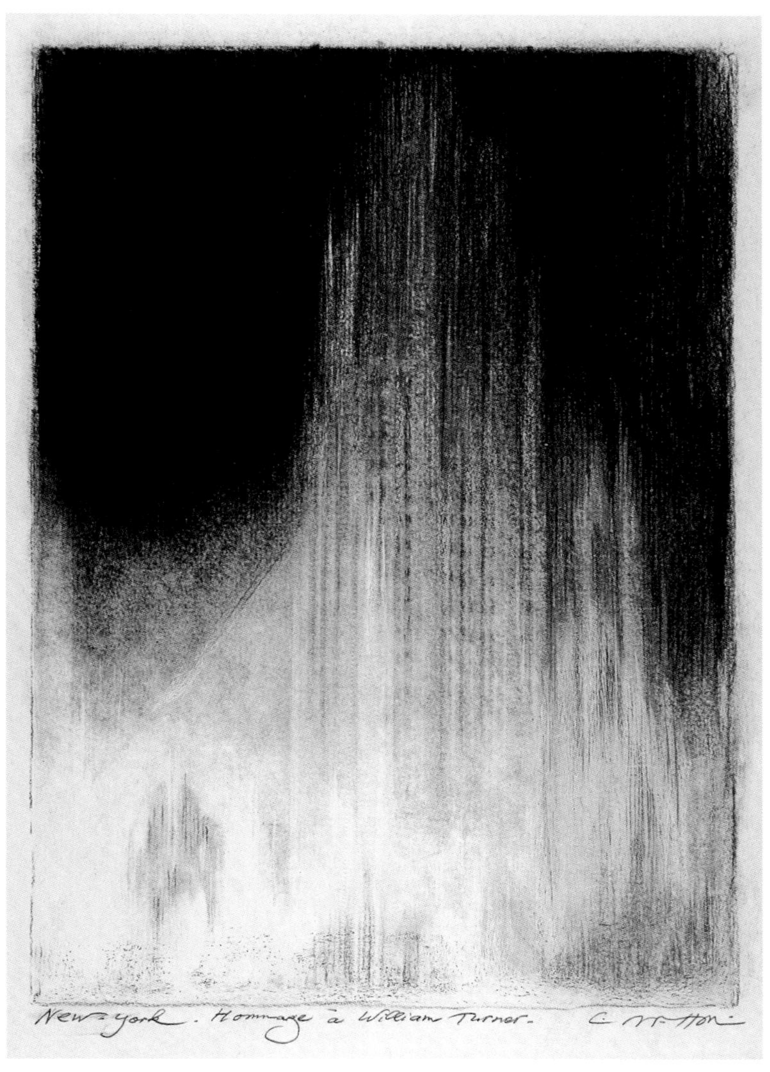

New York, Homage to William Turner, 1986.
Pencil and soft pastel on Ingres paper, 11 ¾ × 8 ¼ in. (29.7 × 21 cm).

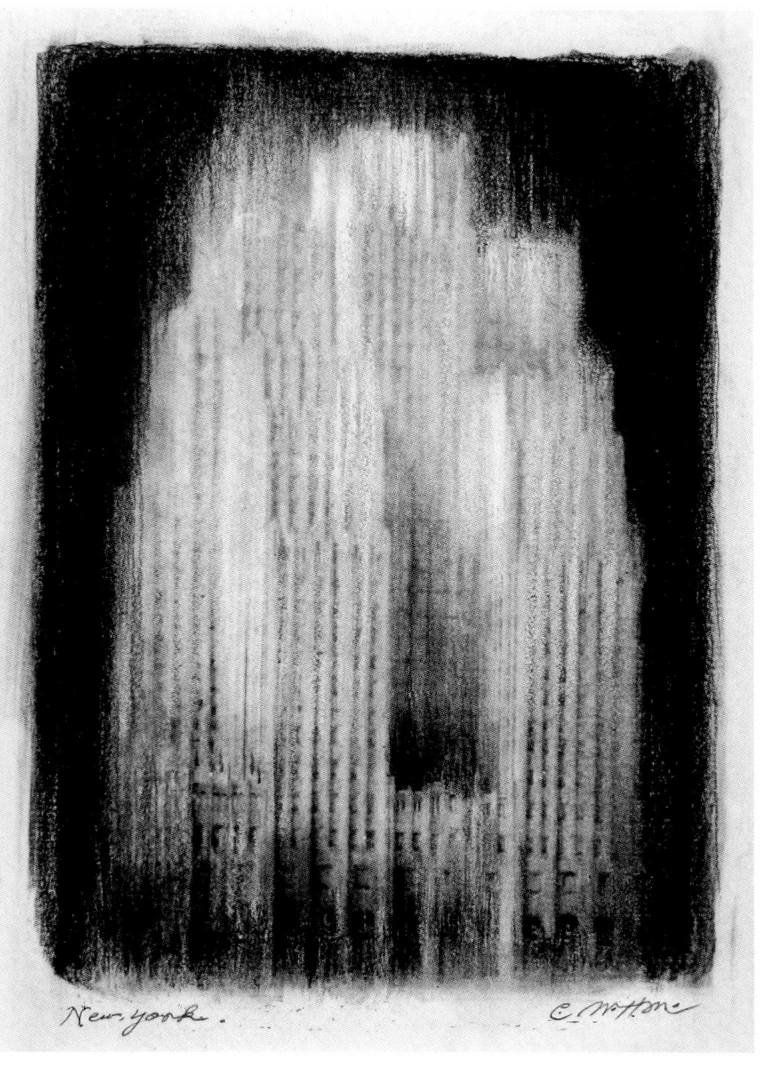

New York 1, 1986.
Pencil and soft pastel on Ingres paper, 11 ¾ × 8 ¼ in. (29.7 × 21 cm).

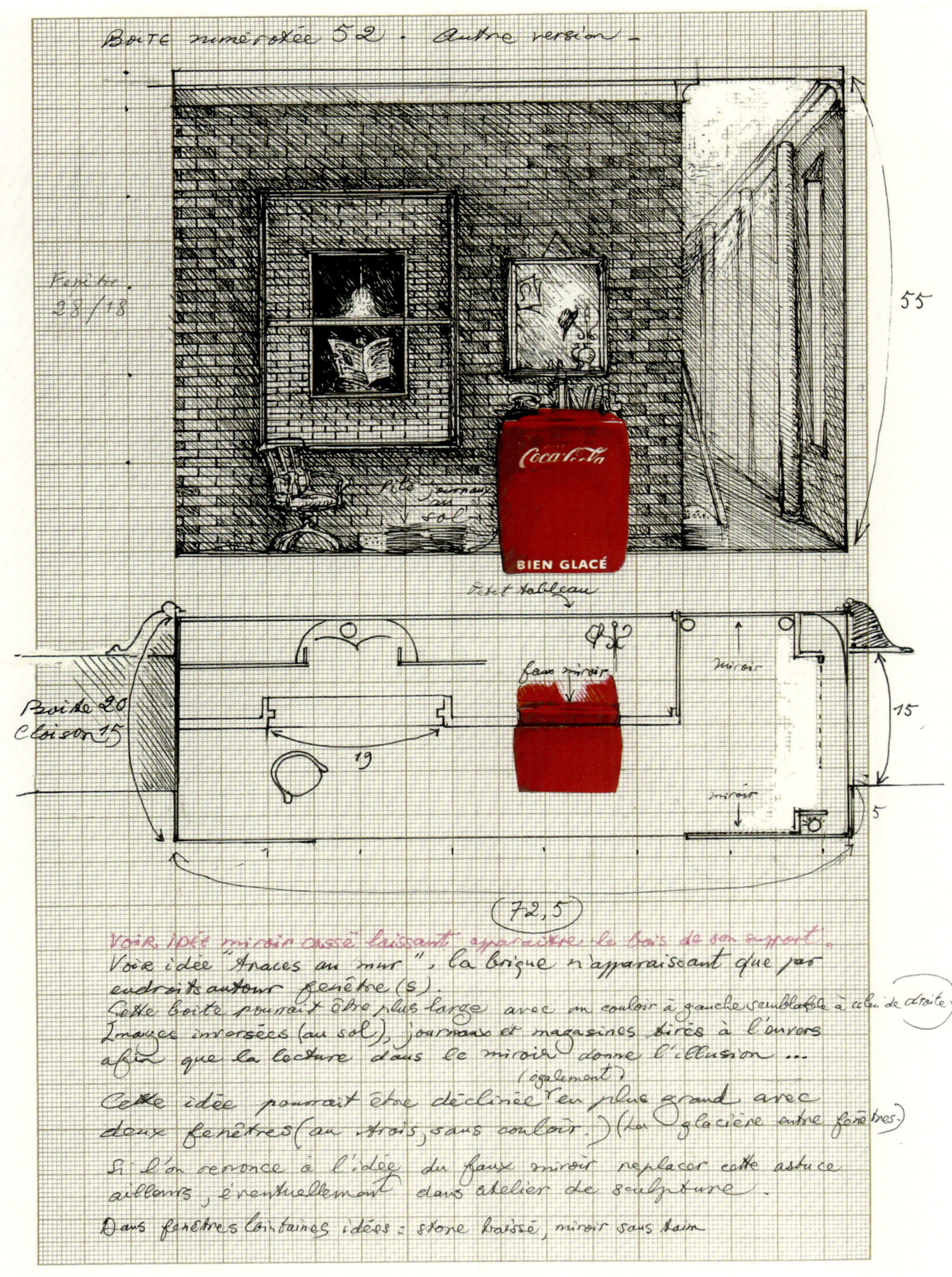

Homage to Edward Hopper, Manhattan I, 1989.
Pencil, felt pen,
and collage on graph paper,
11 ¾ × 8 ¼ in. (29.7 × 21 cm).

See idea: broken mirror allowing its wooden support to be seen.
See idea: "marks on the wall," the brick only appearing in places around the window(s).
This box could be wider with a corridor to the left similar to that on the right.
Reversed images (on the floor), newspapers and magazines printed back to front so that reading in the mirror gives the illusion…
This idea could be varied (similarly) in a larger format with two windows (or three, without the corridor) (the cooler between the windows).

Why so many tributes? Because art is language. And, as I am not the kind to talk to himself, I may as well have a conversation with those I like.

Personal note, October 11, 2000

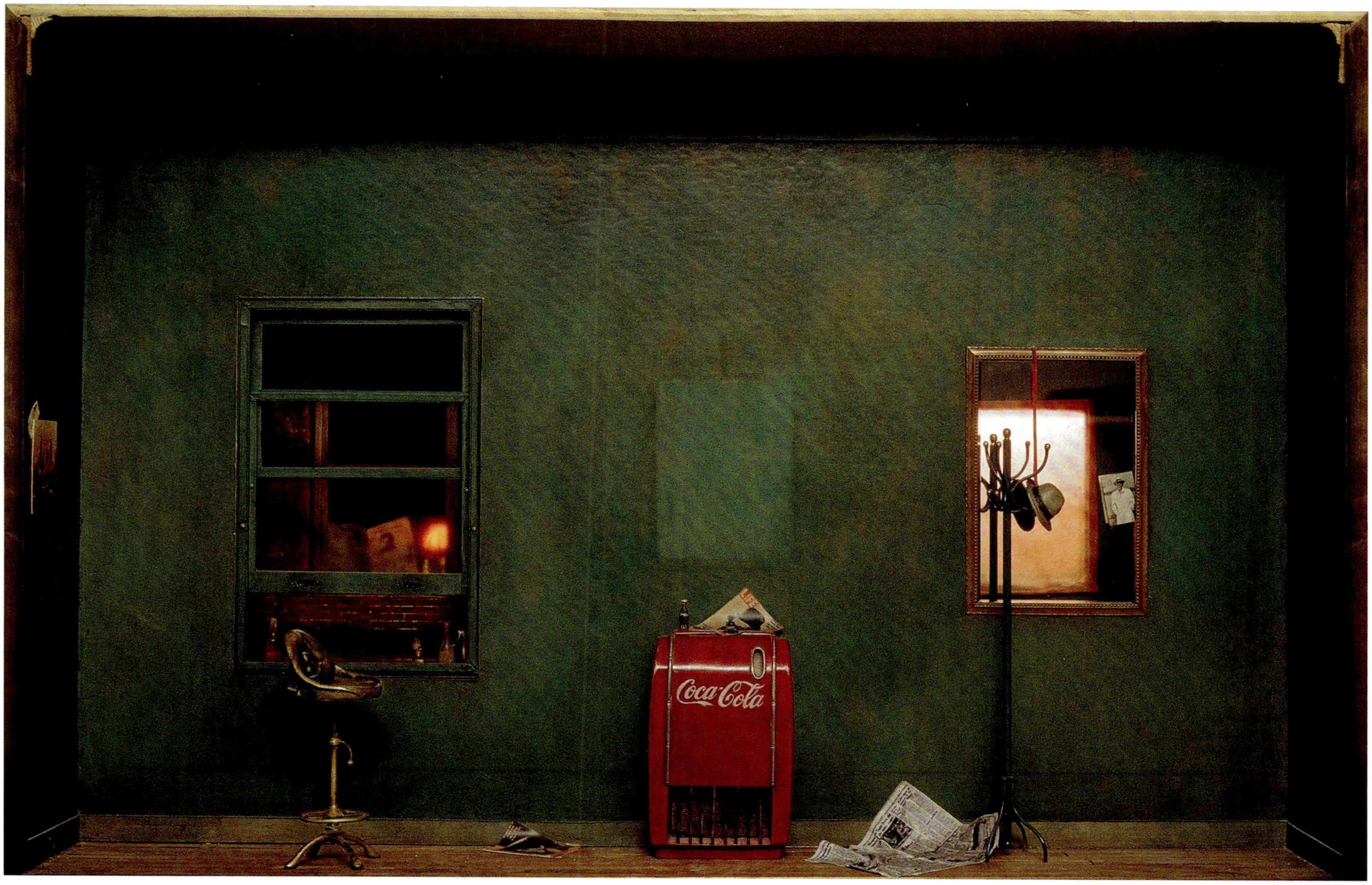

Manhattan III (green wall), 2000.
Mixed media, 23 ¼ × 35 ½ × 12 ¾ in.
(59 × 90 × 32 cm).

Coat Stand for Manhattan Box, 2000.
Pencil on graph paper, 11 ¾ × 8 ¼ in.
(29.7 × 21 cm).

Coca-Cola Coolers, 1989.
Real and reduction, tin hot-dog sculpture.
Photograph.

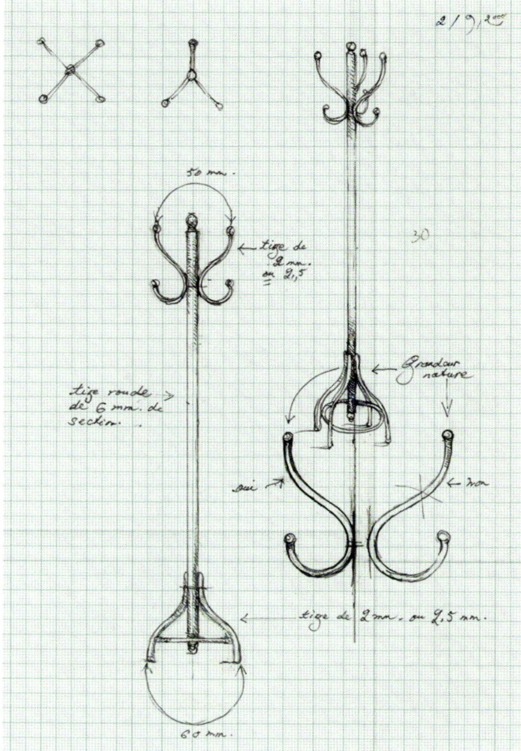

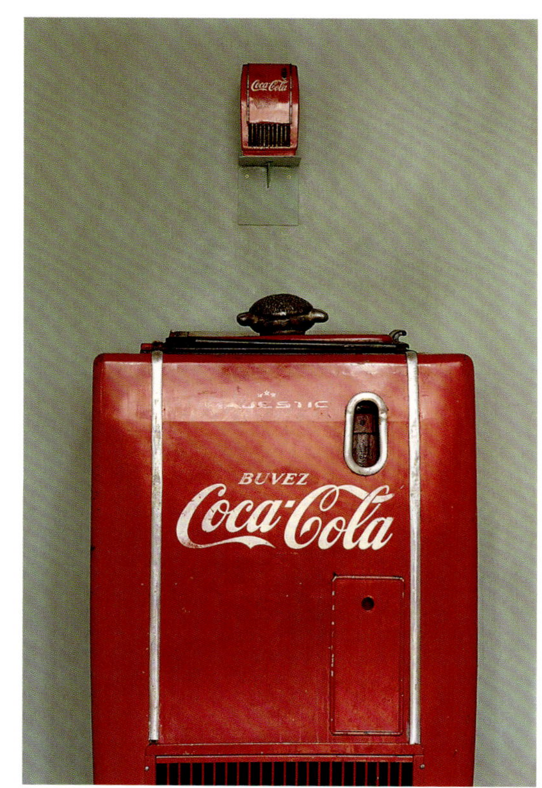

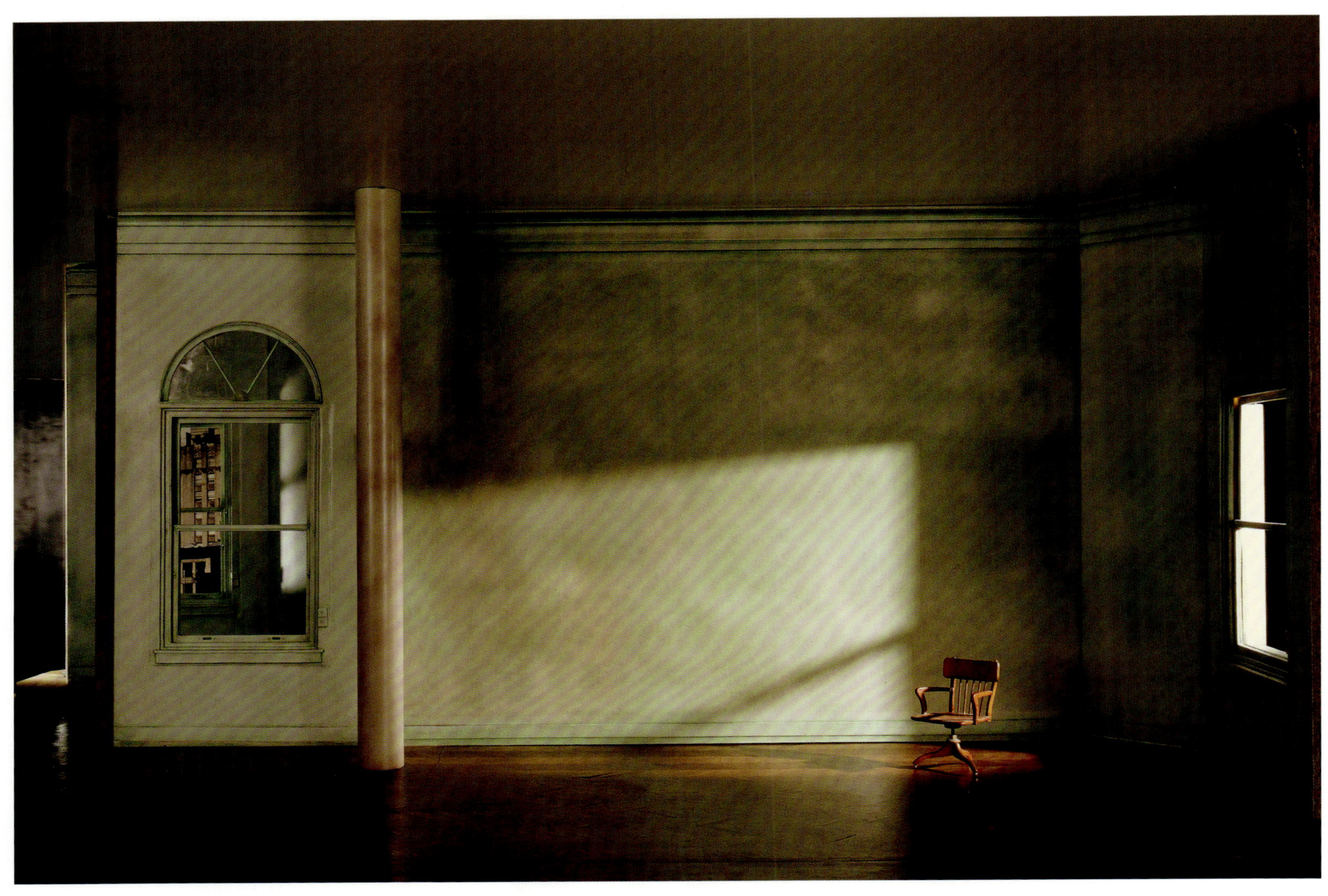

Homage to Edward Hopper I, 1990.
Mixed media, 28 ¼ × 41 ¾ × 24 ½ in. (72 × 106 × 62 cm).

For me, painting is being present at my absence. I was gazing at this New York window that opened, not to the outside, but onto another room in the same locale. The tenant could lean out into his own private world, looking down into the distracted inconsequential intimacy that floats there like a distant memory of himself. He could be there, in the unutterable awareness of his own absence.

Personal note, May 4, 2000

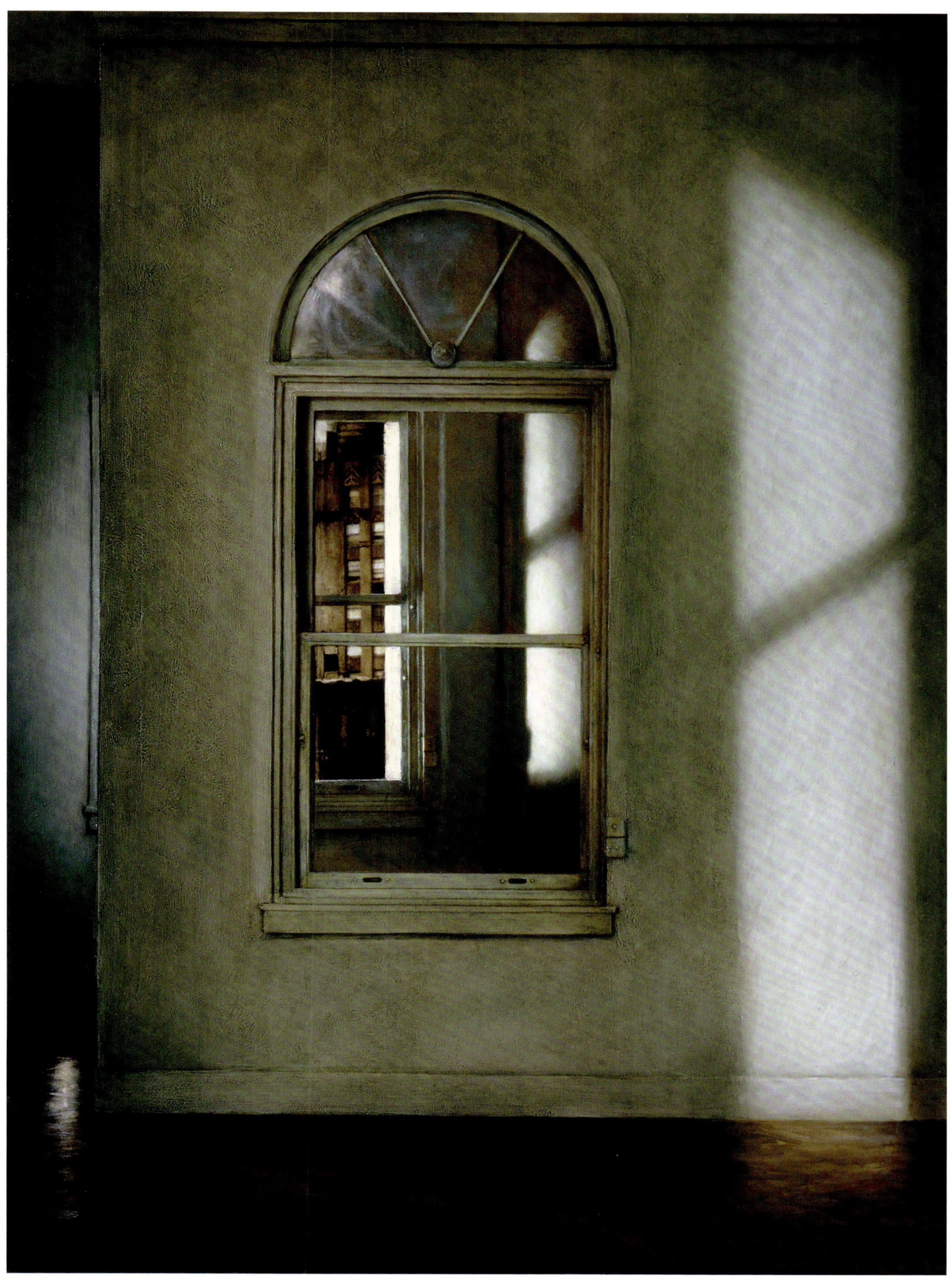

Window Backing on to an Interior, 1990.
Oil on Cibachrome,
33 × 27 ½ in.
(84 × 70 cm).

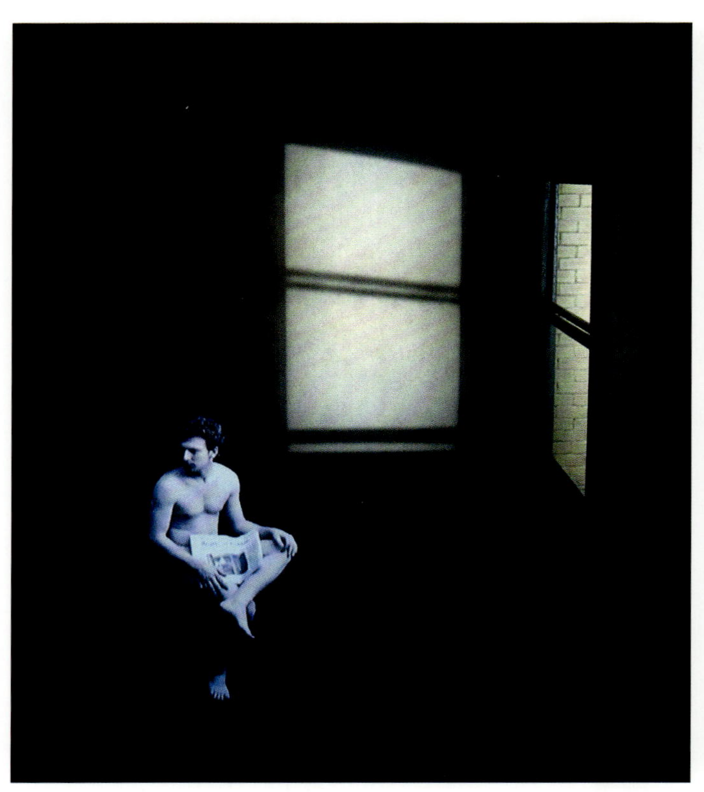

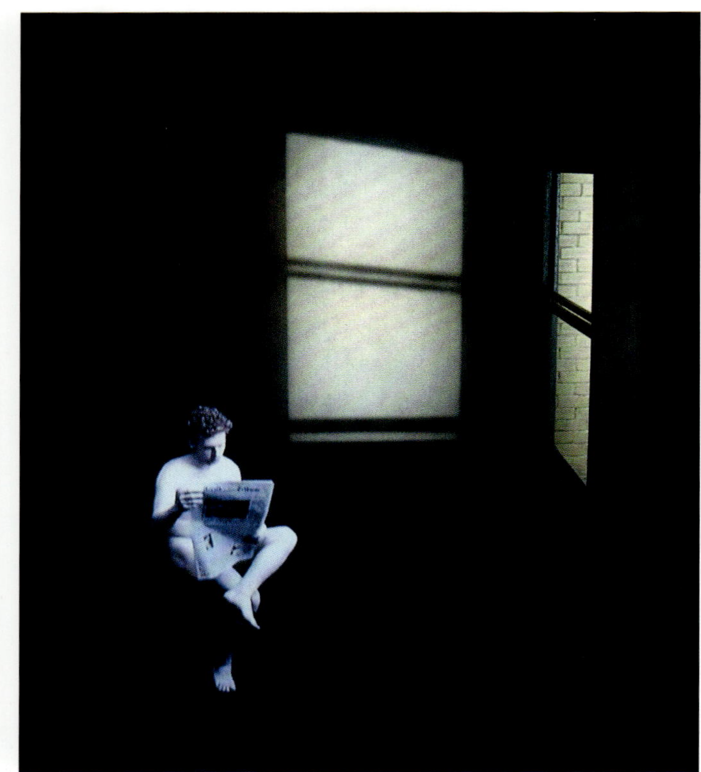

Léonard in New York, 2000.
Mixed media and video, 31 ½ × 30 ¾ × 36 ¼ in. (80 × 78 × 92 cm).

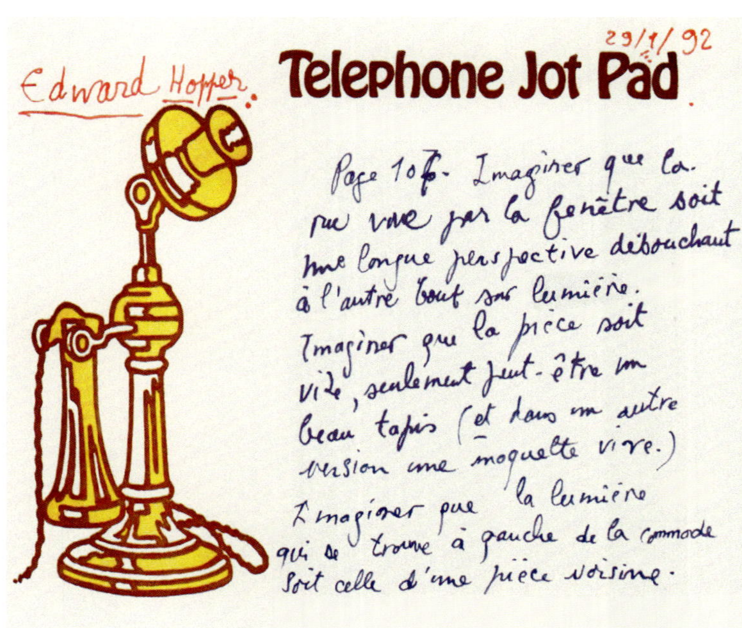

Edward Hopper

Telephone Jot Pad

29/1/92

Page 107 - Imaginer que la rue vue par la fenêtre soit une longue perspective débouchant à l'autre bout sur lumière.
Imaginer que la pièce soit vide, seulement peut-être un beau tapis (et dans un autre version une moquette vive.)
Imaginer que la lumière qui se trouve à gauche de la commode soit celle d'une pièce voisine.

Personal note on a Telephone Jot Pad (*Edward Hopper*). January 29, 1992.

"Page 107. Imagine that the street seen through the window forms a long perspective emerging into the light at the other end. Imagine that the room is empty, perhaps only with a beautiful carpet (and in another version a brightly colored, fitted carpet.) Imagine that the light to the left of the chest of drawers comes from a neighboring room."

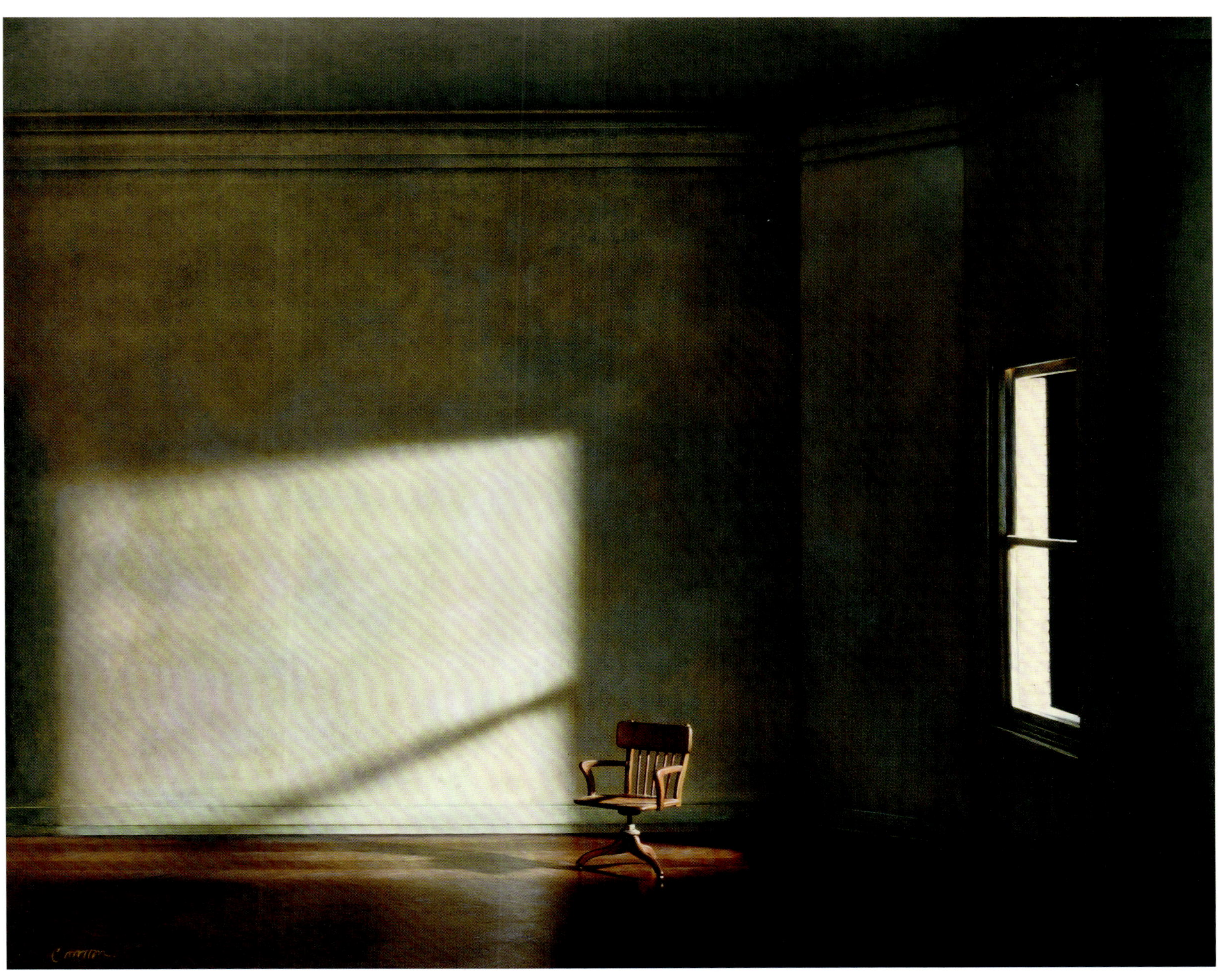

Homage to Edward Hopper I, 1990.
Oil on Cibachrome, 16 × 22 in. (41 × 56 cm).

The white wall and just the window. The angst of the sun.

Imagine a window, a lamp, the light, and almost straight in front, opening onto the blackness with almost nothing, perhaps just the imperceptible presence of a tree, a large window. Here, in the painting of Edward Hopper, it's the black that interests me.

To make color and light come to life.

Some opulent yellow curtains.

Cut out the storytelling, but make the "shininess" of the table more sensual.

Is the beauty of everything a truth that we don't see most of the time, or is it a truth we invent?

Why does a thing become beautiful when it becomes real and true for the person thinking of it?

The whole question is does wisdom invent or does it discover?

Personal note on a Telephone Jot Pad. January 29, 1992

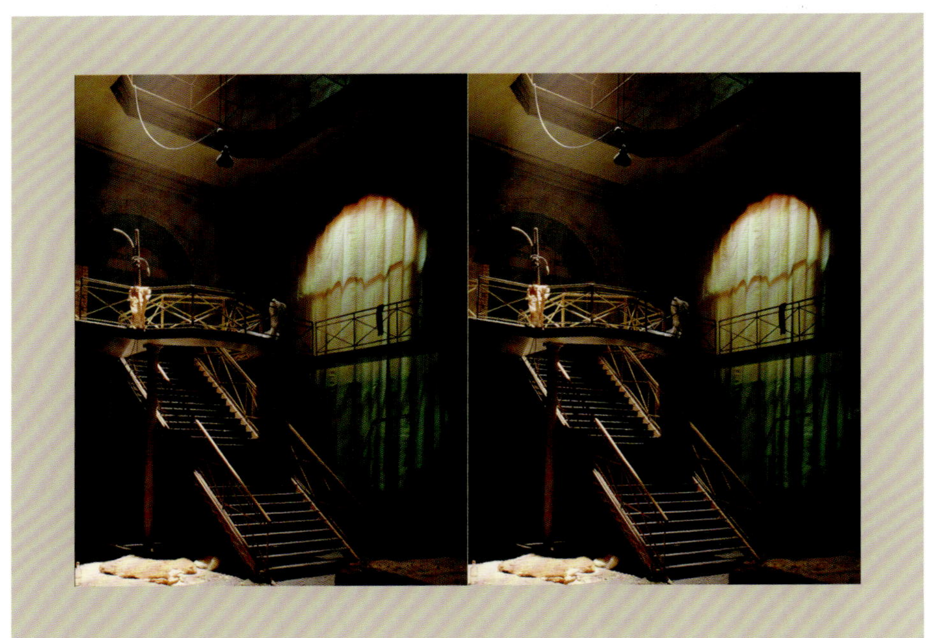

The Loft with the Great Staircase, N.Y.C. (detail 1), 1989.
Photograph.

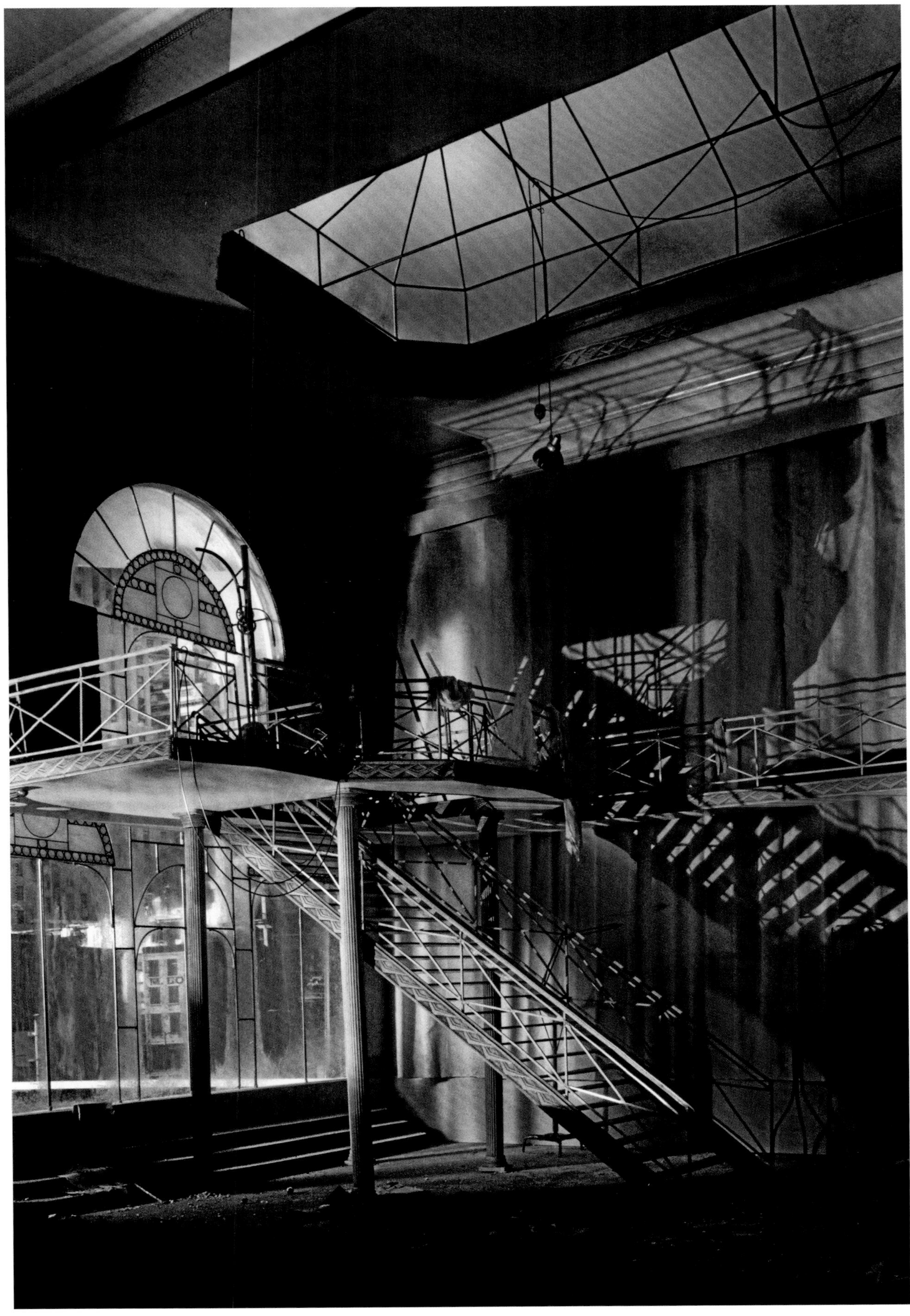

The Loft with the Great Staircase, N.Y.C. (detail 2), 1989.
Photograph.

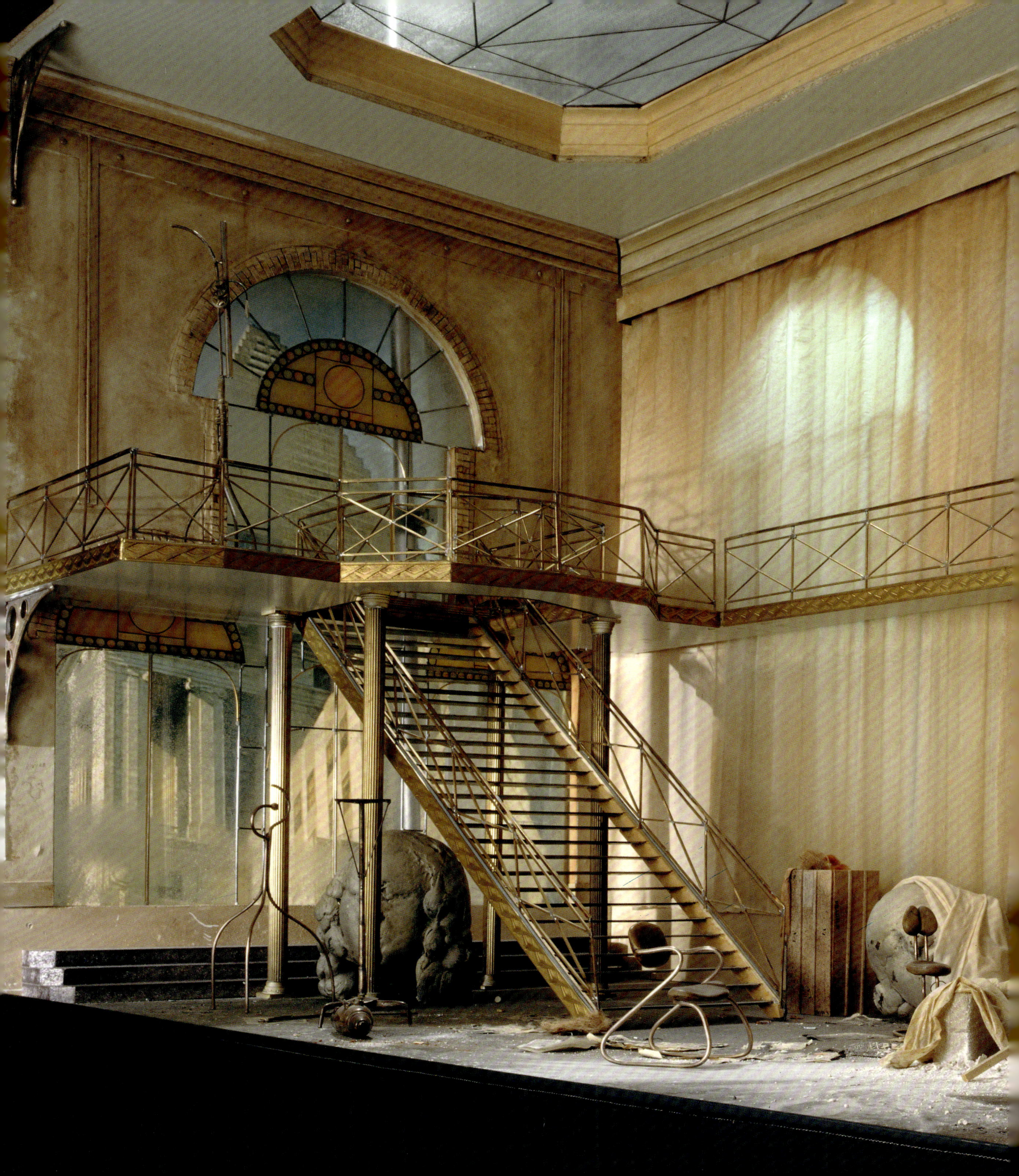

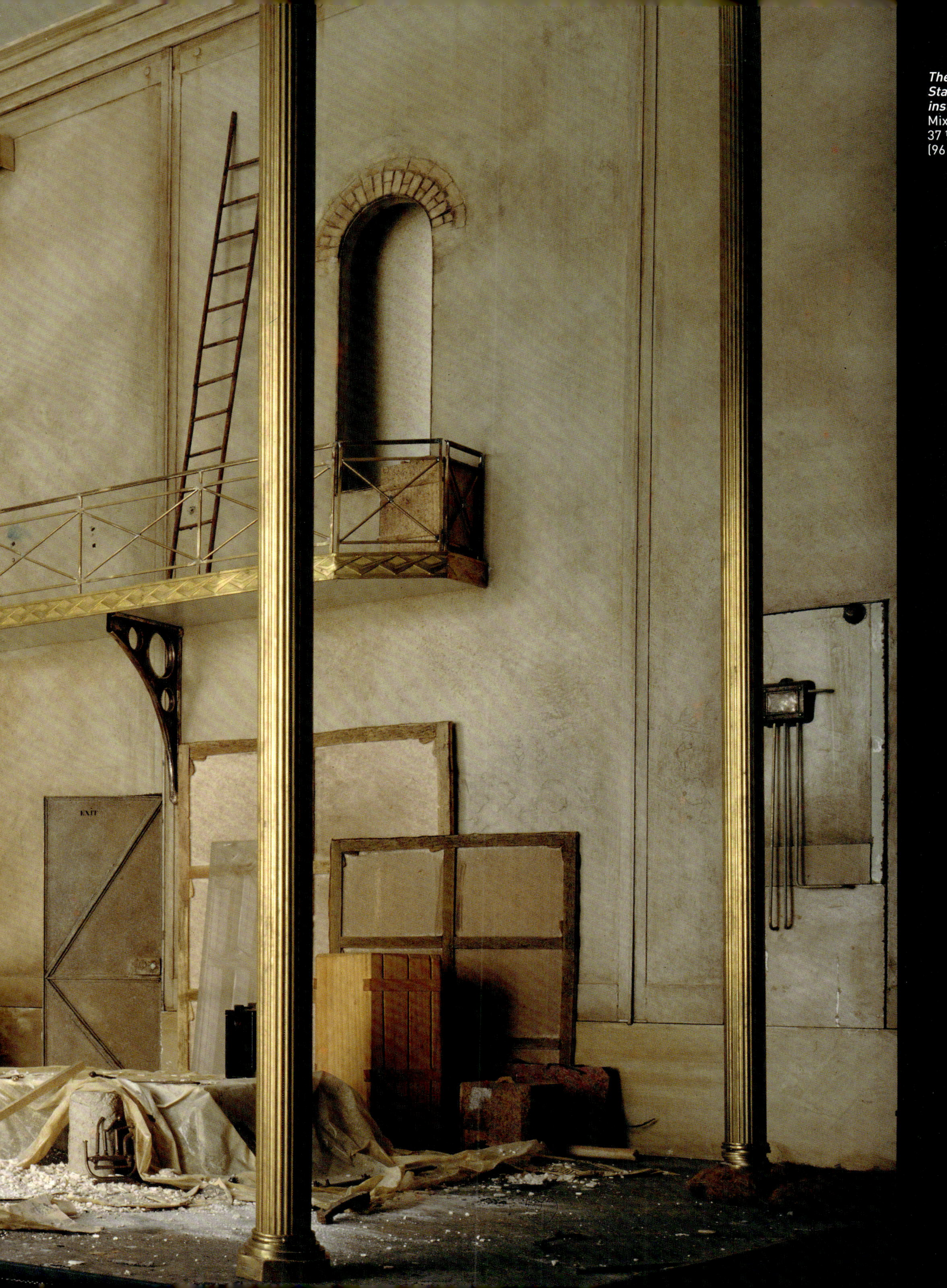

The Loft with the Great Staircase, N.Y.C., installation no. 1, 1988.
Mixed media,
37 ½ × 64 ½ × 30 ¼ in.
(96 × 164 × 77 cm).

Au commencement le propos était de prendre un maximum de décisions plastiques sur la réalité même, une réalité miniaturisée à cet effet.

Le but était de créer plus librement des images picturales (très descriptives) grâce à l'entière liberté de manipulation des lieux reconstitués. A ce moment-là l'objectif était exclusivement la peinture, l'image peinte.

Aujourd'hui il m'arrive d'envisager les reconstitutions de lieux comme des fins en soi, sorte de sculptures polychrômes, synthèses de lieux entrevus ou représentations aussi peu imaginatives que possible d'endroits existant.

Par exemple ce coin d'atelier d'après une photographie parue dans:
« L'atelier d'Alberto Giacometti »
Jean Genet.

At the beginning, the idea was to take the maximum number of visual decisions on reality itself, on a reality miniaturized for the purpose.
The goal was to create (highly descriptive) pictorial images more freely by handling the reconstructed sites utterly without restraint. At that time, the objective was exclusively the painting, the painted image.
Today, I sometimes catch myself thinking of these site reconstitutions as ends in themselves, something like polychrome sculptures, syntheses of places barely seen, or representations, as unimaginative as possible, of actual locations.
For example, this corner of the workshop after a photograph that appeared in The Studio of Alberto Giacometti *by Jean Genet.*

Extract from the catalog to the exhibition *Antipodes*, 1987.

Alberto Giacometti's Studio with the Artist's Hand, 1986.
Photograph.

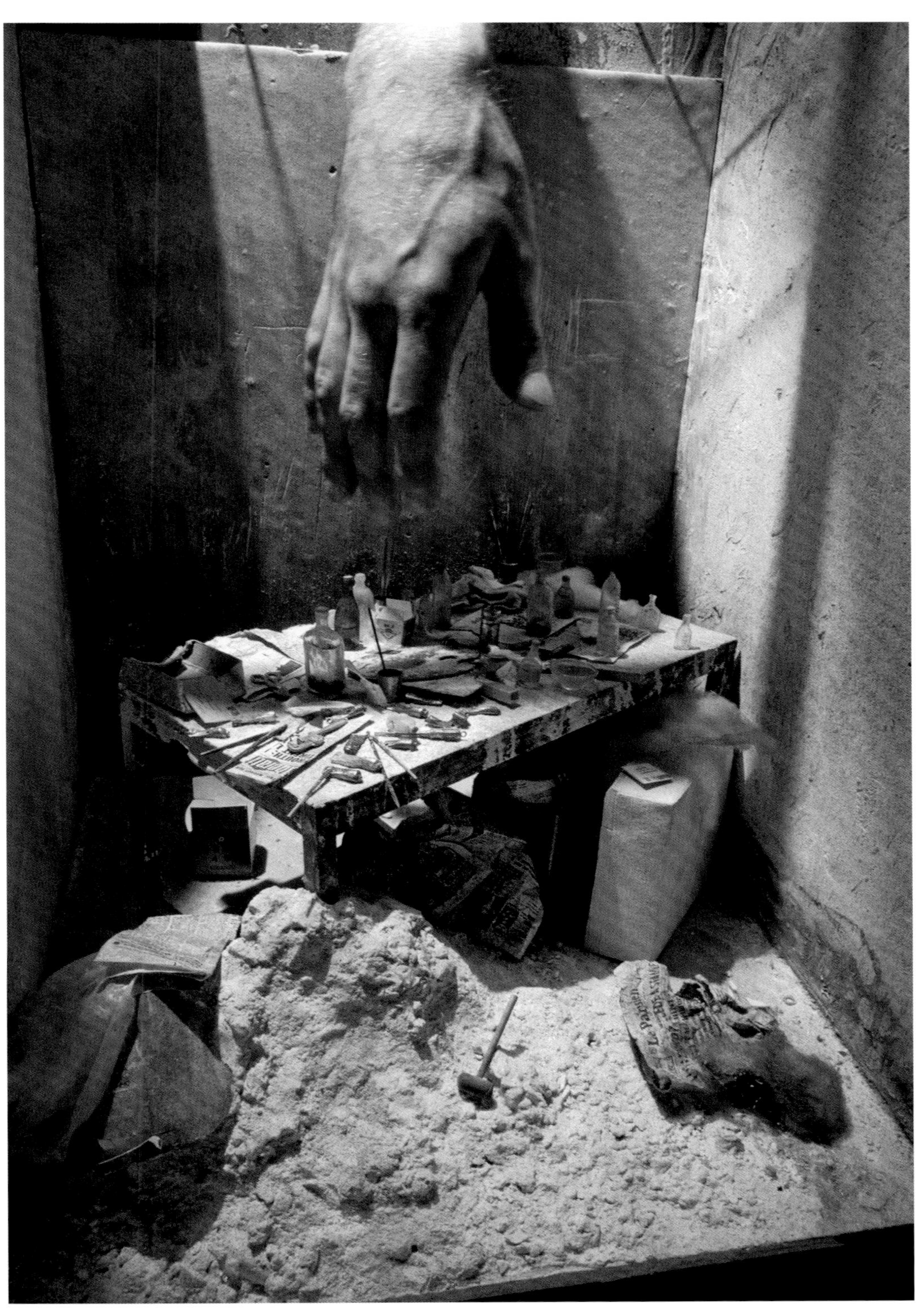

I'm thinking of the wonderful last lines of *L'Atelier d'Alberto Giacometti*, where Jean Genet lets the object speak for itself: "I'm alone, the object seems to say, and therefore caught up in a necessity against which there is nothing you can do. If I am only what I am, I am indestructible. Being what I am, without restraint, my loneliness is aware of yours."
Art, for me, lies in rejecting this loneliness.

C. Matton, *Charles Matton* (Paris: Éditions Hatier, 1991)

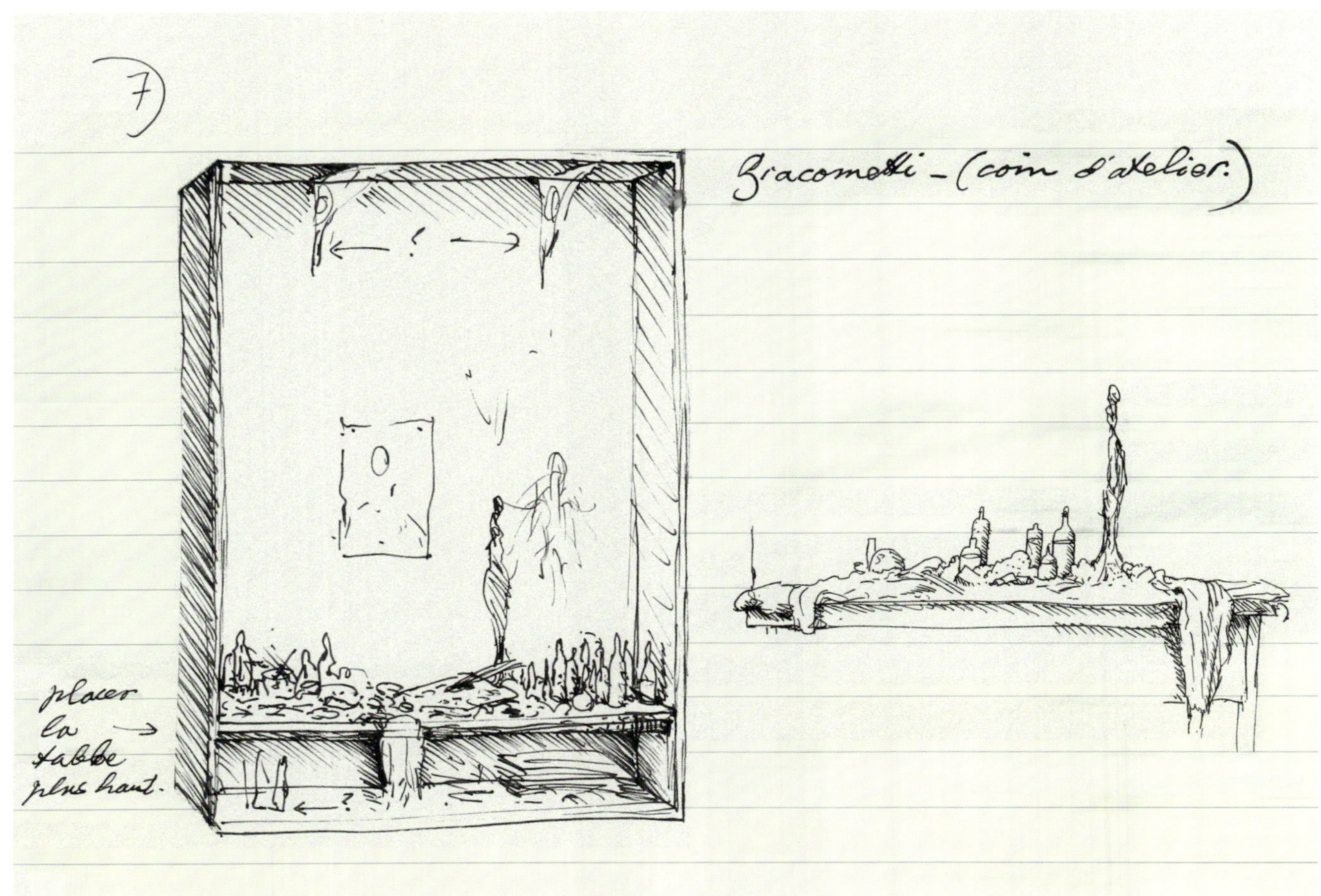
7)
Giacometti - (coin d'atelier.)
placer la table plus haut.

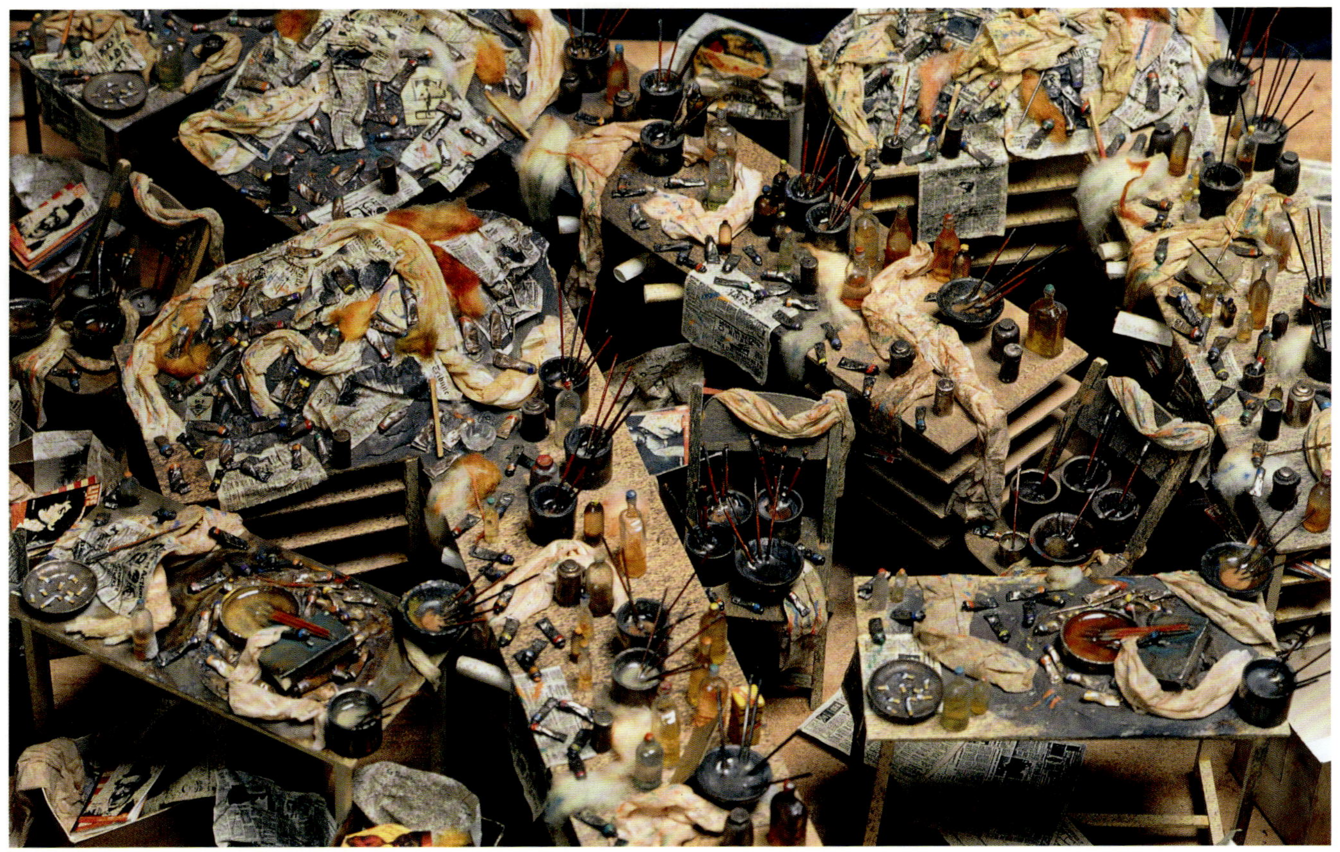

Alberto Giacometti's Studio, 1987.
Mixed media,
19 × 14 ¼ × 13 ½ in.
(48 × 36 × 34 cm).

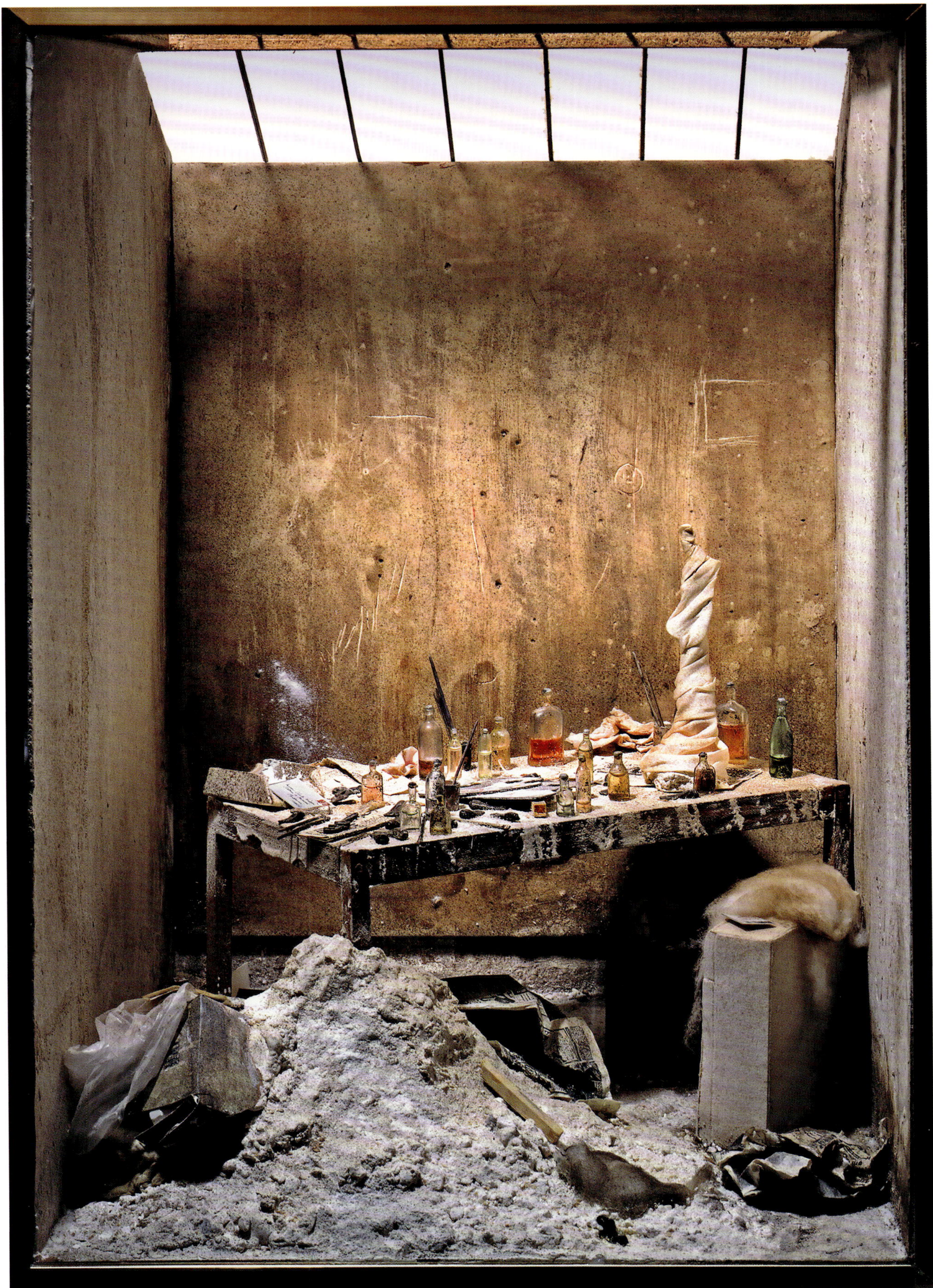

Facing page:
Giacometti (studio corner), 1999.
Felt pen on paper.

Studio Table at Le Coudray-Montceaux, 1987.
Photograph.

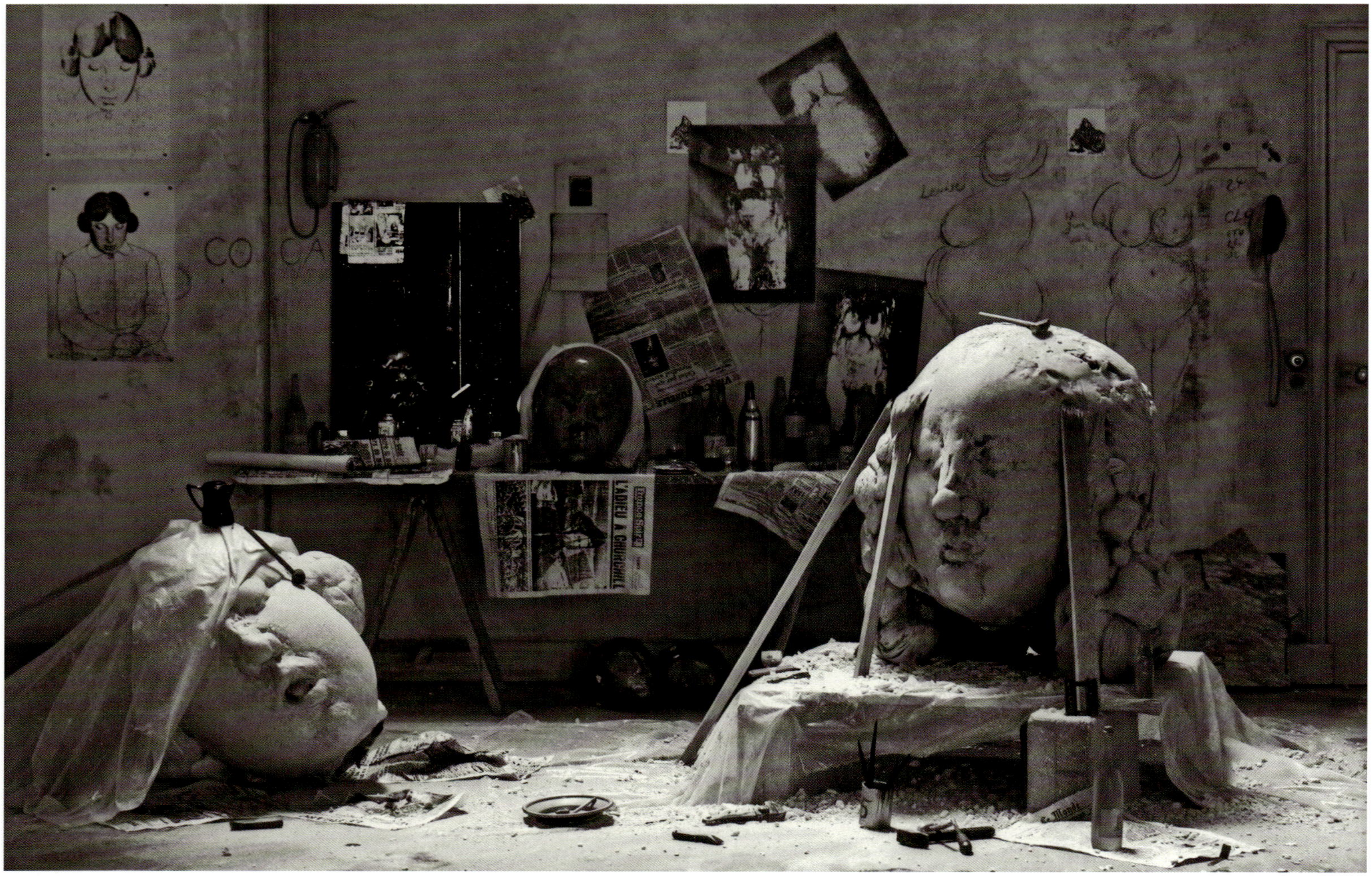

Sculpture Studio with Three Large-scale Portraits of my Sister Christiane I (detail), 1986.
Photograph.

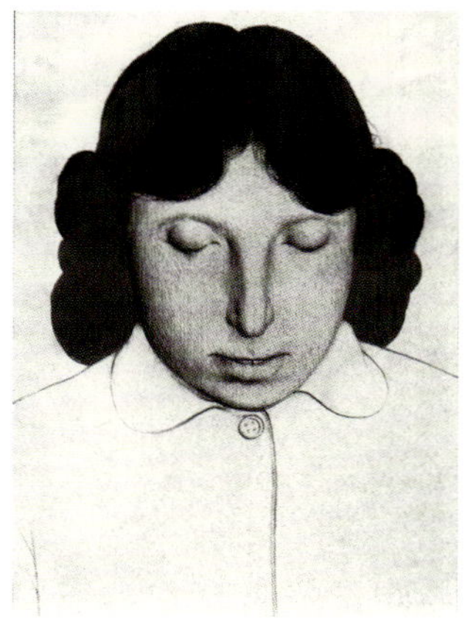

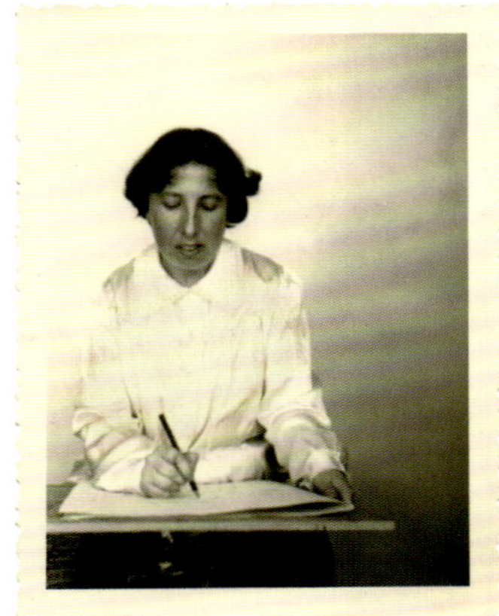

Quita at Prayer, 1957.
Pencil on paper,
8 ¼ × 6 in.
(21 × 15.5 cm).

Christiane Matton Drawing, 1959.
Photograph.

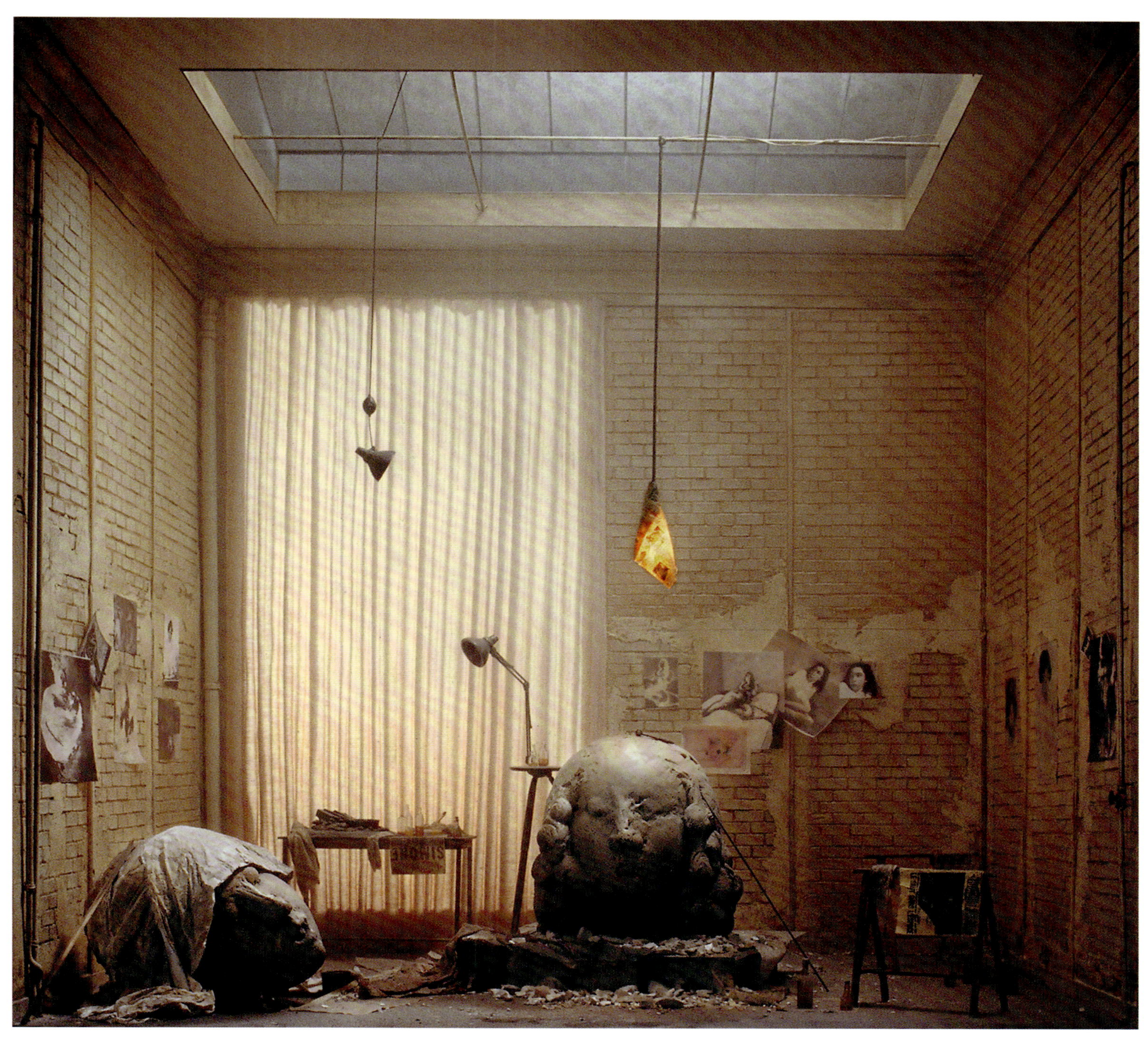

Sculpture Studio with Three Large-scale Portraits of my Sister Christiane III, 1993.
Mixed media, 28 ¾ × 31 × 23 in. (73 × 79 × 59 cm).

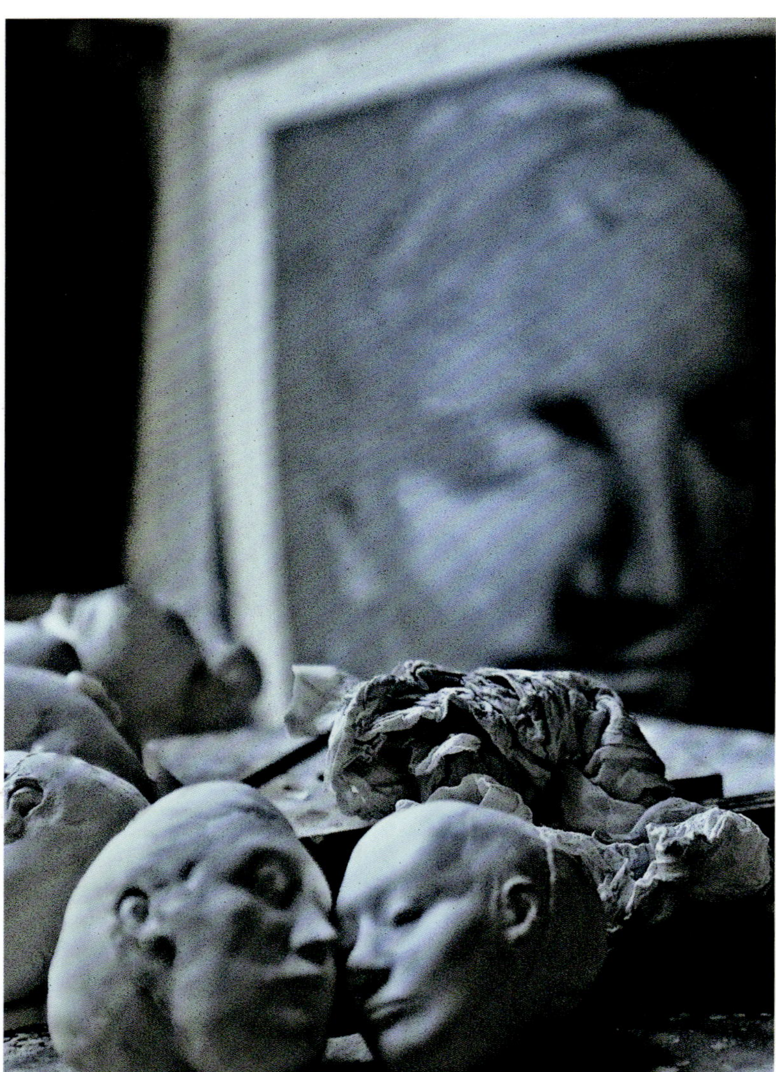

The Lovie-Dovies on the Studio Table, 2001.
Photograph.

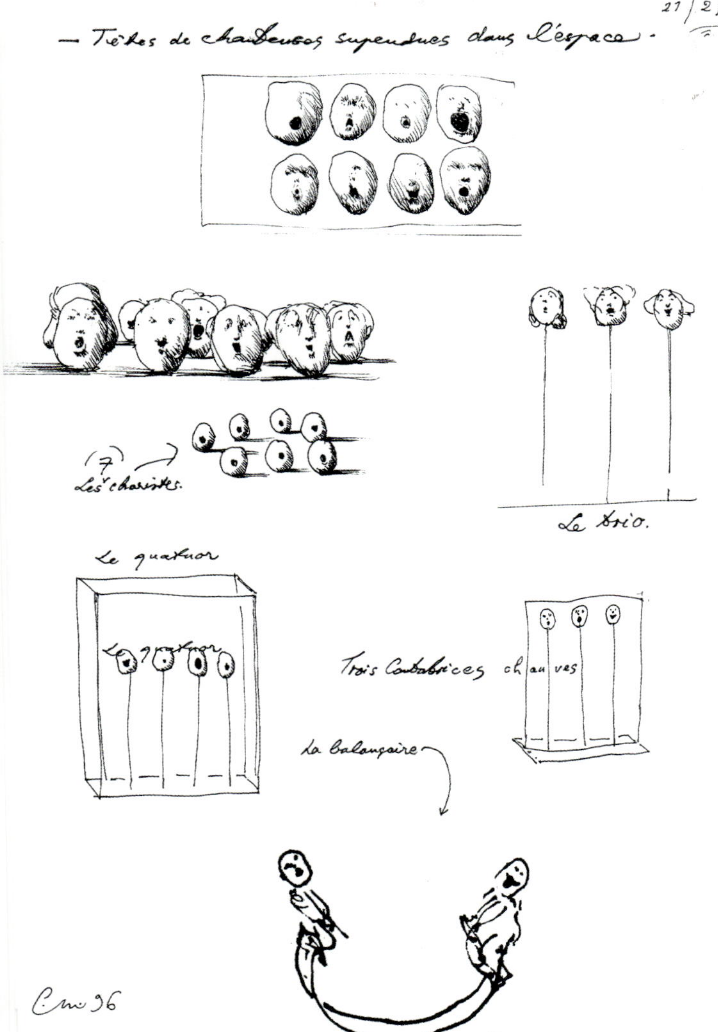

Heads of Female Singers Suspended in Space, 1996.
Felt pen on paper, 11 ¾ × 8 ¼ in. (29.7 × 21 cm).

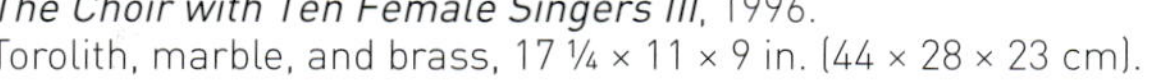

The Choir with Ten Female Singers III, 1996.
Torolith, marble, and brass, 17 ¼ × 11 × 9 in. (44 × 28 × 23 cm).

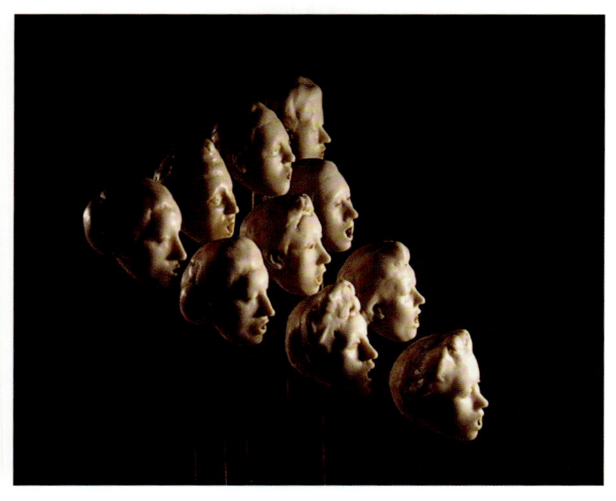

Giacometti was excluded from the surrealist group under the pretext that by carving a head he had reverted to figuration. André Breton exclaimed, "A head! As if we don't know what a head is." And Giacometti is reported to have answered, "Well, no, Mr. Breton, I for one still don't know what a head is."

Breton sought his mysteries in an "elsewhere," whereas for me the mystery lies here—it's very close, in the existence of a head. Appearances have always asked me a question of an almost schizophrenic nature and it's this mystery that for me remains the most pressing.

C. Matton, interview by Frédéric Taddéi, "*Regarde les hommes changer*," Europe 1, November 22, 2007. Radio program

The Choir with Thirty-six Female Singers I, 1997.
Torolith, marble, and brass,
24 × 15 ½ × 15 in.
(61 × 39 × 38 cm).

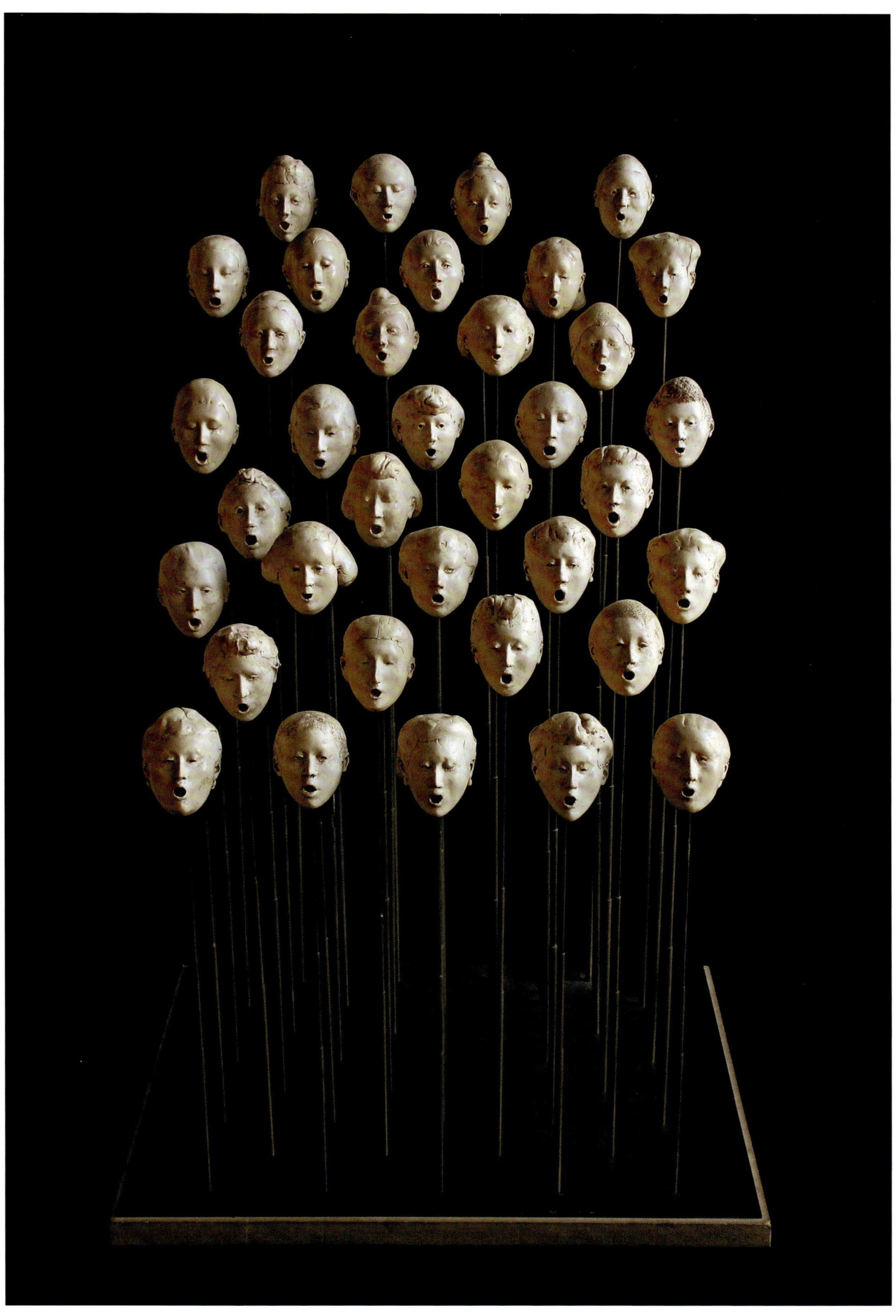

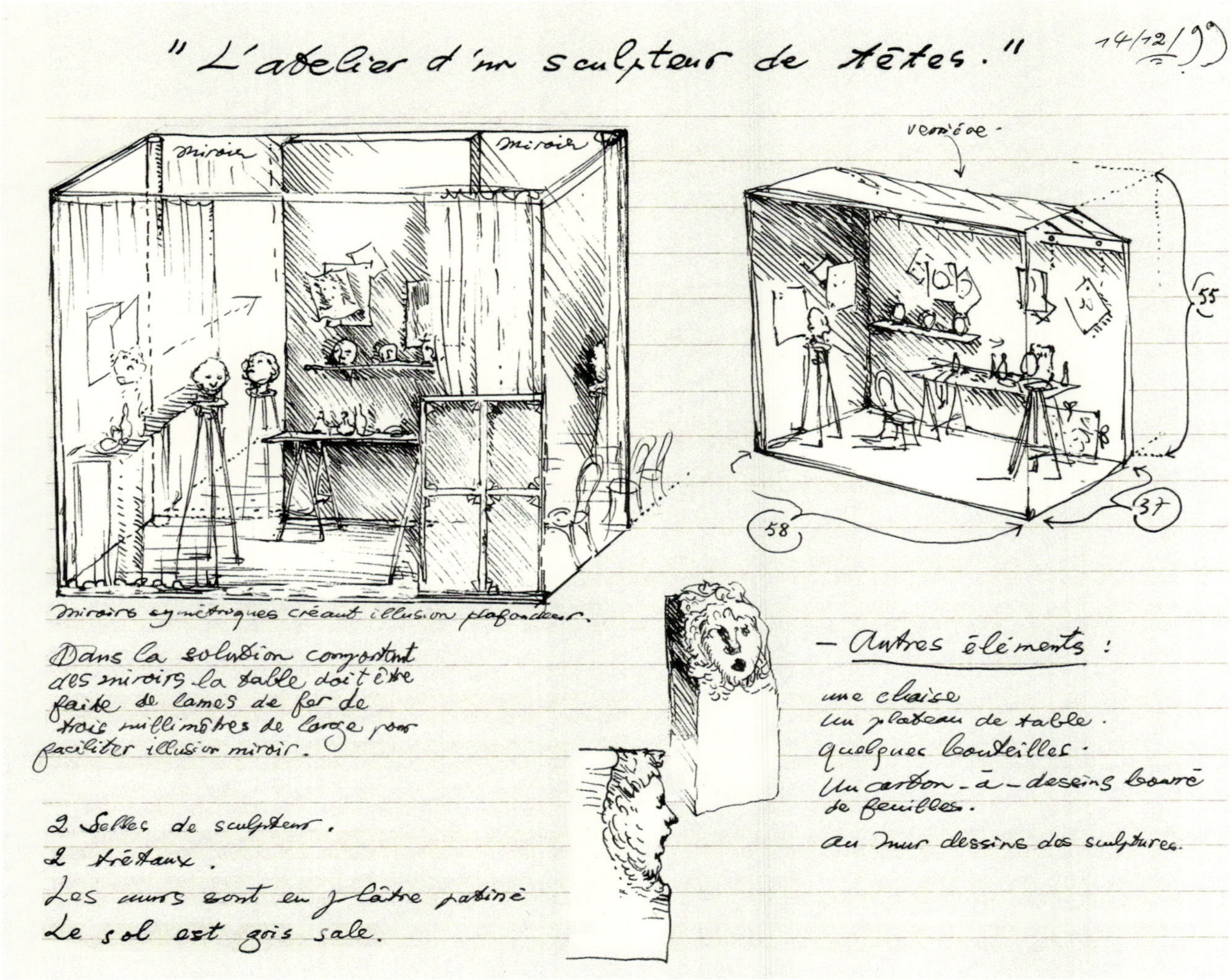

"L'atelier d'un sculpteur de têtes." 14/12/99

miroir — miroir — verrière — 55 — 37 — 58

Miroirs symétriques créant illusion profondeur.

Dans la solution comportant des miroirs la table doit être faite de lames de fer de trois millimètres de large pour faciliter illusion miroir.

2 Selles de sculpteur.
2 tréteaux.
Les murs sont en plâtre patiné
Le sol est gris sale.

— Autres éléments :
une chaise
un plateau de table.
quelques bouteilles.
Un carton-à-dessins bourré de feuilles.
au mur dessins des sculptures.

Studio of a Sculptor of Heads, 1999. Pencil on paper, 6 ½ × 8 ¼ in. (16.5 × 21 cm).

- glass canopy
- mirror
- symetrical mirrors creating an illusion of depth

In the solution with mirrors, the table must be made of metal blades three millimeters across to foster the mirror illusion.

- two sculptor's stands
- two trestles
- the walls are worn plaster
- the floor a dirty gray

Other elements:
- a chair
- a table-top
- some bottles
- a drawing portfolio stuffed with sheets of paper
- on the wall, drawings of the sculptures.

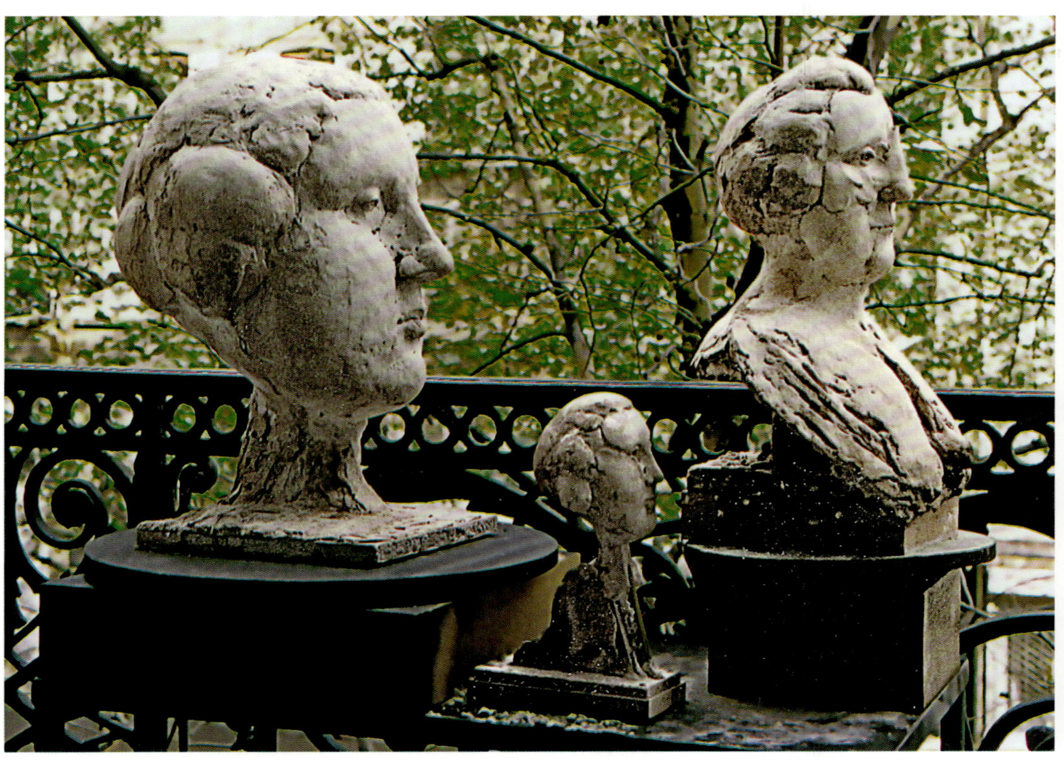

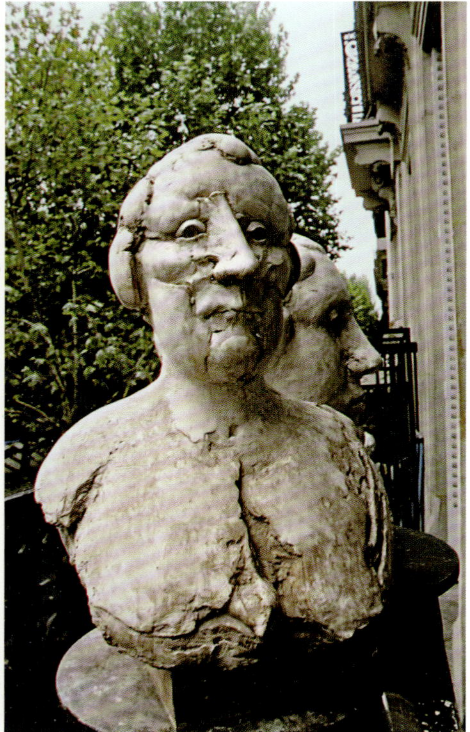

Head I, 1962.
Tin, 2 ½ × 2 ¼ × 3 in.
(6.5 × 5.5 × 7.5 cm).

Head IV, 1962.
Tin, 3 × 2 ¼ × 3 in.
(7.5 × 5.5 × 7.5 cm).

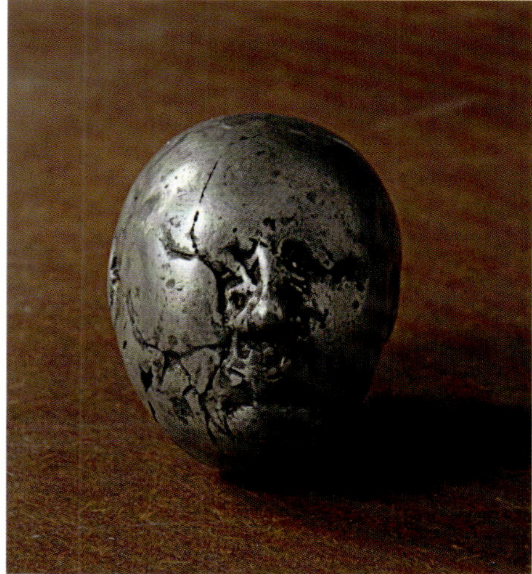

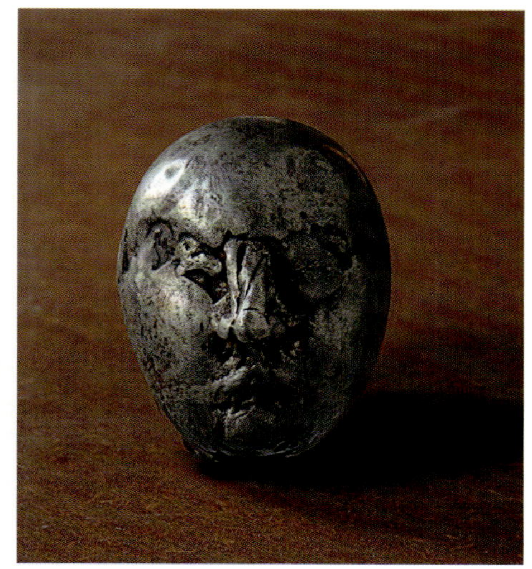

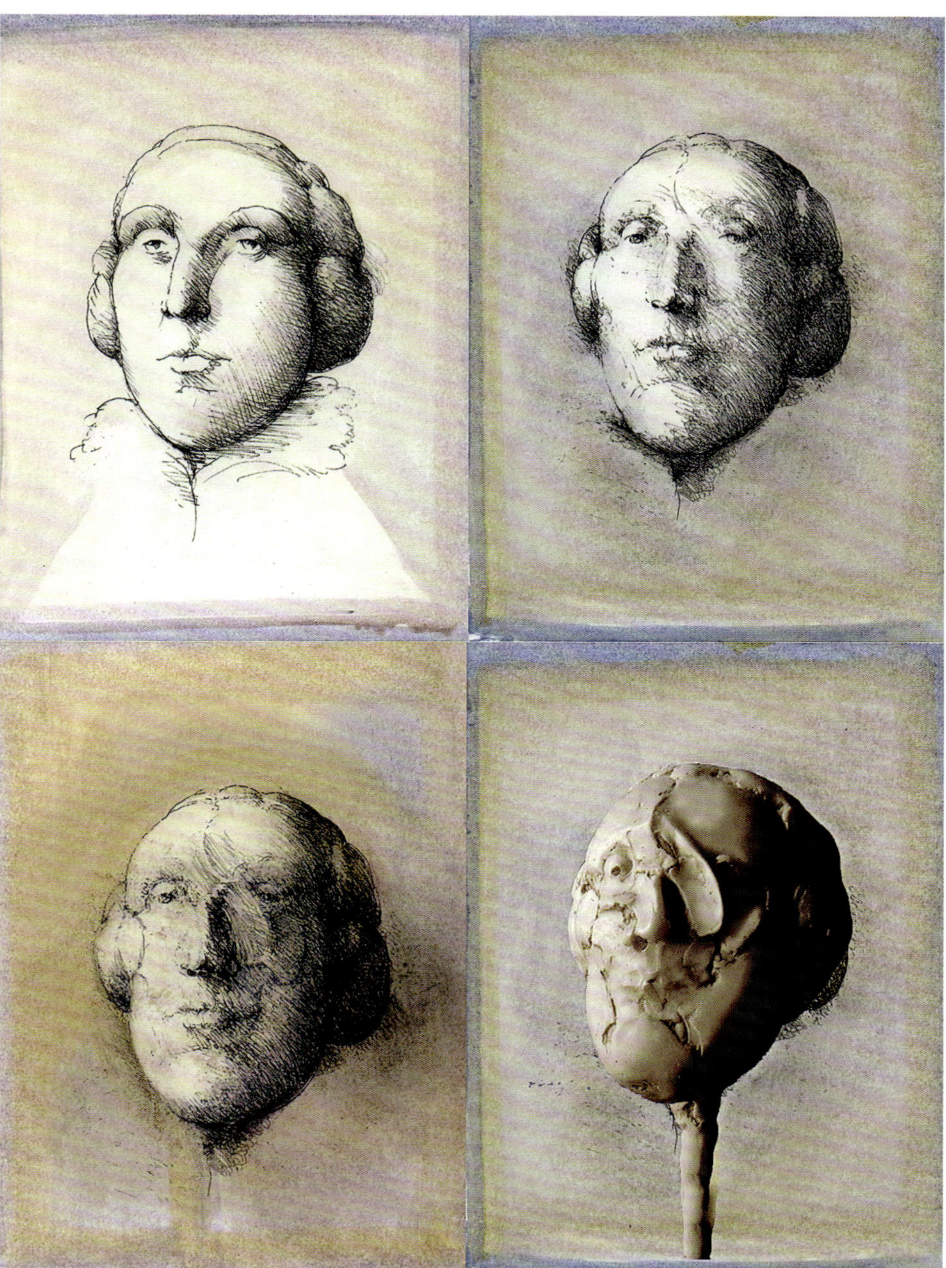

Four variations on *The Duchess*, 2003: Three drawings, 11 ¾ × 8 ¼ in. (29.7 × 21 cm) and one sculpture, 14 ½ × 8 ¼ × 5 ½ in. (37 × 21 × 14 cm).

Facing page:
On the balcony on the boulevard Saint-Germain. From left to right:

The Young Girl, 2003.
Torolith and marble,
22 × 11 × 12 ½ in.
(56 × 28 × 32 cm).

The Sphinx, 2003.
Torolith and marble,
9 × 4 ¼ × 4 ¼ in.
(23 × 11 × 11 cm).

Marie-Thérèse, 2003.
Torolith and marble,
17 ¾ × 11 ¾ × 11 in.
(45 × 30 × 28 cm).

Marie-Thérèse and *The Young Girl*, 2003.
Photograph.

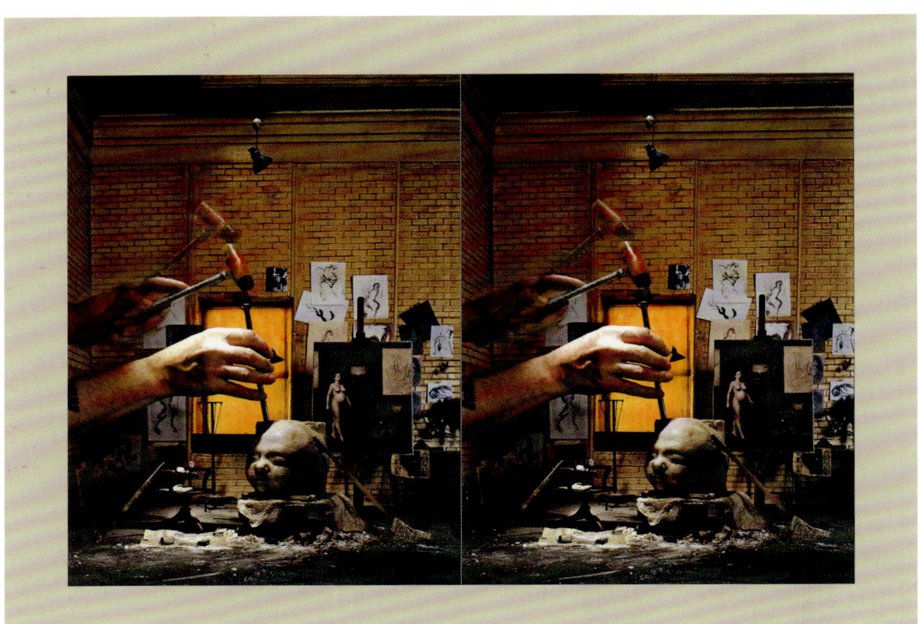

Studio of a Sculptor of Newborns, 1991.
Photograph.

In Giacomo Manzu's sculptures, the epidermis, the surface of the sculpture, is infused by intuition of what lies beneath. I'm not talking about the soul or some other literary, Freudian, or philosophical-mystic lucubration, I'm talking about the existence of a head in itself, I'm talking about its underlying mystery. When its weight, power, its yieldingness, moistness, breath, goodness!, its reality . . . are all translated into sculptural terms, when—as it apprehends the forceful presence of the skeleton, of the bone that stretches the skin, imprinting its swelling outline from within—the merest touch can make a lip or an eyelid shiver inwardly.

Personal note, March 24, 2000

Facing page:
Studio of a Sculptor of Newborns, 1990.
Mixed media, 22 ½ × 17 × 15 ¾ in. (57 × 45.5 × 40 cm).

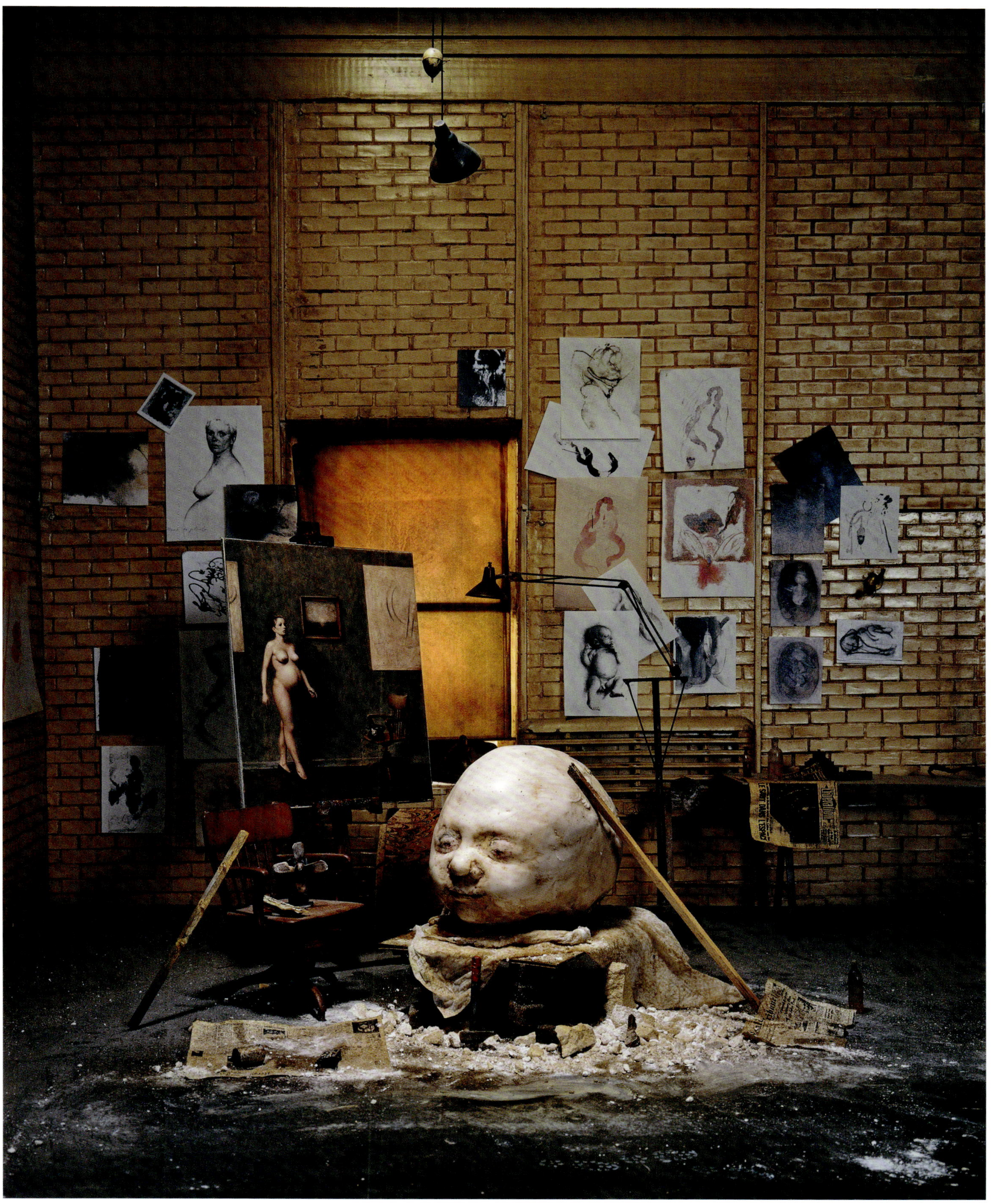

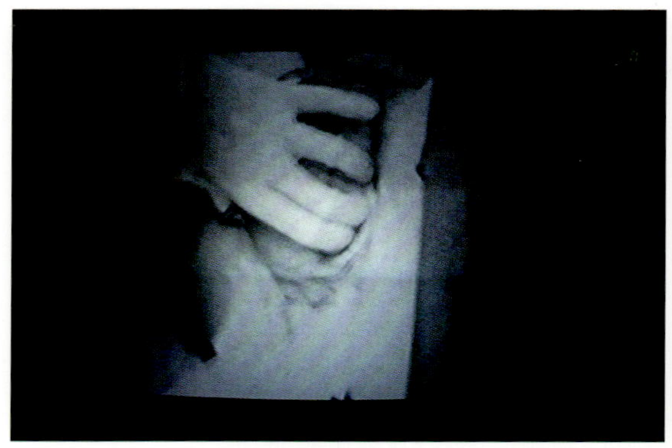

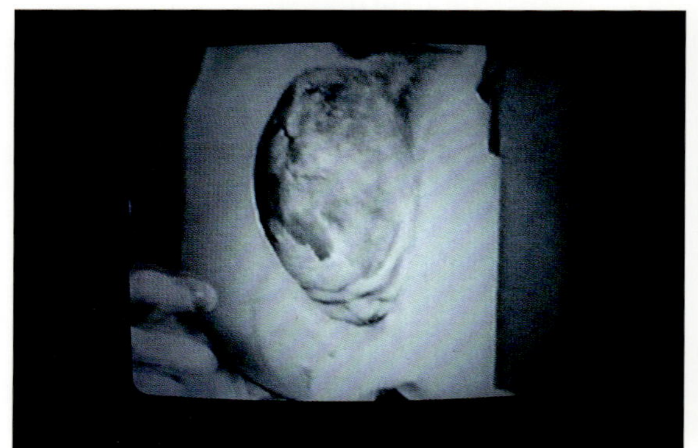

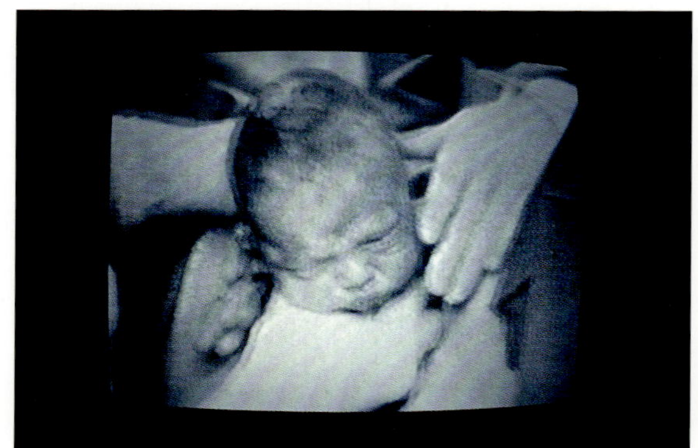

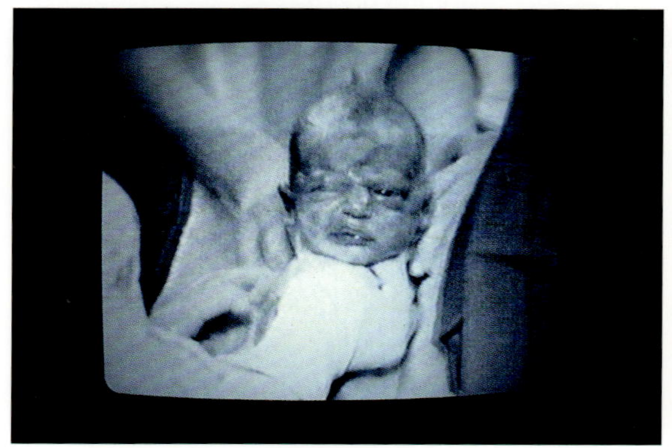

Four moments from Léonard's birth, filmed by Jean-Jacques Flori (stills), September 8, 1983.

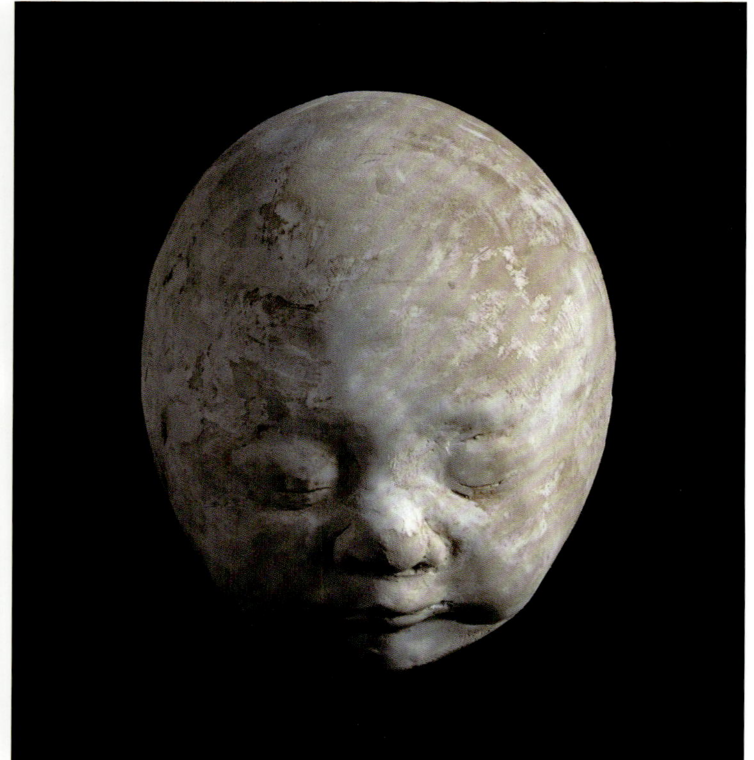

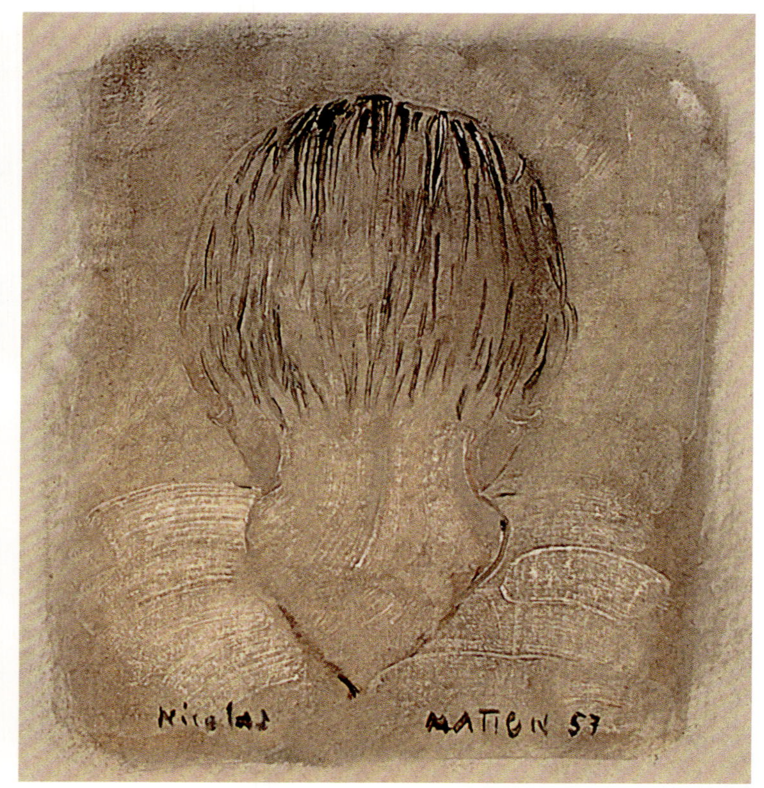

Head of a Newborn II, 1990.
Clay and modeling material, 4 ¾ × 4 × 5 in. (12 × 10 × 13 cm).

Nicolas, 1959.
Oil on canvas, 7 ½ × 6 ¼ in. (19 × 16 cm).

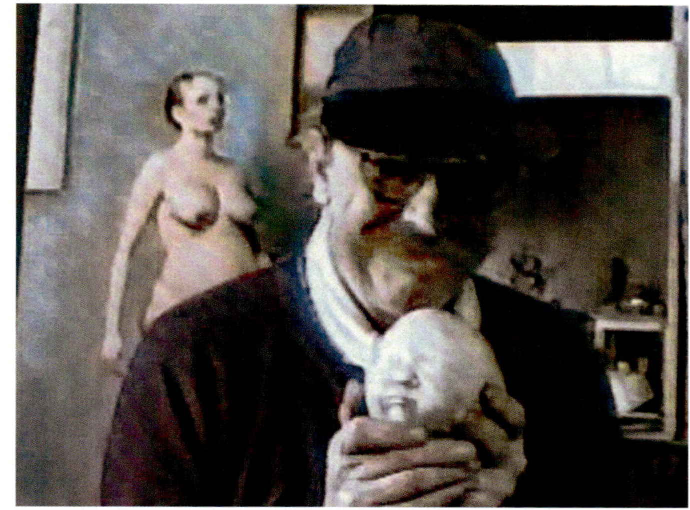

Titus, my son, I've always been so afraid for you. When you were a nursling, a little bean, and I carried you in my arms—I remember your head nestling in the hollow of my hand. It was as though I were gauging the exact weight of my tenderness, yes, that's it—as if I was carrying my love in my arms, all swaddled up.

C. Matton, *Rembrandt*, directed by Charles Matton, script Sylvie Matton (1998). Feature-length film

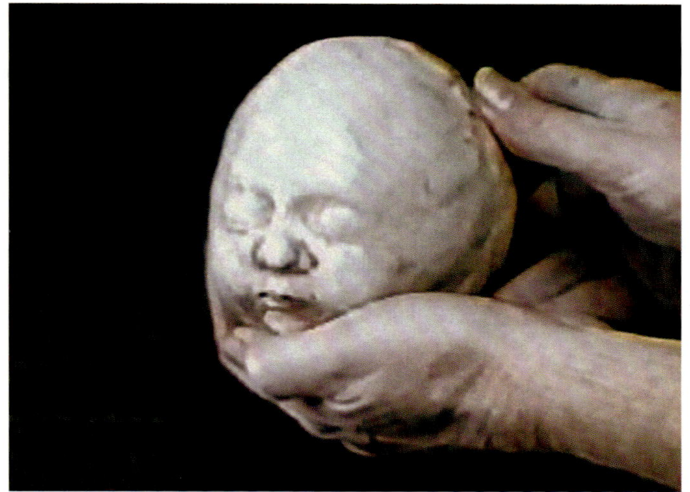

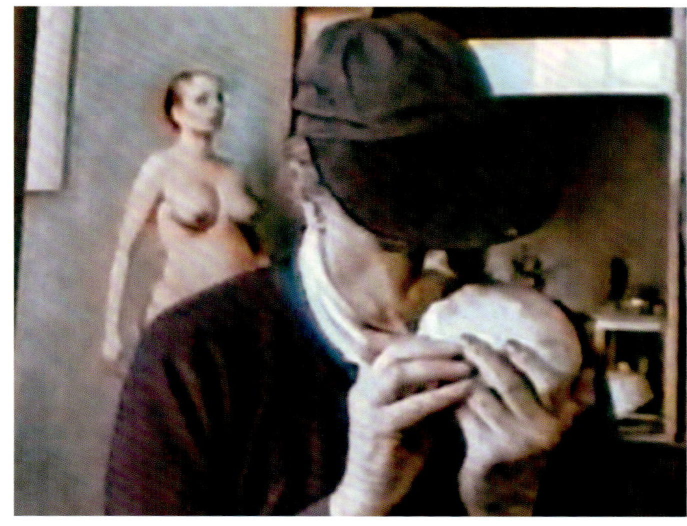

Charles Matton, visiblement (stills), documentary film, written and directed by Sylvie Matton (2009, Production Arte-Kuiv).

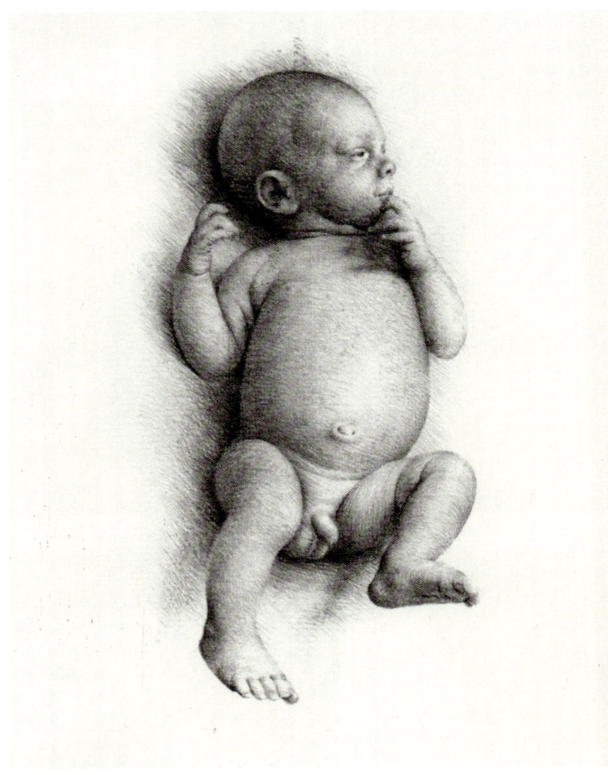

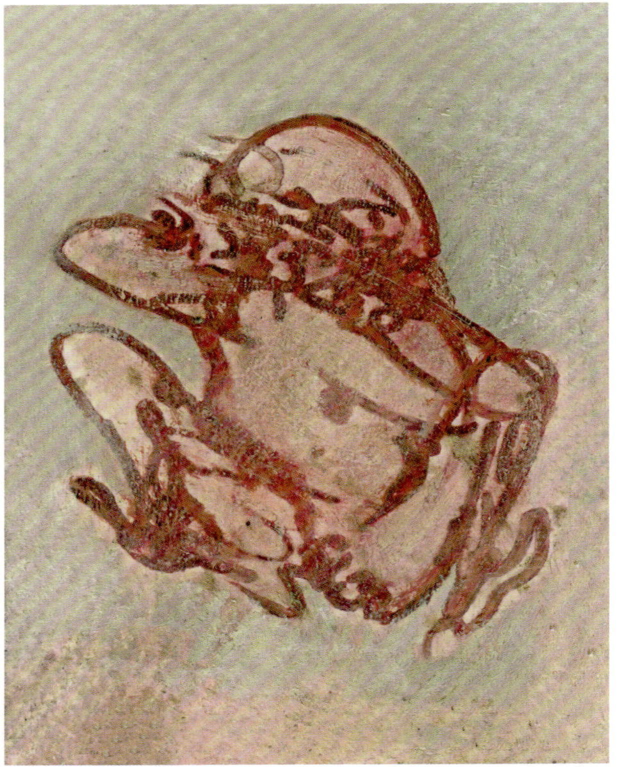

Léonard, 1983.
Pencil on paper,
11 ¾ × 8 ¼ in.
(29.7 × 21 cm).

Léonard, 1983.
Oil, ink, and watercolor
on paper, 6 ¾ × 4 ¾ in.
(17.5 × 12 cm).

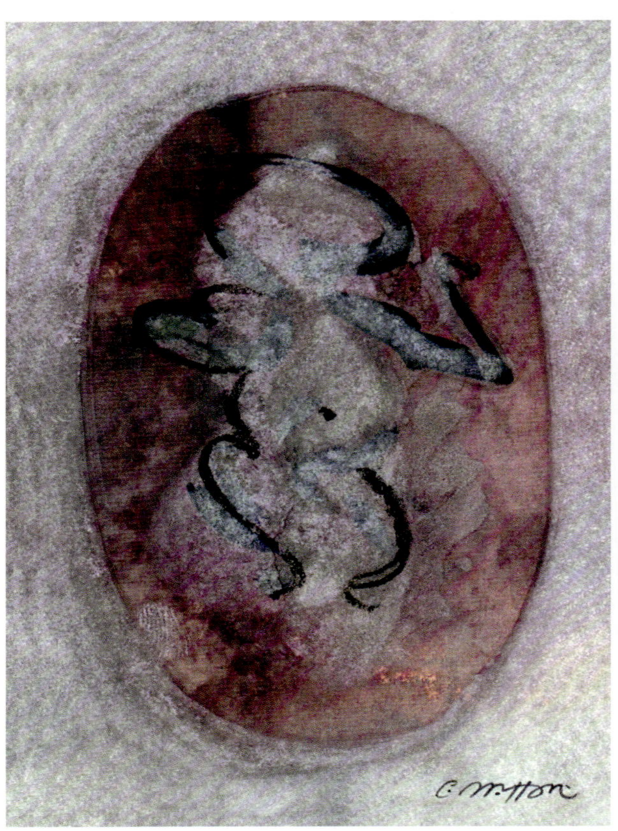

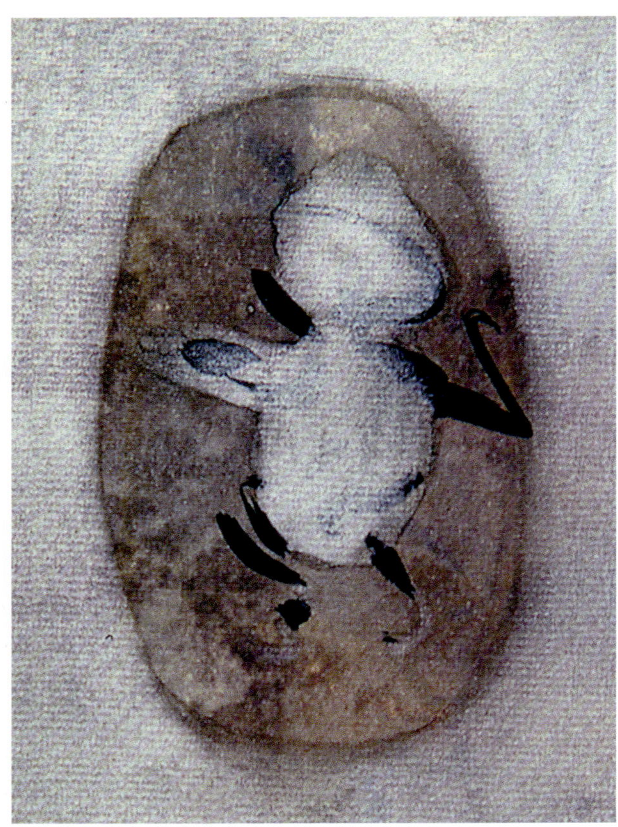

Newborn (Jules) III, 1988.
Watercolor on Ingres paper,
5 ½ × 4 in. (14 × 10 cm).

Newborn (Jules) I, 1988.
Watercolor on Ingres paper,
4 ½ × 3 ¼ in. (11.5 × 8.5 cm).

I love little babies. They're flesh in the pure state. Like life caught in the act of being.

C. Matton, *Charles Matton, visiblement*, op. cit.

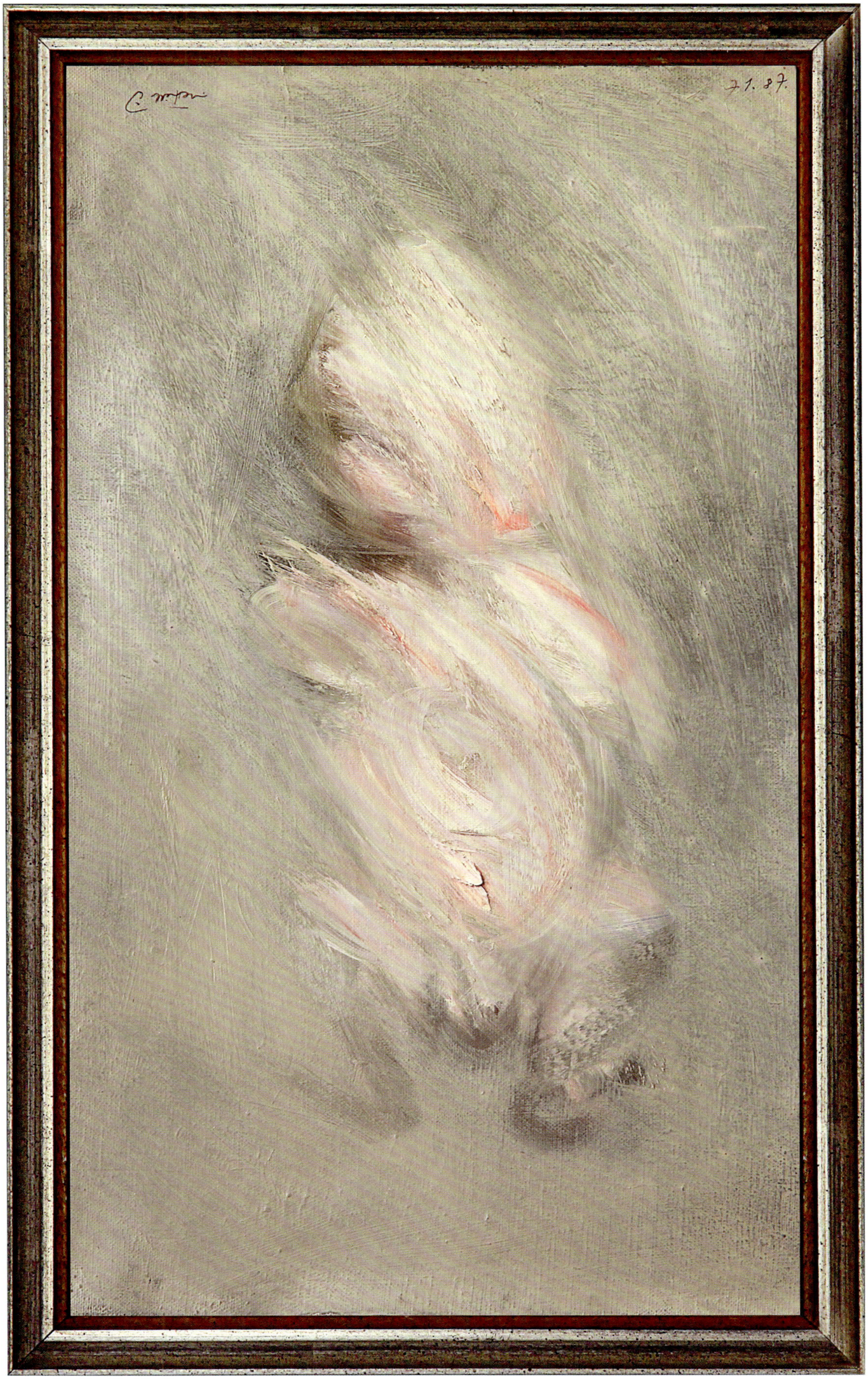

Newborn III, 1987.
Oil on canvas, 16 × 9 ½ in.
(41 × 24 cm).

I think that the word "creation" has always had two meanings. And I believe that both have their own profound significance and raison d'être.

For the first, creating means extracting from nothing, and this can lead to a wide range of undertakings that have in common a belief in innovation as a value in itself. Inventing, escaping, speculating, denunciating, seeking in exotic mysteries an "elsewhere," expressing the unique disorders of the creator's sacred navel, which is more sacrosanct the more unusual, unprecedented, incomparable it is.

The second sense implies, instead, subjecting the self to what appears, striving to conceive of it better—"to conceive" also encompassing the meaning of the verb, "to create." The aim then is to testify to what stands there or, more exactly, to what seems to be there, in order to generate, to produce reality. This meaning opens the door to those for whom an "elsewhere" is no temptation because for them the true mystery lies here below, everywhere: an apple, a body, a tree, a rag left about, a face, the memory of a young man playing the piano, the score he dropped on the carpet.

For these last, and I'm one of them, the most urgent mystery is there because, in the hierarchy of urgency, exploring the "beyond" or some parallel world, when we understand so little of what appears to be here, is putting the cart before the horse. This is what the word "creation" means to me. I see more gravity in it like that.

C. Matton, from the catalog for his one-man exhibition at the Galerie Beaubourg (by Pierre and Marianne Nahon), during the Foire Internationale d'Art Contemporain (FIAC) 2000

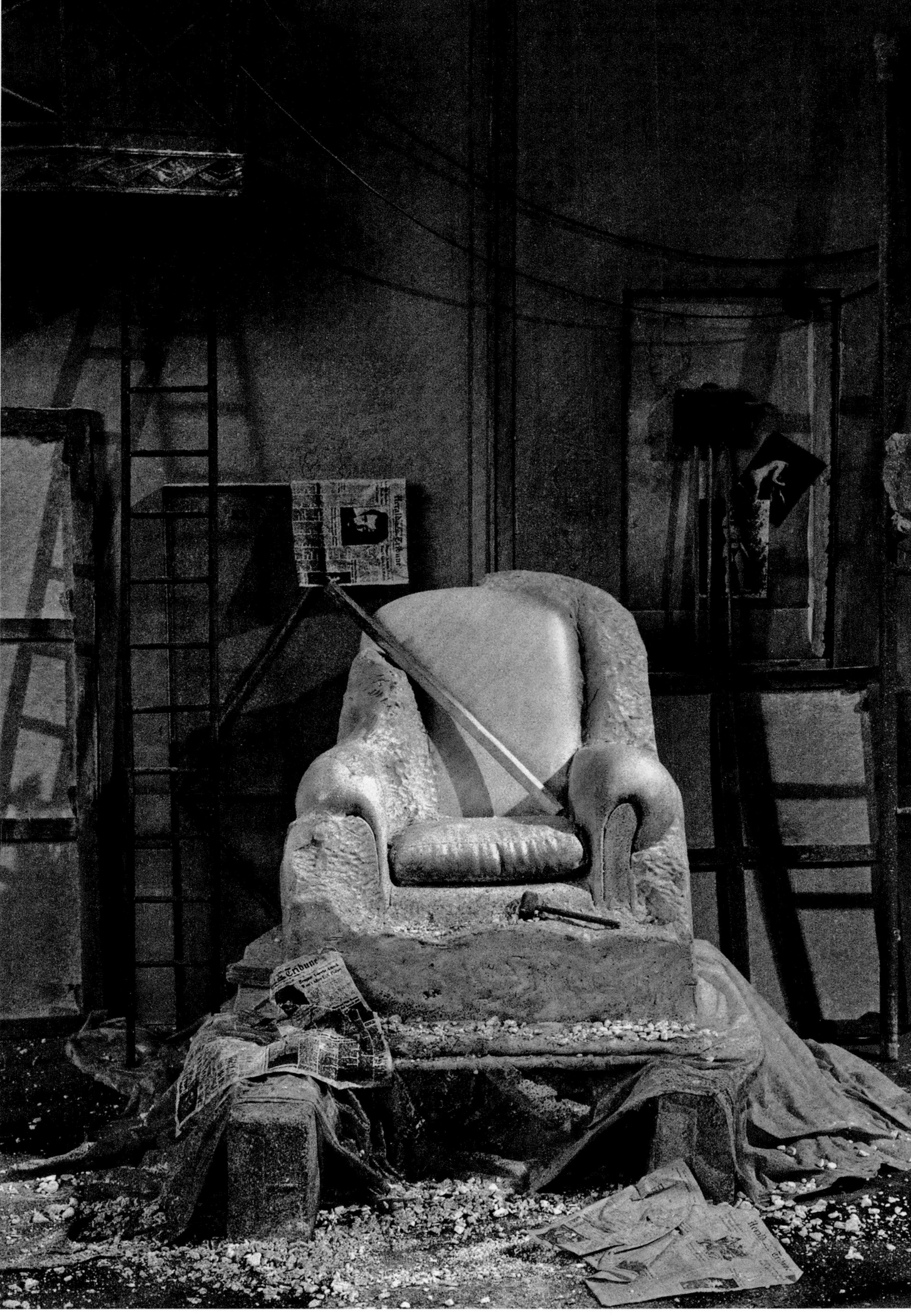

Easy Chair Becoming a Sculpture (set up I), 1989. Photograph.

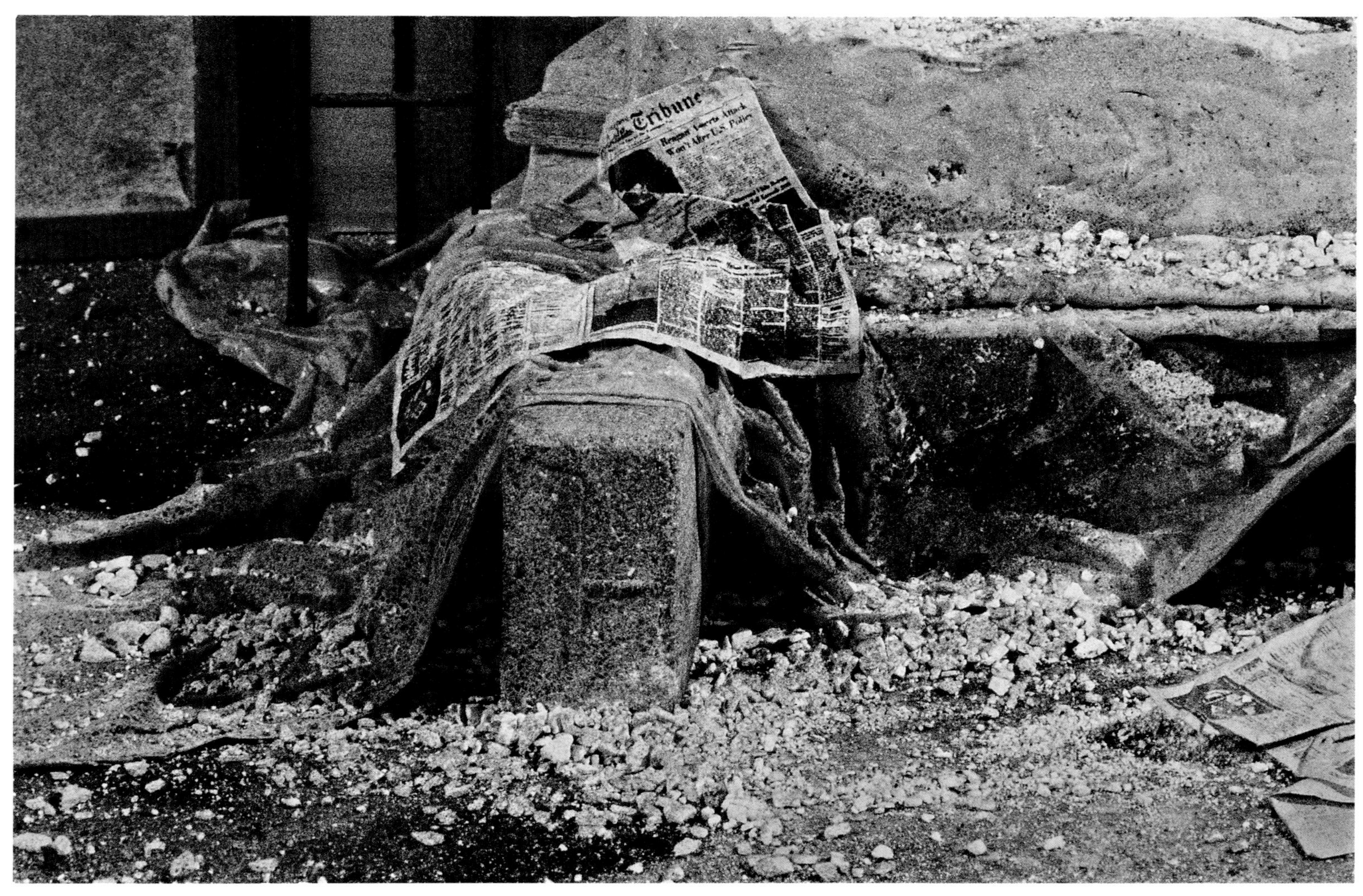

Easy Chair Becoming a Sculpture (set up I)
(detail), 1989.
Photograph.

Following double pages:
Studio of a Sculptor of Beds, 1989.
Mixed media, 28 ¼ × 66 × 27 ½ in.
(72 × 168 × 70 cm).

In "embracing" a different scale with the eye, one augments, one cultivates (the patient recaptures) a more intense level of consciousness.

To "embrace" can signify to "understand," and it can also mean to "hold." And nothing is "held" more surely than something that fits in one's hand. To understand everything I'm trying to say here, the mystery of appearances, that fundamental doubt, has to be an evidence.

I have always regaled in the tiniest detail—to love matter, to take delight in bringing to life the least little rag left about or a hotchpotch of familiar objects, to find the truth behind a smear, behind an oozing, that's what interests me.

C. Matton, comments made during an interview with Laurie Hurwitz, for an article in *Artnews* (June 2008)

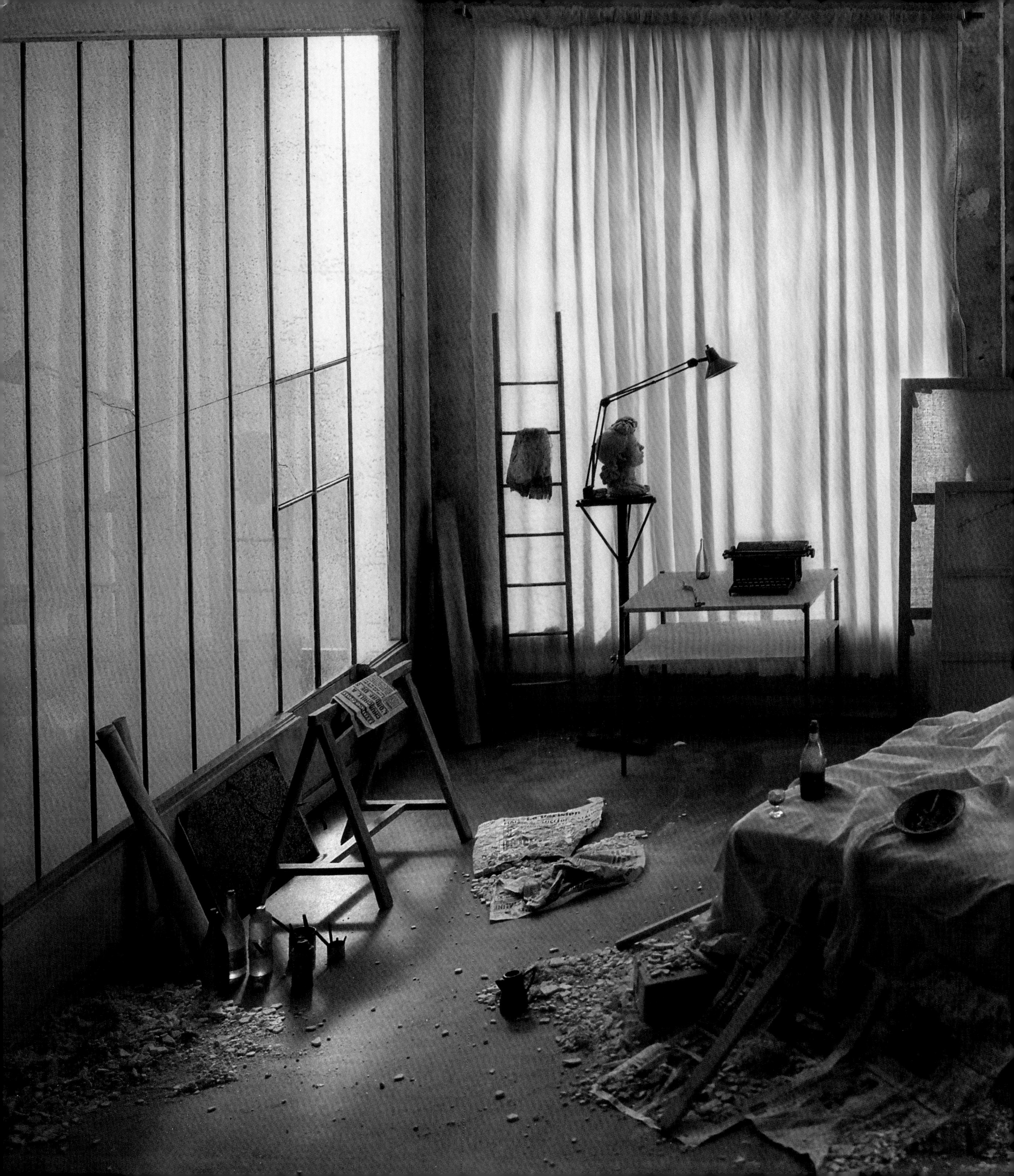

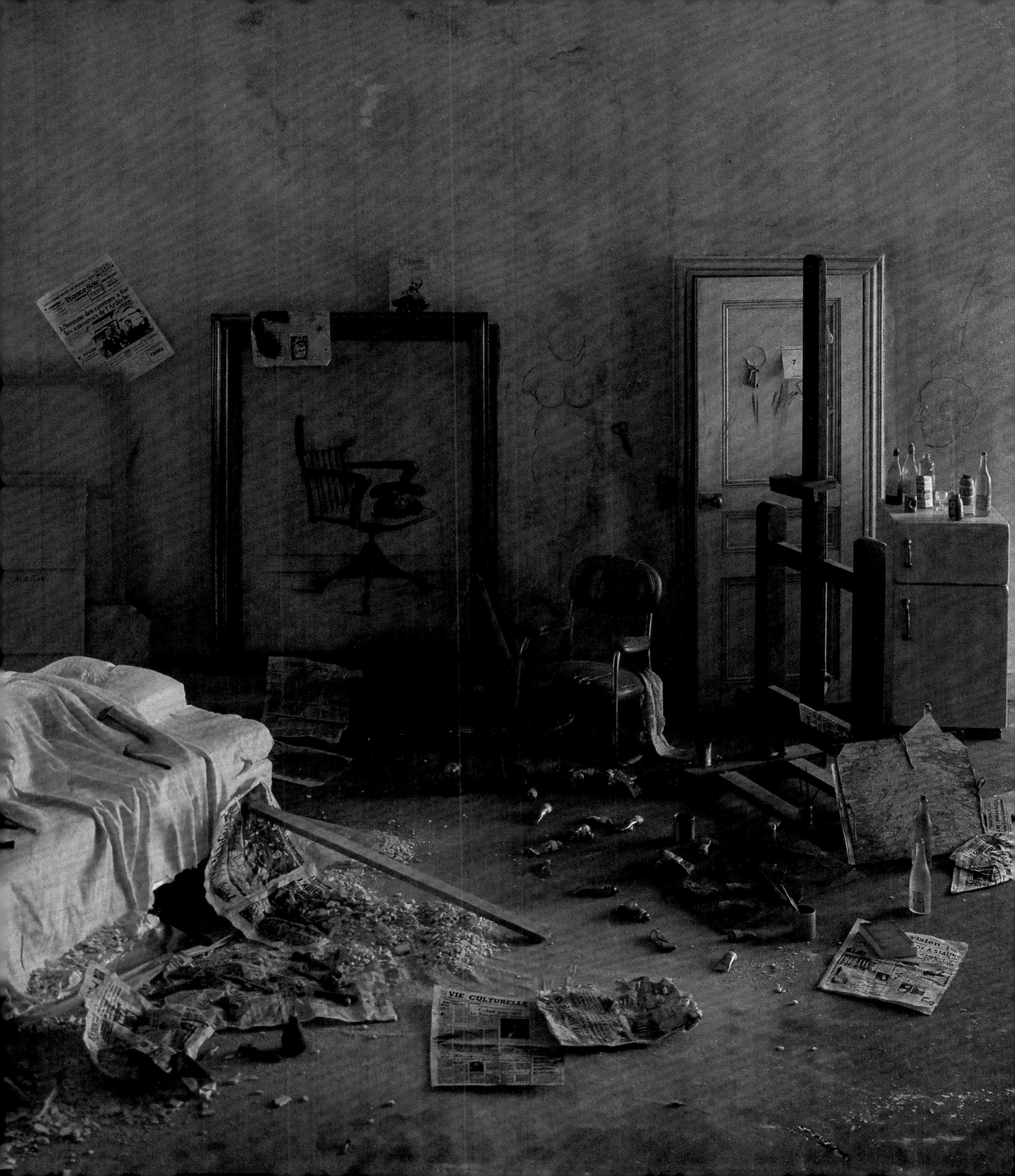
France Soir
L'homme des cavernes a tué
les amoureux de l'Ardèche
VIE CULTURELLE

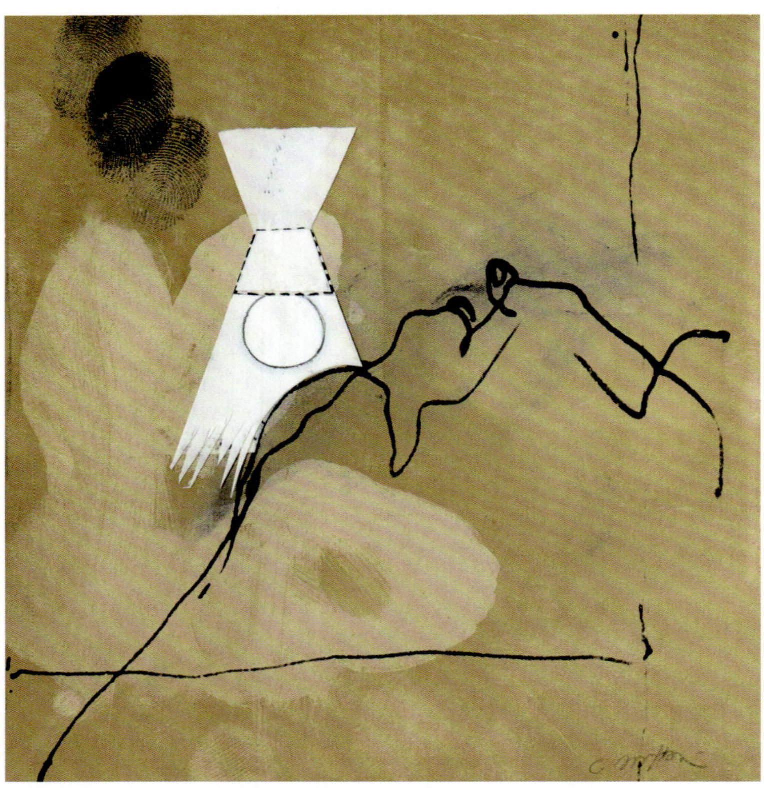

Couple in Bed II, 1989.
Felt pen and collage on paper, and wash,
9 ¼ × 8 ¾ in. (23.5 × 22 cm).

Couple in Bed beneath a Picture Showing a Couple in Bed, 1990.
Pencil, gouache, and pastel on paper, 11 ¾ × 8 ¼ in. (29.7 × 21 cm).

Couple in Bed beneath a Picture in a Bedroom, 1991.
Oil on Cibachrome, 46 ½ × 48 ¾ in. (118 × 124 cm).

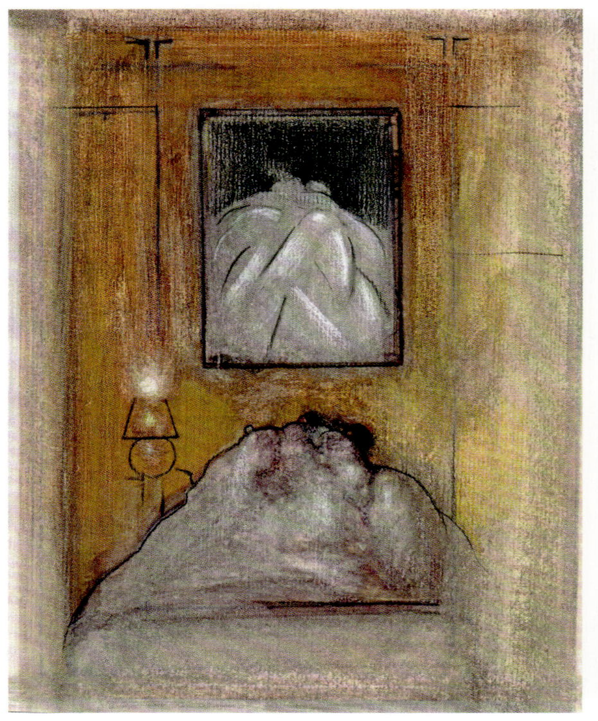

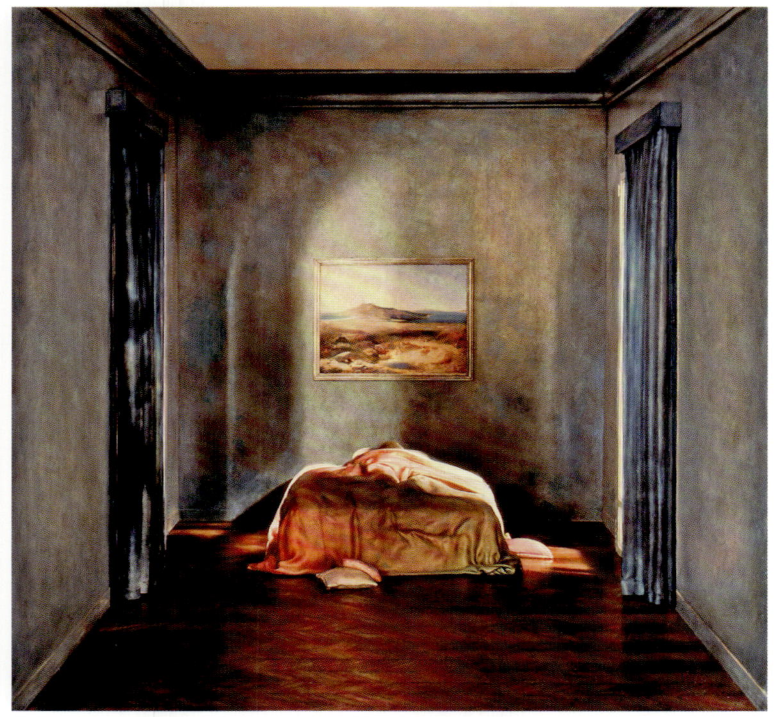

Each art possesses its own specificity and does best on its own terms. I think one can say in sculpture things one can't say in drawing; I think one can say with a photograph things one can't say with a painting, etc. It's passing from one art to another, and it's precisely crossing these borders that interests me whenever I try to express appearances as completely as possible. I didn't say "the real"; I don't know what reality is.

C. Matton, *Charles Matton, visiblement*, op. cit.

Four Variations on a Pillow,
1984.
Black-and-white silver print
(sepia tone).

Still 1 and Still 2
L'Italien des Roses, 1972.
95 min. Script and direction
Charles Matton.

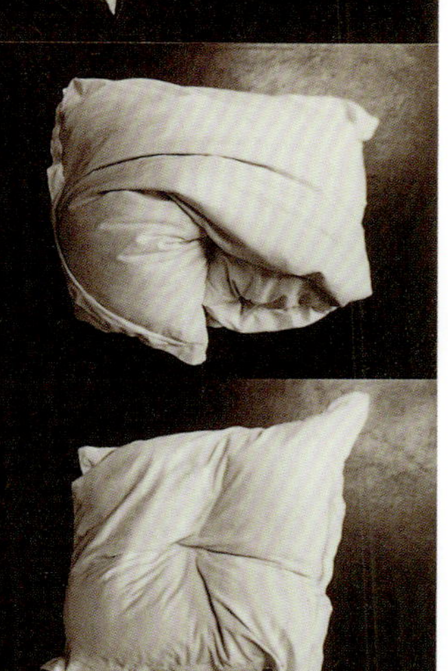

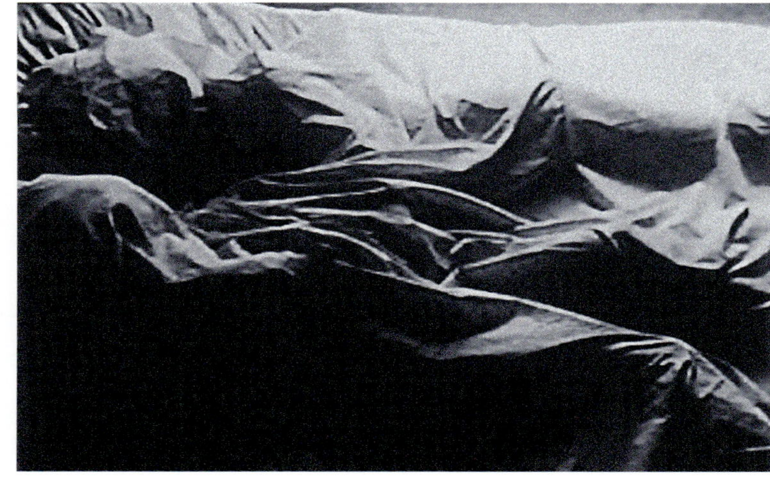

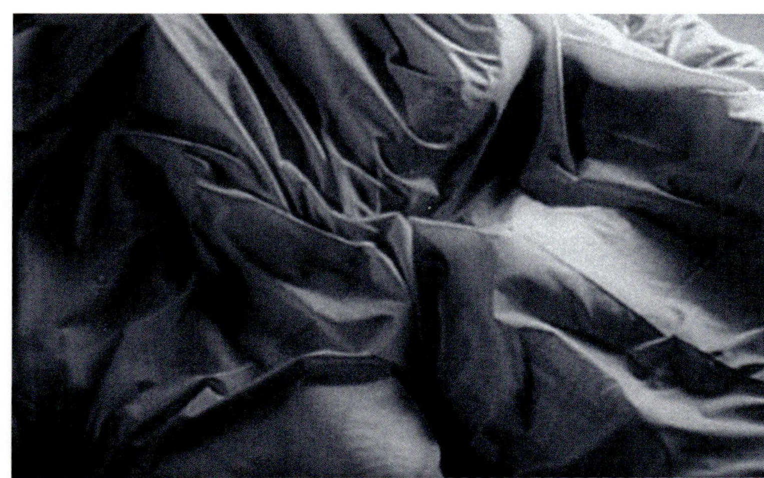

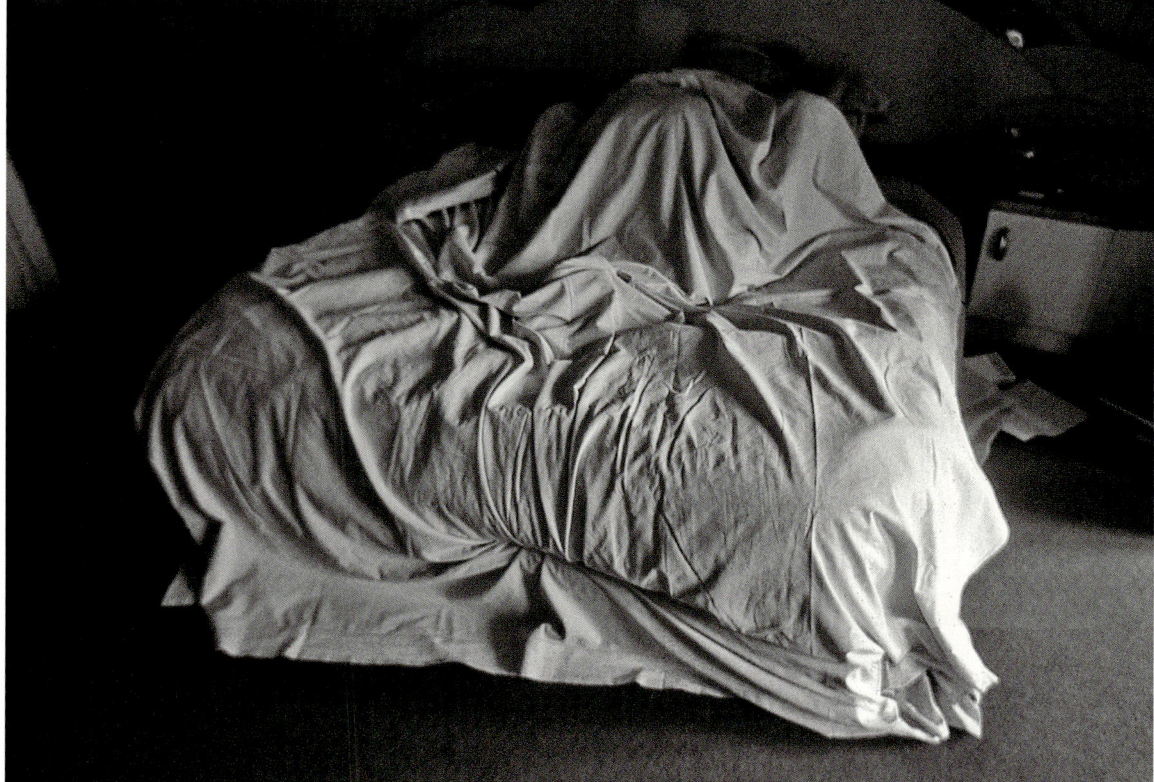

Bedding II [couple in bed,
Le Coudray-Montceaux, France], 1979.
Photograph.

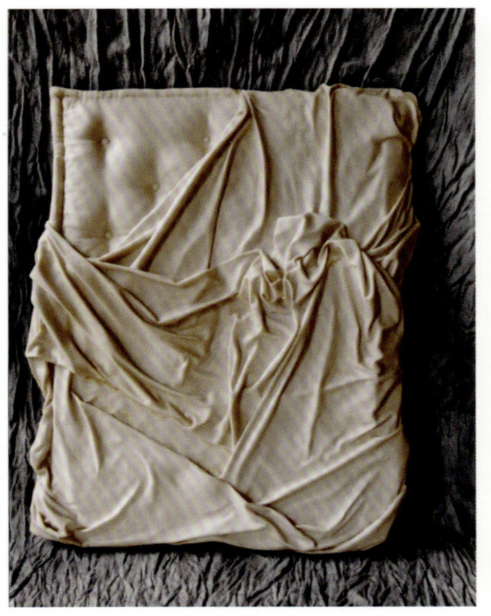

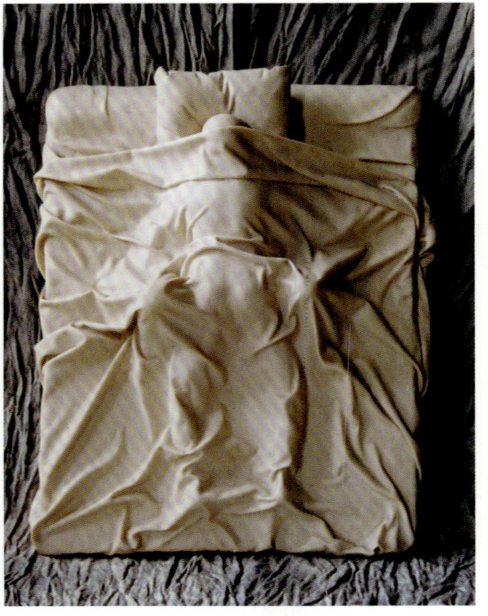

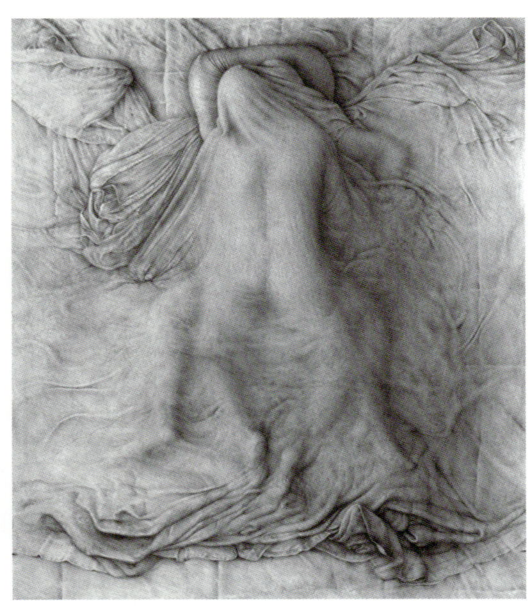

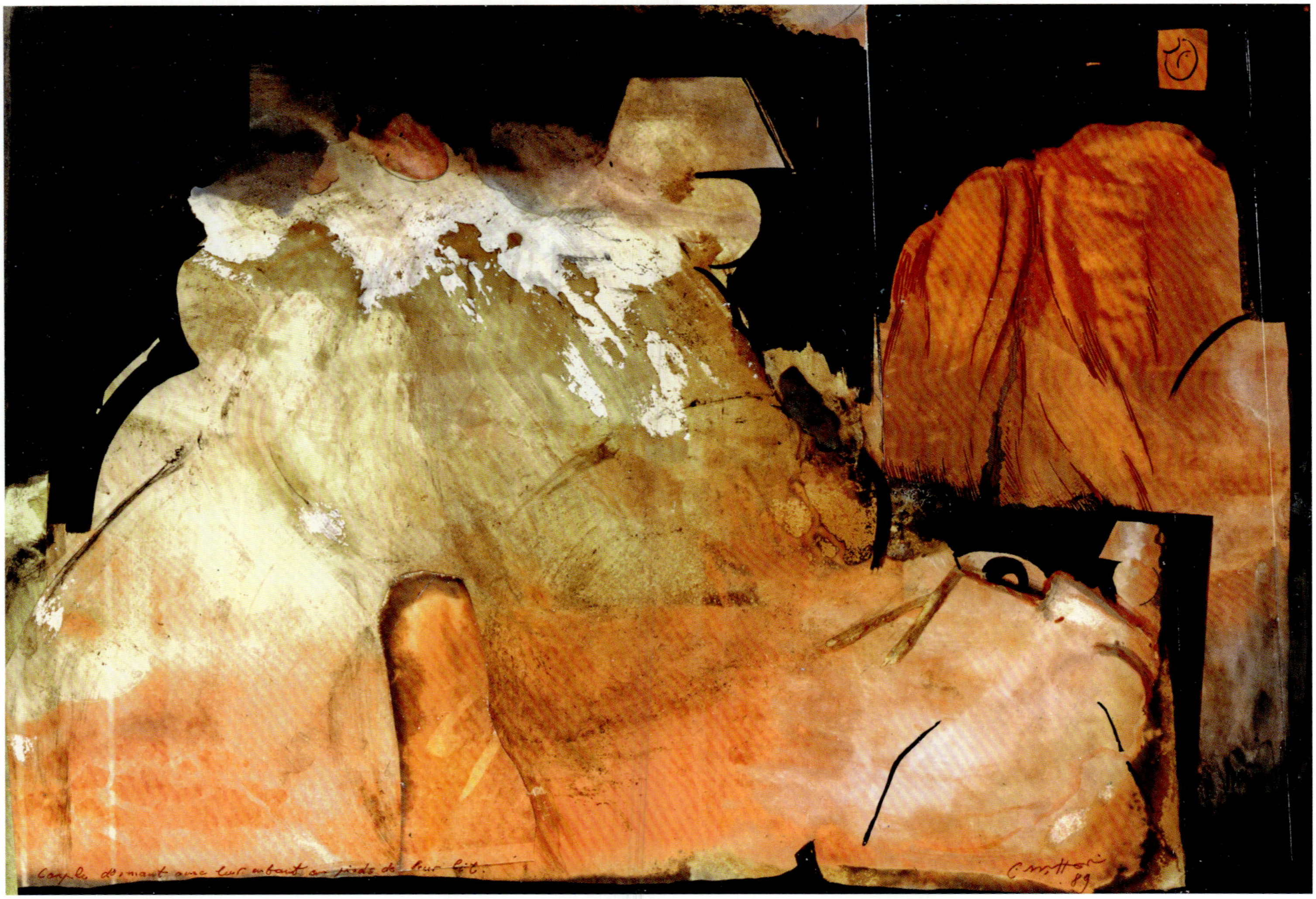

Facing page:
Unmade Bed, 1983.
Torolith and marble,
20 × 16 × 2 ½ in.
(51 × 41 × 6 cm).

Couple in Bed, 1982.
Torolith and marble,
15 ¾ × 12 ¼ × 3 ½ in.
(40 × 31 × 9 cm).

Couple beneath the Sheets, 1972.
Lead pencil on paper,
18 × 15 in. (45.5 × 38 cm).

Couple Asleep, with their Child at the Foot of the Bed, 1989.
Pencil and gouache on cardboard,
11 ½ × 16 ¼ in. (29.5 × 41.5 cm).

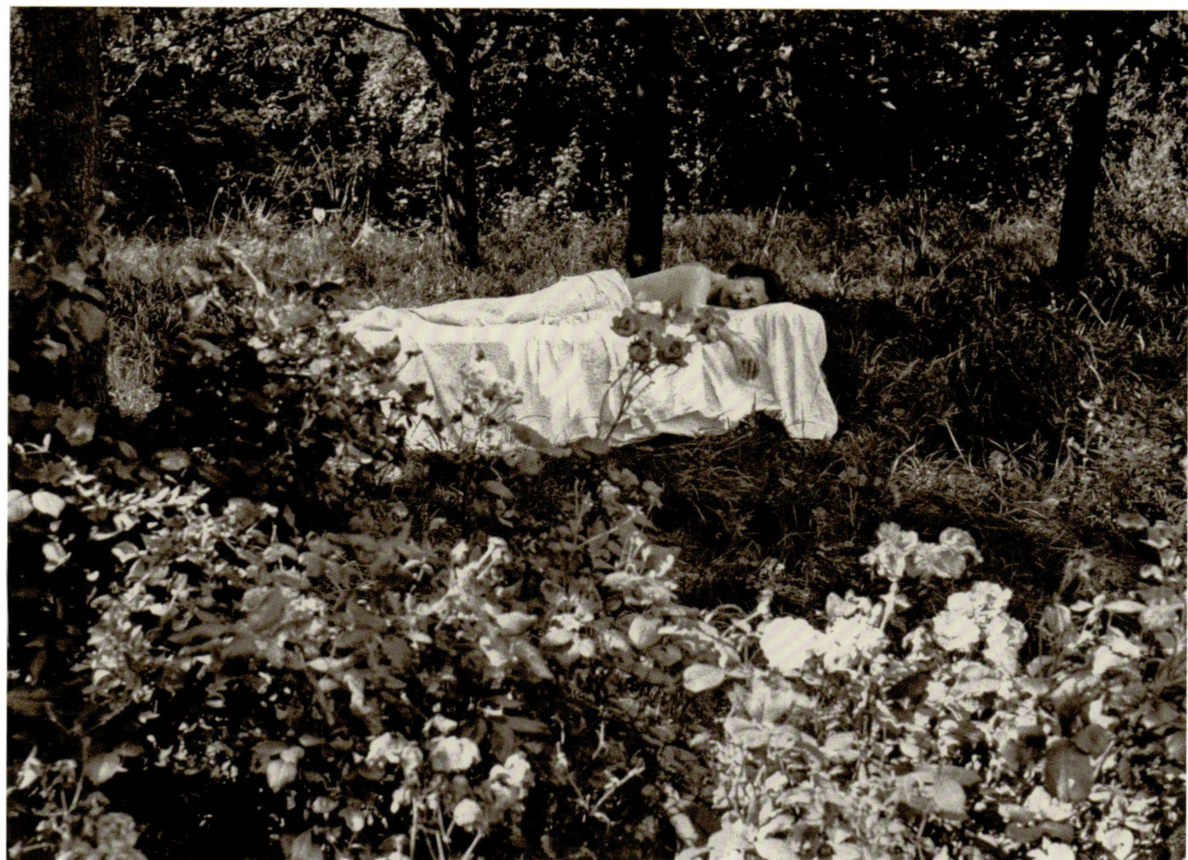

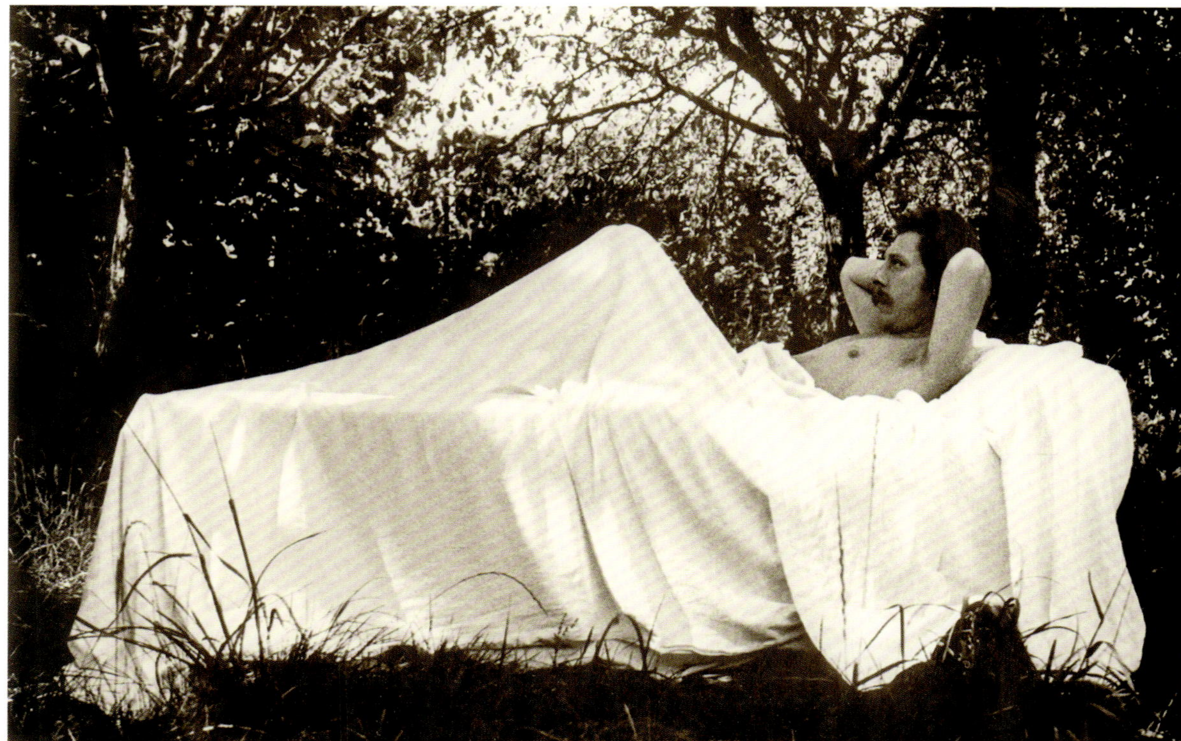

Self-portrait in a Bed in the Countryside III, 1970.
Photograph.

Self-portrait in a Bed in the Countryside II, 1970.
Photograph.

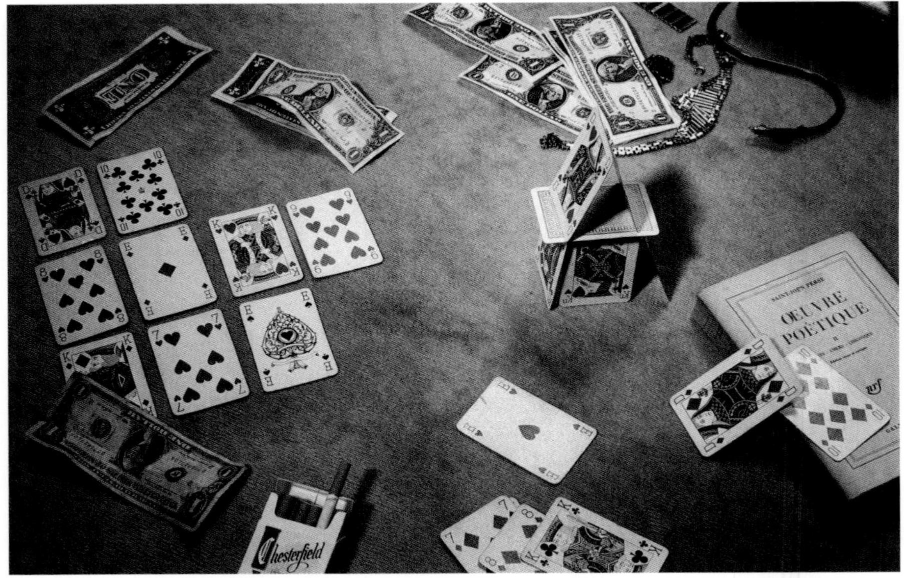

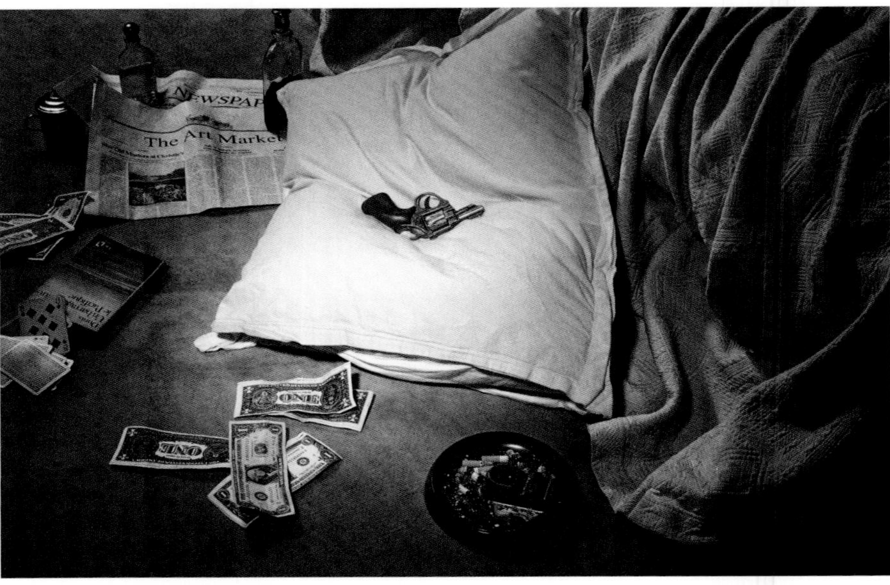

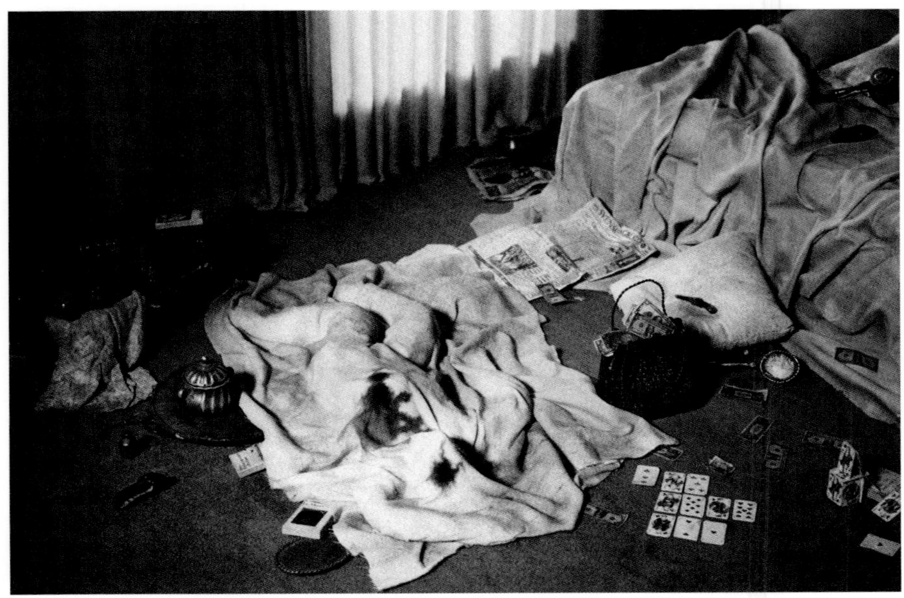

The Bedroom of a Disorderly Woman III, 1996.
Photograph.

The Bedroom of a Disorderly Woman II, 1996.
Photograph.

The Bedroom of a Disorderly Woman I, 1992.
Photograph.

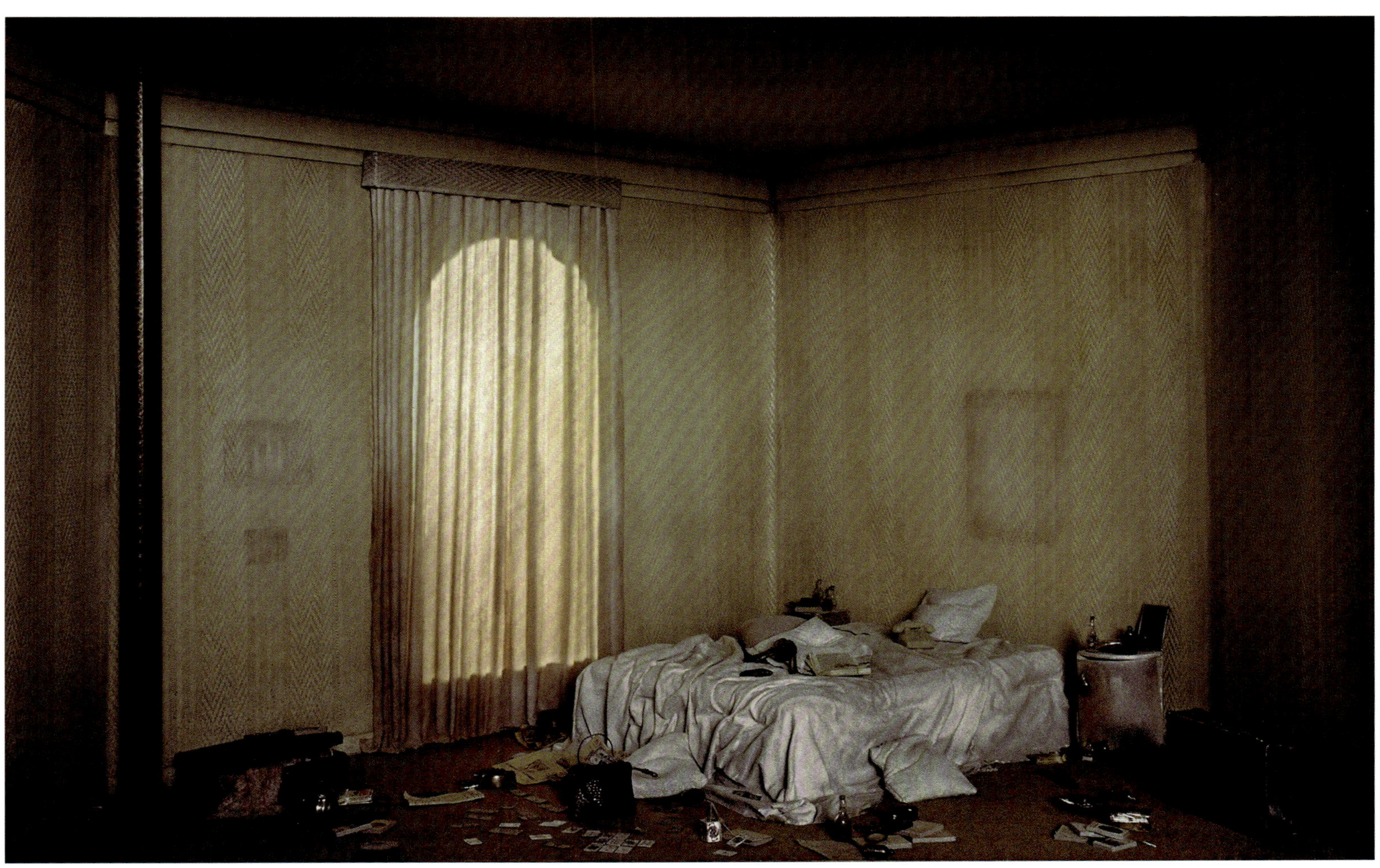

The Bedroom of a Disorderly Woman, 1991.
Mixed media, 20 ½ × 30 × 25 ¾ in. (52 × 76.5 × 65.5 cm).

Personal note, *Disorderly Woman*, September 3, 1991.

(Selected items:) *the bed, the dresser, and coffee table, the knobs on the night-table, the primer or paint on the walls, the fitted carpet, ready-made cushions to be filled, Barbie wigs and lingerie, photographed letter together with books left open, photocopy dollars, playing cards, twisted wires, telephone, newspapers, wire on hairdryer, one or two frames on the wall with Maxfield Parrish, polishing jewel-case and scattered jewelry, cigarette packets, ashtray, acrylic paint for cigarettes in the case, sugar lumps and candy wrappers, the hairbrush, two revolvers, in the frames on the wall there could be a painting like Ferdinand Khnopff or de Nuncques or Gustave Moreau or a pre-Raphaelite or Alma Tadéma or Tamara de Lempika or Caspar Friedrich.... Photographs Cecil Beaton, Duane Michael, Diane Arbus.... The window is almost in darkness, it's nightfall, the little light there is orange, the bedside lamp is lit and "hits" a newspaper shown see-through, is there a disk on the record-player?*

— Ce qui est souligné de rouge est à acheter.
Femme désordre : Le lit, la commode (Didier Falconnet.) et table basse, les poignées table de nuit, revêtement ou peinture des murs, la moquette, (achat et peinture.) le voile (achat et mise en forme.), polissage et oxidation de tous les petits éléments, oreiller coton, coussins déjà fait à remplir, perruques et lingerie Barby, finition valises (peinture bombe kaki clair, orange brûlée, marron foncé.), lettre photographiée, ainsi que livres ouverts, montage loupe, photocopie Dollars, cartes à jouer, fil tortillé et polissage téléphone blanc résine marbre, journaux dont un sur lampe, installation électrique derrière voile et lampe de chevet, + Ponthiéry. Photographies dans cadre, patine de un fauteuil déjà fait soit le 1930 soit le « Normandy (Faith City.), fil sur sèche cheveux, un ou deux cadre au mur avec Maxfield Parish, polissage coffret à bijoux et bijoux épars, paquets de cigarette, [illegible] cendrier, peinture à l'acrylique des cigarettes dans coffret, sucres en morceaux et bonbons papillottes, la brosse à cheveux, finition des deux révolvers, Dans les cadres au mur il pourrait y avoir une peinture genre Ferdinand Knopff ou Nuncques de Villes ? ou Gustave Moreau ou un Préraphaëlique ou un Alma Tadéma ou un Tamara de Lempika ou Gaspard Friedrich.
Photocopies d'étiquettes pour médicament, dentifrice, « signal », finition des chaussures, dans cadres : photographies Cécil Beaton, Duane Michael, Diane Arbus,
Végétation derrière voile, fils pour la radio, miroir souple collé, (à) ADAM, dans cadre et miroir à main.
La fenêtre est presque éteinte, c'est la tombée de la nuit, le peu de lumière est orange, la lampe de chevet est allumée [illegible] et « prend » un journal en transparence, y a-t-il un disque sur un pick up ?
A refaire tirer et métalliser : chaussures, bijoux, oeilleton.
Bricoler chaussures → Piètement table basse.
Gélatine léger rose.
Diminuer le cendrier.

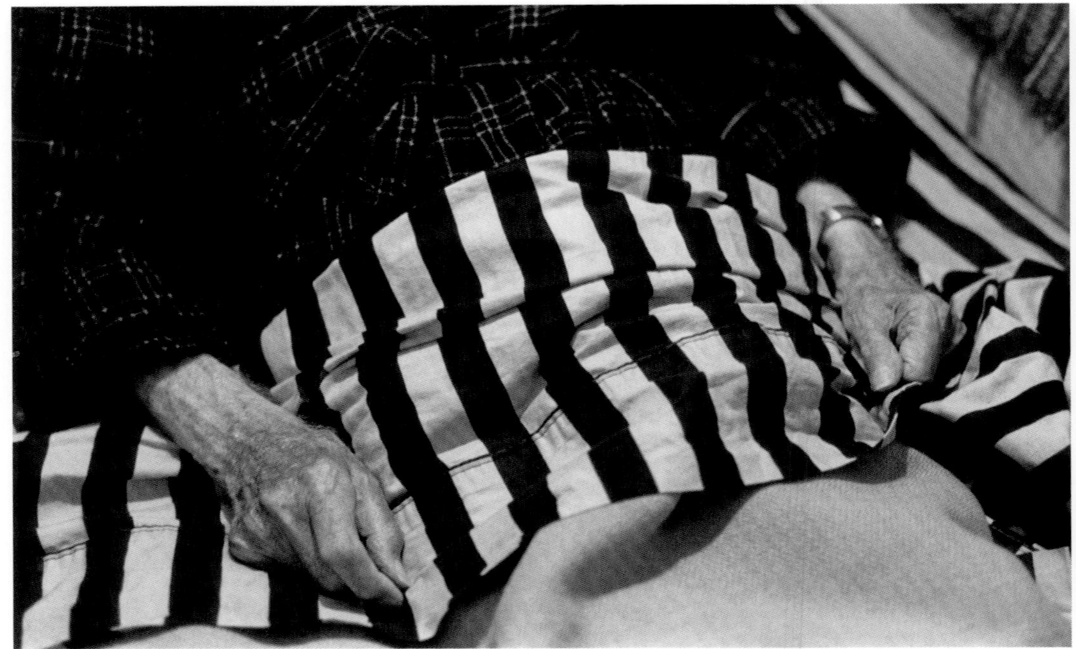

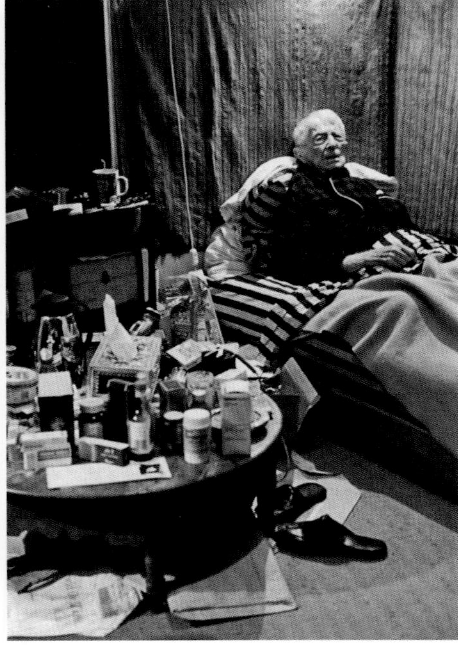

The Hands of Paul Bowles, 1999.
Photograph Hannah Assouline.

Paul Bowles in his Bedroom, Itesa Estate, Tangiers, 1999.
Photograph Hannah Assouline.

The bedroom of Paul Bowles: a dead-end street in a housing project! A housing project! Hemmed in by stray dogs, a housing project cut into pieces by a fascistic, triumphant, cynical sun at the end of the cul-de-sac. He had drawn the curtains against the sun, hoping for only the night-lights above the bed—what am I saying, above the pallet, where, the dandy, he lay shriveled up on a fistful of white hair, there, in the withered heart of his memories. (Find the right word: residua, jetsam, remnants, a medicine-cabinet hodgepodge).

The shoe closet (with John Lobbs and trainers) and some Cunard or Compagnie Transatlantique suitcases doused in perfume by Jane, the woman, funny, so out of her indigent intellectual league. Outside, there are all those Pasolini-type little brats of Vinci, guffawing because they don't give a shit about this old American pansy.

He has probably loved though, and he's stayed here, undone in the moist, fevered hollow of the scattered blandishments of his relics. That awful bad boy Genet came on a visit, the very image of tenderness, a choirboy from the Morvan, as vicious as despair, and *la* Truman Capote, grotesque, a grass harp whose hysterical soprano voice turned turtle peering over the guardrail of Vidal, the gore, spewing out his bile.... Tangiers!

Francis Bacon can't be far away, with his pal the barroom piano-player—who knows, when the hour comes, the Dionysian cordial of jazz might offer solace to all those for whom the nobility of Johann Sebastian Bach is of no avail; I mean, the realists, sick with truth, allergic to the incurable nobility of the spirit. In other words, to those who soak themselves without stint in the unacceptable. So I continue pacing about these fourteen square meters, I wander in their shadows infused with the sunlight that creeps in through the absurd curtain. I skirt round his thigh bones as fragile as crystal flutes, round the table, the packets of tranquilizers, the bottles of syrup, the boxes of Kleenex, gilded, streaked with Moresque arabesques, and catch my feet in the black leather slippers. The whiff of pharmaceuticals sends me into a tizzy; I hover over the old man, his remains, molded into a wretched camel-hair blanket, just to stroke the silvering remnants of his white hair.

Because the light went out for him at the very moment I, a humble manufacturer of microcosms, picked up my crosshead screwdriver to shut the box in which I had the unconscionable presumption to lock up all these scents.

Personal note, 1999

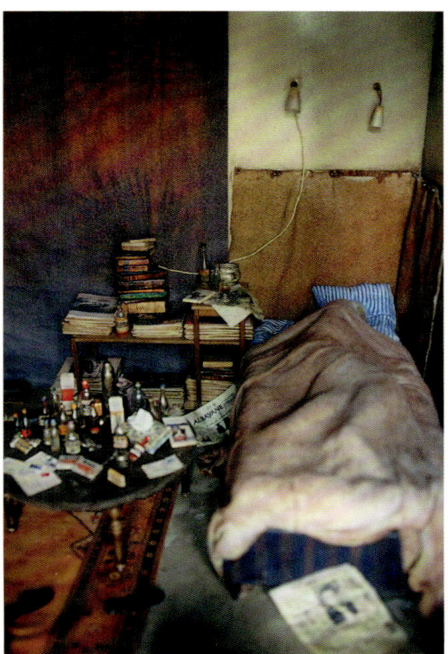

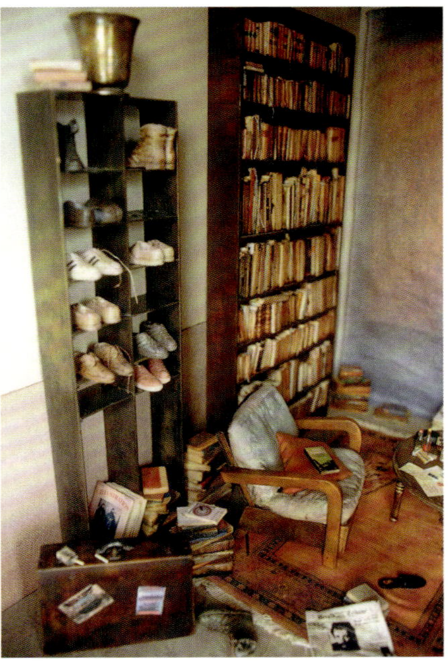

The Bedroom of Paul Bowles in Tangiers (detail 1), 1999.

The Bedroom of Paul Bowles in Tangiers (detail 2), 1999.

The Bedroom of Paul Bowles in Tangiers, 1999.
Mixed media, 22 × 24 ¾ × 17 ¼ in.
(56 × 63 × 44 cm).
(Exhibition "L'Appel de Tanger,"
Institut du Monde Arabe, Paris,
November 9, 1999–January 30, 2000).

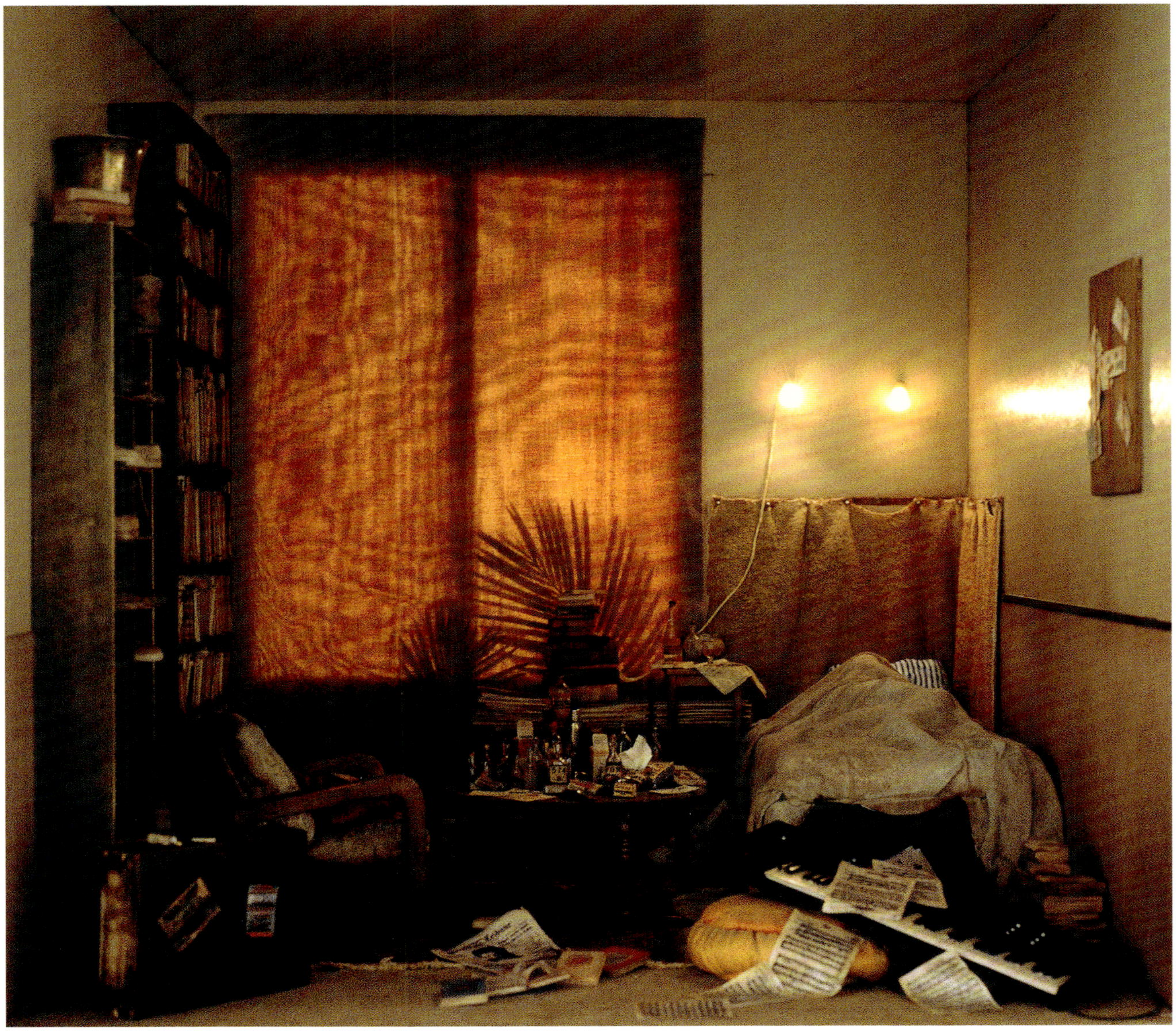

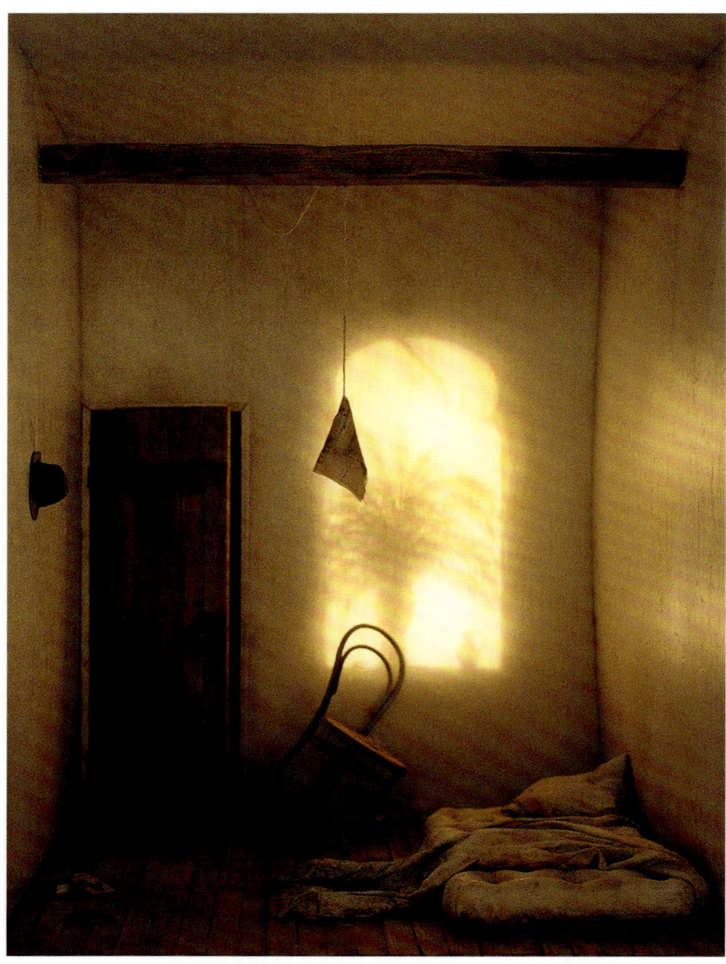

William Burroughs's *Bedroom in Tangiers I*, 1999.
Mixed media, 20 × 16 × 19 ¾ in. (51 × 41 × 50 cm).

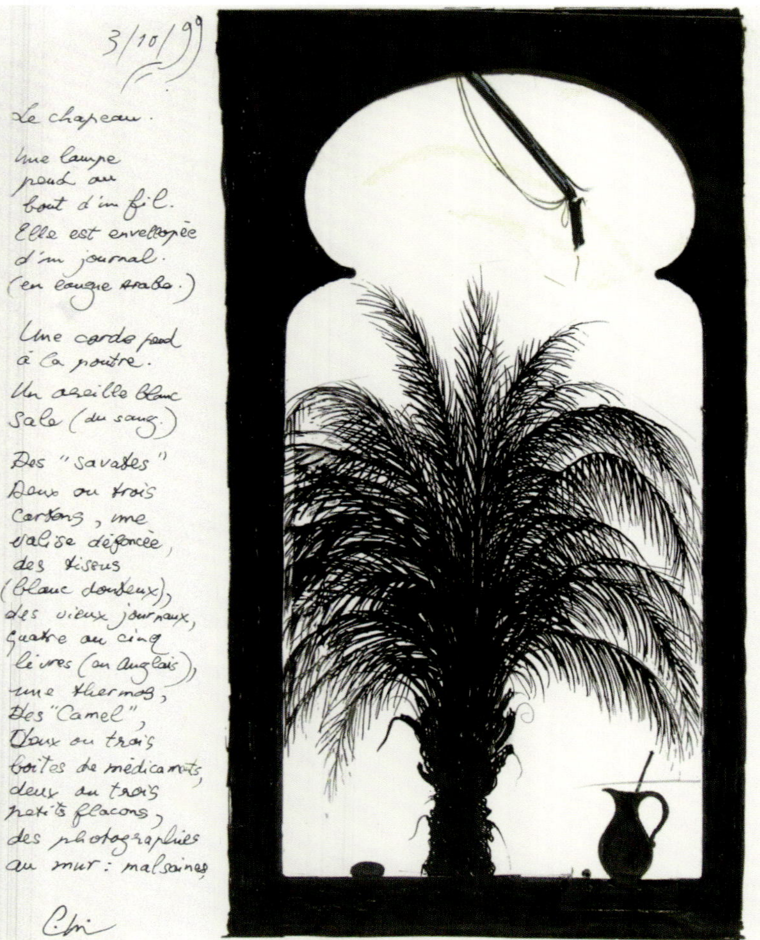

Design for the shadow cast on the window in *William Burroughs's Bedroom in Tangiers I*, 1999.
Felt pen on paper, 11 ¾ × 8 ¼ in. (29.7 × 21 cm).

The hat

A lamp hangs at the end of a wire. It's wrapped in a newspaper (in Arabic.)

A rope hangs from the beam. A dirty white pillow (blood)

"Slip-ons." Two or three cardboard boxes, a bashed up suitcase, cloths (of a dubious white), old newspapers, four or five books (in English), a thermos flask, some Camels, two or three packets of medicines, two or three small bottles, photographs on the wall: unhealthy.

Burroughs

Dandy in camphor, without offspring. Always scampering about after his image. Where is he now? He's gone out to look for it among the neighborhood pushers.

The sun makes the most of his absence to cast a shadow from an outdoors (deliciously) scented with genuine laughter.

He'll be back and, after hanging his fedora on a nail, without having seen the sun, he'll put his skeleton wrapped in an old gray suit to bed in a sheet slashed with dried blood. For an age, he'll gaze down at the end of his shoes bought in New York City, U.S.A., a century ago.

The sun will burn out, and the laughter with it. The sun will wonder what the hell it's doing here, that's for sure. The chair's bust. It's been like that since the day he pretended to hang himself.

Personal note, 1999

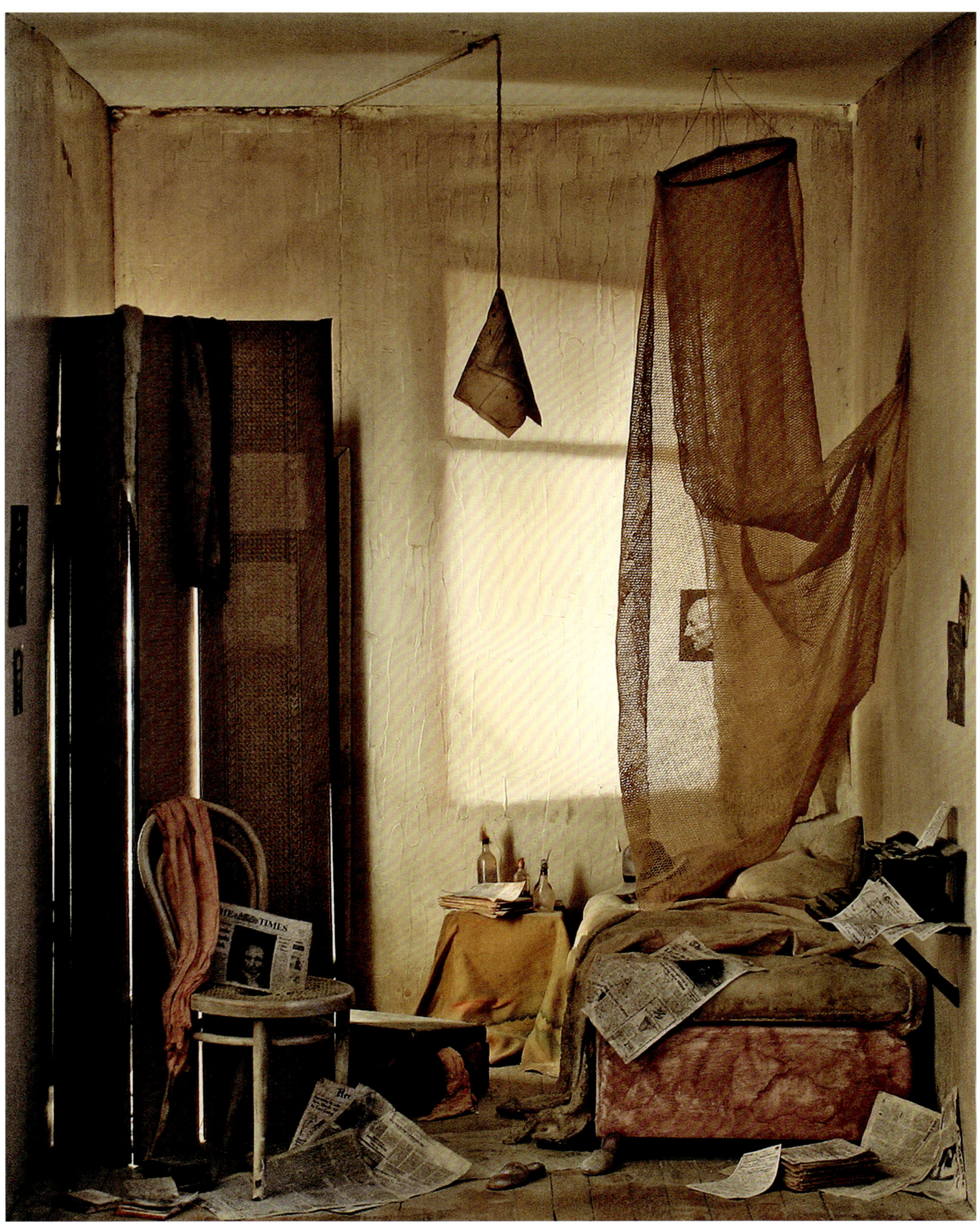

William Burroughs's Bedroom in Tangiers II, 1999. Mixed media, 20 × 16 × 19 ¾ in. (51 × 41 × 50 cm). (Exhibition, "L'Appel de Tanger").

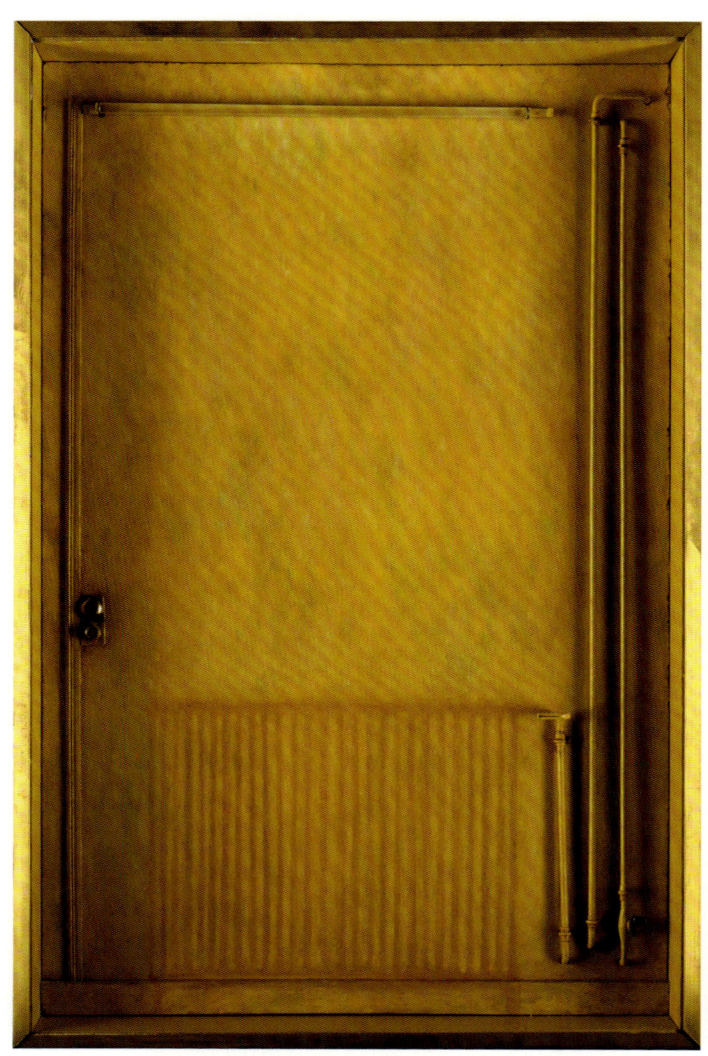

Mark Left by a Radiator on the Wall I, 1989.
Oil on cardboard, metal, electroplated torolith,
20 ½ × 12 × 2 in. (52 × 30 × 5 cm).

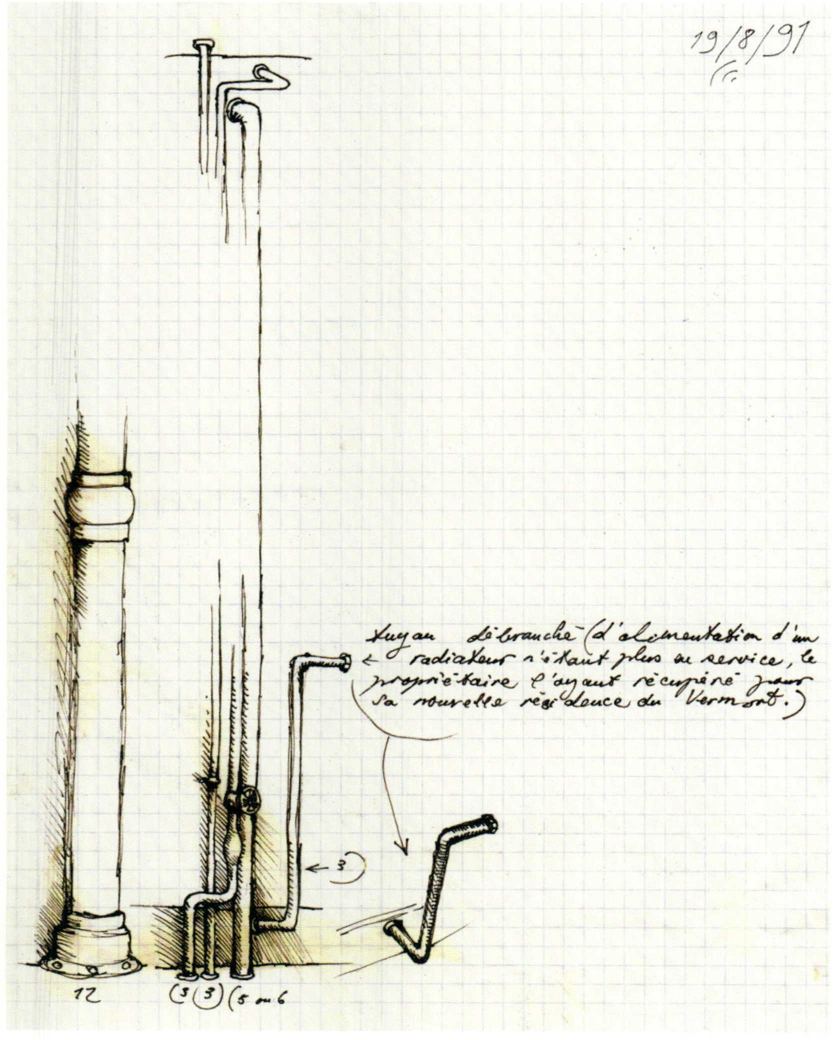

Disconnected Pipe, 1991.
Pencil on paper, 11 ¾ × 8 ¼ in. (29.7 × 21 cm).

Disconnected pipe (supplying a radiator no longer in place, the owner having removed it for his new home in Vermont)

Le Clézio

The Promenade des Anglais (carnival) down which parade the rosy cheeks (Schiaparelli) belonging to cohorts of crumbling old girls, with pursed lips blackened with Rouge Baiser lipstick from a bygone era of fresh breath and kisses. Nice, ghastly city. (Dig out J.M.G. Le Clézio's description.)[1] Long live Vigo, by the way! (*Vive Vigo, à propos!*)[2]

I'm going to leave soon. So as to escape—the indescribable. No, Nice, I do not want to see you; I've pulled the green shutters so as to put out of my mind the frivolous scent of your flowers and your sun, a soporific to help the sated on the brink of death with their siesta.

I've even put my chair on the table to stop myself sitting on it—so I can go and write somewhere else.

Personal note, 1999

1. "Nice, an image of hell? A Sartrean hell of palm trees, rococo buildings, buildings with pink facades." As quoted by *Nice Matin*, from *J.M.G. Le Clézio* by Gérard de Cortanze.
2. Jean Vigo, *À propos de Nice*, directed by Jean Vigo (1930). Short film.

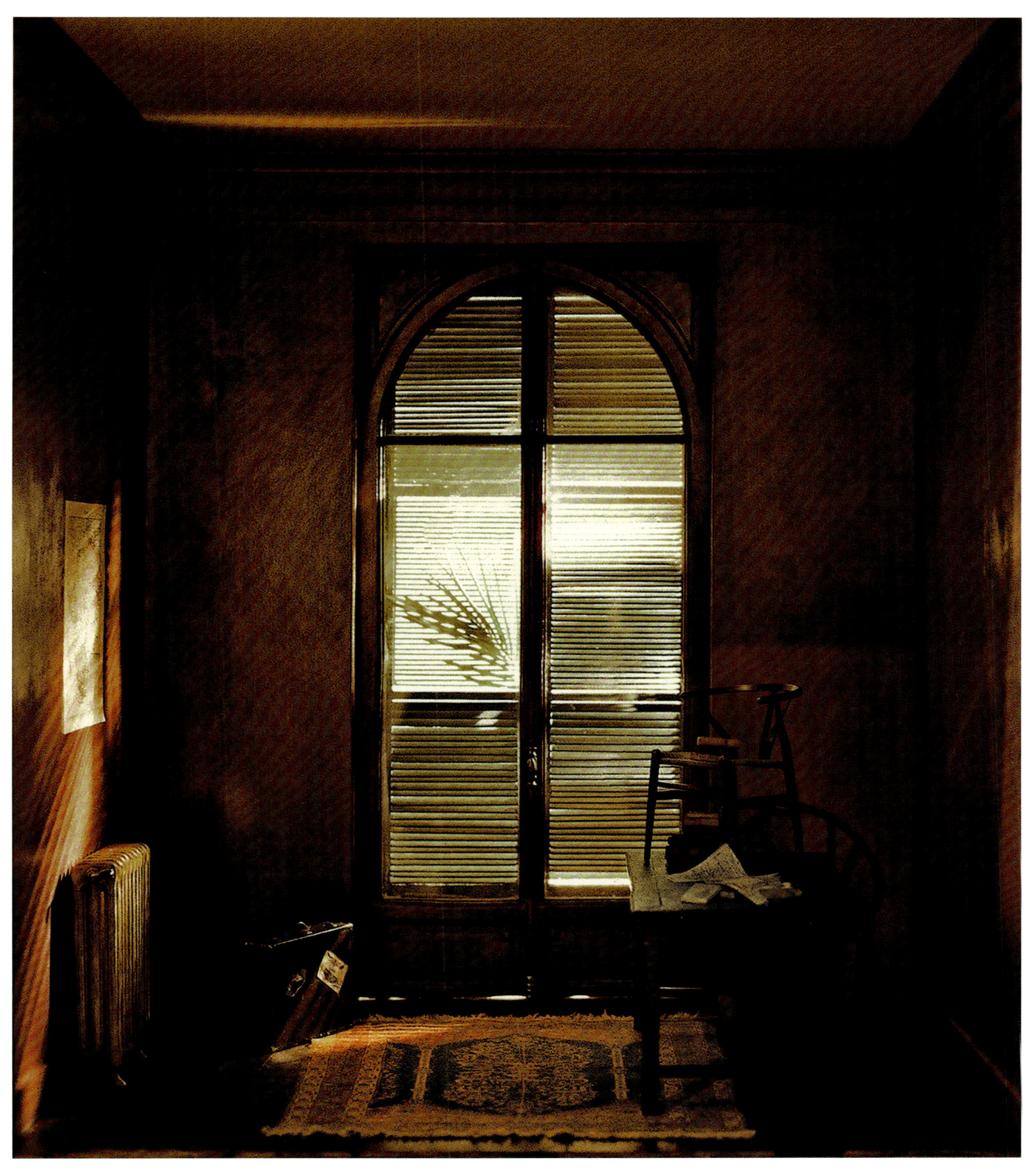

The Bedroom of J.M.G. Le Clézio in Nice, 1999.
Mixed media, 22 × 18 ½ × 17 in. (56 × 47 × 43 cm).
(Exhibition, "L'Appel de Tanger").

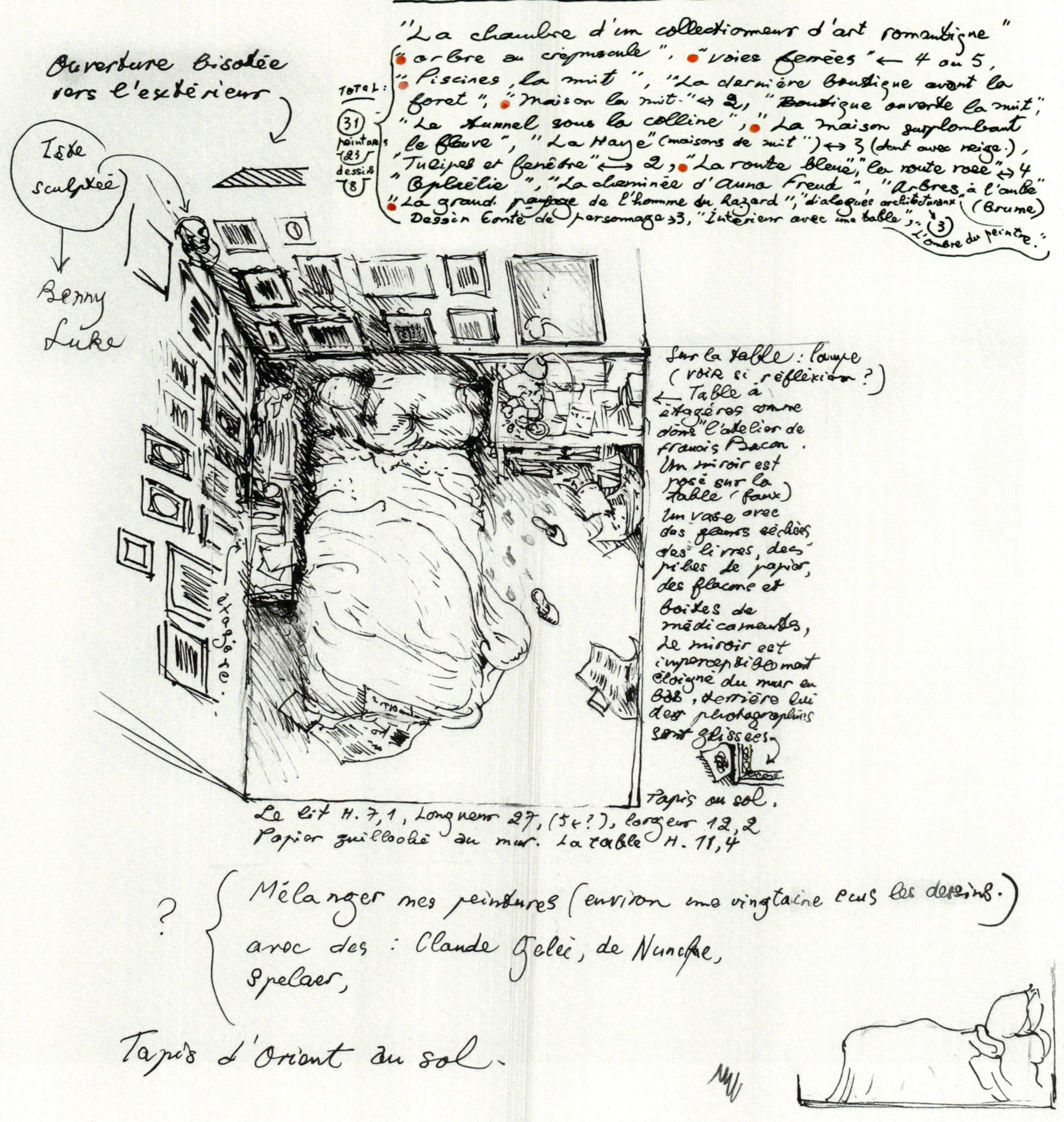

LISTE DES PEINTURES
"La chambre d'un collectionneur d'art romantique"
"arbre au crépuscule", "voies ferrées" ← 4 ou 5,
"Piscines, la nuit", "La dernière boutique avant la forêt", "Maison la nuit" ↔ 2, "Boutique ouverte la nuit",
"Le tunnel sous la colline", "La maison surplombant le fleuve", "La Haye" (maisons de nuit") ↔ 3 (dont avec neige.),
"Tulipes et fenêtre" ↔ 2, "La route bleue", "La route rose" ↔ 4
"Ophélie", "La cheminée d'Anna Freud", "Arbres à l'aube" (Brume)
"Le grand paysage de l'homme du hasard", "dialogues architecturaux"
Dessin Conté de personnage ↔ 3, "Intérieur avec une table" ↔ (3) "L'ombre du peintre".
TOTAL: (31) peintures (23) dessins (8)
Ouverture biseautée vers l'extérieur
Tête sculptée
Benny Luke
exagéré.
Sur la table : lampe (voir si réflexion ?)
← Table à étagères comme dans l'atelier de Francis Bacon. Un miroir est posé sur la table (faux) Un vase avec des fleurs séchées, des livres, des piles de papier, des flacons et boîtes de médicaments, Le miroir est imperceptiblement éloigné du mur en bas, derrière lui des photographies sont glissées.
Tapis au sol.
Le lit H. 7,1, Longueur 27, (54?), largeur 12,2
Papier quillochè au mur. La table H. 11,4
? Mélanger mes peintures (environ une vingtaine sans les dessins.)
avec des : Claude Gelée, de Nunque, Spelaer,
Tapis d'Orient au sol.

The Bedroom of a Romantic Art Collector, 2002. Mixed media, 22 × 16 × 21 in. (56 × 41 × 53 cm).

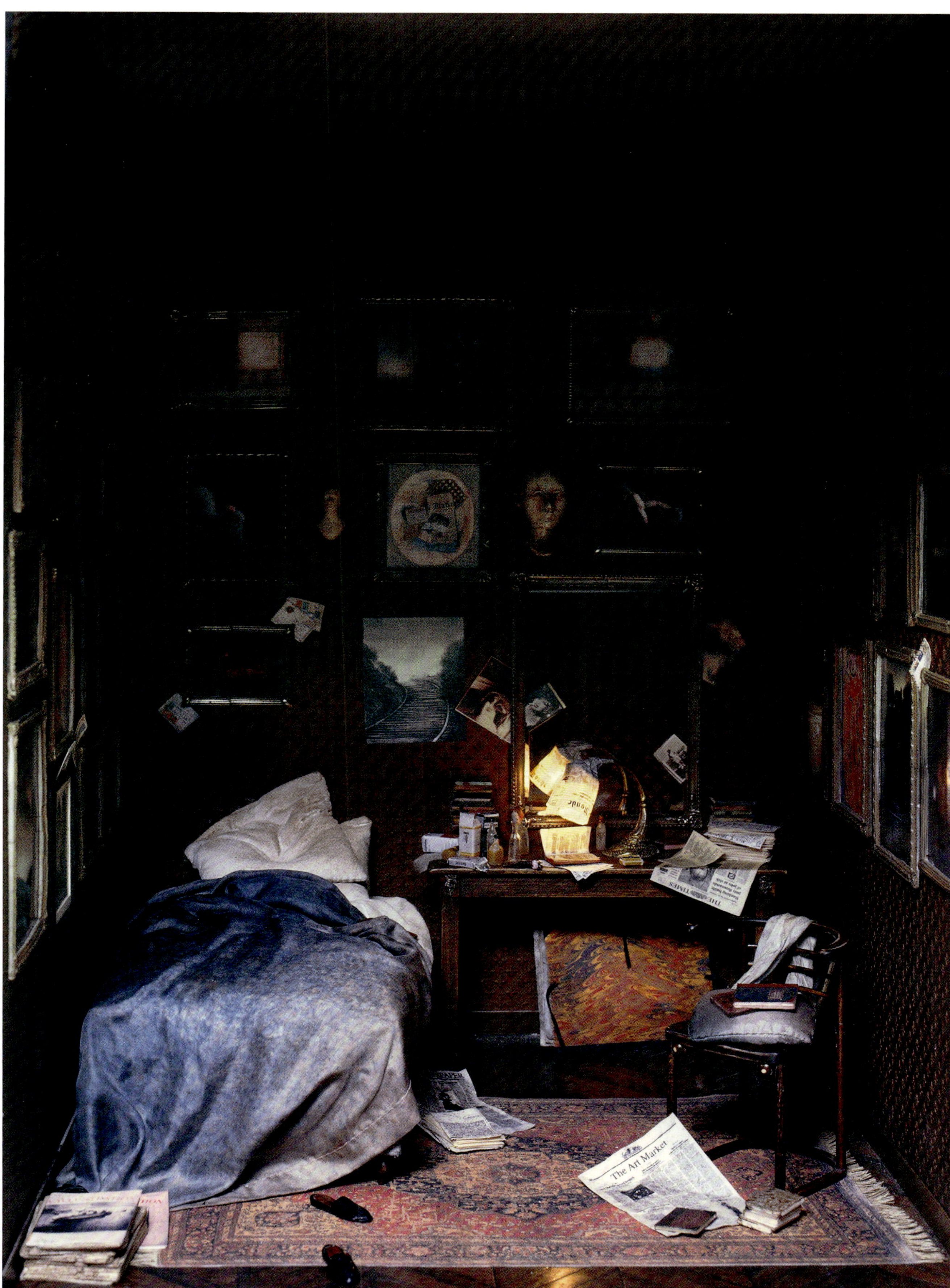

Facing page:
The Bedroom of a Romantic Art Collector, 2001. Pencil and felt pen on paper, 11 ¾ × 8 ¼ in. (29.7 × 21 cm).

-List of paintings [for] The Bedroom of a Romantic Art Collector

Tree at Twilight, *Railroads* 4 or 5, *Swimming Pools at Night*, *The Last Shop before the Forest*, *House at Night* 2, *All-Night Store*, *The Tunnel under the Hill*, *The House Looking down on the River*, *The Hague* (houses at night) 3 (inc. one with snow), *Tulips and Windows* 2, *The Blue Road*, *The Pink Road* 4, *Ophelia*, *Anna Freud's Fireplace*, *Trees at Dawn*, *The Large Landscape of* "The Unexpecting Man", *Architectural Dialogs* 3 (mist), *Conté drawing of figures*, *Interior with a Table*, *The Painter's Shadow*.

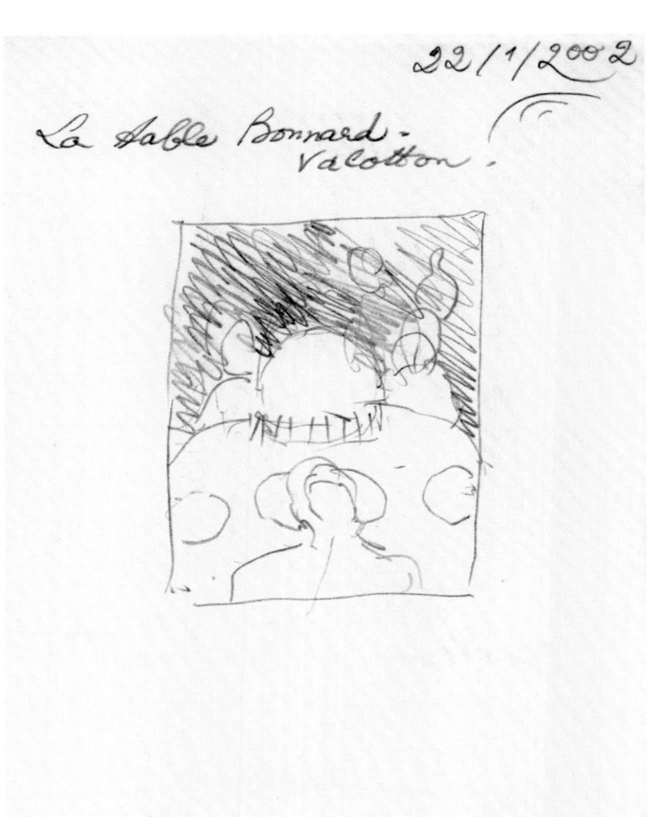

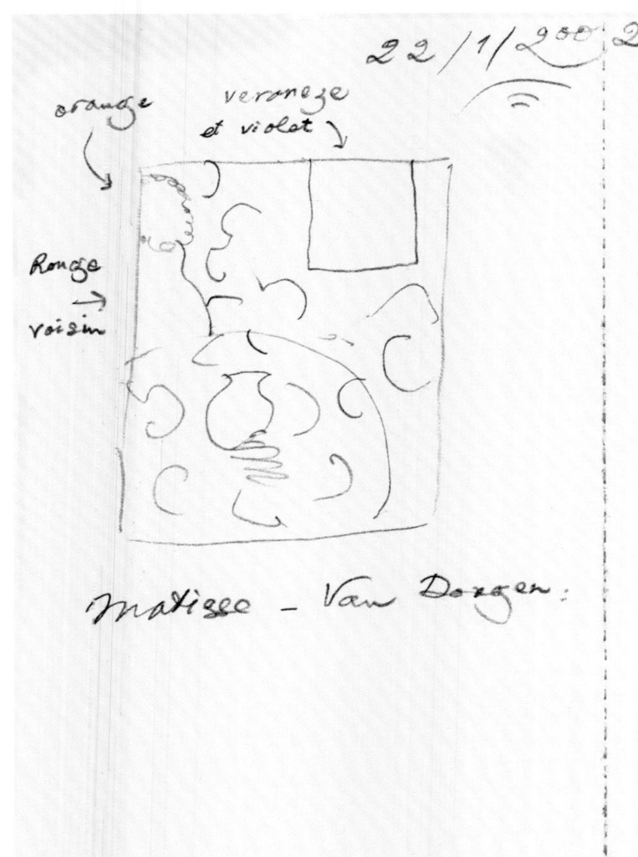

The Bonnard—Vallotton Table, 2002. Pencil on paper in a Moleskine notebook, 5 ¼ × 3 ¾ in. (13.2 × 9.8 cm).

Matisse—Van Dongen, 2002. Pencil on paper.

Hockney—Ritz, 2002. Pencil on paper.

Facing page: ***Ridiculously Sentimental Picture for a Seriously Reactionary Art Lover***, 2001. Pencil on paper, 11 ¾ × 8 ¼ in. (29.7 × 21 cm).

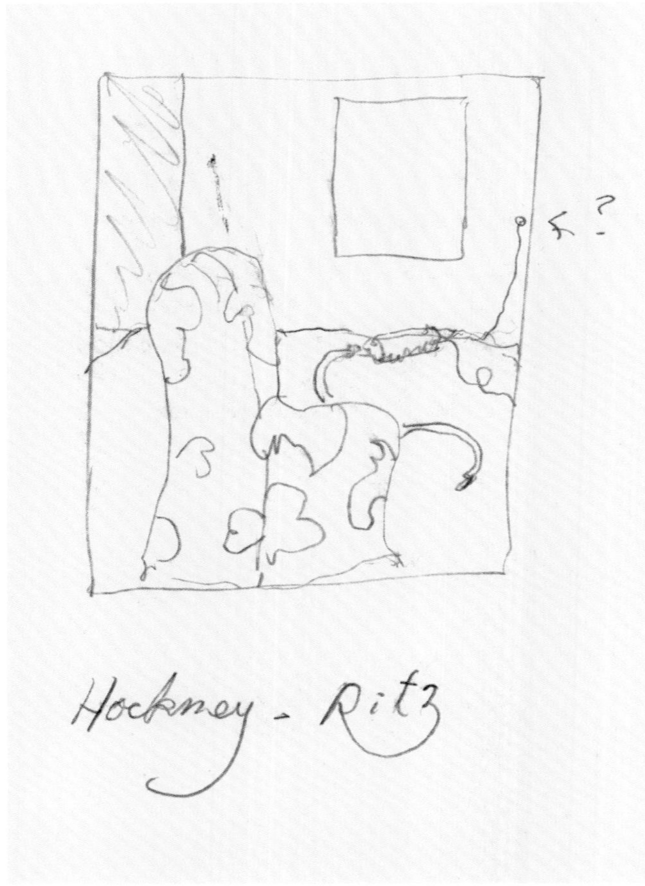

The Bedroom of a Collector required a great deal of work because I was determined that all the collector's pieces be original works made especially for the occasion. I enjoyed imagining an art lover who could appreciate pieces inspired by romantic art as much as by impressionist or nabi works. So, first I had to paint full-size the thirty pictures that would hang on the walls, and then reduce them to the proportions of the box. I really had to concentrate hard on the character of this collector so as to get a complete idea of his tastes.

However eclectic they may appear, I'm of the opinion that the choices an art lover makes have their coherence. It's obvious that this one is close to me. Romantic painting—when it's not waylaid by symbolism or, worse, by esotericism—really touches me and, as I've realized, I've always been prone to a desire to paint in this style. The same goes for impressionism and post-impressionism, which call upon more narrowly pictorial talents.

Personal note in a notebook, January 1, 2002

((ou Décembre))

-C. Mitton. Hiver 1937 – 7/2/2001

Image ridiculement sentimentale pour un auteur gravement réactionnaire.

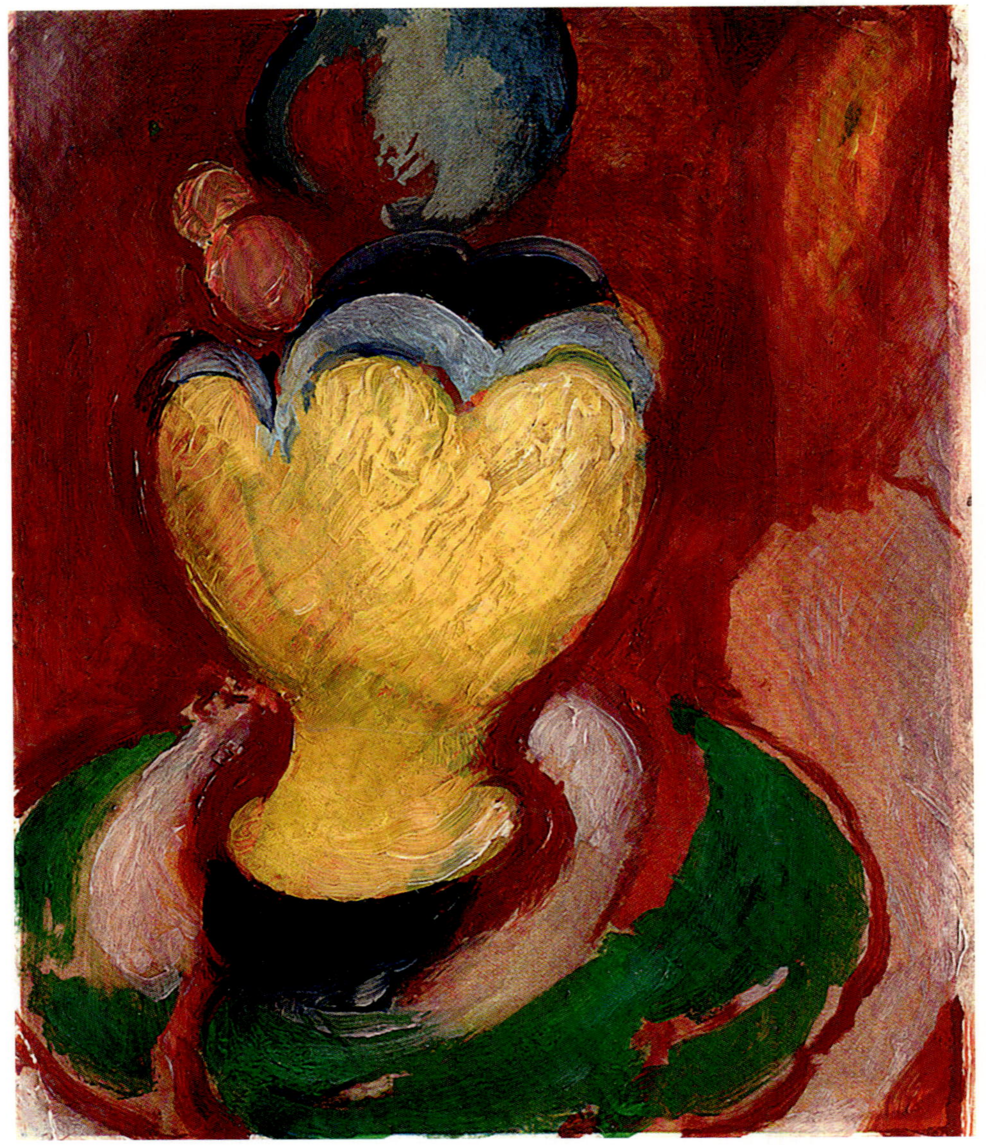

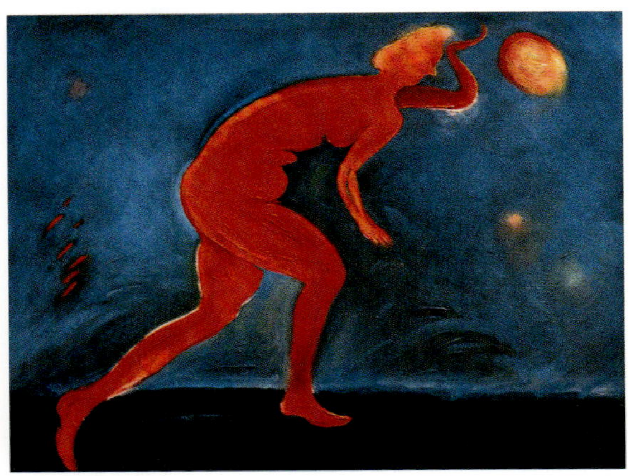

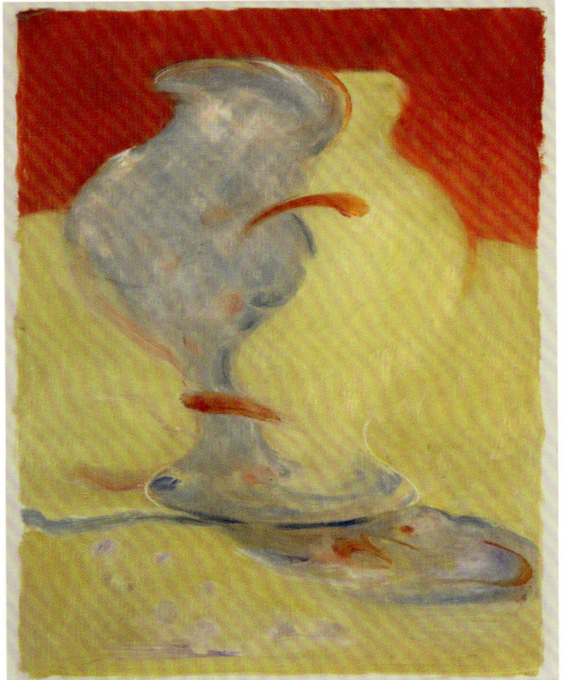

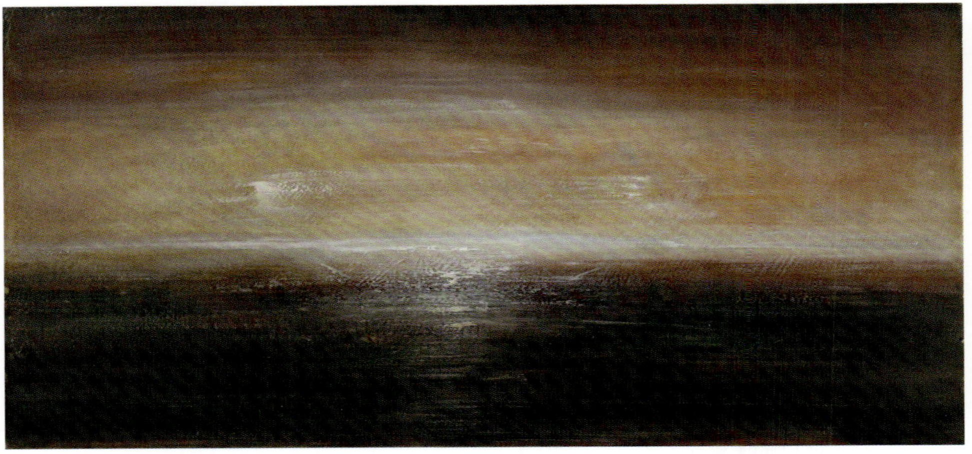

Vase on a Side Table, 2001.
Oil on Bristol board, 5 ½ × 4 ¼ in. (14 × 11 cm.).

Homage to William Turner VII, 1995.
Oil on cardboard, 8 × 16 in. (20.5 × 40.5 cm).

This Sun's Really Beating Down, 2000.
Oil on canvas, 14 ¾ × 18 in. (37.7 × 45.5 cm).

A Carafe on a Table, 2001.
Oil on canvas, 12 ½ × 9 in. (31.8 × 23 cm).

The Last Store before the Forest, 2001.
Oil on Bristol board, 11 ½ × 14 ¾ in. (29.6 × 37.7 cm).

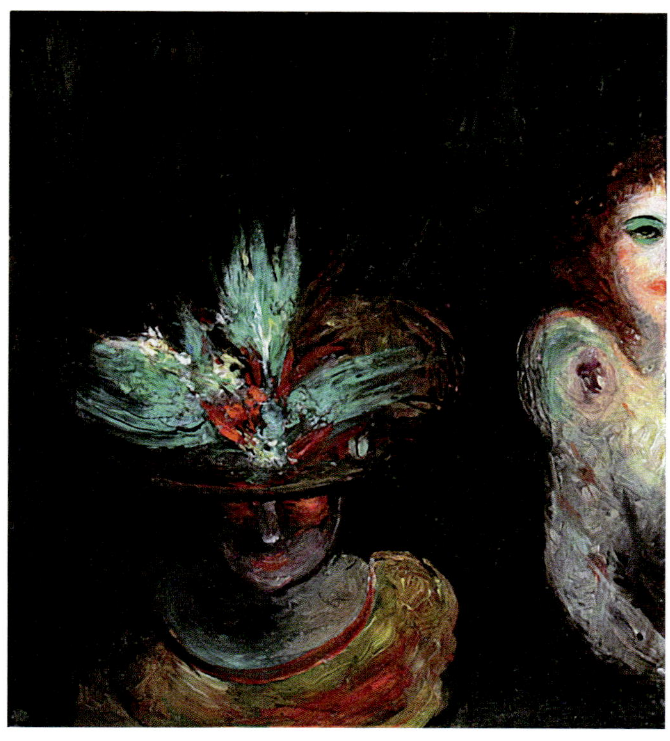

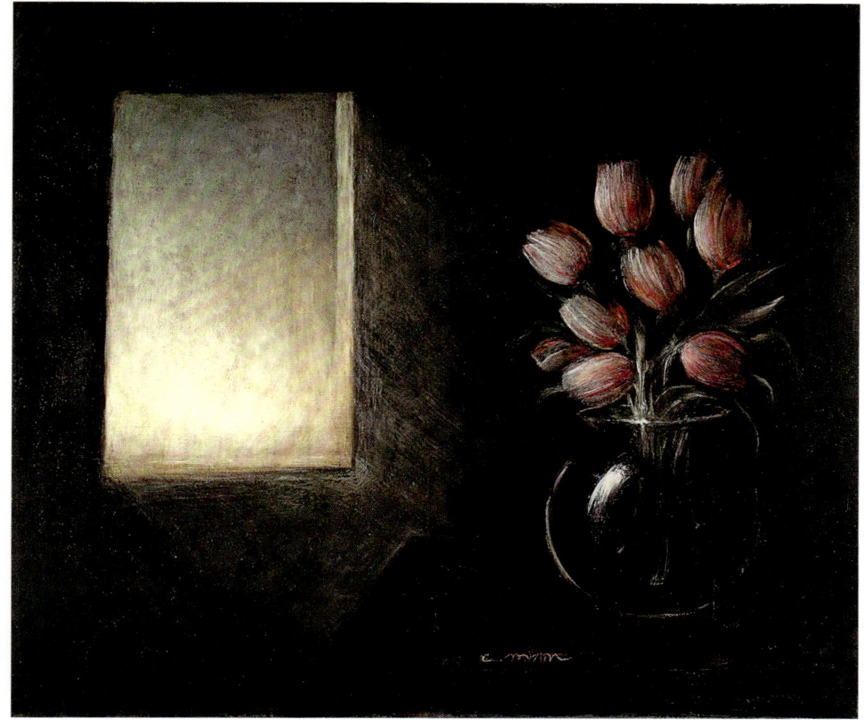

Two Women in Hats, 2001.
Oil on Bristol board,
6 ¼ × 6 in. (15.9 × 15.6 cm).

Tulips and Window, 2001.
Oil on Bristol board,
11 ½ × 13 ½ in. (29.6 × 34.3 cm).

The Blue Road, 2001.
Oil on Bristol board,
11 ¾ × 10 ½ in. (30 × 27 cm).

The Hague (Houses at Night), 2001.
Oil on Bristol board,
12 ¼ × 10 ½ in. (31 × 26.5 cm).

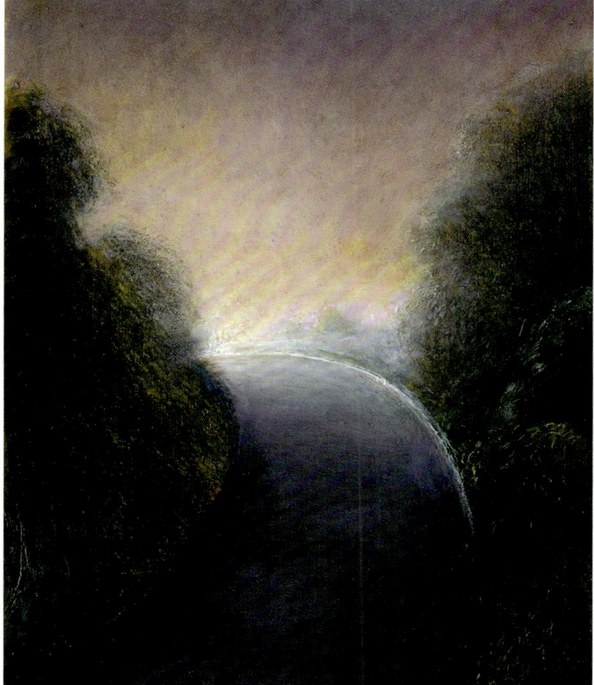

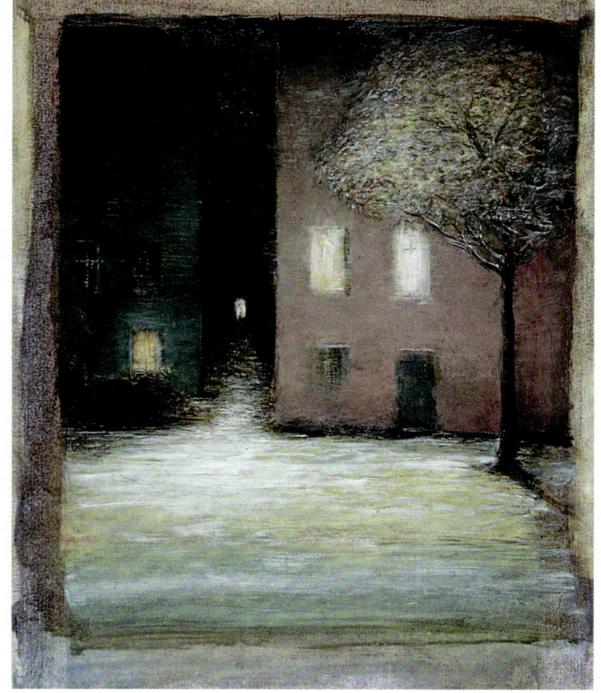

Nine pictures among those created for *The Bedroom of a Romantic Art Collector* prior to reduction. S.M.

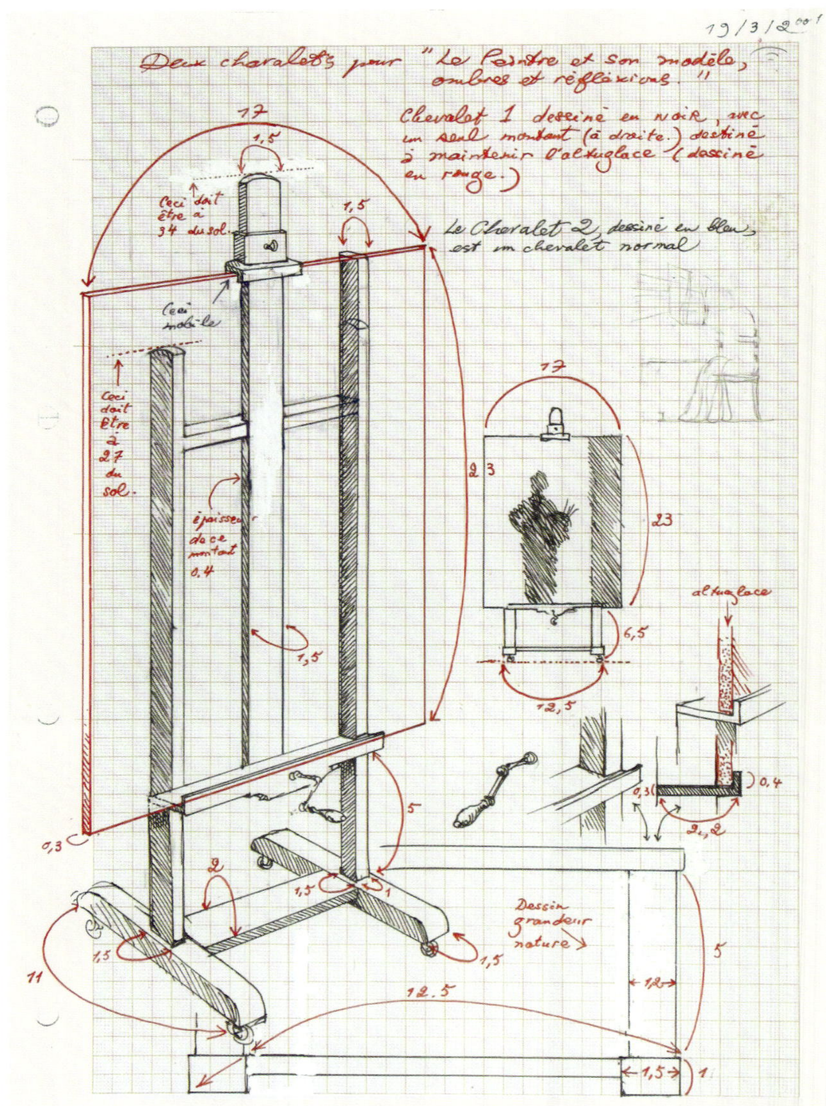

Two Easels for *The Painter and His Model, Shadows and Reflections*, 2001.
Pencil and felt pen on graph paper, 11 ¾ × 8 ¼ in. (29.7 × 21 cm).

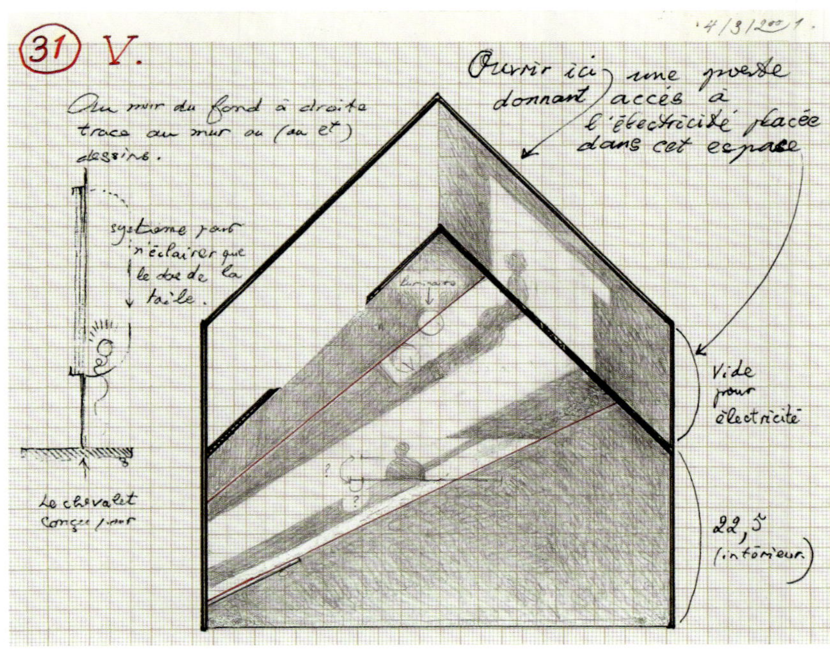

The Painter's Shadow (study), 2001.
Pencil on graph paper, 5 ½ × 8 ¼ in. (14 × 21 cm).

- for the wall at the back and to the right—a mark on the wall and (or) drawn
- a system to only shed light on the back of the waist
- an easel
- open a door here for the electricity installed in this space

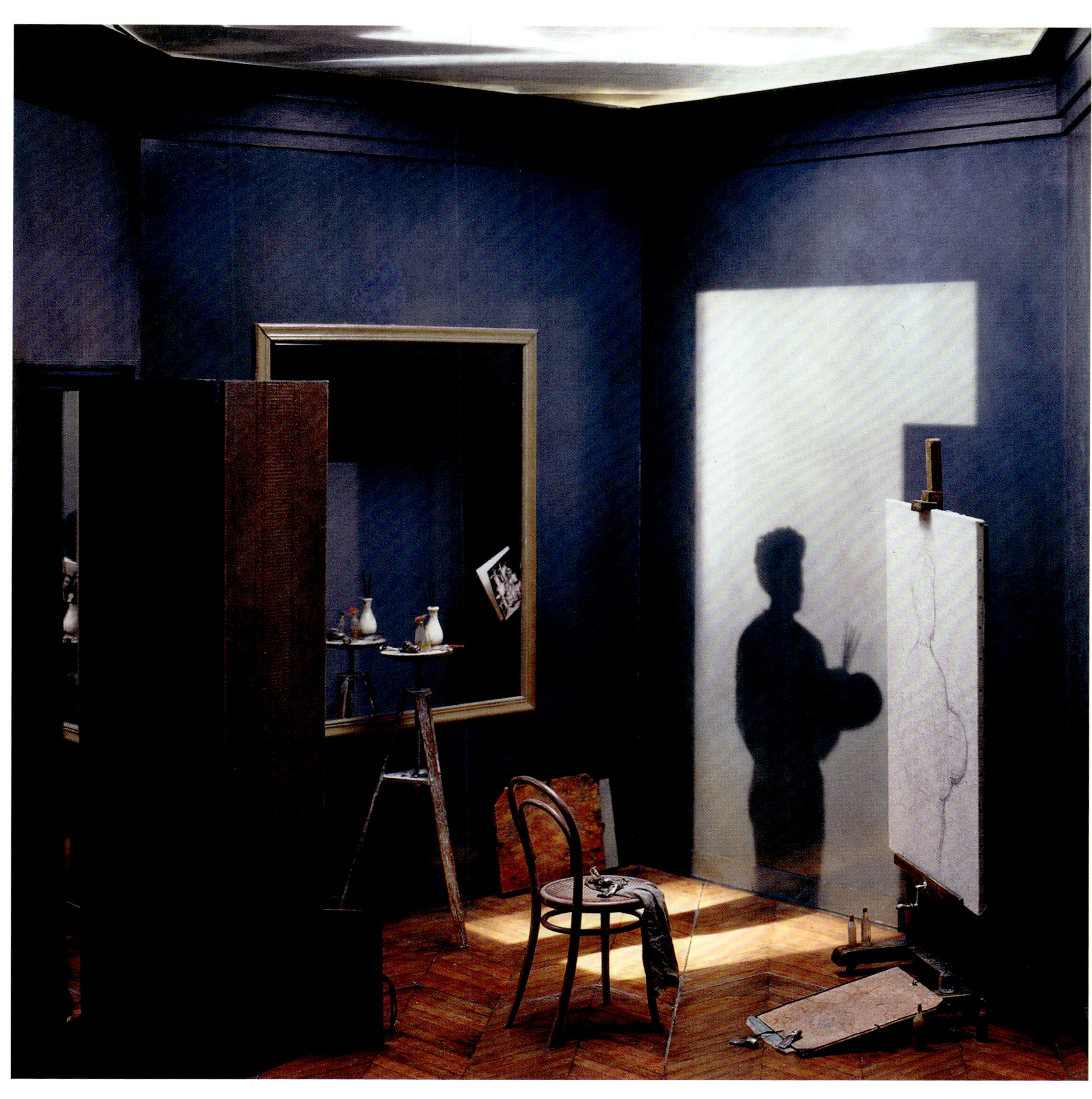

The Painter's Shadow II, 2002.
Mixed media, 26 ¾ × 23 ¼ × 24 ½ in. (68 × 59 × 62 cm).

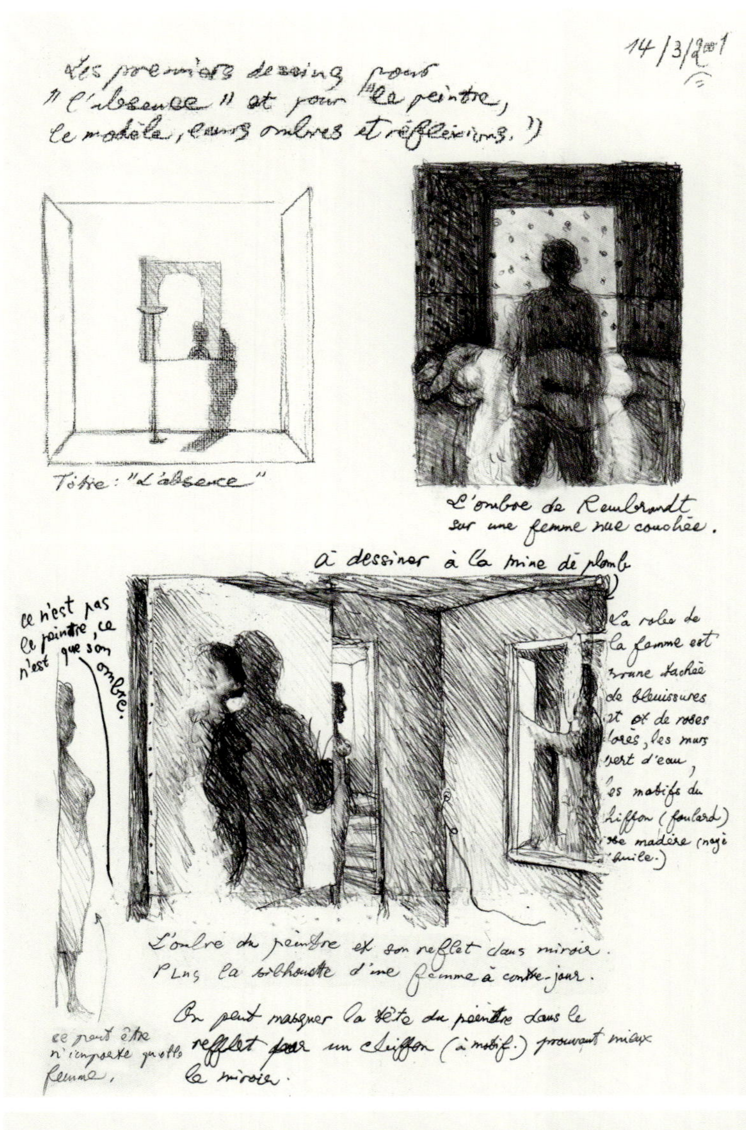

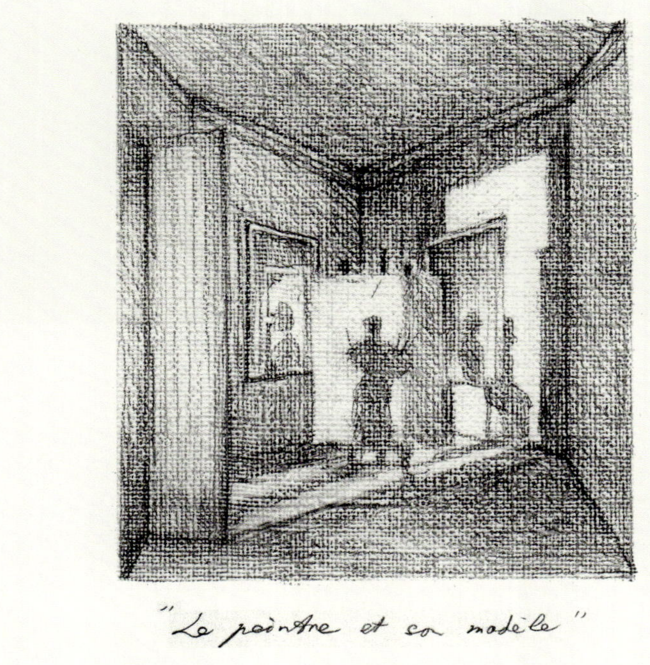

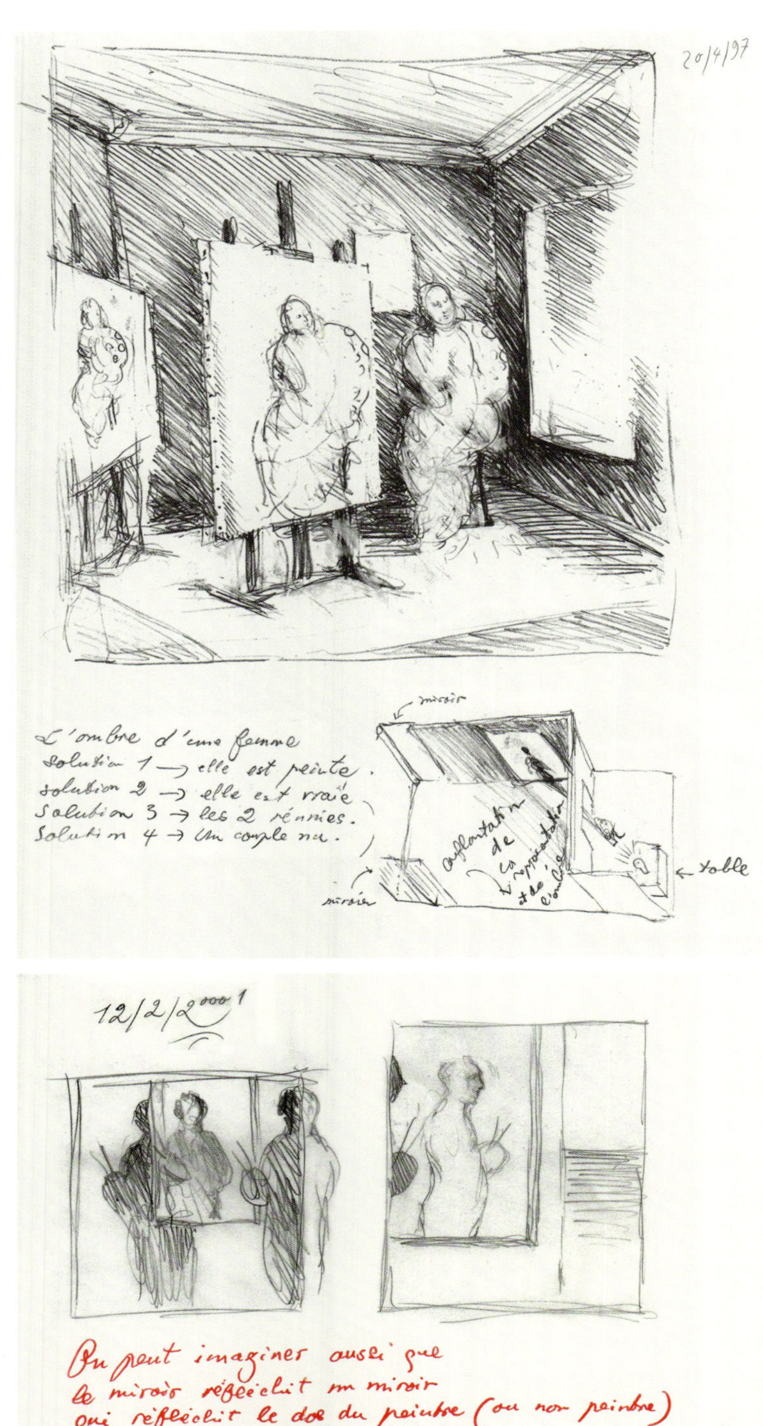

For a long time, shadows have had a bad press. I think it's time they were rehabilitated: an over-long daydream, captivated by the pure colors of an innocence supposedly regained, has confused them with evil. Yes, I think that it would be a good idea to turn some light on this shadow business.

C. Matton, *Charles Matton, visiblement*, op. cit.

The Model, the Painter's Shadow, and his Double Reflection, 2001.
Pencil on paper,
8 ¼ × 11 ¾ in. (21 × 29.7 cm).

The Painter, the Shadow, and the Model, 2001.
Pencil on pasteboard,
8 ¼ × 11 ¾ in. (21 × 29.7 cm).

The Painter, his Model, Shadows and Reflections, 2004.
Pencil on paper,
6 × 8 ¼ in. (15 × 21 cm).

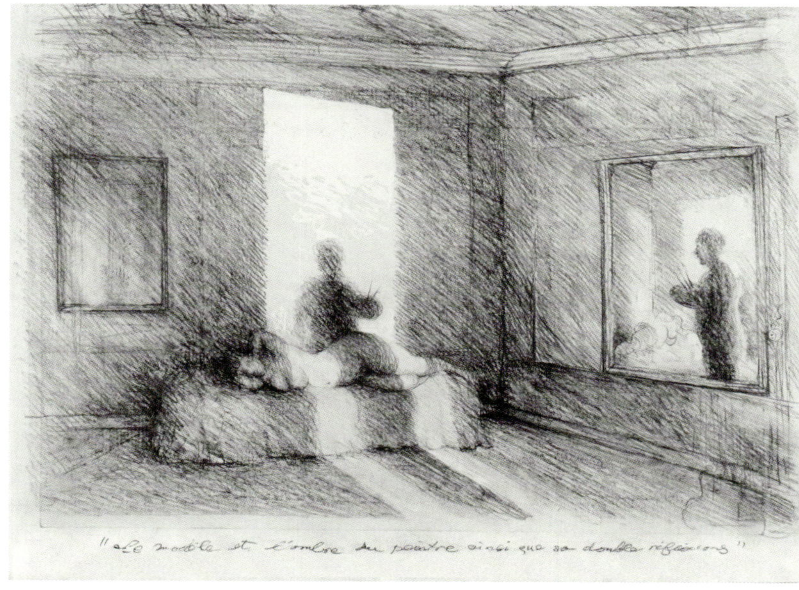

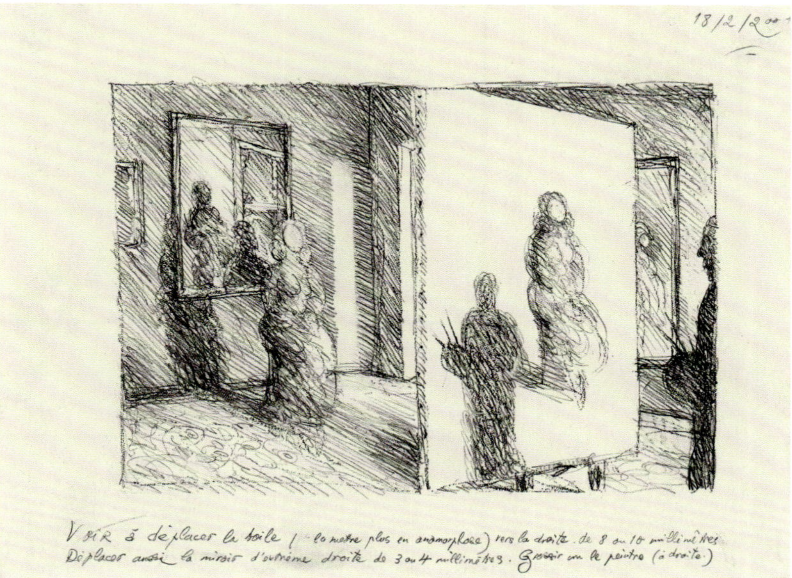

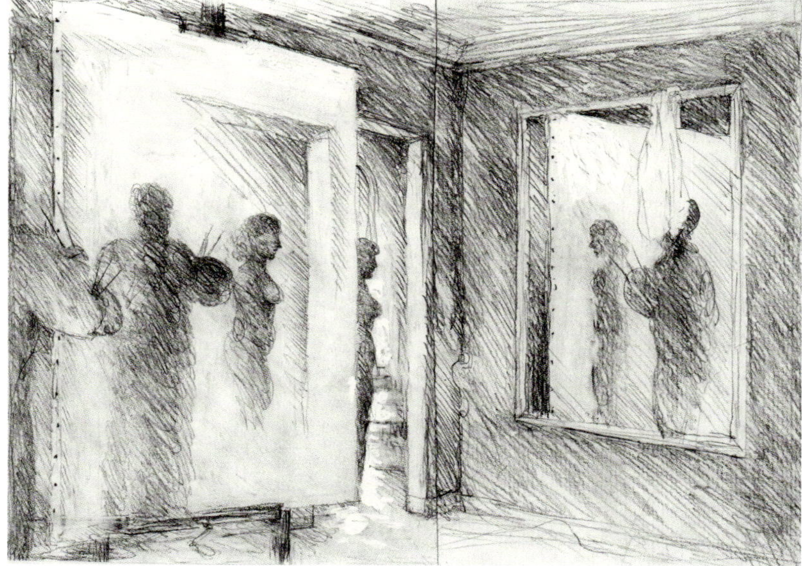

Facing page (clockwise from top left):
Earliest drawings for *Absence* and *The Painter, the Model, their Shadows and Reflections*,
1995–2001. Pencil on paper,
various dimensions on loose leaves,
11 ¾ × 8 ¼ in. (29.7 × 21 cm).

14/03/2001
- Title Absence.
- Rembrandt's shadow reflected on a naked woman in bed.
- This is not the painter, but only his shadow.
- It can be any woman.
- The shadow of the painter and its reflection in the mirror plus a woman's silhouette against the light.
- To make a better use of the mirror, the painter's head can be blurred in the reflection using a (printed) scarf.

20/4/97
Shadow of a woman
Solution 1: painted
Solution 2: real
Solution 3: both together
Solution 4: a naked couple

12/2/2000-1
One can also imagine that the mirror reflects a mirror that reflects the back of the painter (or non-painter) who one sees directly to the right.

Bottom left:
The painter and his model.

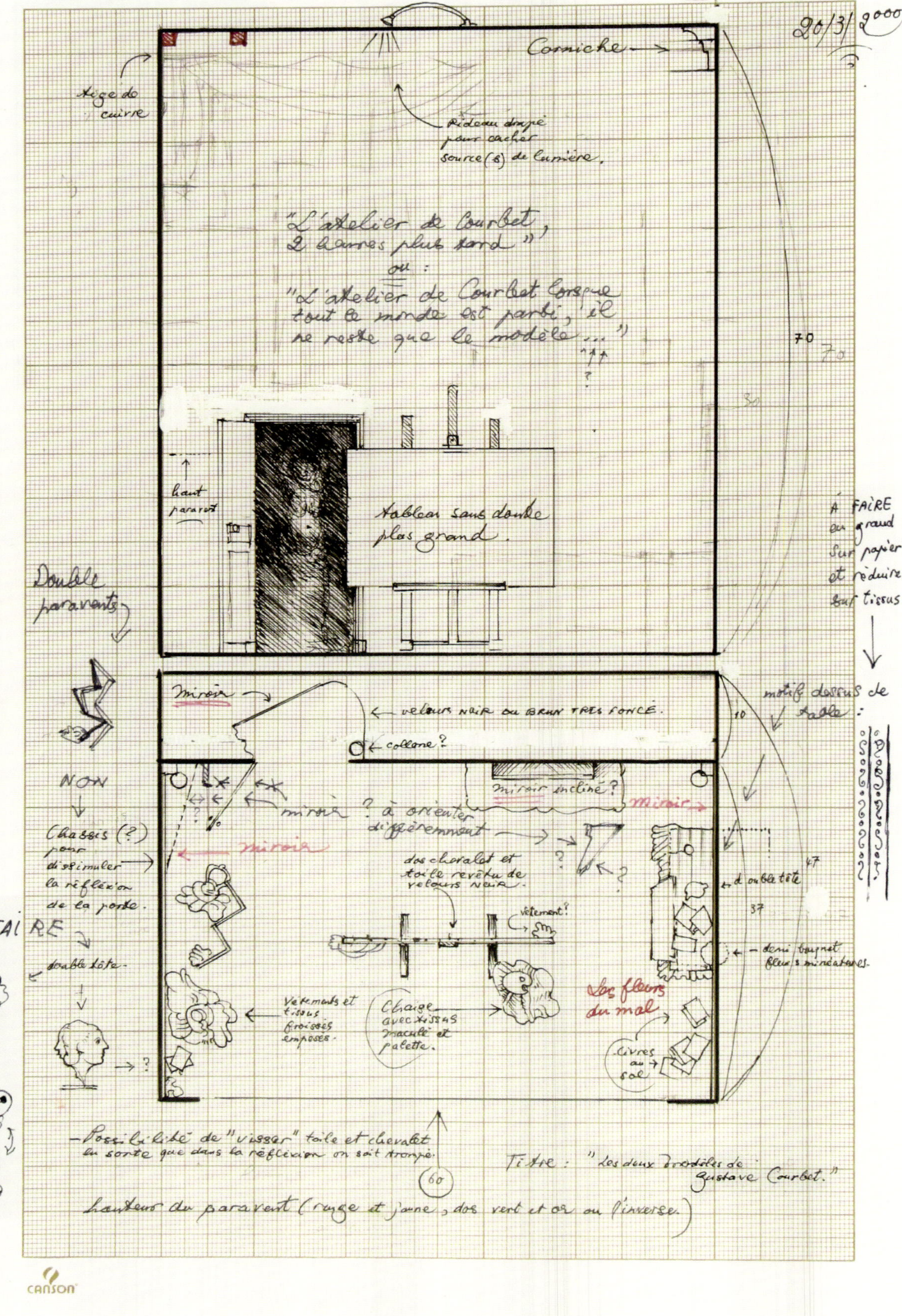

Courbet's Studio Two Hours Later, or *Courbet's Studio, when all have gone, only the model remains*. 2000. Pencil and felt pen on graph paper, 11 ¾ × 8 ¼ in. (29.7 × 21 cm).

Two variations of *The Caryatid I (Courbet's Model)*, 1999.
Torolith and marble,
11 ½ × 3 ½ × 3 ½ in.
(29 × 9 × 9 cm).
Photographs.

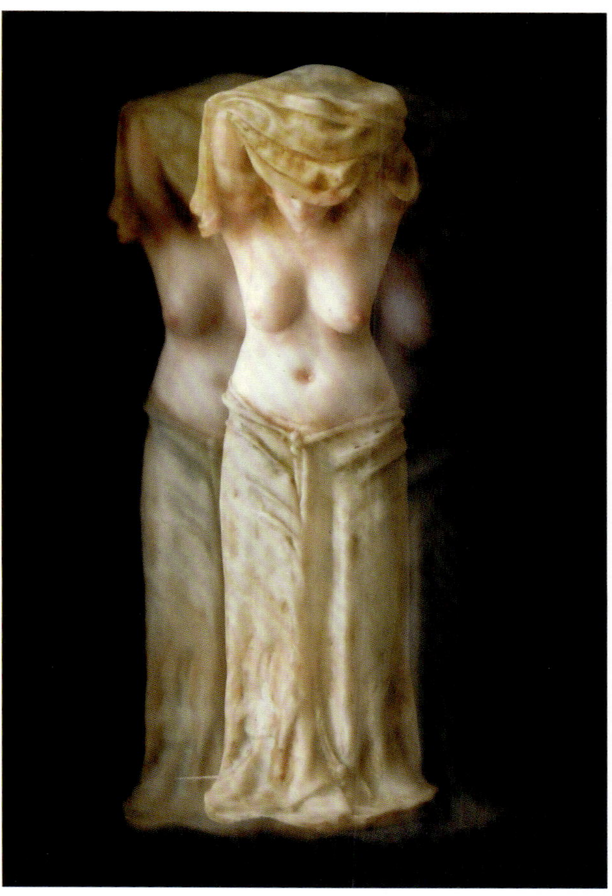

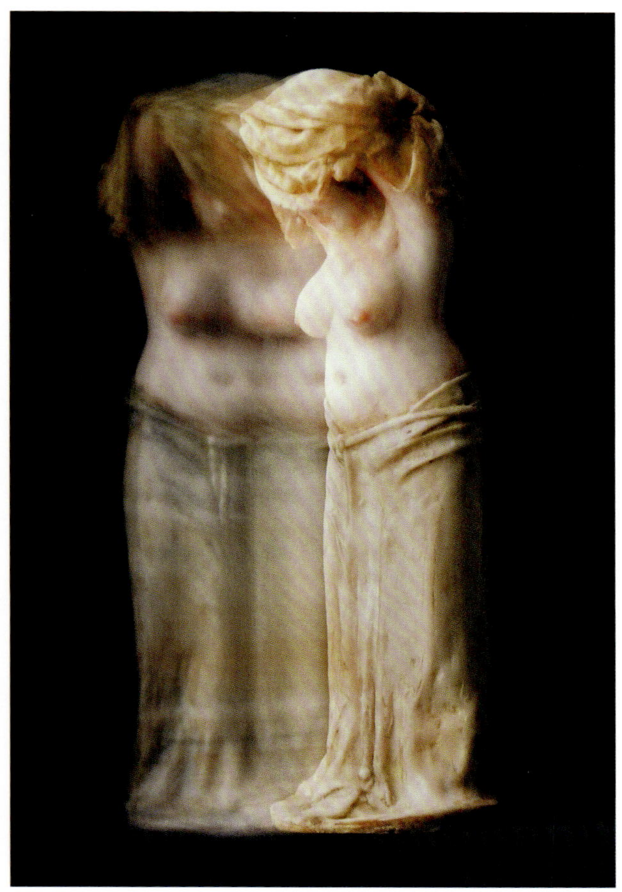

The Model, study I, 2007.
Pencil on paper,
11 ¾ × 8 ¼ in.
(29.7 × 21 cm).

The Model, study III, 2007.
Pencil on paper,
16 ½ × 11 ¾ in.
(42 × 29.7 cm).

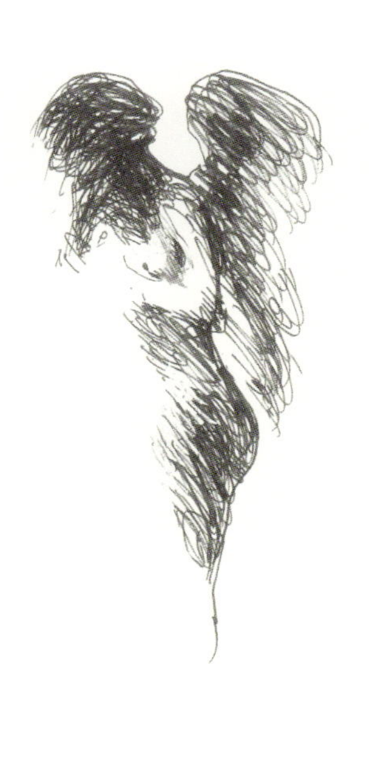

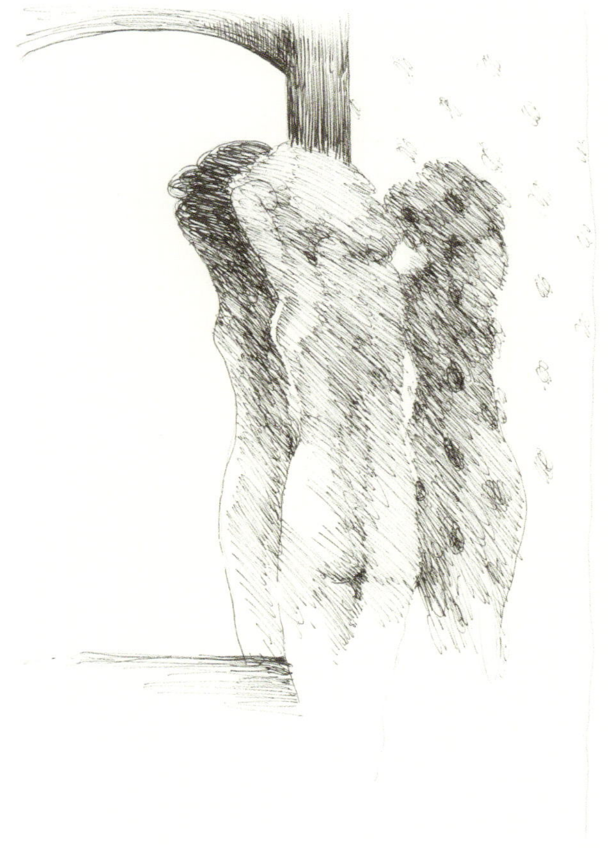

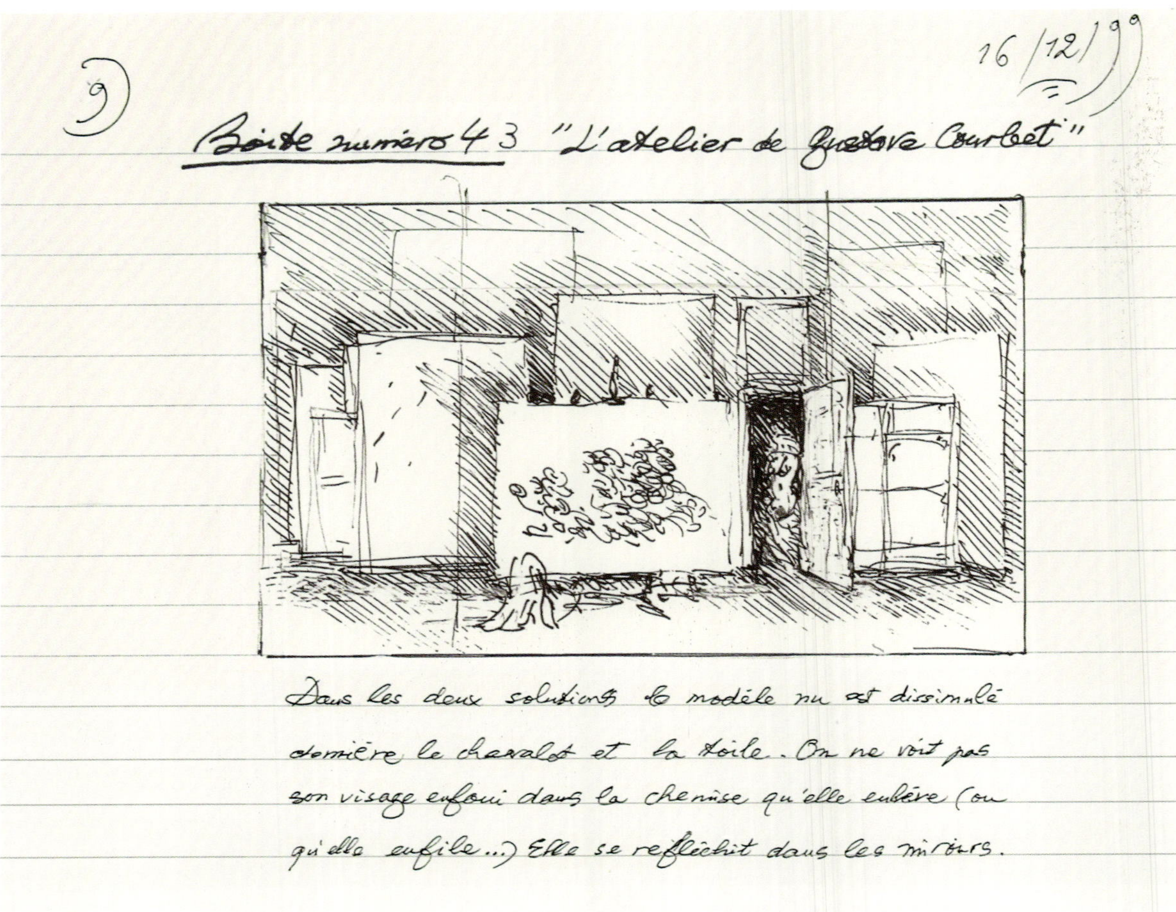

Gustave Courbet's Studio I, 1999.
Pencil on paper,
6 × 8 ¼ in. (15 × 21 cm).

9) Box number 43
Gustave Courbet's Studio
In both solutions, the naked model is hidden behind the easel and the canvas. One can't see her face buried in the shirt she's taking off (or throwing on...). She's reflected in the mirrors.

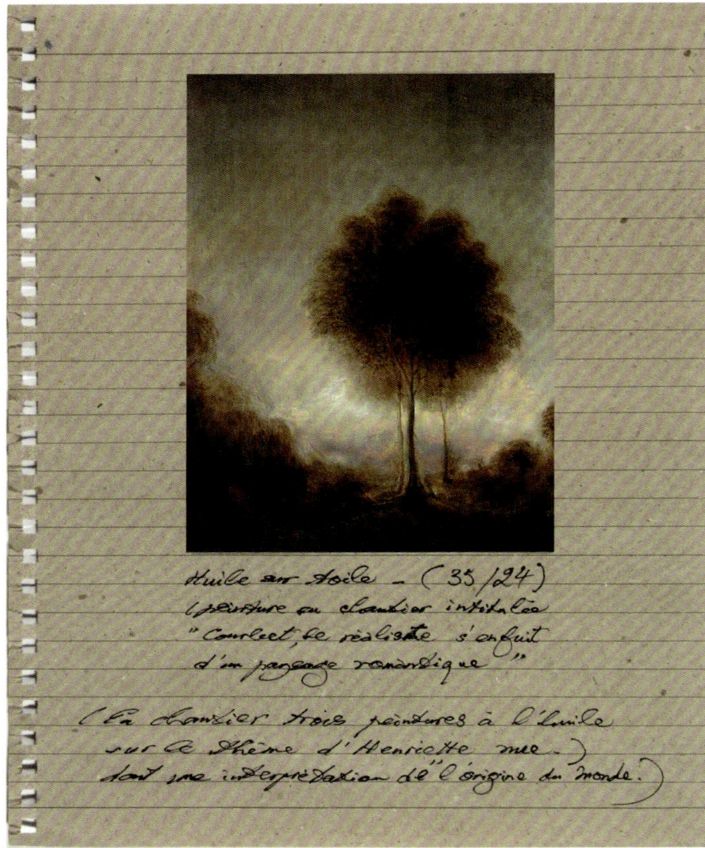

The Realist Courbet Flees a Romantic Landscape, 2000.
Collage and felt pen on cardboard,
11 ¾ × 8 ¼ in. (29.7 × 21 cm).

Oil on canvas _ (35/24)
Painting in progress entitled The Realist Courbet Flees a Romantic Landscape *(three oil paintings in progress on the theme of Henriette nude, including an interpretation of* The Origin of the World).

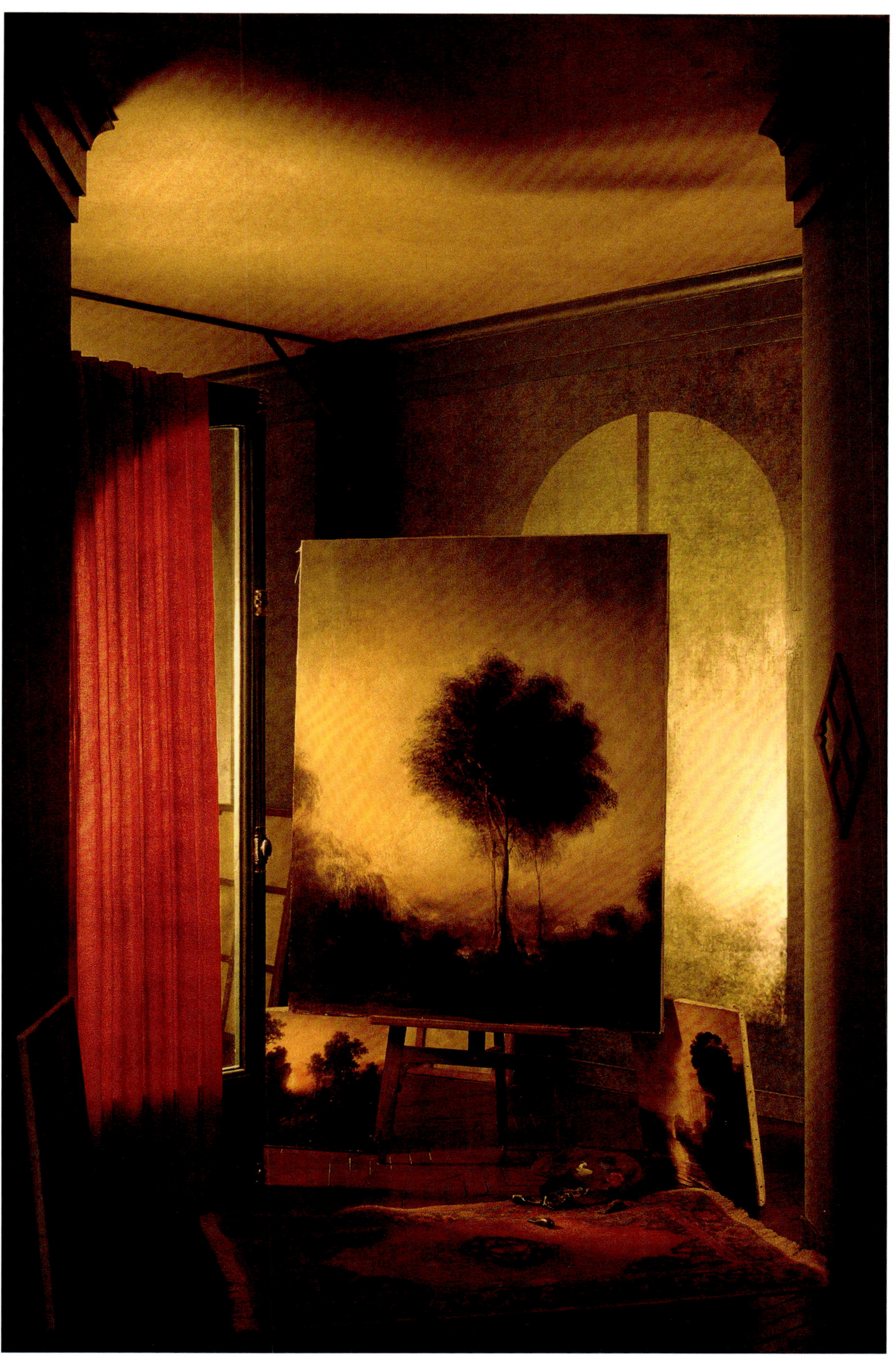

The Studio of a Romantic Painter, 2000.
Mixed media,
32 ¼ × 25 ½ × 33 in.
(82 × 65 × 84 cm).

Alain Finkielkraut: "You will love art only when you love what it reflects more." How unlikely Ruskin's phrase sounds at a time when it's out of the question for art to reflect anything agreeable at all [...] It's odd because, when I think of this dichotomy, which you share, Charles Matton, it reminds me of the split in poetry, between, on the one side, the vein of Mallarmé and, on the other, that of Saint-John Perse. Mallarmé, who writes in a letter to Casalis, "The here and now smells of the kitchen." A Gnostic rejection of the world in favor of the book. Then, Saint-John Perse, on the contrary, a kind of nomenclature, in love with the world and with things.
Charles Matton: What you've just said is very strange because when I was talking to you just now about tracing things back to Cézanne to find out who's to blame, if one can talk of blaming—let's say instead, trying to get to the bottom of it all—I had Mallarmé in the back of my mind, as I hold him chiefly responsible for the loss of meaning. Or rather, for this Cézanne-like remoteness that has, paradoxically, led to the conceptual castration Roland Barthes denounced shortly before his death.

C. Matton and Alain Finkielkraut, Interview by Alain Finkielkraut, "Être artiste aujourd'hui," *Répliques*, France Culture (December 16, 2000)

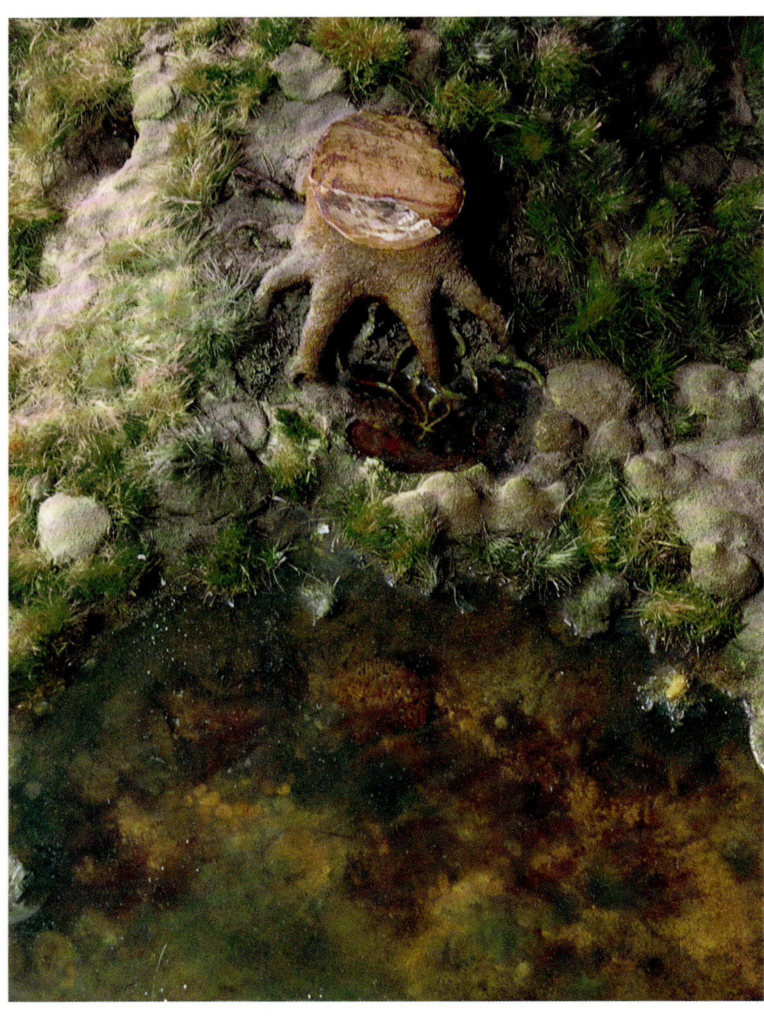

63 m² of Nature, 1997.
Mixed media, 6 × 21 ¾ × 31 ½ in. (15 × 55 × 80 cm).

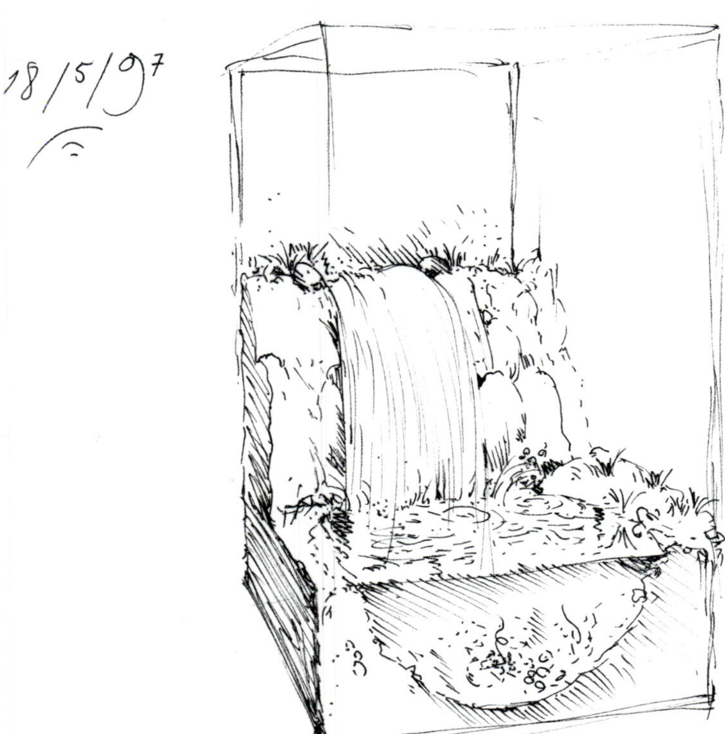

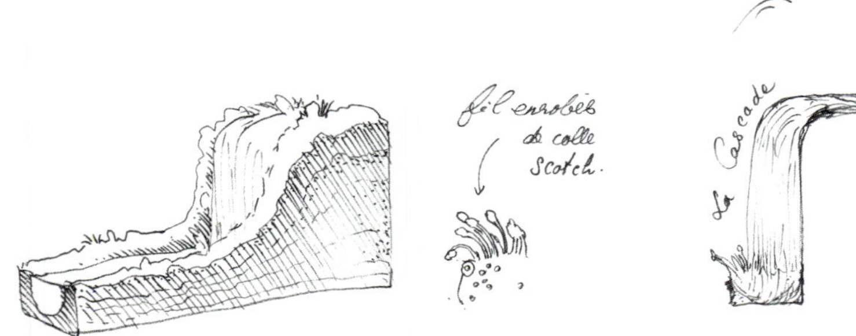

Art Story *The Waterfall*

I worked and worked with plaster soaked in coffee and ink, or dipped in sand from the Seychelles, with supermarket nylon feather-dusters (to make the grass, set with hot air from a hairdryer). I modeled the rocks, the tree roots out of painted plastolith; I added stones collected on the beaches of the Côte d'Opale, gravel from the little Saint-Germain Square, and real roots of basil. In this kind of work, one is always feeling one's way; there's no guarantee in advance. Above all one mustn't lose courage, must one?

The waterfall itself is made of crystal epoxy resin laid down in layers, because it is very difficult to control as it has to be deployed as it catalyzes, and that happens very fast, in ten seconds at the most. I would go to bed pretty pleased in the evening but be disappointed next morning; the weight of the liquid, its vigor, its logic would be missing. The days passed. I stopped when I heard the noise of water. Then I knew.

Personal note, November 7, 1997

The Waterfall, 1997.
Mixed media,
17 ¾ × 21 ¾ × 31 ½ in.
(45 × 55 × 80 cm).

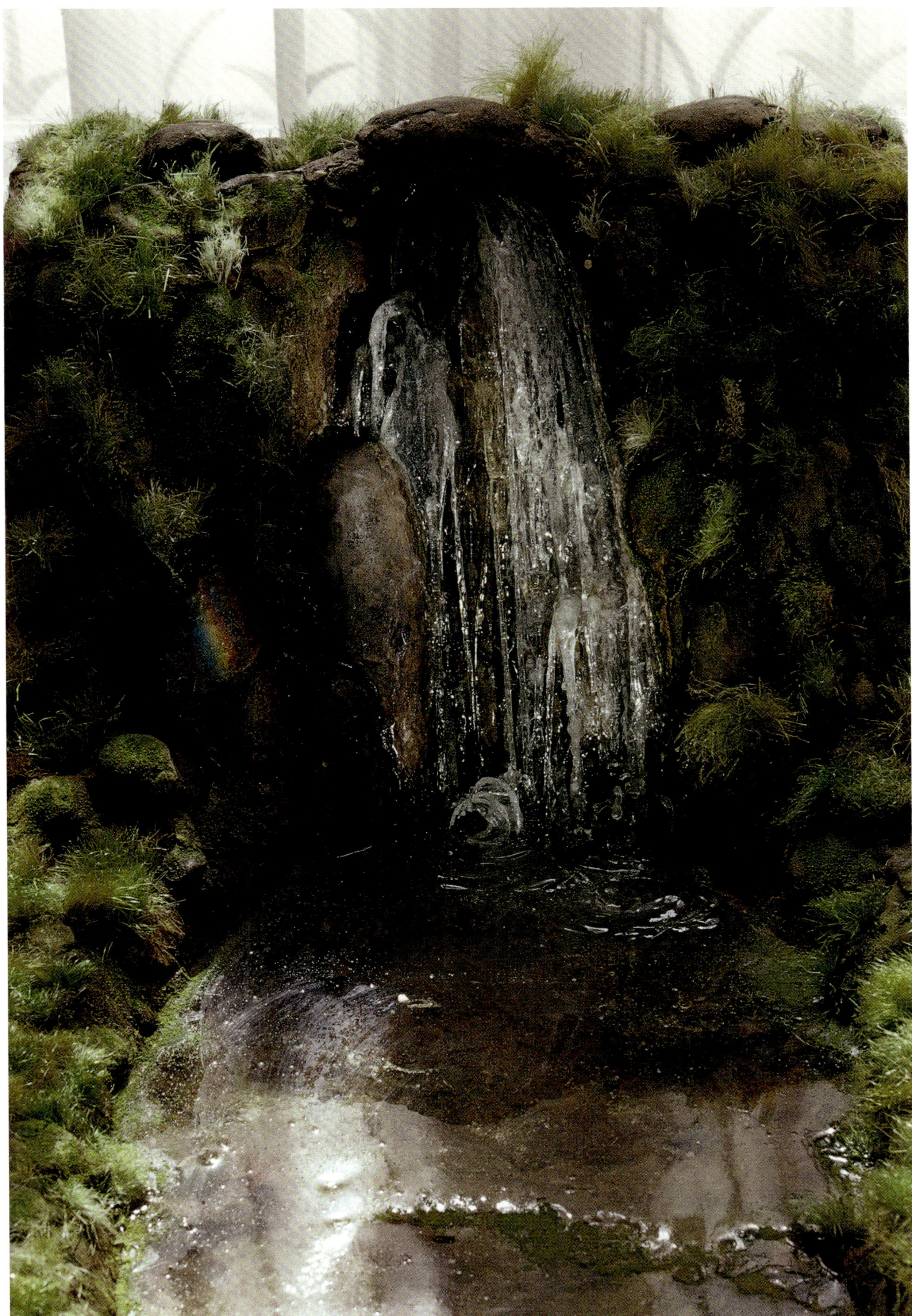

Facing page:
The Waterfall (studies),
1997.
Pencil on paper,
3 ¾ × 2 ½ in. (9.5 × 6.7 cm)
and 1 ½ × 3 ¾ in. (4 × 9.5 cm).

Buy stacks of little glass balls.
Try to mix mother-of-pearl.
Try to widen the pond.

Wire coated with Scotch glue

1/2/2001

ACHATS:

Gel médium pour épaissir la peinture.
Toile lisse au mètre.

"Le jaune, le jaune du safran au citron acide. Safran lourd onctueux (en) grasse pâte, citron (et) fluide, juteux, transparent (Comme de l'aquarelle), Lors du passage de l'un à l'autre des roses violacés s'immiscent, s'immiscent c'est le mot. Le territoire est finement marqué, délimité par une ligne franche à un brun doré, là, après le rouge, éteint de (exogène mais) gris, s'en donne à coeur-joie dans ses propres limites du tyrien à la mandarine confite, crevé, çà et là, de taches en contradiction (de tons insurgés), ponctuée de virgules (ceruleum véronèze et turquoise)
Vaste Plage dont l'éclat est garanti par une savante retenue, qui figure les parois d'une chambre....
Au mur un tableau d'esprit sentimental?

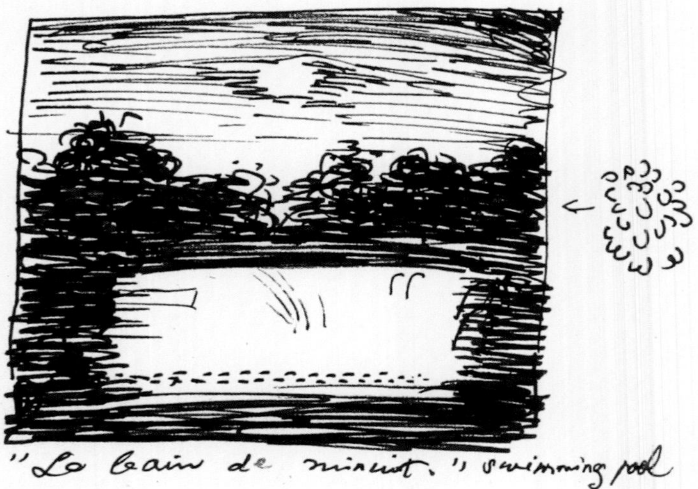

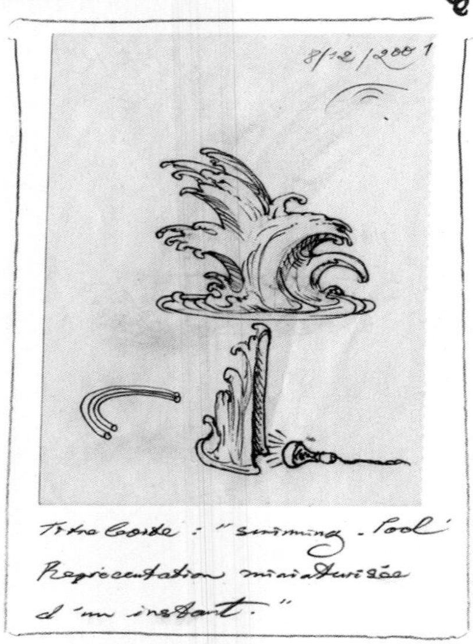

Personal note and sketches, 2001.
Pencil on paper, 6 ½ × 8 ½ in. (17 × 21 cm).

Yellow, from saffron yellow to acid lemon. Unctuous heavy saffron in stiff paste, juicy and fluid lemon, transparent like watercolor, lean, as one color passes into the other the purplish pinks encroach, encroach, that's the word.
The territory is finely marked, delimited by a line, faint but clear, in golden brown, there, after the red dulled with gray exalts within its limits of Tyrian crystallized tangerine, punctuated here and there by contradictory (insurgent tones) patches, studded with commas (ceruleum, Veronese, and turquoise).
Vast expanse whose sheen is ensured by a calculated restraint, depicting bedroom walls....
On the wall a picture in the sentimental vein?

Box title:
Swimming Pool.
Miniaturized representation of an instant.

Facing page:
Swimming Pool at Night III, 2007.
Mixed media, 28 × 19 ¾ × 20 ¼ in. (71 × 50 × 58.5 cm).

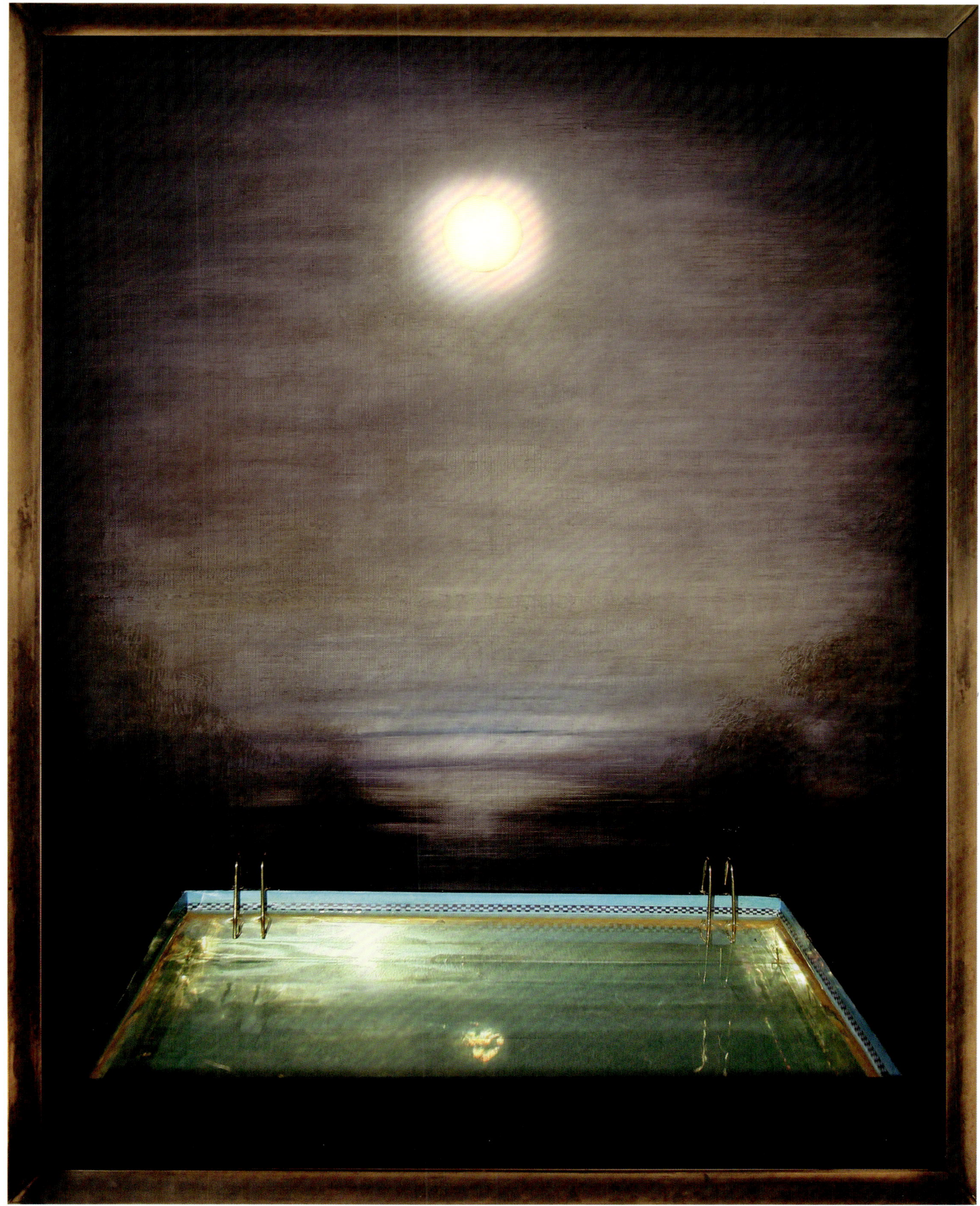

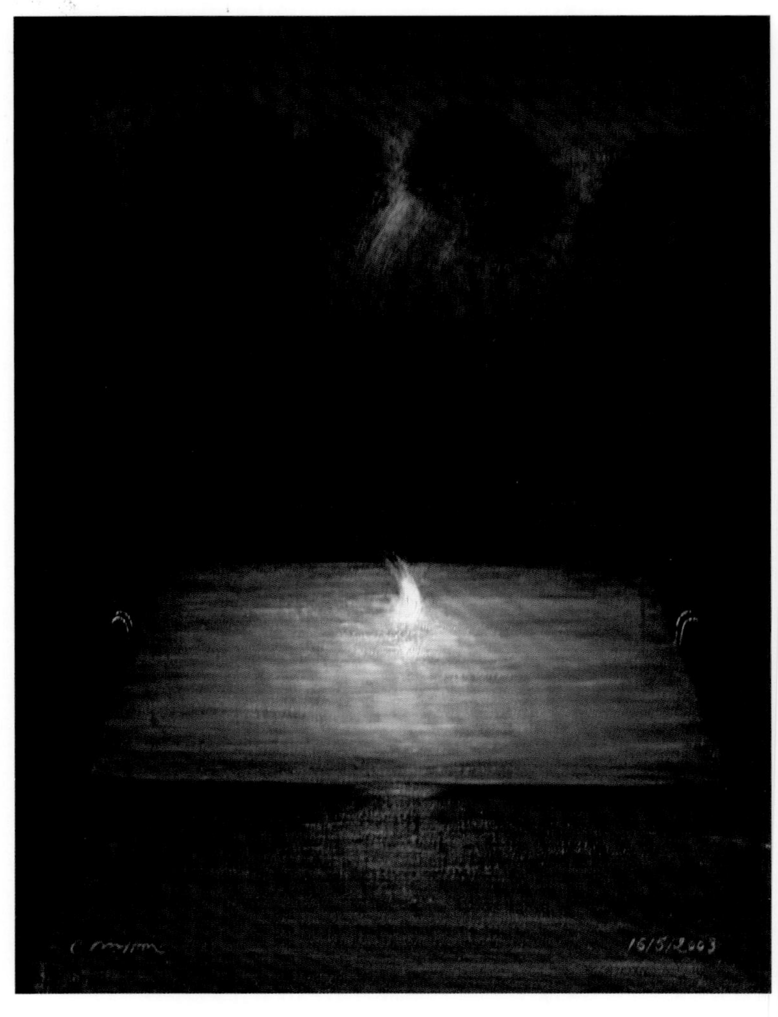
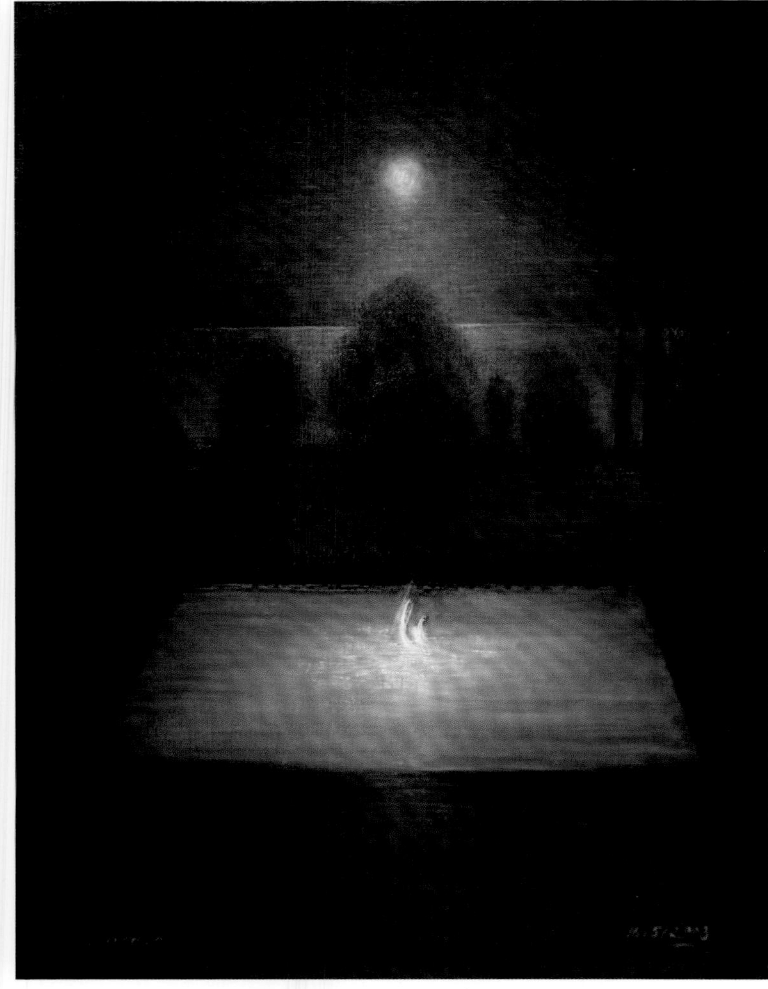

The Midnight Dip I, II, III, IV, 2003.
Oil on canvas, 24 × 18 in. (61 × 46 cm).

Painting idea: Night, tree completely black, gray-pink sky, blue (find which) around the moon the sky's lighter, the moon, pale yellow, yellow white.

Personal note, June 11, 1977

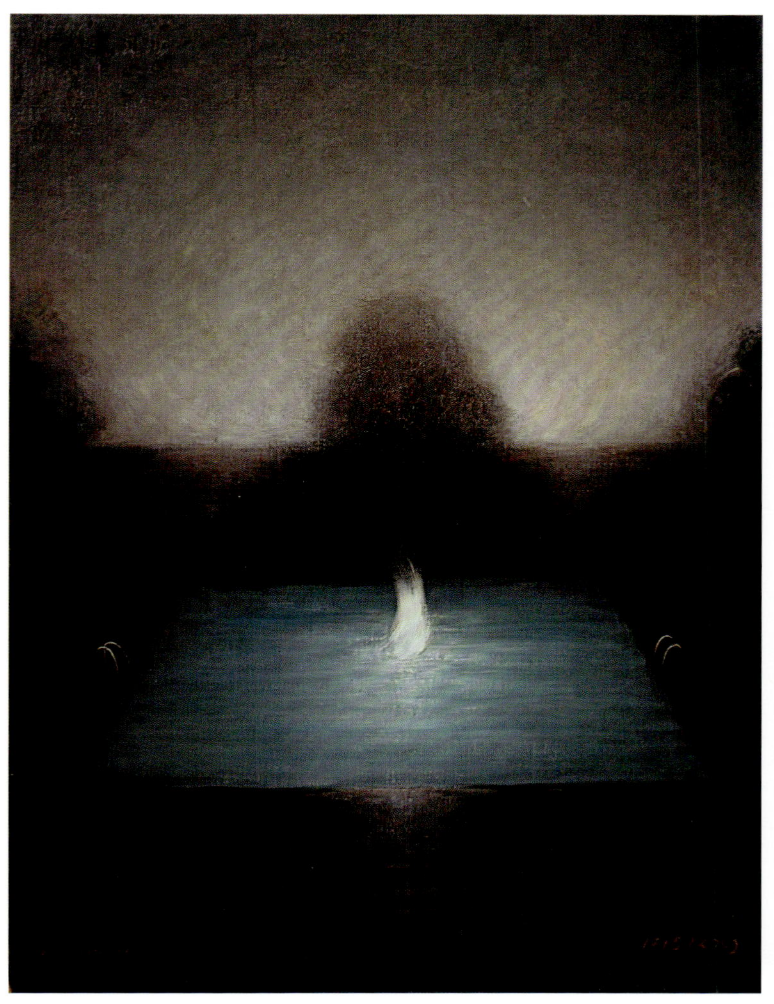

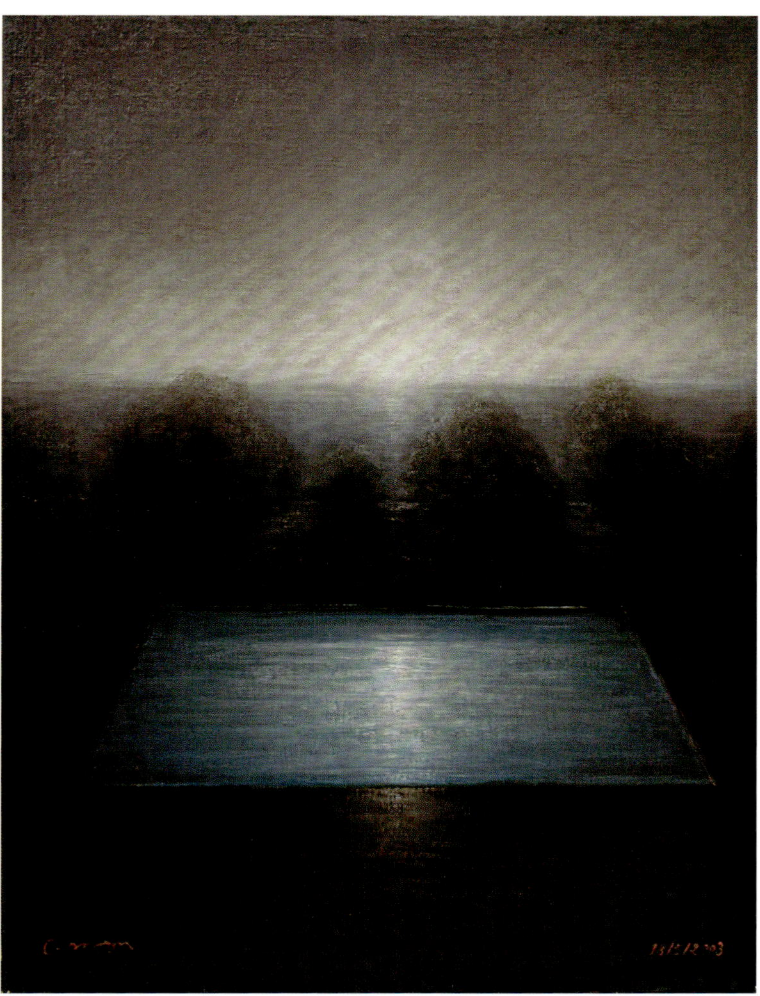

Guideline for thought: What interests me in descriptive painting is the poetry; now this poetry can exist without description (Turner). So I'm less concerned with the trajectory "from story to gesture," and my aim now is to fuse poetry and pure painting in a single image.

Personal note, March 30, 1997

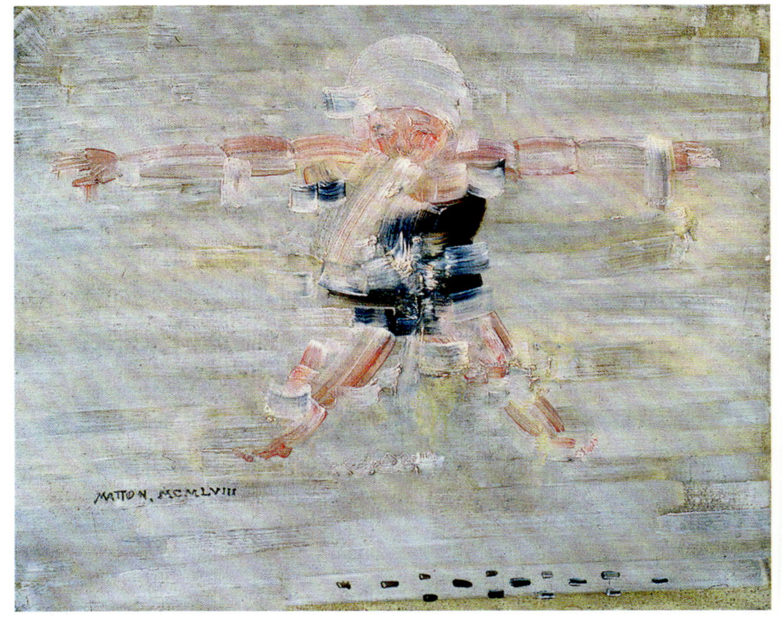

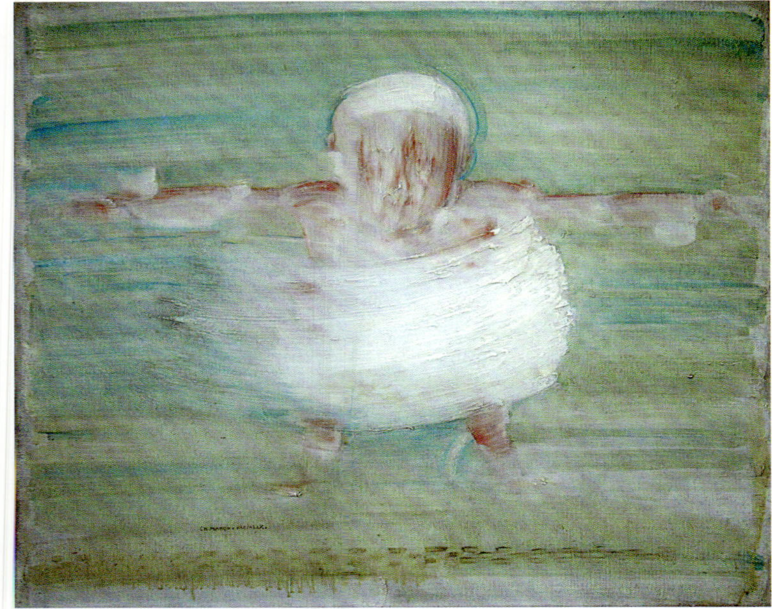

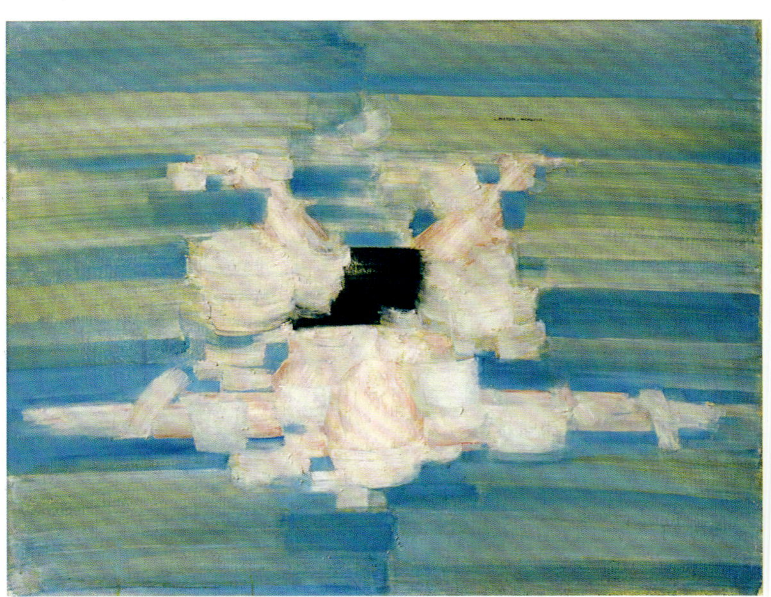

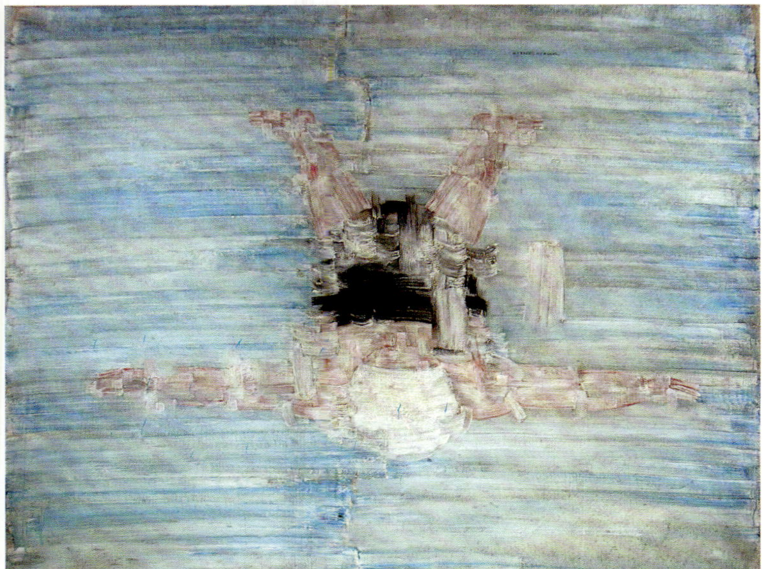

Bather IV, 1958.
Oil on canvas, 8 ¾ × 10 ½ in.
(22 × 27 cm).

The Grand Bather II, 1958.
Oil on canvas, 28 ¾ × 36 ¼ in.
(73 × 92 cm).

The Large Trail of Water, 1958.
Oil on canvas, 18 × 21 ¾ in. (46 × 55 cm).

The Grand Bather I, 1958.
Oil on canvas, 28 ¾ × 36 ¼ in.
(73 × 92 cm).

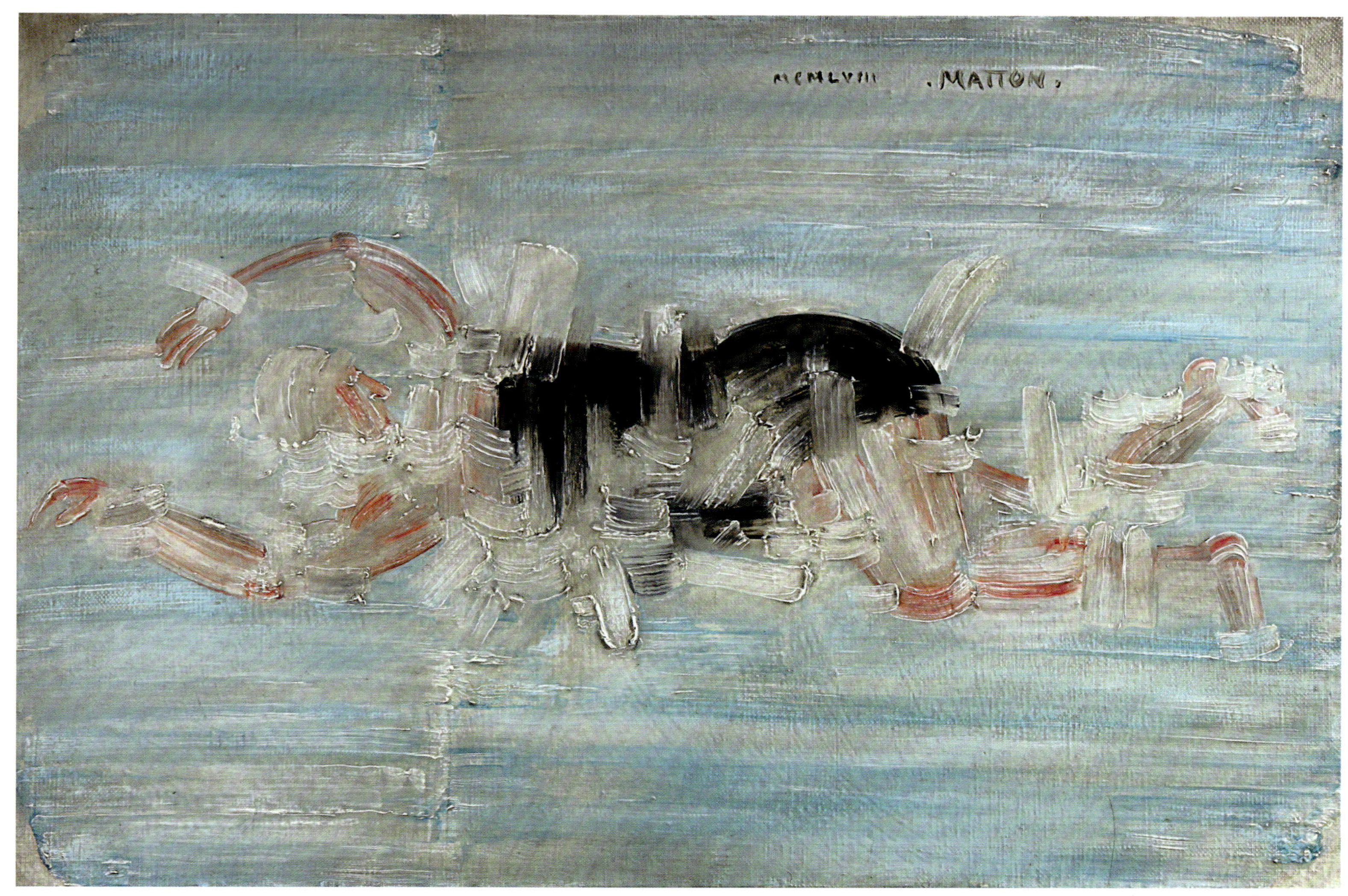

I wanted to use what had been gained from non-figuration to "re-figure," to extract the form of the figure from the informal chaos, yet without describing it. The water in the swimming pools, by diluting the bodies, made my task easier. It met me, as it were, halfway.

C. Matton, *Charles Matton, visiblement*, op. cit.

Crawl II, 1958.
Oil on canvas, 12 ¾ × 18 in.
(32.5 × 46 cm).

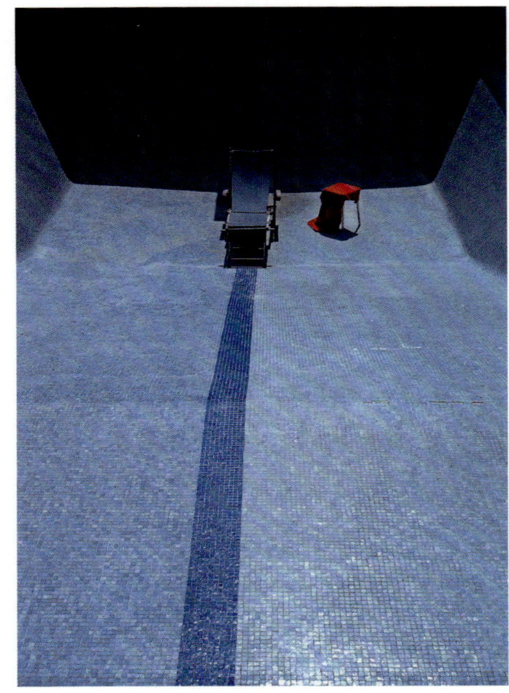

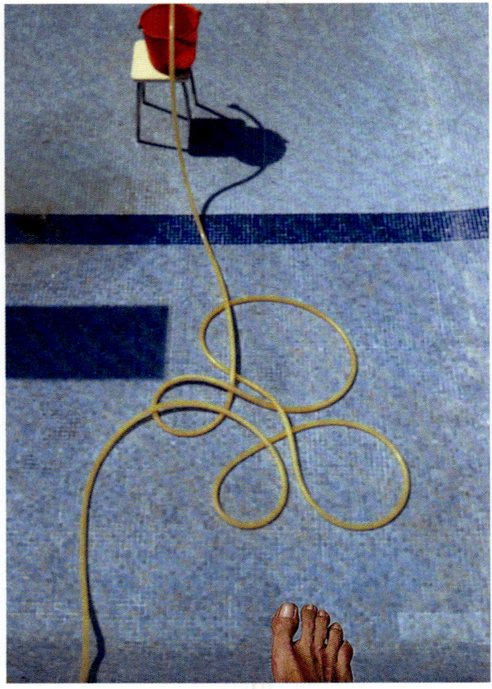

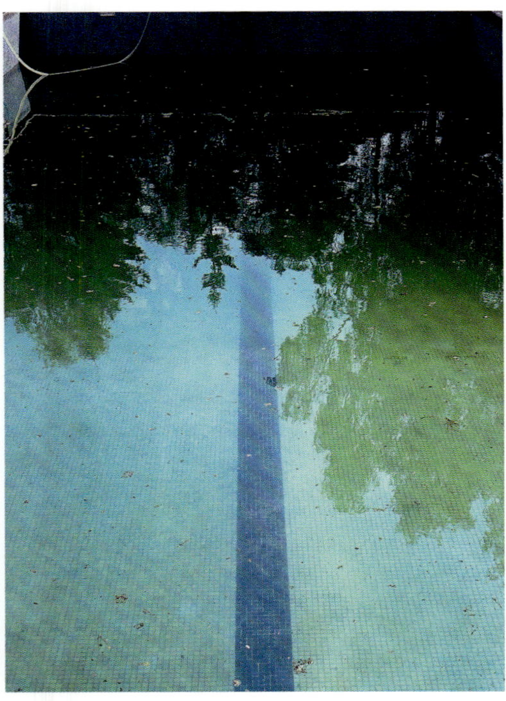

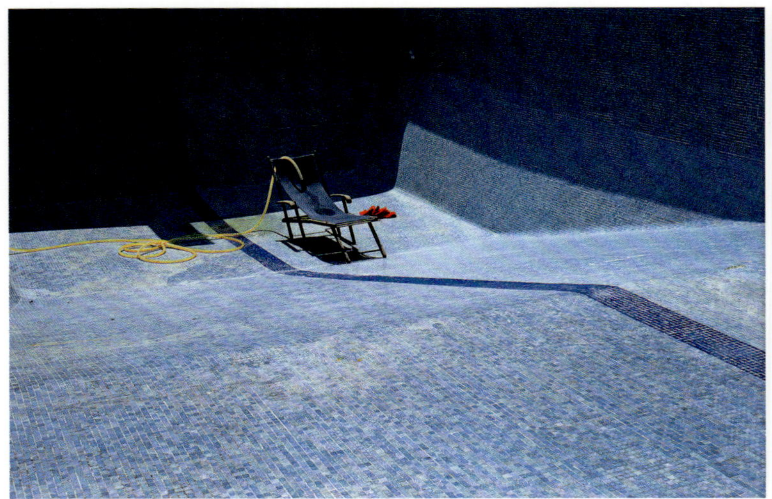

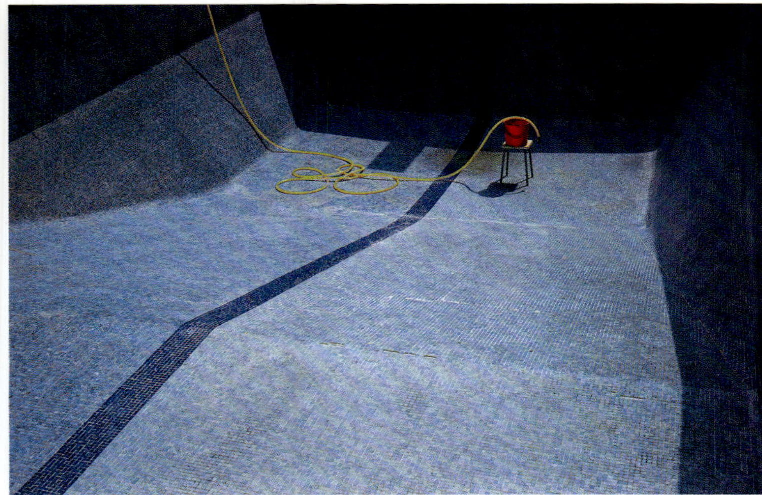

Swimming Pool VII, 1974.
Photograph.

Self-portrait with Foot. 1974.
Photograph.

Swimming Pool X, 1974.
Photograph.

Swimming Pool I, 1974.
Photograph.

Swimming Pool II. 1974.
Photograph.

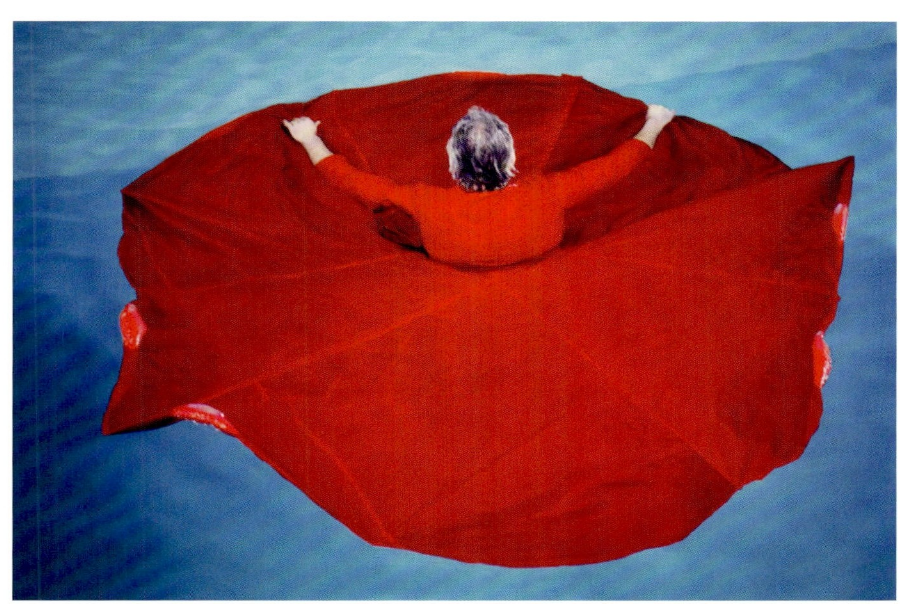

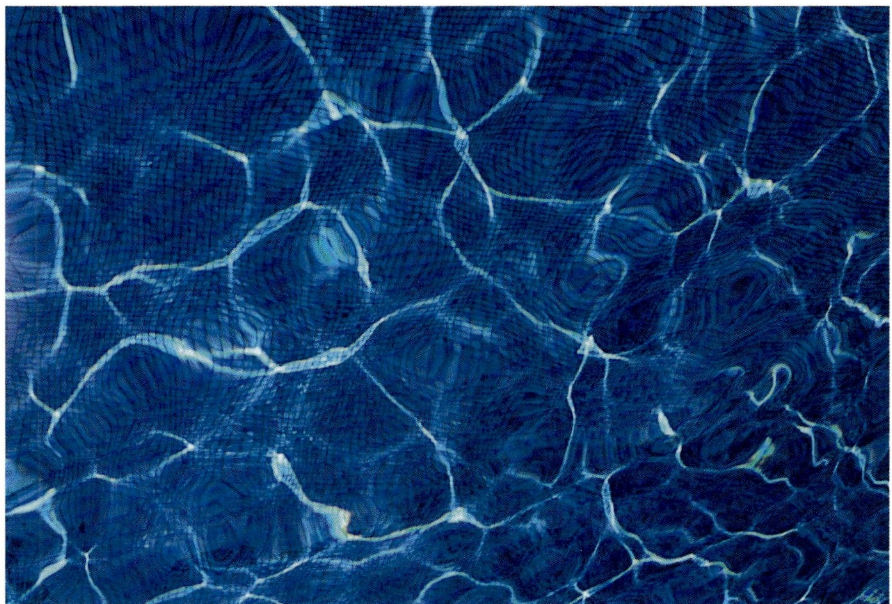

Priest in the Swimming Pool (from the shoot of *L'Amour est un fleuve en Russie* directed by Charles Matton), 1976. Photograph.

Swimming Pool (detail), 1975. Photograph.

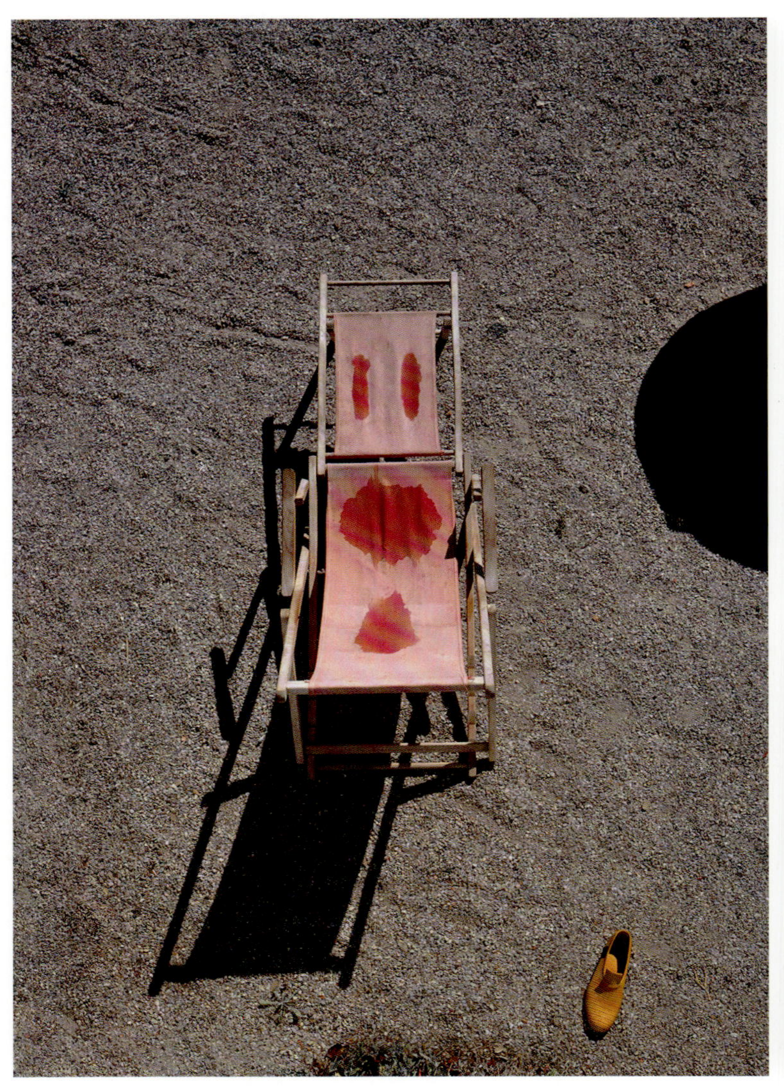

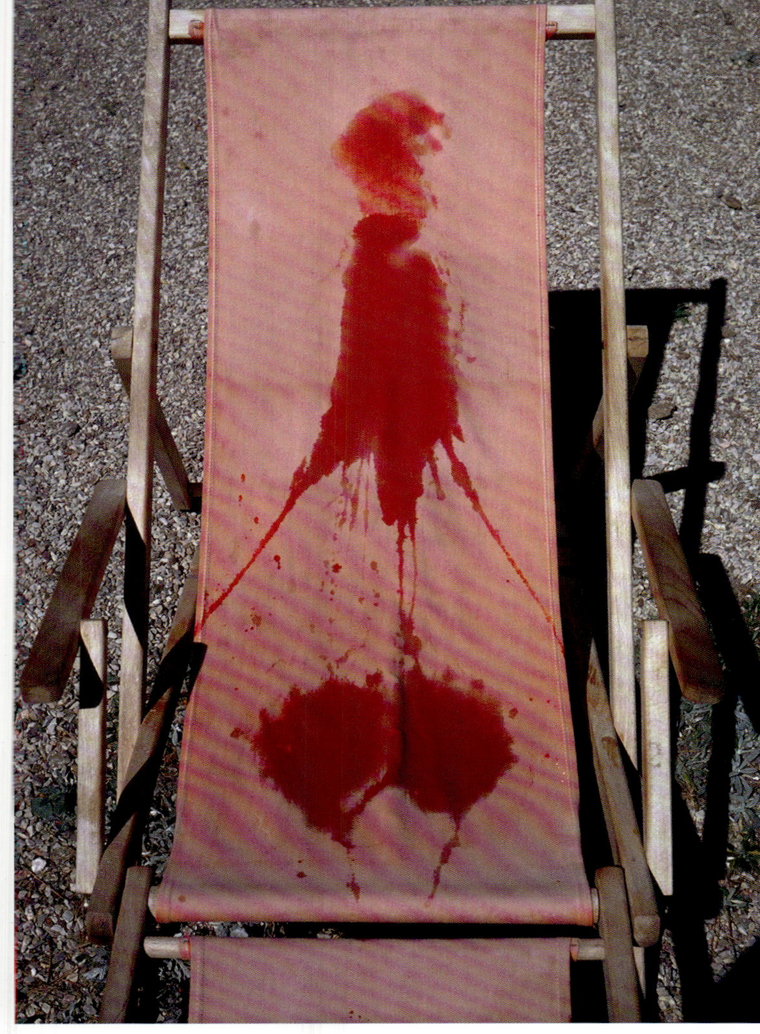

The Deck Chair in Absence, I, II, III, 1978.
Photographs.

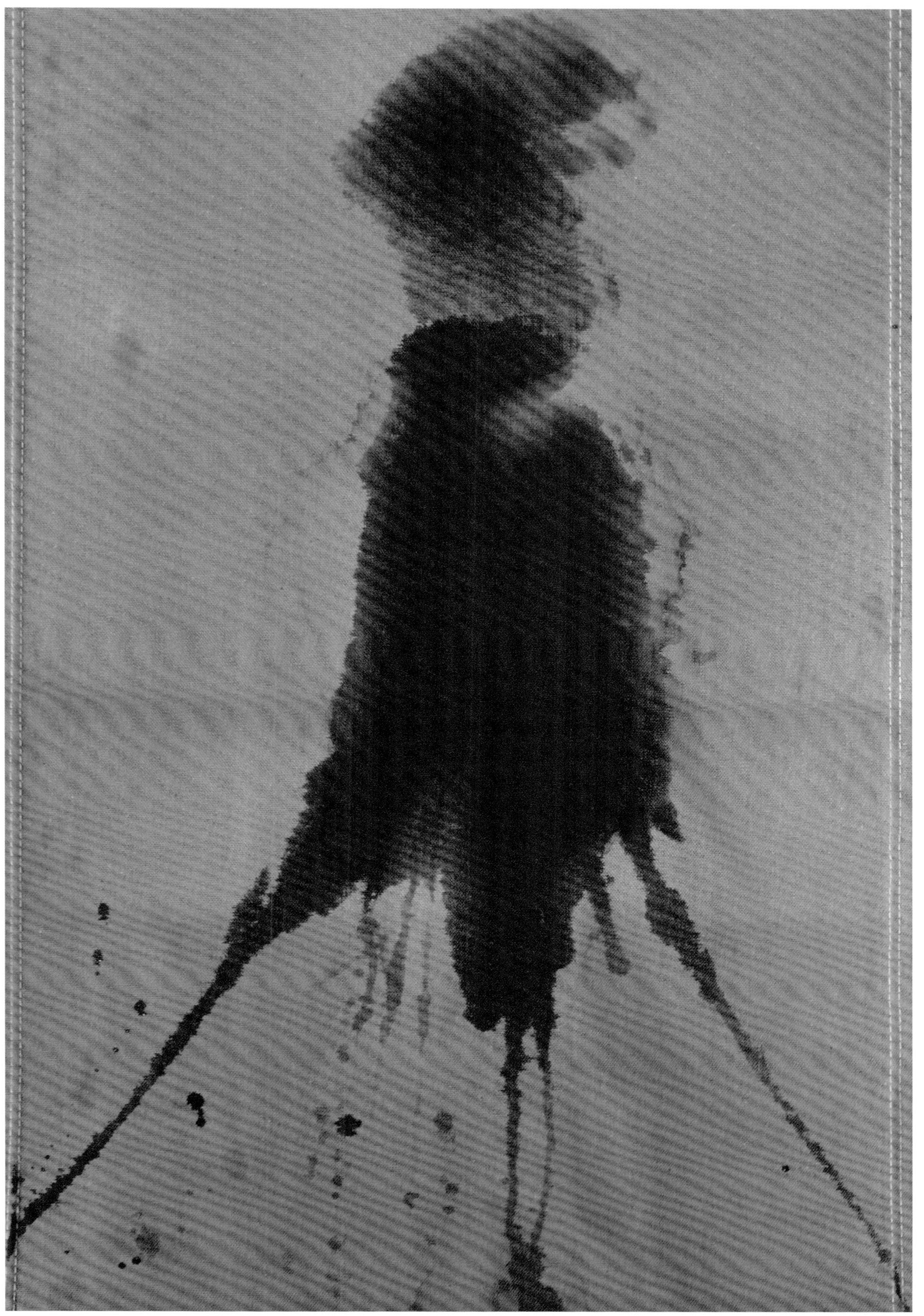

In the visible, everything is reading, but we only learn how to read words. Generally, we look at things only in so far as we need them, so as not to bang into them, so as not to trip up on a step, to tell if it'll rain. May as well say that things aren't seen at all. To turn an eye absolutely devoid of all practical interest onto creatures and things, that's love, perhaps.
To include in that way the greatest amount of the visible possible, therein, probably, lies my ambition.

C. Matton, *Rembrandt* (Paris: Éditions J'ai lu, 1999)

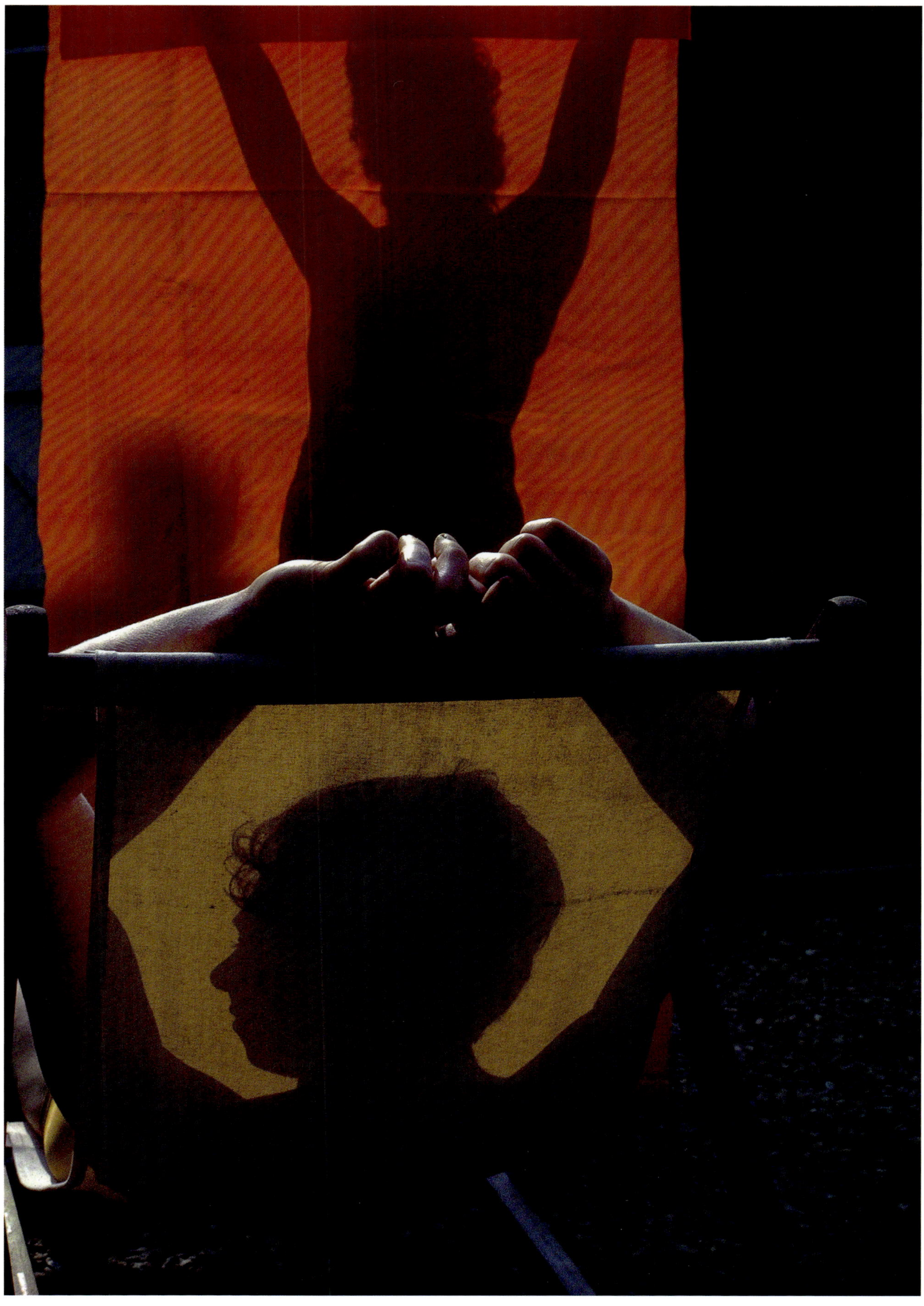

Nicolas in the Deck Chair, 1978.
Photograph.

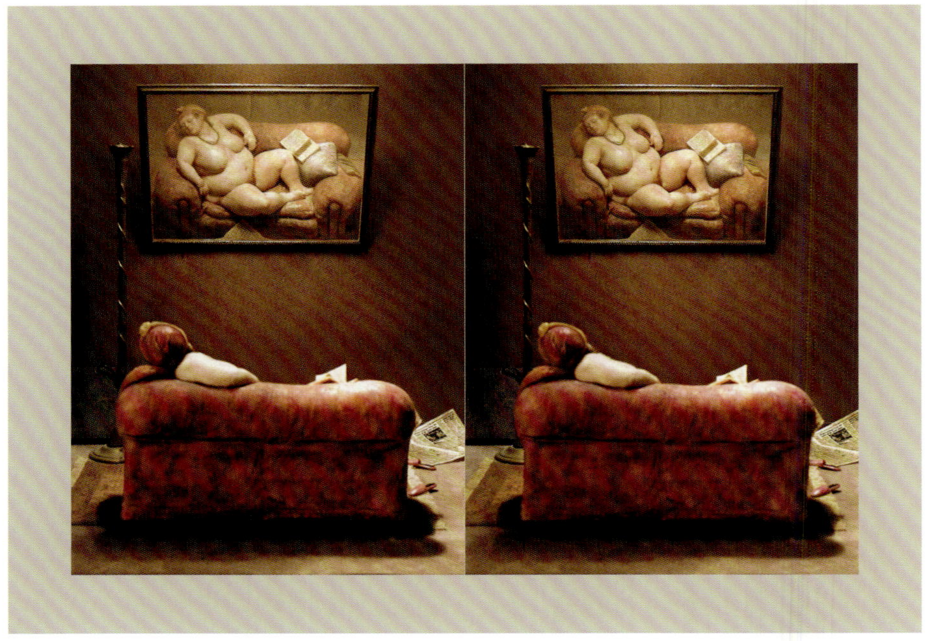

The Painter's Studio, Sue on Sofa I [detail], 2000.

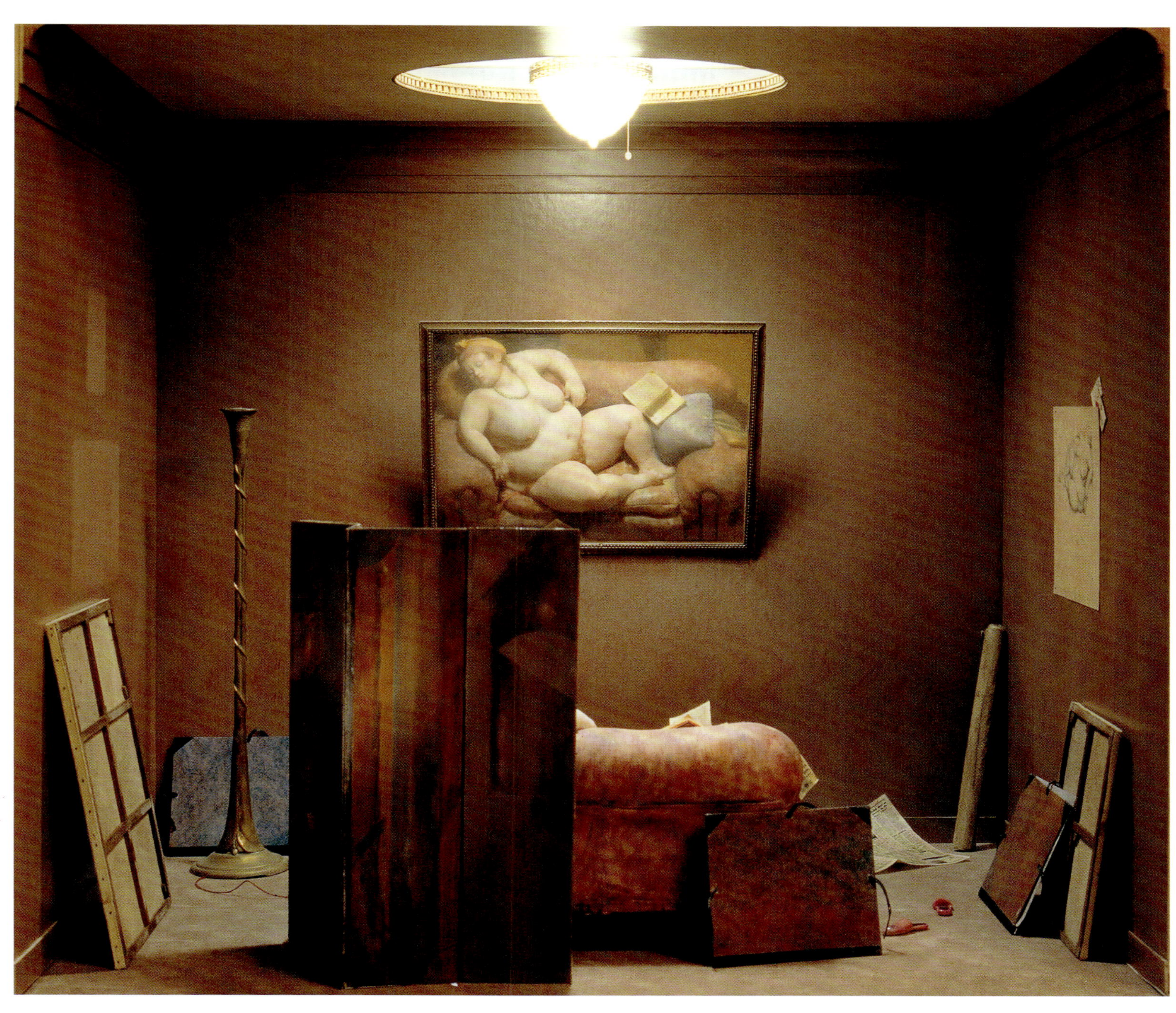

The Painter's Studio, Sue on Sofa I, 2000.
Mixed media, 22 ¾ × 26 × 17 in.
(58 × 66 × 43 cm).

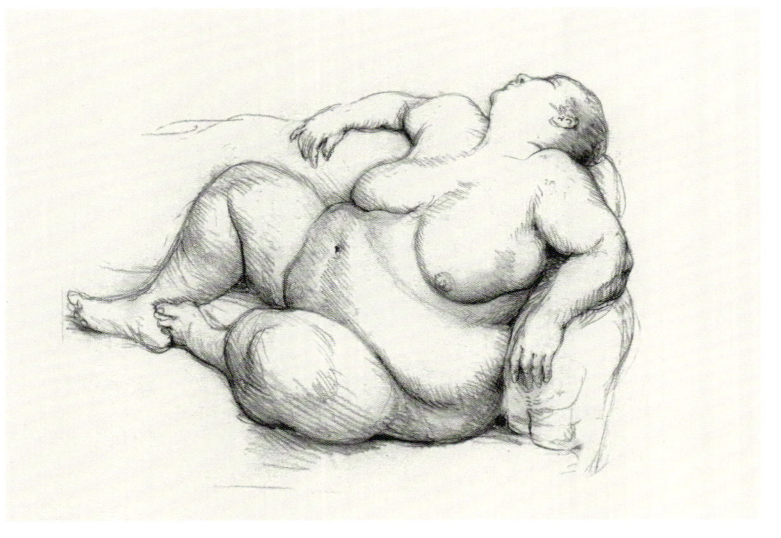

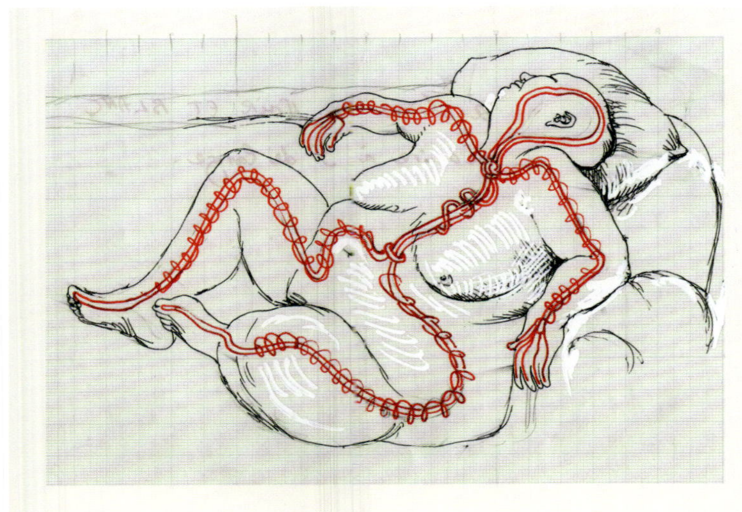

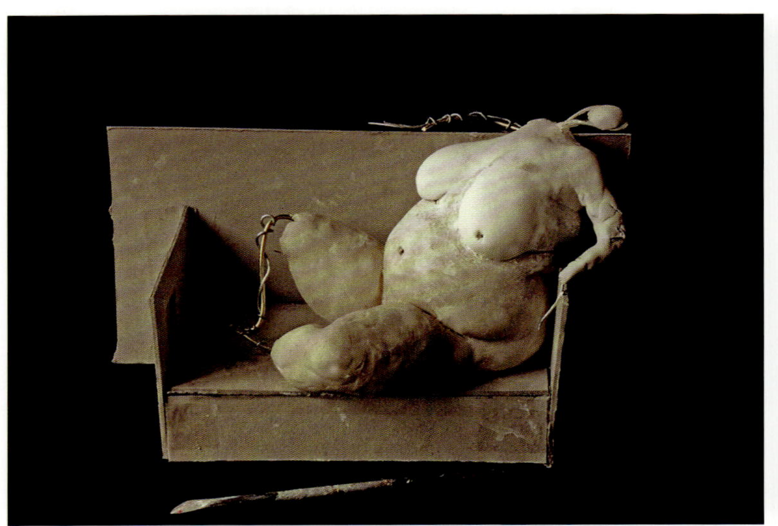

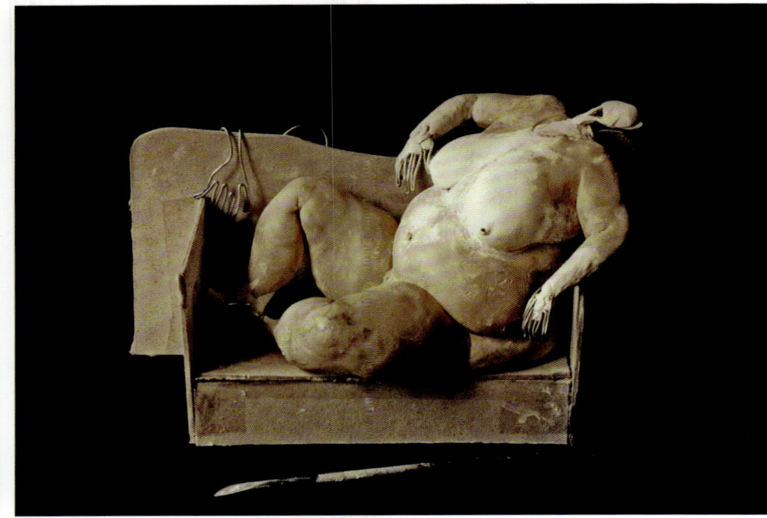

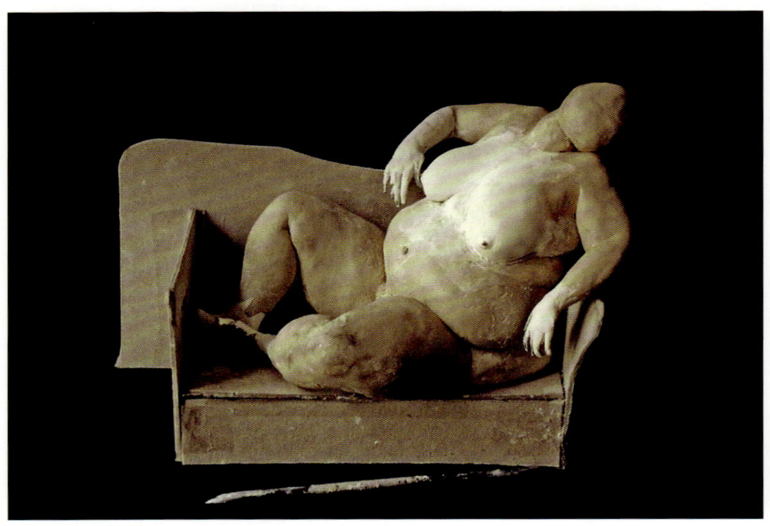

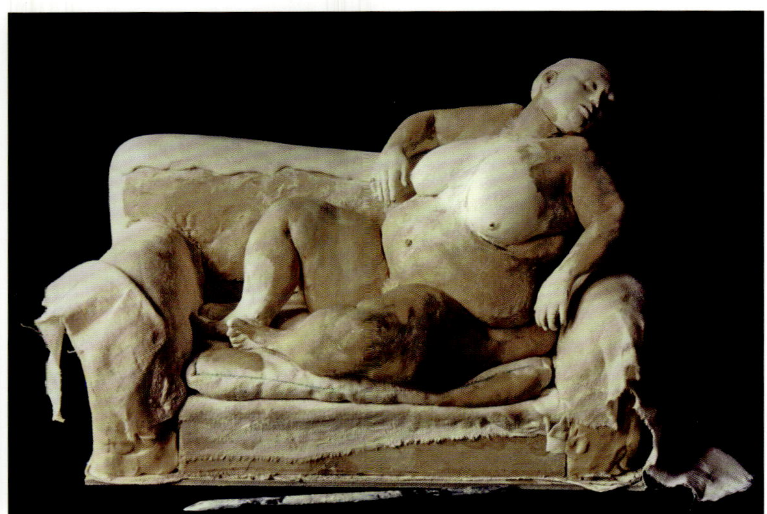

Sue on Sofa I, 1999.
Pencil on paper, 8 ¼ × 11 ¾ in. (21 × 29.7 cm).

Sue, preparatory drawing for a sculpture, 1999.
Pencil and felt pen on graph paper, 8 ¼ × 11 ¾ in. (21 × 29.7 cm).

Elaboration for a sculpture in four movements (Sue on Sofa), 1999.
Photographs.

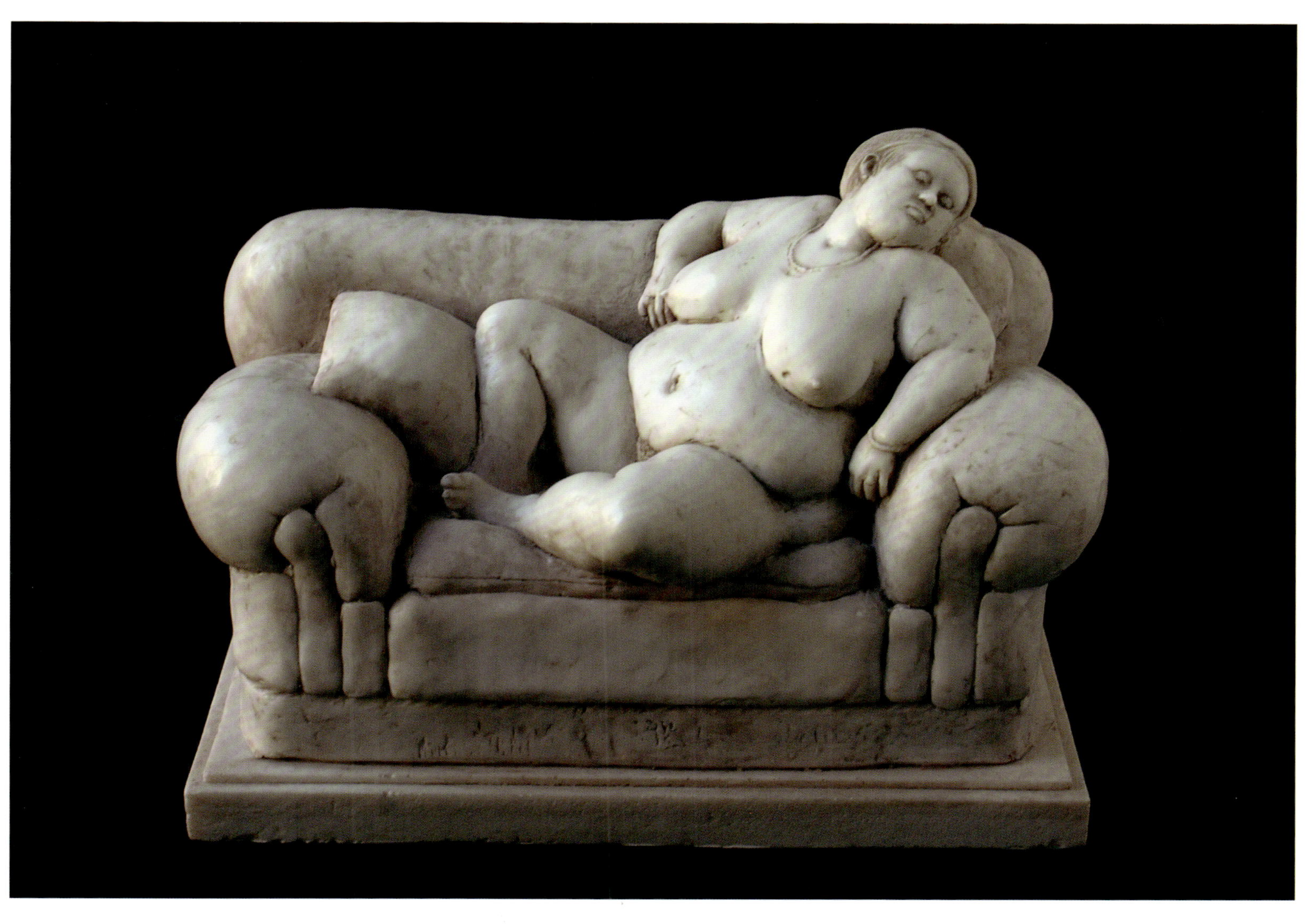

Sue on Sofa II, 2001.
Torolith and marble, 8 ¼ × 11 × 7 in. (21 × 28 × 18 cm).

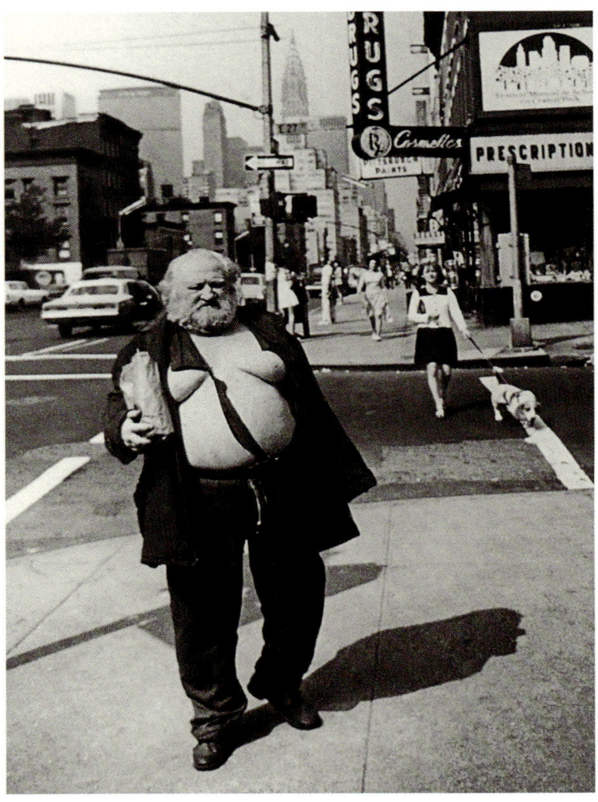

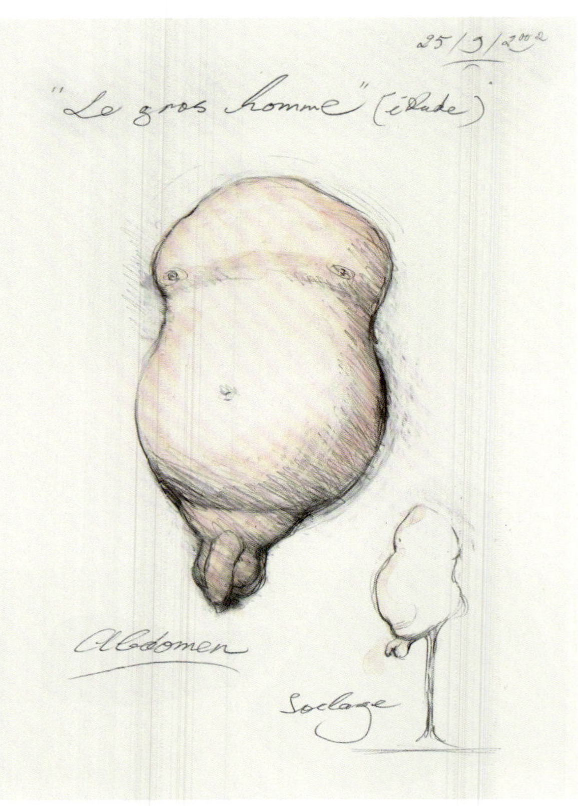

Poussine and Romeo the Dog, New York, 27th Street, 1972.
Photograph.

The Fat Man (study), 2002.
Pencil with watercolor on paper, 11 ¾ × 8 ¼ in. (29.7 × 21 cm).

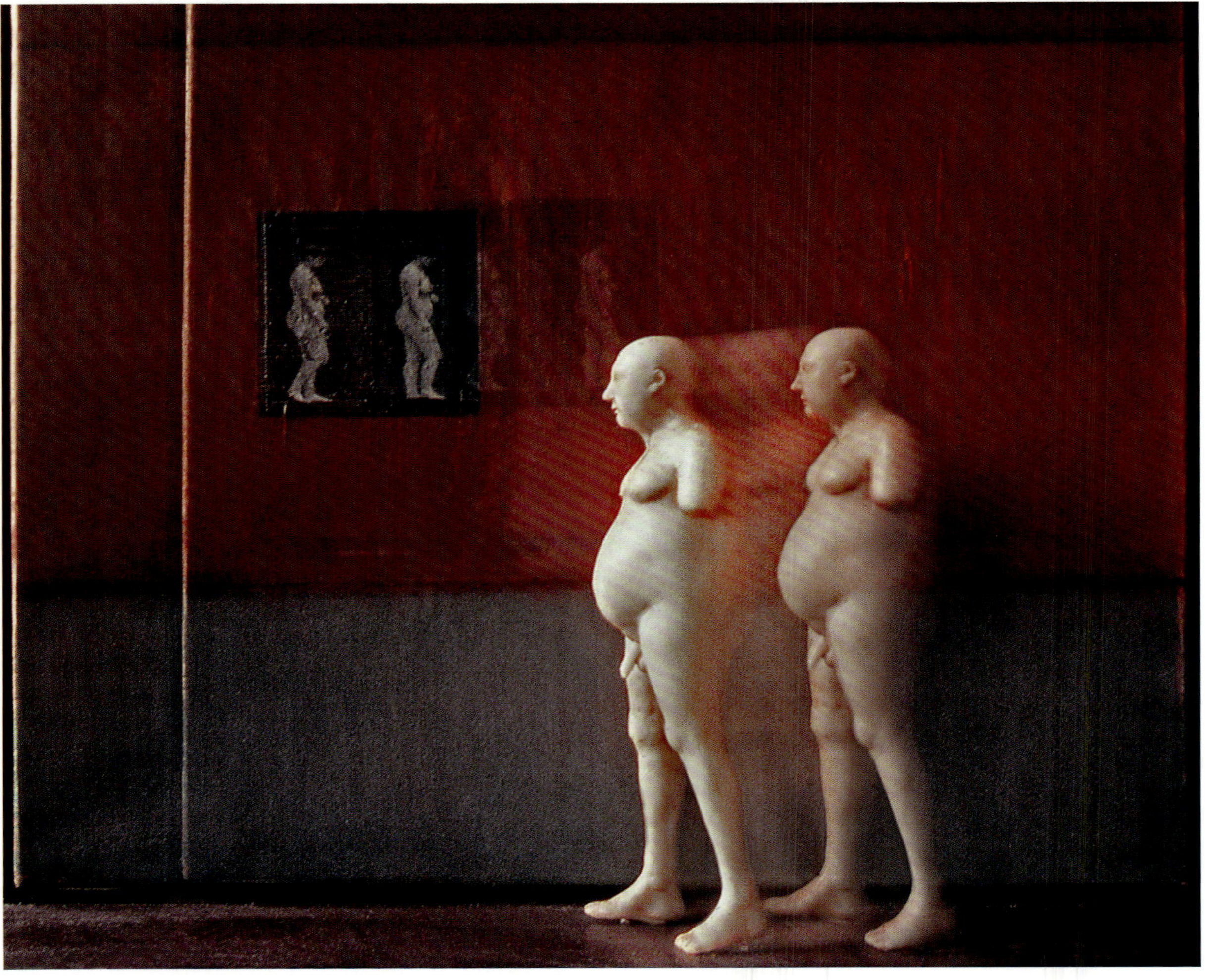

Louis the Little One Walking, 2003.
Picture-sculpture, torolith, and marble, 9 × 2 ¾ × 3 in. (23 × 7 × 7.5 cm), oil on canvas, painted steel, 15 × 18 in. (38 × 46 cm).

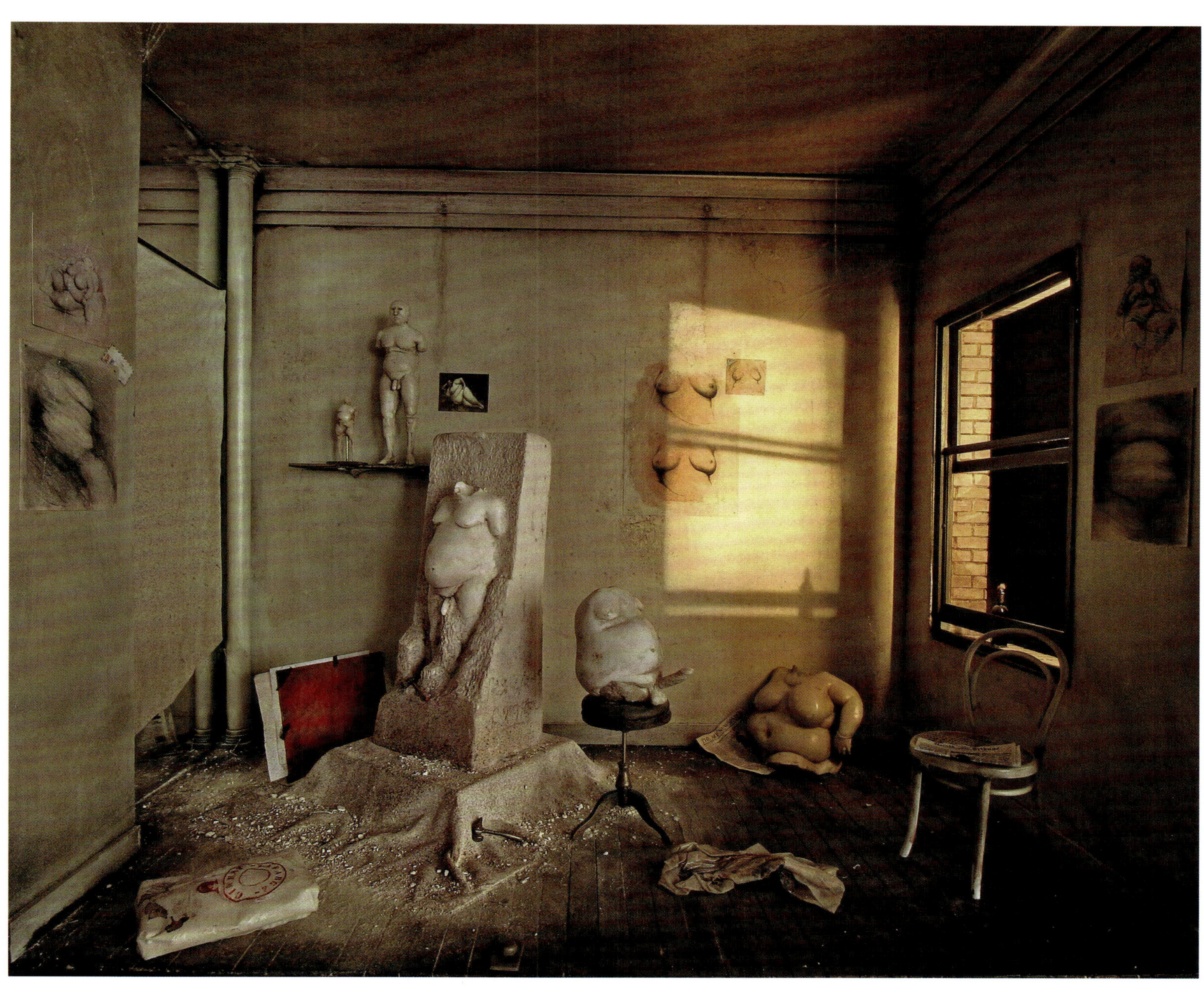

The Studio of a Sculptor of Fat People, 2006.
Mixed media, 27 × 28 ¾ × 16 ½ in.
(69 × 73 × 42 cm).

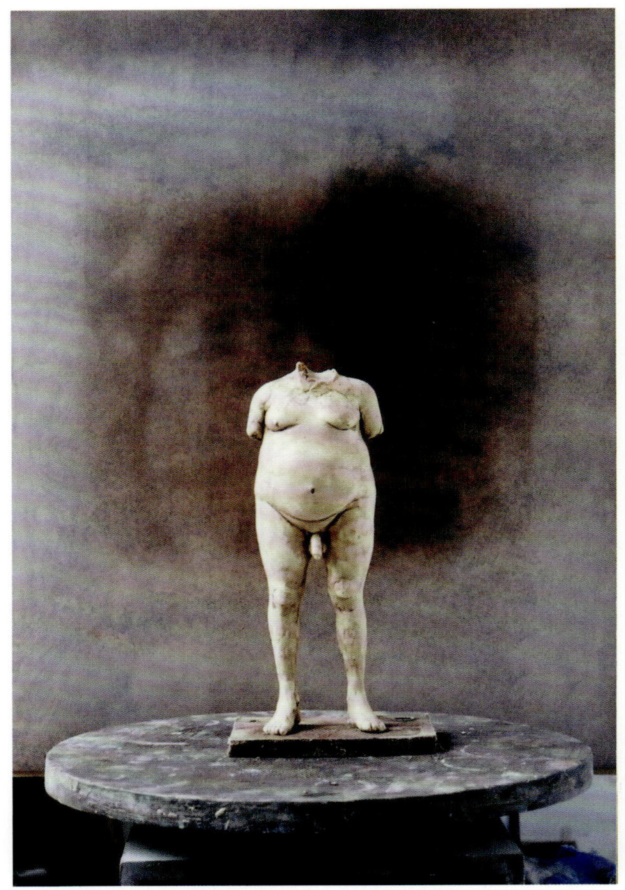

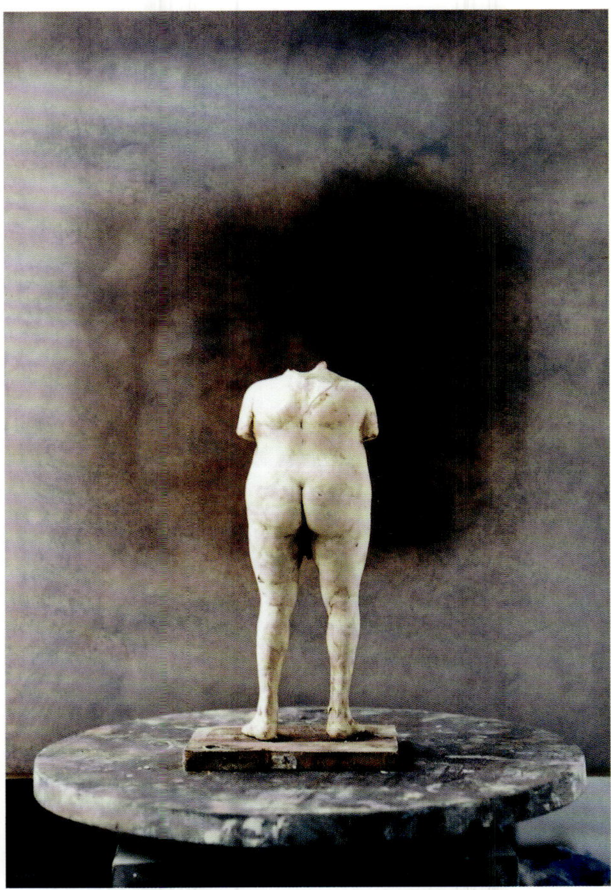

Louis the Little One I (headless), 2001.
Torolith and marble,
7 ½ × 2 ½ × 3 in.
(19.5 × 6.5 × 7.5 cm).

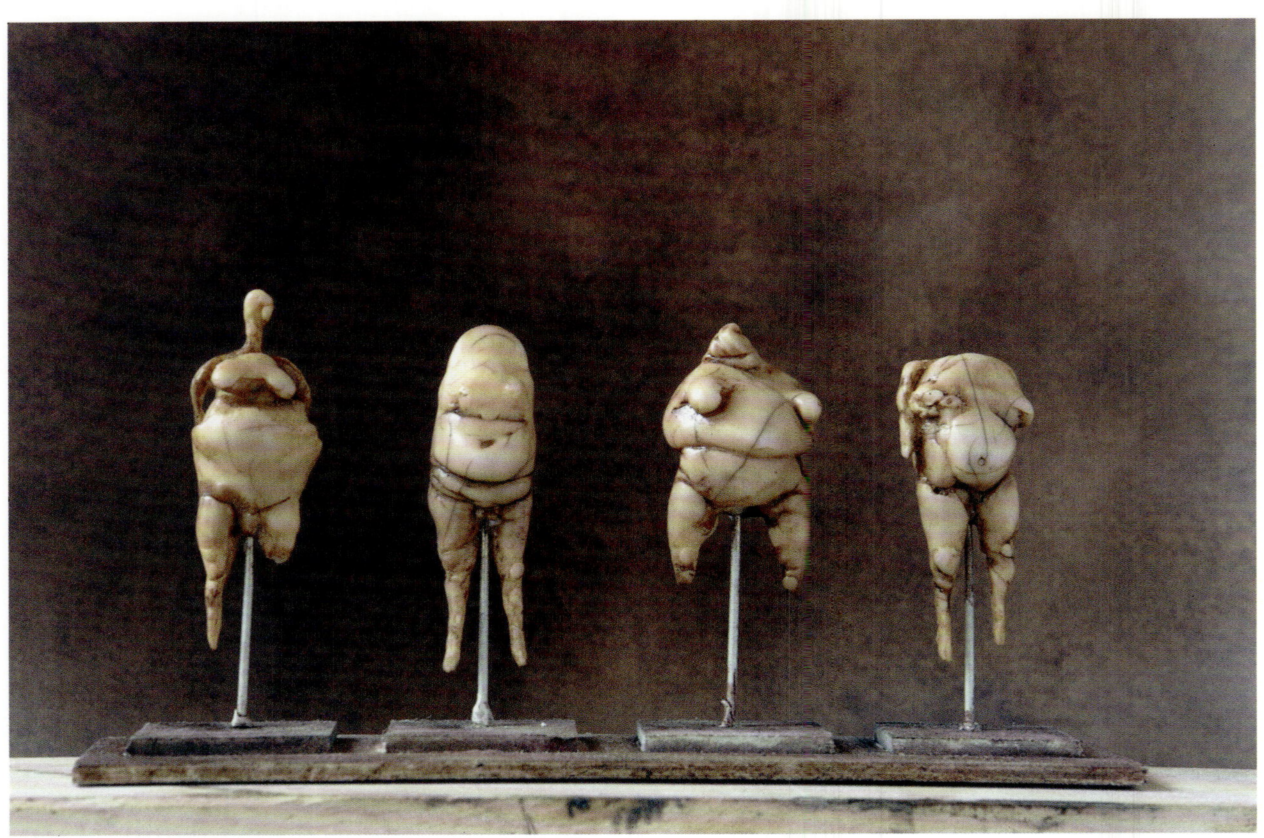

Gestural Little Fatty, I, II, III, IV, 1991.
Torolith and marble,
2–2 ¾ in. (5.2–7 cm) h.

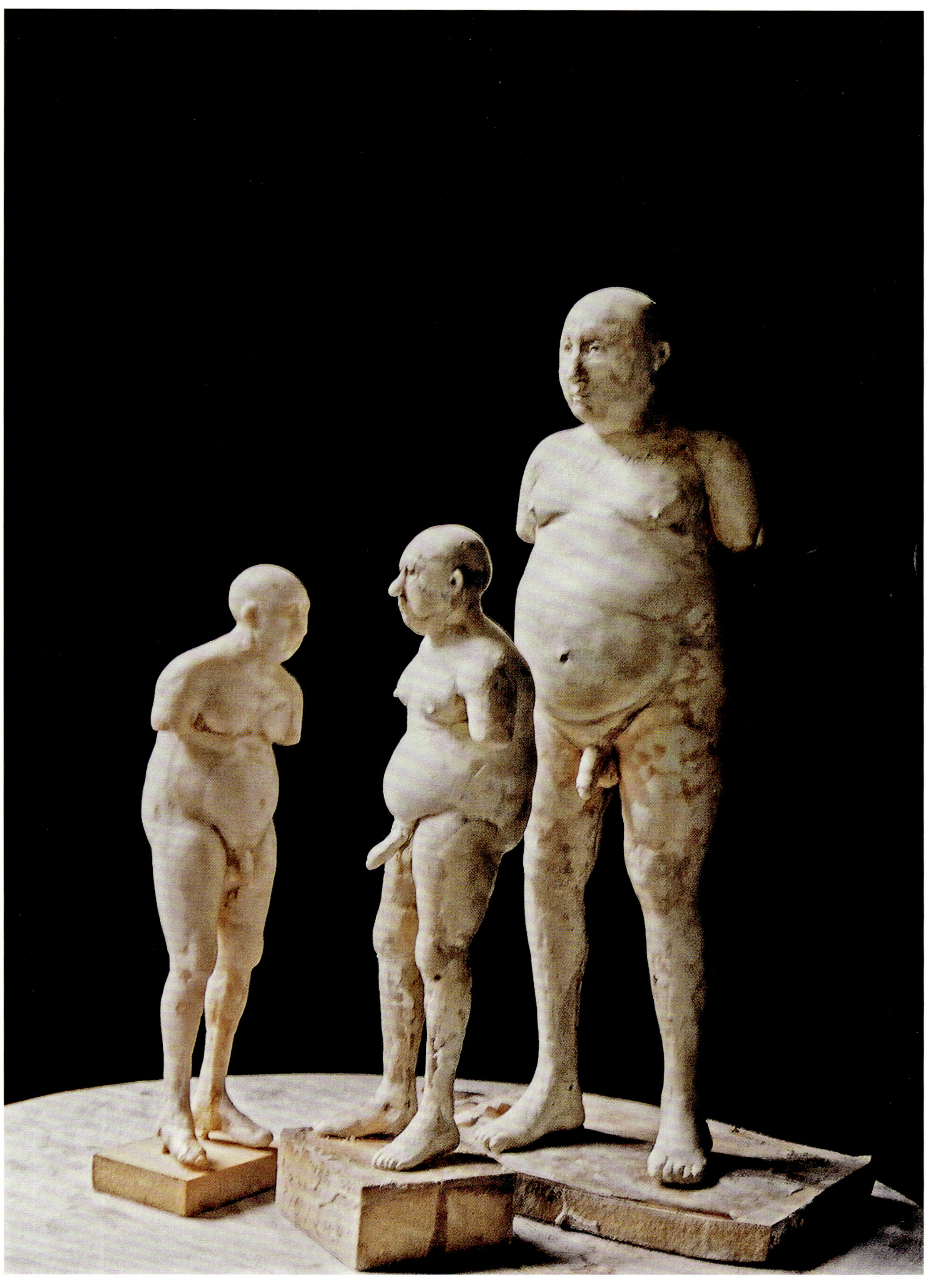

Louis the Little One III, IV, II, 2003.
Photograph,
6 × 1 ½ × 1 ¾ in.
(15 × 3.5 × 3.8 cm);
6 × 1 ½ × 1 ½ in.
(15 × 3.7 × 3.7 cm);
8 ¾ × 2 ¾ × 2 ½ in.
(22.5 × 7 × 6.7 cm).

Happiness terrifies me because, if one calculates the probabilities, if it's going too well then normally it can't last! It never occurs to me that I could have it all; I mean that the balance might be reached, not with my life alone, but with every life—that I could actually be "spoiled" without risk, and that others might "pay" in my stead.

I'd find that unfair, inelegant.

Yet I love nothing more than strength, joy, victory, life! The insolence of the advantage of strength and beauty. Those who don't feel this are the winners, now I understand how: money follows money, seduction the seducer, good luck the lucky, because others feel their assurance, their confidence. They're fascinated by it, they bow to it, overcome they take a backseat, and they love that. So, I'm sure there's a great deal of fear in my tottering on the edge of failure. But there's also a bit of pride at being the most elegant, and this elegance is conveyed through my taste for the absurd.

Personal note, October 16, 1979

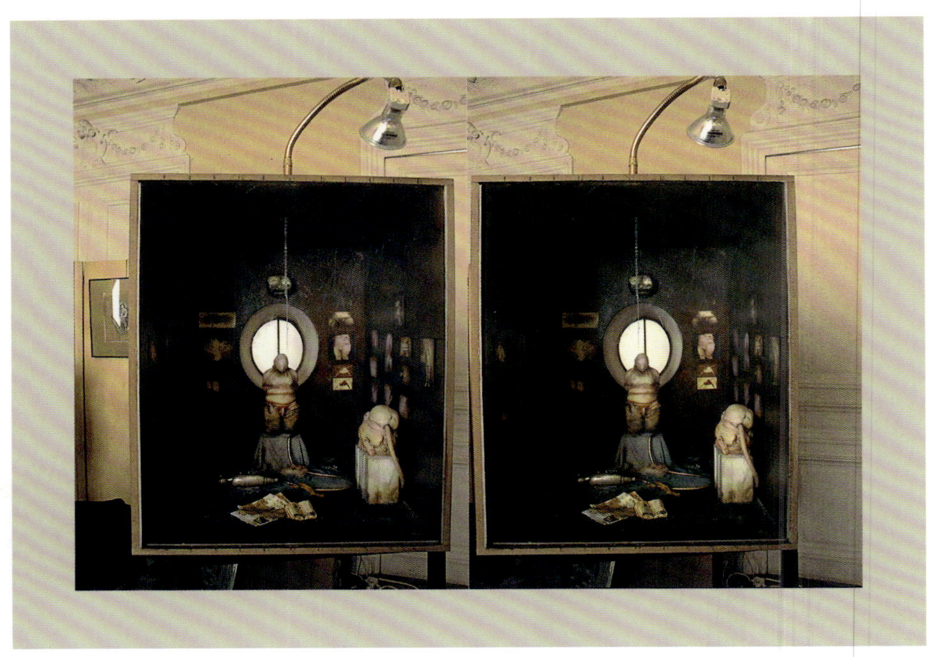

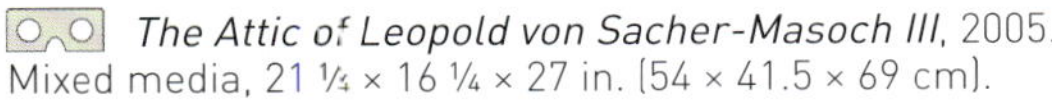 *The Attic of Leopold von Sacher-Masoch III*, 2005.
Mixed media, 21 ¼ × 16 ¼ × 27 in. (54 × 41.5 × 69 cm).

Facing page, top:
Projects for sculptures, 1971.
Felt pen on paper, 11 ¾ × 8 ¼ in.
(29.7 × 21 cm).

Mute Mask, 1982.
Silver-plated torolith, 7 ½ × 5 ¼ × 2 ¼ in.
(19 × 13.5 × 6.5 cm).

Self-portrait with Mute Mask, 1982.
Photograph.

Facing page, bottom:
The Attic of Leopold von Sacher-Masoch III (details 3 and 1), 2005.

Masoch.

6/3/2006

— Re-placer l'image à droite (en bas) mur du fond. (pour cela rephotographier dernières prises de vues.)
— Jus sur oeil de boeuf.
— Le cadenas.
— Jus sur les murs pour noyer les images
— Couler en plâtre la sculpture, la ~~poser~~
percer pour le tube en caoutchouc rose.
la faire sécher puis gomme laque plus jus et (socle.)
— Fixer la barre à gauche.
— Tissus gris bleu sur socle et fixer l'homme.
— mettre en forme tige filetée → tuyau aspirateur.
— Carton gris au sol et salissures, détritus, journaux
— Toile d'araignée, chaine à la grille et au plafond.
— Embuer oeil de boeuf, détériorer les murs.

Masoch

- Colorwash on bull's-eye window.
- The padlock.
- Colorwash on the walls to blur the images.

Cast the sculpture in plaster, bore a hole for the pink rubber tube. Dry it, then varnished gum then colorwash and plinth.
- Blue-gray fabric on base and fix the man.
- Give shape to filleted rod (vacuum-cleaner pipe).
- Gray cardboard on the floor and stains, refuse, newspapers
- Cobweb, chains on the bars and on the ceiling.
- Mist the bull's-eye, distress the walls.

Personal note, March 6, 2006.

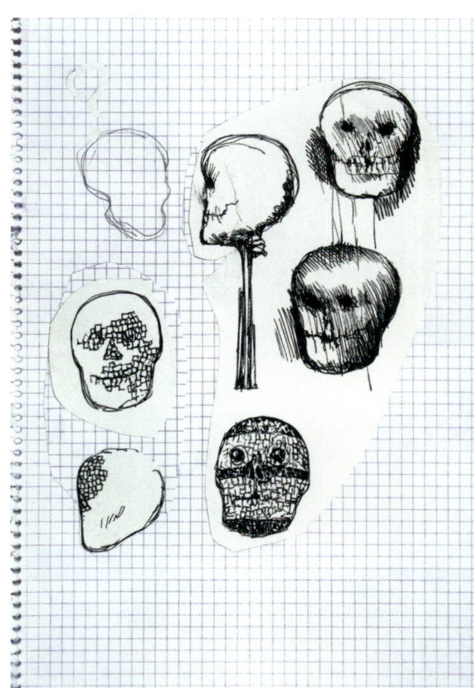
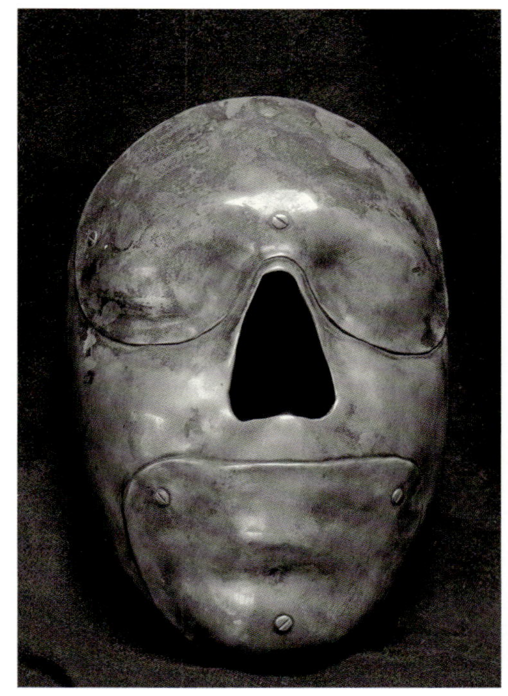
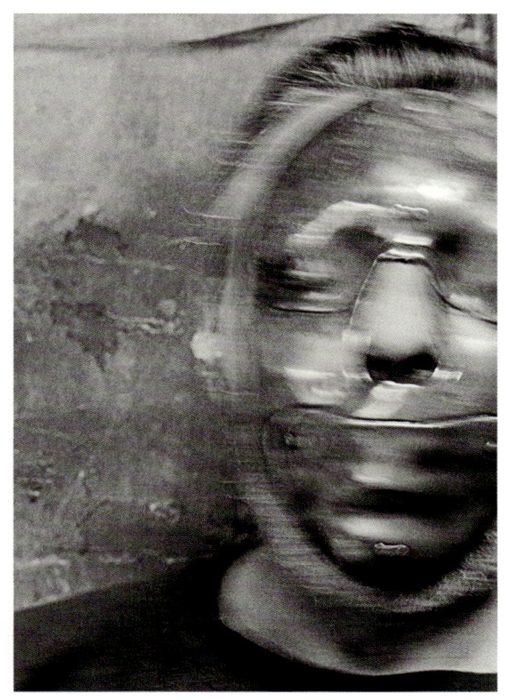
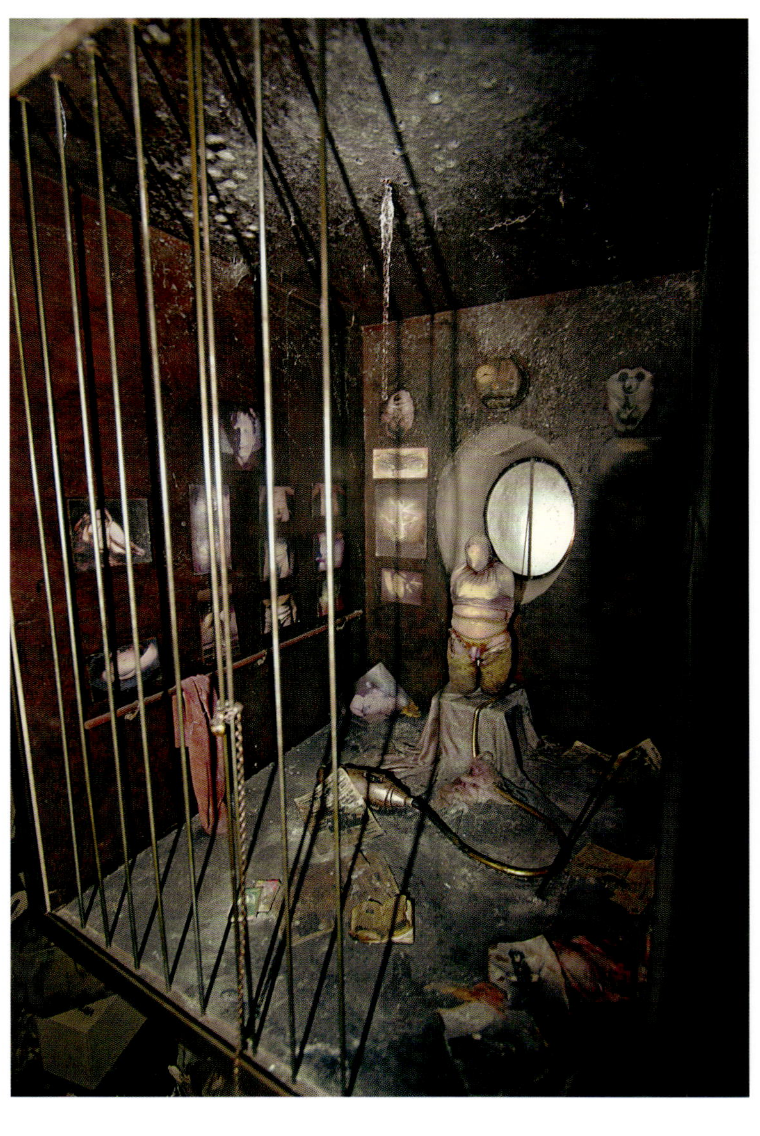
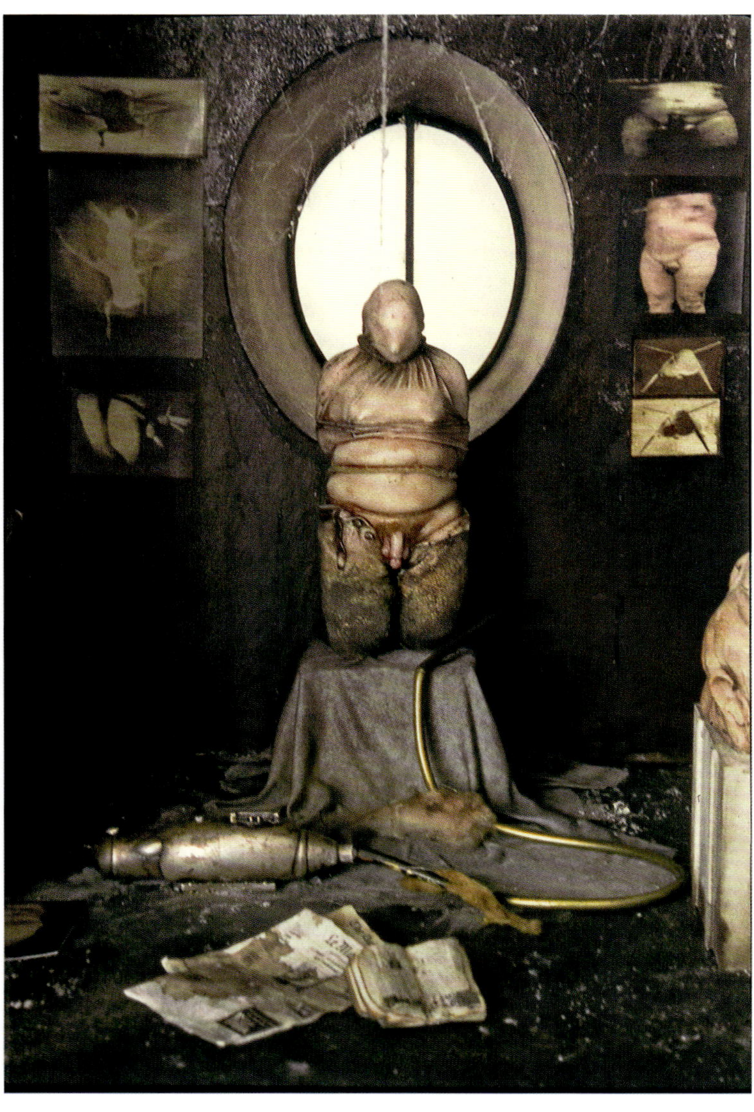

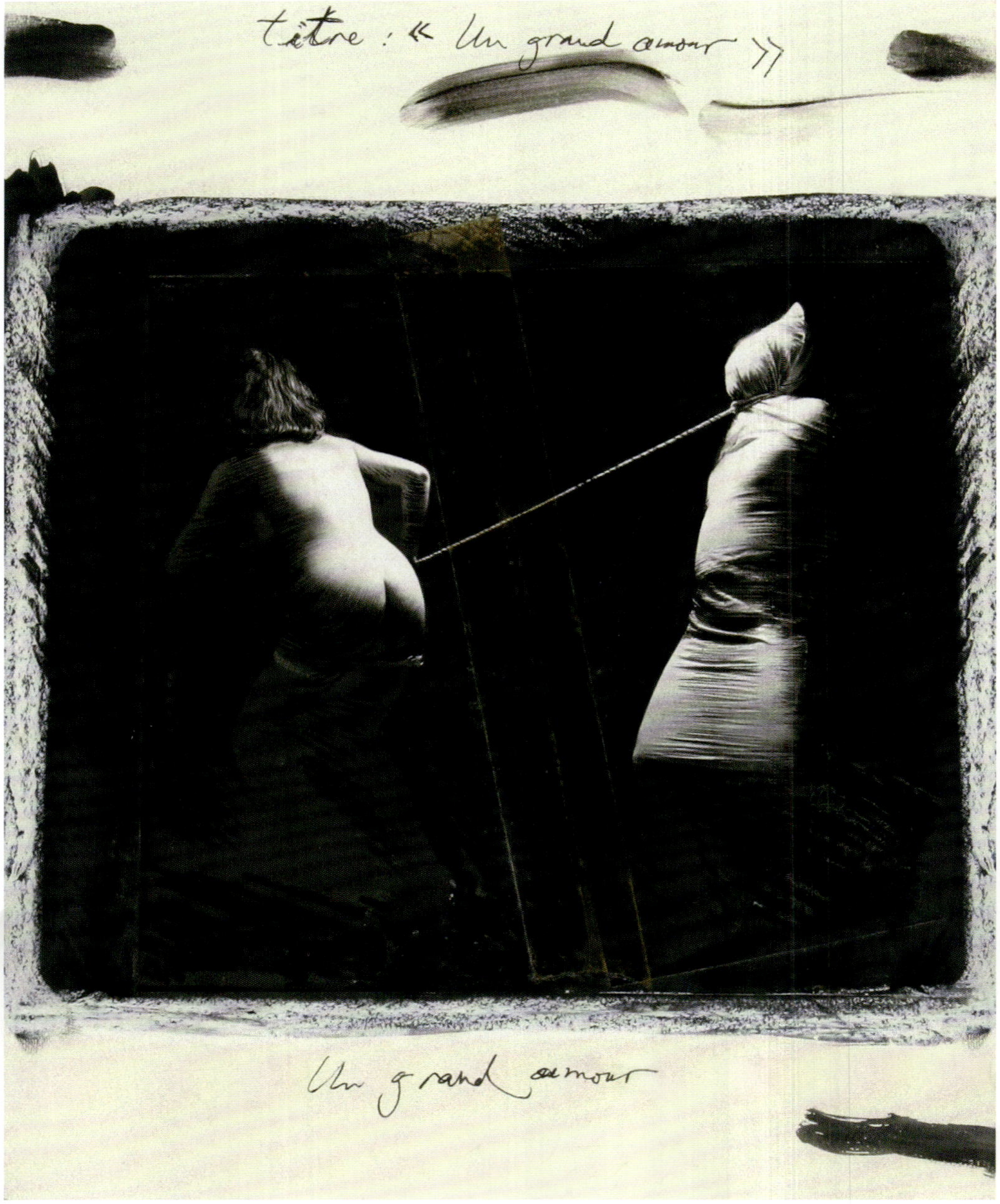

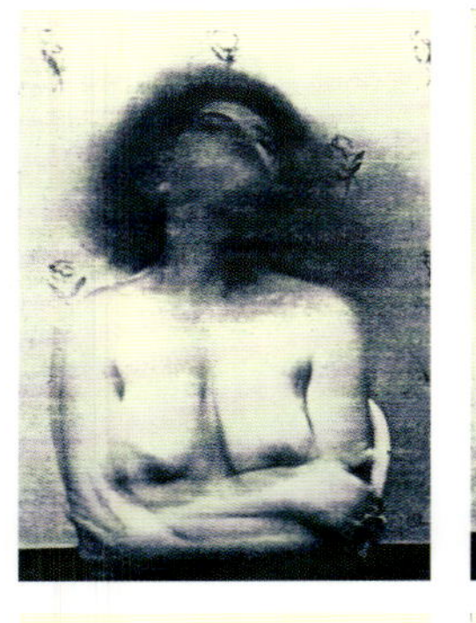
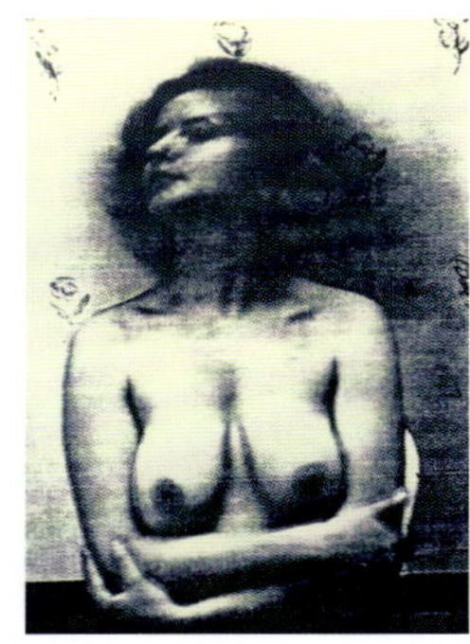
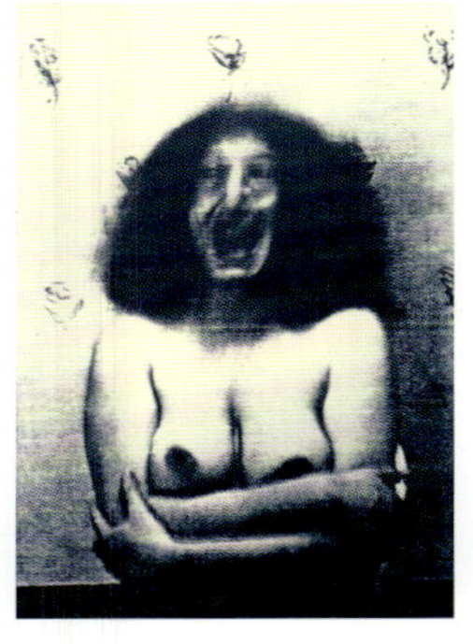
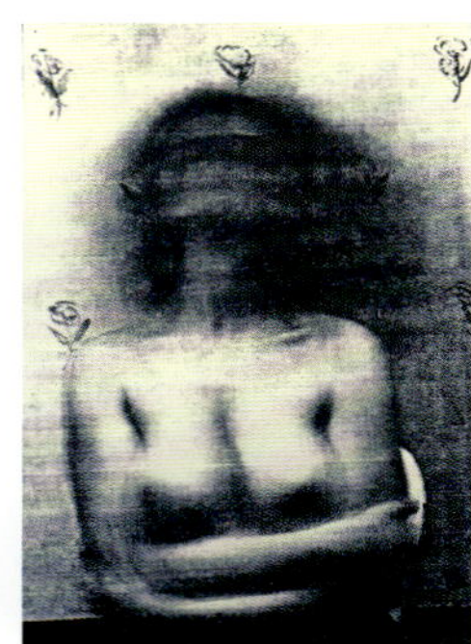
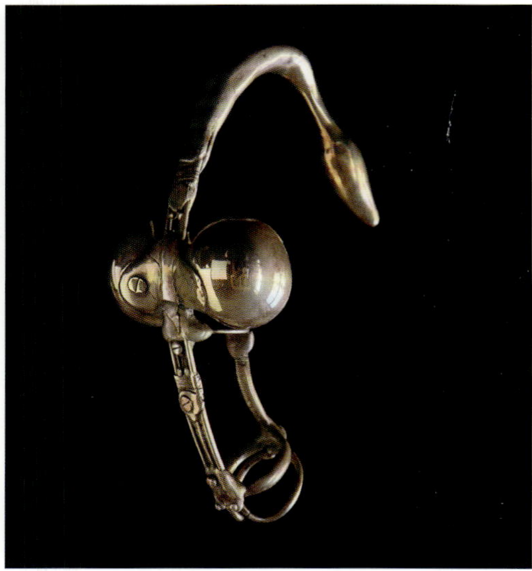

A Great Love, 1984.
Black chalk and soft pastel on silver print, 8 ¼ × 7 ½ in. (21 × 19 cm).

Four Variations of Louise (the shout), 1979.
Photographs.

The Grasshopper (jewelry for men), 1984.
Silver-plated metal and resin, 9 ¼ × 5 × 5 ¾ in. (24 × 12.5 × 14.5 cm).

Masochism has played a significant role in my story, in my life, with cash, women, definitely with women, one might say with my behavior in the social sphere. It's complicated. In art history, for example, Michelangelo is a masochist who slept sprawled on the barrel chests of hefty stonebreakers oozing with sweat. On the other hand, Leonardo da Vinci is a typical invert. He draws boys who look like girls; he likes them pretty. No meeting is possible between these two, no more than between a masochist and a sadist. For me, Proust is a masochist. Bacon is a masochist, who liked to be whacked by lowlife types in specialized locales. On the other hand, Cocteau is a real homosexual, an invert, who feels for a man the same sensations a man does for a woman. It's not a perversion; it's an inversion. But masochism is much more complex.

C. Matton, *Entretiens avec Isabelle Sobelman* (forthcoming)

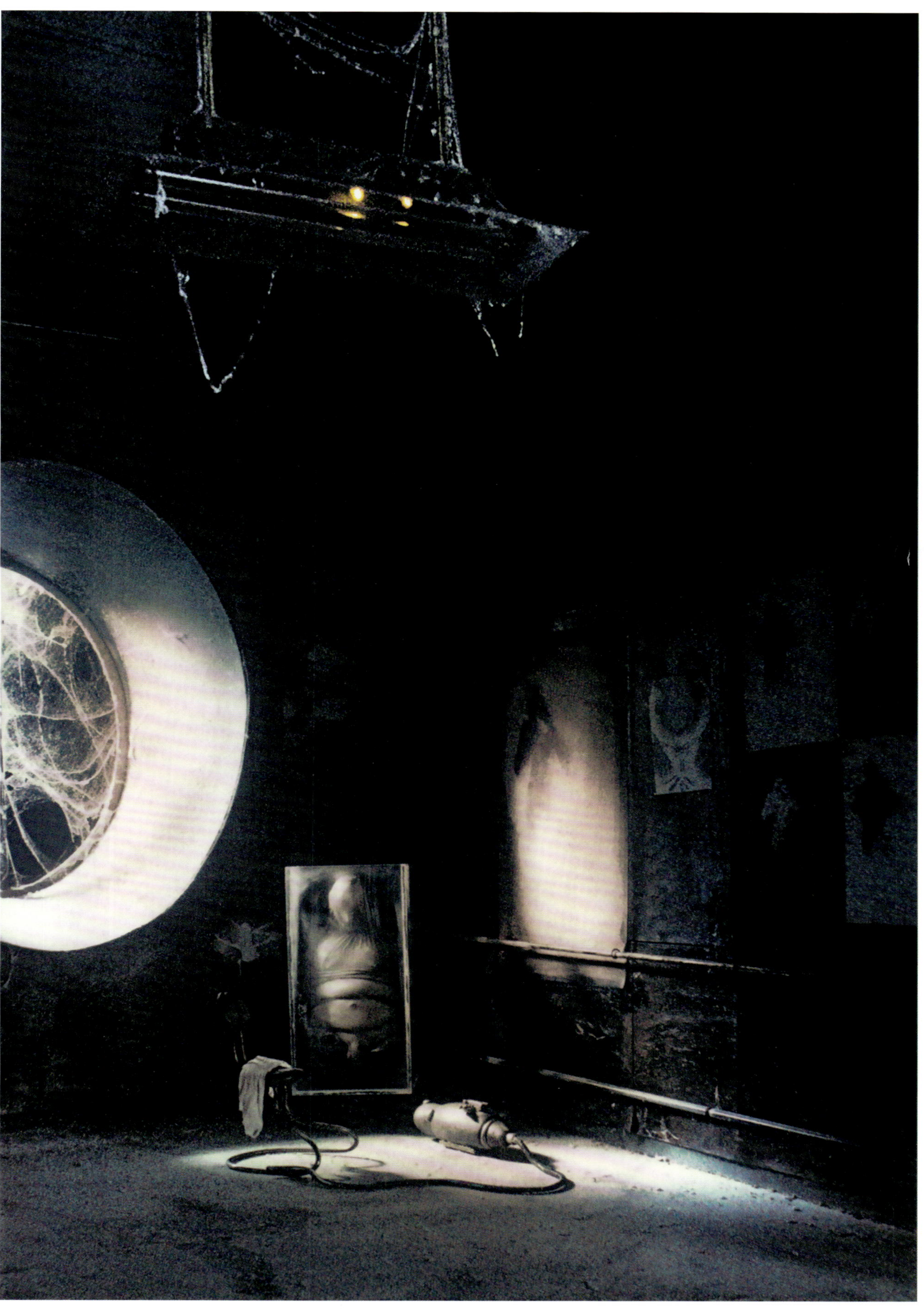

The Attic of Leopold von Sacher-Masoch I (detail), 1990. Photograph (Polacolor).

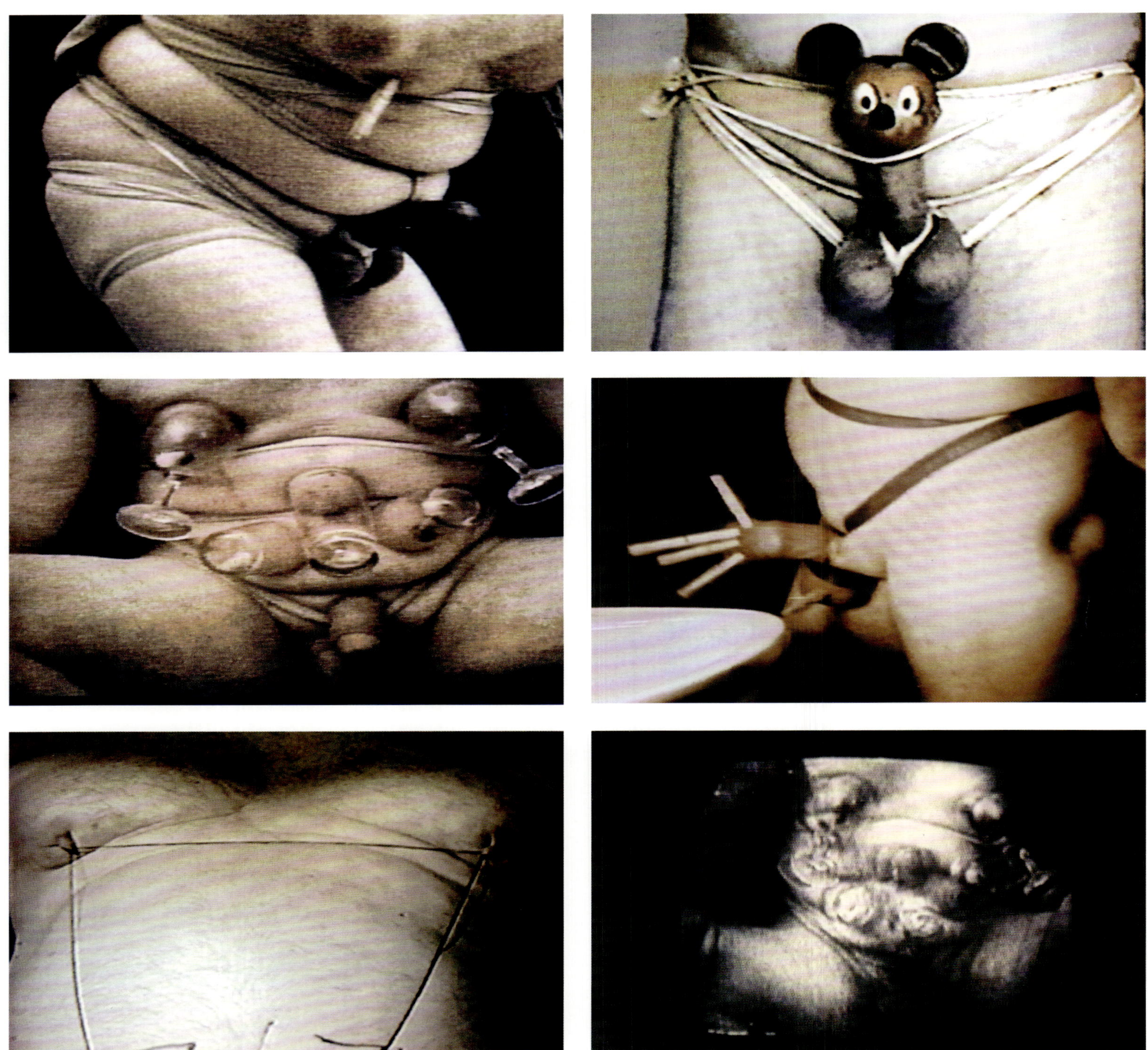

From left to right and from top to bottom:
Screen shots, Masochism III, IV, II, I, VI, VIII, 2004.
Photographs.

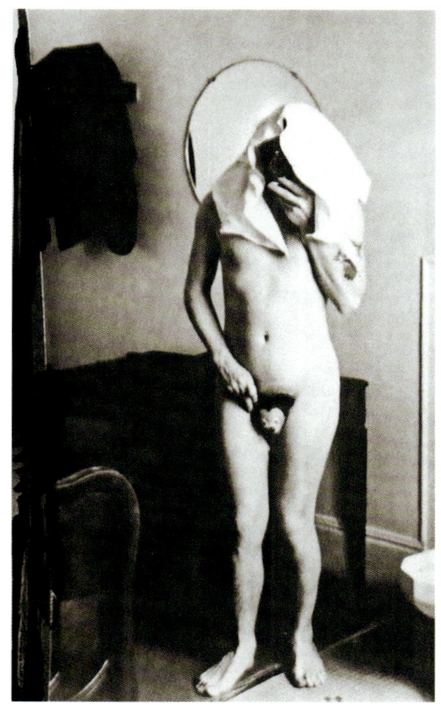

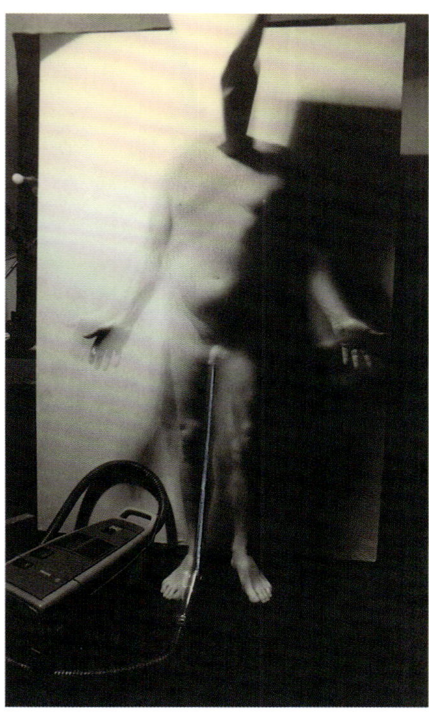

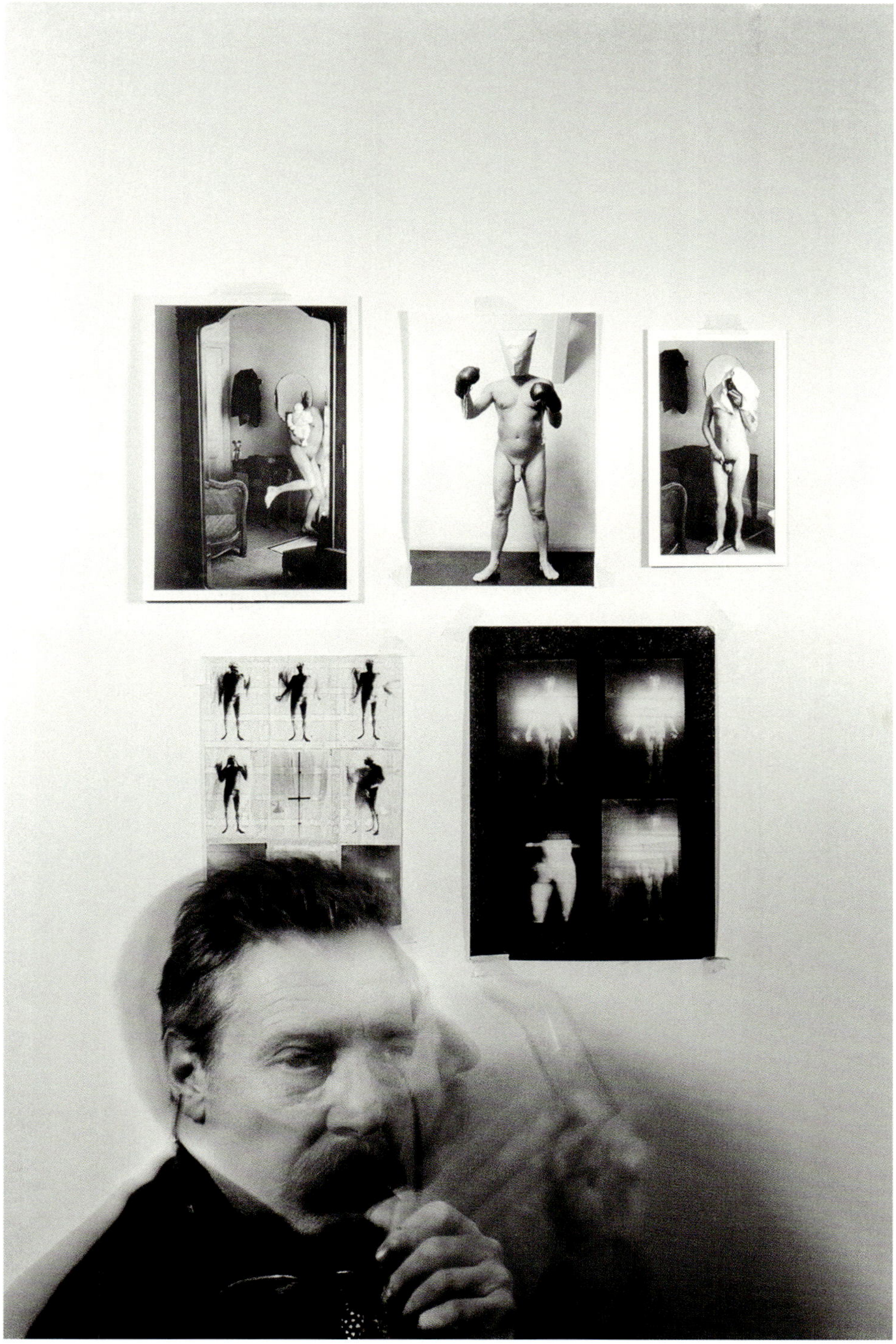

Self-portrait with Mickey Mouse, 1975.
Photograph.

Tornado Self-portrait, 1980.
Soft pastel on photostat, photograph.

Self-portrait before a Wall of Photographs, 1994.
Photograph.

The Wine Cellar II (detail), 2006.
Photograph.

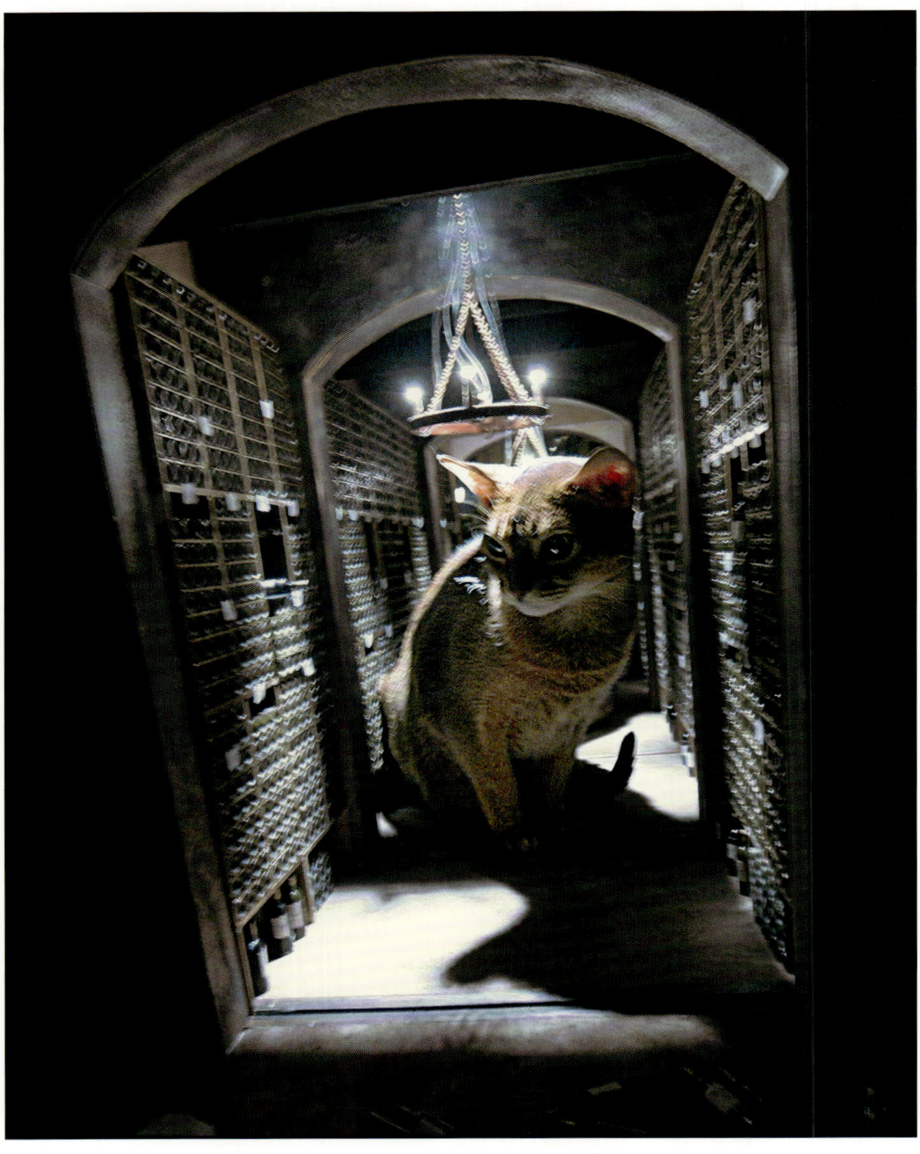

The Abyssinian Cat Lancaster in the Wine Cellar II, 2007.

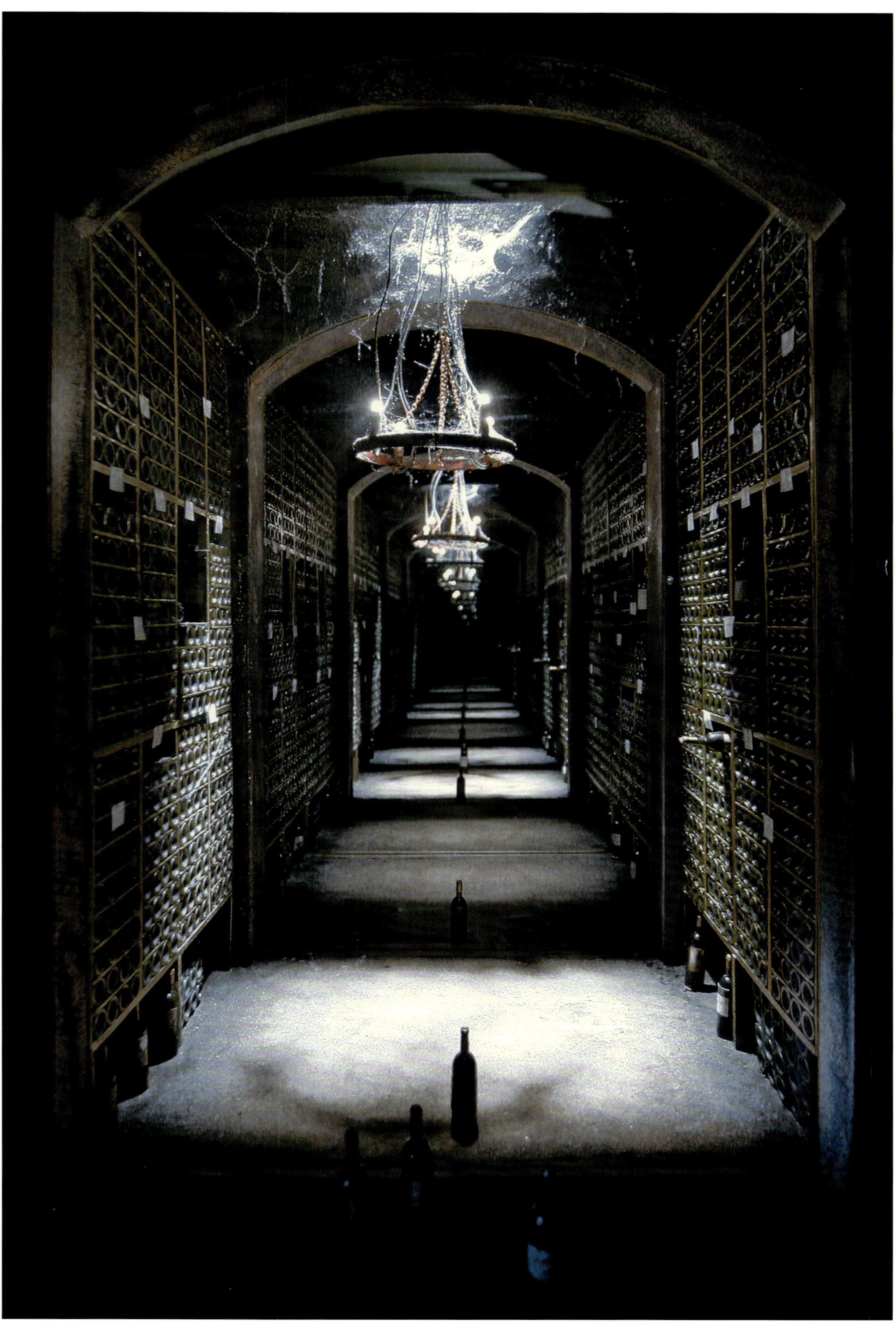

The Wine-cellar II, 2006.
Mixed media,
24 ¾ × 16 × 20 ¾ in.
(63 × 41 × 53 cm).

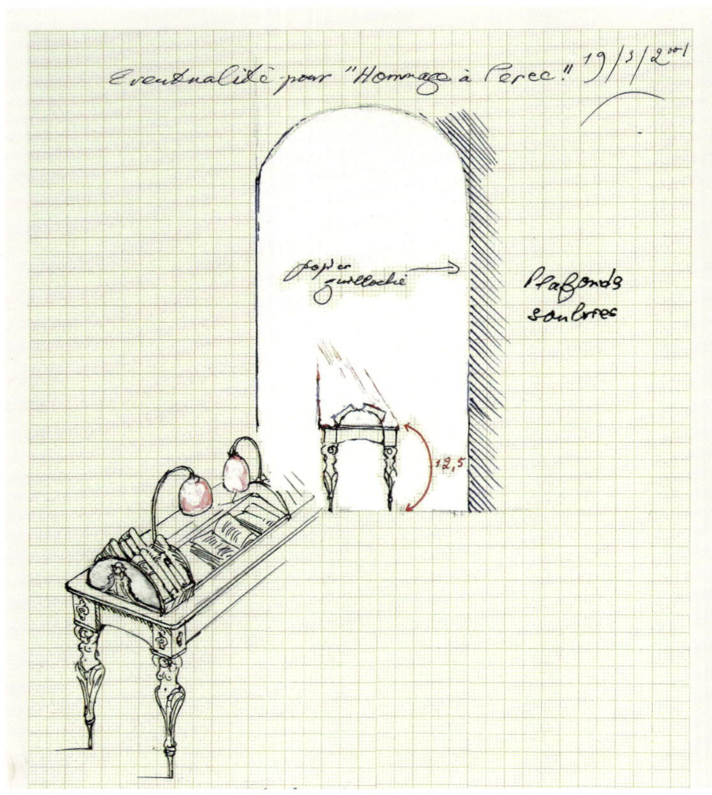

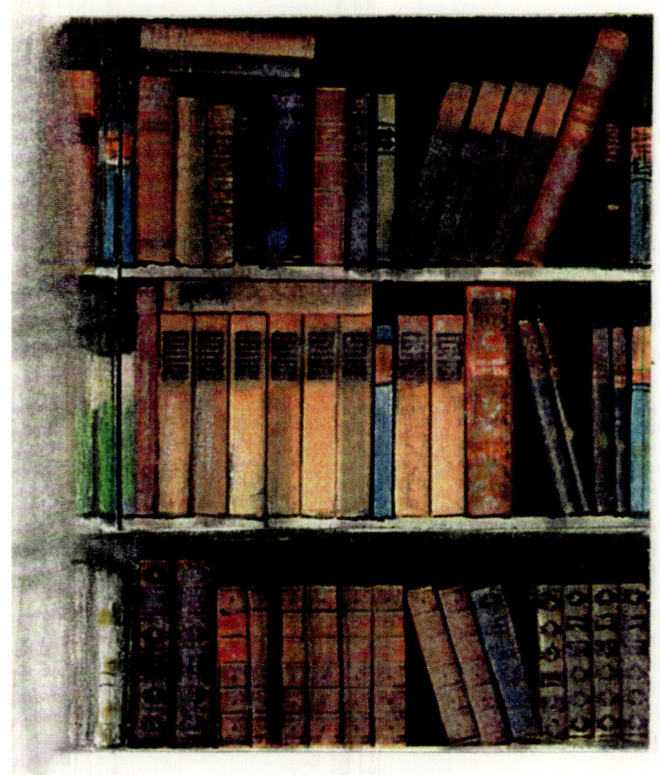

Study for a Homage to Perec, 2001.
Pencil, felt pen, and watercolor on graph paper, 9 ½ × 8 ¼ in. (24 × 21 cm).

Three Shelves, 2003.
Gouache on paper, 12 ½ × 10 ¼ in. (32 × 26 cm).

Study for a Library, 2001.
Pencil on paper, 6 × 4 ¼ in. (15 × 11 cm).

I concur wholeheartedly with Georges Perec's remark: "How is one to account for, to question, to describe what happens every day—the banal, the quotidian, the obvious, the routine, the ordinary, the background noise, the usual?" The aim of this box, *Homage to Georges Perec*, is to investigate, as objectively as possible, the silence and the immobility of this library. Nothing else.

Personal note, December 11, 2001

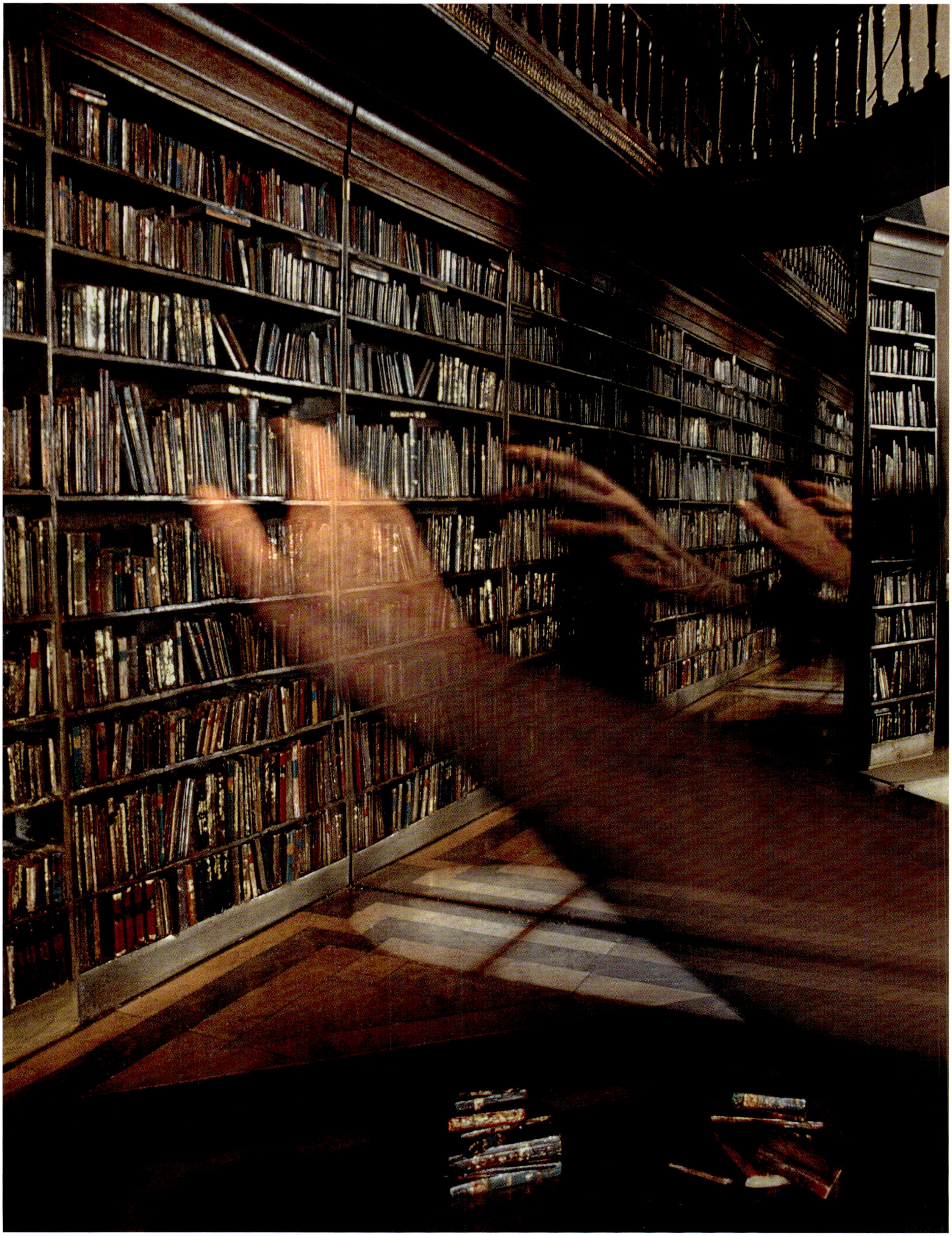

Library in Homage to Georges Perec III (with the artist's hand), 2004.
Mixed media,
33 ¾ × 27 × 28 ¼ in.
(86 × 69 × 72 cm).

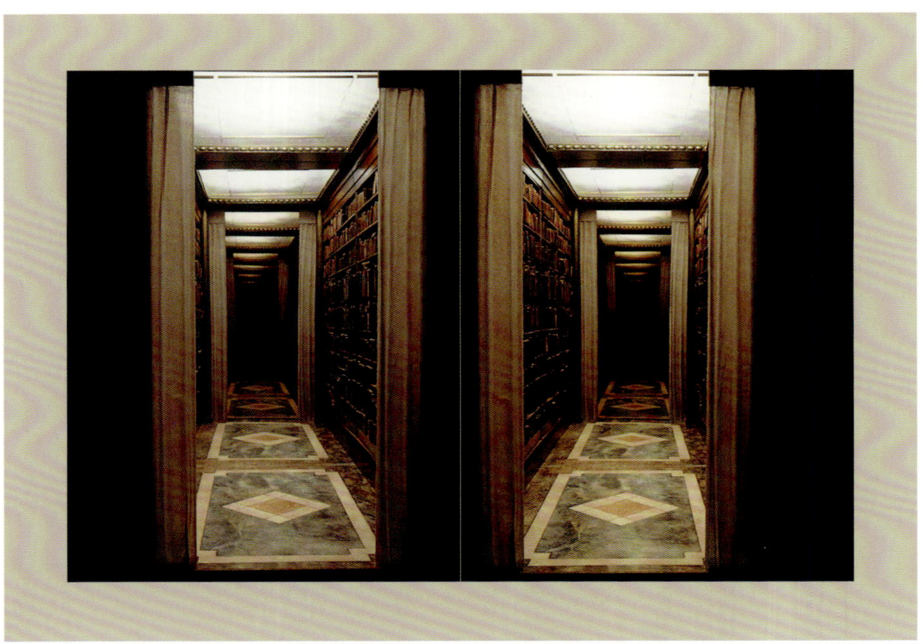

Book-lined Corridor, 2000.
Mixed media, 22 ¾ × 15 × 14 ¼ in. (58 × 38 × 36 cm).

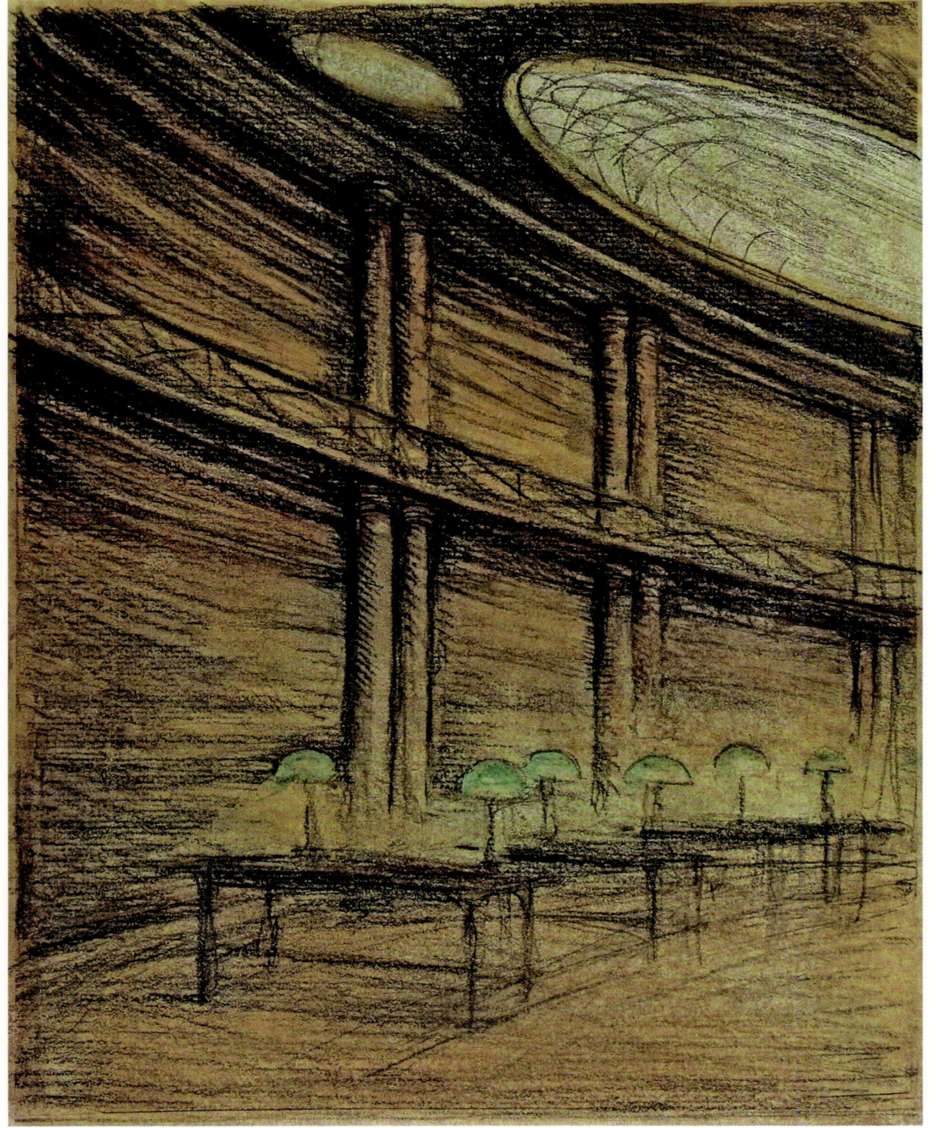

The National Library, 2005.
Pencil, watercolor, and wash on cardboard, 9 × 7 in. (22.5 × 17.5 cm).

Certain boxes might easily be the fruit of the skills of an architect or an illusionist. I devise these looking-glass games, whose goal is to spark minor mental tremors in the viewer's consciousness, on paper. Thus, these tricks, these decoys, these spatial illusions, these simulacra create an unease that brings the viewer back to reality, so that he loses his self-awareness and thus is able to perceive what is before his eyes even more strongly.

C. Matton, interview by Frédéric Mitterand, "Ça me dit, l'après-midi," France Culture (September 1, 2007). Radio program

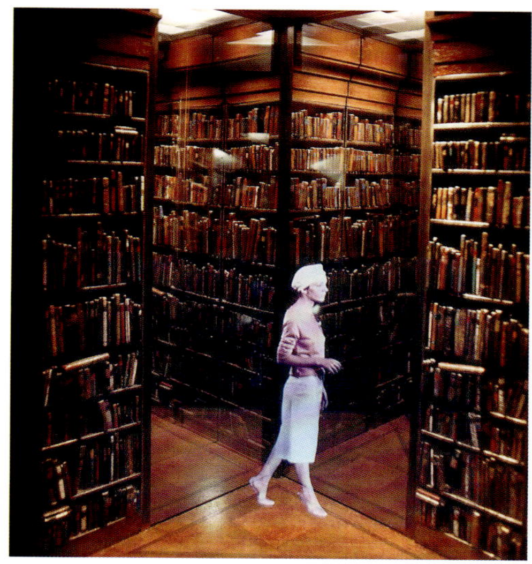
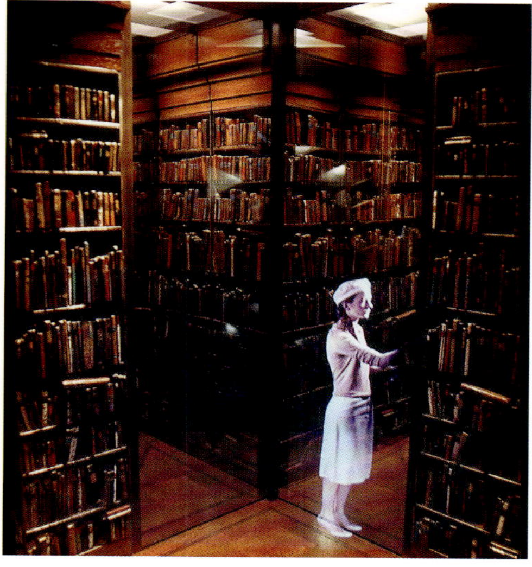
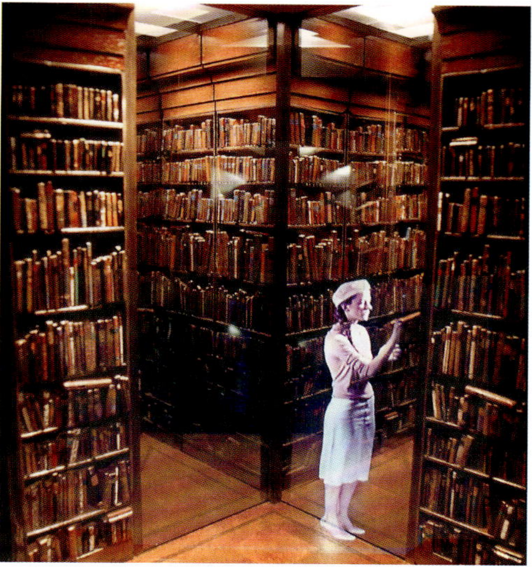
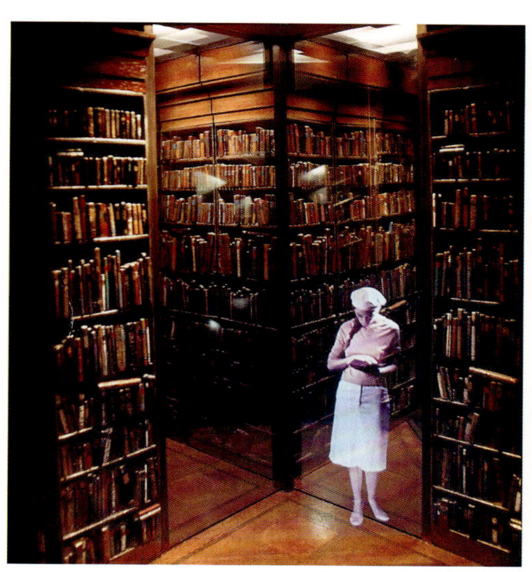
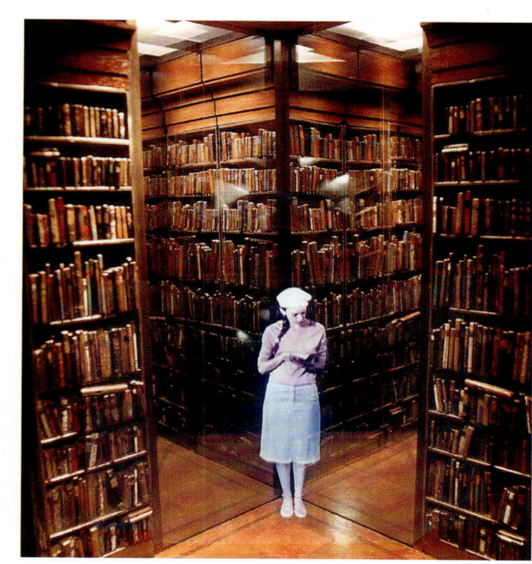
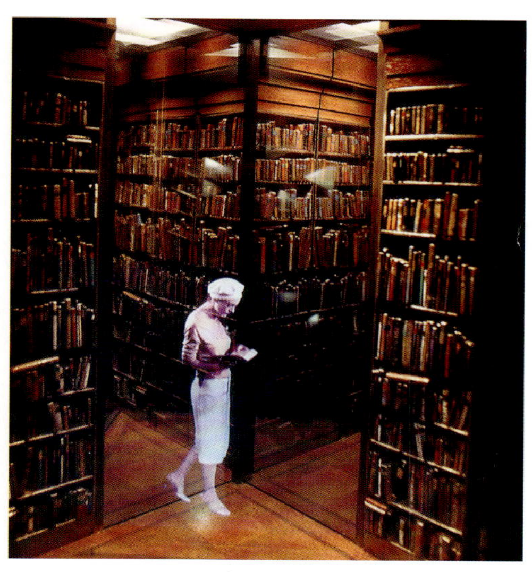
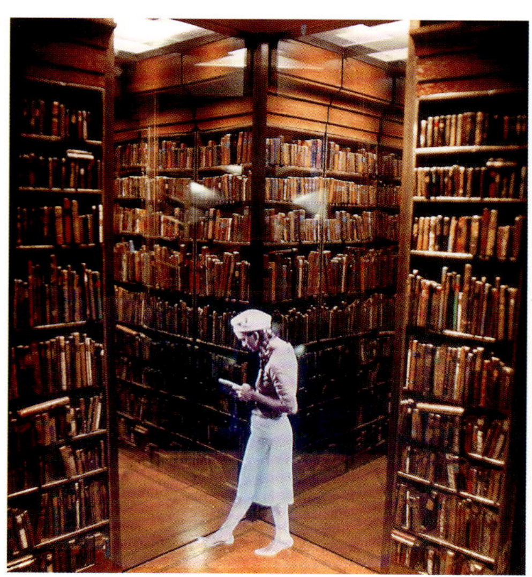
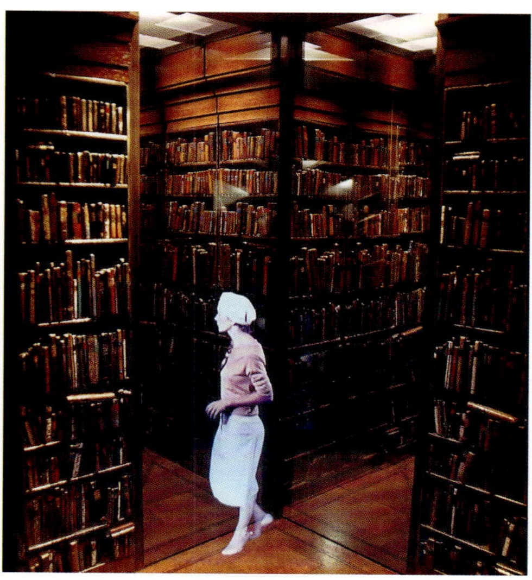
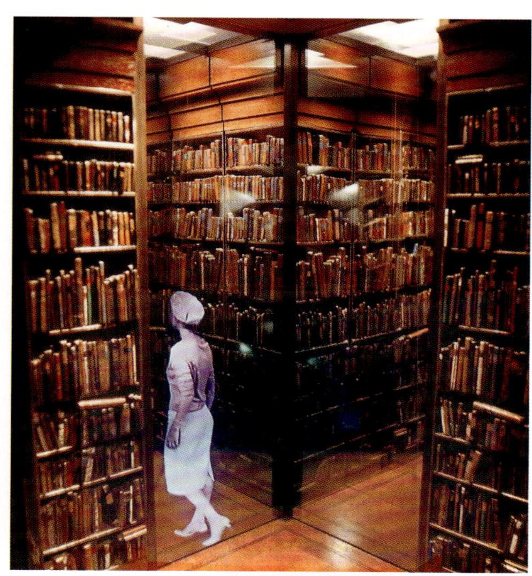

Library with Memory of Anna (9 instants), 2004.
Mixed media with video, 22 ½ × 19 ¼ × 21 ½ in. (57 × 49 × 55 cm).

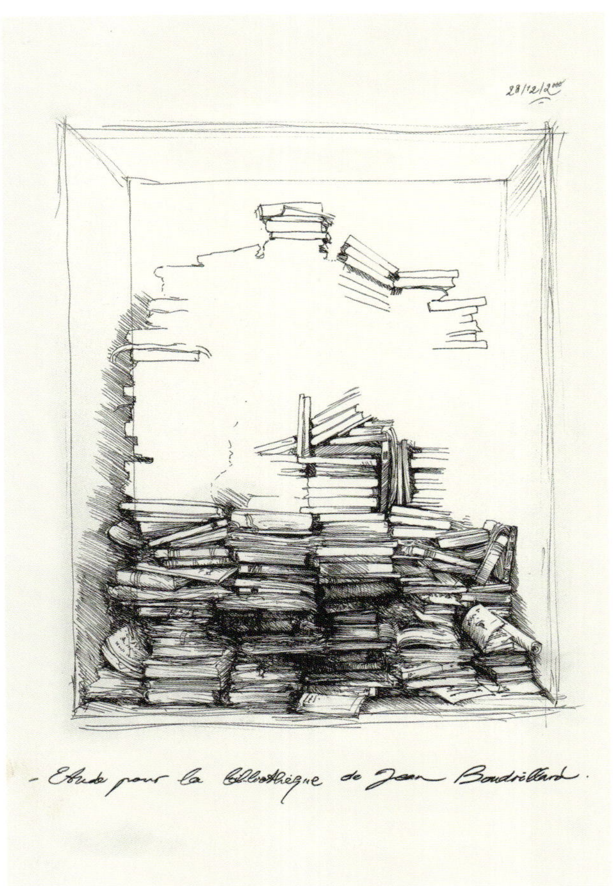

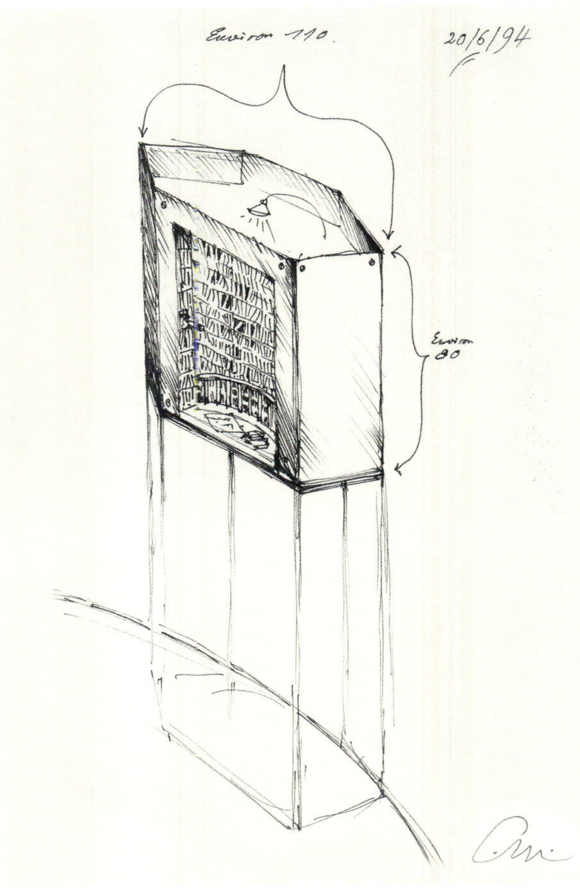

Jean Baudrillard's Library (study), 2000.
Pencil on paper,
11 ¾ × 8 ½ in.
(29.7 × 21 cm).

Library with a Balcony I, 1994.
Pencil on paper,
5 ½ × 3 in. (14 × 8 cm).

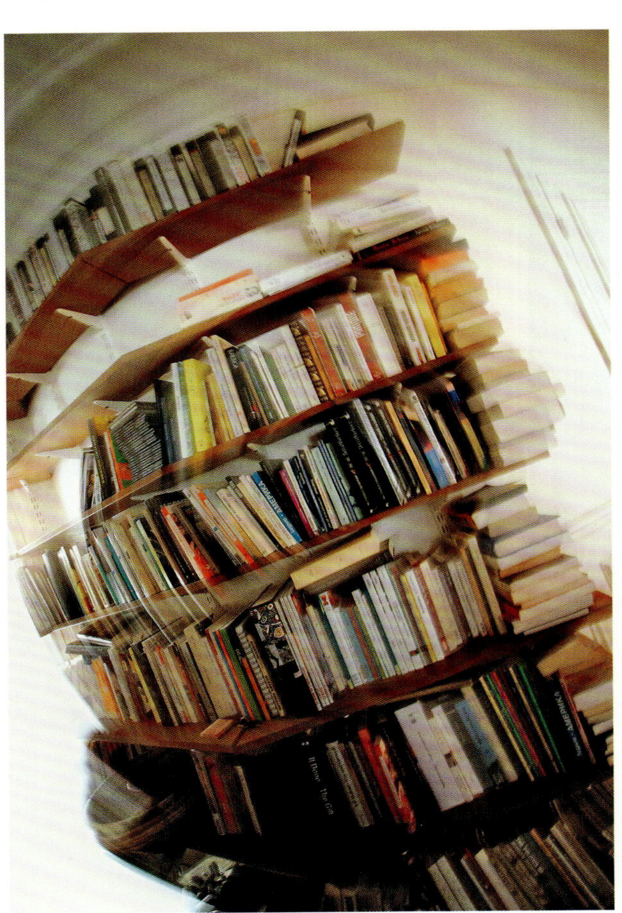

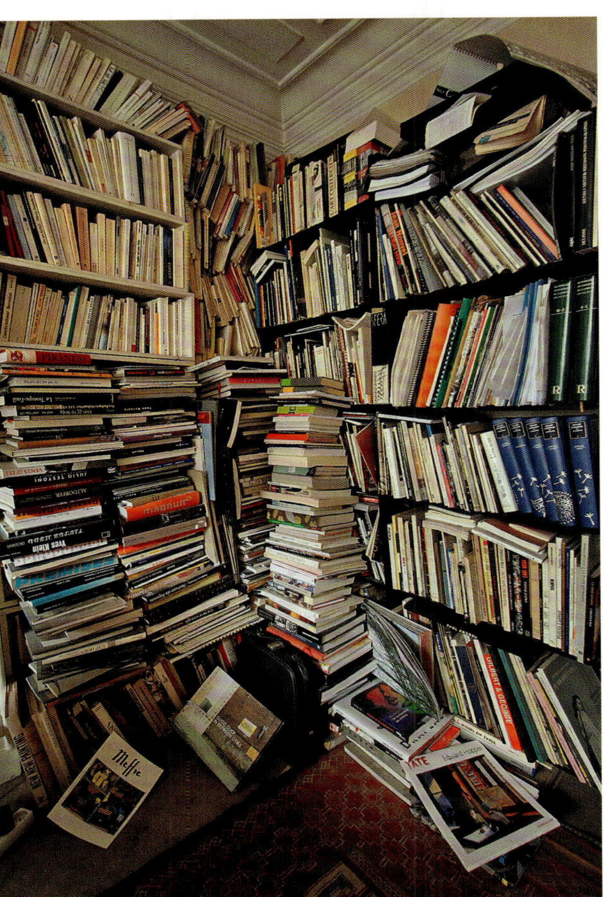

Jean Baudrillard's Library II (on the Curved Wall), 2007.
Photograph.

Jean Baudrillard's Library I (in his Study), 2007.
Photograph.

Library *Shelves, Paintbrush, and the Artist's Hand*, 2004. Photograph.

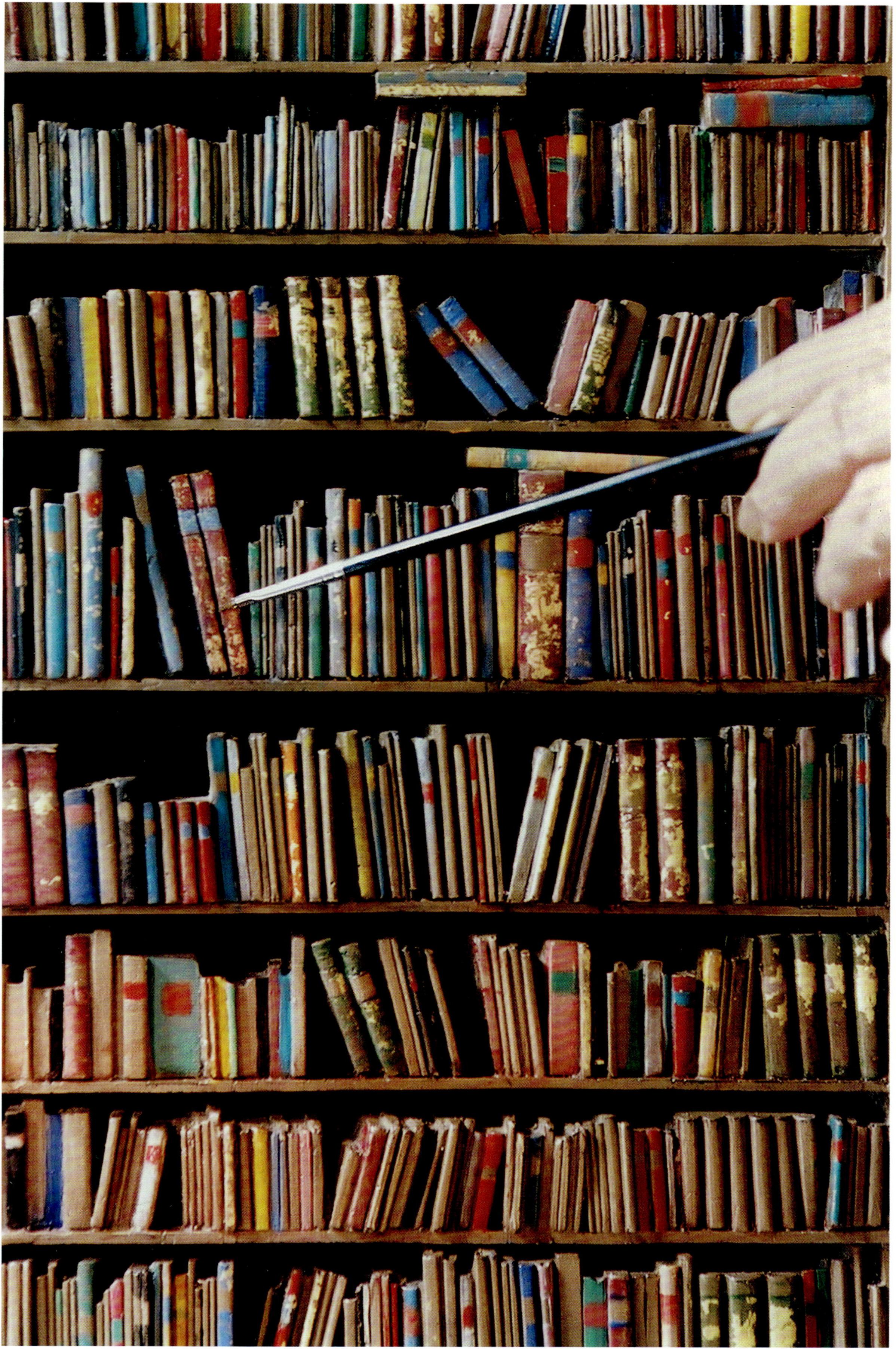

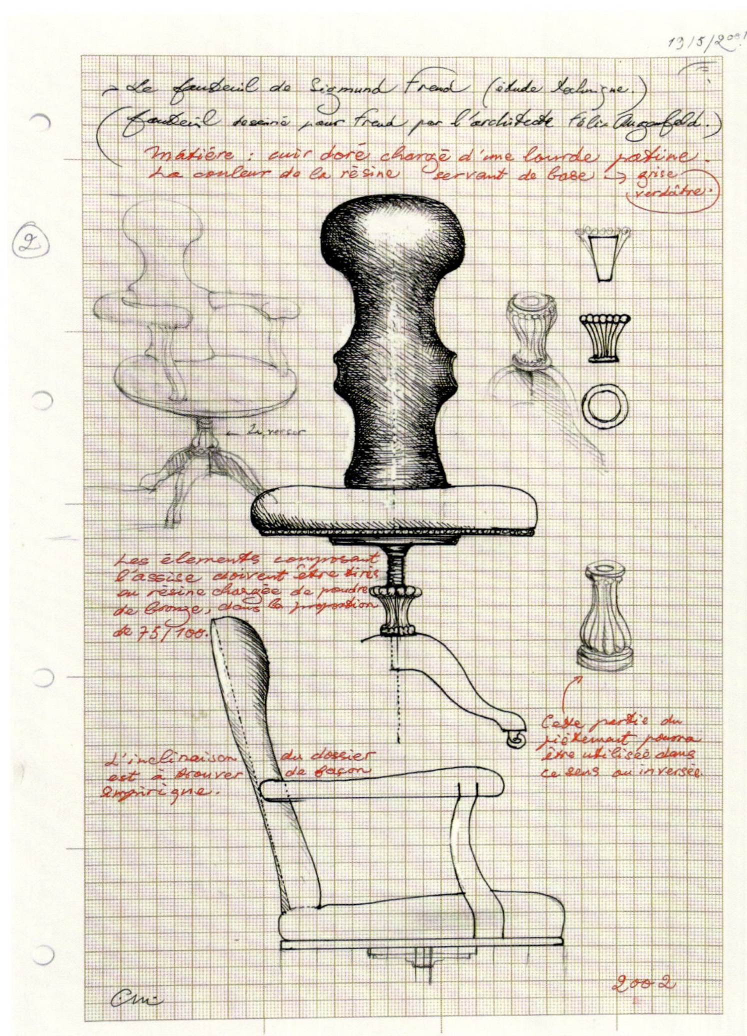
13/5/2001
Le fauteuil de Sigmund Freud (étude technique.)
(fauteuil dessiné pour Freud par l'architecte Felix Augenfeld.)
Matière : cuir doré chargé d'une lourde patine.
La couleur de la résine servant de base → grise verdâtre.
Les éléments composant l'assise doivent être tirés en résine chargée de poudre de bronze, dans la proportion de 75/100.
Cette partie du piètement pourra être utilisée dans ce sens ou inversée.
L'inclinaison du dossier est à trouver de façon empirique.
2002

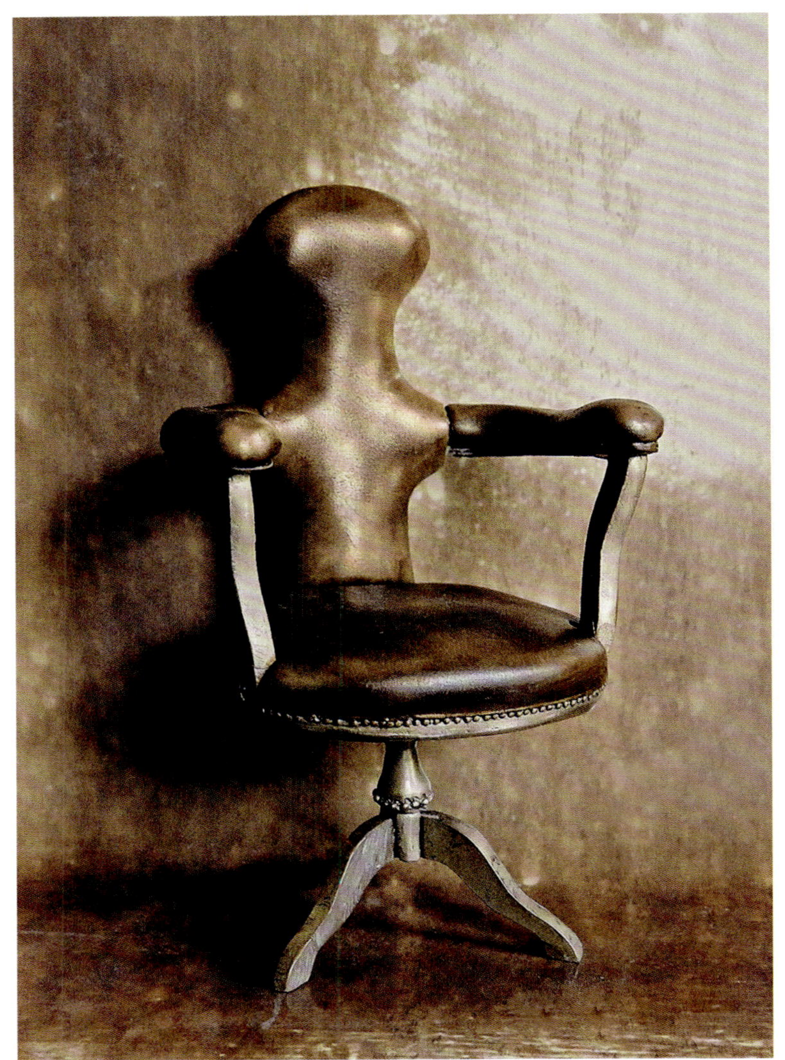

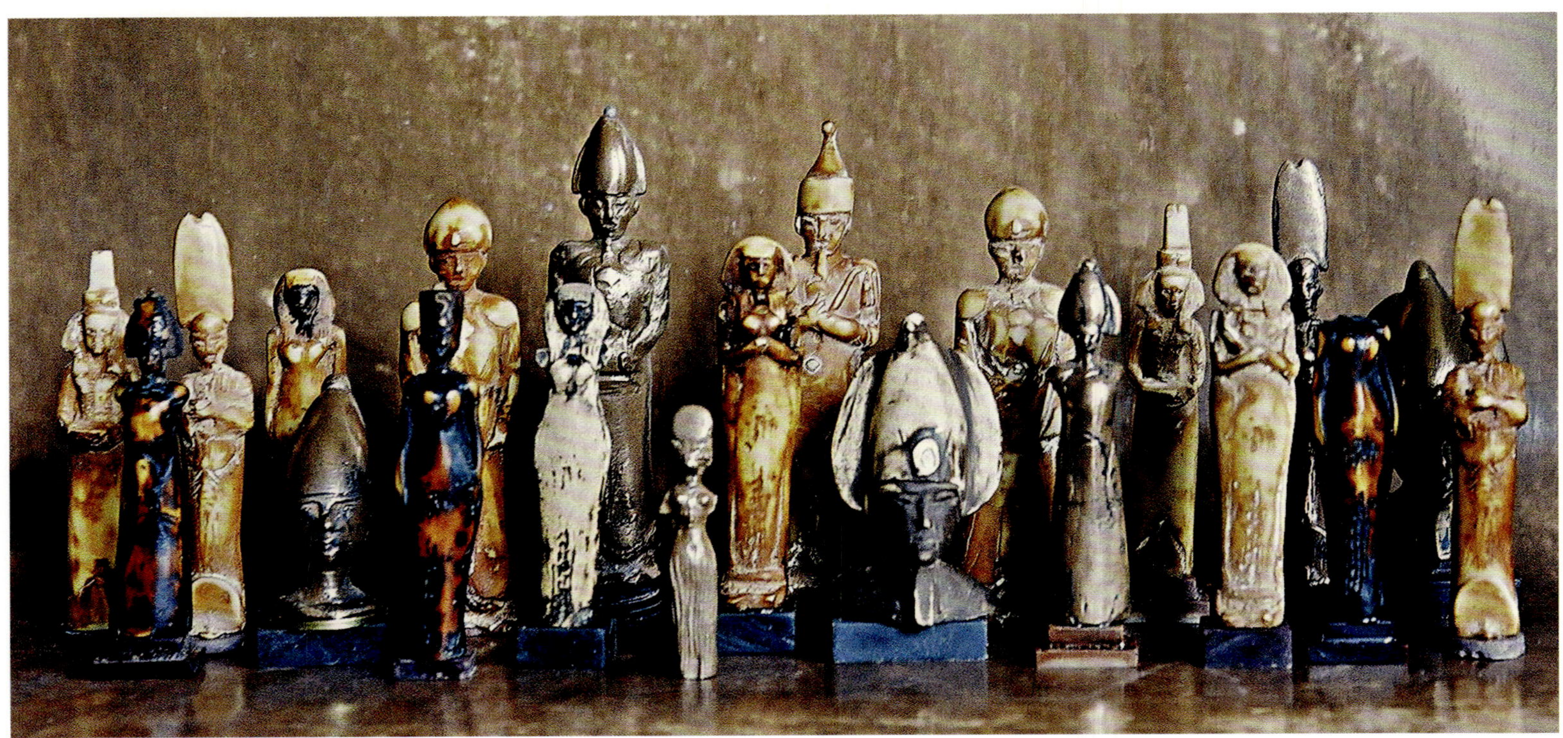

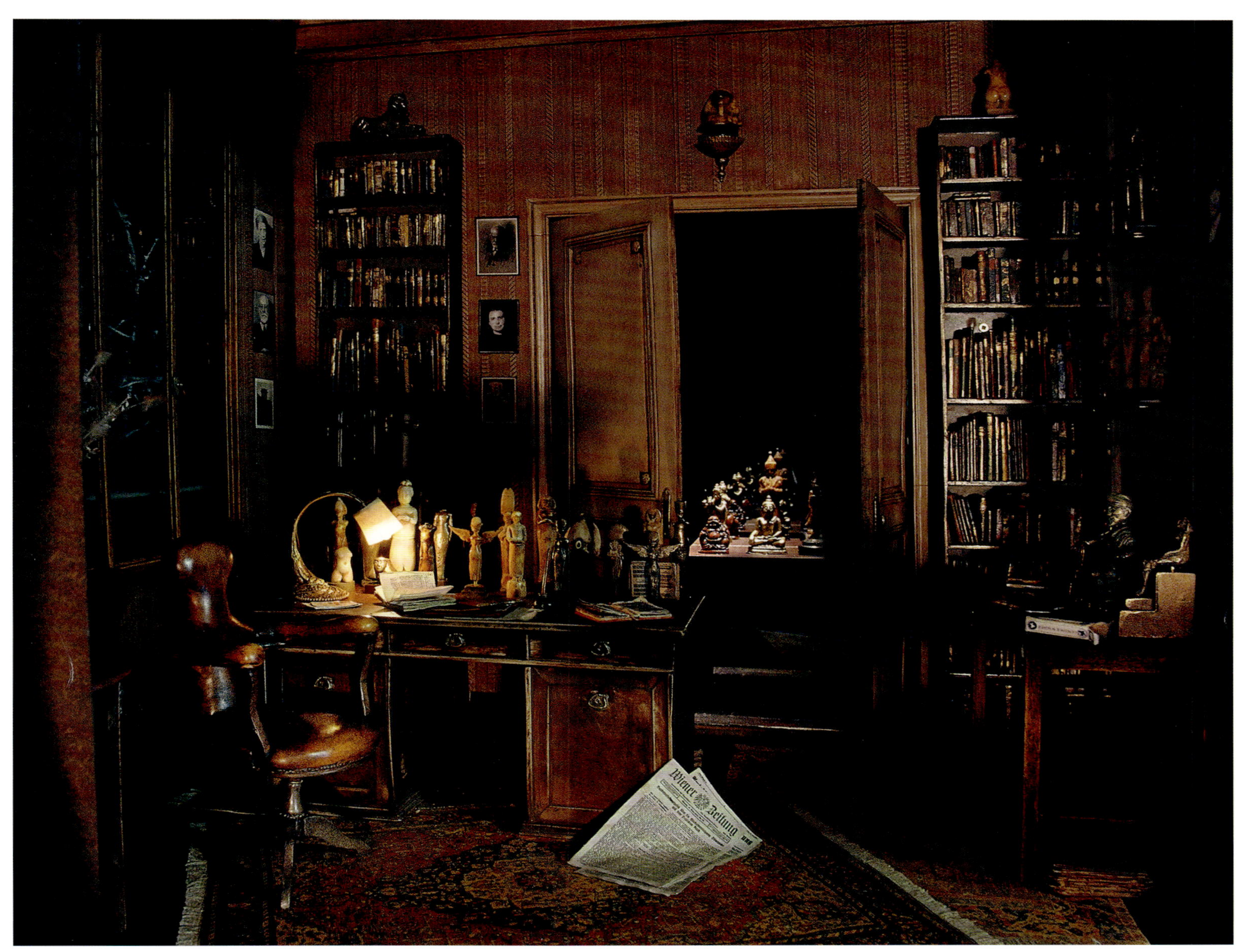

Sigmund Freud's Study I, 2002.
Mixed media, 22 ¼ × 28 × 21 ½ in. (56.5 × 71 × 55 cm).

Facing page:
Sigmund Freud's Armchair (technical study), 2001–02.
Pencil and felt pen on graph paper,
11 ¾ × 8 ½ in. (29.7 × 21 cm).

Sigmund Freud's Armchair in his Study, 2002.
Torolith and oil, 6 ¼ × 3 ½ × 3 ½ in.
(16 × 9 × 9 cm).

Twenty-one Sculptures Belonging to Sigmund Freud's Study, 2001–02.
Fired torolith and marble, oil,
1–2 in. (2.5–6.3 cm) h.

I had in my hands a photography book by a friend of Freud's, who took photographs all over Freud's house: the consulting room, his study, large numbers of sculptures (there are twenty-one on his desk). This box is as objective a reconstitution as possible. At the same time, the view through the door is fairly dreamlike. I wanted to express the collecting mania that characterized Freud. An extraordinary accumulation of sculpture, mainly Egyptian, Greco-Roman, Chinese, Far Eastern in general, large in size, small in size; the house was chock-a-block with sculpture. Fascinating. It meant a lot of work.

C. Matton, in "Ça me dit, l'après-midi," op. cit.

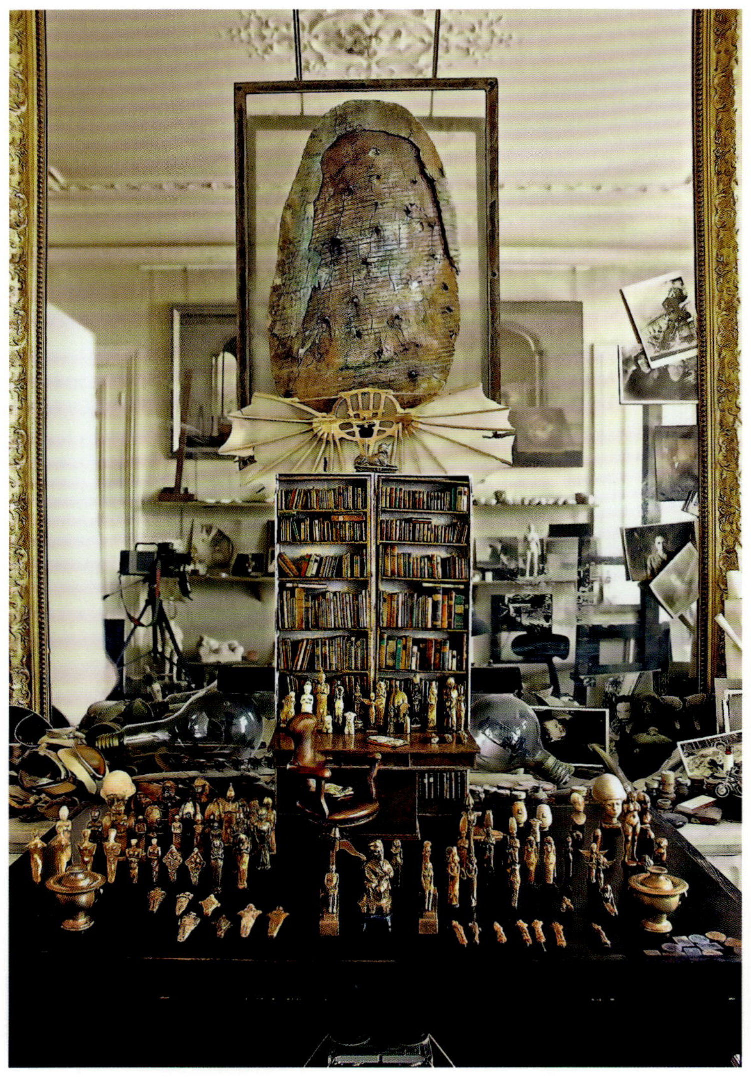

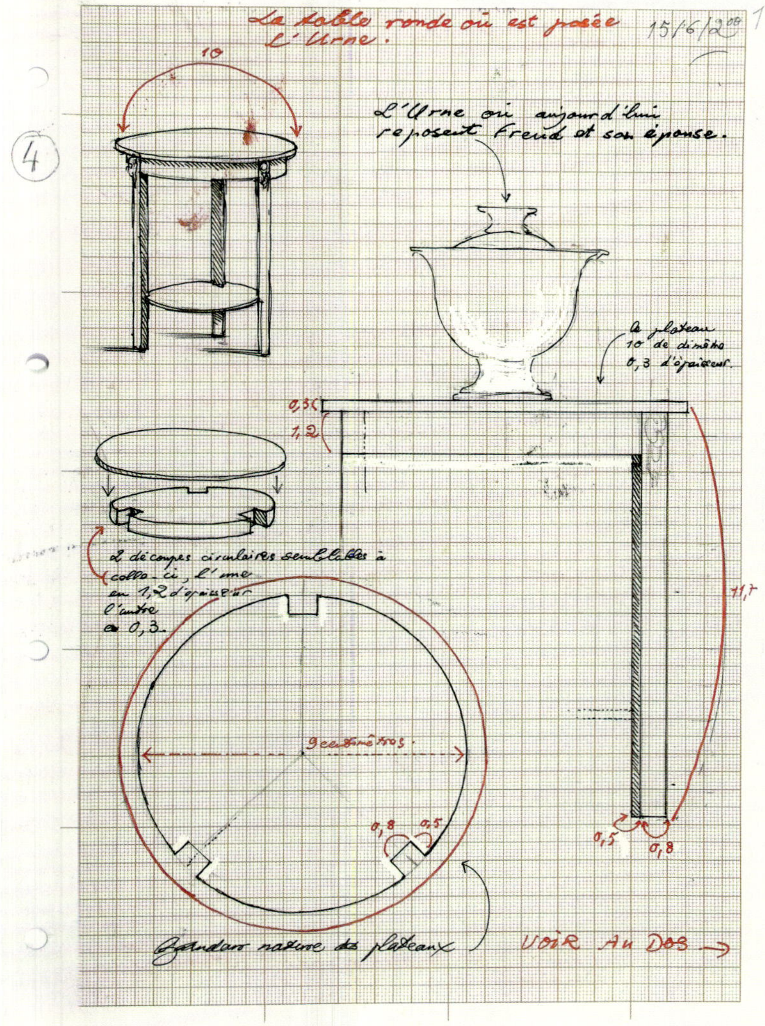

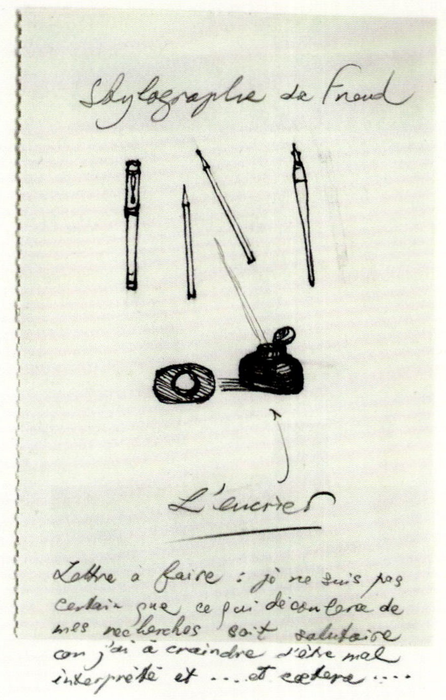

In front of the Mirror in the Studio on boulevard Saint-Germain, 2002. Photograph.

The Round Table on which the Urn Stands, 2001. Pencil and felt pen on graph paper, 11 ½ × 8 ¼ in. (29.7 × 21 cm).

Fountain Pen, Inkpot, and a Fake Draft of a Letter by Freud, 2001. Pencil on paper, 4 ¼ × 2 ¾ in. (11 × 7 cm).

Freud's stylograph
Inkpot
Letter to write: I'm not sure that what will result from my research will be worthwhile as I'm worried about being wrongly interpreted and… et cetera…

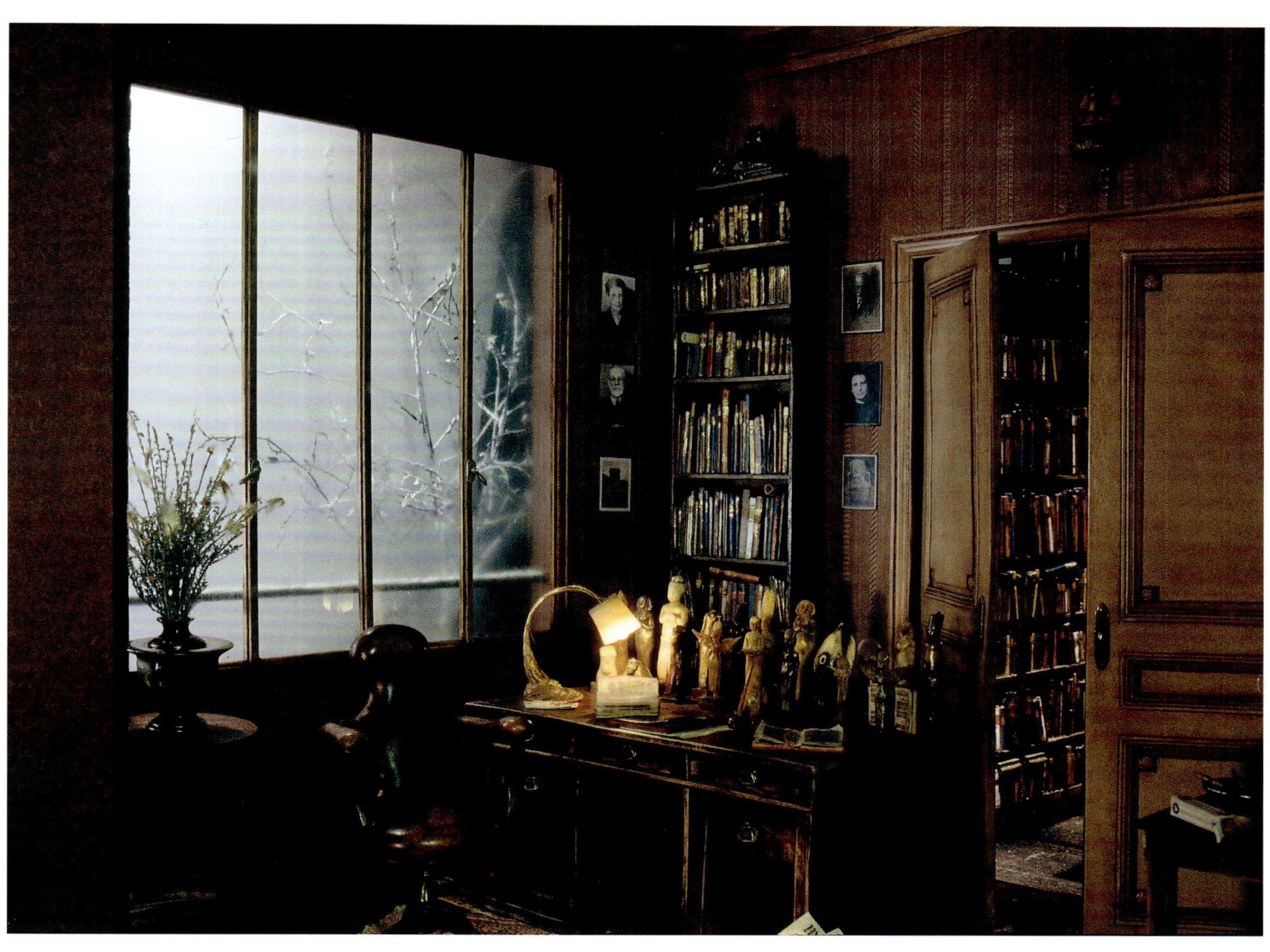

Sigmund Freud's *Study II*, 2007.
Mixed media, 22 ¼ × 28 × 21 ½ in. (56.5 × 71 × 55 cm).

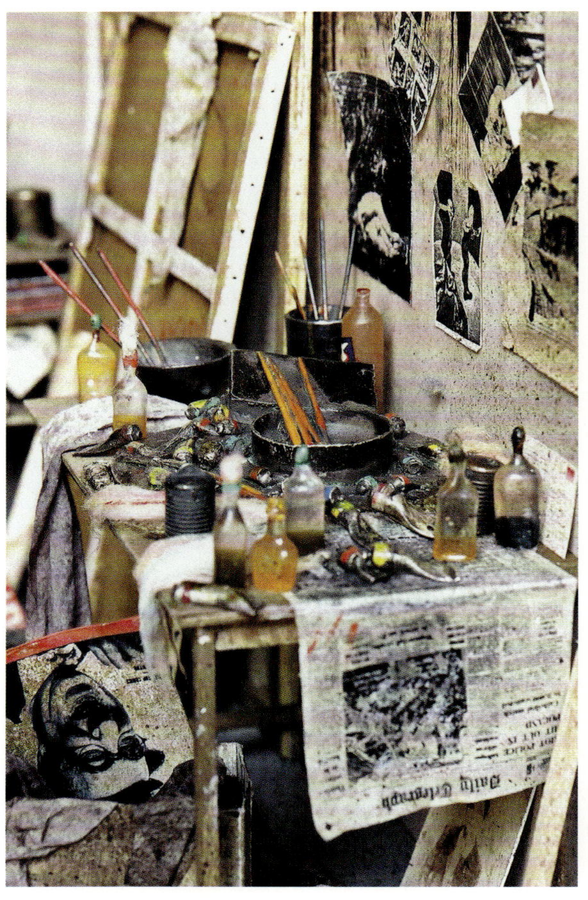

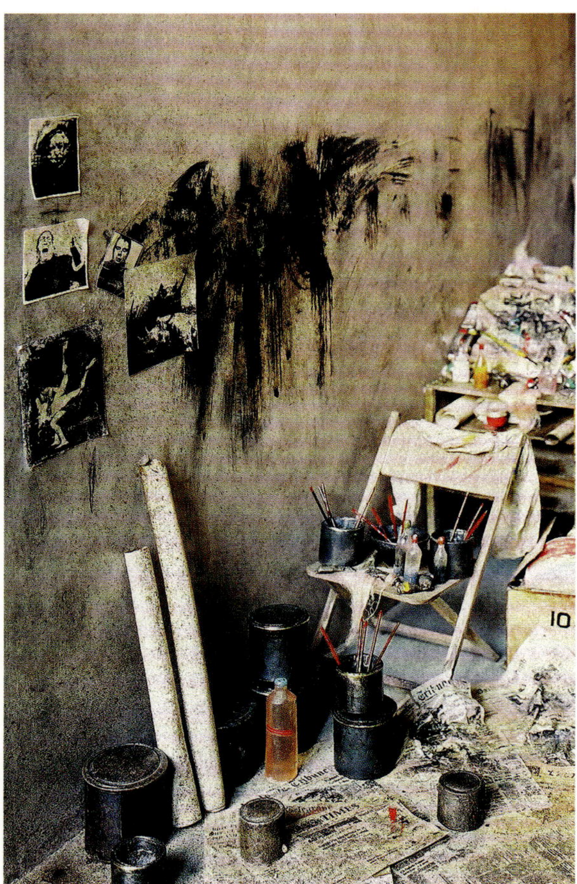

Francis Bacon's Studio (detail 1), 1987.
Photograph.

Francis Bacon's Studio (detail 2), 1987.
Photograph.

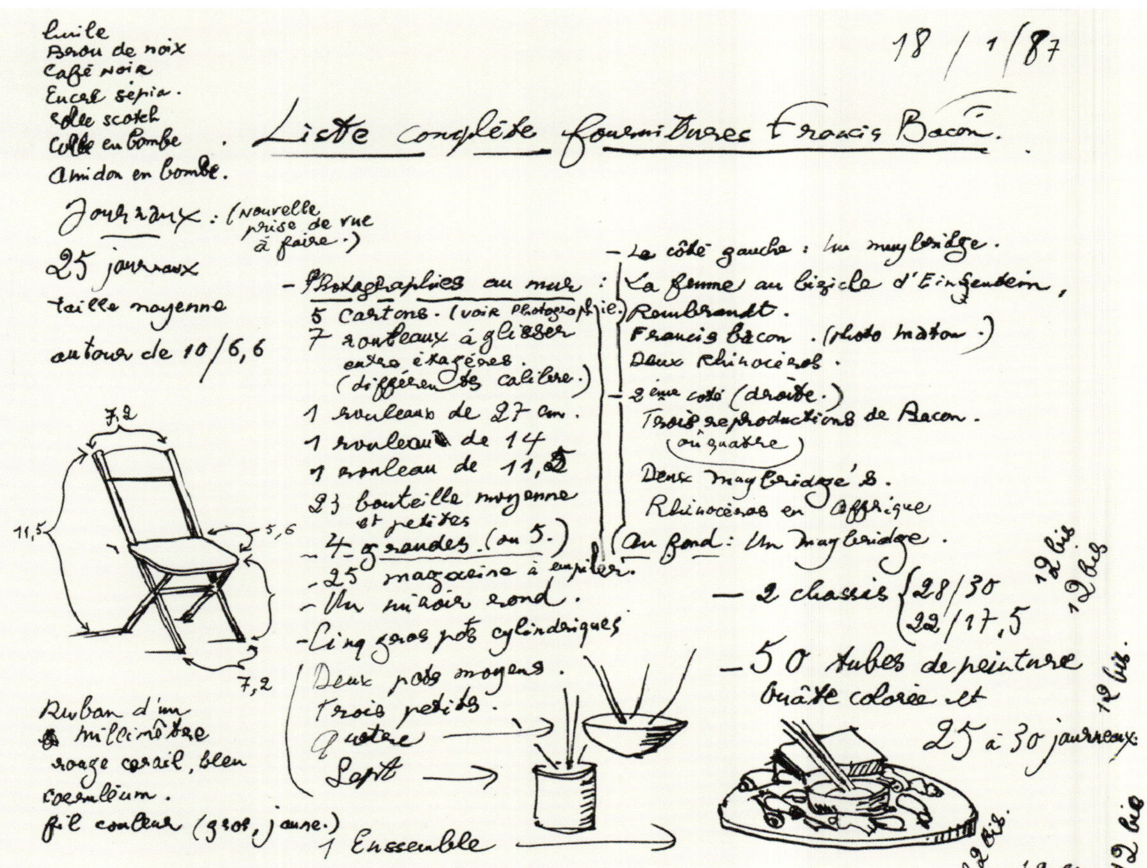

18 / 1 / 87

Liste complète fournitures Francis Bacon.

huile
Brou de noix
Café noir
Encre sépia.
colle scotch
Colle en bombe
Amidon en bombe.

Journaux : (nouvelle prise de vue à faire.)
25 journaux
taille moyenne
autour de 10/6,6

7,2
11,5
5,6
7,2

Ruban d'un millimètre rouge corail, bleu coeruleum.
fil couleur (gros, jaune.)

– Photographies au mur : 5 cartons. (voir photographie.)
7 rouleaux à glisser entre étagères. (différents calibre.)
1 rouleau de 27 cm.
1 rouleau de 14
1 rouleau de 11,5
23 bouteille moyenne et petites
– 4 grandes. (ou 5.)
– 25 magazine à empiler.
– Un miroir rond.
– Cinq gros pots cylindriques
Deux pots moyens.
Trois petits.
Quatre
Sept
1 Ensemble

– Le côté gauche : Un muybridge.
La femme au bizicle d'Einzenstein,
Rembrandt.
Francis Bacon. (photo maton.)
Deux Rhinocéros.
– 2ème coté (droite.)
Trois reproductions de Bacon. (ou quatre)
Deux muybridge's.
Rhinocéros en Affrique
(Au fond : Un muybridge.

– 2 chassis {28/30 12 bis
22/17,5 12 bis
– 50 tubes de peinture 12 bis.
ouate colorée et
25 à 30 journaux.
12 bis. 12 bis 12 bis

Complete List Supplies Francis Bacon, 1987.
Felt pen on paper, 6 ¾ × 8 ¼ in. (17 × 21 cm).

Selected supplies:

- *oil*
- *walnut stain*
- *black coffee*
- *sepia ink*
- *Scotch glue*
- *spray adhesive*
- *spray starch*

- *Newspapers*

- *Millimeter ribbon*

- *Photographs on the wall*
- *twenty-three medium and small bottles*
- *twenty-five magazines to pile up*
- *one round mirror*
- *five large cylindrical pots*

Left side: a Muybridge
- *Eisenstein's woman with glasses*
- *Rembrandt*
- *Francis Bacon (ID photo)*
- *two rhinoceroses*

- *fifty tubes of paint, colored cotton wool and between twenty-five and thirty newspapers.*

Francis Bacon's Studio, 1987.
Mixed media,
22 ¾ × 17 ¼ × 20 ¼ in.
(58 × 44 × 51.5 cm).

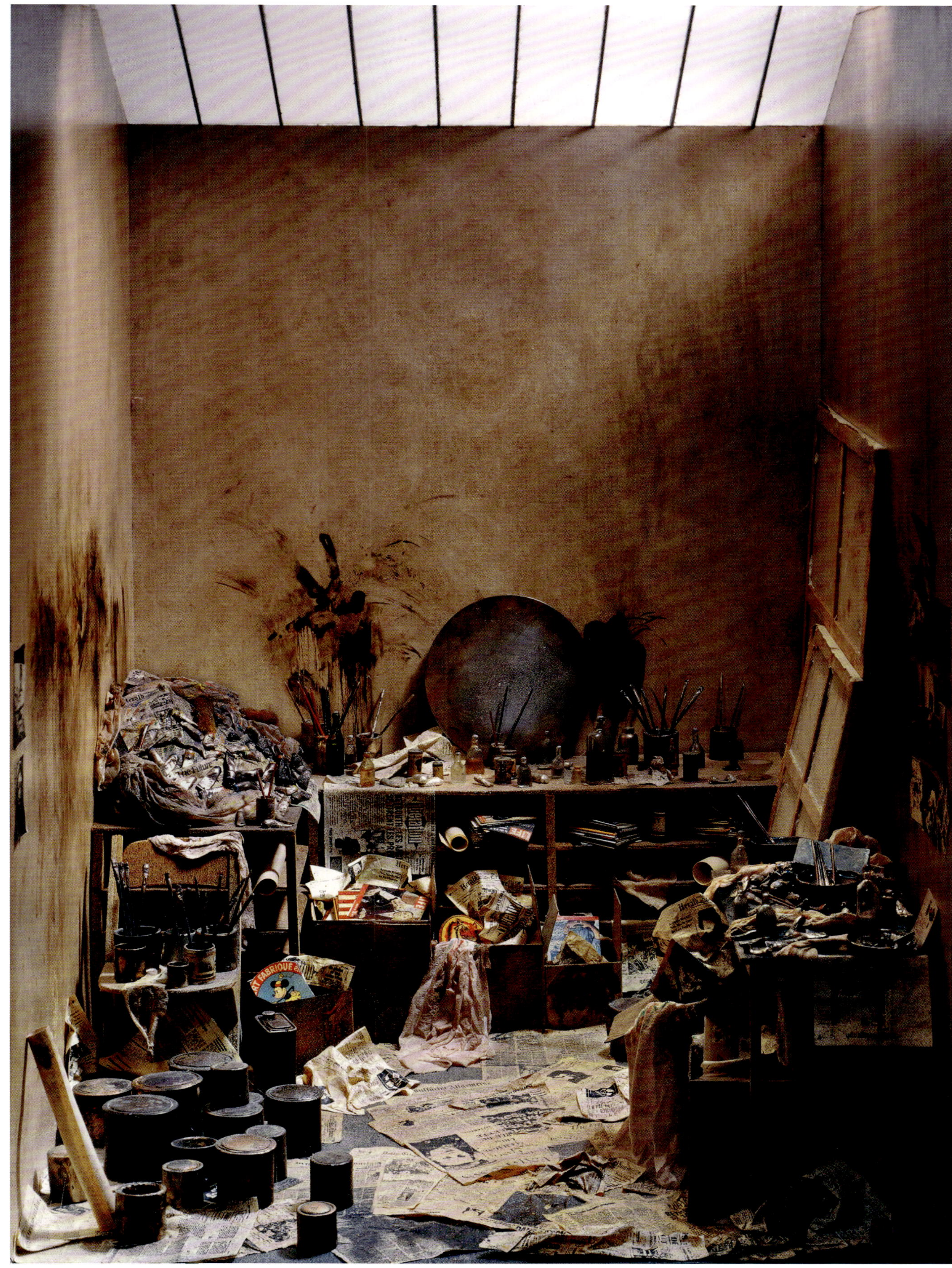

Following double pages:
Francis Bacon's Studio Wall (detail).
Photograph.

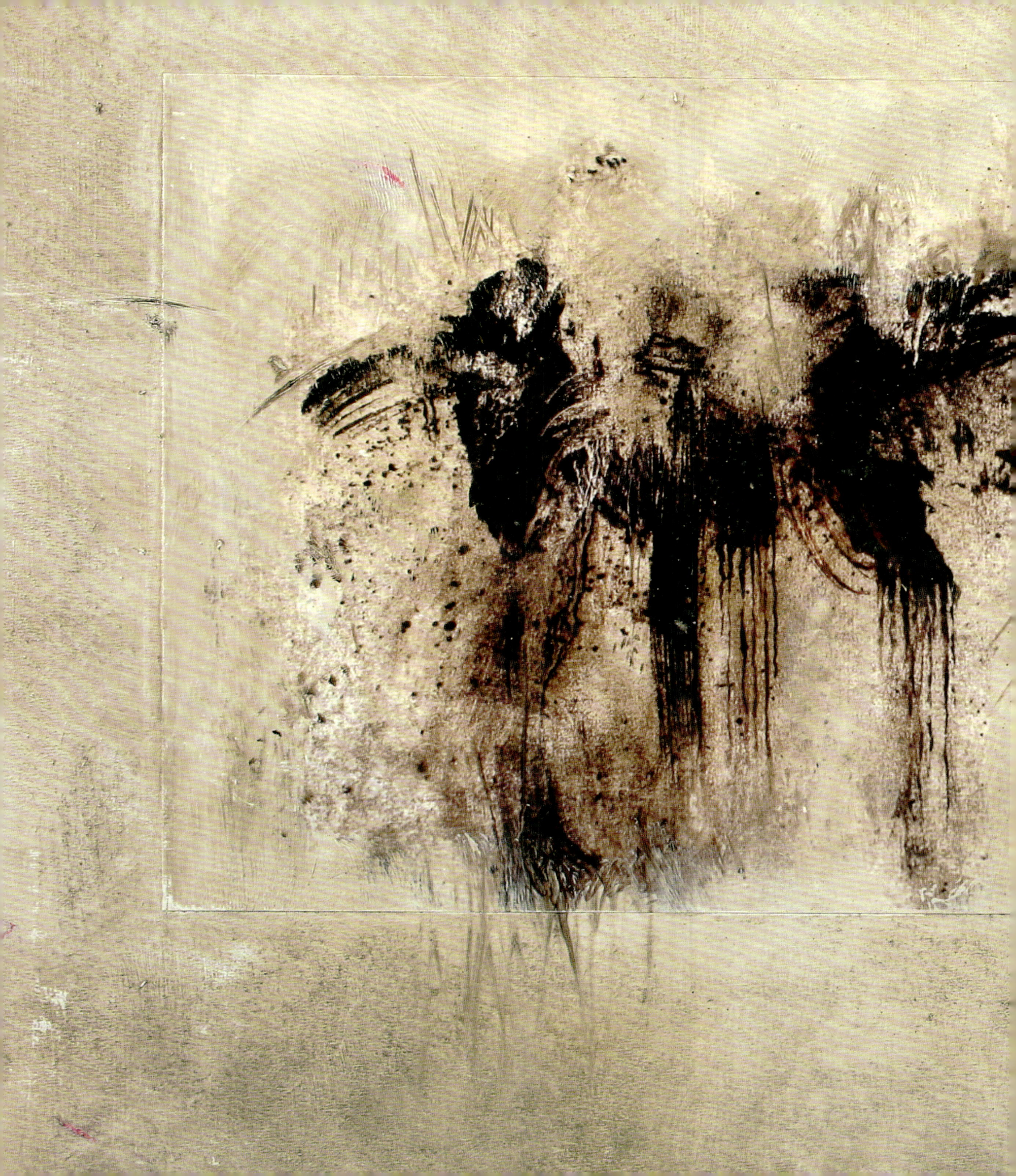

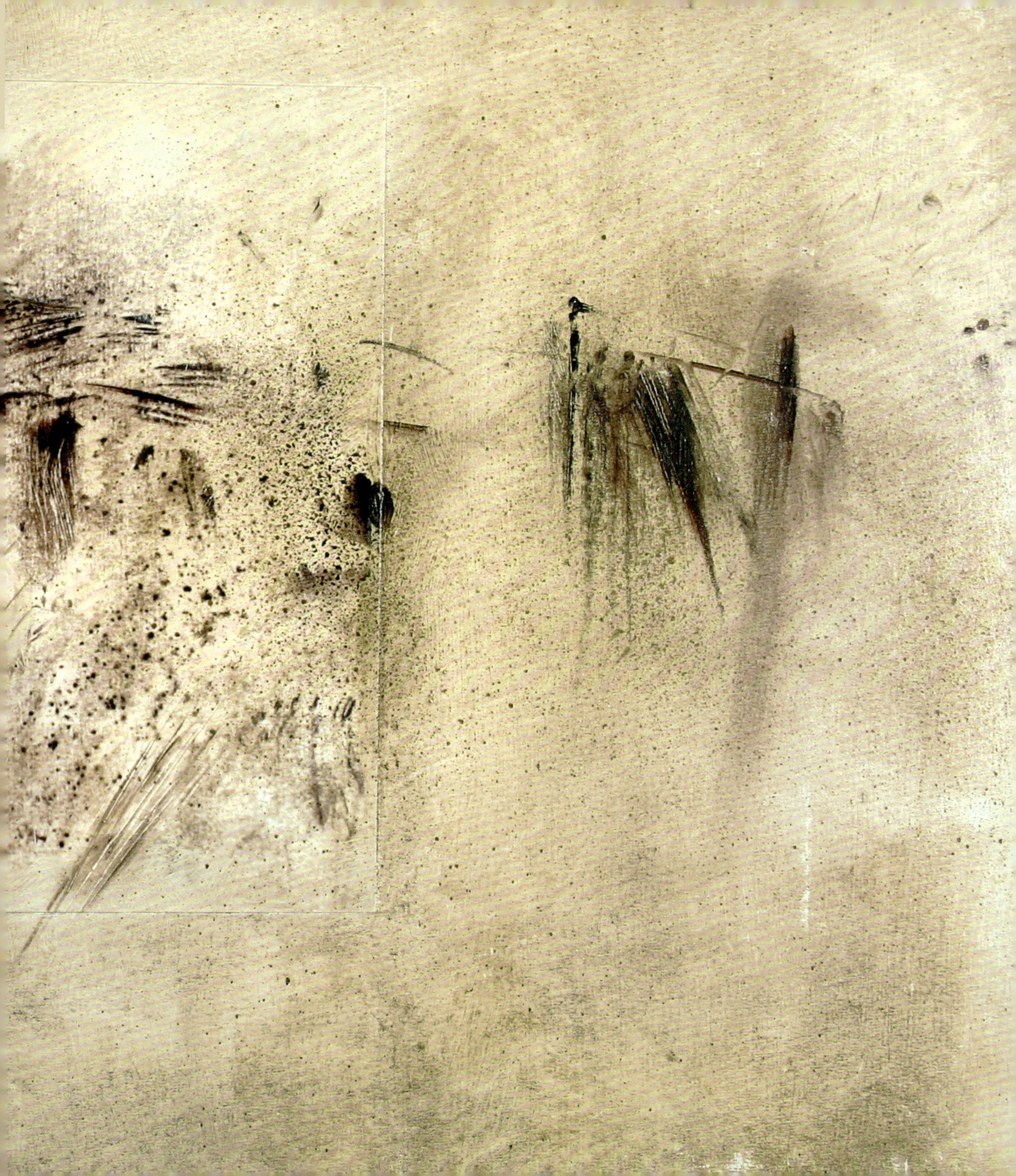

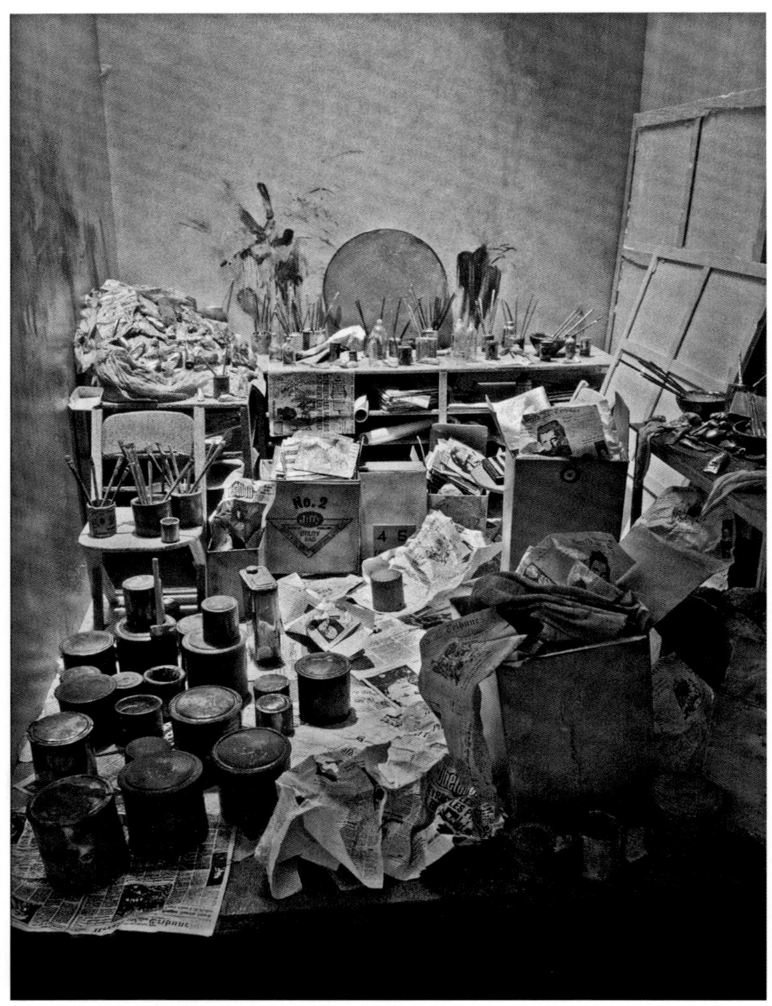

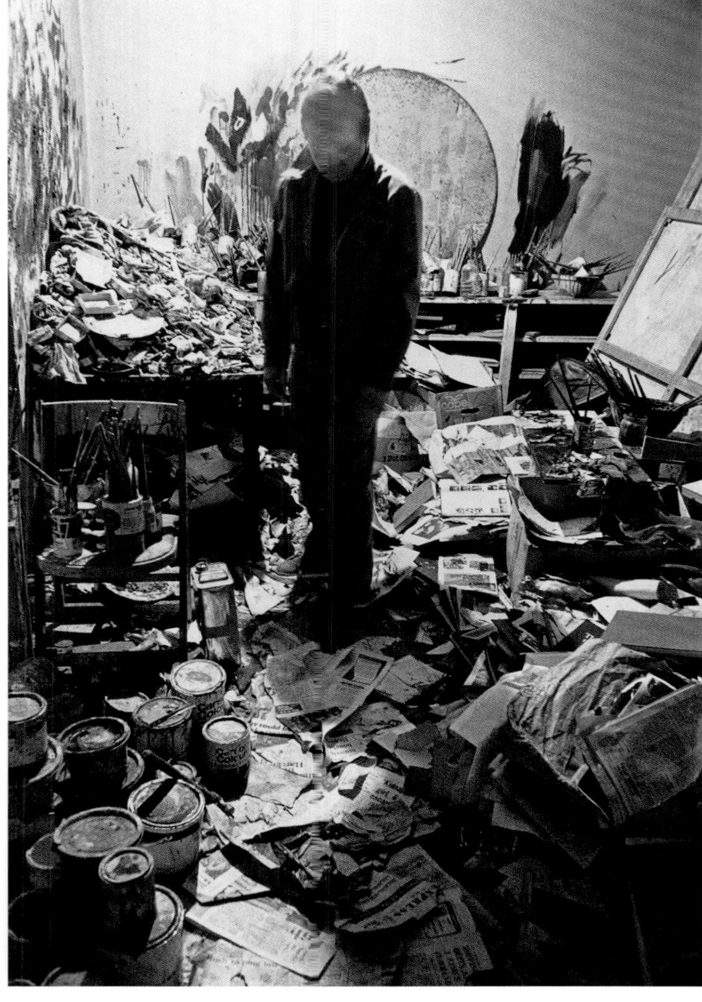

Francis Bacon's Studio, 1987.
Photograph.

Francis Bacon in his Compost Heap Studio, 7 Reece Mews, 1972.
Photograph © Peter Beard, courtesy of the Peter Beard Studio.

I carried out this miniature reconstitution of Francis Bacon's studio in 1987. A photograph of him had haunted me for a long time; a fuzzy, ghostly outline, anchored in the middle of his studio, an indescribable heap of pots, brushes, rags, magazines, and unidentifiable treasures. This is my first tribute to Bacon. I've made others—paintings and sculptures—since. I paid homage to him even though I had to break into his place, uninvited. I know he saw the box in the window of the bookshop *La Hune* in Paris in October, 1991, and, intrigued, went round my exhibition at the École des Beaux-Arts. We were never to meet, but that blurred silhouette and those paintings will always haunt me. I'd love it if the perfect order of the studio were left intact, if no one ever tried to set its ritual disorder to rights by applying some rational order. I'd love it if it became a "listed building," an untouchable space with a large glass front in place of the door, so that those who know that the greatest contemporary painter has just left this planet could all gather there.

C. Matton, "L'hommage de Charles Matton à Francis Bacon," *Paris-Match*, May 14, 1992

Facing page:
Homage to Francis Bacon III, 1992.
Oil on canvas, 62 ¾ × 45 in. (160 × 114 cm).

Installation with the Princess Margareth *Painting*, 1991.
Oil on Cibachrome, 75 ½ × 49 ¼ in. (192 × 125 cm).

Charles Matton applying the finishing touches to Homage to Francis Bacon I *while installing his exhibition* Rétrospective et Citations *in front of* Triptych 1976 *by Francis Bacon*, 1992.
Photograph Toby Gilbert.

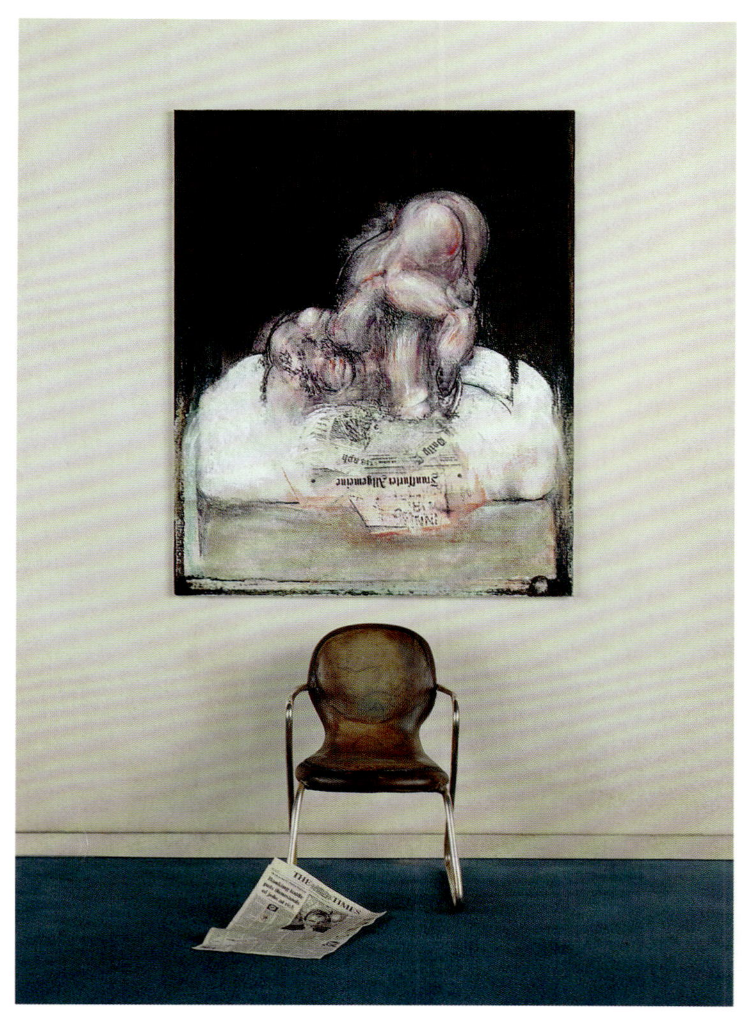

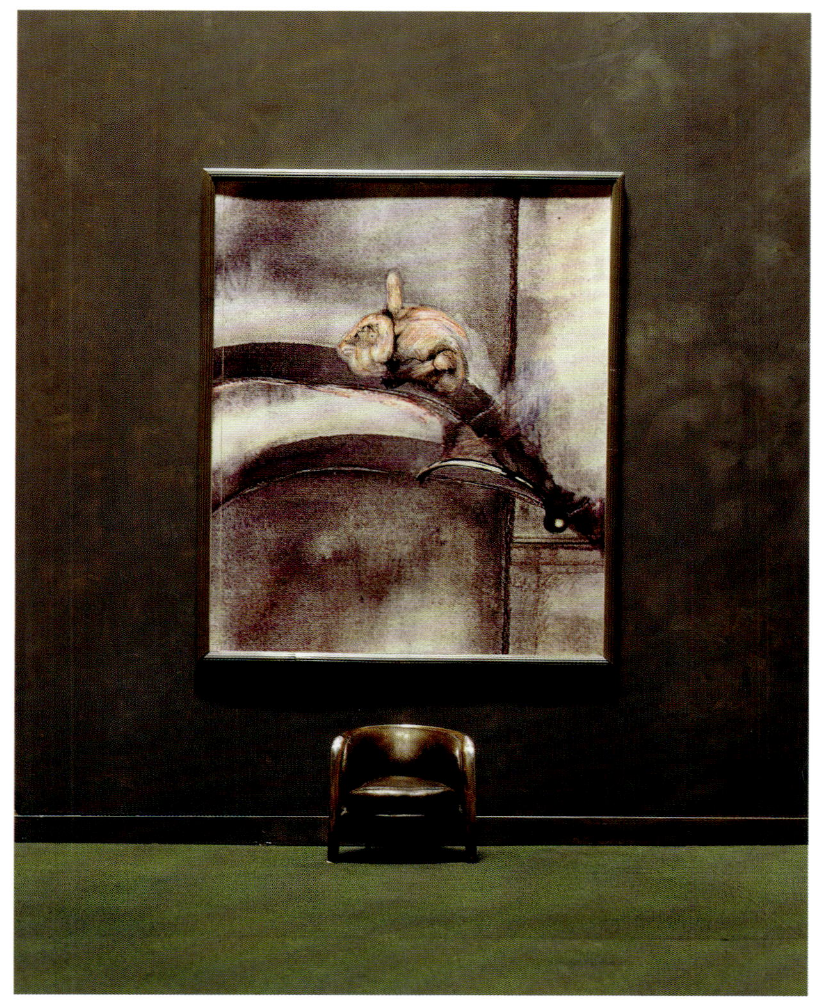

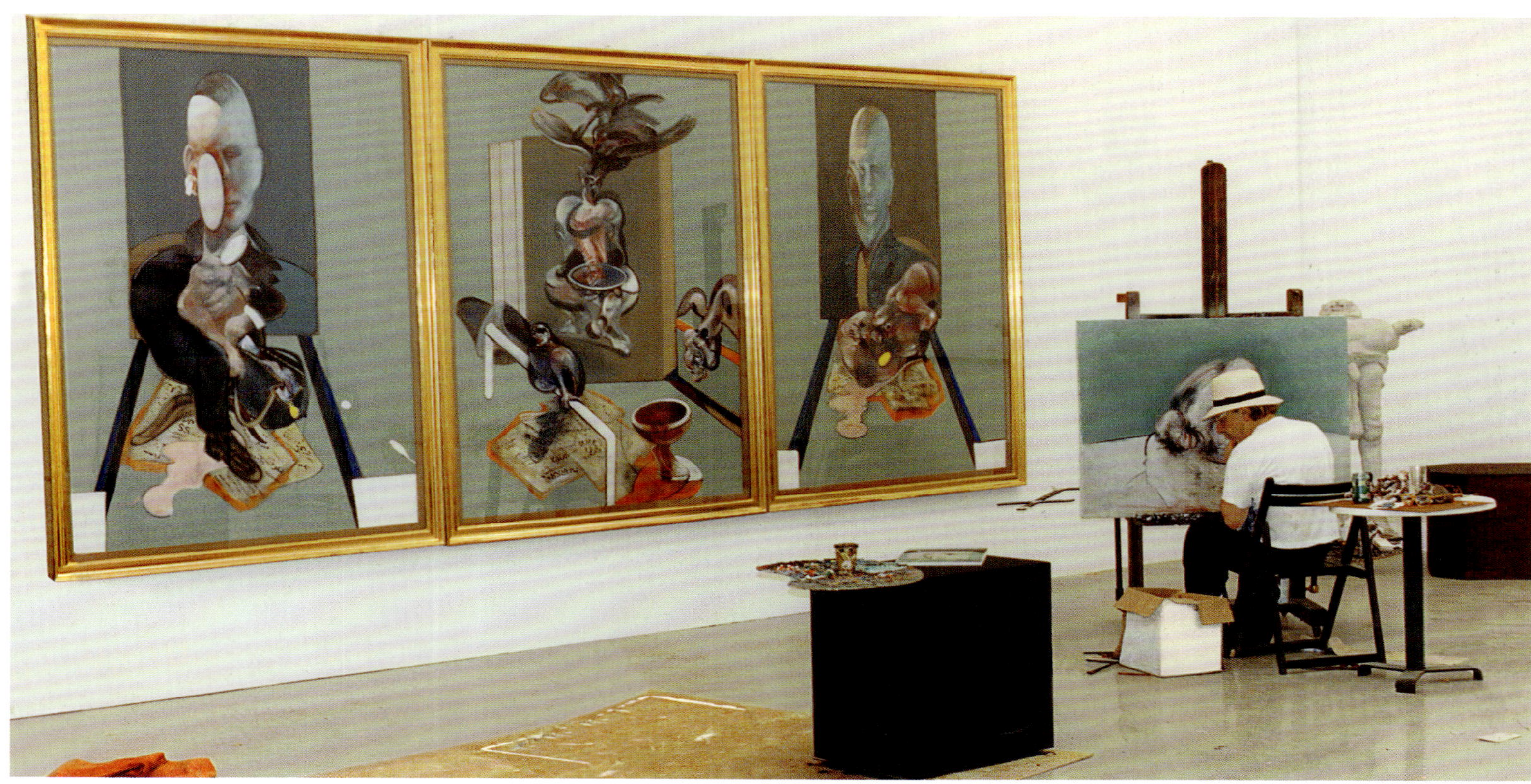

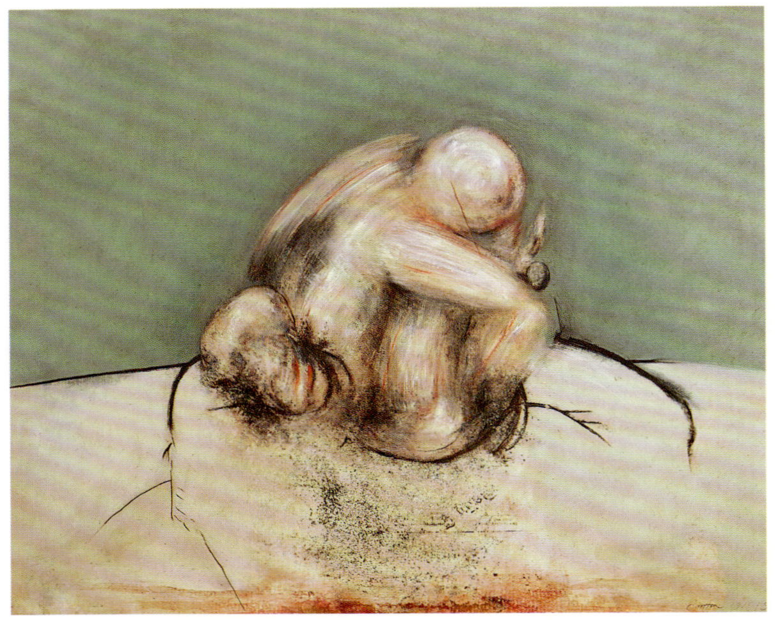

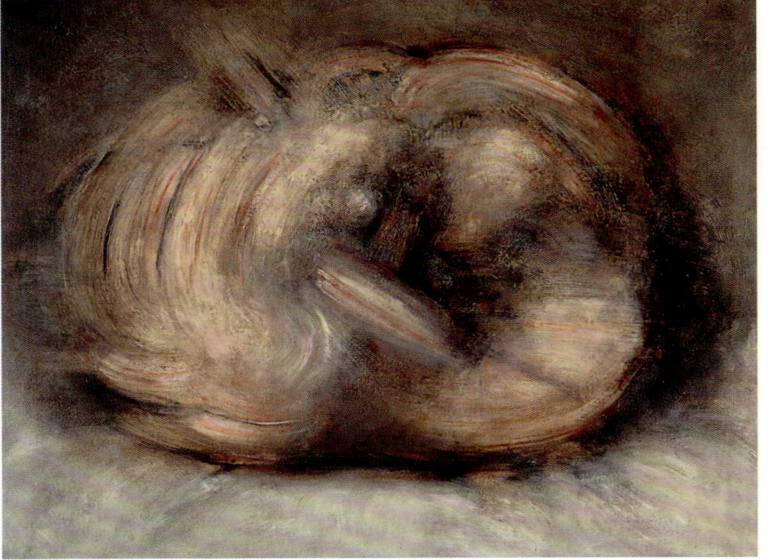

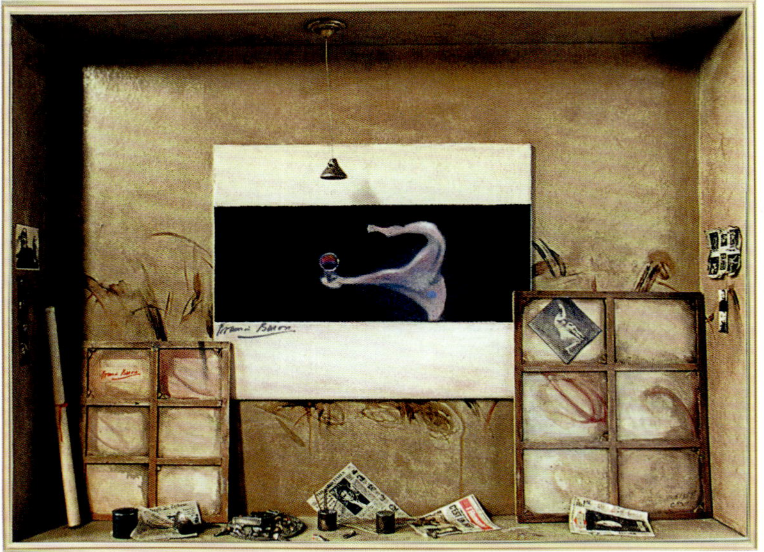

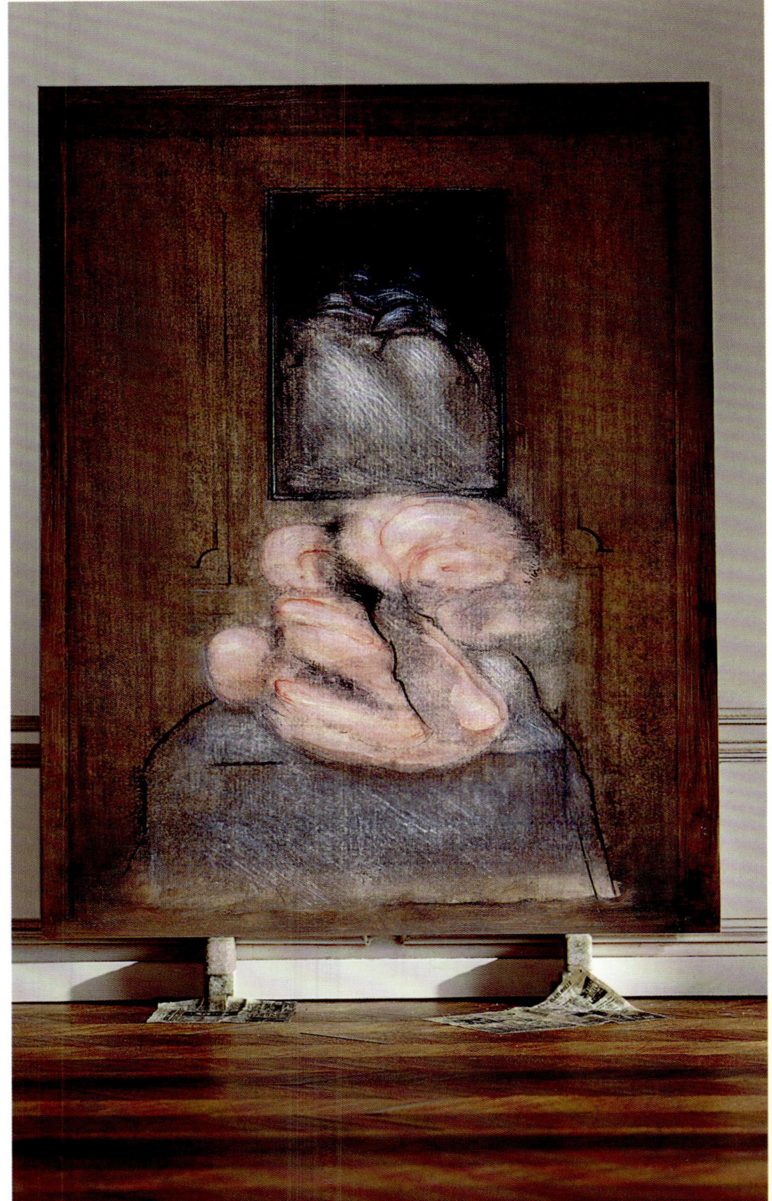

Homage to Francis Bacon I, 1992.
Oil on canvas, 26 ¾ × 35 ½ in. (68 × 90 cm).

Coupling, 1970-1991.
Oil on canvas, 23 ¾ × 30 in. (60.5 × 76.5 cm).

The Painting *Body on a Bed beneath a Painting Representing a Couple in Bed* in a Situation Scenario, 1991.
Oil on Cibachrome, 63 × 45 in.
(160 × 114 cm).

Installation Created around an Original Francis Bacon Illustrating the label of Château Mouton Rothschild 1990, 1995.
22 ½ × 29 ½ × 3 ¼ in. (57.5 × 75 × 8.5 cm).

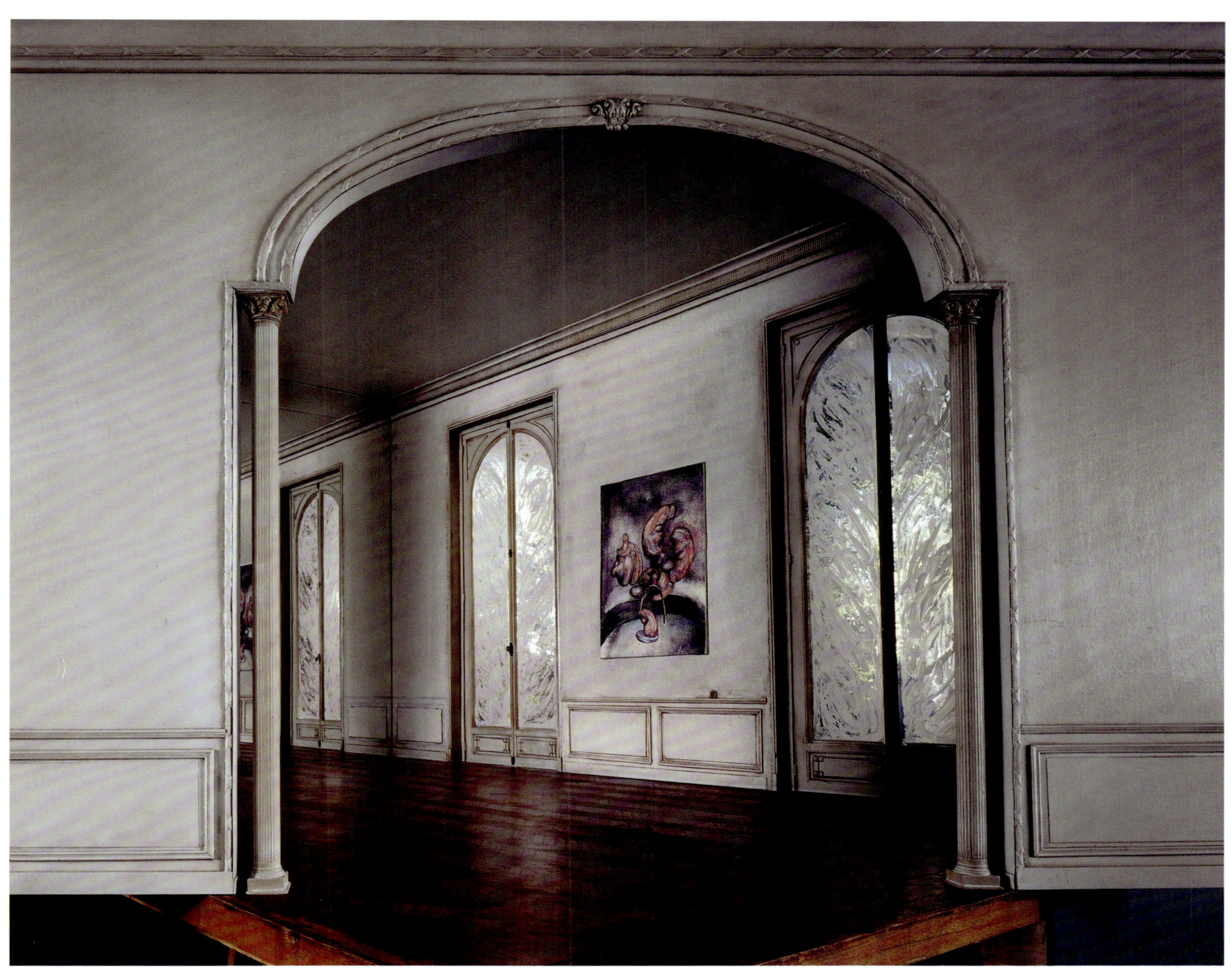

Installation of The Homage to Francis Bacon VI *in The White Drawing-room*, 1991.
Photograph.

I first discovered Bacon in 1966, but even more so in 1972, at his great Paris exhibition at the Grand Palais. Encountering his work was highly significant for me, because it confirmed my belief that one can still today make one's own the liberation of visual vocabulary, which has been in such upheaval since the beginning of the twentieth century, precisely so as to return to figuration. There's a misunderstanding with regard to Bacon. I'm knocking on an open door here, in that he was forever saying how he hated being taken, first for a surrealist, then for an expressionist painter, or told he was betraying the faces he observed, when all he wanted to do was to express the person before him, the model.

When he started out painting, it was at a point in history when it was impossible to do figuration in the sense that Balthus did figuration. He was, thus, forced to invent a new language, to pummel the paint, to torture it. His sole aim was to testify to reality. Bacon's pictures have been seen as images of torture, while in fact it's the brushwork that's tortured. Why? Because he rejects description. He feels impelled to come to grips with matter until he gets the face to emerge. Bacon doesn't disfigure; he refigures.

C. Matton, in "Ça me dit, l'après-midi," op. cit.

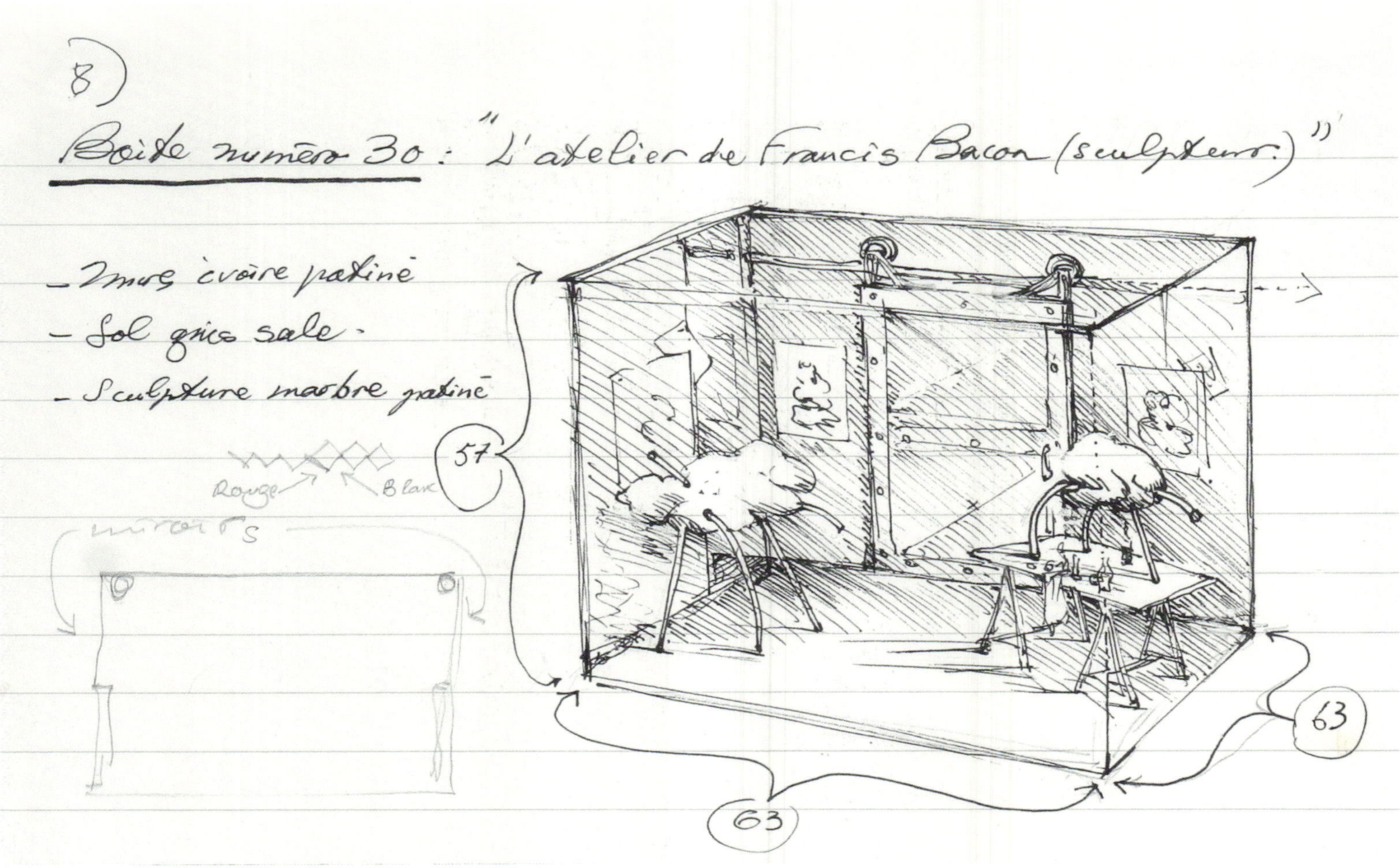

8)

Boite numéro 30 : "L'atelier de Francis Bacon (sculpteur.)"

- Murs ivoire patiné
- Sol gris sale.
- Sculpture marbre patiné

Rouge

Blanc

miroirs

57

63

63

Francis Bacon's Studio (sculptor), 1990.
Pencil on paper, 5 ½ × 8 ¼ in. (14 × 21 cm).

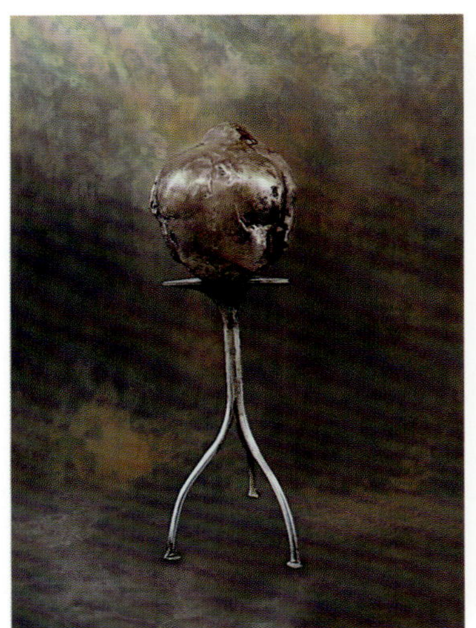

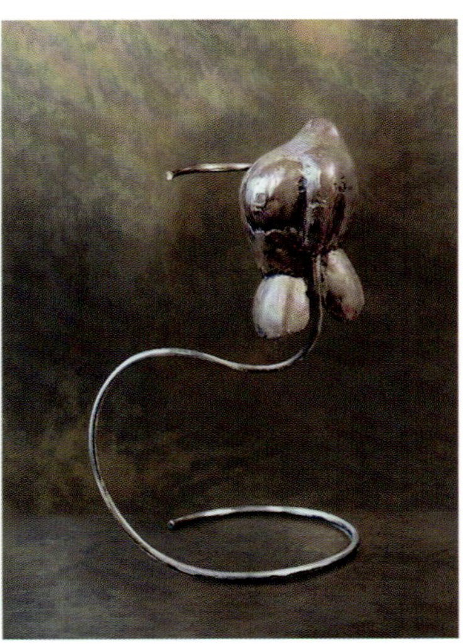

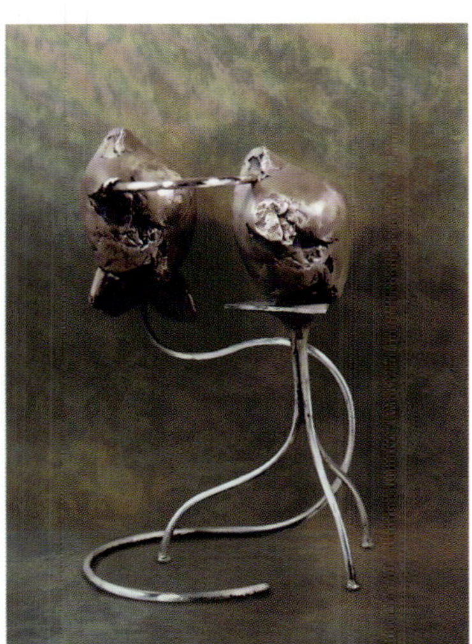

"Bacon-ian" Sculptures I, II, and I and II, 1990.
Resin and metal, silver electroplating,
9 ¾ in. (25 cm) and 10 ½ in. (27 cm) h.

I produced my first *Studio of a Contemporary Sculptor* after reading the book of conversations between Francis Bacon and David Sylvester (1), a hugely important book if one wants to understand Bacon anc, still more so, art. Bacon describes sculptures he never made, he never sculpted, he knew he'd never do. He describes exactly the sculptures I felt the desire to make.

Personal note, September 14, 1993

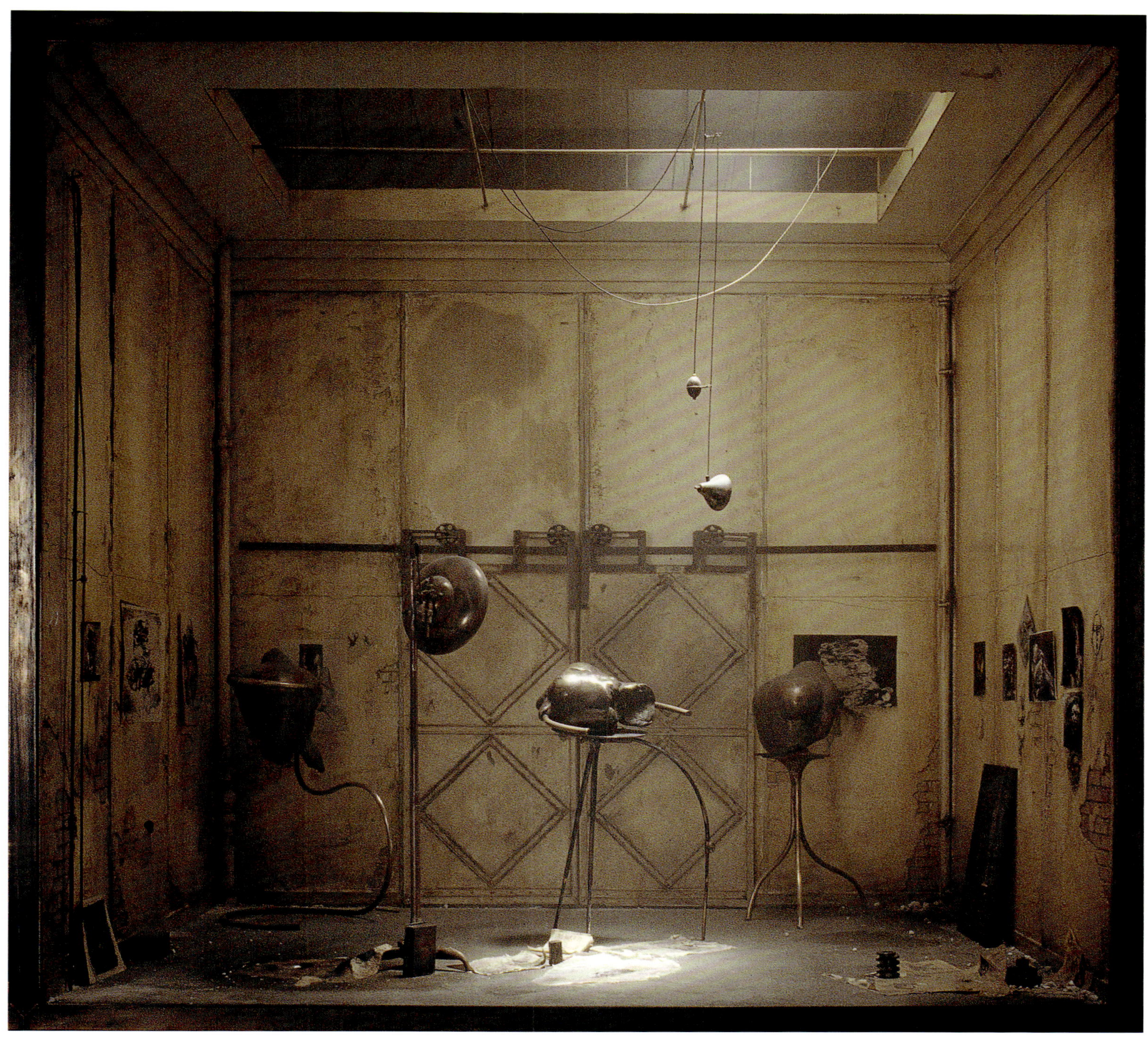

Studio of a Contemporary Sculptor, 1990.
Mixed media, 23 ¼ × 24 ¾ × 24 ½ in. (59 × 63 × 62 cm).

Francis Bacon: "In thinking about them as sculptures, it suddenly came to me how I could make them in paint, and do them much better in paint. It would be a kind of structured painting in which images, as it were, would arise from a river of flesh. [...] I've thought about sculptures on a kind of armature, a very large armature made so that the sculpture could slide along it and people could even alter the positions of the sculpture as they wanted."

David Sylvester, *Interviews with Francis Bacon: The Brutality of Fact* (London: Thames & Hudson, 1993 [1975], p. 83

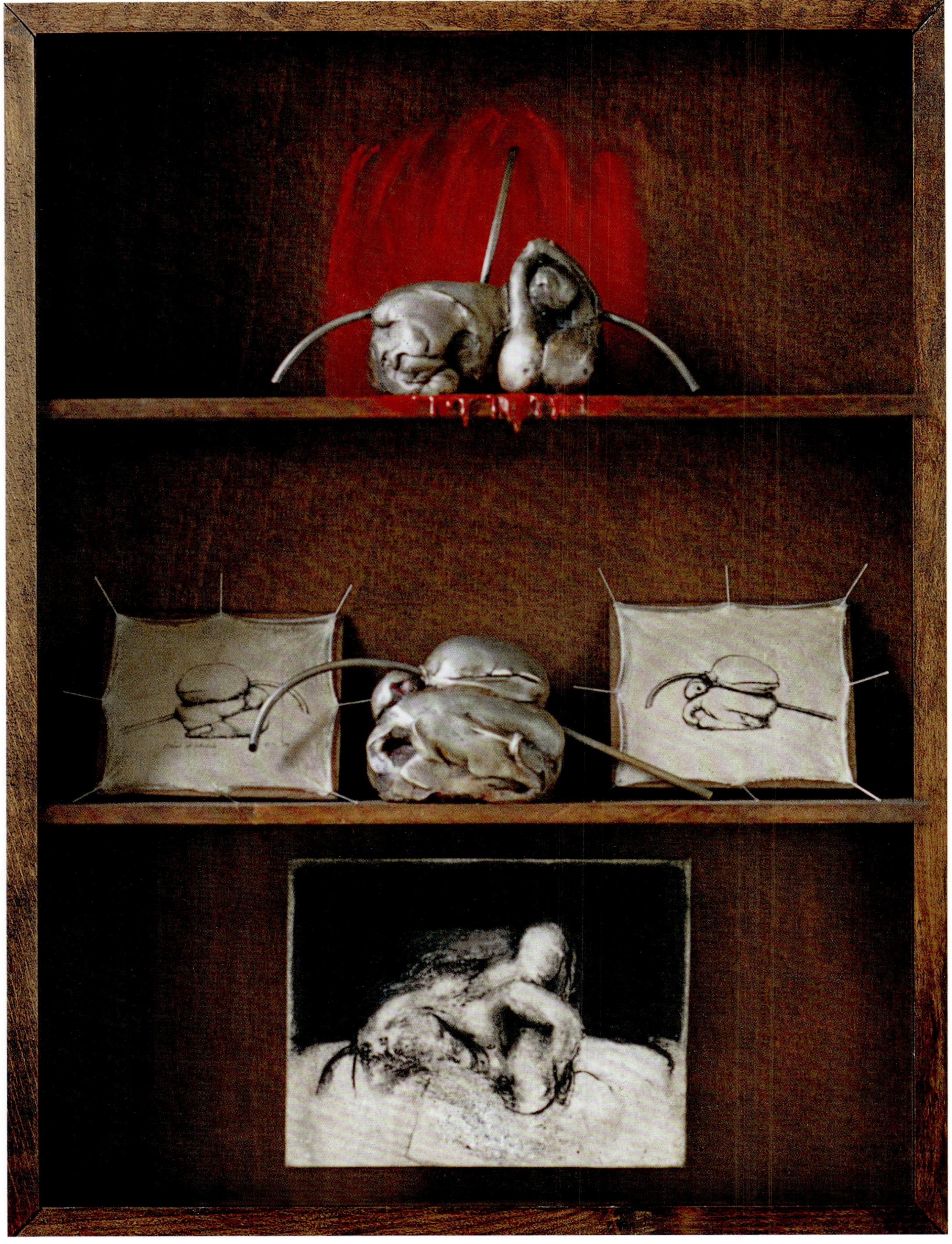

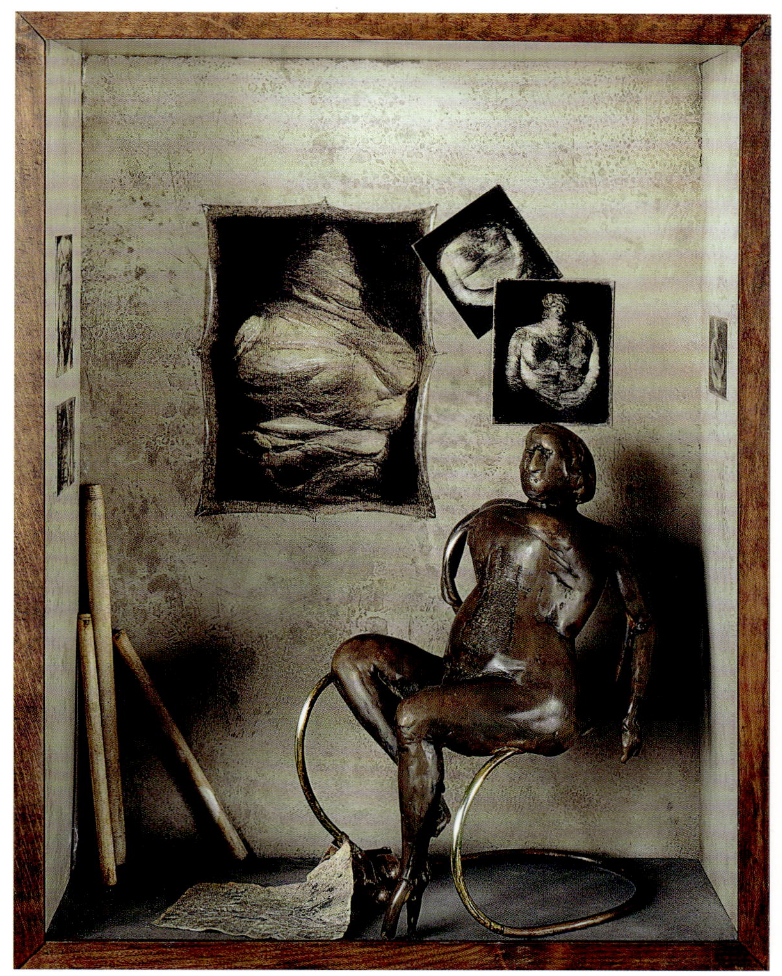

Flesh and Chromium Comprising a Narrative Zone at the Height of the Girdle, 1987.
Silver-plated synthetic polyester resin and brass, papers, transfer gel, cardboard, oil, and wood, 22 ¾ × 17 × 5 ¾ in. (58 × 43.5 × 14.5 cm).

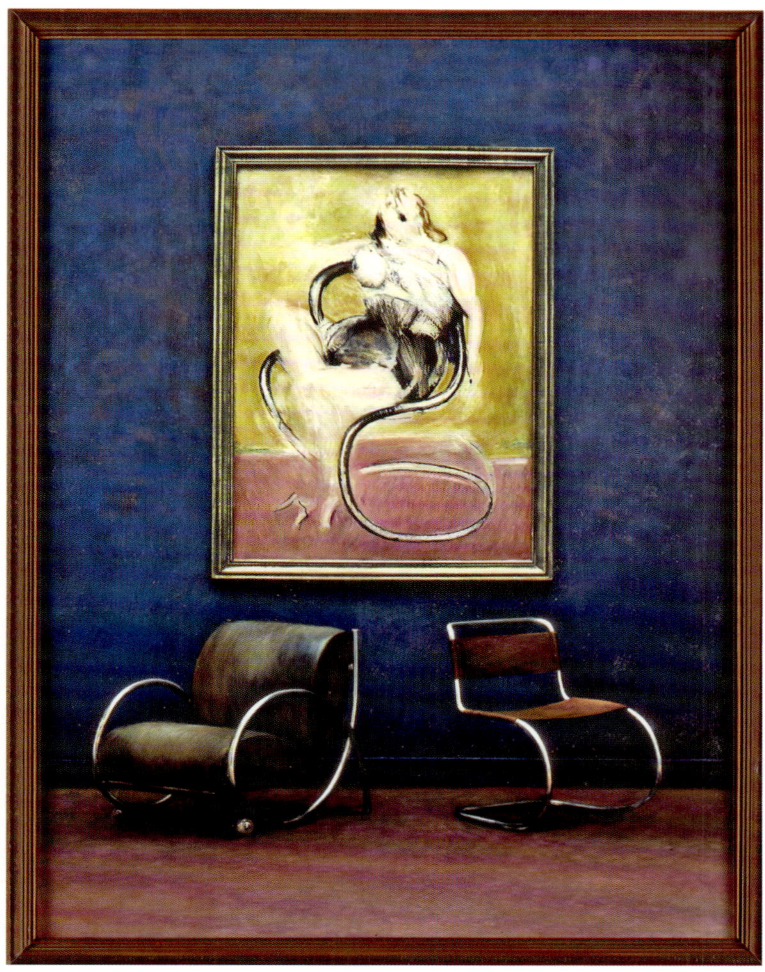

Attempted Reconciliation between a Story concerning Two Tubular Steel Chairs and the Gestural Equivalence of a Fat Woman in a Girdle, 1987.
Oil on Cibachrome, 75 ½ × 46 ½ in. (192 × 118 cm).

Facing page:
Reflections on Bacon-ian Sculptures, 1990.
Silver-plated torolith and brass, black chalk, and pastel on pasteboard, transfer gel, and pins on cardboard, wax, and wood, 17 × 12 ½ in. (43.5 × 32 cm).

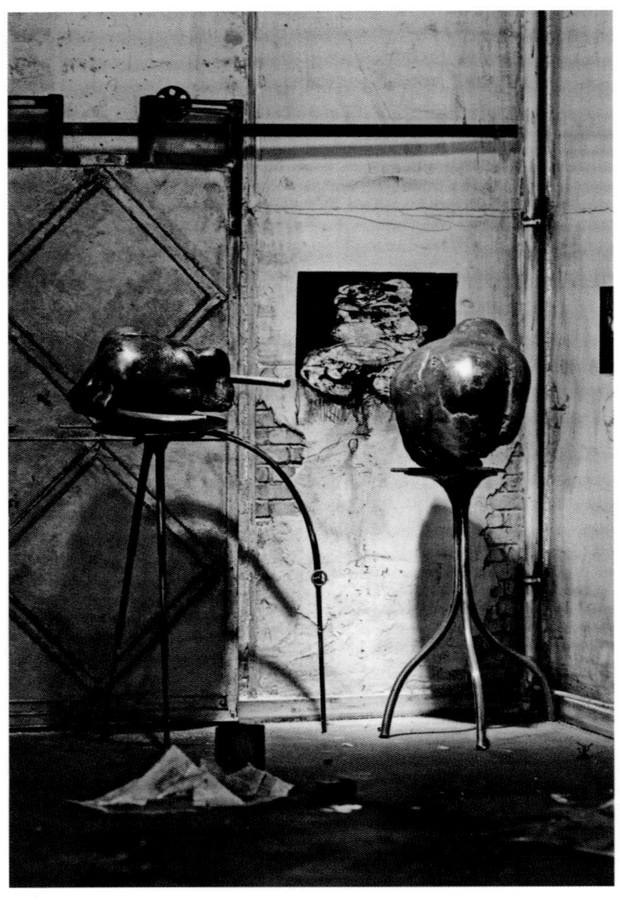

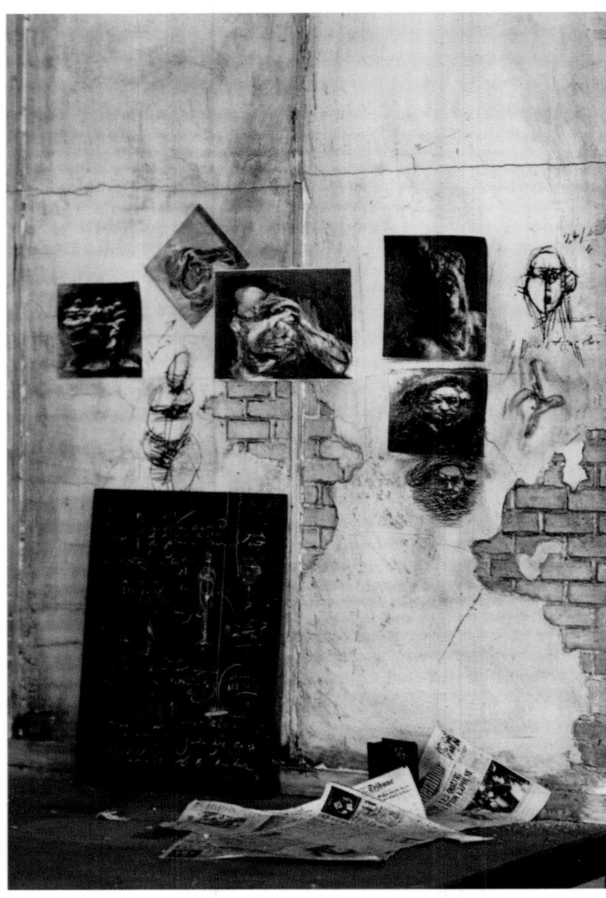

Studio of a Contemporary Sculptor (detail 1, sculptures and marks on the wall), 1990. Photograph.

Studio of a Contemporary Sculptor (detail 2, marks on the wall), 1990. Photograph.

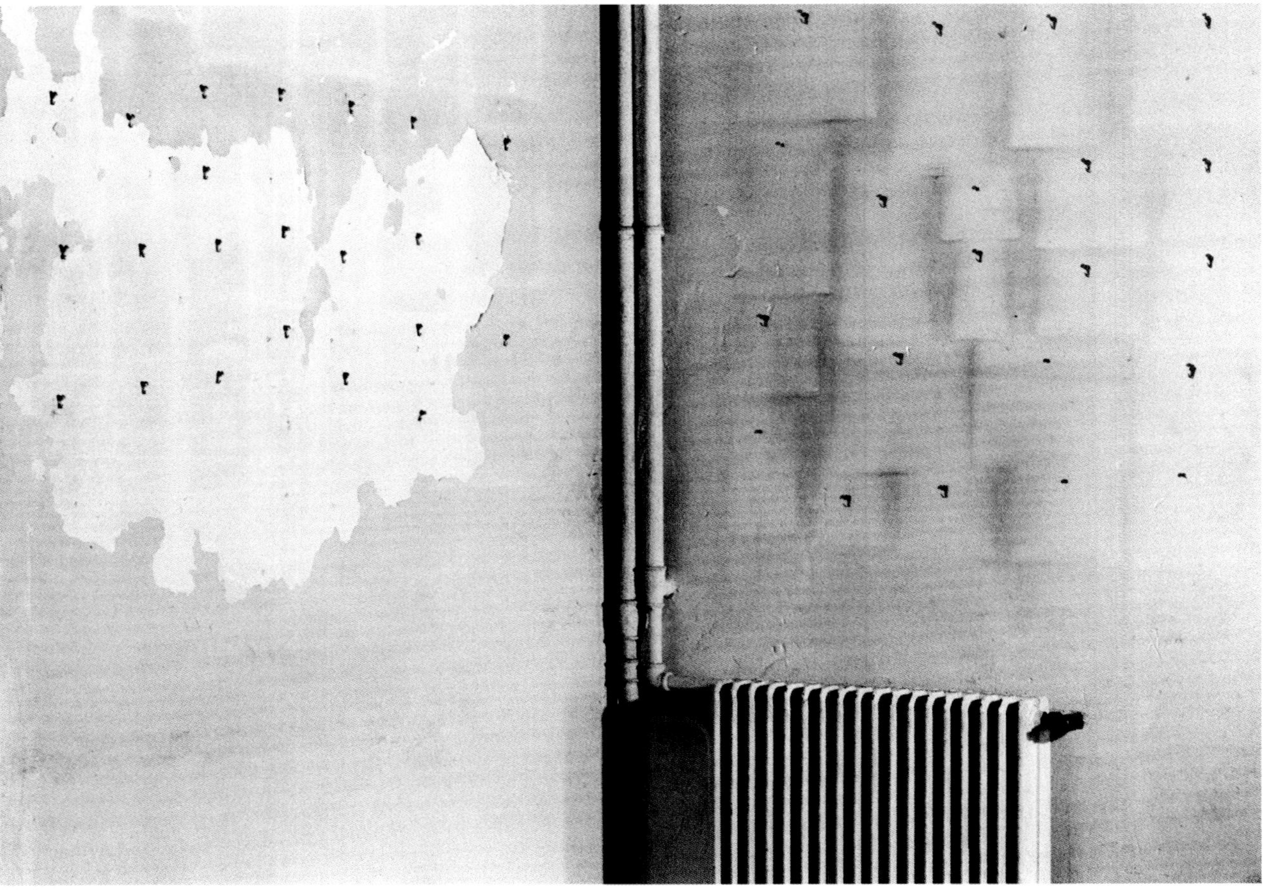

Marks on the Wall, Moving out, Le Coudray-Montceaux II, 1988. Photograph.

Marks on the Wall and Picture Hangers, 1988.
Photograph.

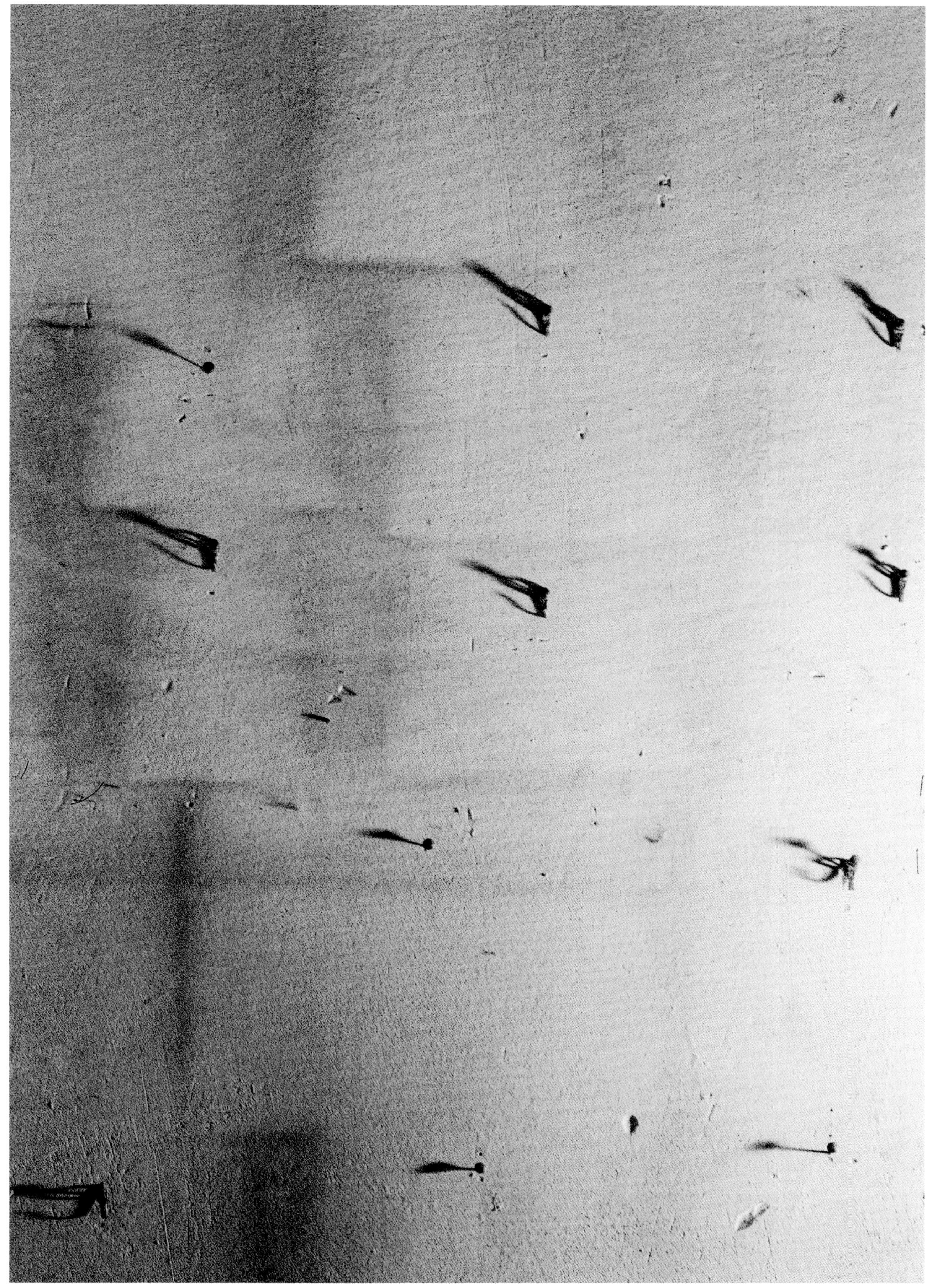

Sometimes I wonder whether, rather than being a painter, somebody who quite simply does painting, I'm using it to analyze it. To psychoanalyze art, to go back in time so as to uncover the origin of each style, their raisons d'être, and to philosophize about my discoveries, to arrange them into hierarchies.

Personal note, October 9, 2006

"Magic" boxes and metaphysical boxes. I'd like people to enter my boxes as they go round an exhibition.

Personal note, December 6, 2004

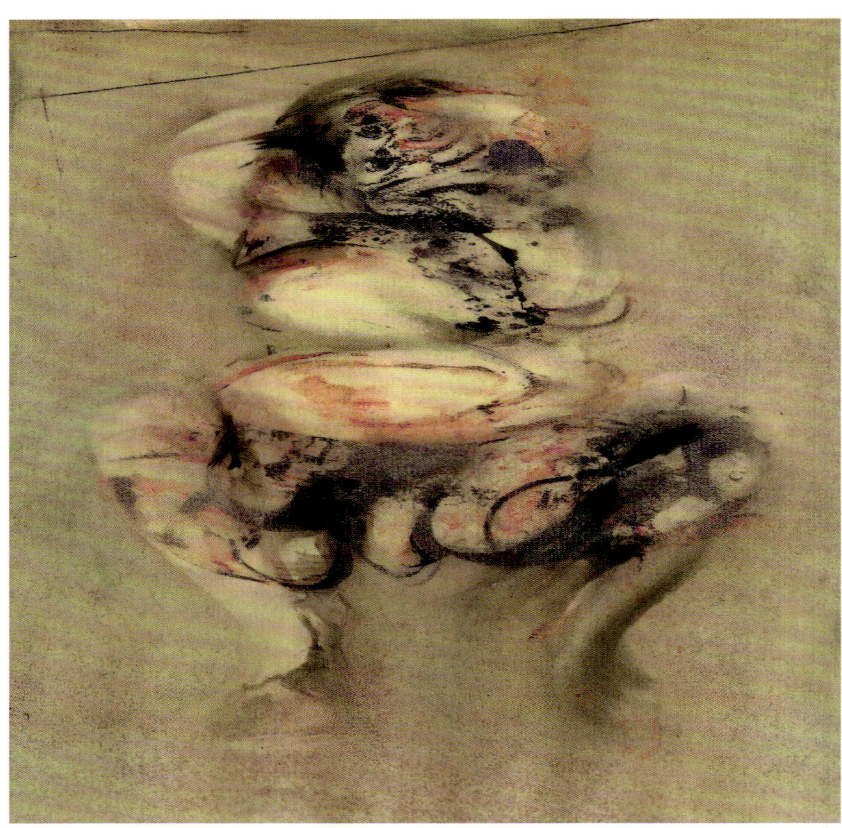

The Great Expansive II, 2003.
Pencil and watercolor on paper,
6 ¼ × 6 ¼ in. (16 × 16 cm).

Facing page:
Studio of a Contemporary Sculptor III, 2004.
Mixed media,
28 × 39 ½ × 38 ¾ in.
(71.5 × 100.5 × 98.5 cm).

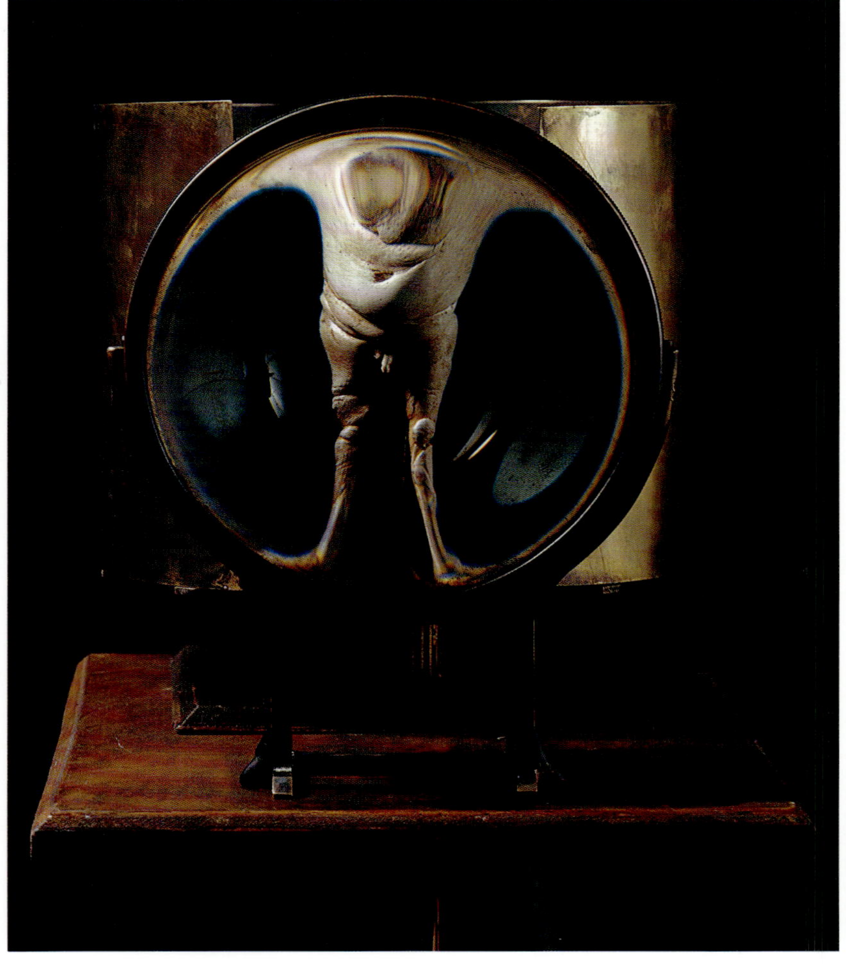

A Gestural Little Fatty behind the magnifying-glass in *The Little Fatties' Merry-go-round*, 1992.
Torolith and marble, brass, magnifying-glass, and wood,
6 ¼ × 6 × 9 ¾ in. (16 × 15.5 × 25 cm).

I've always shuttled back and forth between a descriptive representation of things and a gestural representation. I tend to call "gestural work" a form, drawn, painted, or sculpted, which expresses itself through its color, its material, and the spirit of its form, through its own means, as it were.

C. Matton, in *Charles Matton, visiblement*, op. cit.

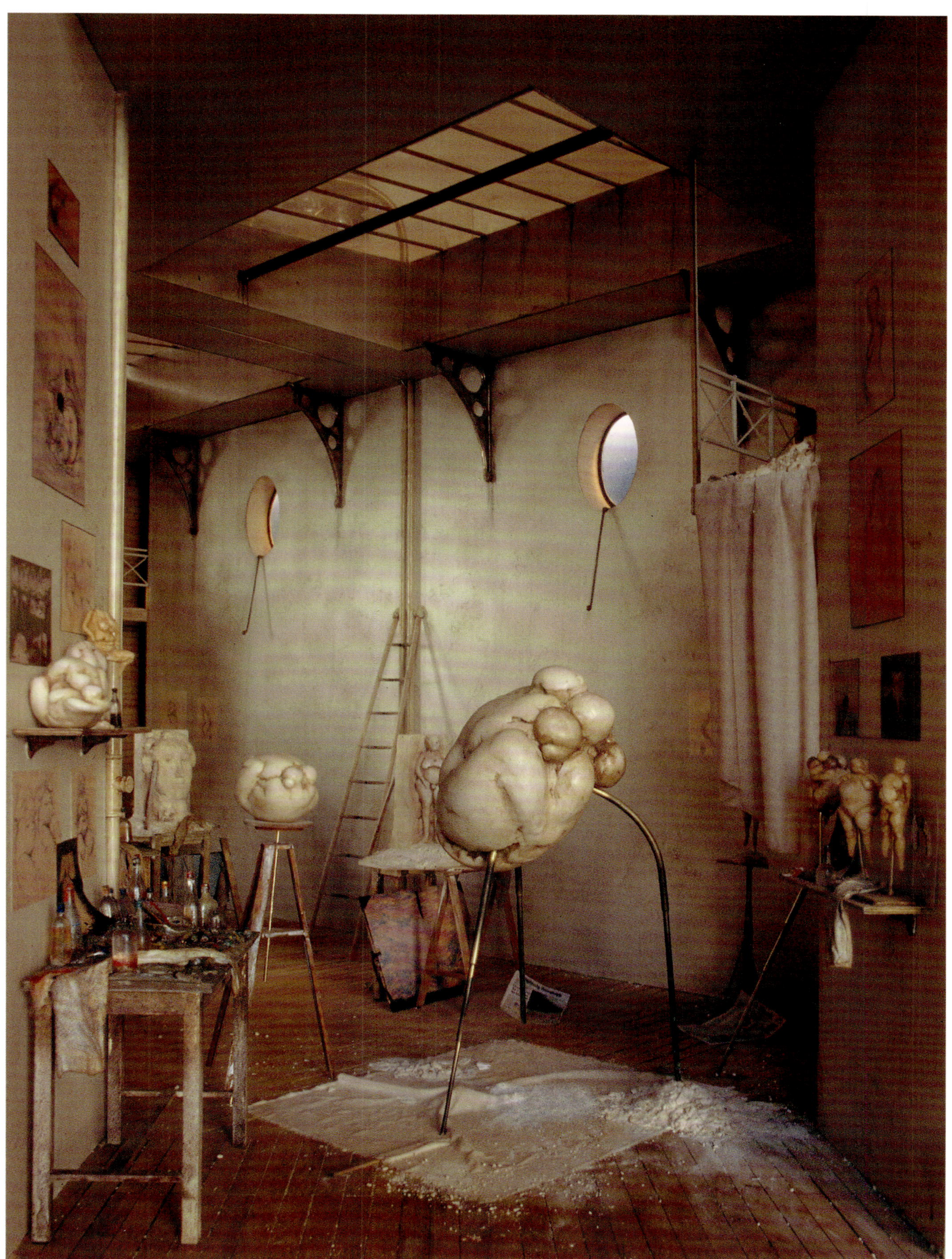

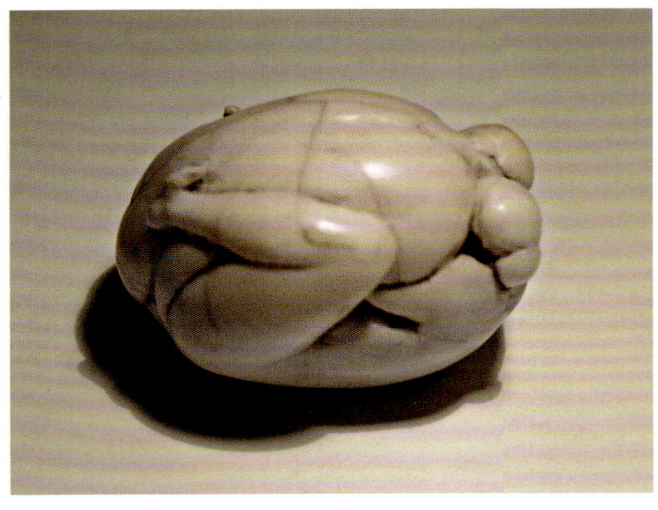

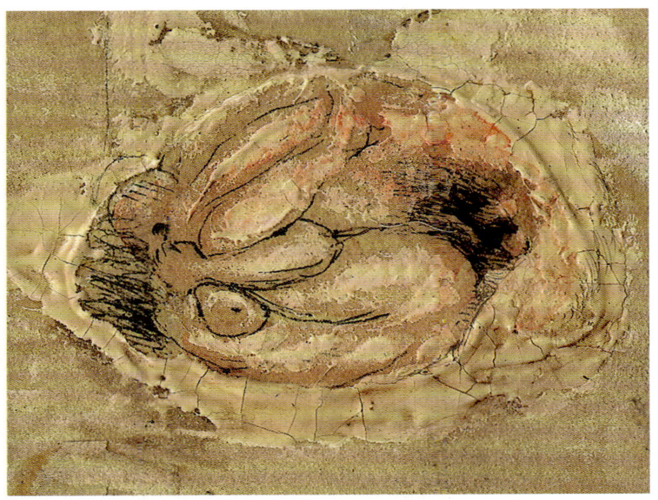

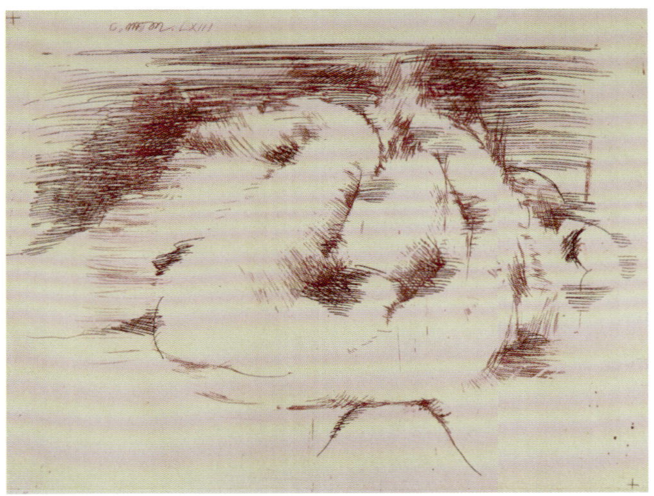

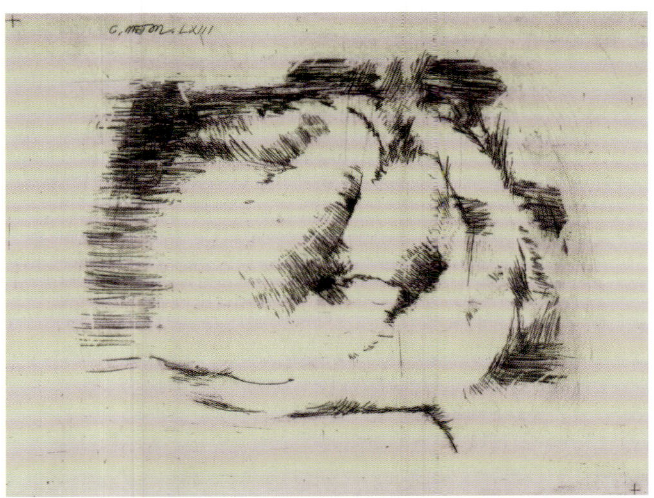

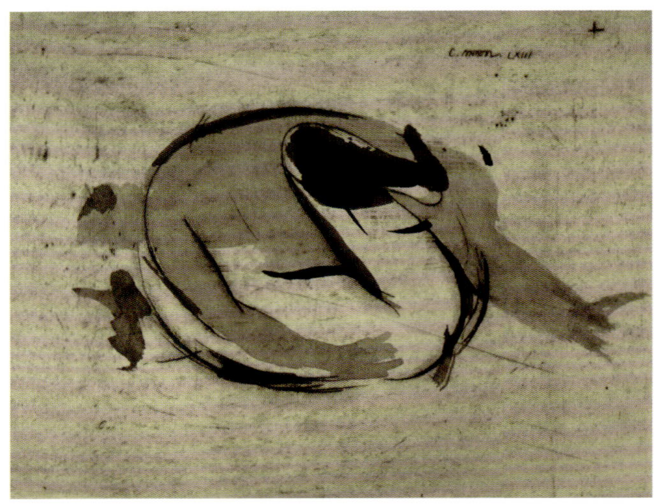

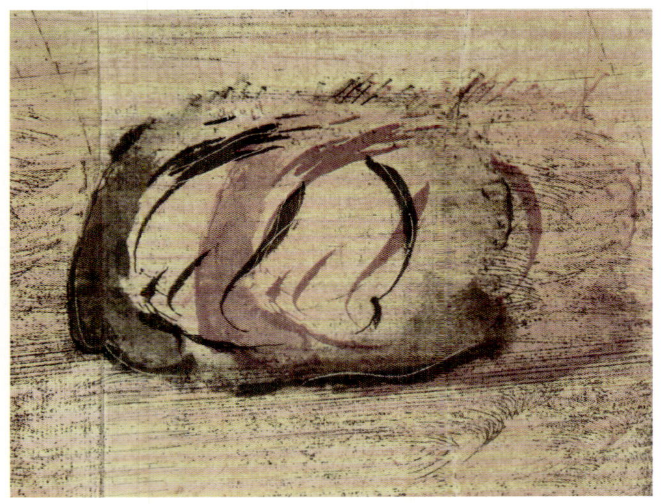

Coupling, 2003.
Torolith and marble, 2 × 2 ¾ × 2 ¼ in. (5.3 × 6.8 × 5.8 cm).

Coupling, 1953.
Etching in sanguine, 7 × 9 ¼ in. (18 × 23.7 cm).

Coupling, 1953.
Ink and wash on paper, 4 × 8 in. (10.5 × 20.5 cm).

Coupling, 1970–90.
Pencil and gouache on pasteboard, 4 ¼ × 5 ¾ in. (11 × 14.5 cm).

Coupling, 1953.
Etching, 7 × 9 ¼ in. (18 × 23.7 cm).

Coupling, 1953.
Ink and wash on paper, 7 × 9 ½ in. (18 × 23.5 cm).

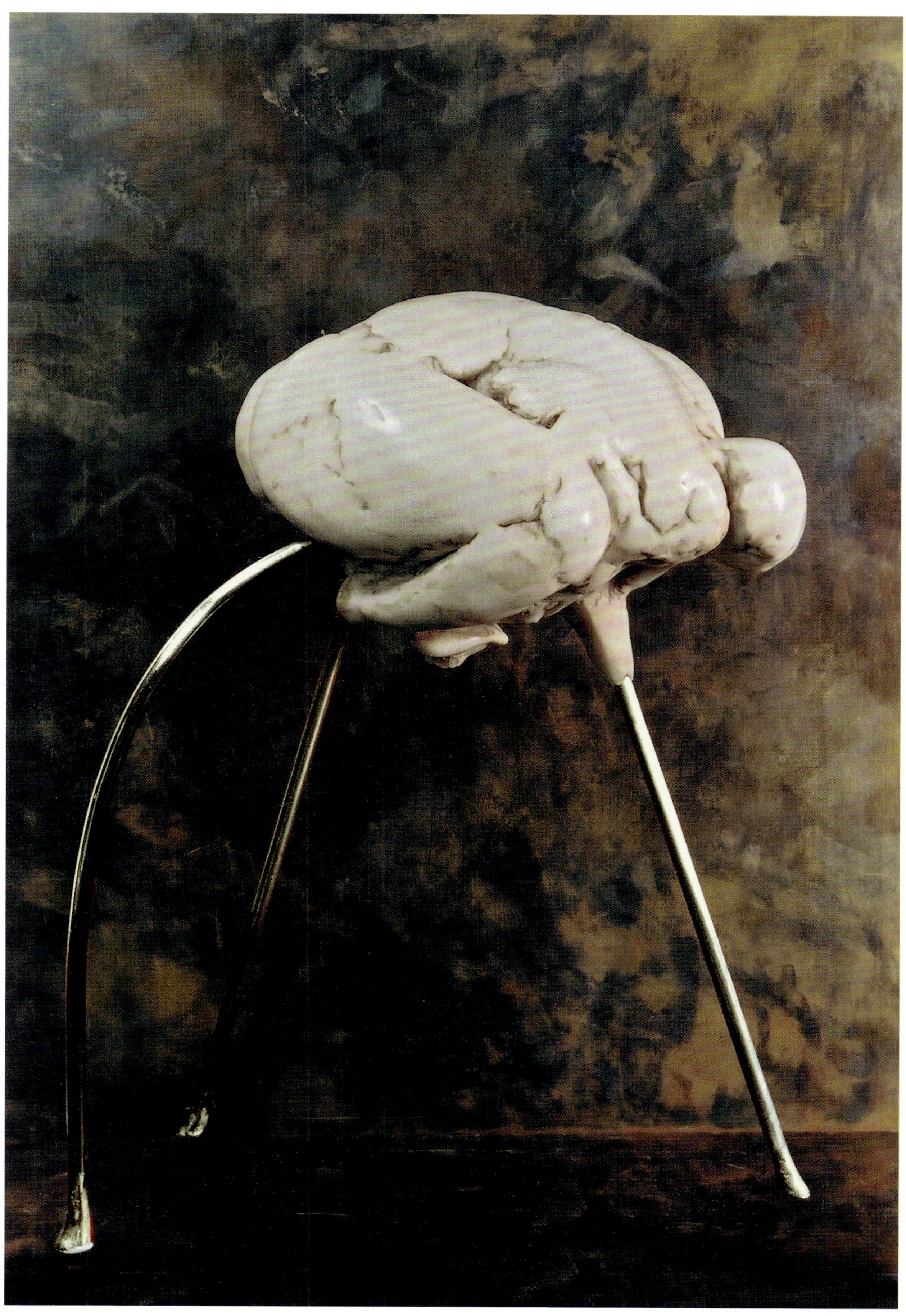

The Boxers, 2003.
Torolith, marble, and metal,
10 ½ × 6 × 4 in.
(27 × 15 × 10.5 cm).

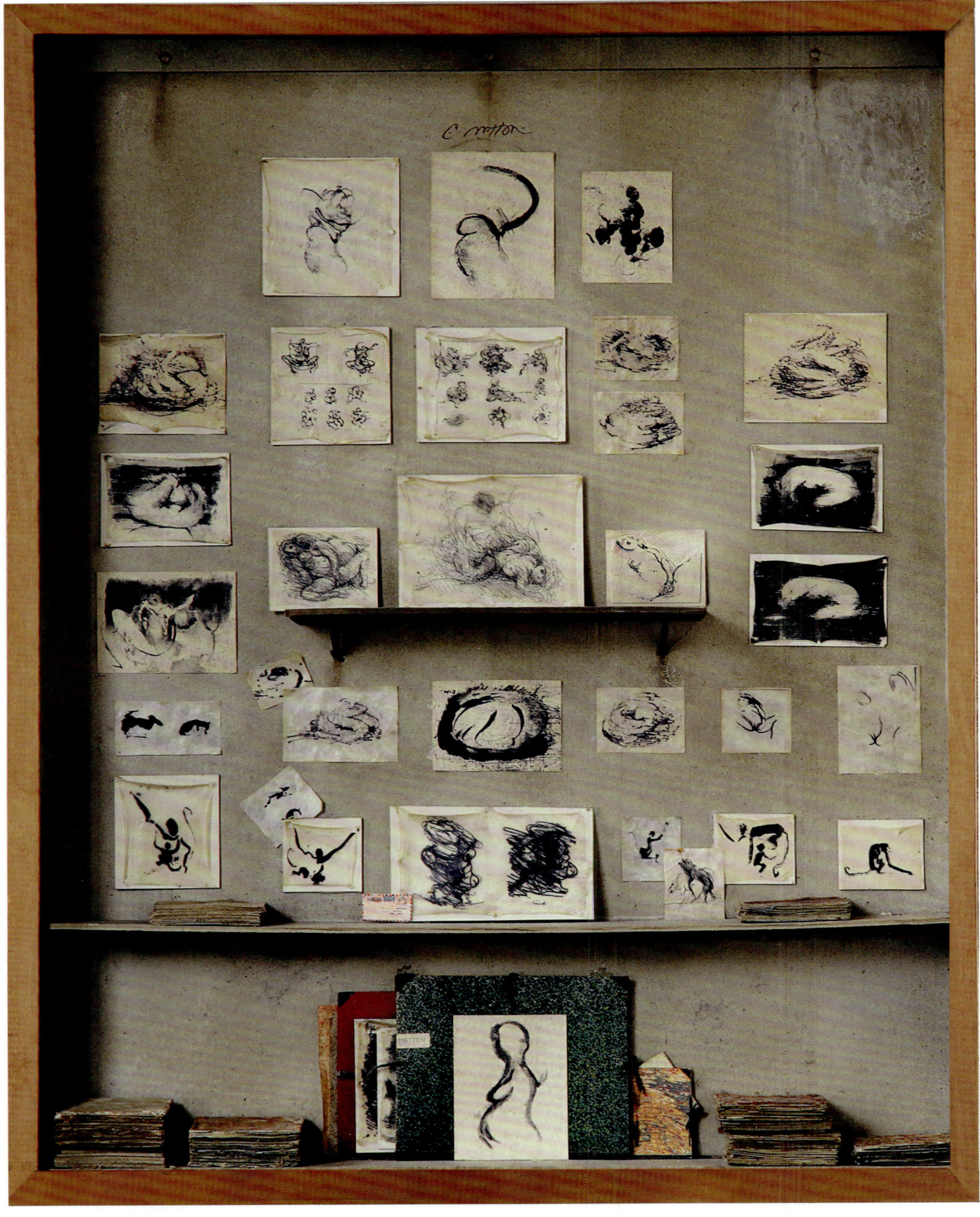

Wall by a Gestural Draftsman, 1999. Wood, pencil, and wash on paper, transfer gel on cardboard, torolith, and oil paint, 22 ¾ × 18 × 2 ¼ in. (58 × 45.5 × 6 cm).

For some time now, I've been striving to convey those comings and goings that lie at the core of my explorations in art, between a descriptive enterprise and one that offers, I think, a more intuitive way of capturing appearances.

Personal note, May 4, 1997

Wall by a Classical Draftsman, 2000.
Wood, pencil, and wash on paper, transfer gel on cardboard, torolith, marble, and oil, 25 × 19 ¾ × 2 ½ in. (66 × 50 × 6.5 cm).

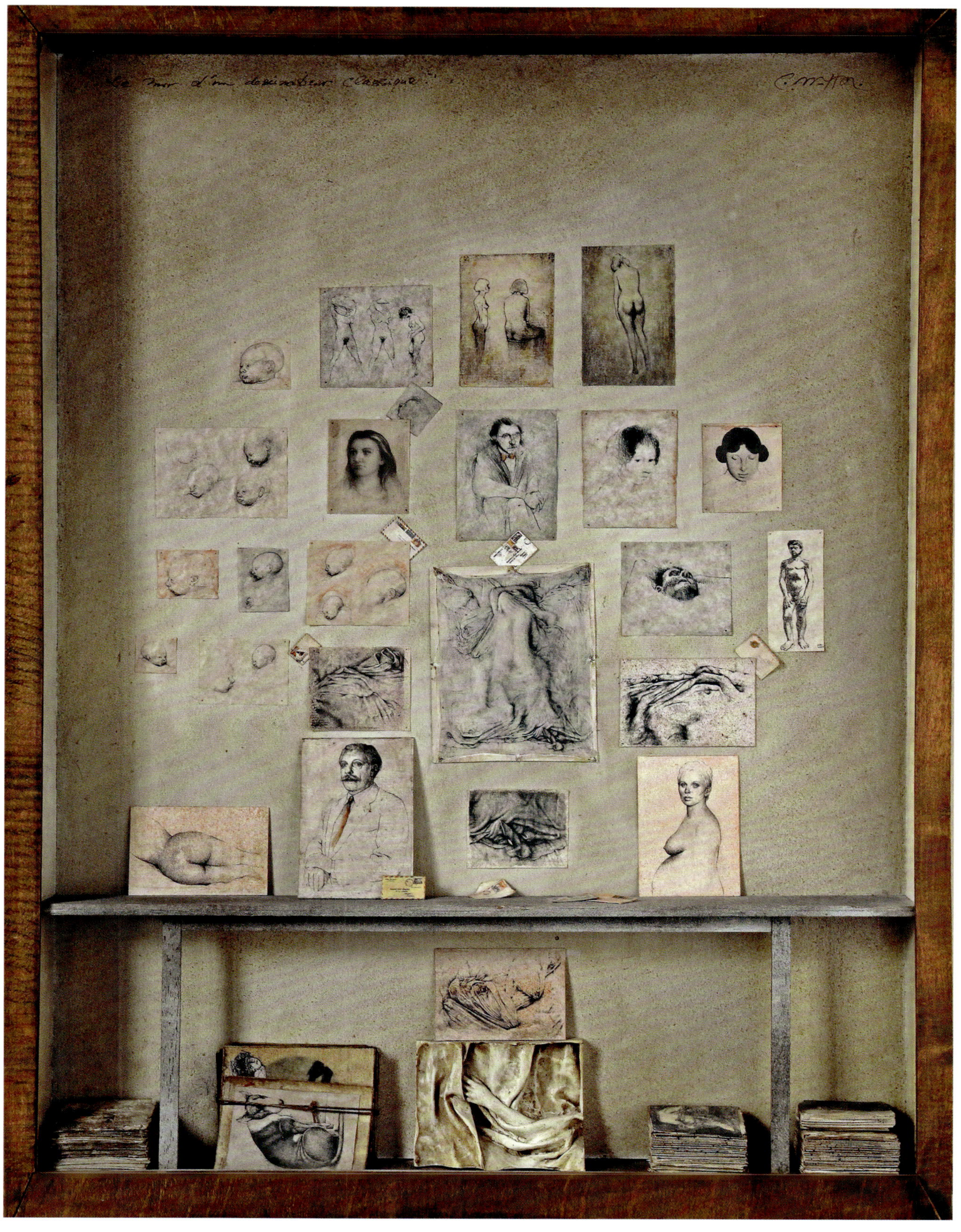

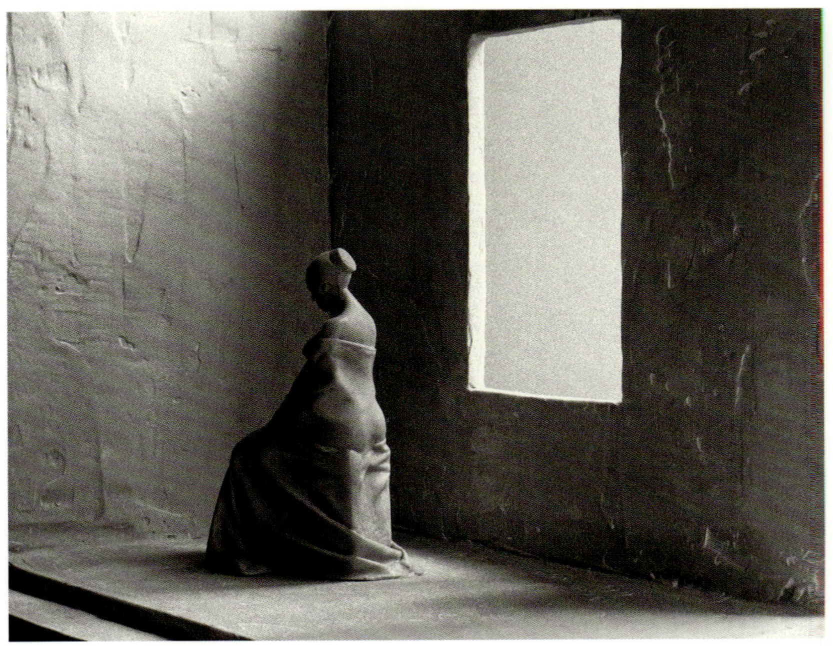

Saskia Pregnant with Titus in the Corner by a Wall, installation no. III, 1999.
Torolith and marble,
19 × 21 × 14 ¼ in.
(48.5 × 53.5 × 36 cm).

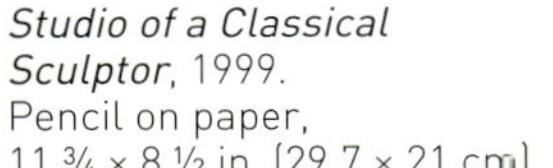

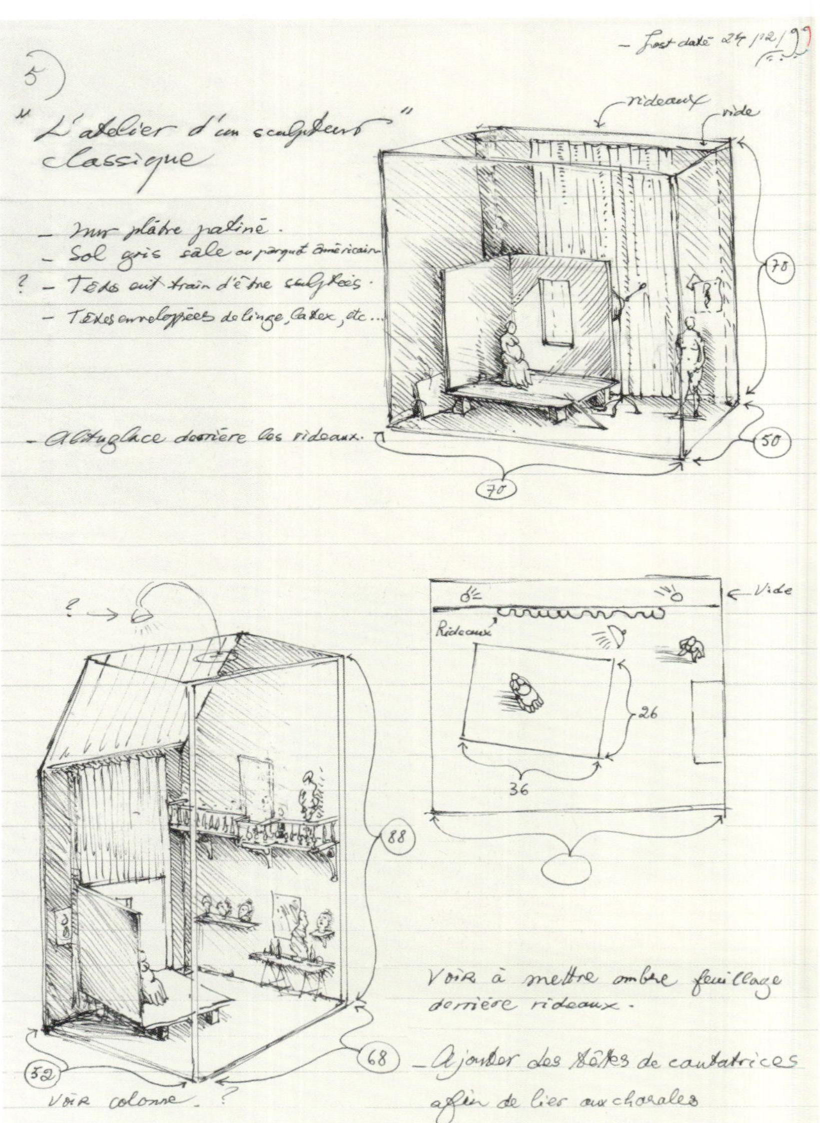

Studio of a Classical Sculptor, 1999.
Pencil on paper,
11 ¾ × 8 ½ in. (29.7 × 21 cm).

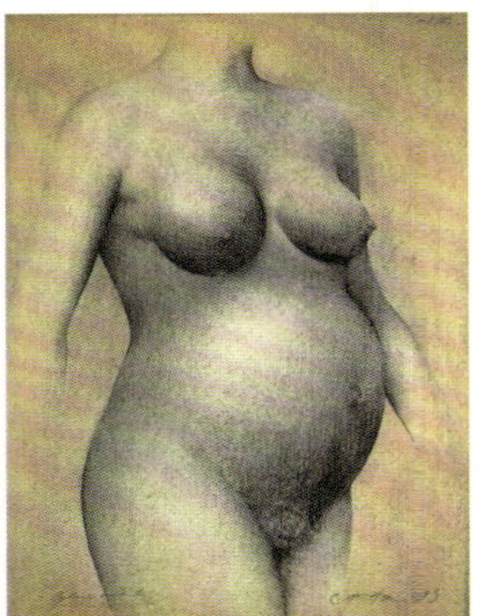

Sylvie Pregnant, 1983.
Lead pencil and ink on pasteboard, 16 ½ × 11 ¾ in.
(42 × 29.7 cm).

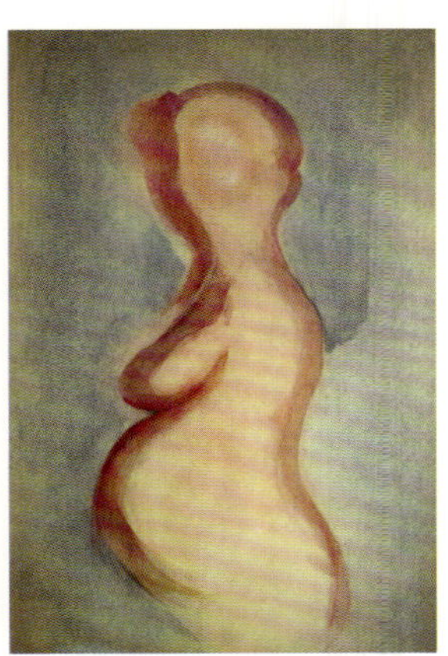

Sylvie Pregnant, 1983.
Watercolor and wash on paper, 16 ½ × 11 ¾ in.
(42 × 29.7 cm).

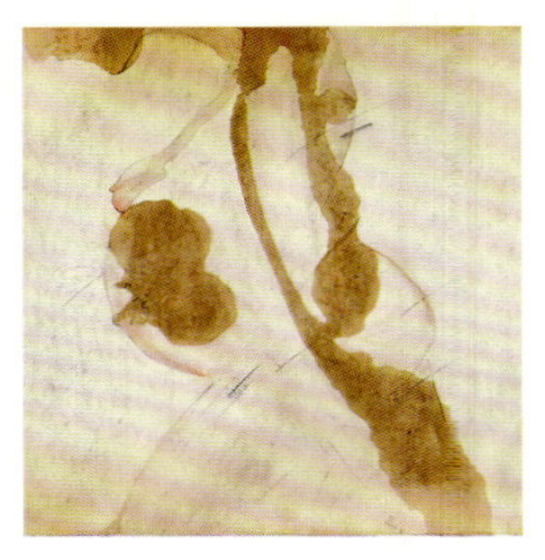

Pregnancy. Exploitation of a Coffee Stain on a Piece of Glossy Bristol Card, 1985.
6 × 5 ½ in. (15 × 14 cm).

Facing page:
Studio of a Classical Sculptor V (*Saskia Pregnant with Titus* II), 2003.
Mixed media, 32 ¼ × 27 ½ × 32 ¼ in.
(82 × 70 × 82 cm).

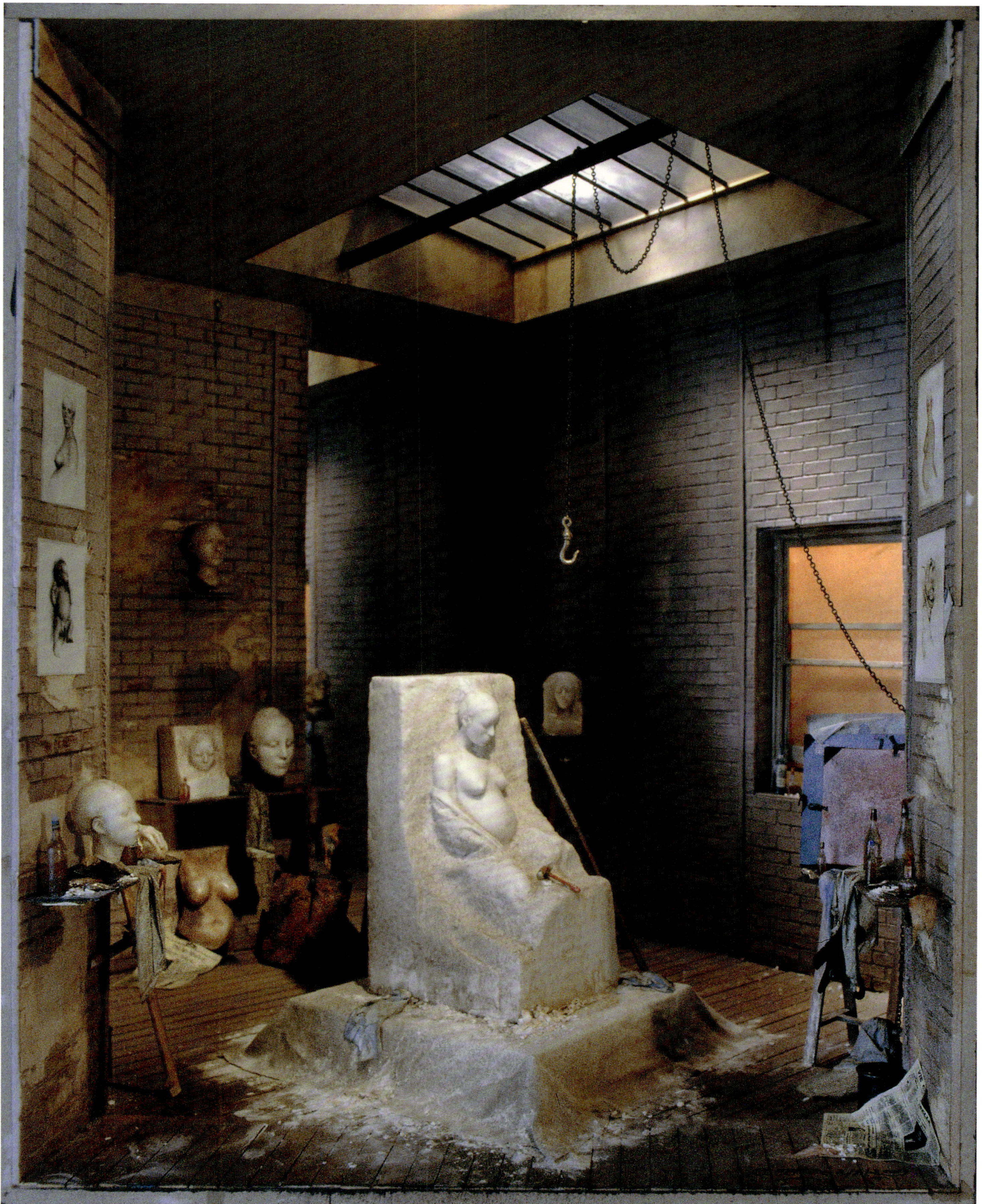

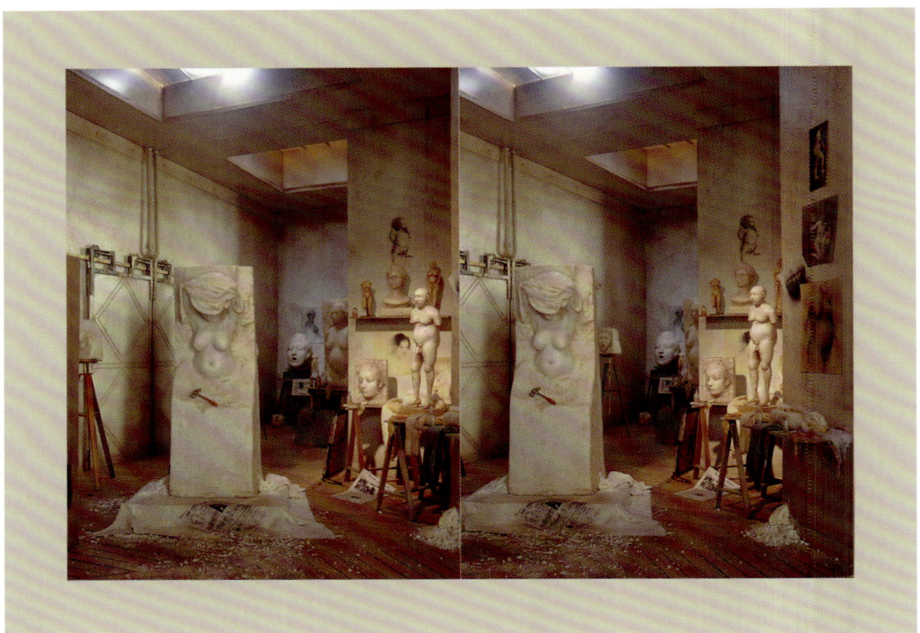

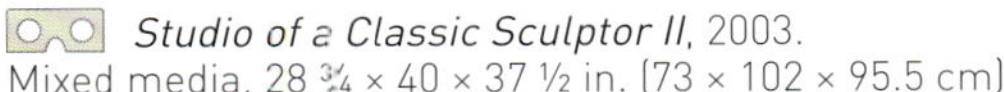 *Studio of a Classic Sculptor II*, 2003.
Mixed media, 28 ¾ × 40 × 37 ½ in. (73 × 102 × 95.5 cm).

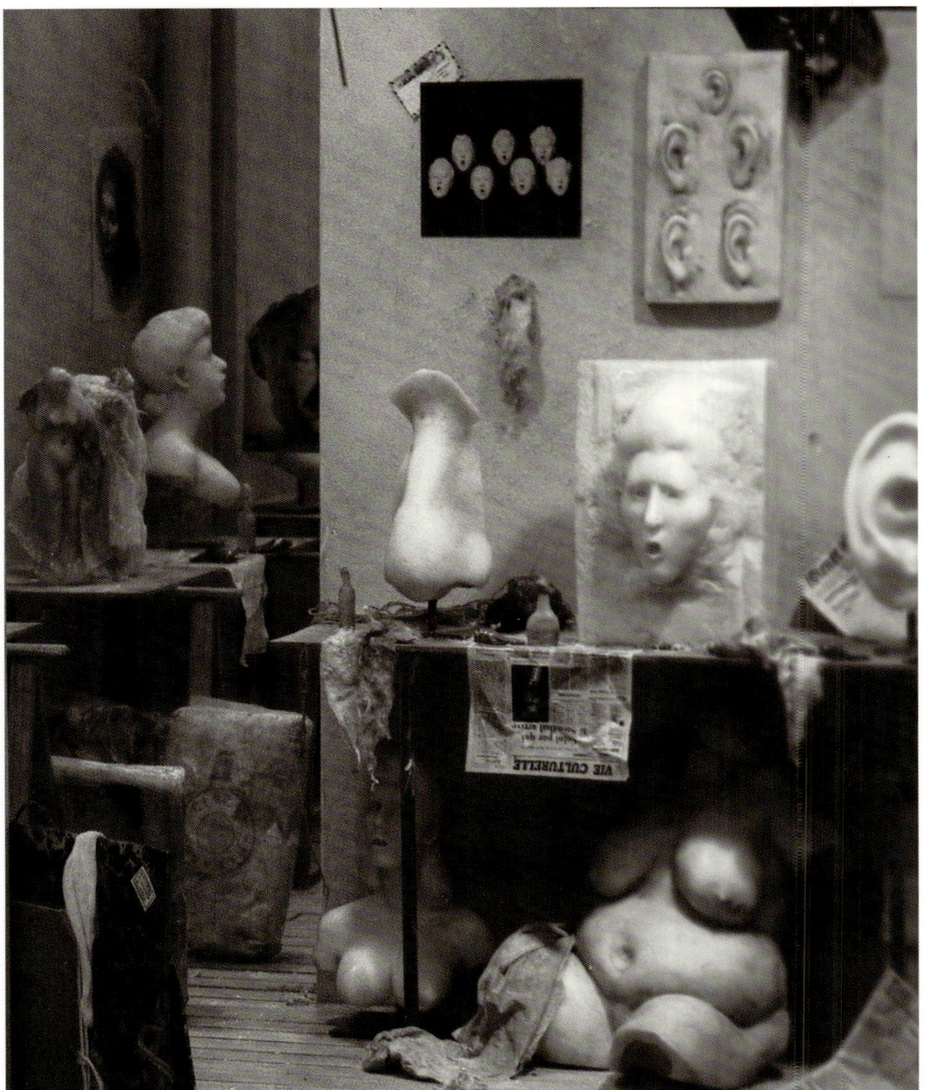

Sculptor's Storage I (detail), 2003.
Photograph, 28 ¾ × 40 × 37 ½ in. (73 × 102 × 95.5 cm).

Facing page:
Personal note, *Sculptor's Storage*, January 17, 2001.

The Sculptor's Storage (bric-a-brac)

- List of various elements liable to enter the box: Louise, Radiah standing, Radiah: head, Tooky: head, Tooky: legs, Radiah and Tooky retouched as white women, large head of the Infanta, small head of the Infanta, the head of the dwarf, the small "large Lulu" wrapped, the "large Lulu" reclining (detail), the Infanta's dog, some noses from the 36 female singers, some of the "intercourses," "Sue" (detail), head of cereal packet man, head of a black man, details of the man and the woman tied up, Courbet's model, bedlinen details, cushions from the Turkish bath by Charles Marie Hilpert, known as Cody, details of the Rhinoceros (the large one), detail of the small Rhinoceros, 2 or 3 noses.

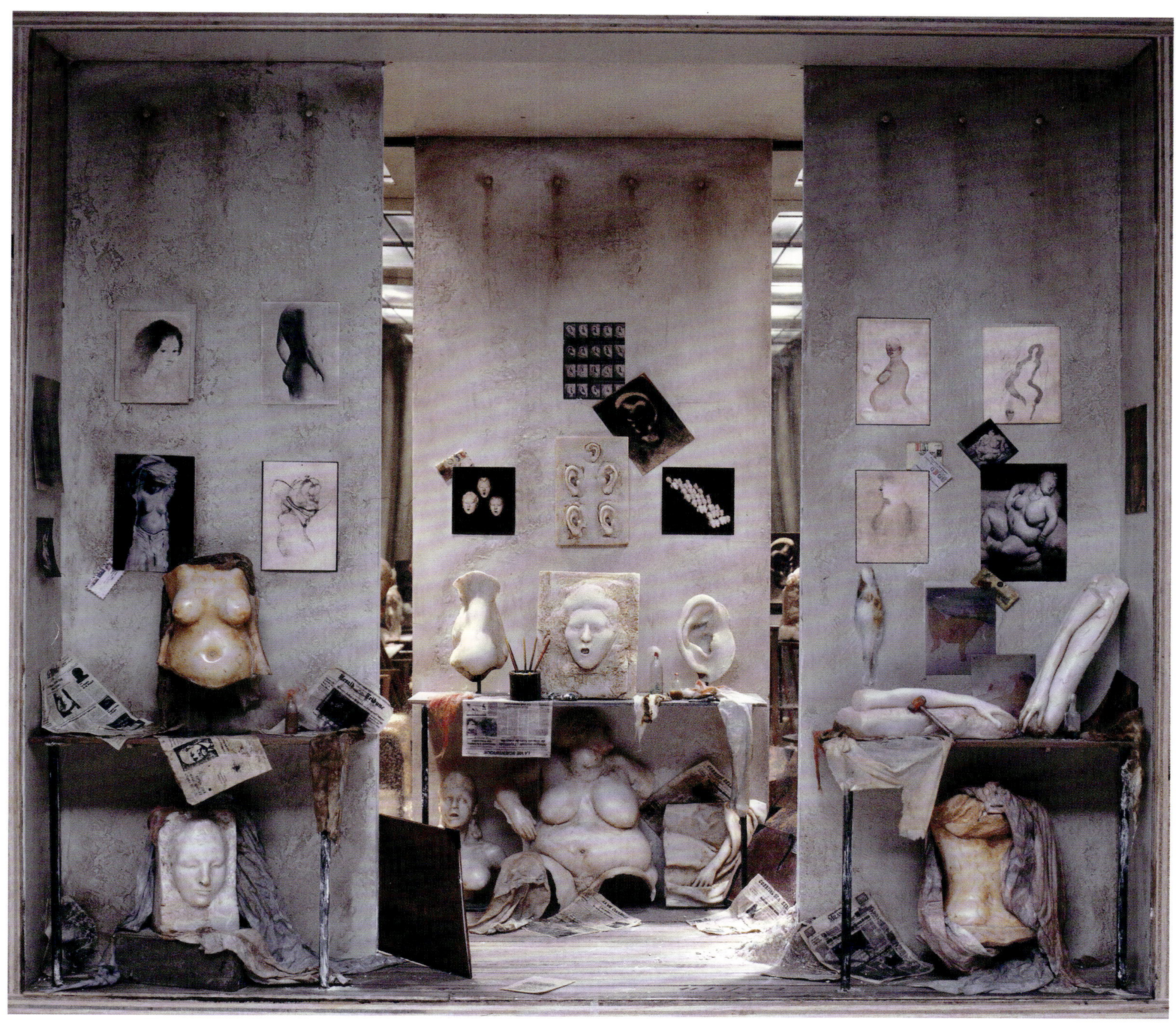

"La remise d'un sculpteur (bric-à-brac)

— Liste des différents éléments susceptibles d'entrer dans la boîte :
Louise, Radiah debout, Radiah : la tête, Tooky : la tête, Tooky : les jambes,
Radiah et Tooky retouchées en femmes blanches, grosse tête d'Infante,
petites tête d'Infante, la tête de la Naine, la petit "grande Lulu" enveloppée,
la "grande Lulu" (couchée) (détail), le chien de l'Infante, quelques unes des 36
cantatrices, quelques unes de "coites", "Sue" (détail), tête
d'homme du paquet de céréales, tête d'homme NOIR, détails de l'homme
et de la femme ficelés, "le modèle de Courbet, détails literie,
les coussins du bain Turc de Charles Marie Hilpert, dit Cody.
détails du Rhynocéros (le grand), détail du petit Rhinocéros, 2 ou 3 nez.

Sculptor's Storage II, 2002.
Mixed media,
29 × 22 ¾ × 28 ¼ in.
(73.5 × 58 × 72 cm).

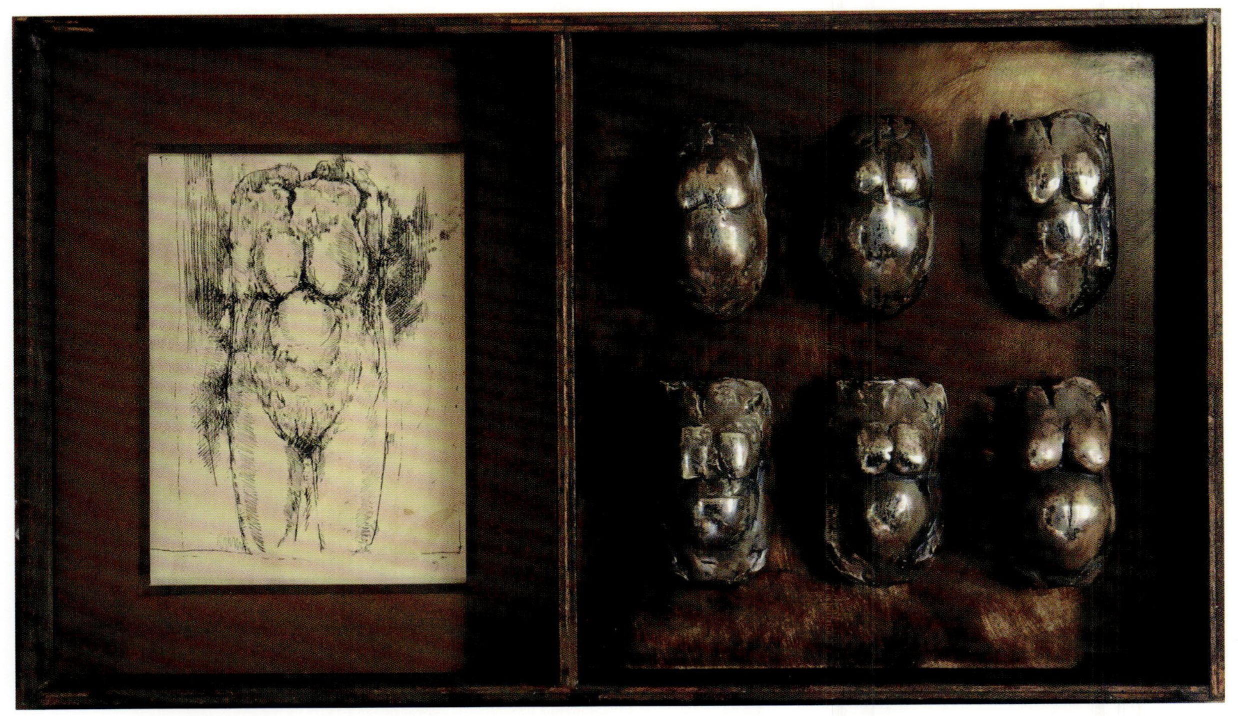

Sequence of Six Sculptures Confronted with an Engraving, Zeugma, 1967–86.
Etching, tin, steel, and wood,
12 ½ × 20 ¾ × 2 in.
(31.5 × 53 × 5 cm).

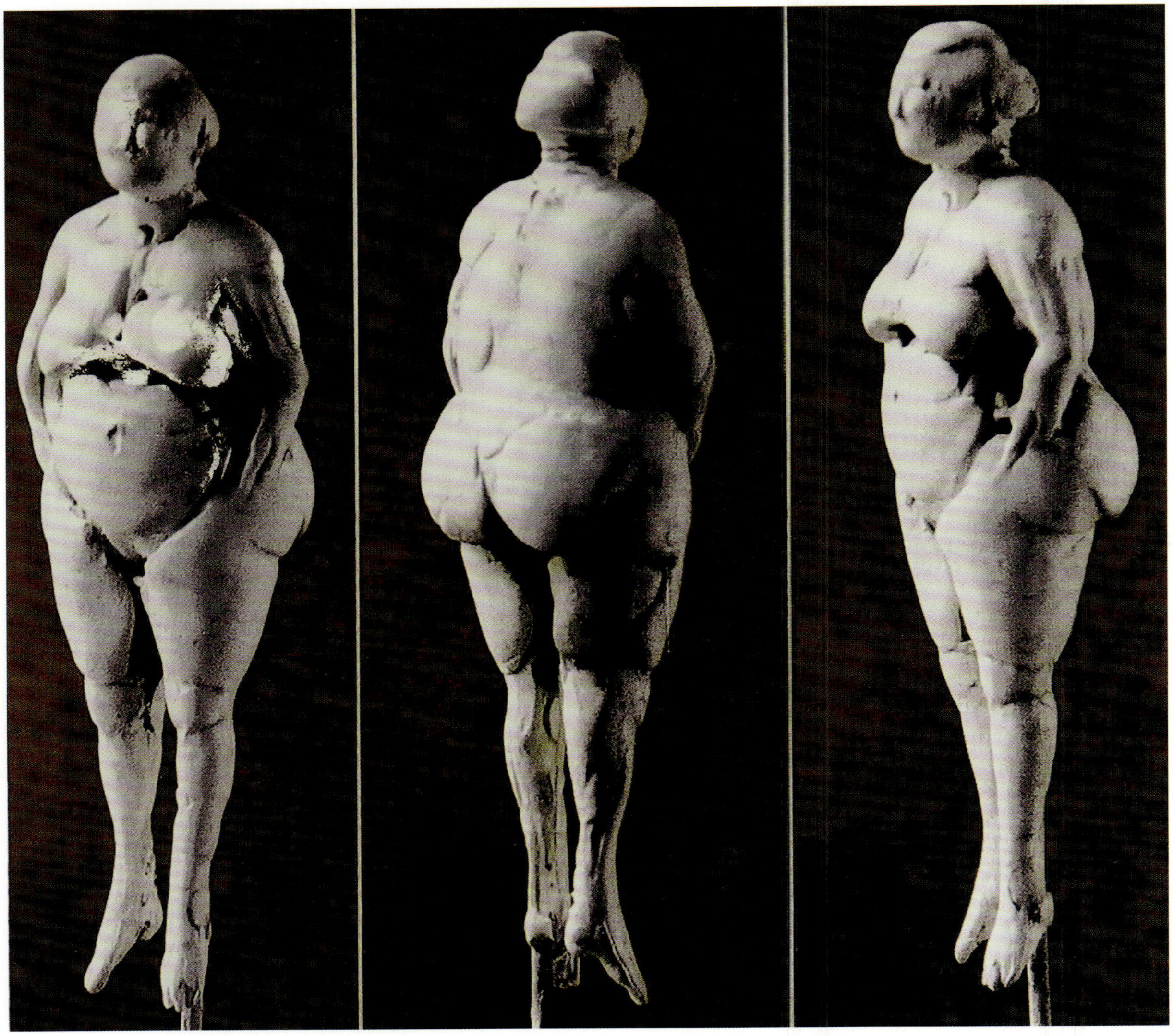

Sue Standing (in preparation),
2003.
Sculptulite and plaster,
16 × 5 ¼ × 3 ½ in.
(41 × 13.5 × 8.5 cm).

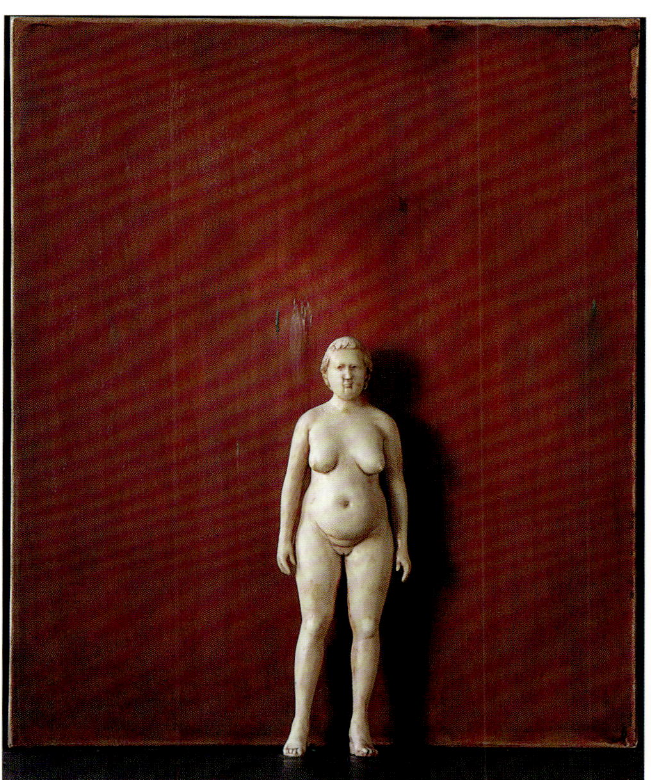

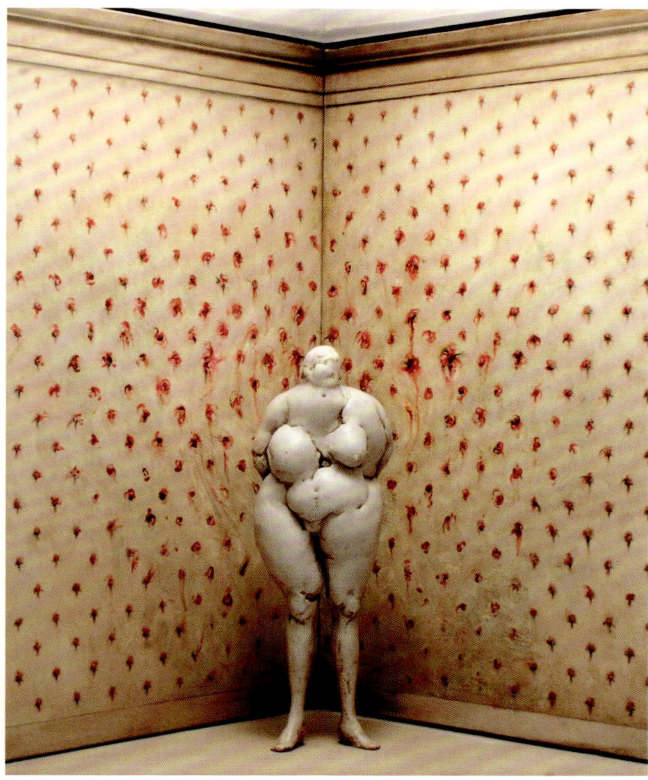

Louise II in front of a Wall, 2003.
Torolith and marble, 12 in.
(31.5 cm) h. and oil on canvas,
22 × 18 ½ in. (56 × 47 cm).

Sue with her Arms behind her Back in a Wallpapered Corner, 2000.
Torolith and marble,
13 ¾ in. (35 cm) h., corner-piece
pictures 26 × 26 ¾ in.
(66 × 68 cm), and plinth
in painted steel.

The Gestural Caryatid in a Blue Wallpapered Corner, 2002.
Torolith and marble, 14 ½ in.
(37 cm) h., corner-piece
pictures, 29 × 30 in.
(74 × 76 cm) h., plinth
in painted steel.

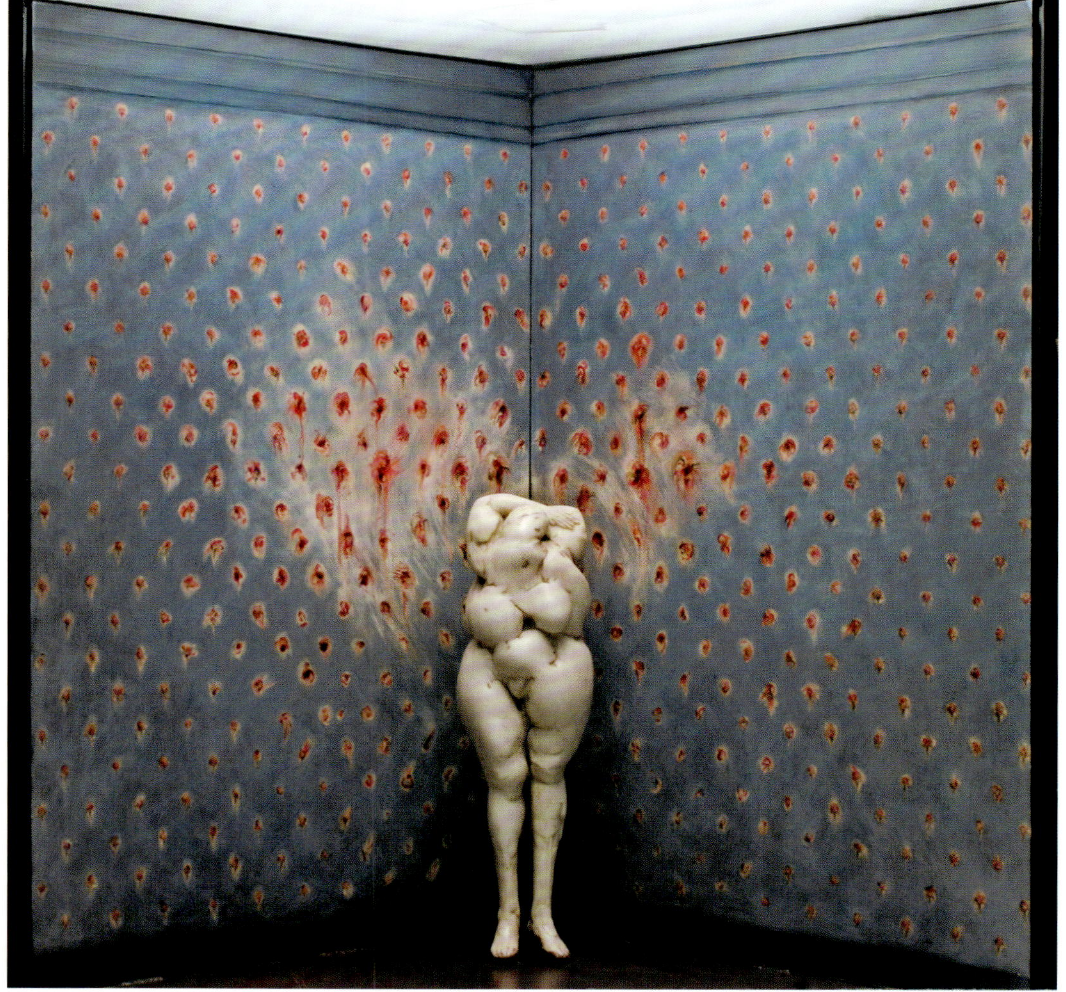

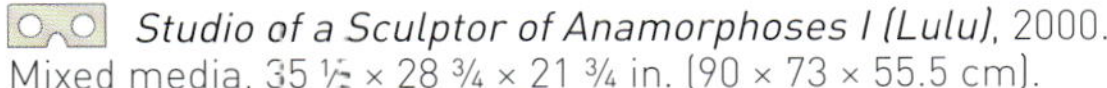
Studio of a Sculptor of Anamorphoses I (Lulu), 2000.
Mixed media, 35 ½ × 28 ¾ × 21 ¾ in. (90 × 73 × 55.5 cm).

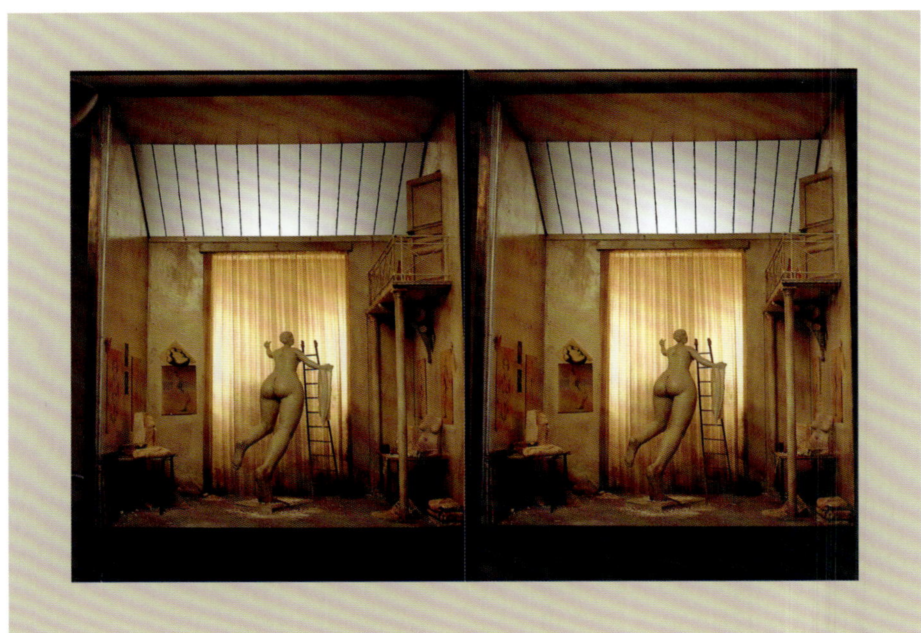

In the studio on rue du Temple, Paris, 2000.
Photograph Yann Matton.

Charles and his assistant, Isabelle Blanc, working on *The Large Lulu*, 2000.
Photograph Yann Matton.

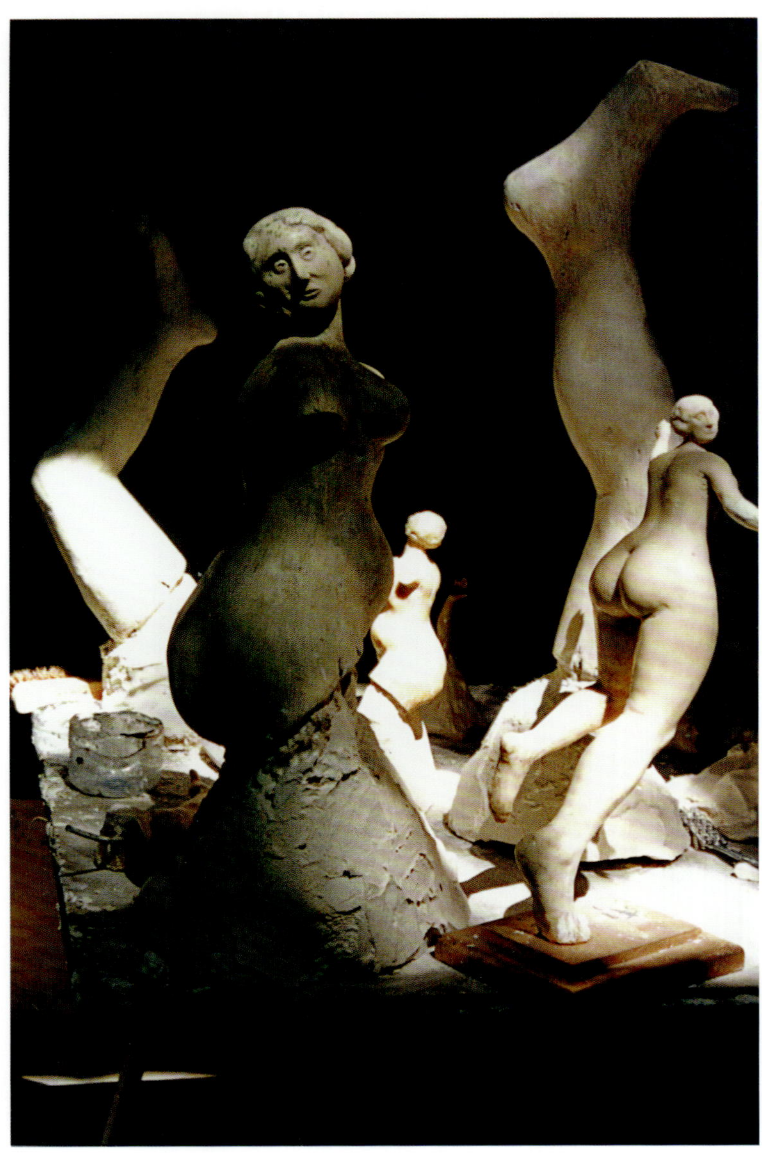

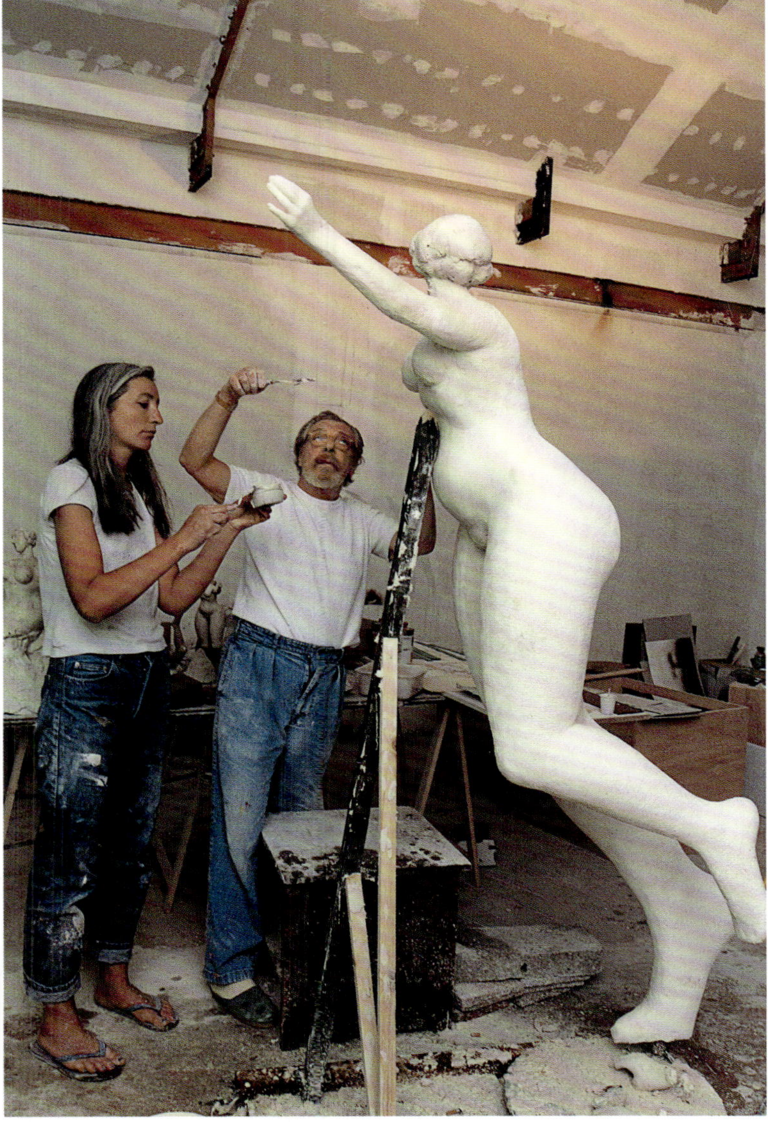

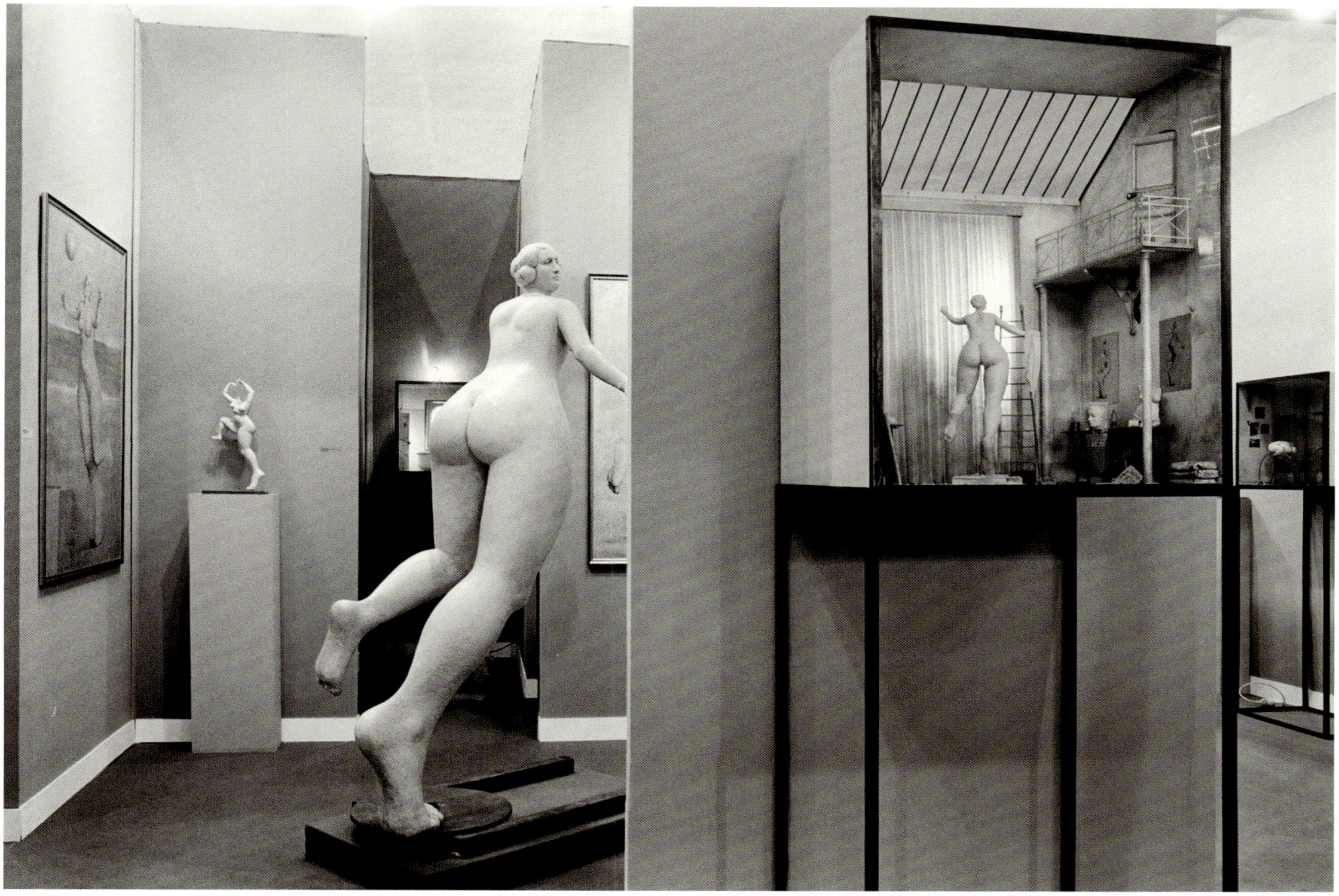

Solo display by Charles Matton at the FIAC 2000
(with Galerie Beaubourg, Pierre and Marianne Nahon).
Photograph Léonard Matton.

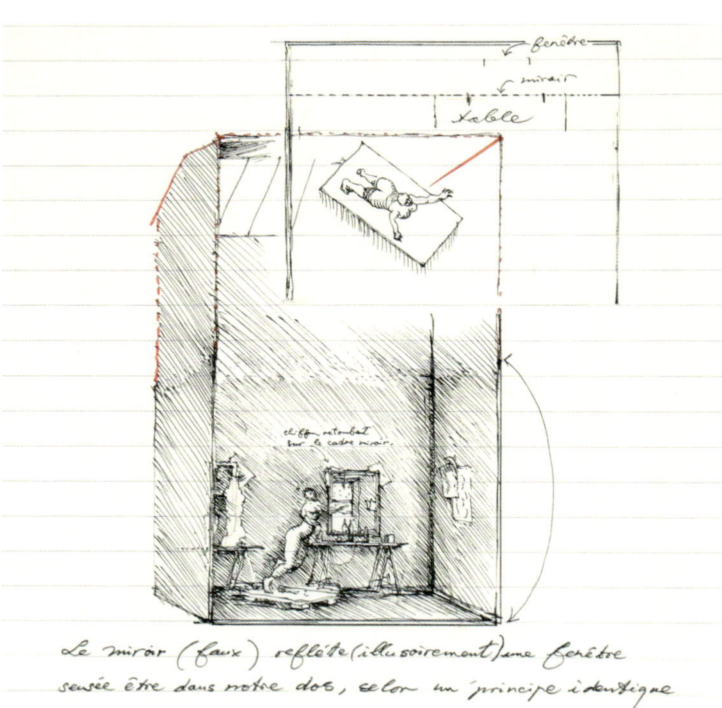

Studio of a Sculptor of Anamorphoses III, 2001.
Pencil on paper, 8 ½ × 8 ¼ in. (22 × 21 cm).

The (false) mirror reflects (an illusion) a window meant to be behind us in accordance with a principle identical to that already used in the mirrored wardrobe.

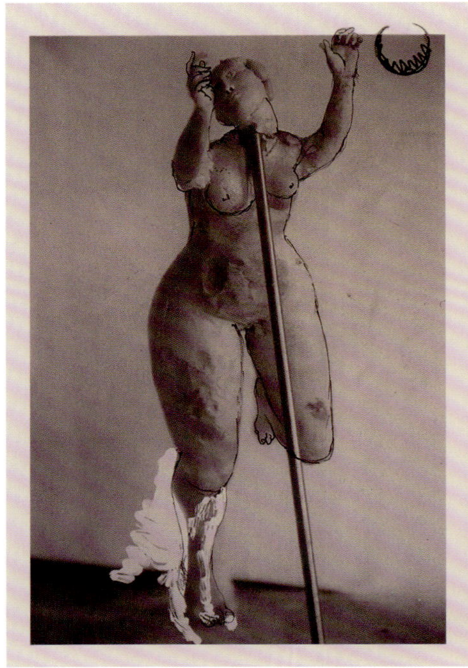

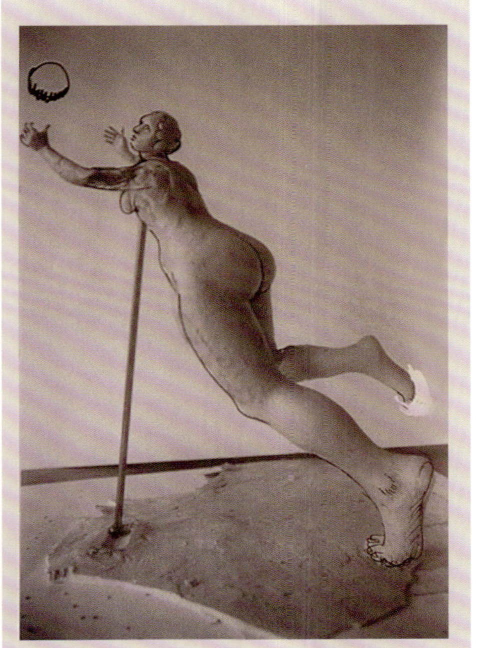

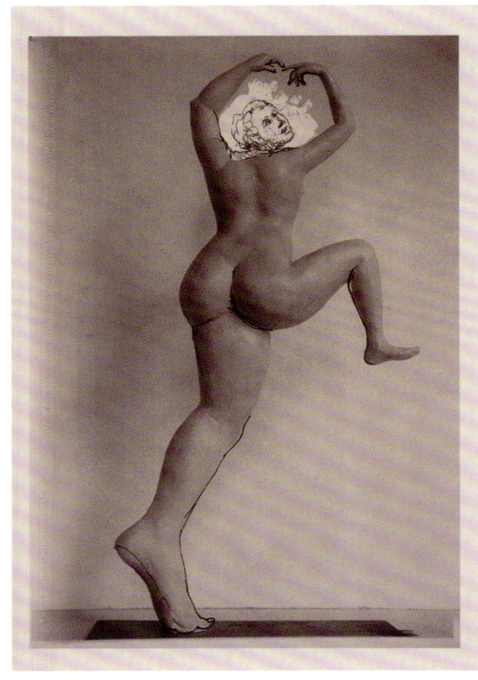

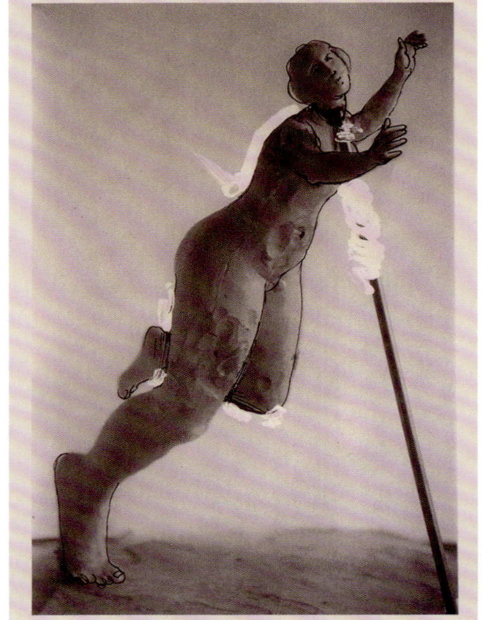

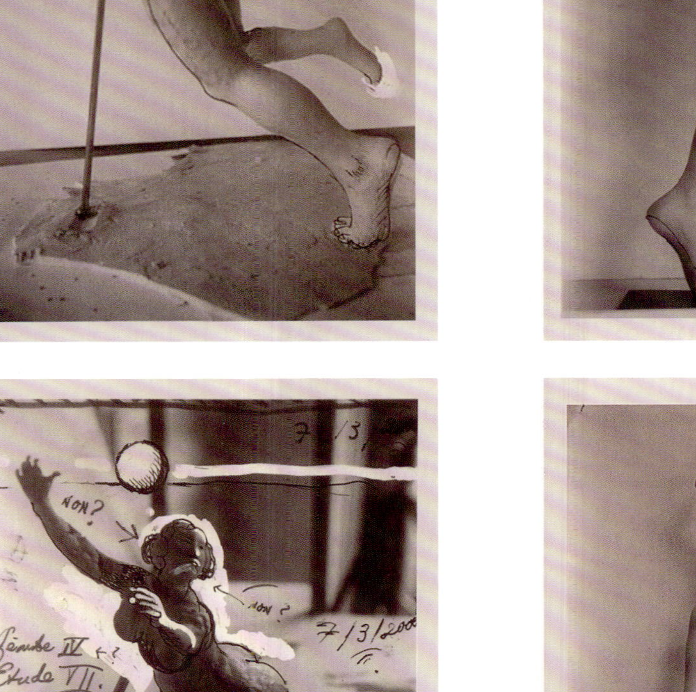

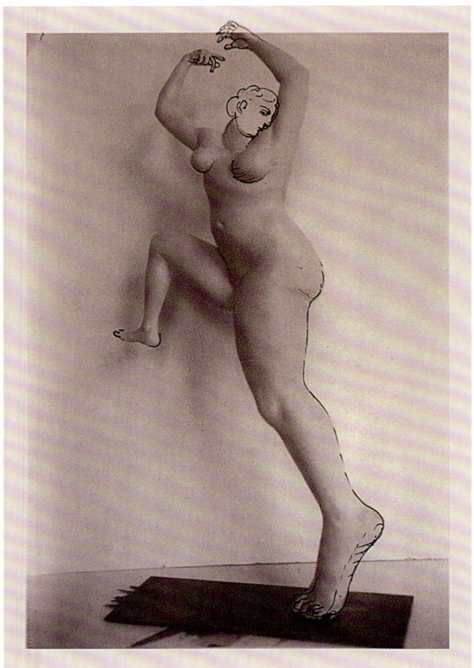

Lulu, Anamorphosis I (four phases), 2000.
Pencil, felt pen, and white corrector fluid on photographic prints, 4 ¾ × 3 ½ in. (12 × 9 cm).

The Dancer, Anamorphosis III (two phases), 2000.
Pencil, felt pen, and white corrector fluid on photographic prints, 4 ¾ × 3 ½ in. (12 × 9 cm).

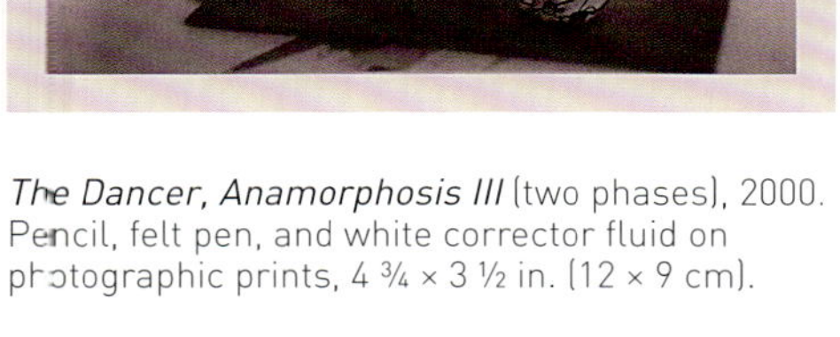

It is the beautiful Emma Thingamabob,
Who dances the abracadabra,
A dance she invented,
Whom I treated in anamorphosis.

Personal note, June 19, 2002

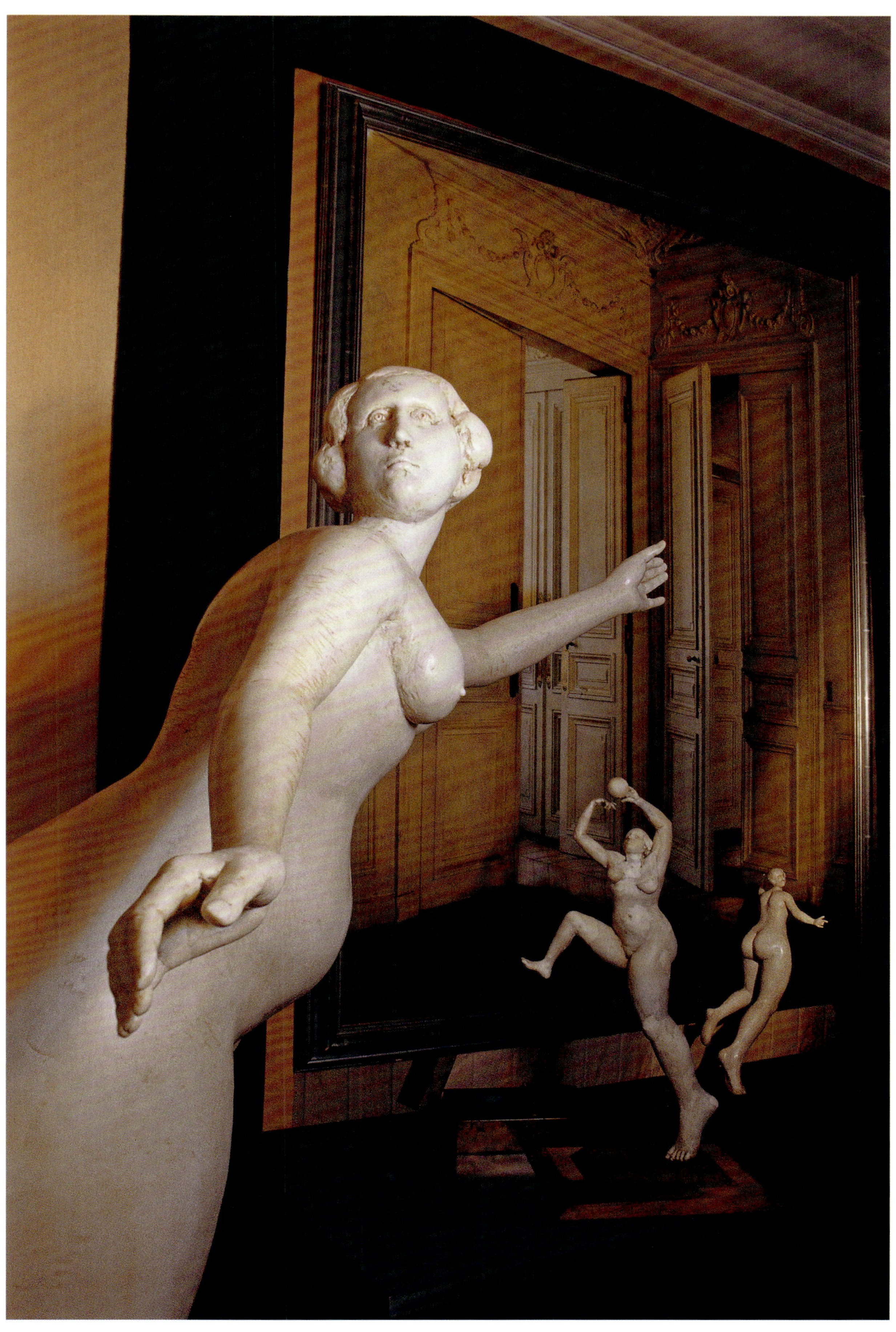

The Large Lulu, The Dancer with Ball, and *Lulu I* in front of the picture *The Three Doors*, 2000. Photograph.

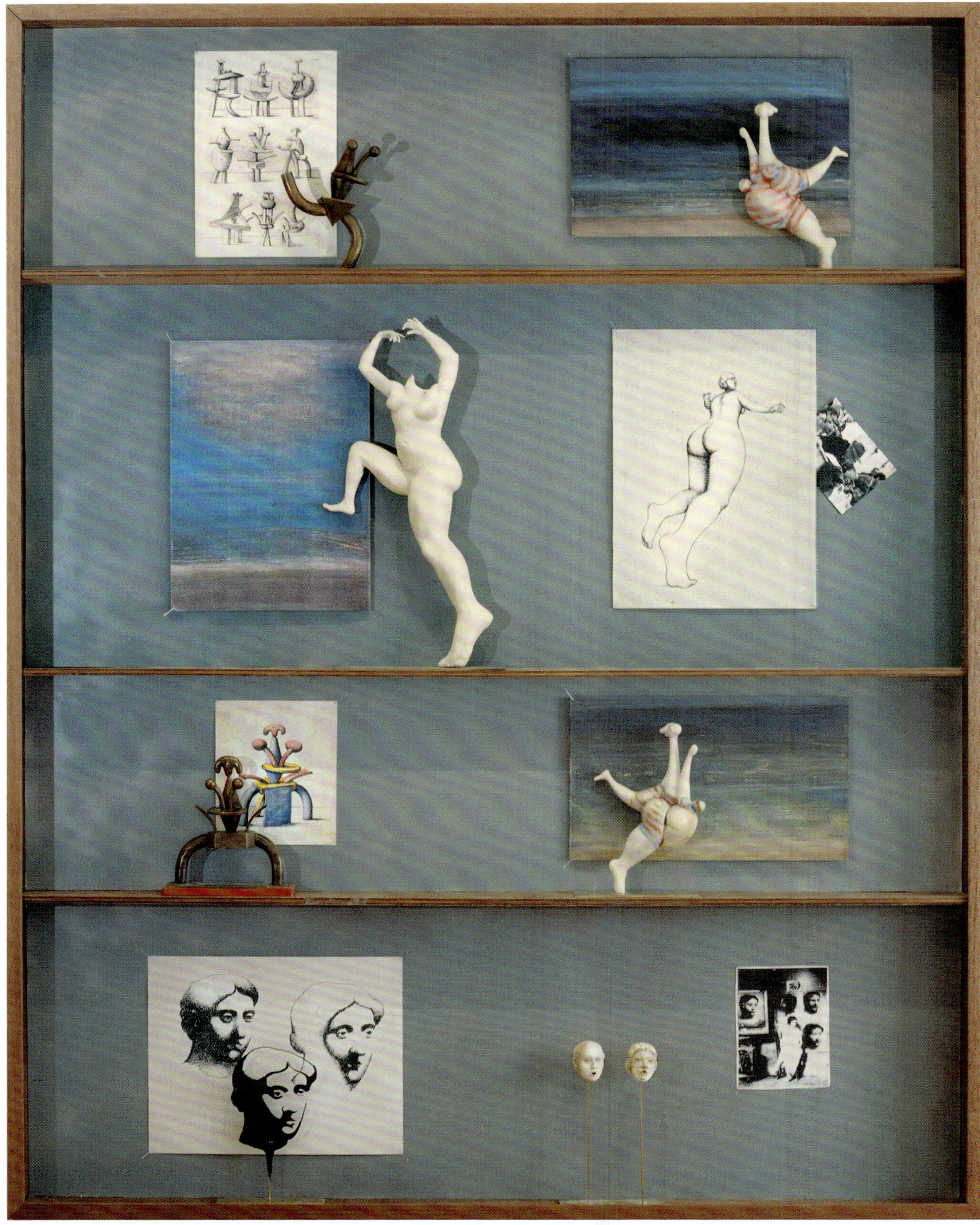

Bathers, encirclement (homage to Picasso), 1999.
Wood, oil on canvas, torolith, marble, brass, pencil, and black chalk on paper, photographs, and tin, 58 ½ × 42 ½ × 4 ¾ in. (149 × 108 × 12 cm).

Picasso puts on disguises to be more than one. I put on disguises to prove I don't exist.

Personal note, February 18, 1998

Meninas, encirclement (homage to Velásquez), 1998.
Wood, oils on canvas, torolith, marble, brass, pencil, and black chalk on paper, and photograph, 58 ½ × 42 ½ × 4 ¾ in. (149 × 108 × 12 cm).

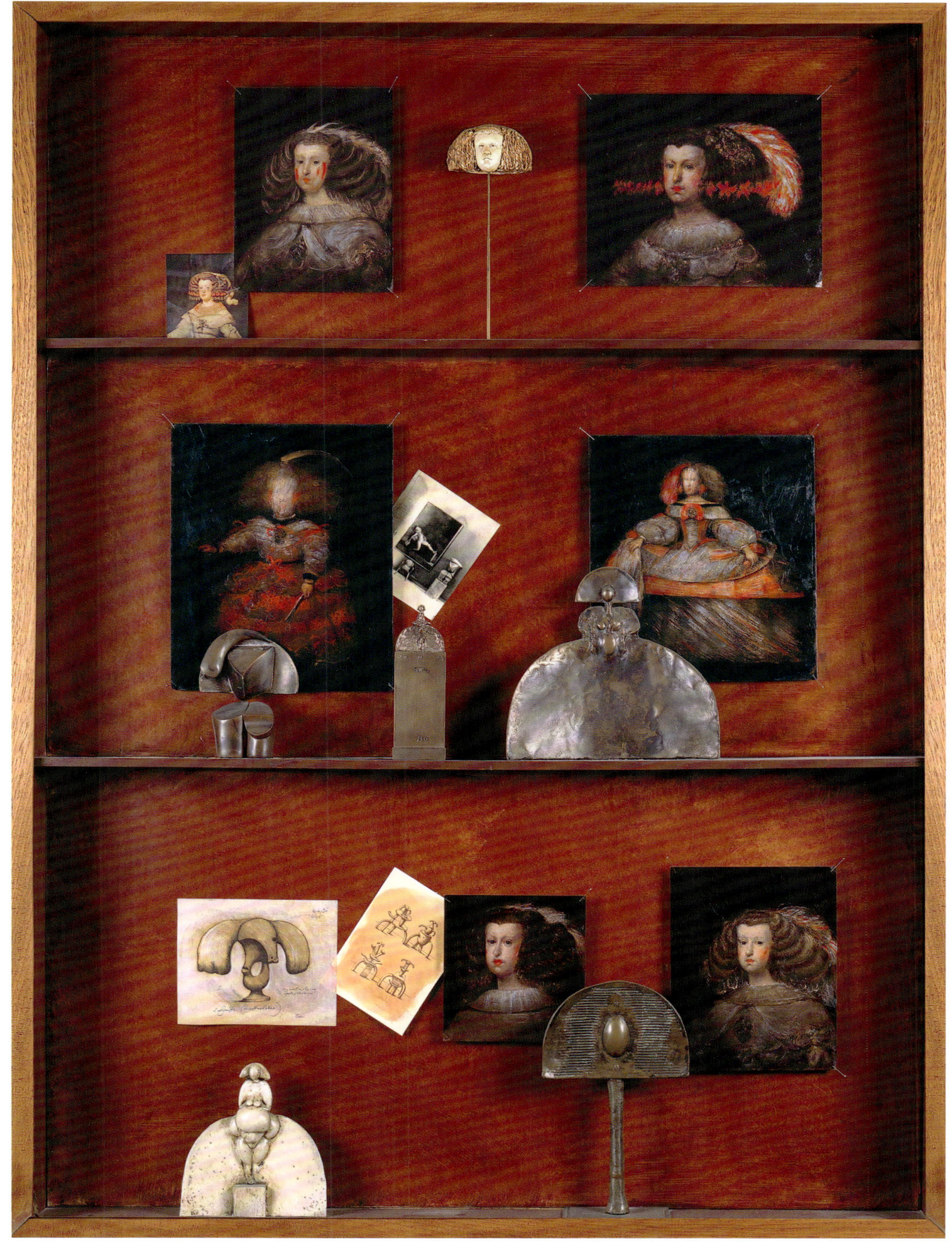

[. . .] a few reflections on what are in my opinion the affiliations between Rembrandt, Velásquez, Bacon, and Picasso.

Personal note, May 7, 1998

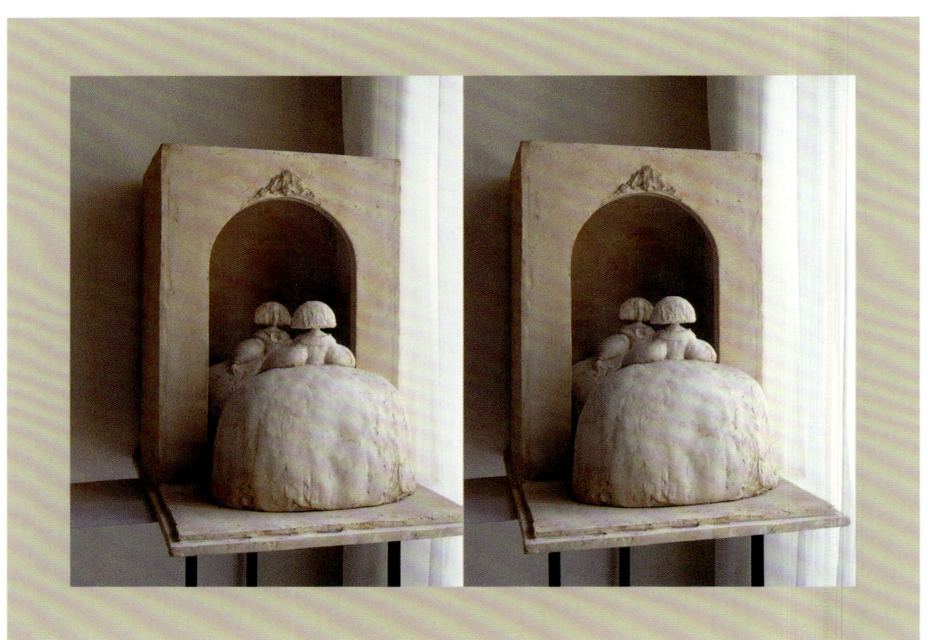

The Double Infanta (in a Mirror), 1997.
Torolith and marble, 27 ¼ × 20 ½ × 26 ½ in.
(69 × 52 × 67.5 cm).

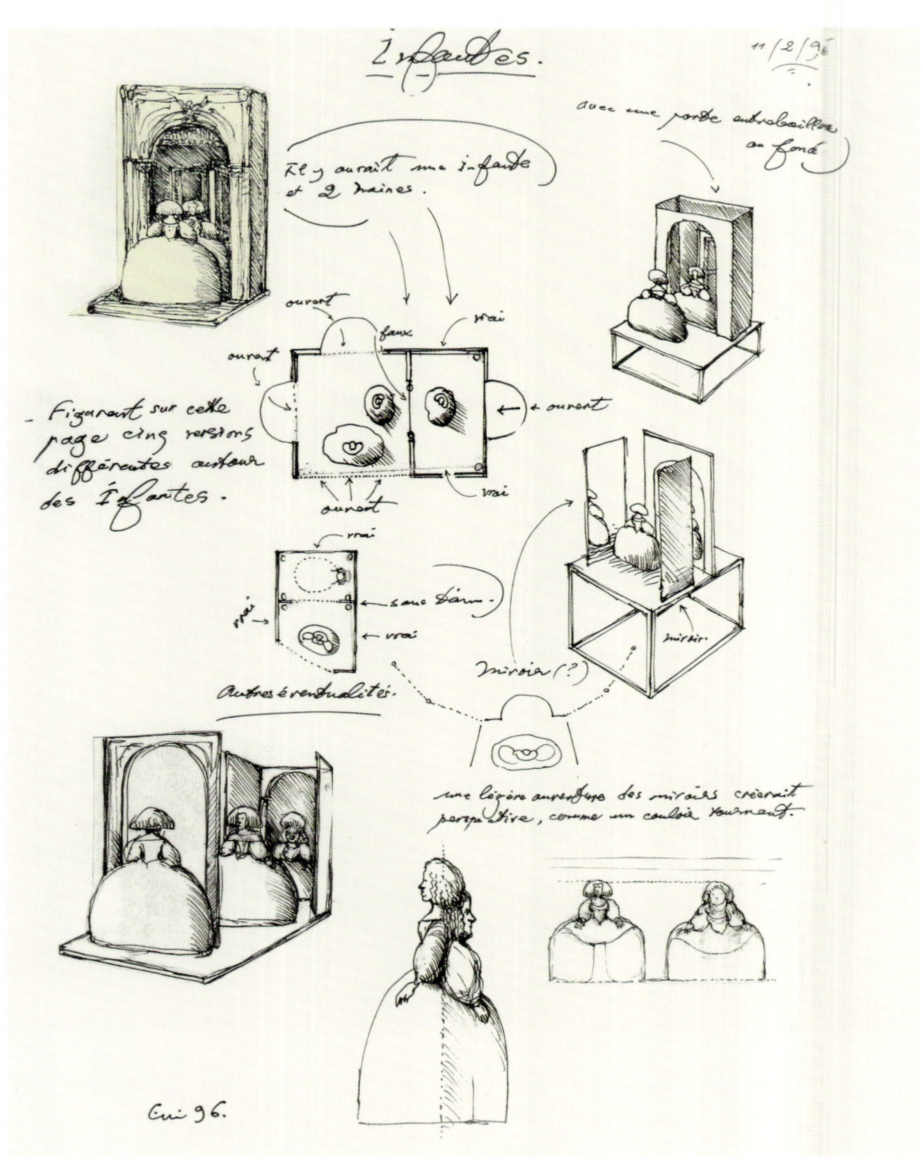

Infantas, 1996.
Pencil and felt pen on paper,
16 ½ × 11 ¾ in. (42 × 29.7 cm).

The Infanta Margarita and her Dwarf Lady-in-waiting in an Interior, 2003.
Torolith, marble, and oil paint, 31 × 28 ¼ × 22 ½ in. (79 × 72 × 57 cm).

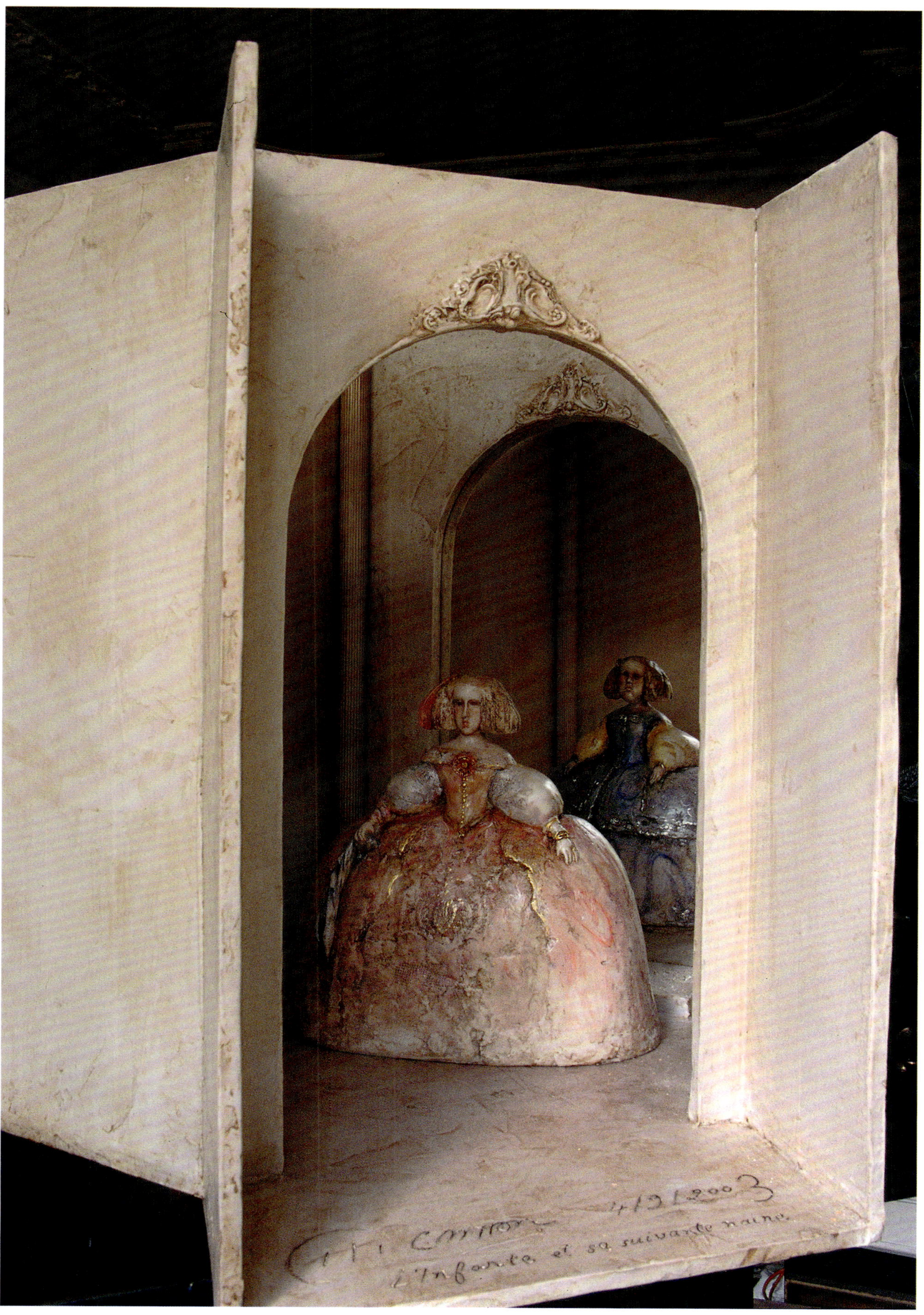

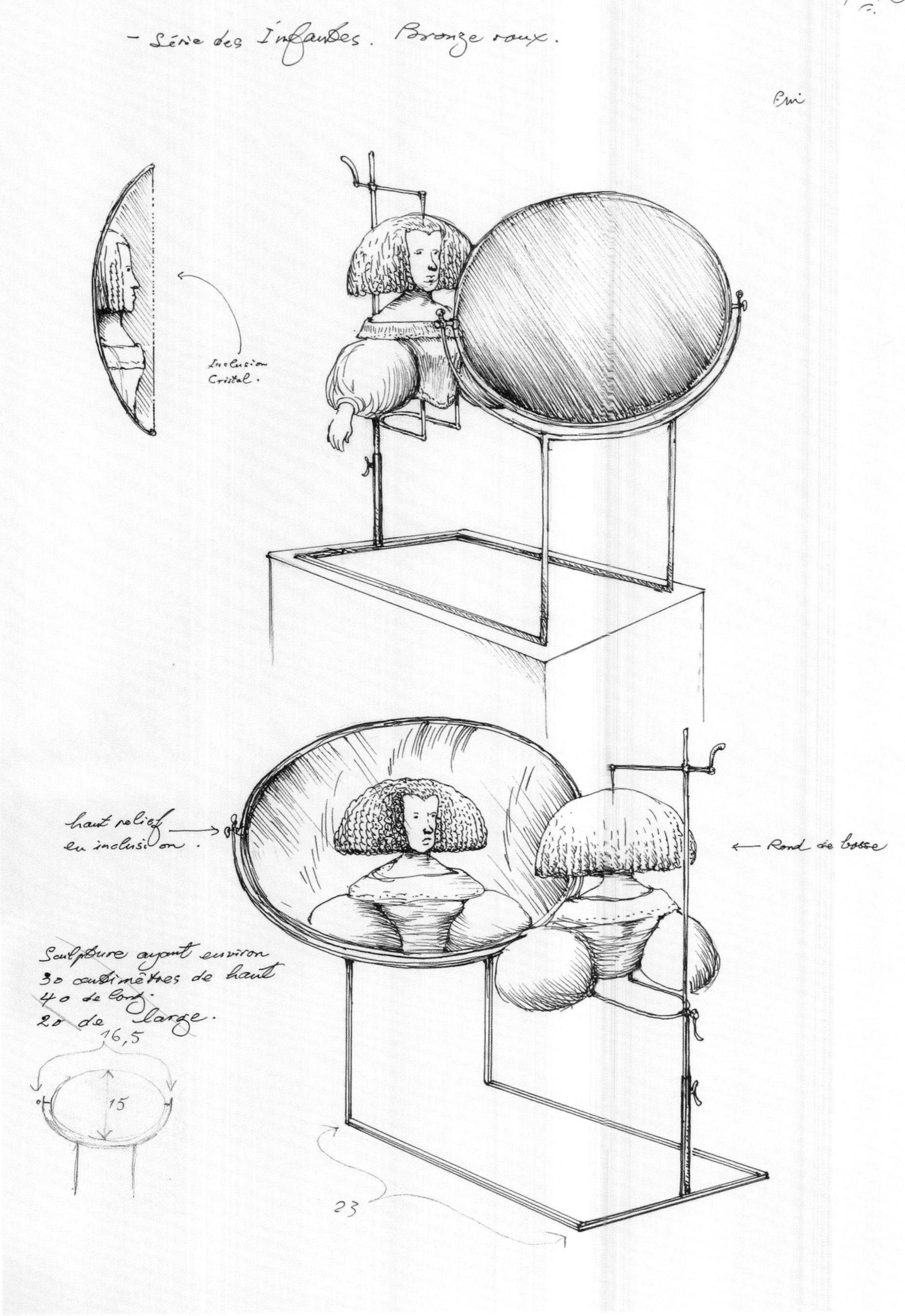

The Infanta's Mirror, 1996.
Pencil on paper,
16 ½ × 11 ¾ in.
(42 × 29.7 cm).

Maria Tesselschade II, 1998. Torolith and marble, 11 × 10 ¼ × 2 in. (28 × 26 × 5 cm).

Maria Tesselschade I, 1998. Original, in Sculptulite, plaster, and coffee spoons, 9 ¾ × 10 ¼ × 2 ¾ in. (25 × 26 × 7 cm).

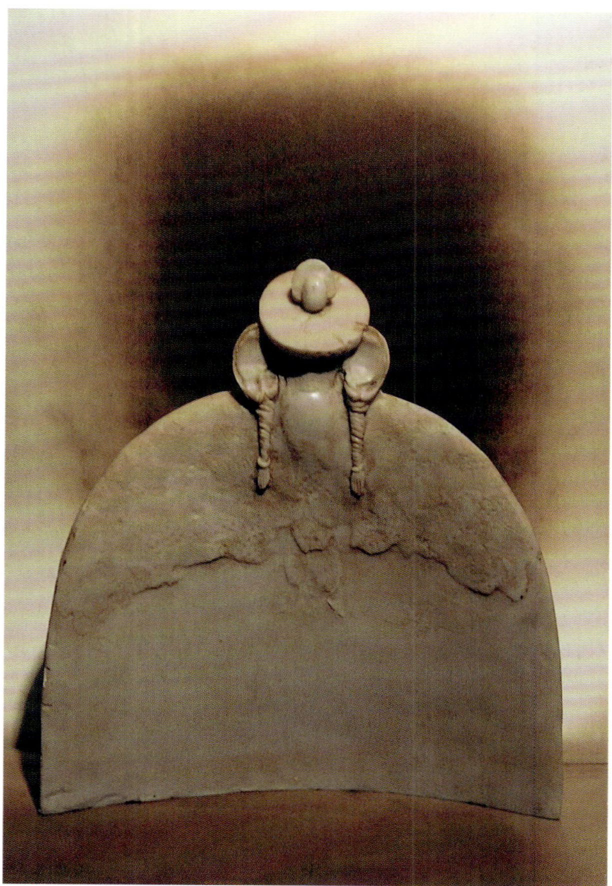

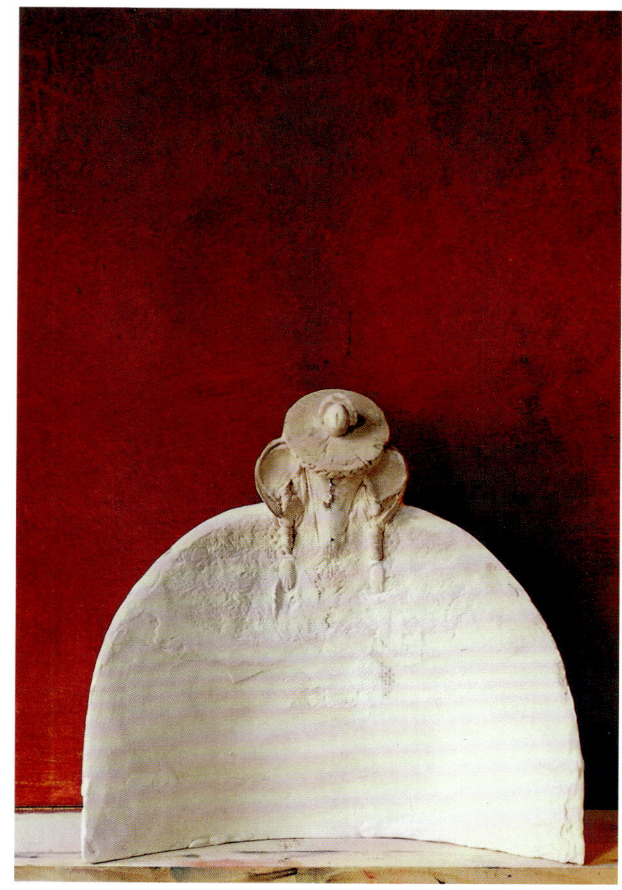

Infanta II, 1997. Torolith and bronze, 9 ½ × 9 ¾ × 22 in. (24 × 25 × 56 cm).

The Infanta of Lespug, 1995. Torolith and marble, 6 ¾ × 6 ½ in. (17.5 × 16.5 cm), beneath a *Picasian Infanta*, pencil, ink, watercolor, and wash on paper.

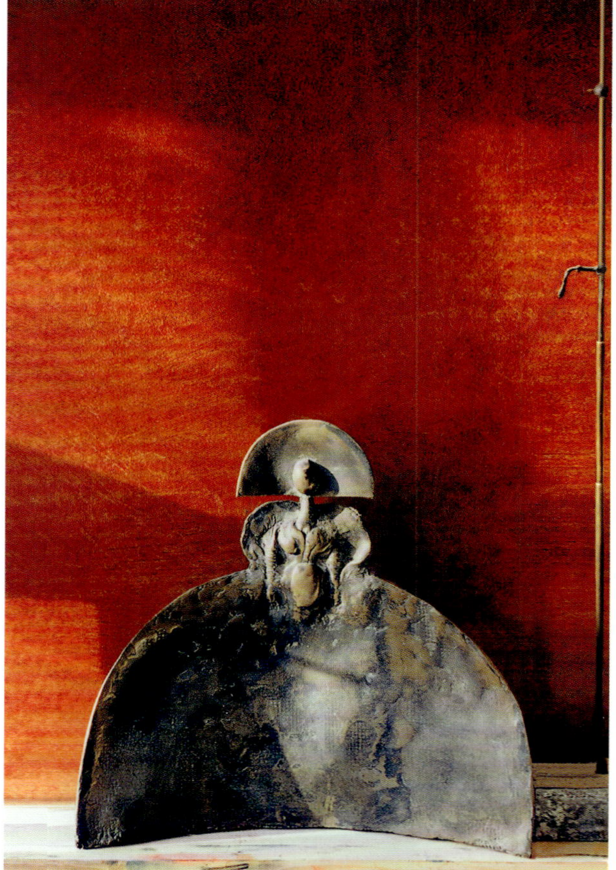

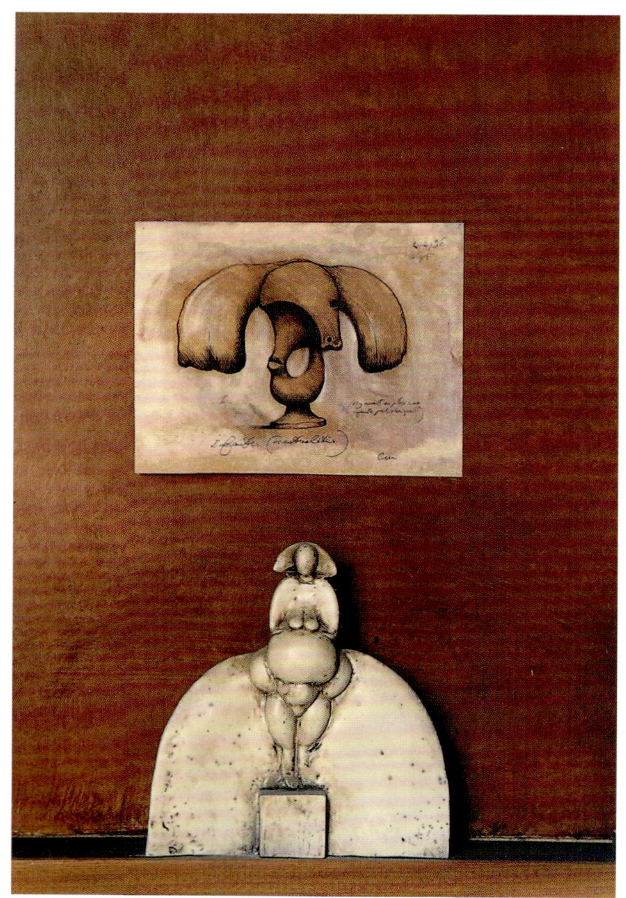

The boxes are primarily intended to immortalize "slices of life," to half the flow of time. I consider my work complete once the clocks have stopped in those spaces that I prefer as unexotic as possible, completely realistic, completely lifelike.

Personal note, June 12 bis, 2002

- Recently Paul Virilio, a specialist in the concepts of duration and destruction, referred to timelessness, to the suspension of time in respect of my works.
- At bottom, you're only too pleased when people see eternity in what you've made, one can boil it down to that.
- And just to that!
- That's marvelous. One here reaches the most elevated function of the art, where one creates pieces, even highly fragmented ones, of eternity.

C. Matton, in a conversation with Yasmina Reza, September 9, 2009

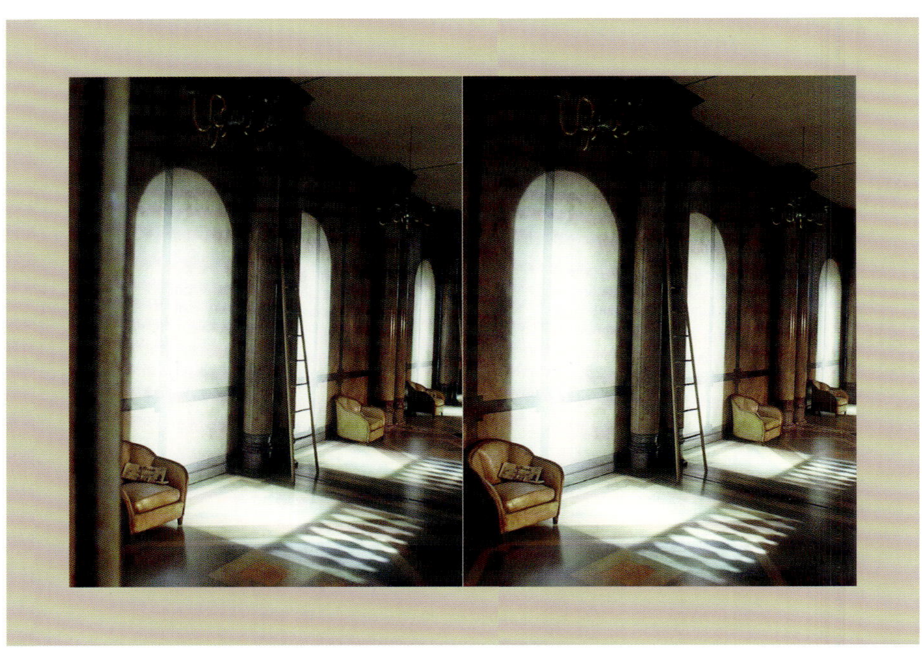

The Hotel Hall III, 2003.
Mixed media, 31 × 36 ¼ × 37 ½ in. (79 × 92 × 95 cm).

This hotel hall derives from a memory of Italy. It's an attempt to recollect the space, with its silence, its light, the setting sun casting shadows of the banister rail on the pink marble floor, that abandoned sense of the "annual closure," right down to the dust sent up by some building work. Invent nothing, just attest to the place, make it reappear, the armchair on which lies a newspaper from last season, from that time when footsteps, women's voices, children's laughter, when music resounded down these endless corridors, to make all that exist again, forever.

Personal note, May 4, 2003

Hôtel du Lac, 1994.
Mixed media, 29 ½ × 39 ¼ × 24 ½ in. (75 × 100 × 62 cm).

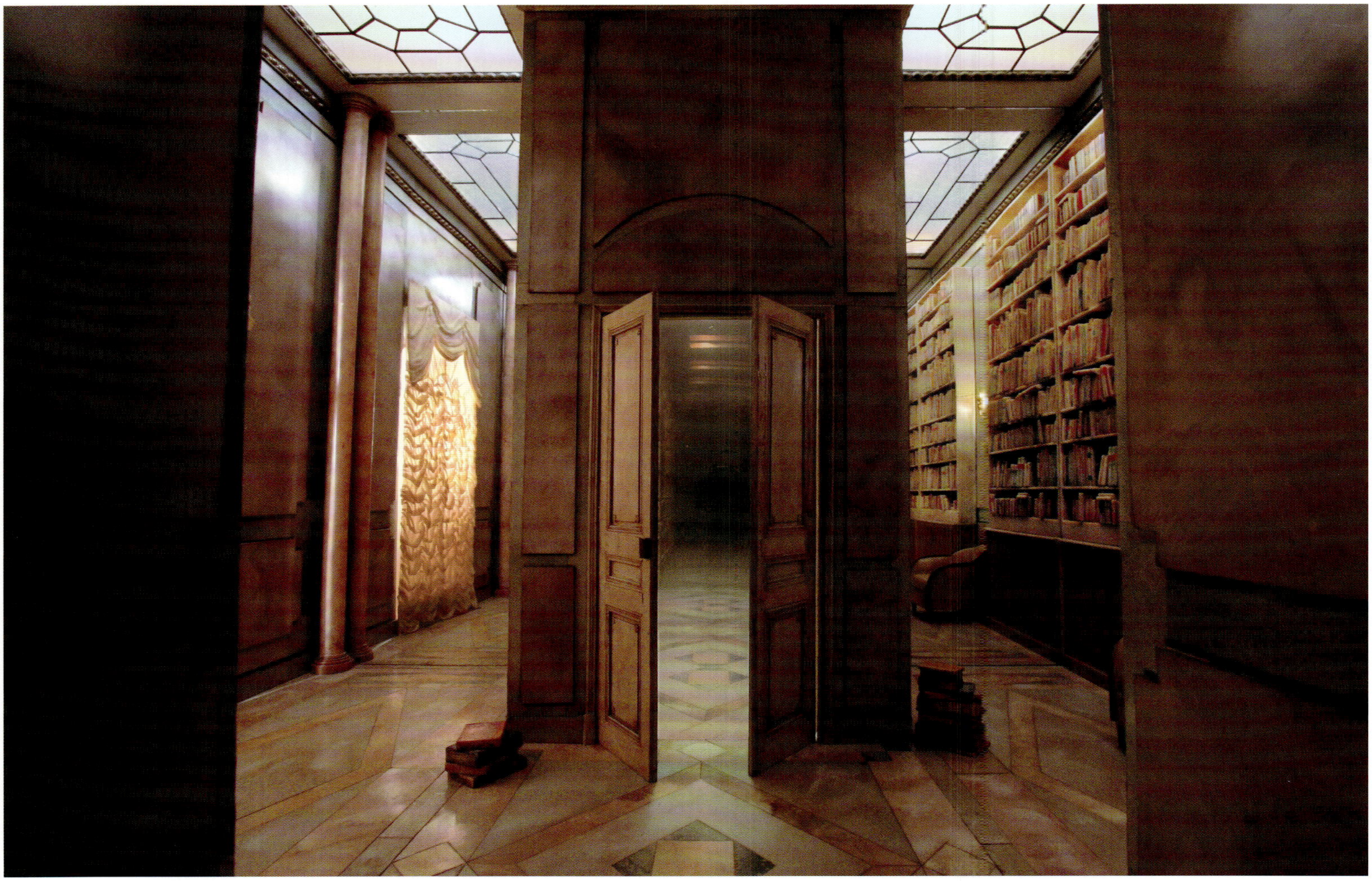

Hôtel de l'Esplanade, Annual Closure II, 2005.
Mixed media,
31 ½ × 37 × 37 ¾ in.
(80 × 94 × 96 cm).

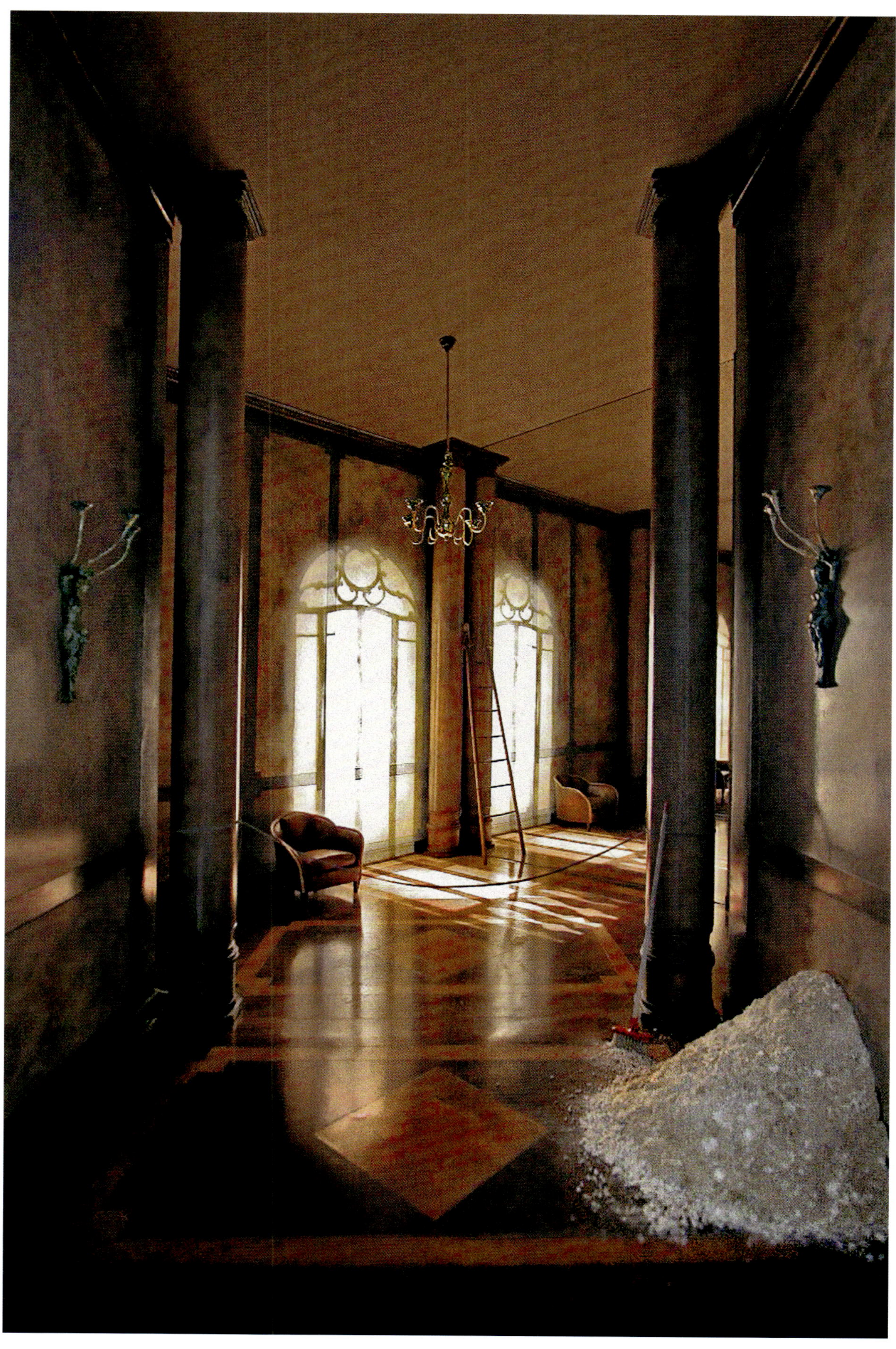

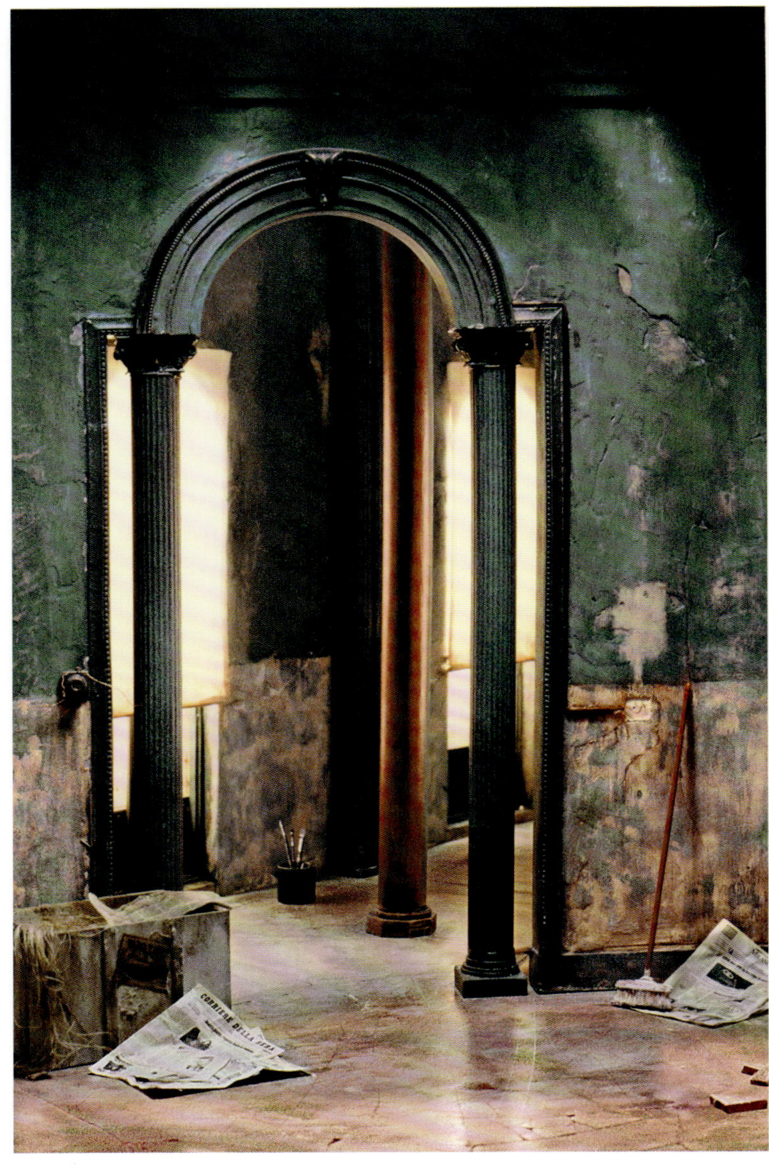

Hôtel Yverdon, 2001.
Mixed media, 20 × 25 ½ × 21 ¼ in. (51 × 64.5 × 54 cm).

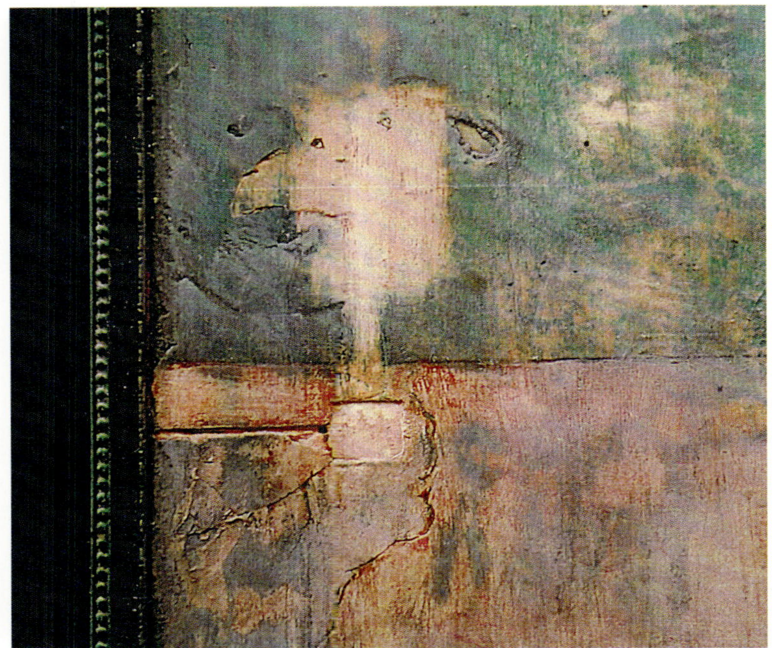

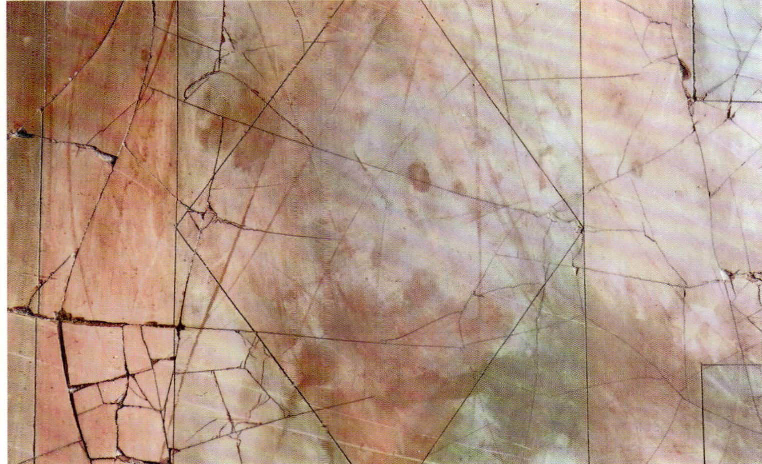

Hôtel Yverdon (detail of the wall), 2001.
Photograph.

Hôtel Yverdon (detail of the floor), 2001.
Photograph.

In the hall stood two brass and gilded-leather suitcases, a little out of shape—and elegant because out of shape. They bore witness to the opulence of traveling in the past, their tiredness served to excuse the hubbub. Beyond their reflection in the mirror, one catches sight of a greenish-and-pink marble gallery. This gallery seemed to go on and on, to plunge into the very heart of the endless palatial hotel, a hotel for always.

Personal note, January 7, 1989

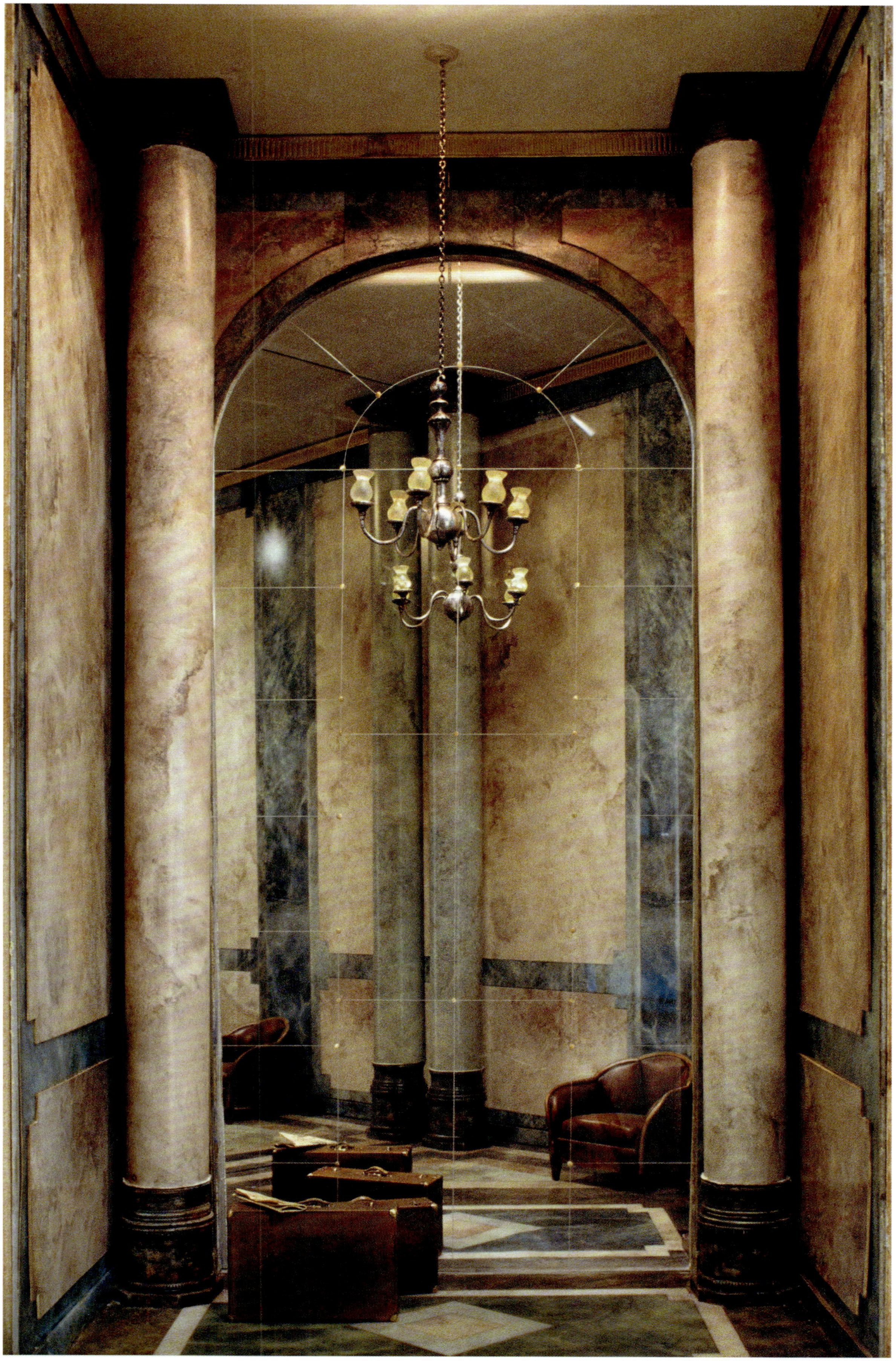

The Hotel Hall I, 1989.
Mixed media,
35 ¾ × 35 × 35 ¾ in.
(91 × 89 × 91 cm).

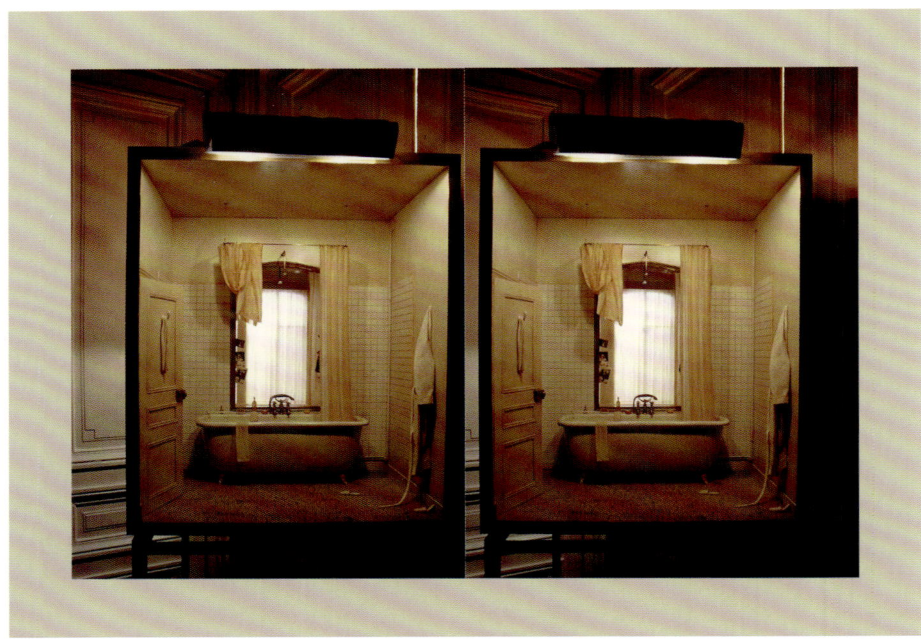

The Bathroom at Mariefried, 2001.
Mixed media,
22 ¾ × 19 ¾ × 26 ½ in.
(58 × 50 × 67.5 cm).

Facing page:
Bathroom II, 1987.
Mixed media,
23 ½ × 17 ¾ × 21 ¼ in.
(60 × 45.5 × 54 cm).

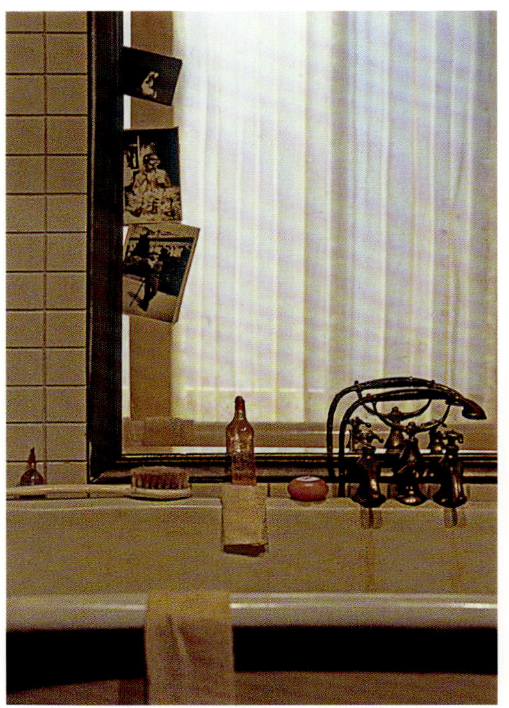

The Bathroom at Mariefried (detail).

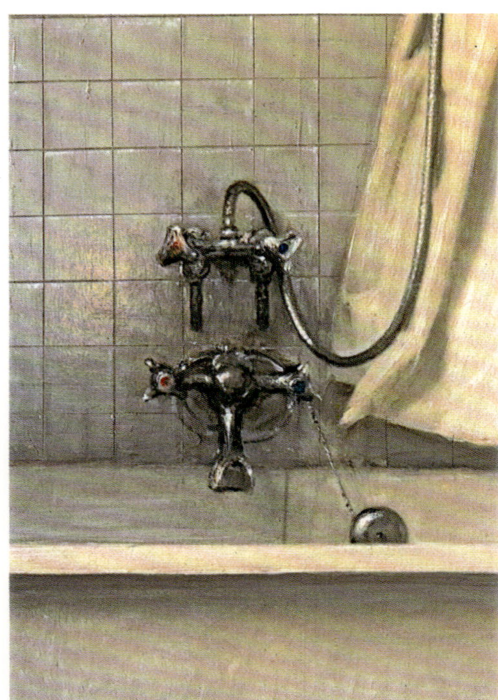

The Bathroom with the White Curtain (detail).

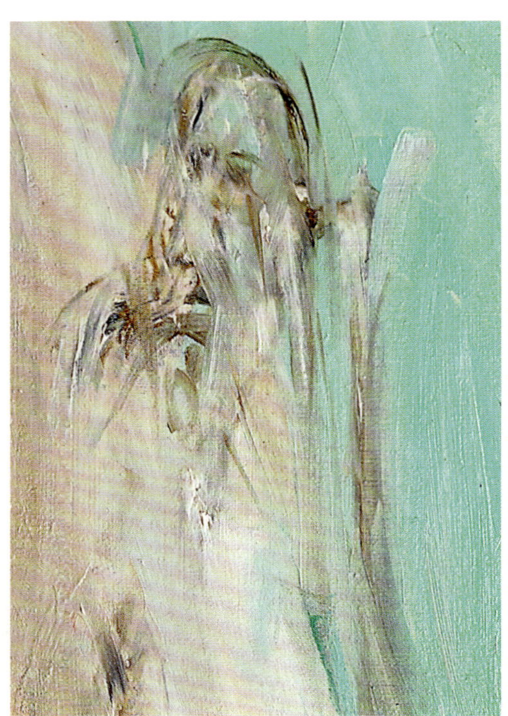

The Large Bathtub on a Veronese Green Ground (detail).

Dealing with "overworked" images, images so familiar no one sees them anymore, can be very rewarding. There's something bad about living without "knowing," about looking without seeing; it's like a "sin." I'm not actually a painter as such, rather a kind of aesthetic priest who employs the vocabulary of the plastic arts to gain understanding.

Personal note, October 18, 1987

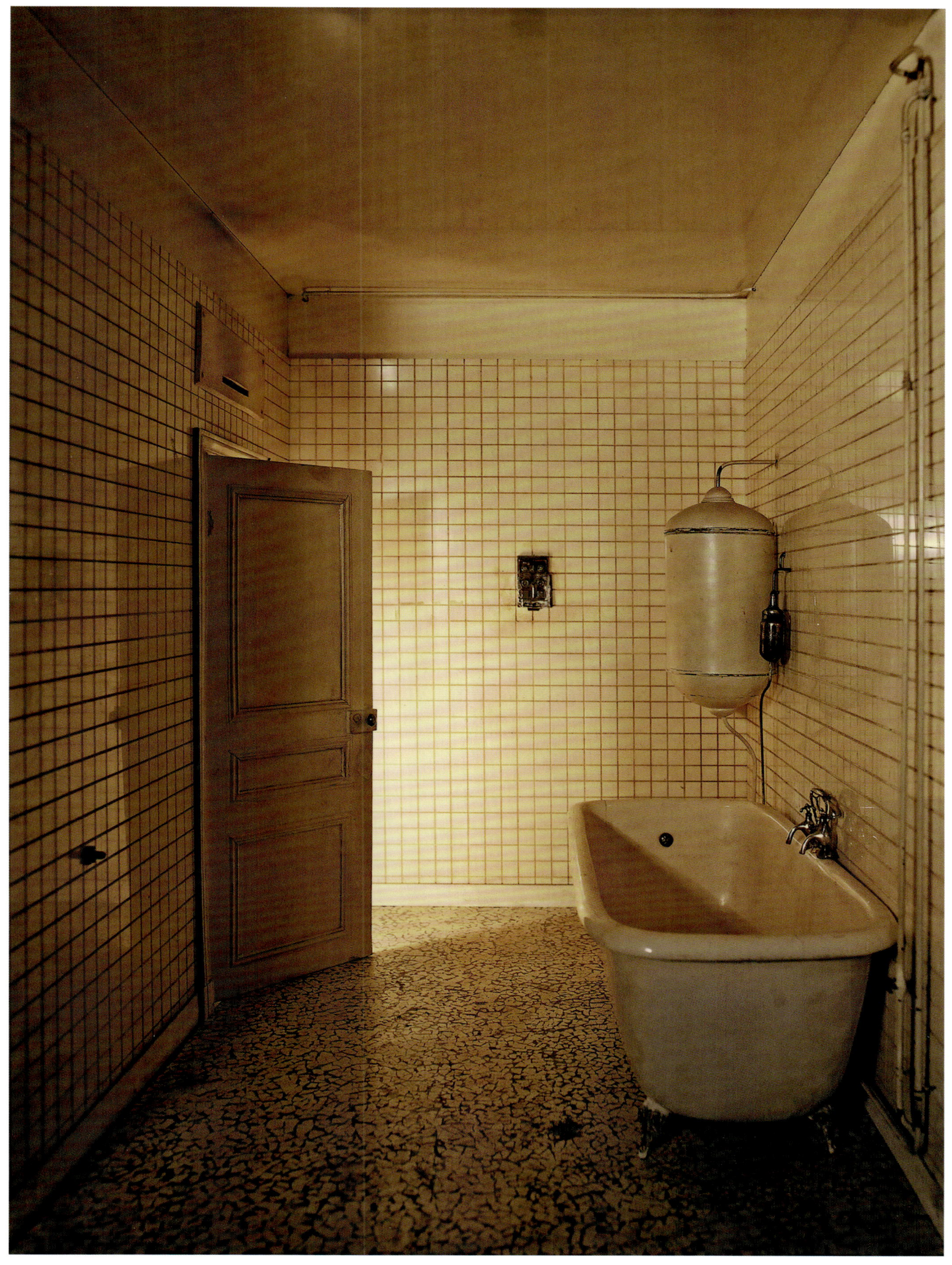

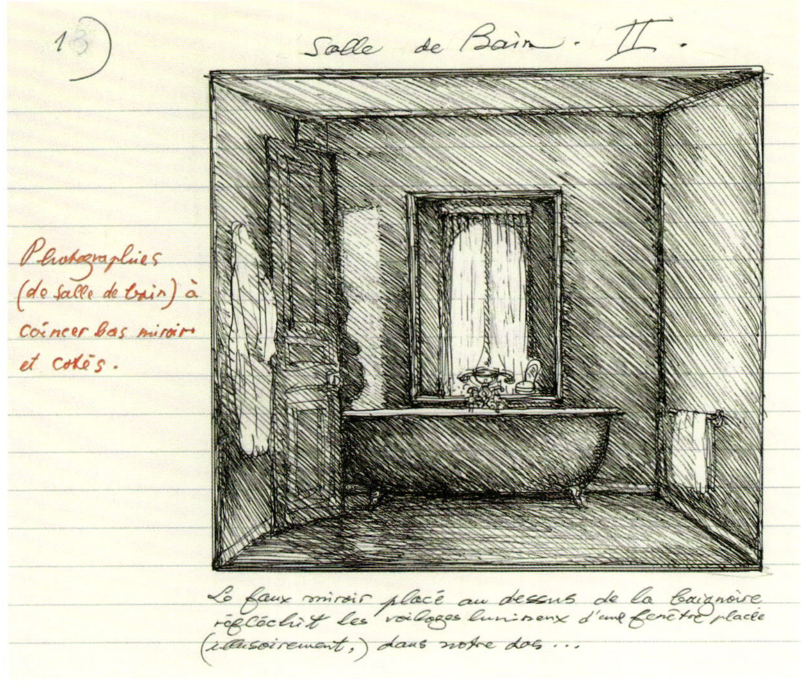

The Bathroom at Mariefried, 2001.
Pencil on paper, 7 × 8 ¼ in. (17.5 × 21 cm).

Photographs (bathroom) wedged below mirror and the sides.

The false mirror placed above the bathtub reflects the brightly lit net curtain over a window placed (an illusion) behind us...

What I like about Charles Matton is the obsessive familiarity he maintains with objects, a sense of their obviousness that is more than an aesthetic sense—that has something of an exorcism, something magical. To get the object to emerge, that's more important than making it *mean*. To take up with the object at its source, to exorcize its every nuance, does not inevitably mean returning to some lost secret of art or of painting. It means inventing another. Here, it's the object that generates its own fiction.

Jean Baudrillard, *Antipodes* (Paris: Palais de Tokyo, 1987). Exhibition catalog

[...] Oddly, Jean taught me something about my work, because even if I might have managed to intuit the sentence "To get the object to emerge, that's more important than making it mean," I'd never have been able to put it into words. One day I asked him what sense did he attribute to the word "important"? An answer did not come. He just grabbed me by the tie, saying, "Don't you ever do that to me again!"

C. Matton, in "Ça me dit, l'après-midi," op. cit.

The Bathroom, 1965.
Etching, 11 ½ × 9 ½ in. (29.5 × 24 cm).

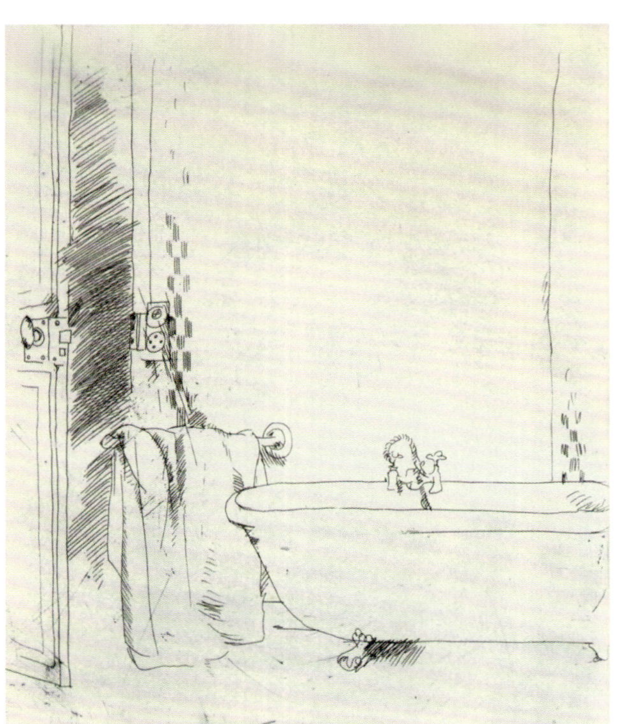

The Bathroom, Morning, 1965.
Etching and wash, 23 × 19 ½ in. (58.8 × 49.8 cm).

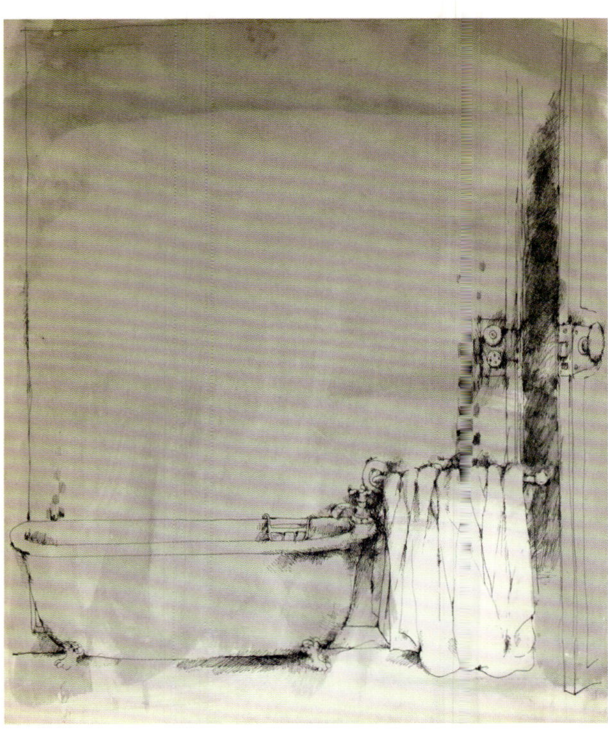

"Things mislead us, that's for sure, but always in the same way. That's reassuring."

C. Matton, *La Pomme ou l'Histoire d'une histoire* directed by Charles Matton (1966). Short film

Facing page:
The Bathroom at Mariefried, 2001.
Mixed media,
22 ¾ × 19 ¾ × 26 ½ in.
(58 × 50 × 67.5 cm).

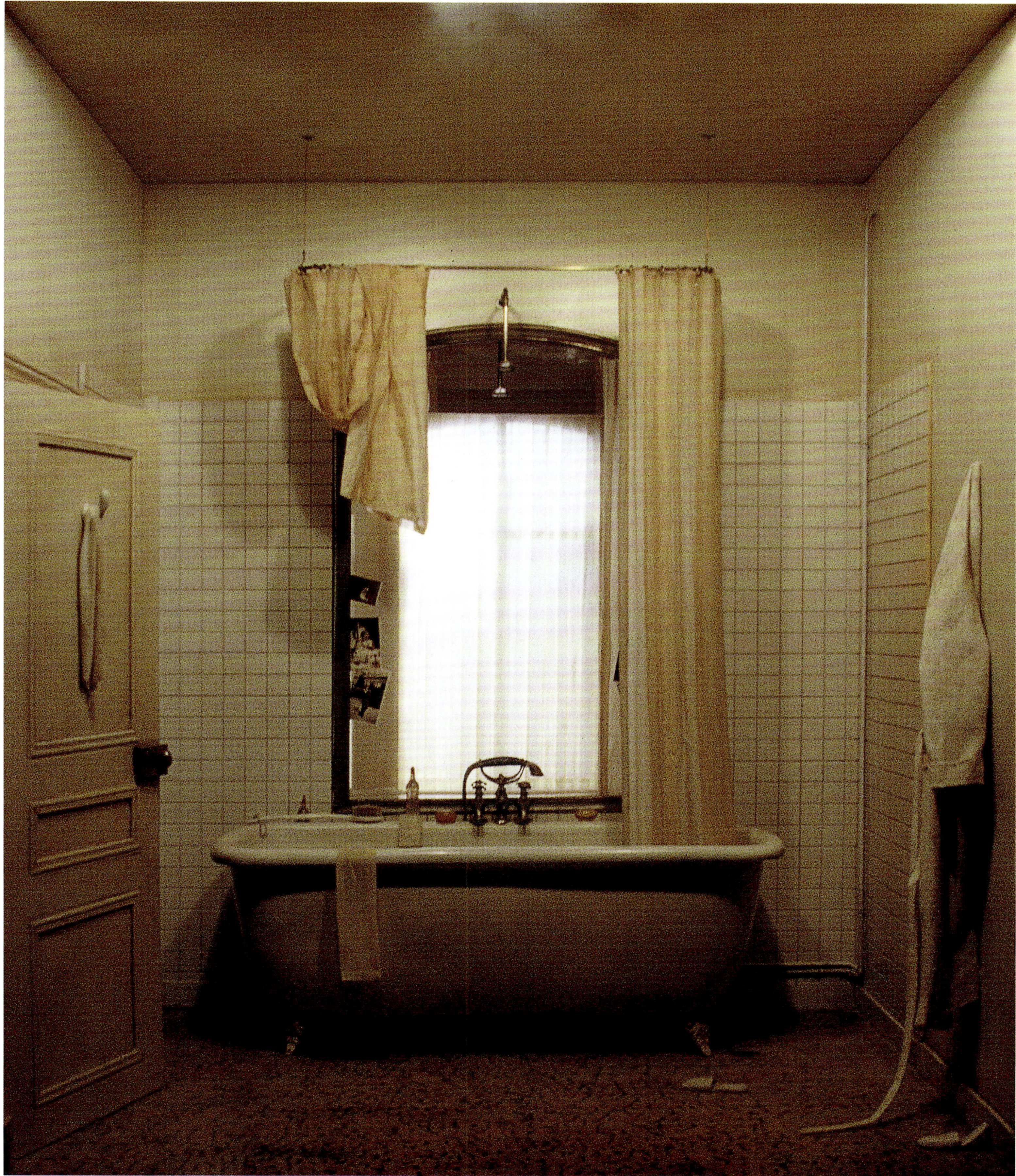

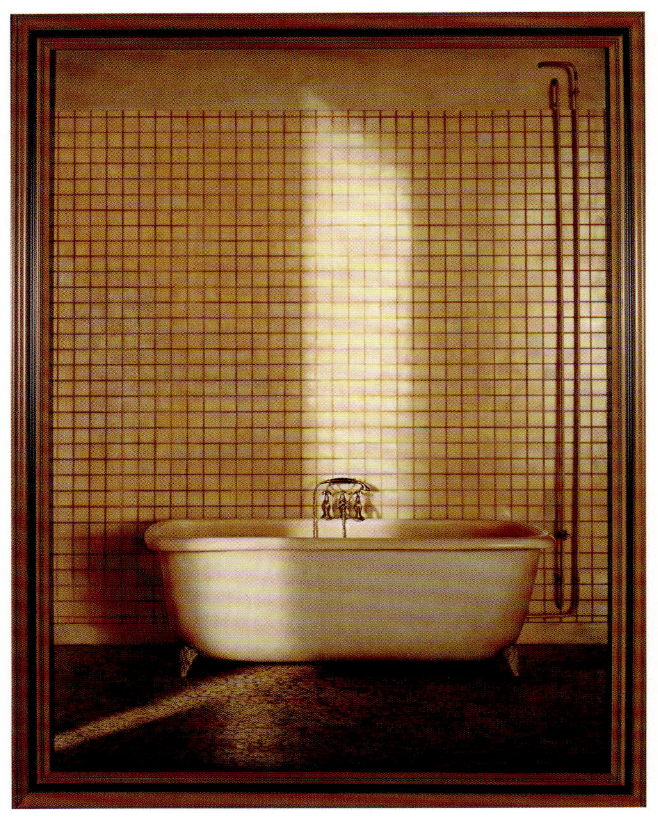

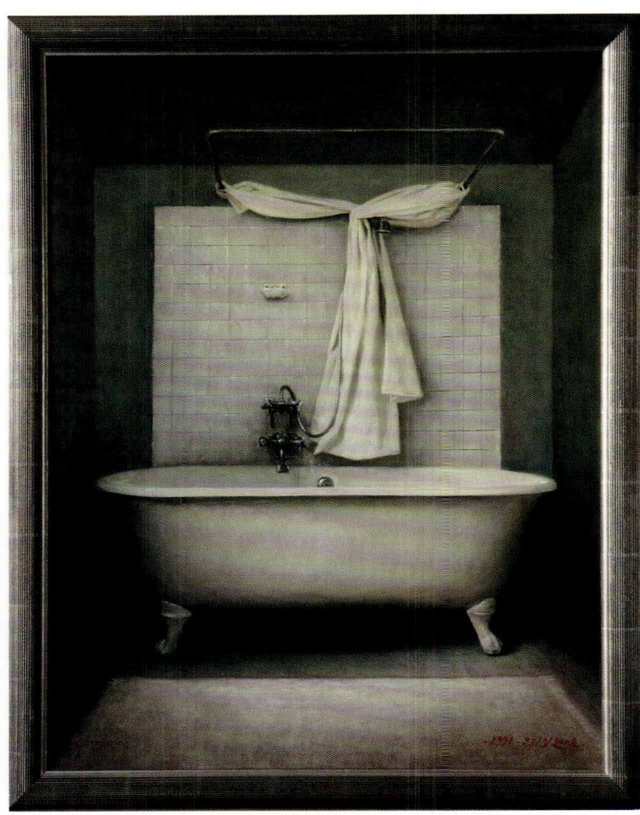

The Tiled Bathroom, 1989. Oil on Cibachrome, 31 ½ × 23 ½ in. (80 × 60 cm).

The Bathroom with the White Curtain, 1987. Oil on canvas, 31 ½ × 23 ½ in. (80 × 60 cm).

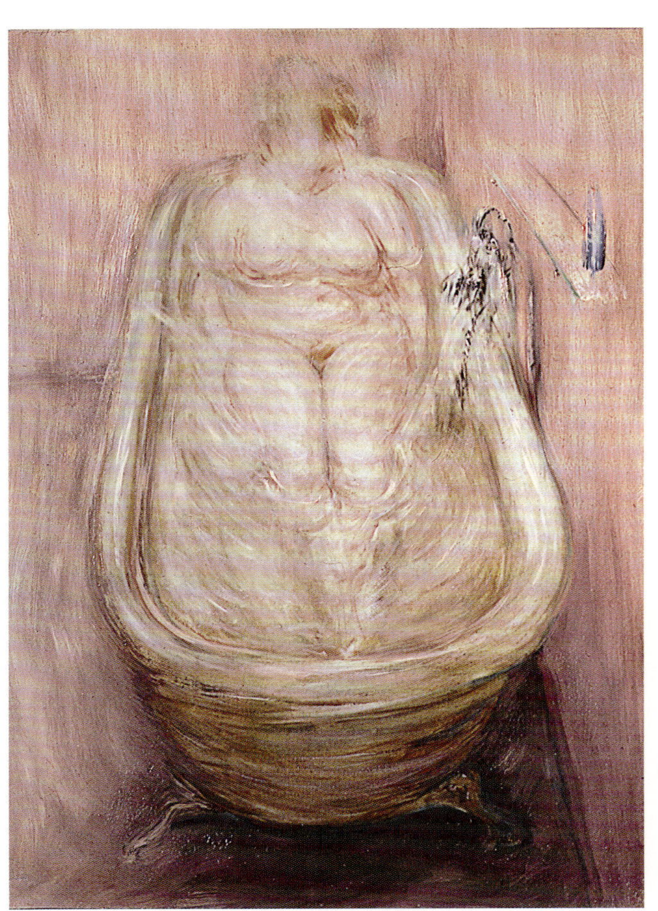

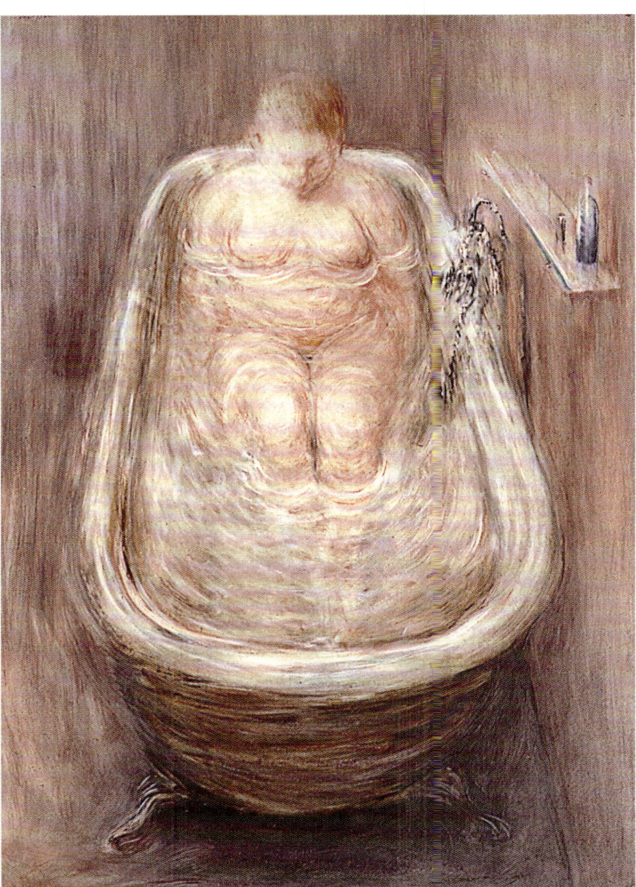

The Pink Bathroom III, 1987. Oil on Cibachrome, 15 ¾ × 11 ½ in. (40 × 29 cm).

The Pink Bathroom V, 1987. Oil on Cibachrome, 15 ¾ × 11 ½ in. (40 × 29 cm).

Facing page: *The Large Bathroom on a Veronese Green Ground*, 1991-2002. Oil on canvas, 45 × 33 ½ in. (114 × 85.5 cm).

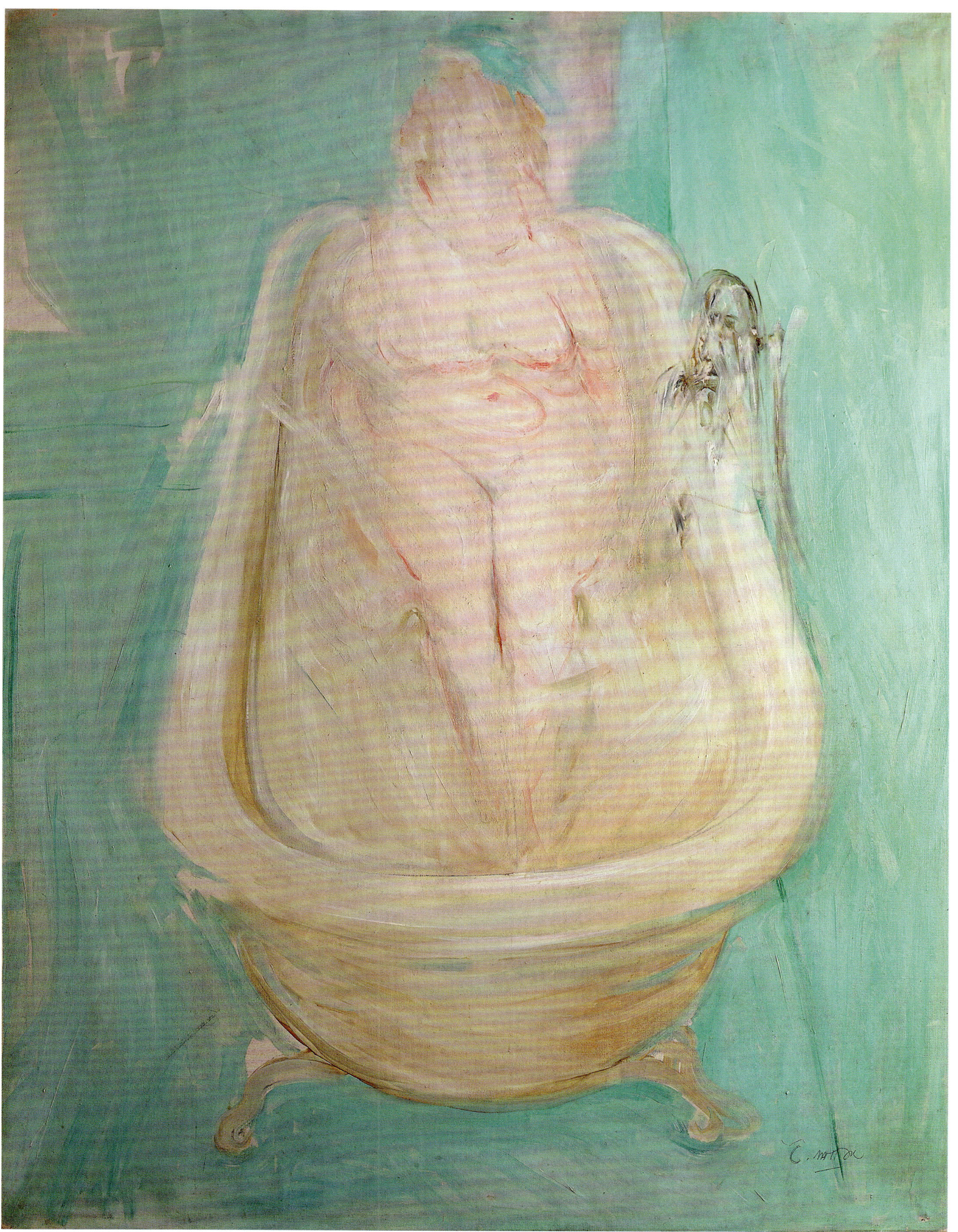

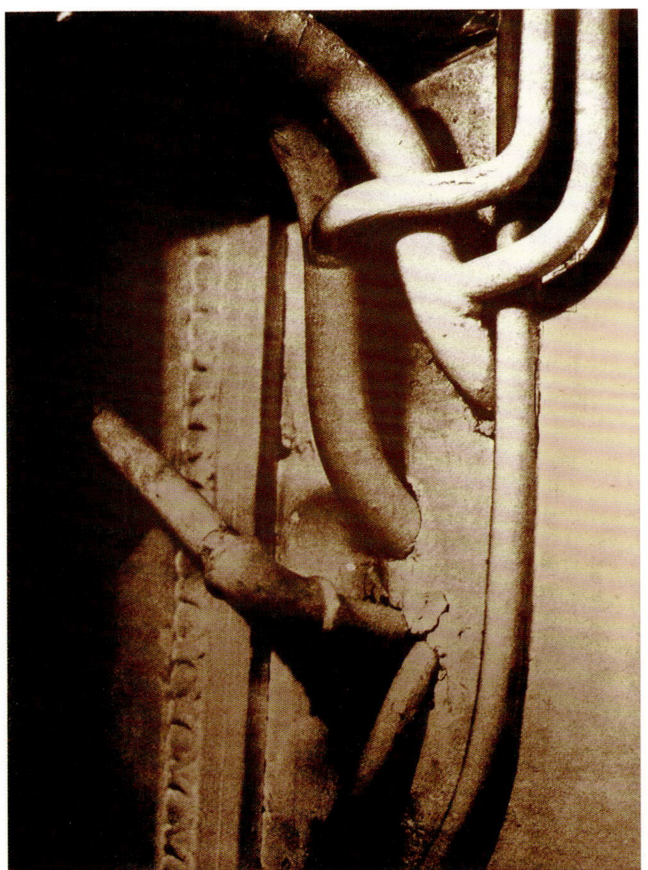

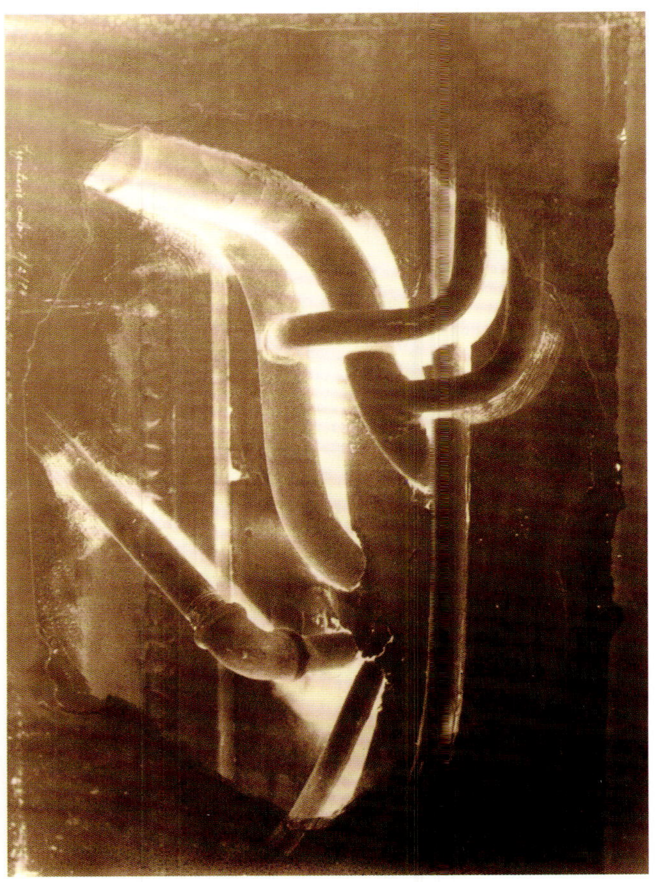

Pipe Nodes III, 1975.
Photograph.

Pipe Nodes IV, 1975.
Photograph.

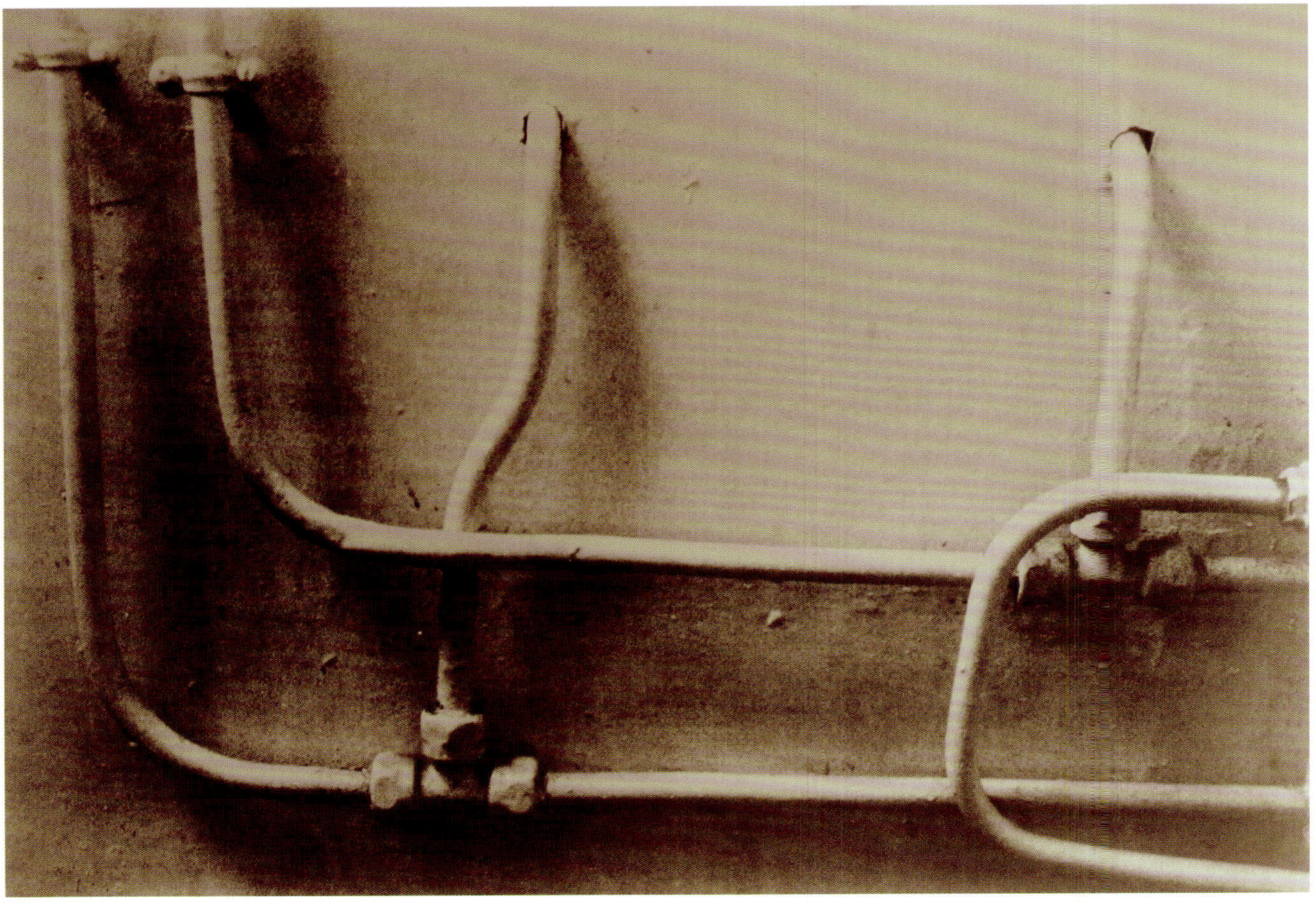

Pipe Nodes II, 1975.
Photograph.

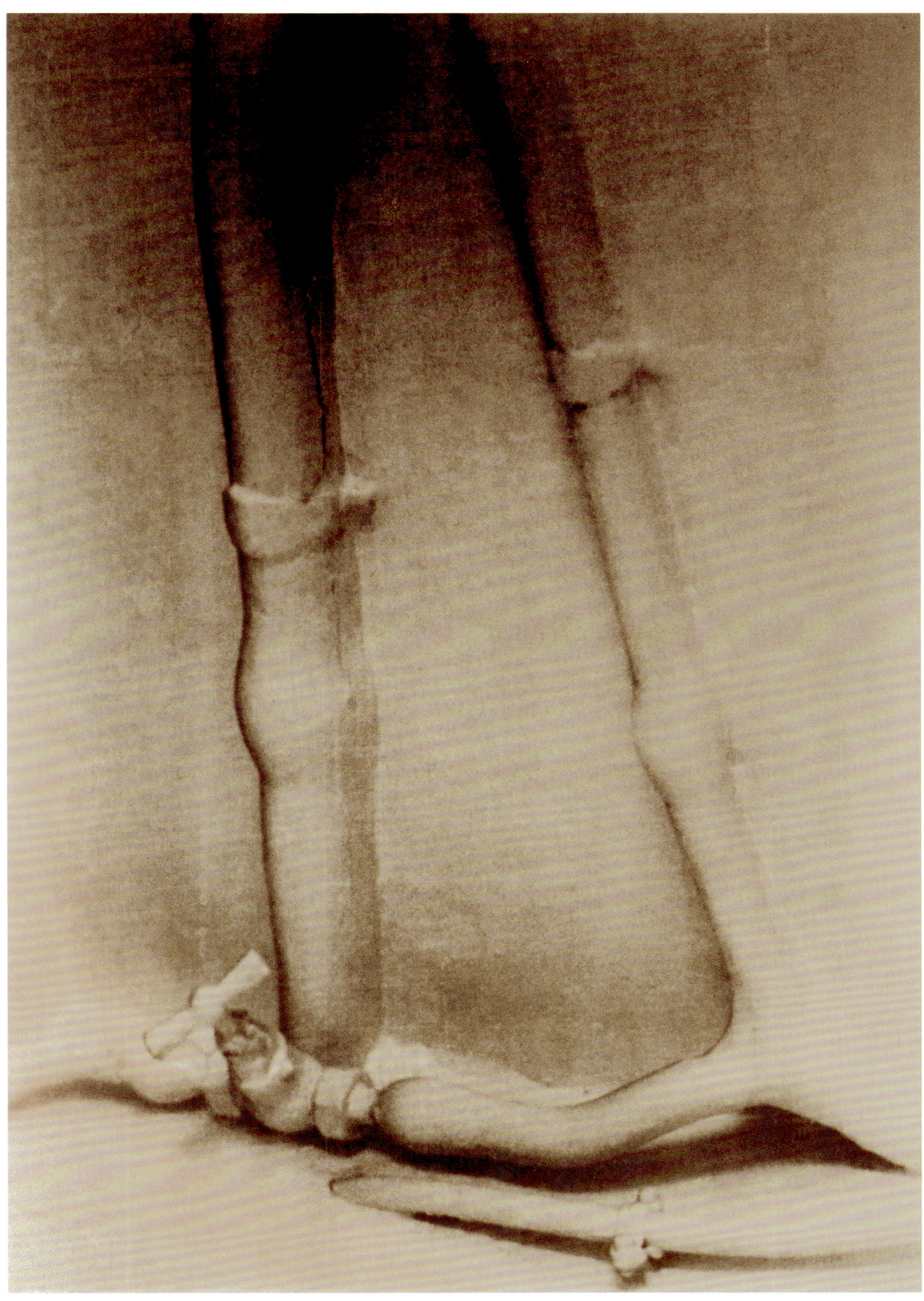

Pipe Nodes I, 1975.
Photograph.

Facing page:
The Delivery Room II, 1987.
Mixed media, 23 ½ × 17 ¼ × 21 ¼ in.
(59.5 × 44 × 54 cm).

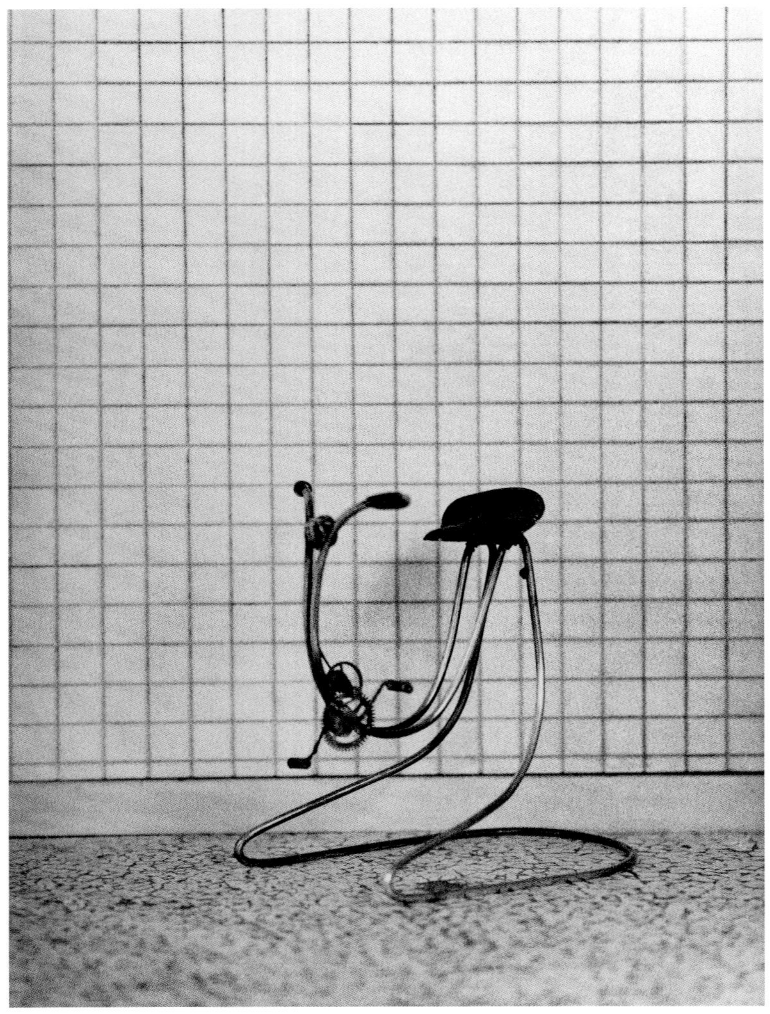

The Exercise Bike, 1987.
Mixed media, 17 ¼ × 29 ¾ × 11 ¼ in. (44 × 75.5 × 28.5 cm).

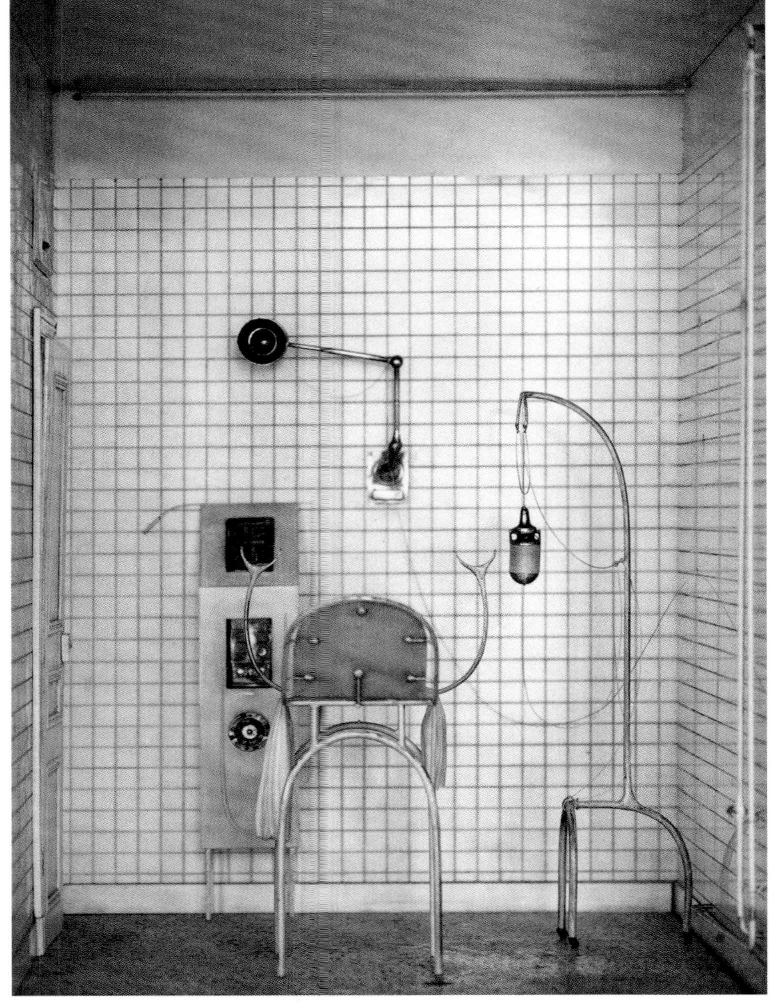

The Delivery Room at Pontoise Hospital in 1952, 1987.
Mixed media, 23 ½ × 17 ¼ × 21 ¼ in. (59.5 × 44 × 54 cm).

Dear Jean, [...] I'm working at the moment on a small room, all-white and tiled, in the middle of which there'll be nothing but an exercise bike. An opening in one of the walls will let in a bright ray of light casting the shadow of my profile on the tiles,

I'll photograph the whole thing and, using the expediency of varnish and patina, I'll turn it into a painting. For, in an era of simulacra, isn't it by simulacra that we will know them? I think I improved my approach and reached what you already referred to in your foreword to my exhibition, *Séductions utopiques*[1]: "an effect of objective irony, in which art too, at the same time as everyday objects, discovers the most elegant way of disappearing." [...]

C. Matton, draft of a letter to Jean Baudrillard, March 18, 1987

1. Exhibition held at Galerie Idéodis (Robert Delpire), Paris, May–June 1983.

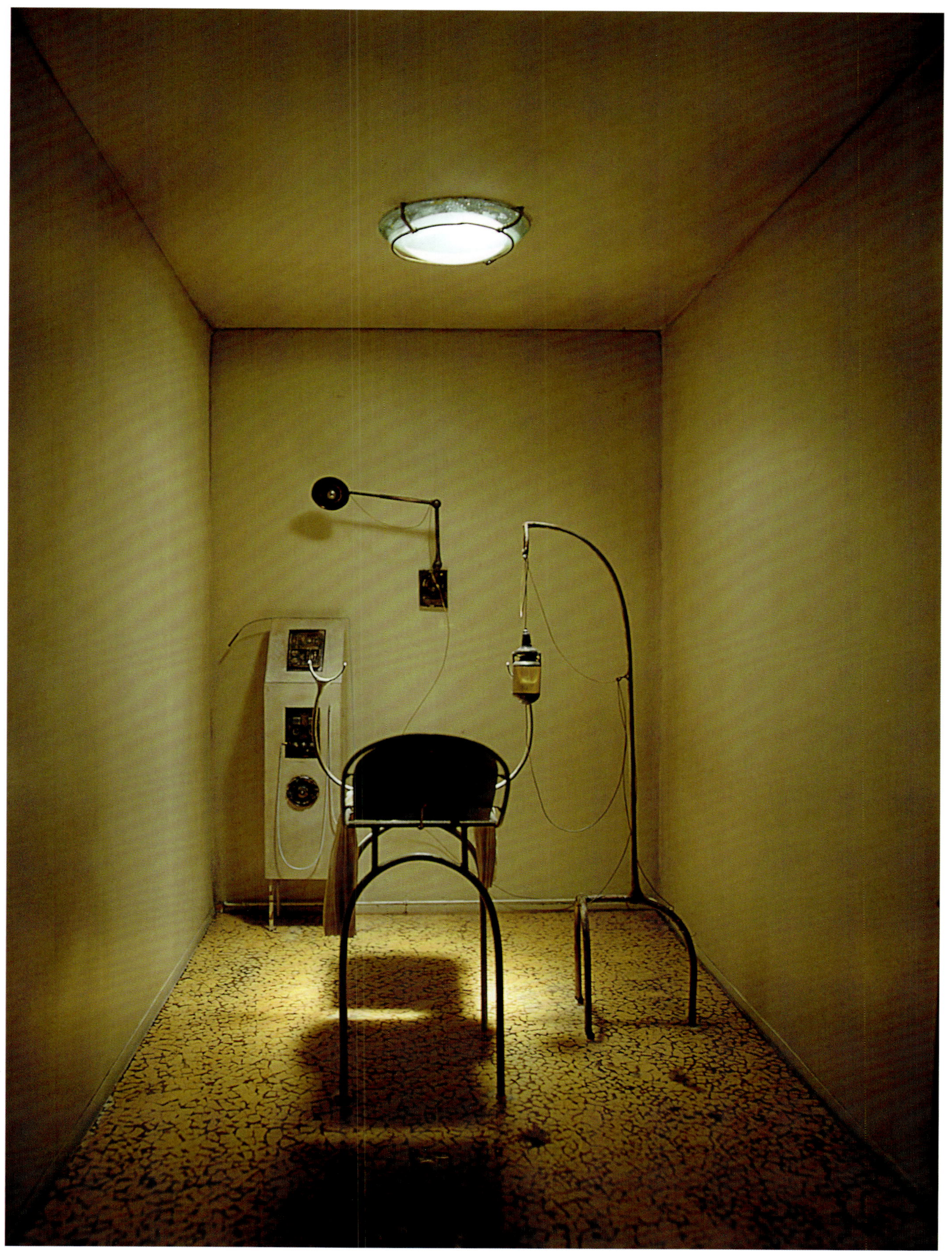

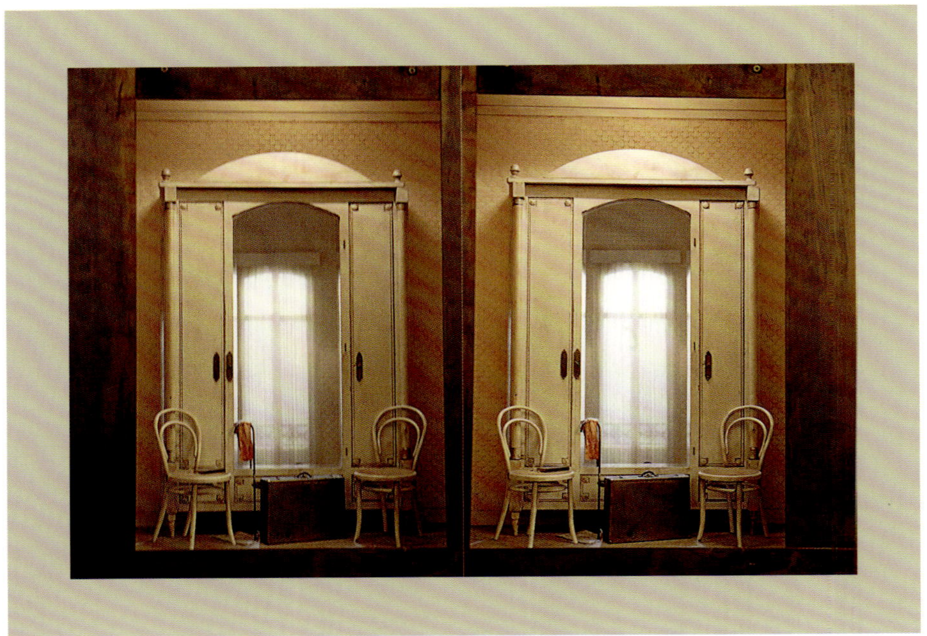

The Mirrored Wardrobe III,
1999.
Mixed media,
29 × 19 ½ × 21 ¾ in.
(74 × 49.5 × 55 cm).

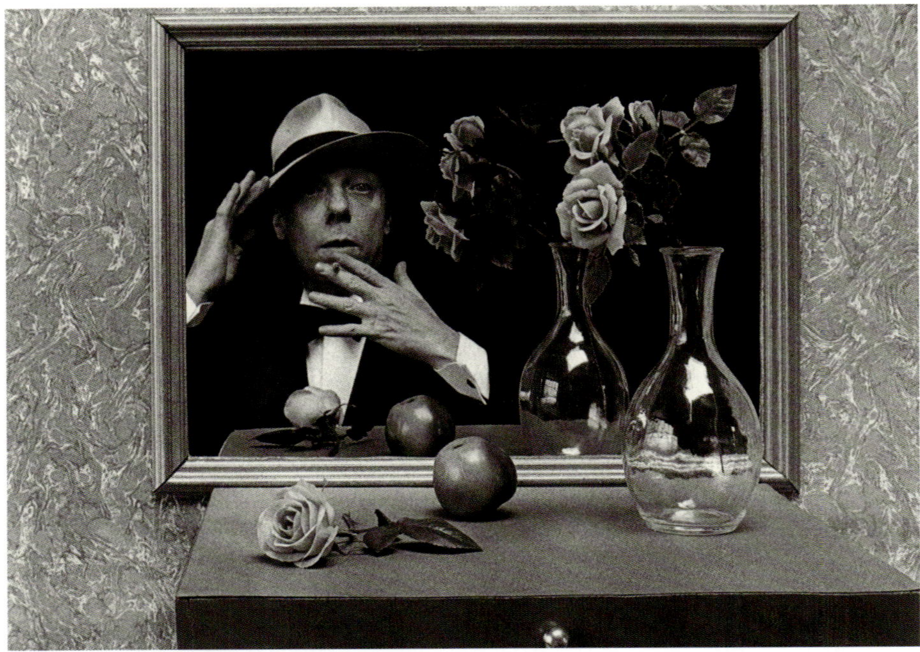

Self-portrait with False Mirror,
1981.
Photograph.

I often fall to making false mirrors, illusions of mirrors, where there is in fact no mirror. I think they can return the viewer to an awareness of reality, so he loses his sense of self and perceives what stands before his eyes more forcefully.

C. Matton, in "Ça me dit, l'après-midi," op. cit.

On paper, I create sets of mirrors and false mirrors where in fact there is no mirror. I use real mirrors, but also two-way mirrors. I've worked a lot on this reflection business, creating illusions of perspective.

C. Matton, in "Regarde les hommes changer," op. cit.

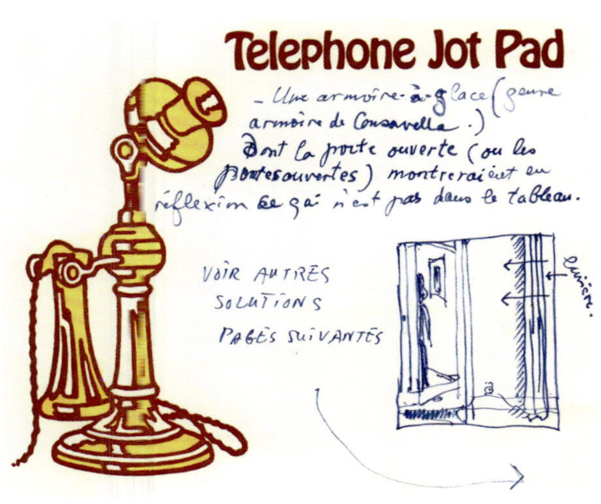

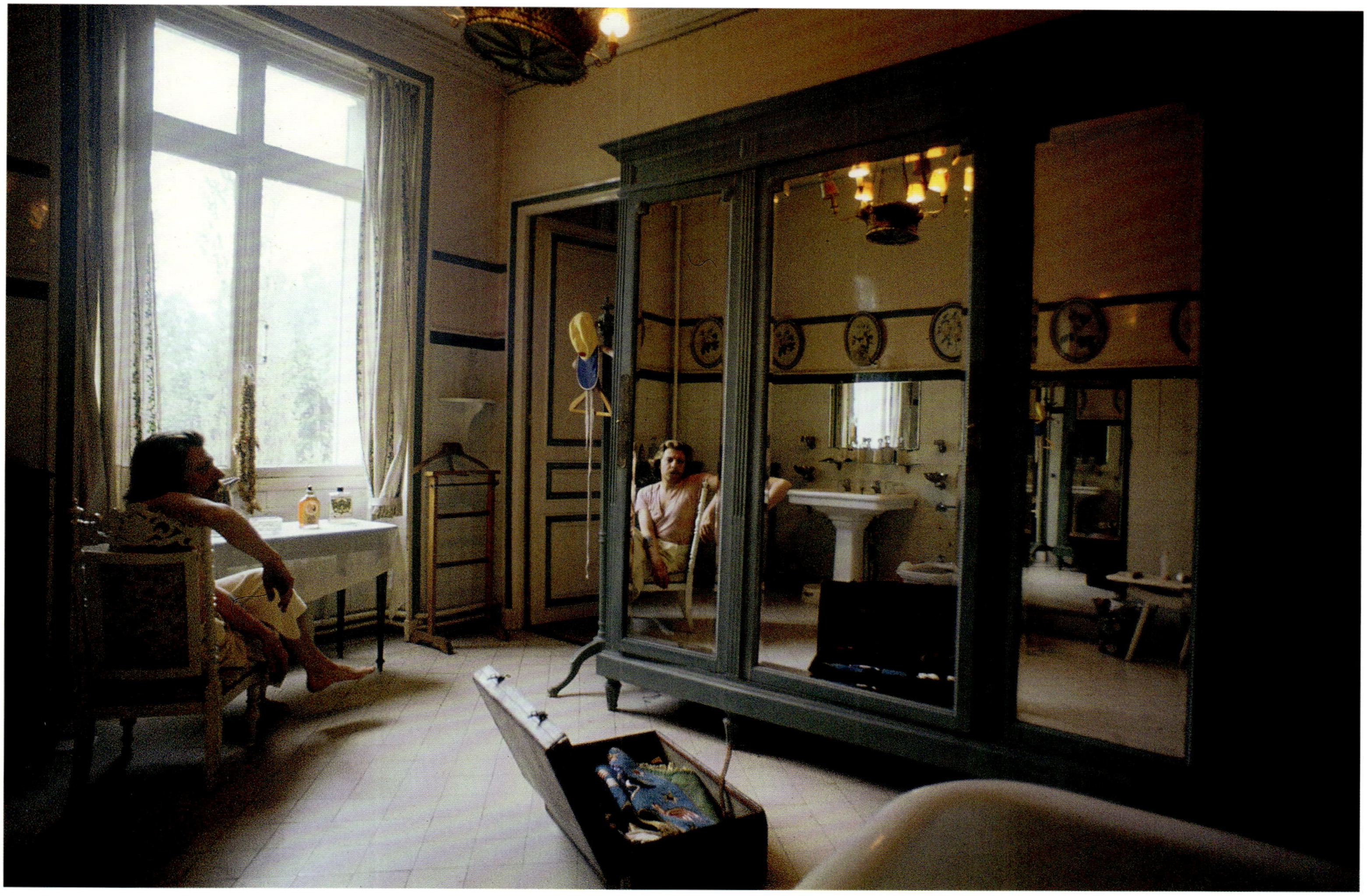

Facing page bottom right, and below:
Personal notes. Five pages
of the Telephone Jot Pad, February 3, 1992

Self-portrait in front of the Mirrored Wardrobe, 1973.
Photograph.

A mirrored wardrobe (same as Consavella's), whose open door (or open doors) show in reflection what does not appear in the picture. Other solutions on the following pages.

What can be seen in the mirror.

Inside the wardrobe. Studies: 1. pen and ink drawing, 2. watercolor.
For the watercolor, thin stripes of orange, yellow, green, and blue.

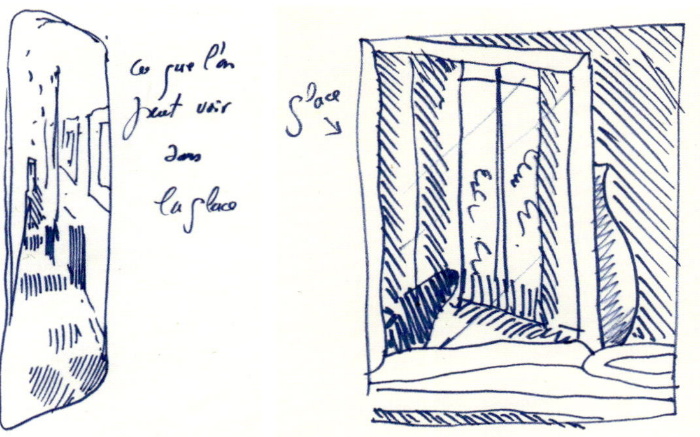

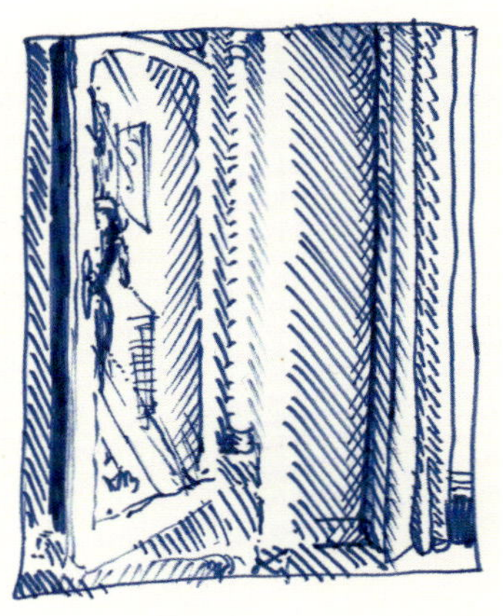

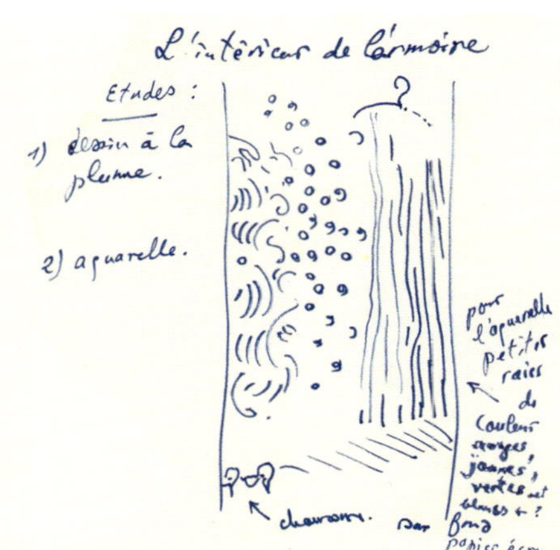

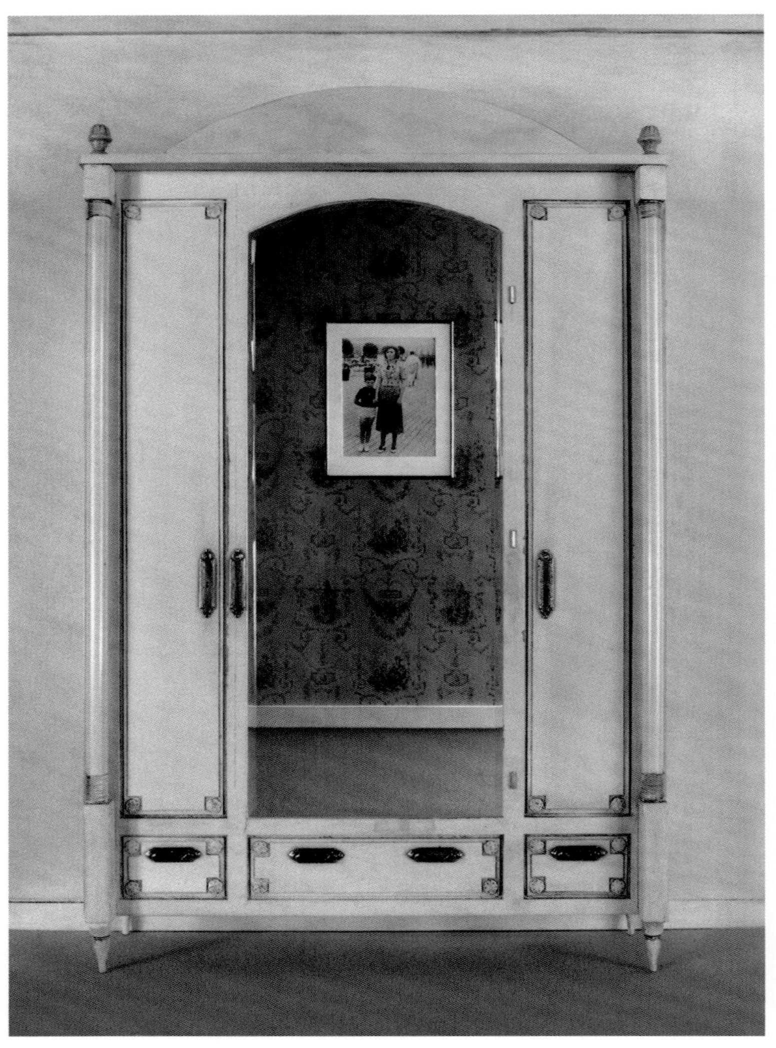

Mirrored Wardrobe, installation no. I, 1987.
Photograph.

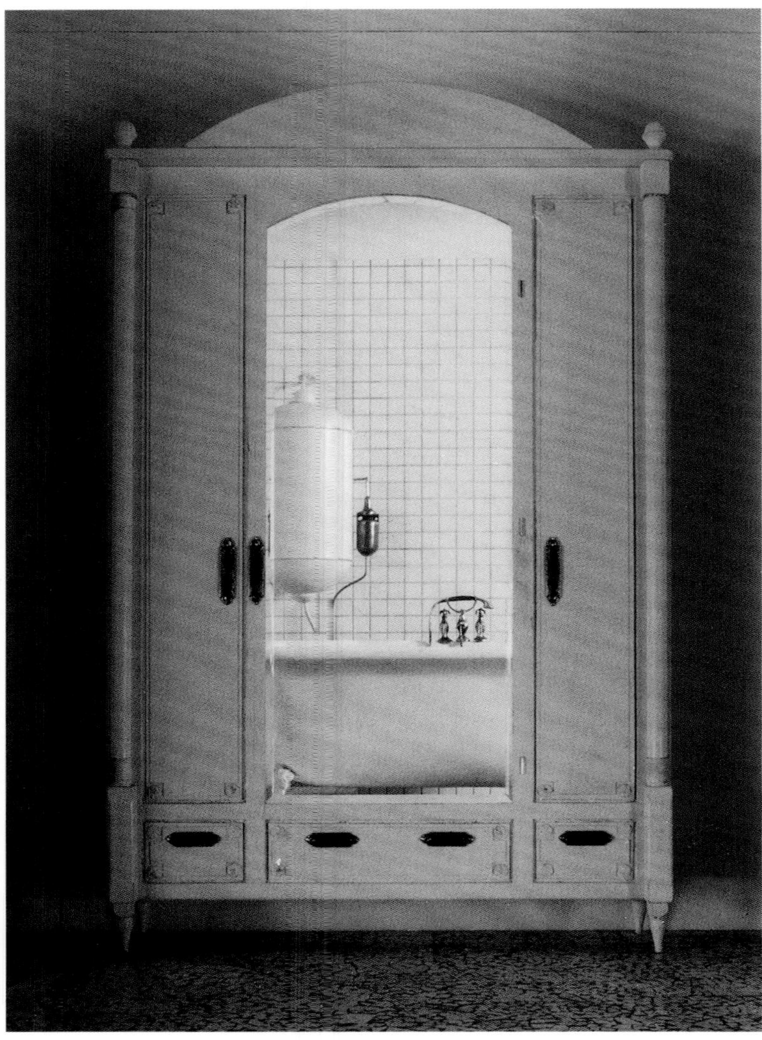

Hôtel Métropole, Mirrored Wardrobe II, 1987.
Photograph.

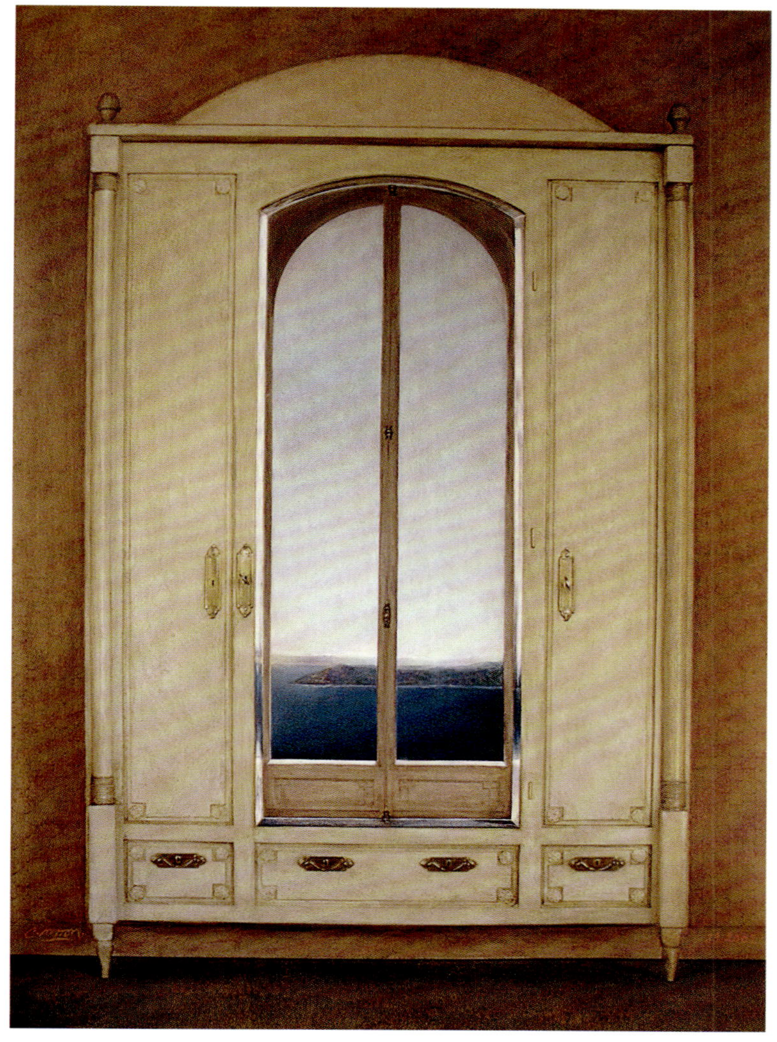
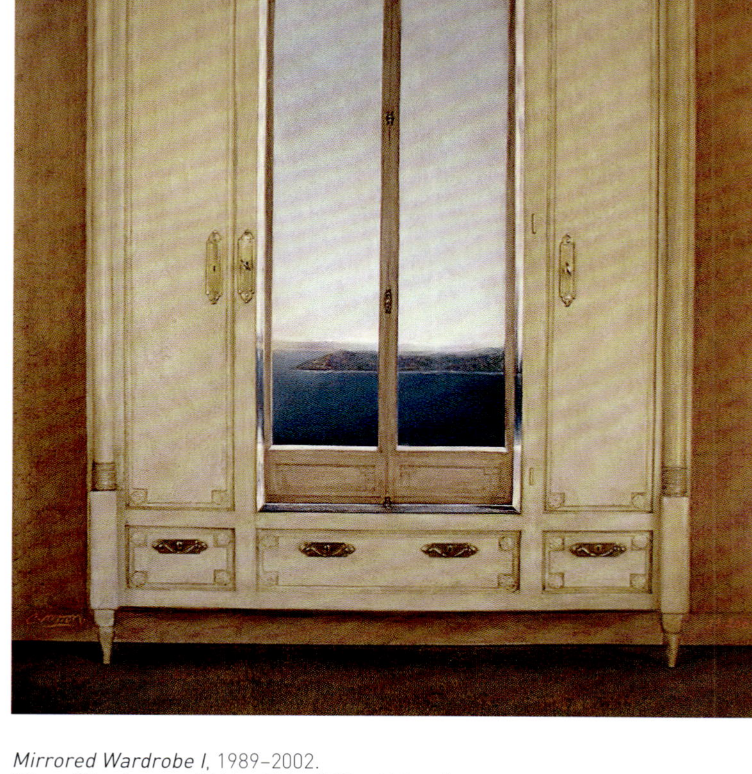

Mirrored Wardrobe I, 1989–2002.
Oil on Cibachrome, 71 ½ × 50 in. (182 × 127 cm).

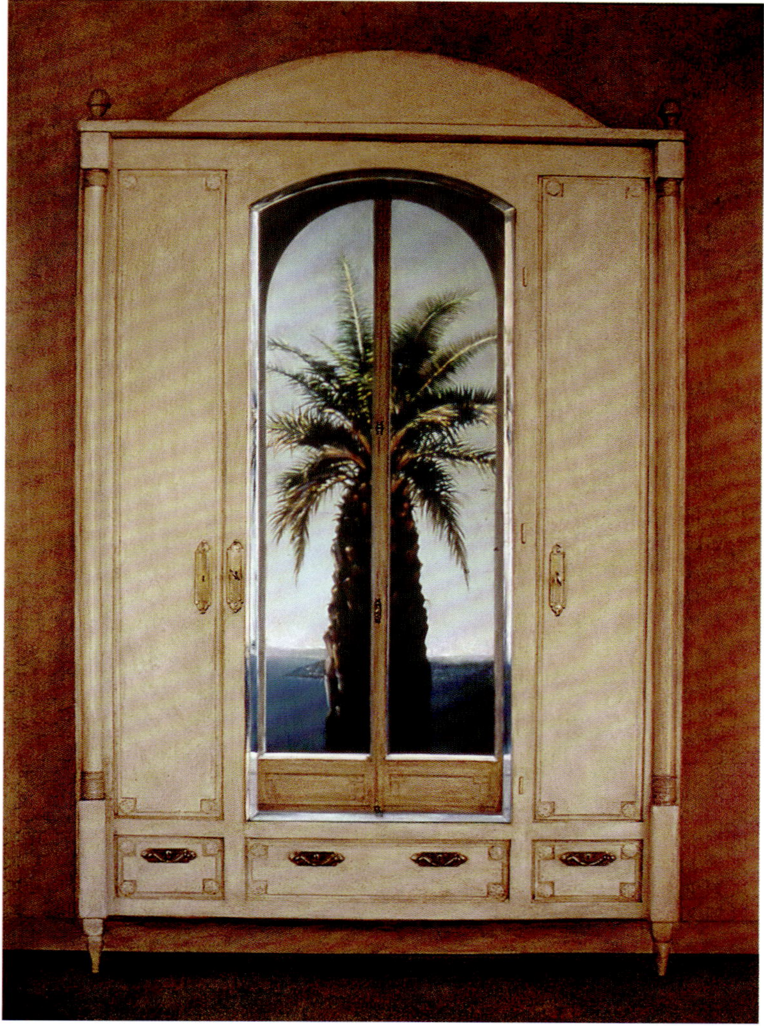

Miami Bow-window, Mirrored Wardrobe III, 2002.
Oil on Cibachrome, 31 ½ × 23 ½ in. (80 × 60 cm).

Charles (the child): Come and play mirrors with me.
Karl (the German soldier): I know exactly why you do that. You think the room you see in the mirror is really there. And, since everything is the wrong way round, you can't recognize it. You'll never be able to get there.
Charles: Why do I like it?
Karl: Because you can see the room as if you weren't there. It lies outside your time, your space, you understand?
Charles: Yes, but why do I like it?
Karl: It gives you the illusion that in that world where there's no time nothing can die.

Narrator [Charles Matton]: Thus, we bore witness to our own absence. It's like a moment from the past lived in the present. Nothing can threaten the past.

La Lumière des étoiles mortes, directed and written by Charles Matton (1994). Feature-length film

Facing page:
Anna Freud's Living Room,
2002.
Mixed media,
22 ½ × 19 ¼ × 21 ½ in.
(57 × 49 × 55 cm).

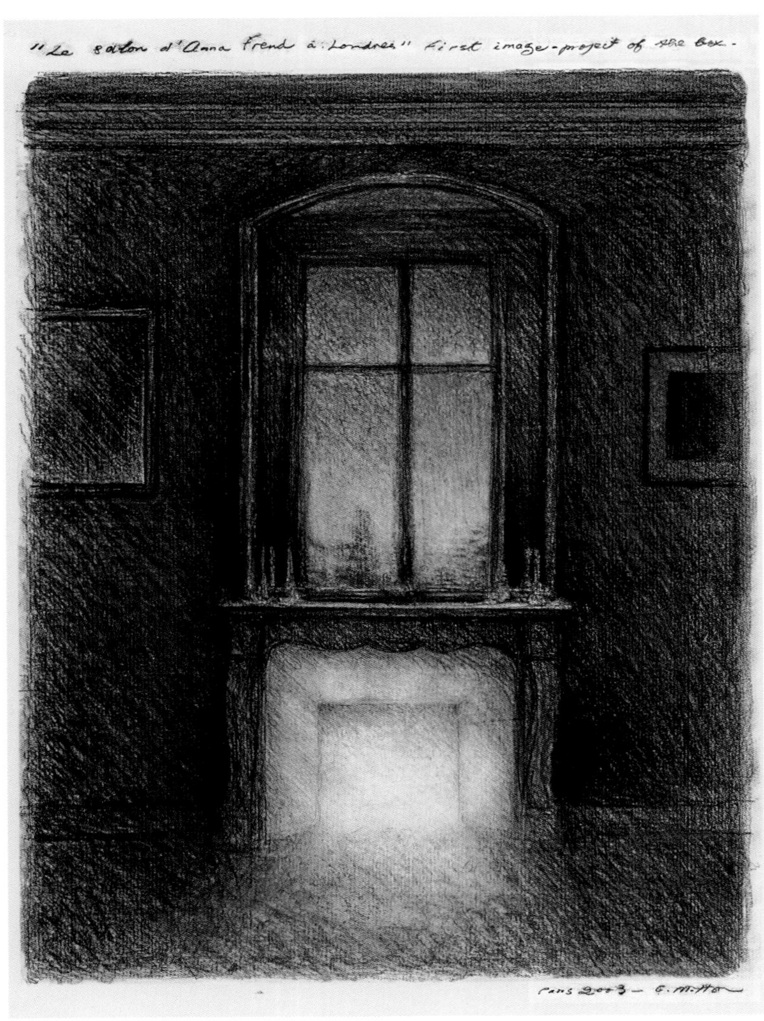

Anna Freud's Living Room, 2001.
Pencil and charcoal on paper, 11 ¾ × 8 ¼ in. (29.7 × 21 cm).

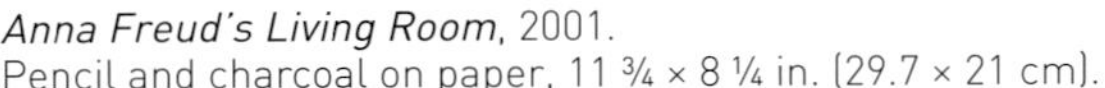

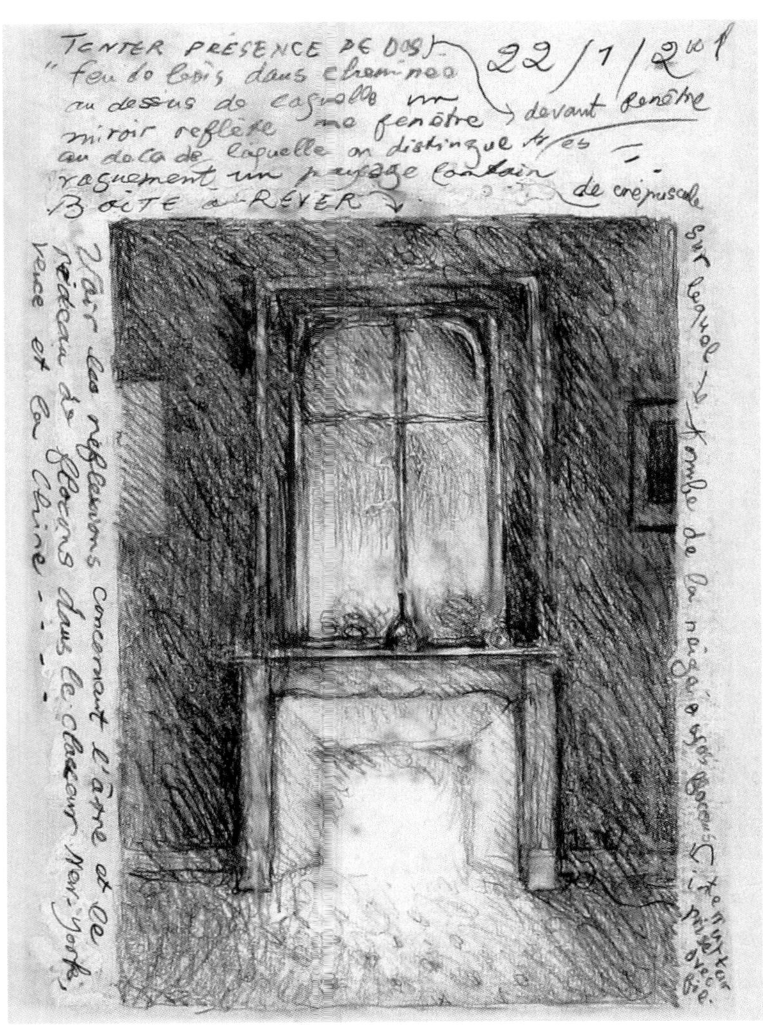

Anna Freud's Living Room, Dream Box, 2001.
Pencil on paper, 11 ¾ × 8 ¼ in. (29.7 × 21 cm).

Try showing a back in front of the window.
Try a wood fire in the fireplace with above a mirror reflecting a window beyond which can vaguely be made out in the distance a crepuscular landscape on which fall big snowflakes.
Dream box.

I believe that realistic drawing, observational drawing, is the toughest exercise for testifying to appearances. It makes it impossible for us to dodge the questions they raise, to be led astray by the charms of color or material. To an extent, drawing forces us to forget ourselves more completely than any other discipline of the visual arts. Because there one has to attest to every last detail, and this presupposes one has to love each of them to the point of disregarding the self, and that without effort—it resembles a really gentle pleasure . . . that of succumbing without misgivings.

Personal note, February 5, 2002

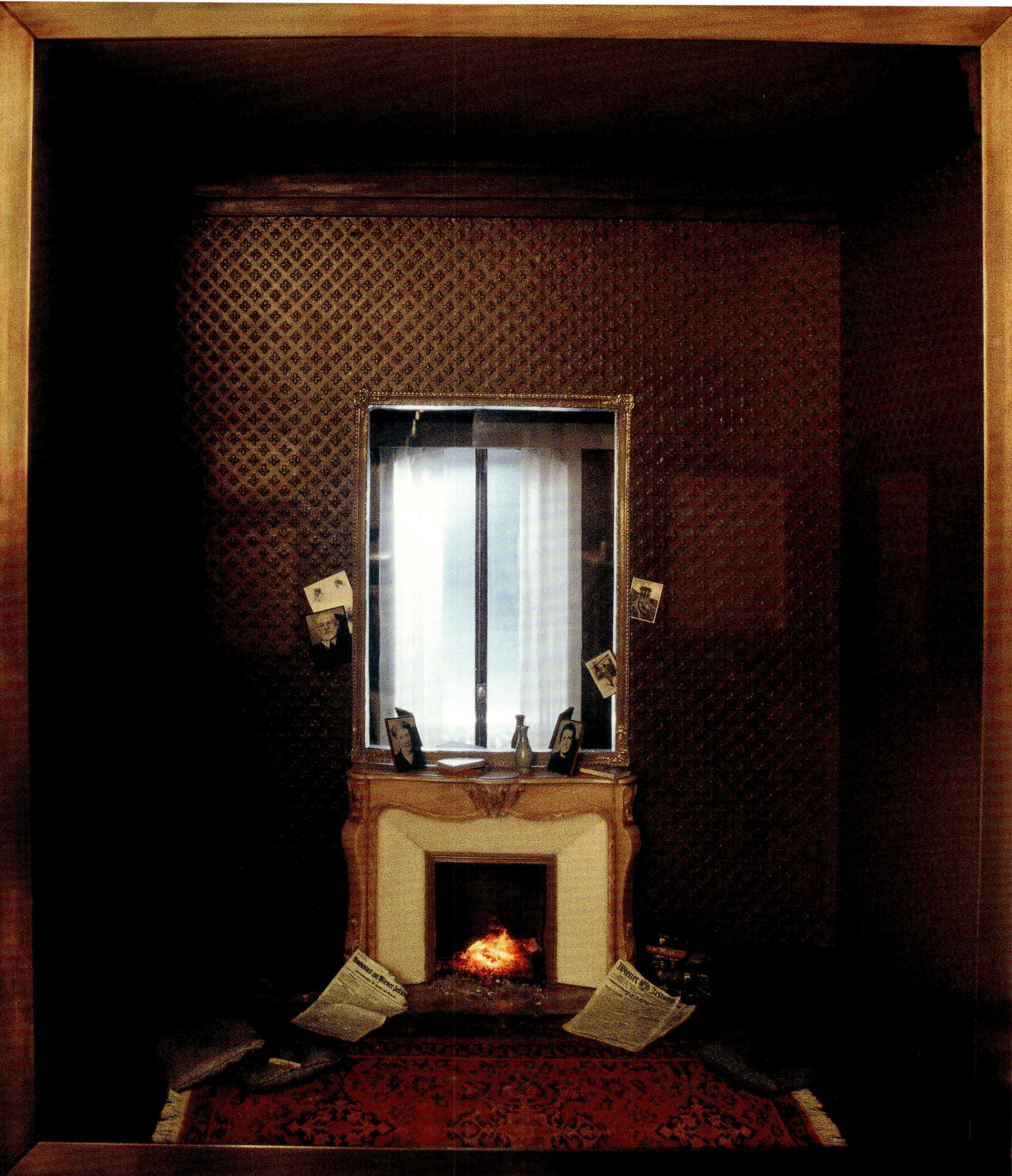

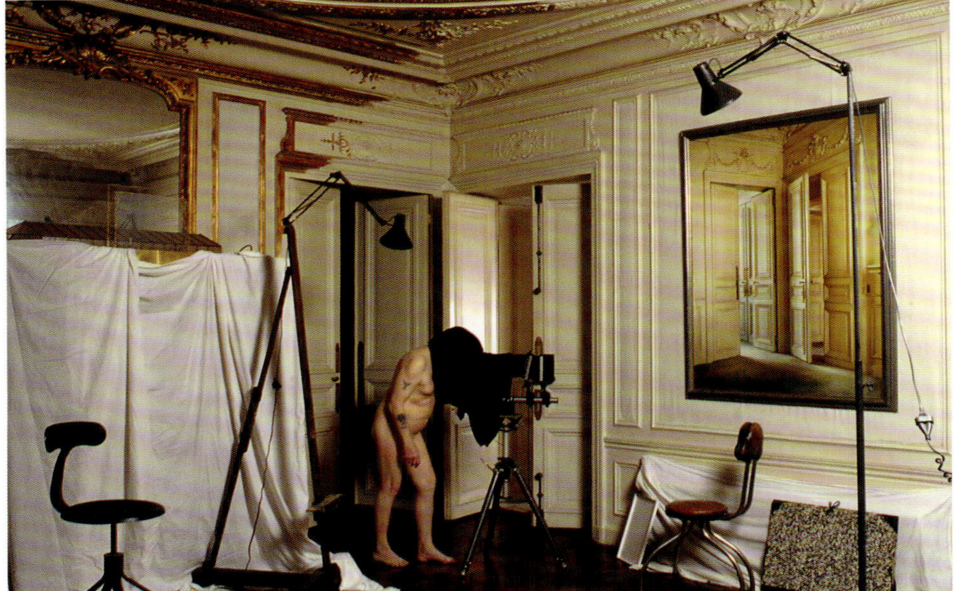

Self-portrait Photographing the Picture The Three Doors, 1990. Photograph.

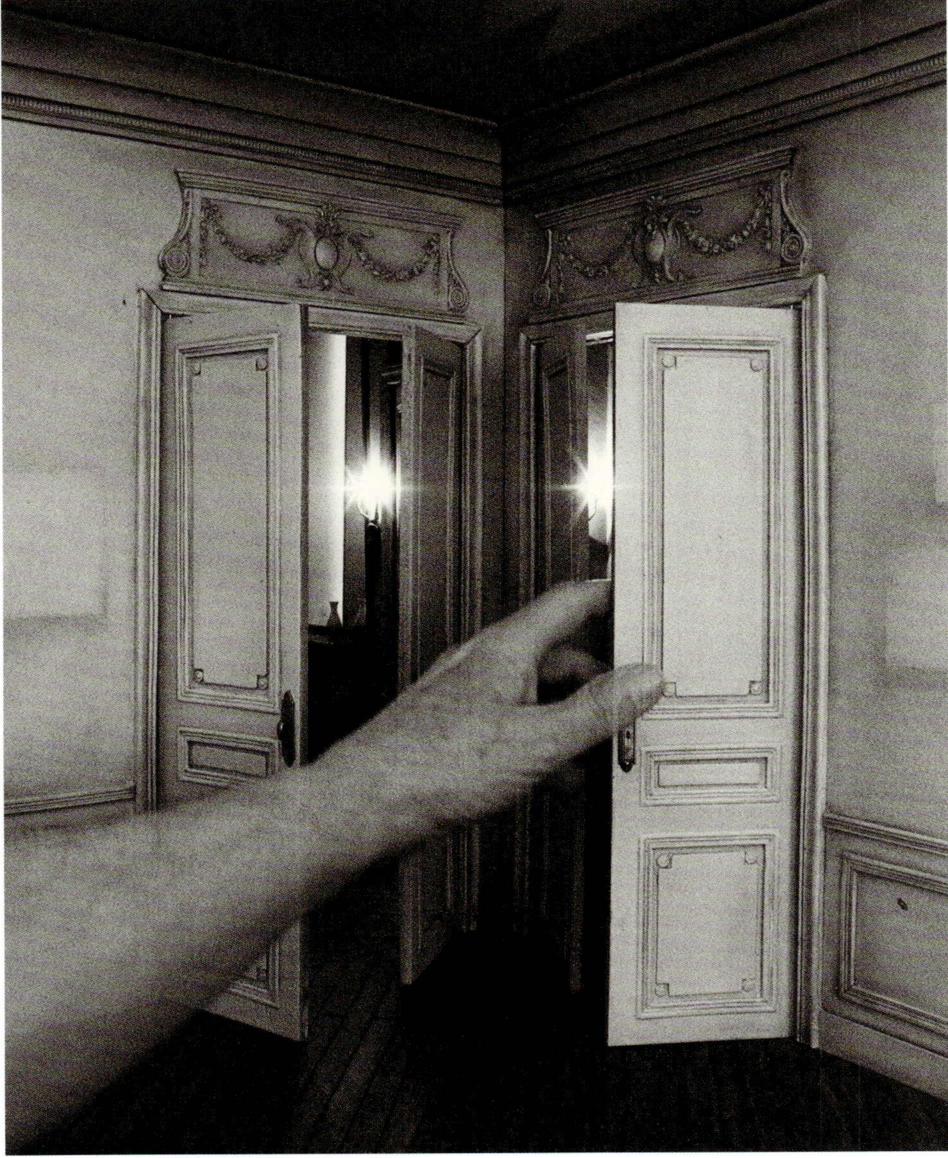

The Three Doors, boulevard Saint-Germain and the Artist's Hand, 1991. Photograph.

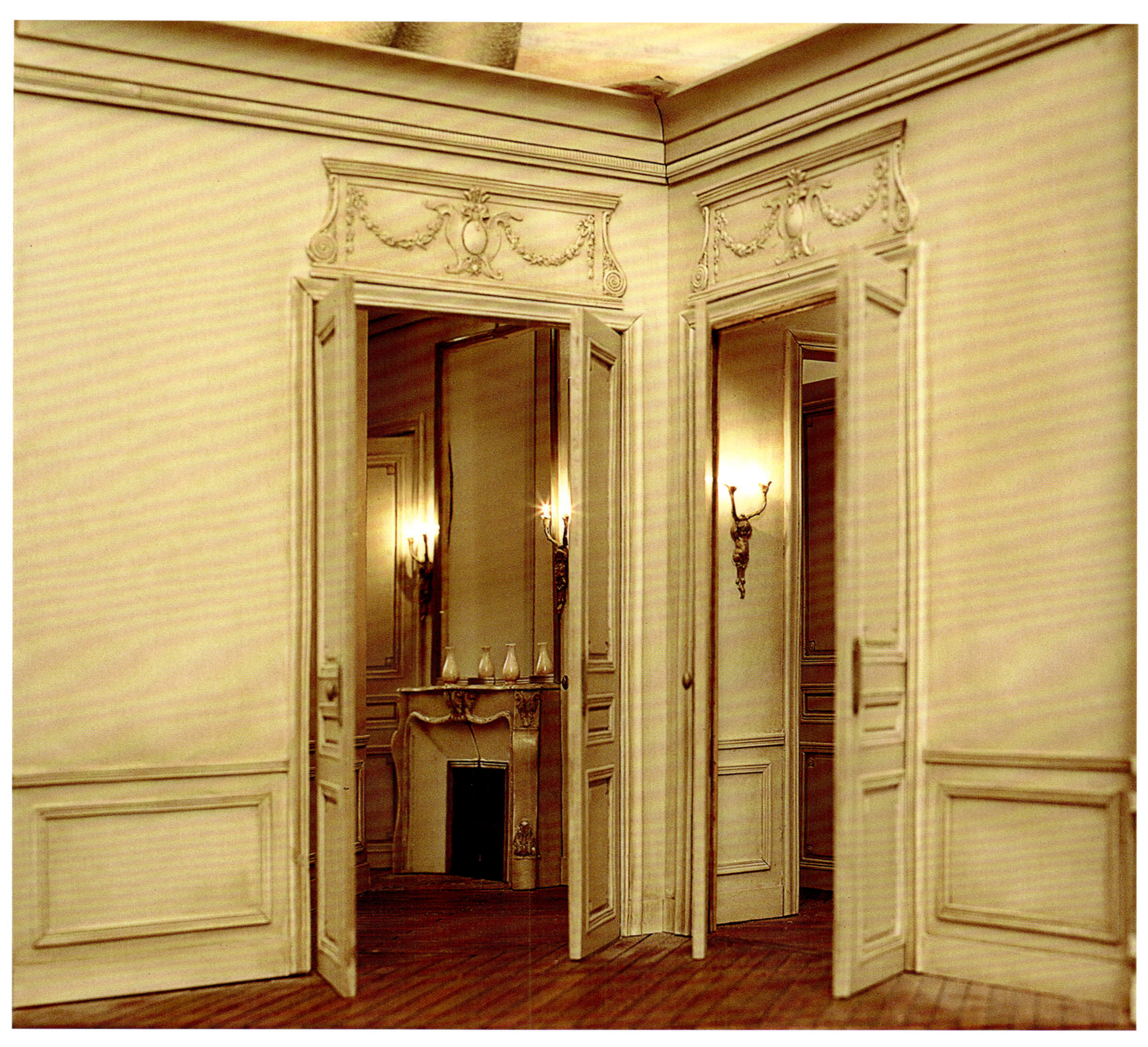

The Three Doors, boulevard Saint-Germain, 1991.
Mixed media, 19 × 20 ¾ × 24 ½ in. (48.5 × 52.5 × 62 cm).

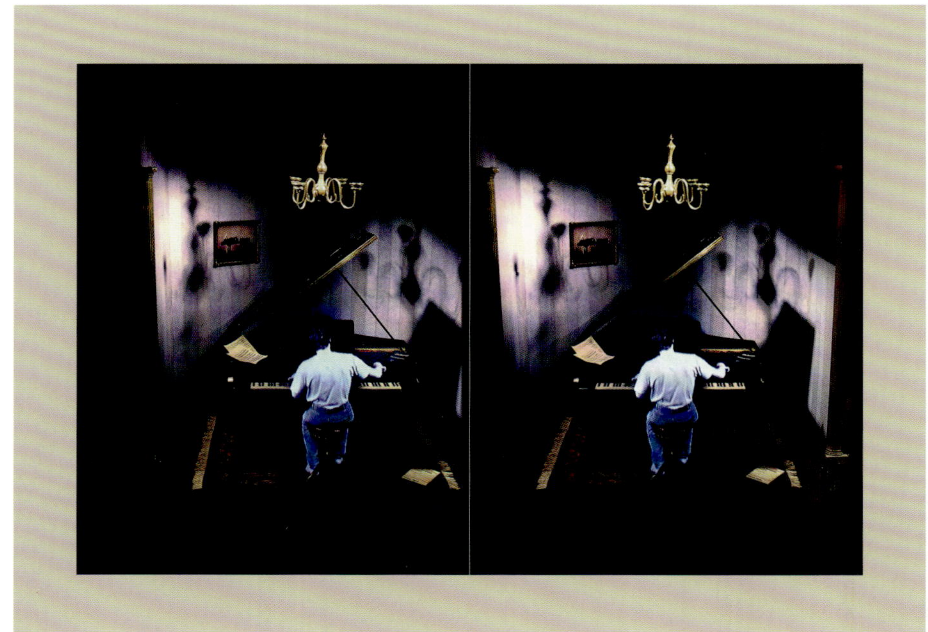

Poisson d'Or, Jules at the Piano II, 2004.
Mixed media and video,
34 ½ × 21 ¼ × 36 ¼ in.
(88 × 54 × 92 cm).

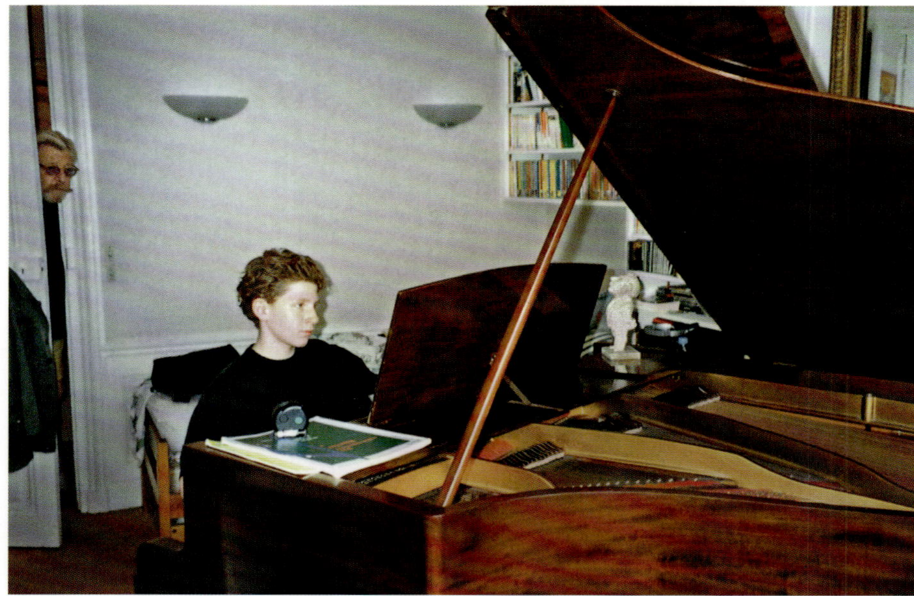

Charles at the Door to Jules's Bedroom, 1992.
Photograph Léonard Matton.

Debussy, *Poisson d'Or*

My son Jules is a pianist. He'd been studying this piece by Debussy for a long time. I had the pleasure of living and working for weeks in the company of this music. I often went to watch him in his little room entirely taken up with his piano. Slowly, on tiptoe, I'd walk up close to the half-open door and hover there without moving, holding my breath, so he wouldn't notice I was looking at him. I wanted these minutes, these moments, to last. I needed to do a fair amount of research before arriving at the correct technical solution. I think I've managed to preserve this memory, capturing it, as it were, in a box.

C. Matton, Introduction to *Within These Walls* (NY: Forum Gallery, 2004). Exhibition

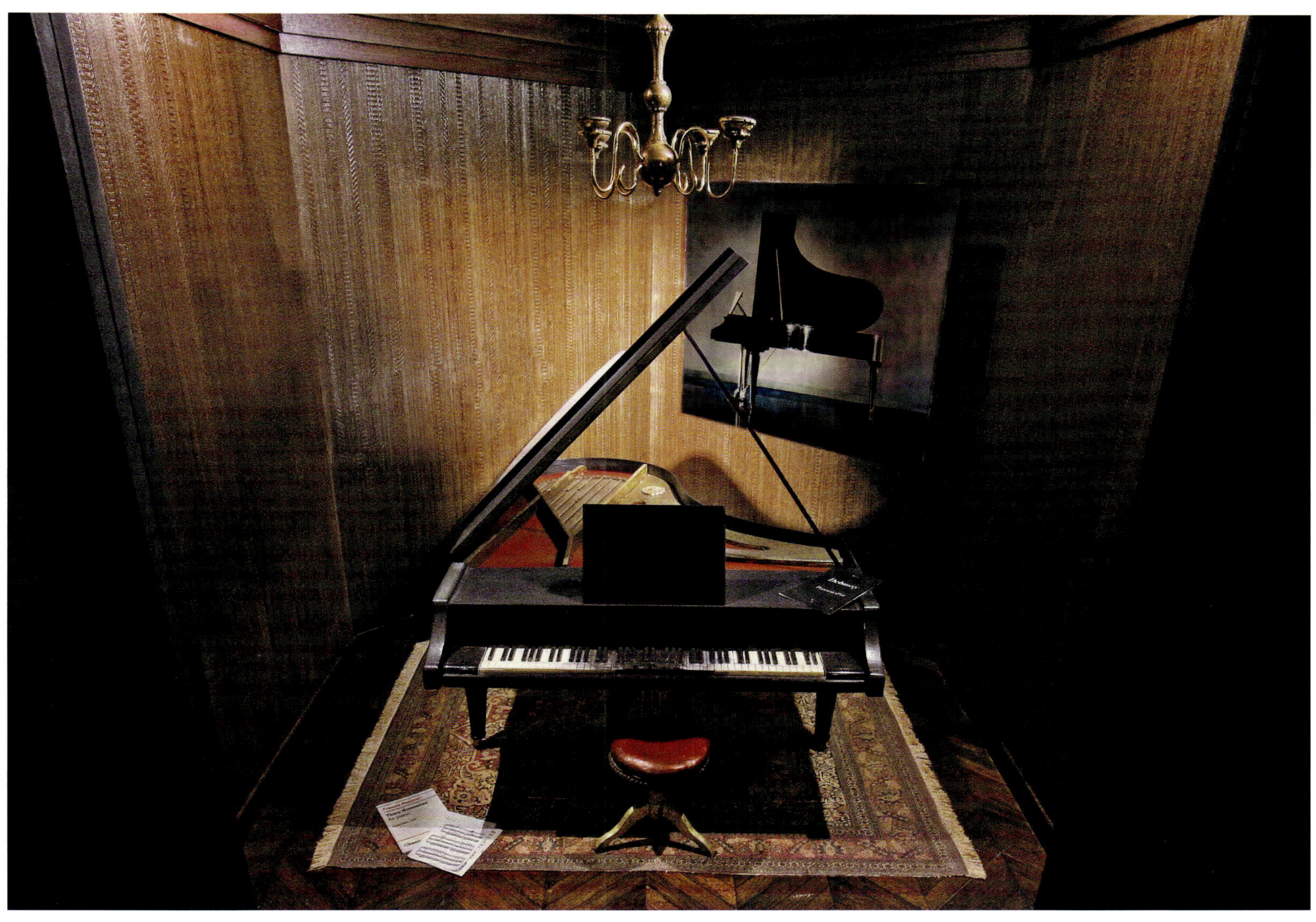

Poisson d'Or (detail), 2004.

Poisson d'Or,
Jules at the Piano
(detail), 2004.

Léonard plays Shakespeare. Jules plays the piano.
How joyful is a home where music is studied!

Personal note, December 3, 2004

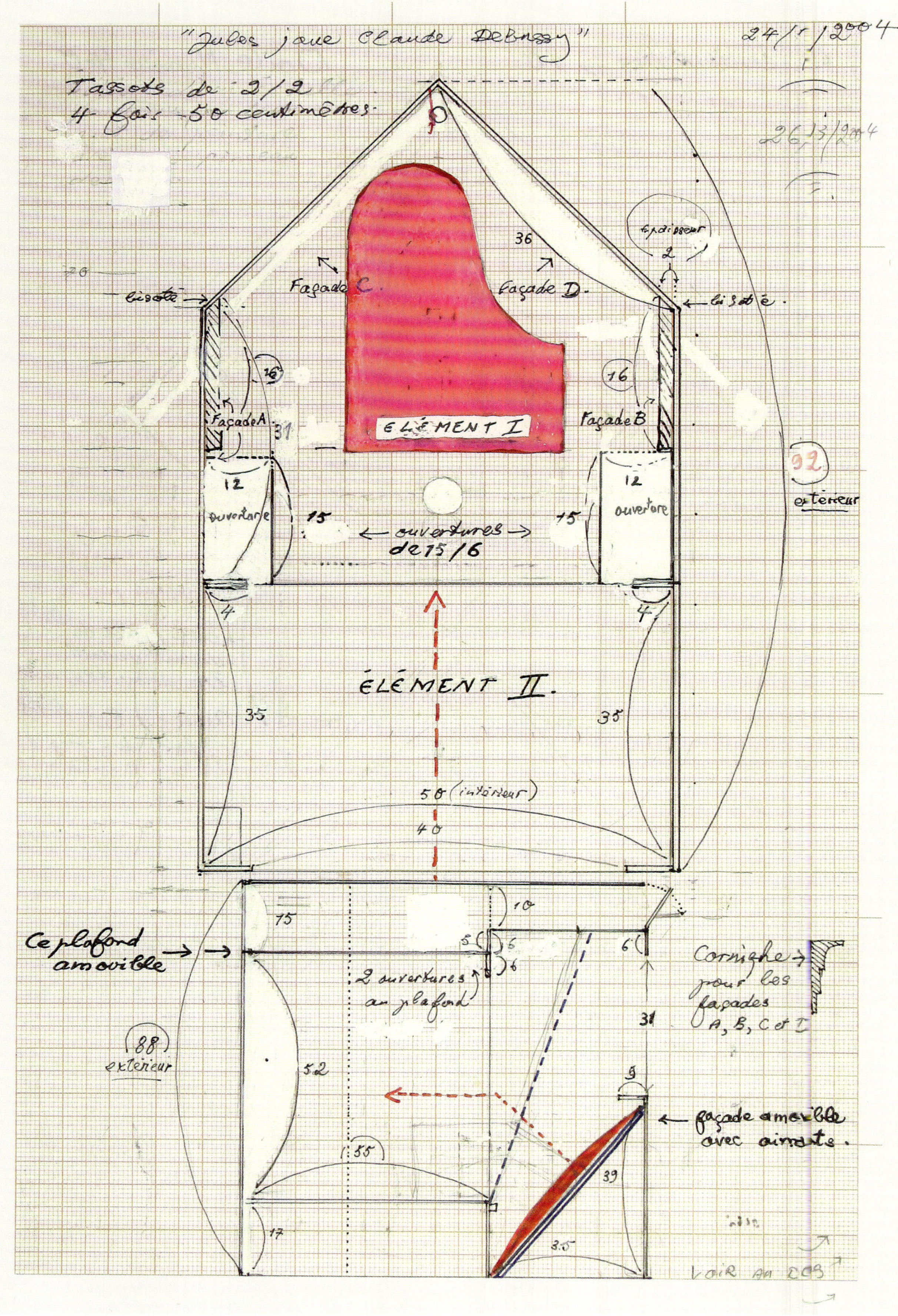

Jules Playing Claude Debussy, 2004.
Pencil and felt pen on graph paper, 11 ¾ × 8 ¼ in. (29.7 × 21 cm).

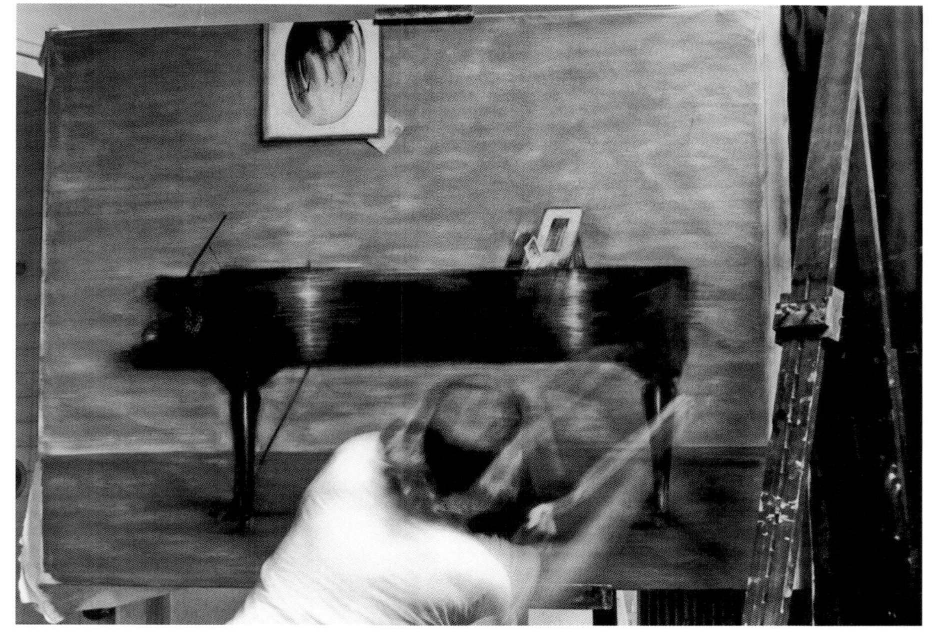

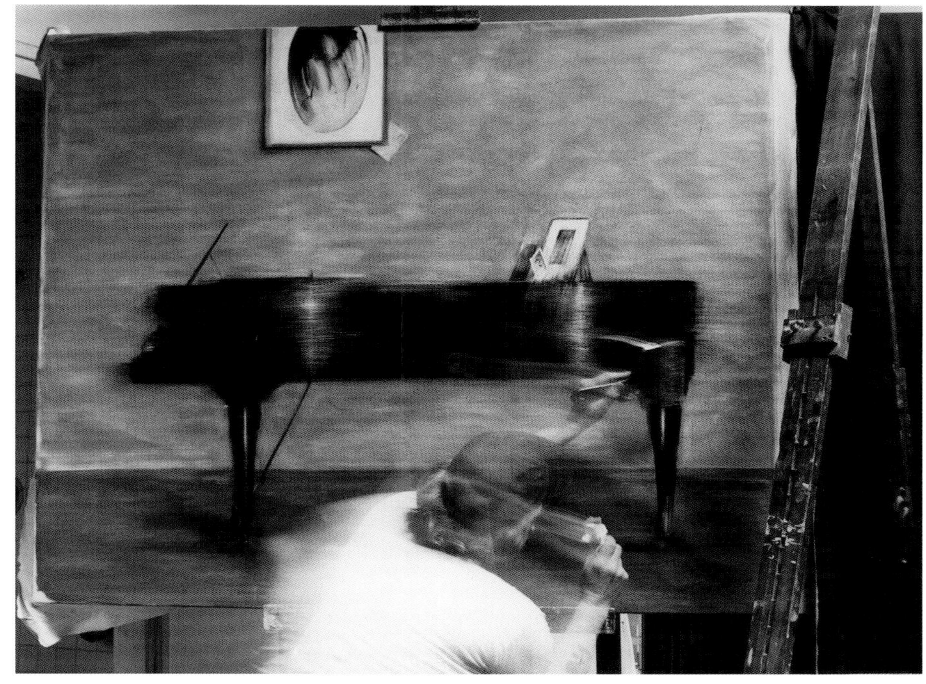

Self-portrait Painting The Grand Piano, I *and* IV, 1987. Photographs.

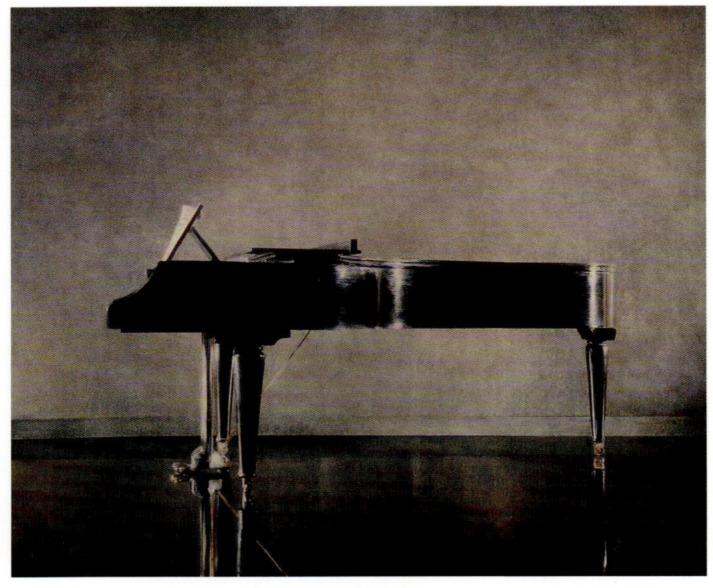

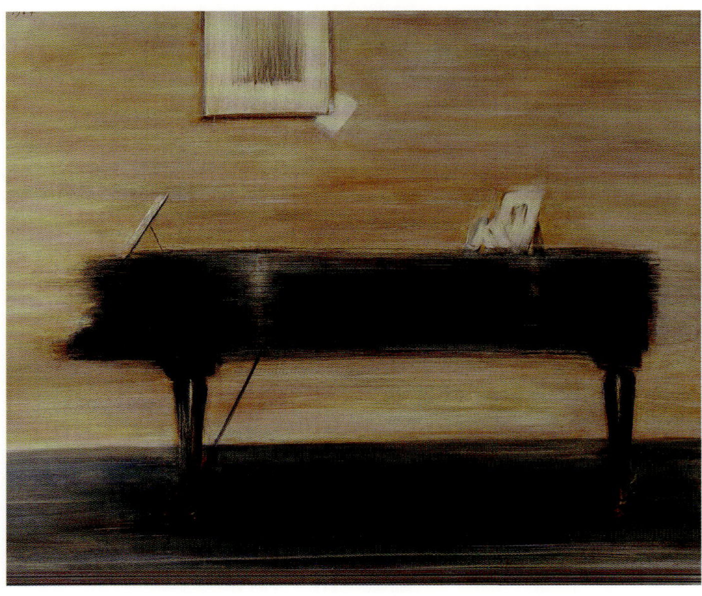

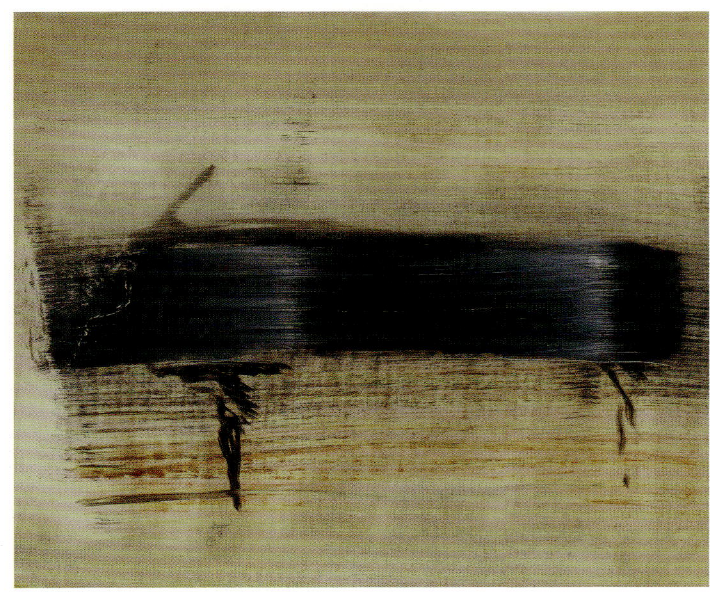

Diptych, Piano I, 1988.
Oil on Cibachrome,
35 × 45 ½ in. (89 × 116 cm).

Gestural Piano II, 1988.
Oil on canvas,
23 ¾ × 26 in. (60.5 × 66 cm).

Succinct Piano, 1986.
Oil on canvas,
15 × 18 in. (38 × 46 cm).

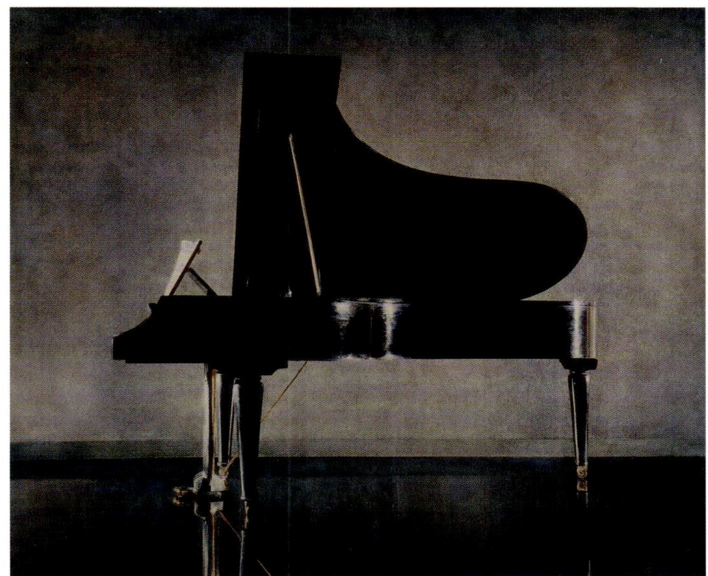

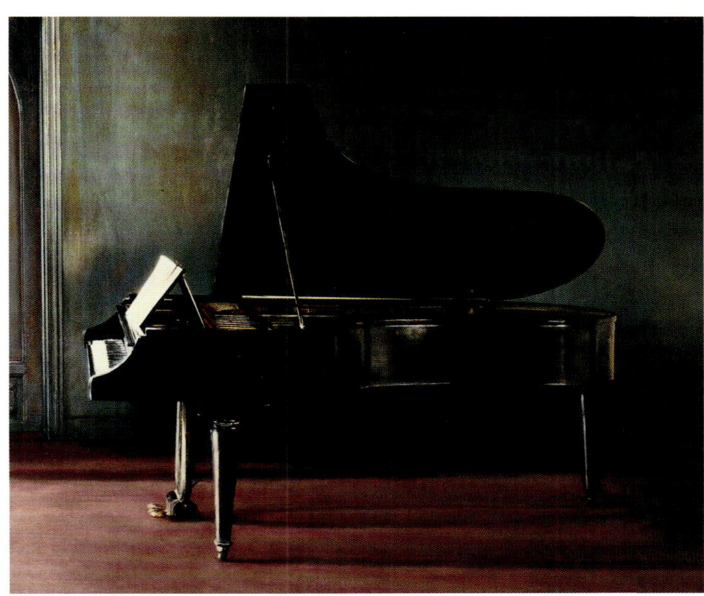

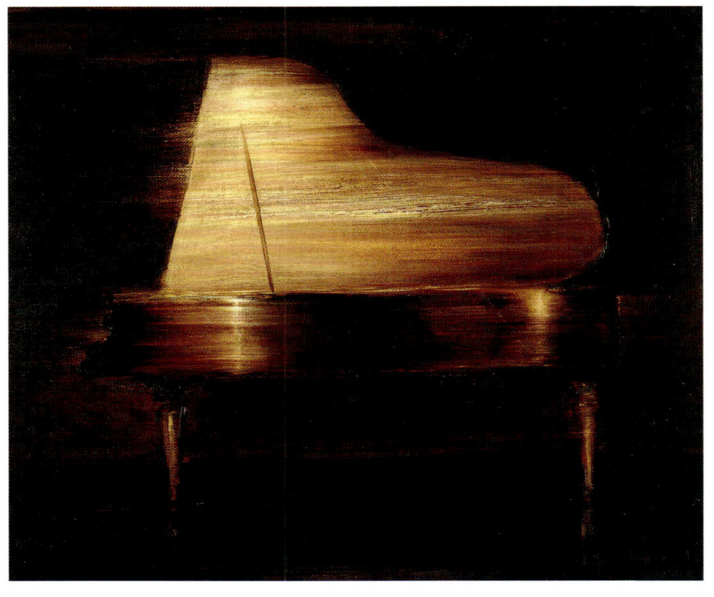

Diptych, Piano II, 1988.
Oil on Cibachrome,
35 × 45 ¾ in. (89 × 116 cm).

Gabriel García Márquez's Piano,
1987.
Oil on Cibachrome,
36 ¼ × 45 ¼ in. (92 × 115 cm).

Little Reddish-brown Piano,
1967–1988.
Oil on canvas,
12 ¼ × 16 in. (33 × 41 cm).

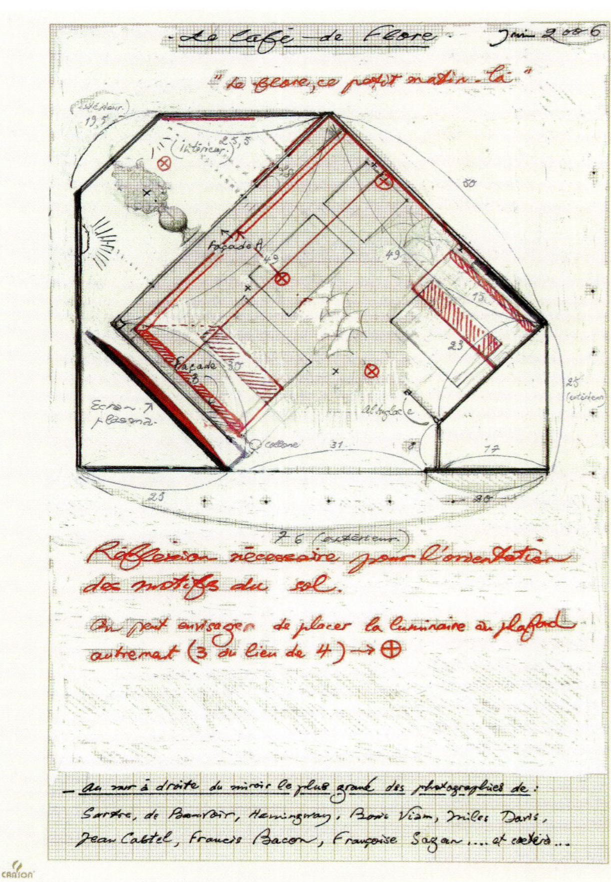

The Café de Flore, 2006.
Pencil and felt pen on graph paper,
11 ¾ × 8 ¼ in. (29.7 × 21 cm).

"The Flore, early that morning"

Reflection necessary to line up the motifs on the floor.

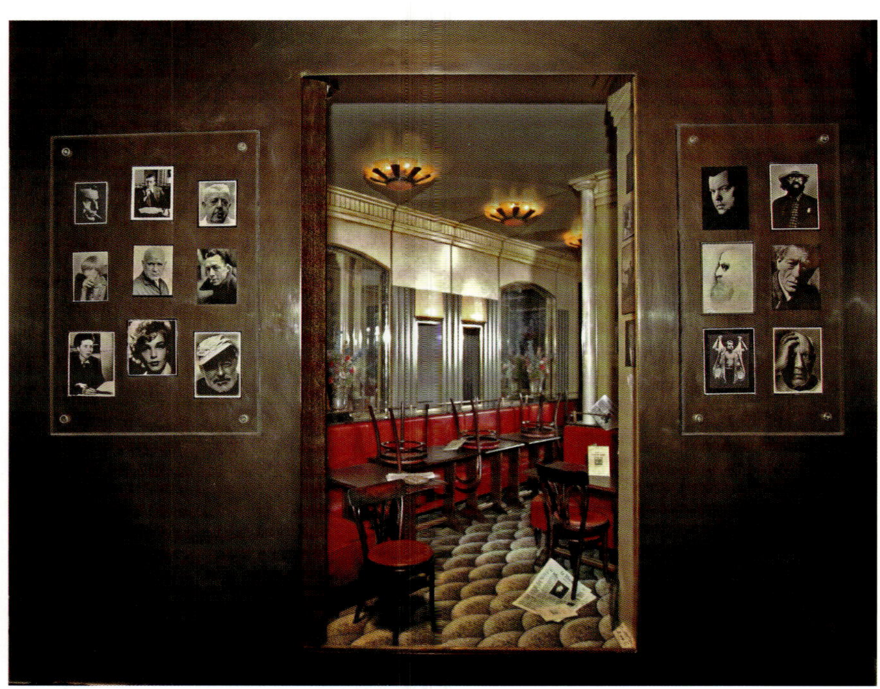

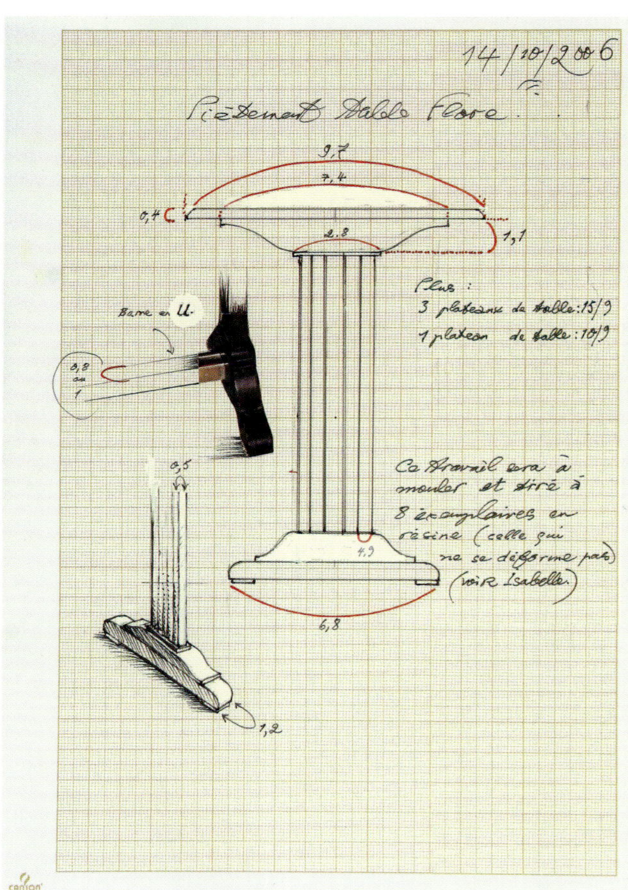

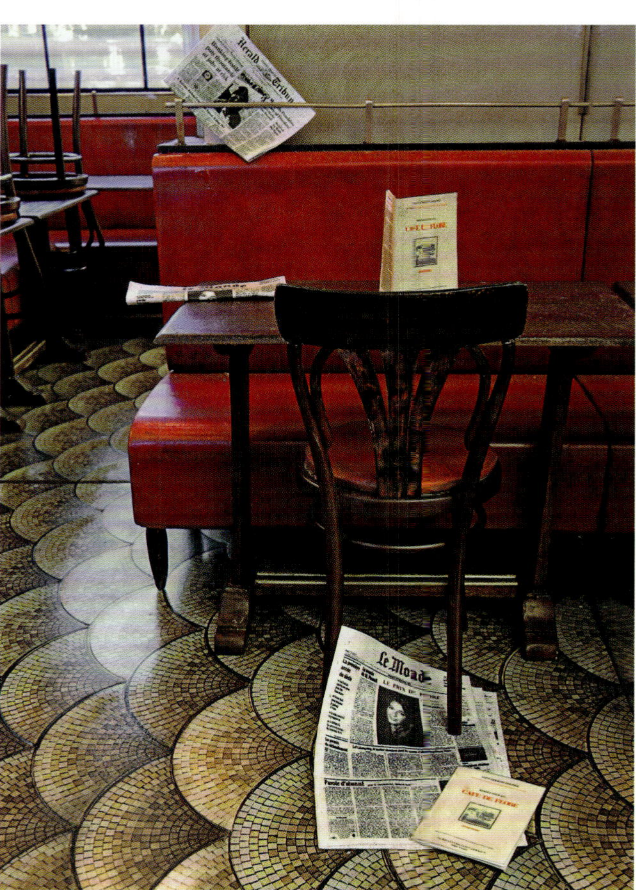

Early Morning at the Café de Flore, 2006.
Mixed media,
26 ¼ × 33 ½ × 32 ¾ in.
(66.5 × 86 × 83 cm).

Table Base, Café de Flore, 2006.
Pencil and felt pen on graph paper,
11 ¾ × 8 ¼ in.
(29.7 × 21 cm).

Early Morning at the Café de Flore (detail), 2006.

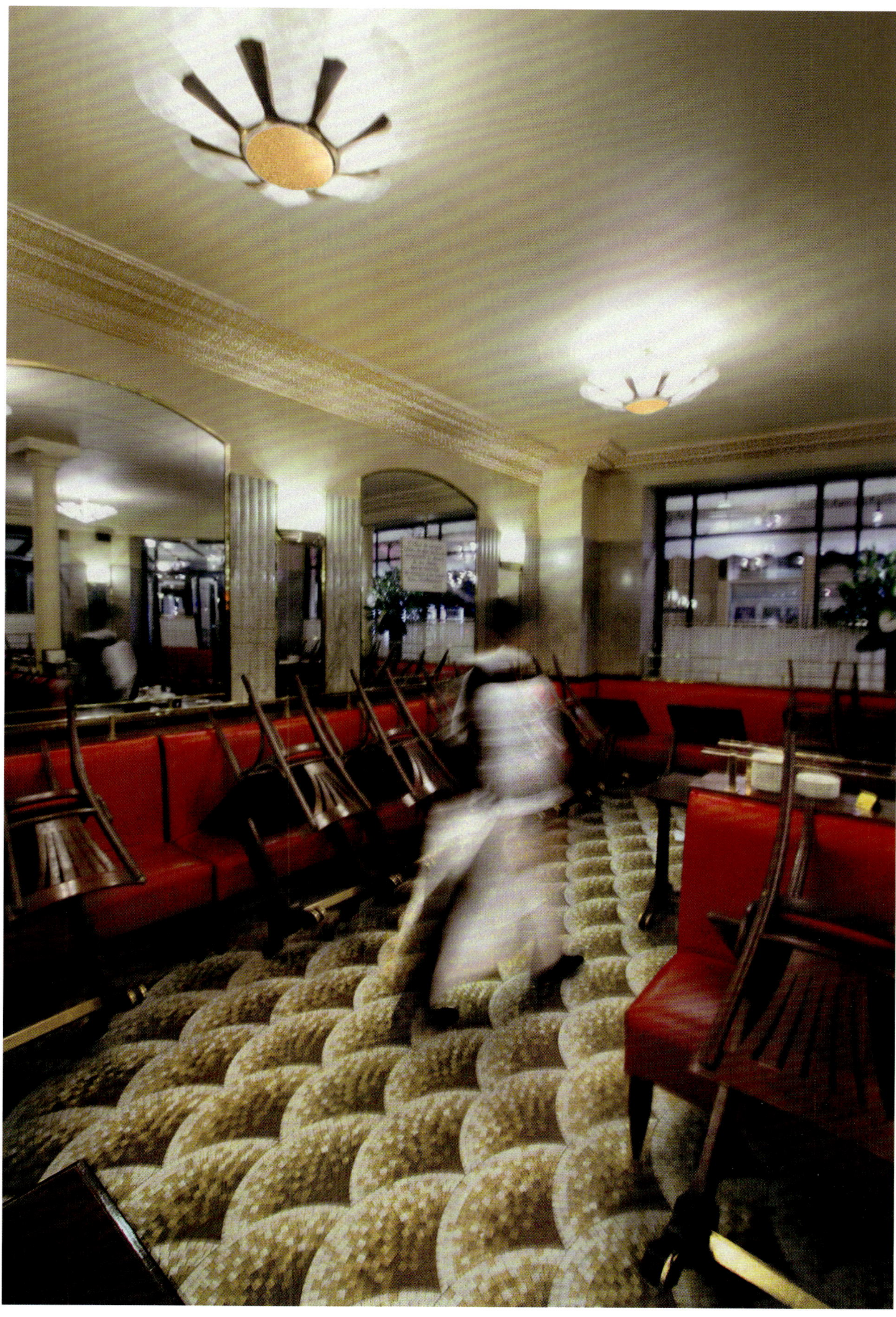

The Café de Flore, Paris, November 9, 2006, 1 o'clock in the Morning, 2006. Photograph.

Ah yes, that's for sure, the Café de Flore forms part of my life, it's like a piece of me.

I went in for the first time almost fifty years ago. I was doing my military service at the Ministry for War (today, of Defense) on rue Saint-Dominique; fifteen months away from my Swedish wife whom I'd married shortly before being called up. Fifteen months duly noting petitions submitted to "good offices" of the Deputies, requests for Legions of Honor, for job transfers. By the time evening came, I felt an overriding need for a change of scene. The Flore was my own private America, the opposite of days stuck in front of my Remington, the opposite of all that gray. I entered the well-lit, noisy cave filled with rather effeminate boys and dippy goddesses. The ashtrays, I remember well, were brimful of Lucky Strike cigarette butts stained with Rouge Baiser lipstick. At the Café de Flore, I would often enjoy a round or two with César, Jean Castel, immediately by the entrance to the left, the mischievous Pomerand, the ambiguous Hugues de Géorgis. And the actresses: Bernadette Lafont, Isabelle Huppert, Bulle Ogier, Catherine Deneuve, Anouk Aimée, Lauren Bacall, all beautiful, just like at the cinema. And the periods overlap; at the Flore I remember seeing Boris Vian, Juliette Gréco, Jean-Paul Sartre, Françoise Sagan, Jean Genet, Violette Leduc, Michel Warren. The mad, birdlike laugh of Roland Topor still rings through images that come back to me from another time. Simone Signoret gives me a kiss. . . .

Remoteness makes things look grander. Over time, figures from the past acquire a brighter sheen, myth fuses with reality. Mulling over it, the charm of Le Flore is that, whatever the hour, one is sure to see faces there, friends or unknowns, that reflect a state of mind close to one's own—a certain elegance, humor, and, especially, a spirit of tolerance.

C. Matton, publication by Carole Chrétionnot, *Hommage au Café de Flore, making of*, December 2006

Early Morning at the Flore is the only work on permanent exhibition (since 2006) at the Café de Flore, Paris. S.M.

Early Morning at the Flore (detail).

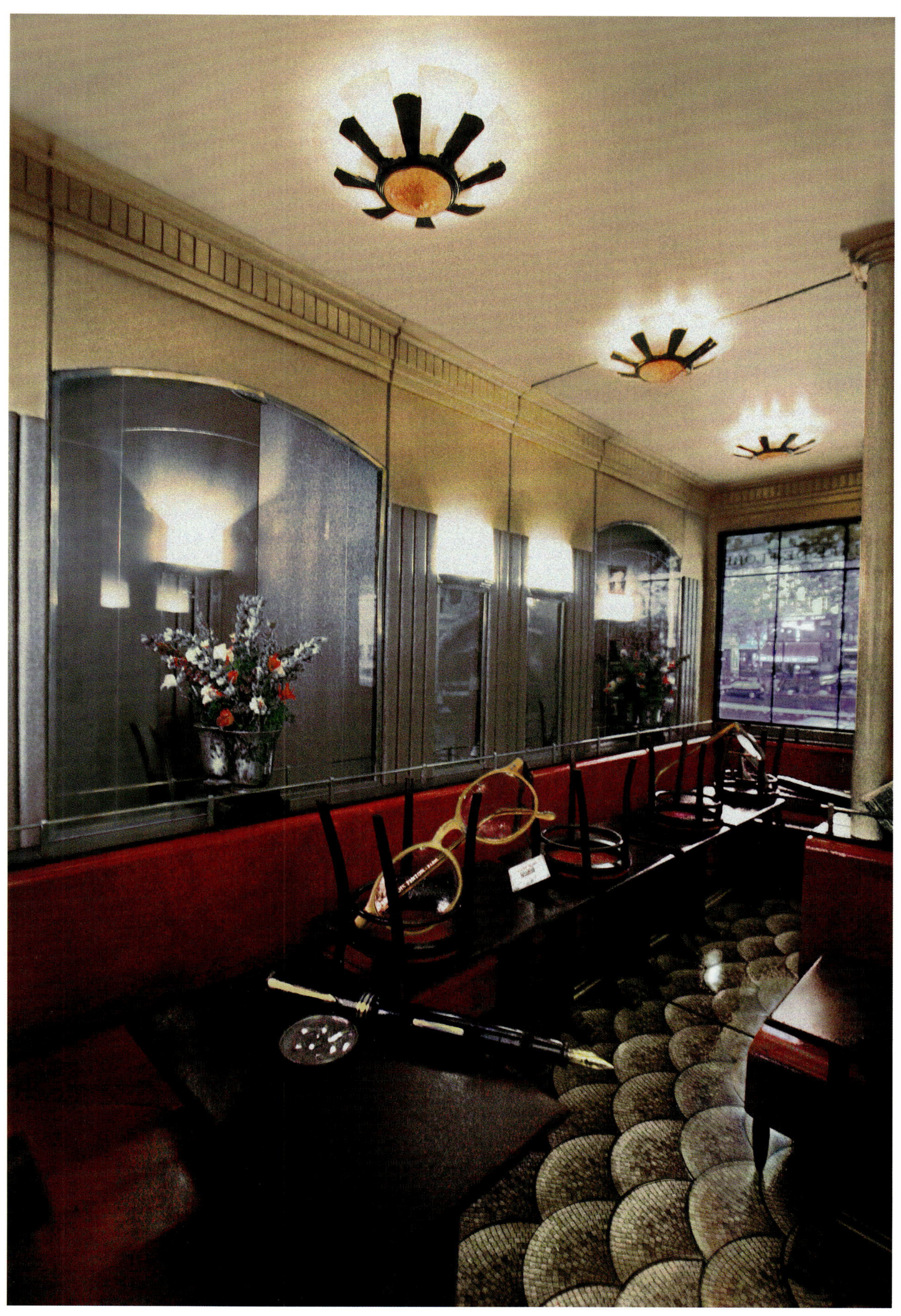

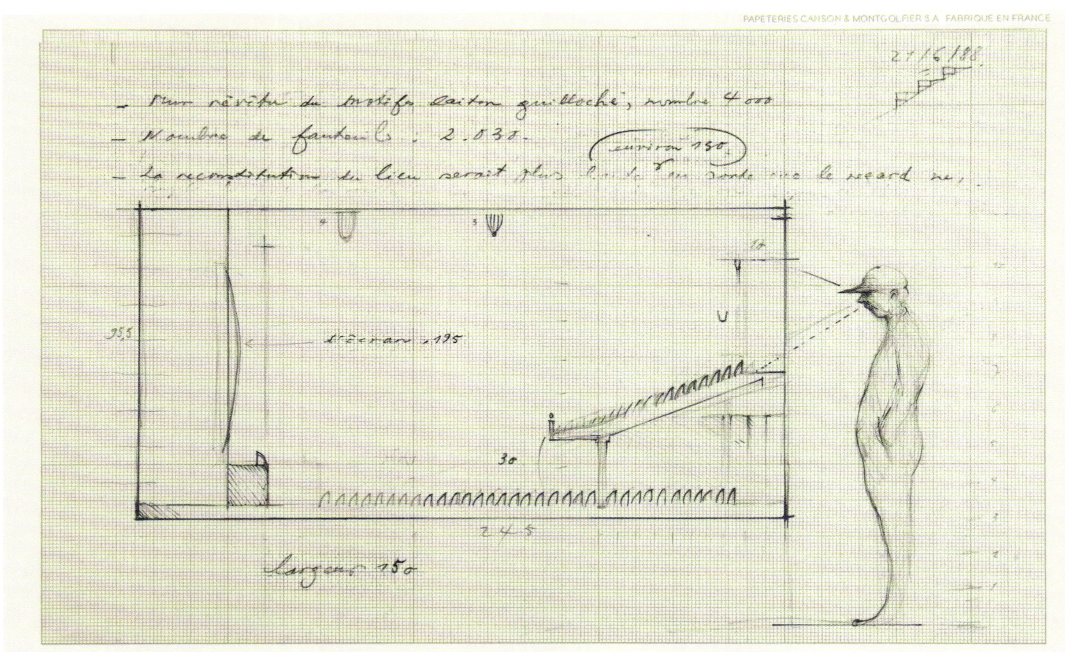

Theater Palace, first study, 1988.
Pencil on graph paper,
11 ¾ × 8 ¼ in. (29.7 × 21 cm).

– wall clad with engraved brass filigree
– number of seats: 2,038
– the reconstitution of the space will be higher, approximately 60 in. h.

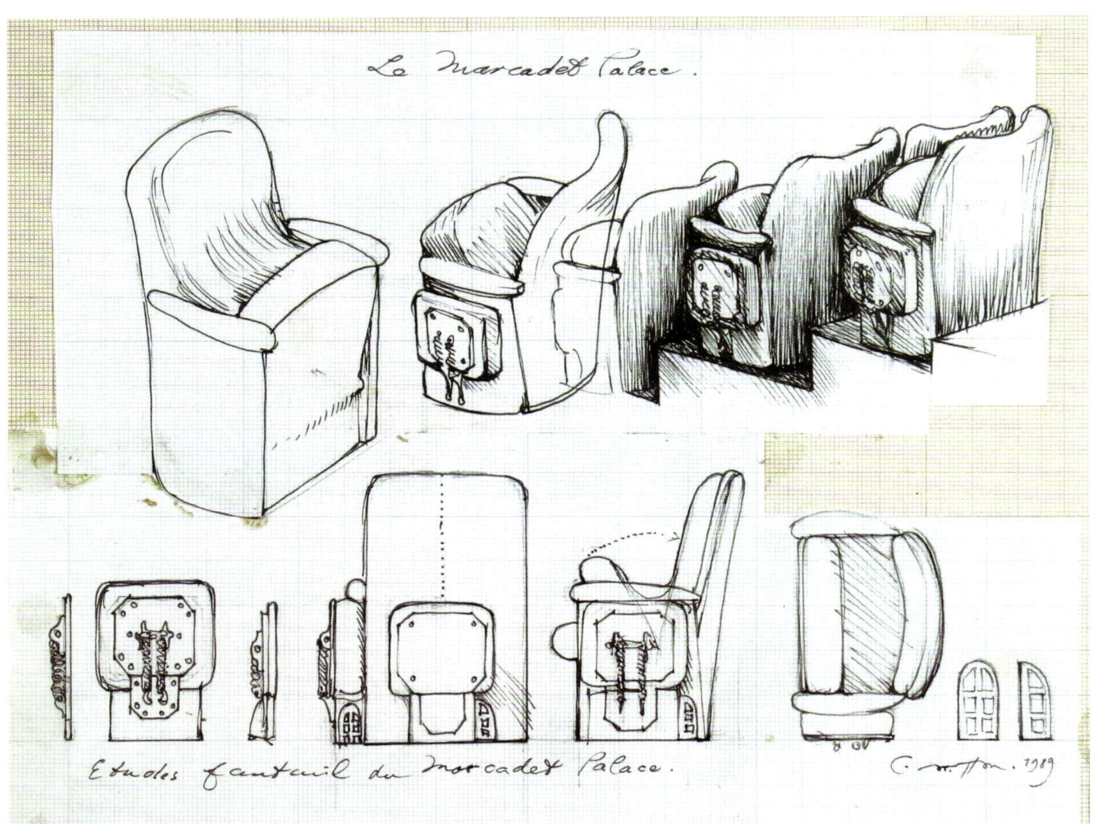

The Marcadet Palace, Stalls, 1989.
Felt pen on paper,
4 ¾ × 6 ½ in. (12 × 16.2 cm).

To take up with the object at its source, to exorcize its every nuance, does not inevitably mean returning to some lost secret of art or of painting. It means inventing another. Here, it's the object that generates its own fiction. [...] Matton knows the strategy of the moderns inside out, since he's deployed their tricks and ruses. But he uses these modern means to leap over the shadow of modernity. His experimentation is modern.

Jean Baudrillard, 1987

The Theater Palace, 1989.
Mixed media,
37 ¾ × 59 × 96 ½ in.
(95.5 × 150 × 245 cm).

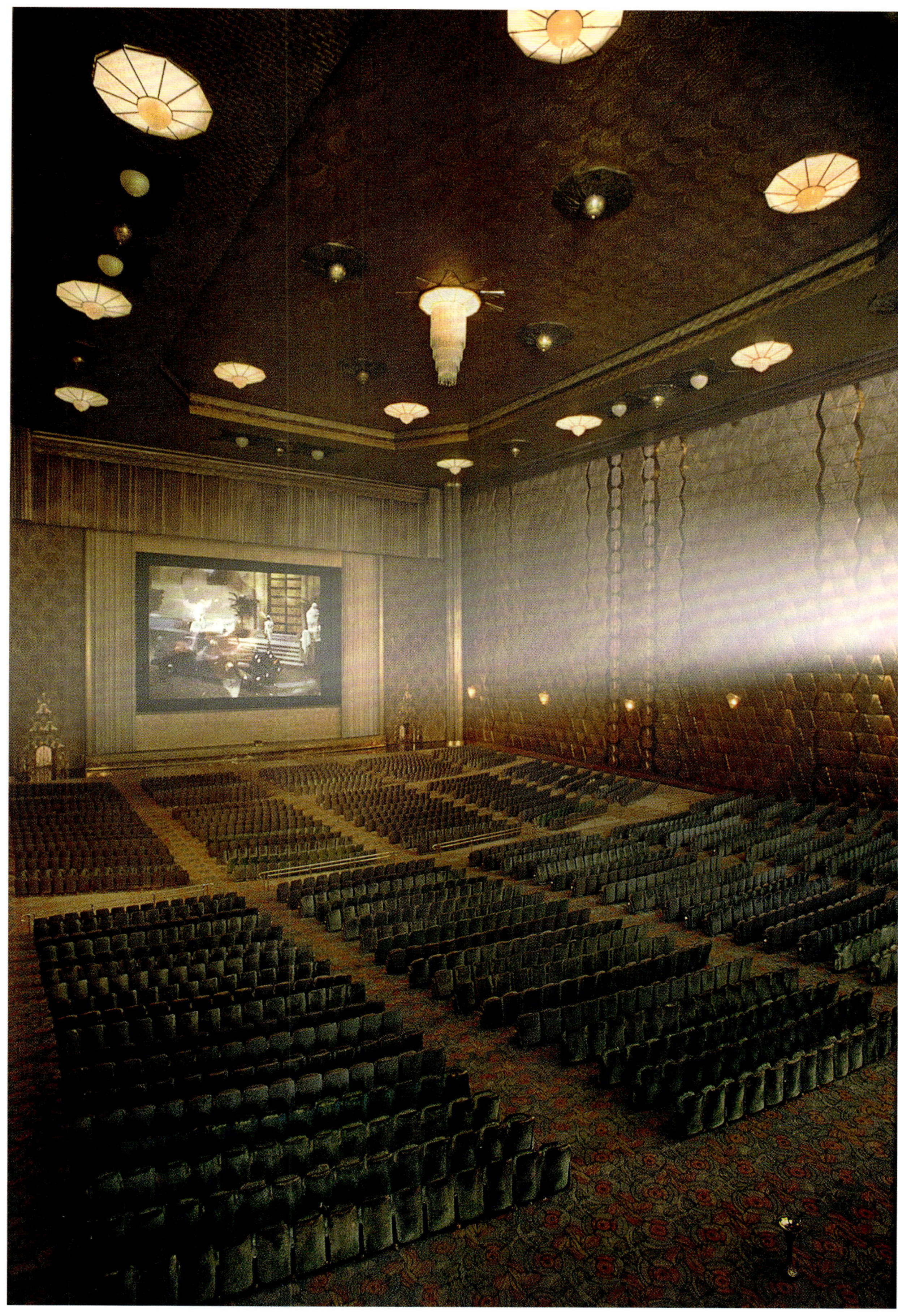

Following double page:
The Theater Palace (detail),
1989.

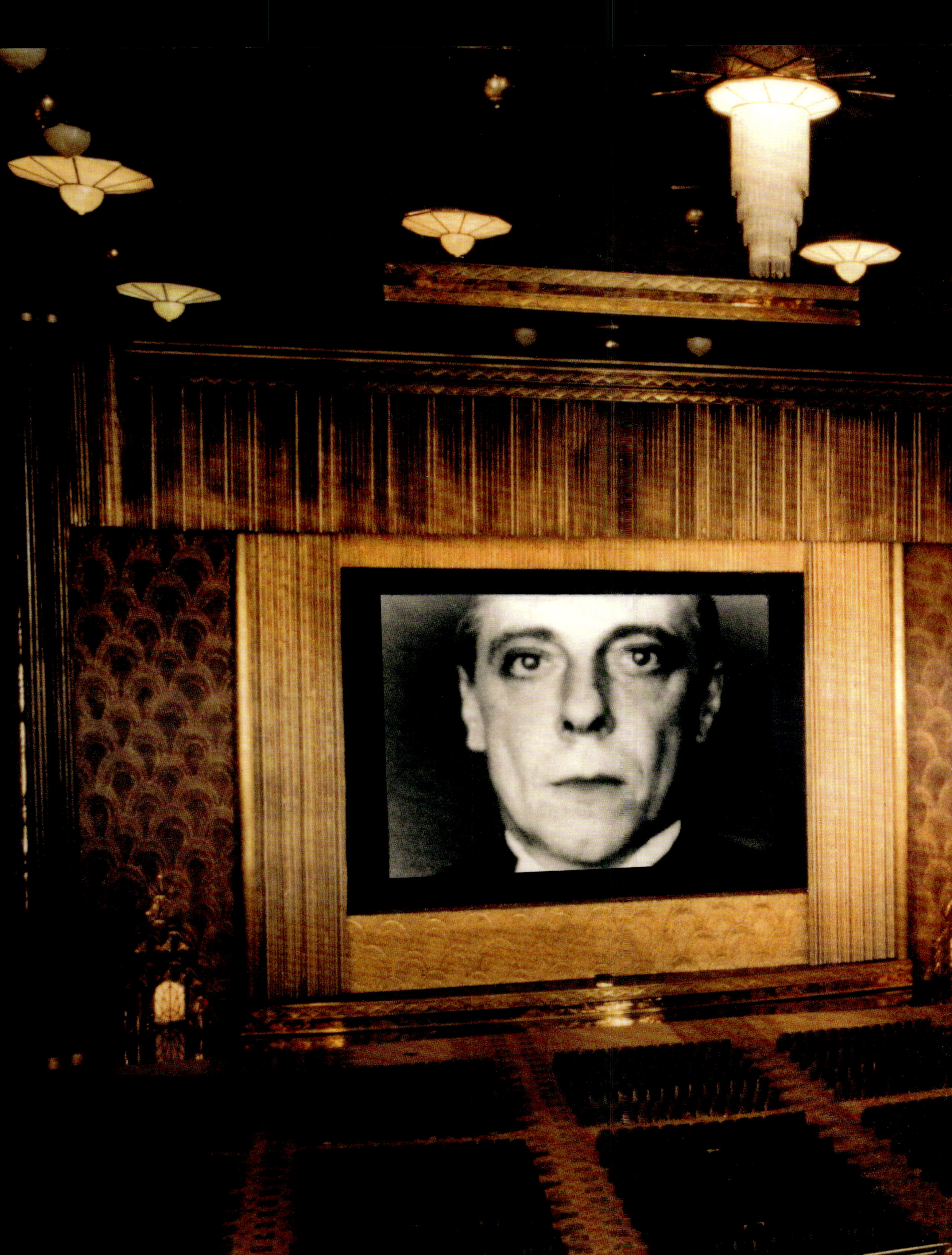

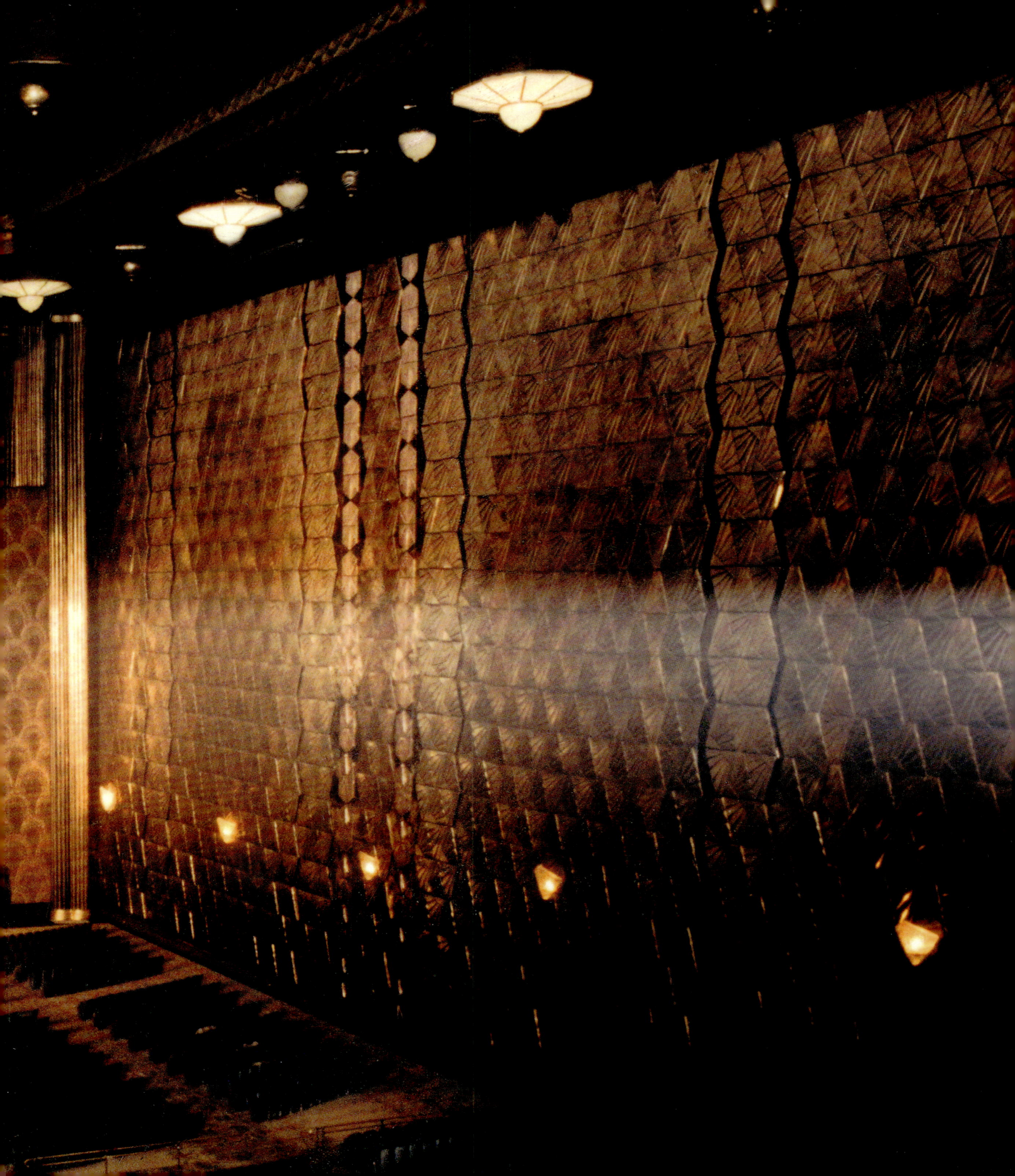

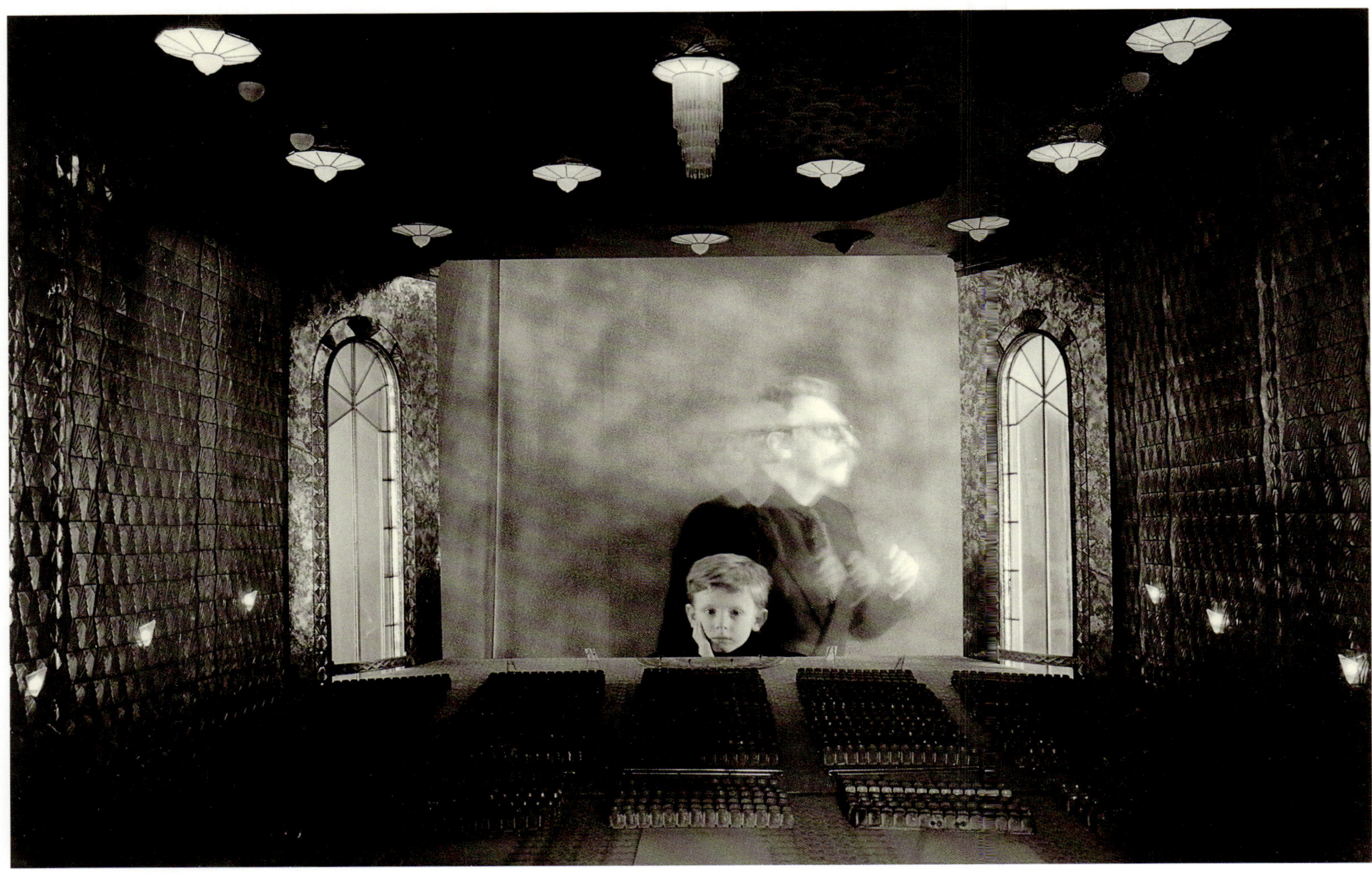

Self-portrait behind Léonard, in front of the Theater Palace, 1989.
Photograph.

Facing page:
The Drive-in, 1989.
Mixed media, 16 × 24 ½ × 14 ¼ in. (41 × 62 × 36 cm).

Car Cemetery, 1989.
Silver-plated torolith and black paint on steel, 12 ¼ × 17 × 13 in. (31 × 43 × 33 cm).

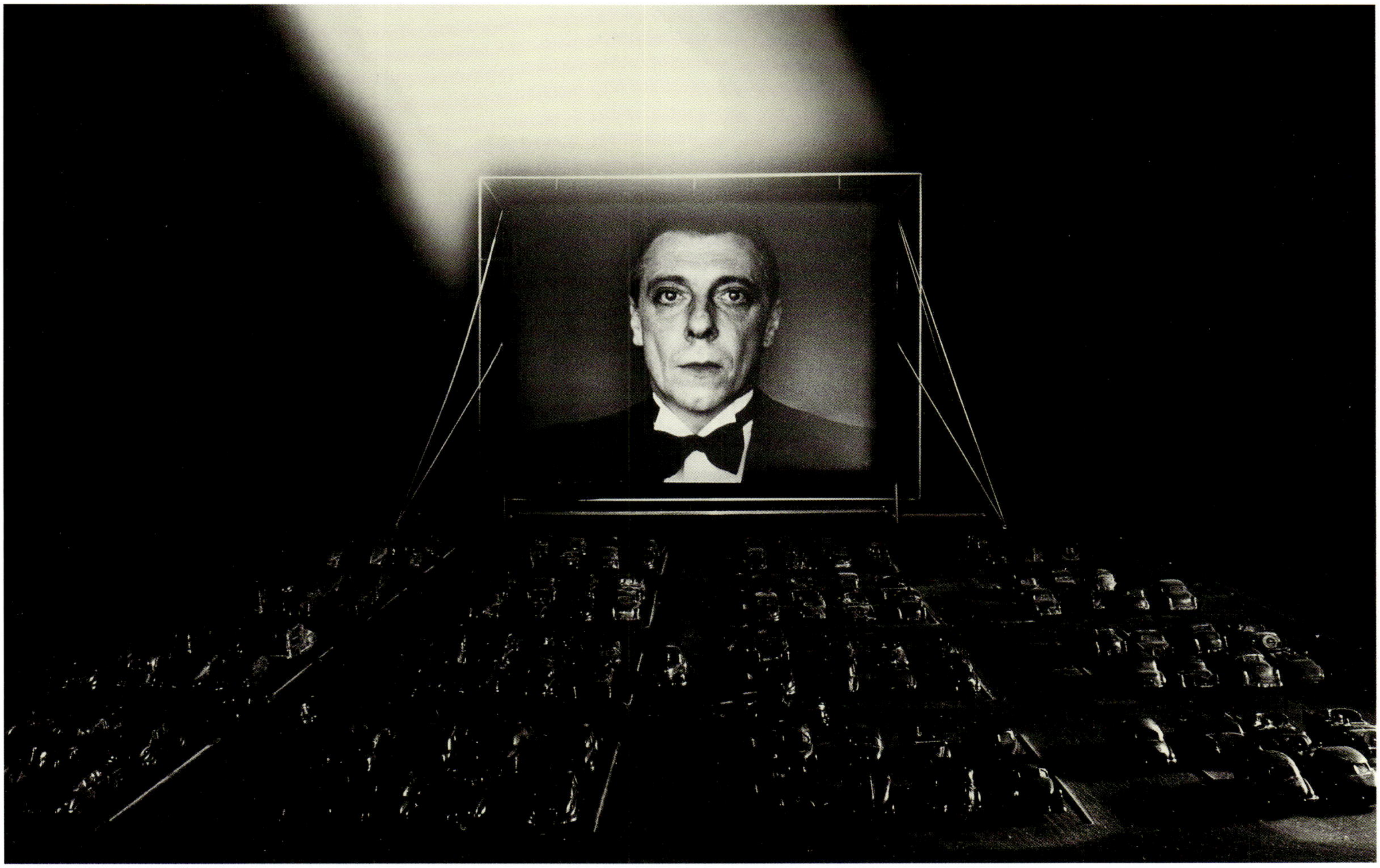

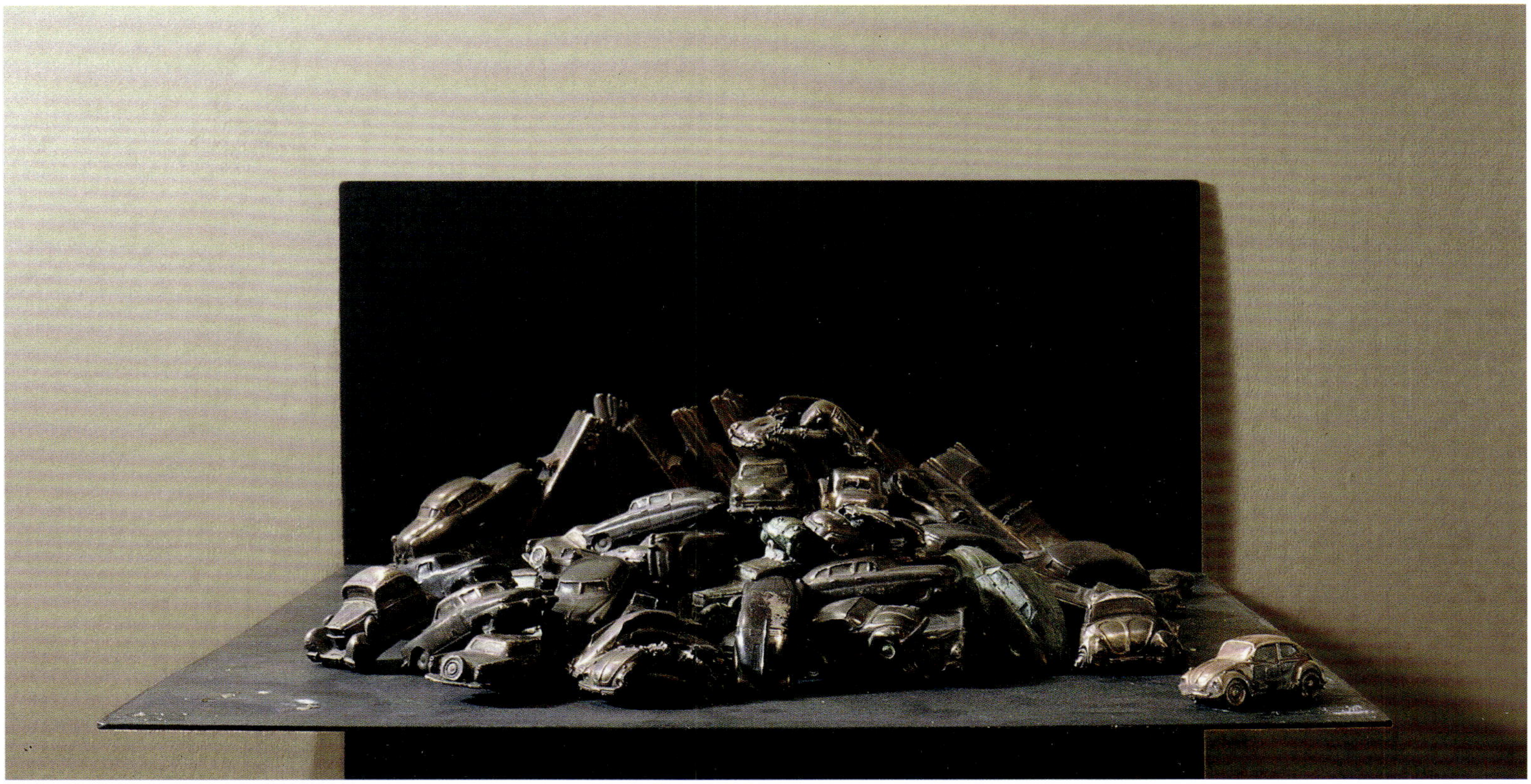

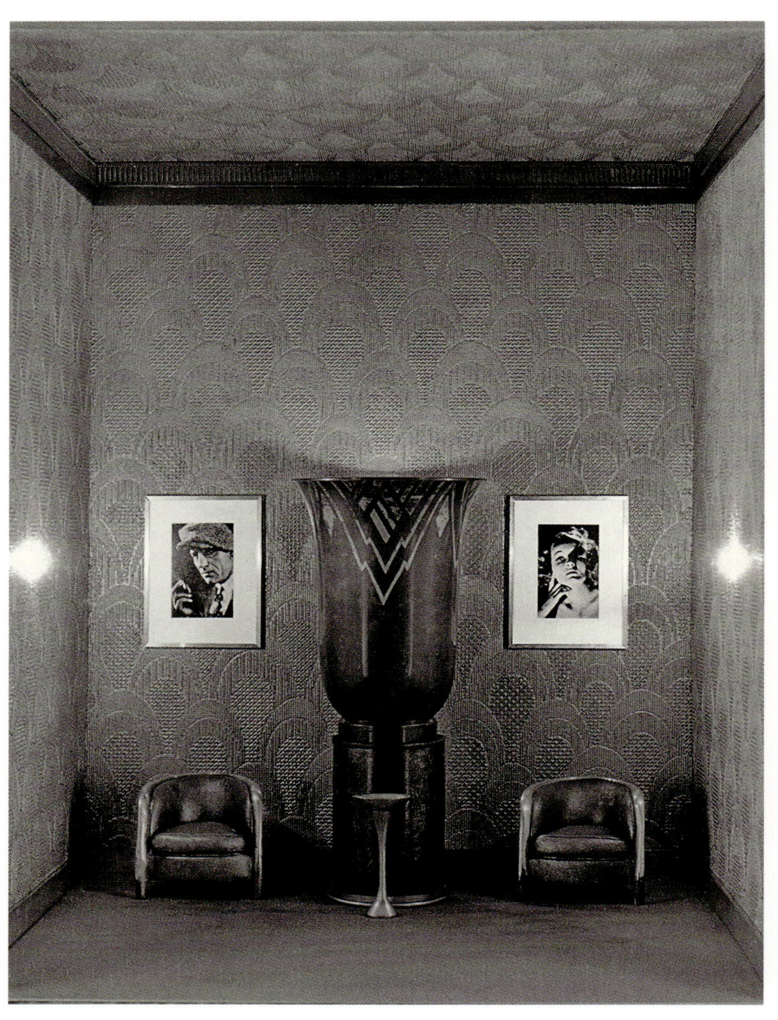

Ladies' Room, 1989.
Mixed media, 20 ½ × 17 ½ × 14 in. [52 × 44.5 × 35.5 cm].

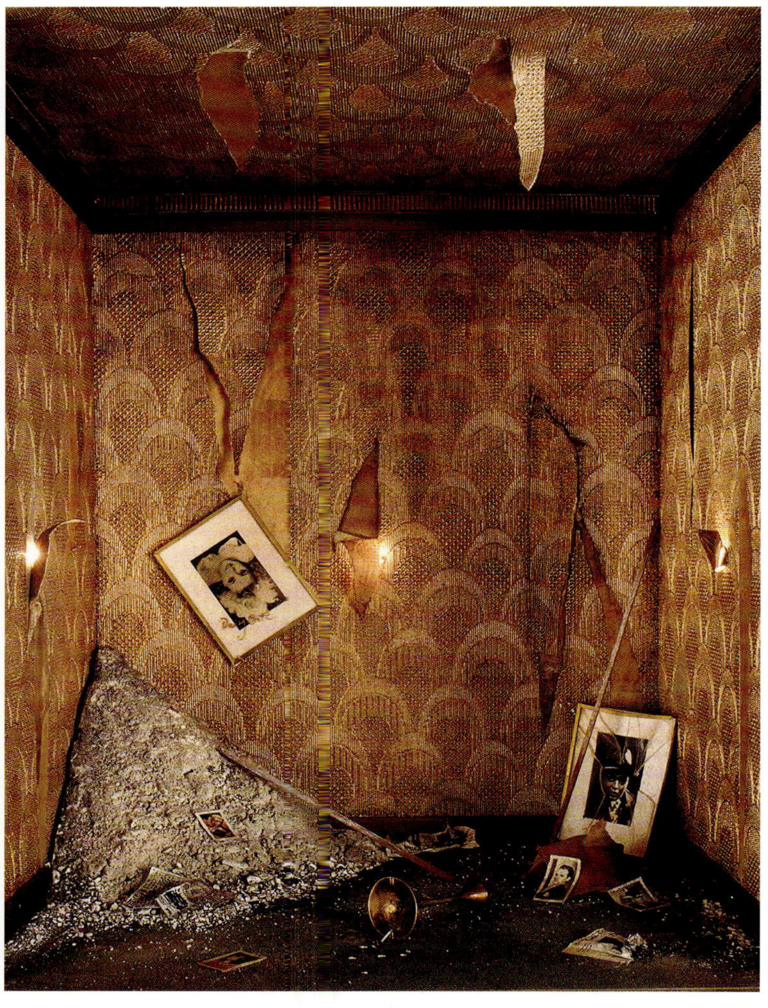

Ladies' Room, 20 Years After, 1989.
Mixed media, 20 ½ × 17 ½ × 14 in. [52 × 44.5 × 35.5 cm].

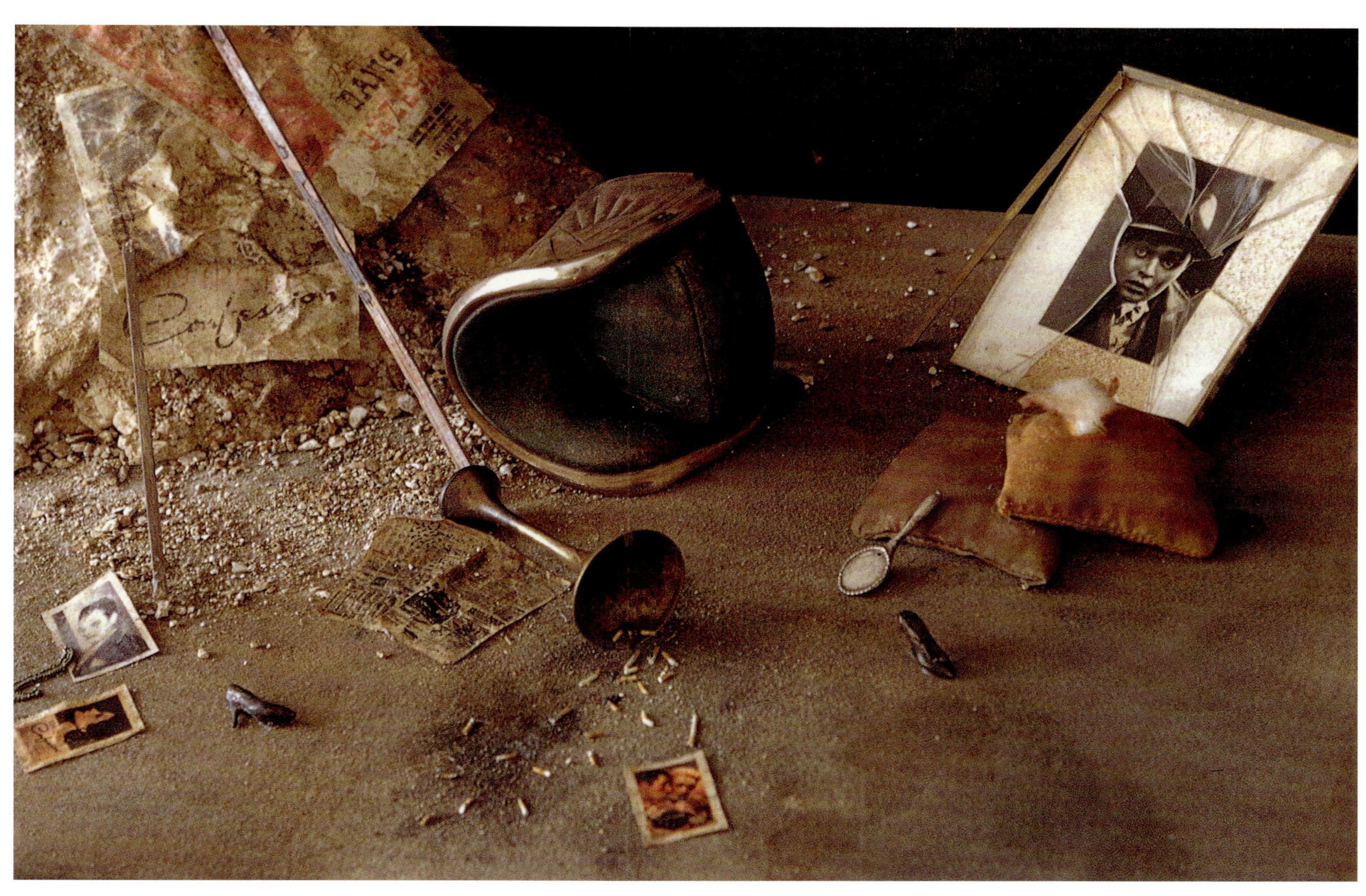

Ladies' Room, 20 Years After, installation II (detail), 2003.
Photograph.

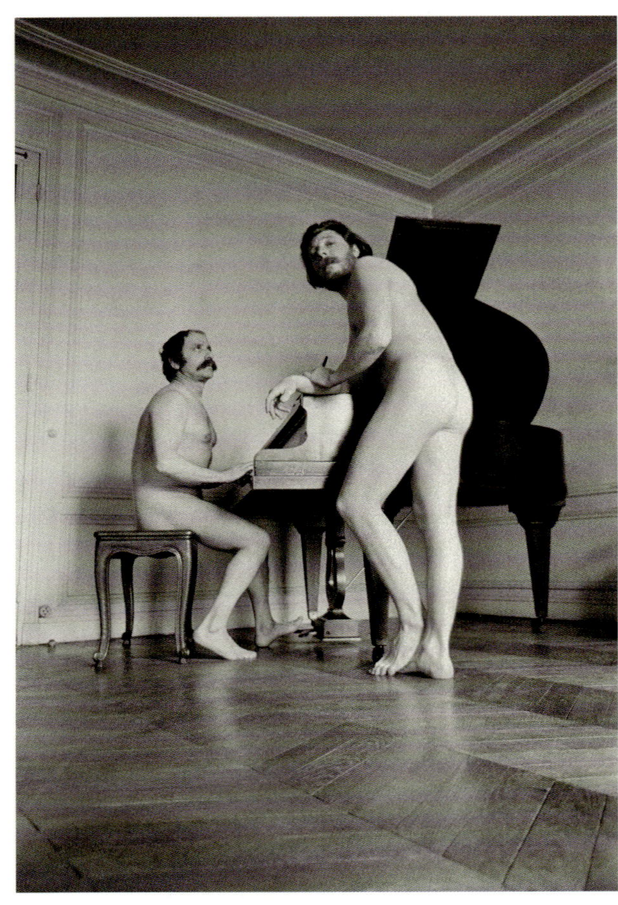

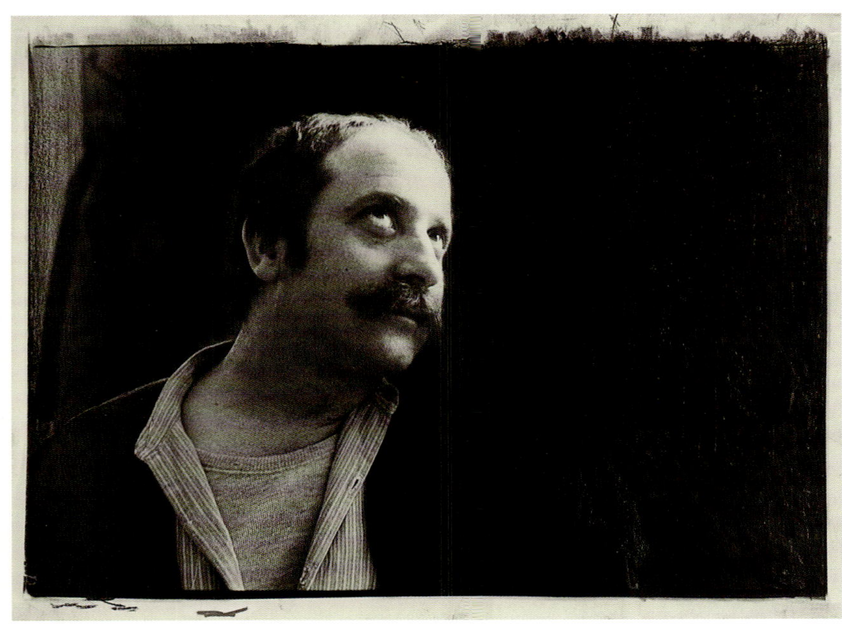

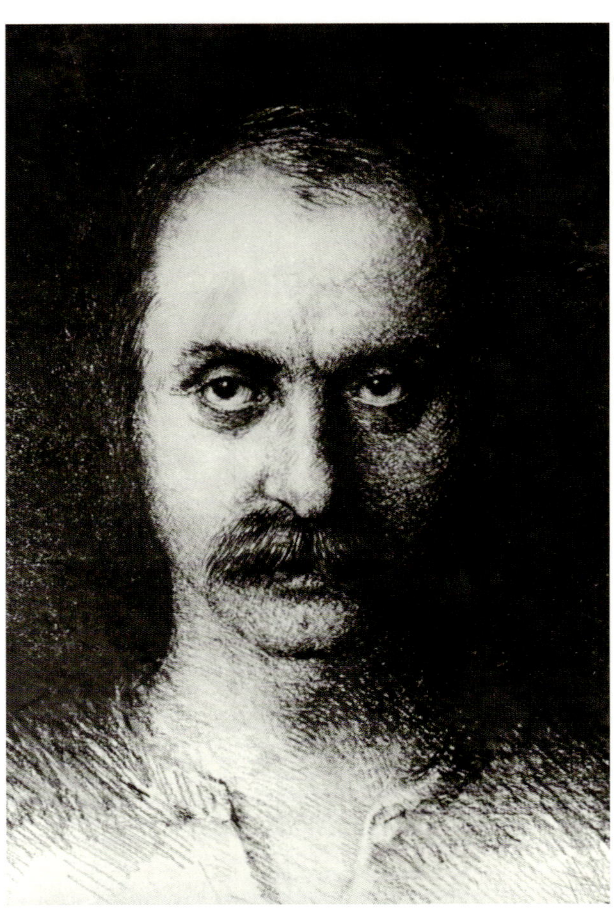

14/12/2004
1/II.

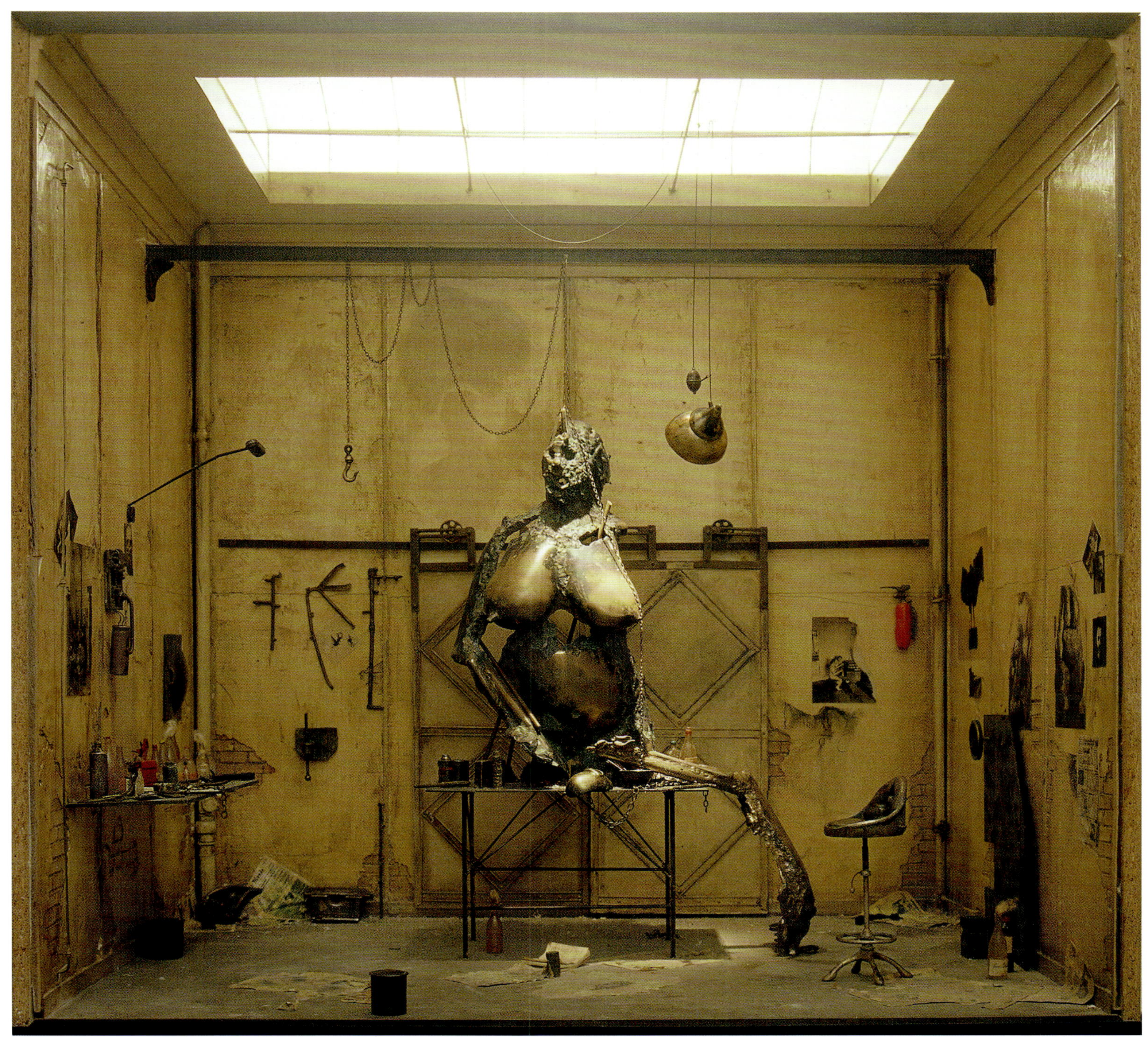

César's Studio II, 1999.
Mixed media, 29 × 26 × 17 ¾ in. (74 × 66 × 45 cm).

Facing page:
Charles and César at the piano, boulevard du Montparnasse, Paris, 1968.
Photograph Yann Matton.

César, with his Eyes to Heaven, 1967.
Black chalk on silver print, 7 ¼ × 9 ½ in. (18.3 × 24.3 cm).

César, 1968.
Pencil and charcoal on paper, 9 ½ × 7 ¼ in. (24.3 × 18.3 cm).

César, the Friend, 2004.
Lead pencil, Conté pencil, black chalk, and wash on paper, 15 ¼ × 15 in. (39 × 38 cm).

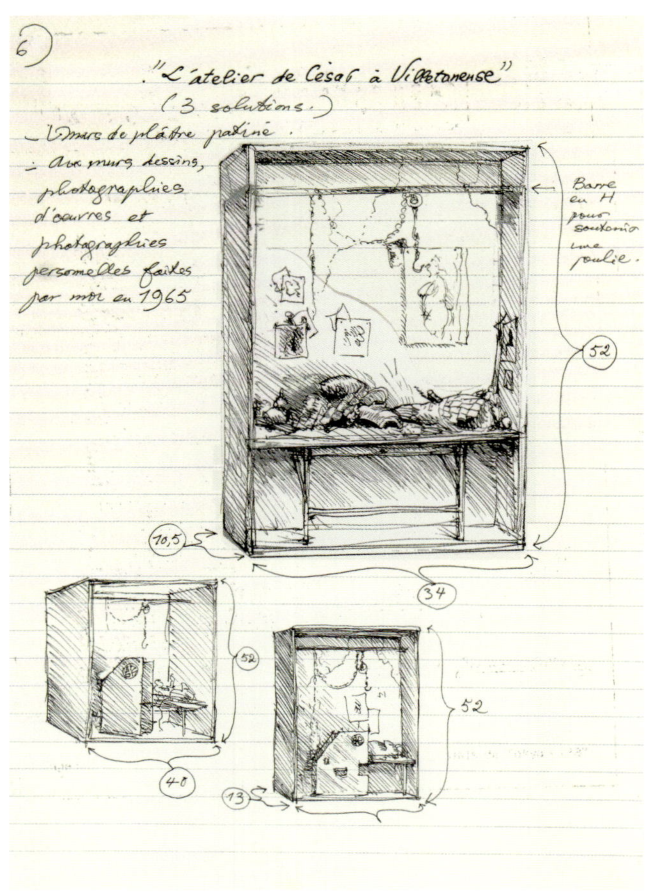

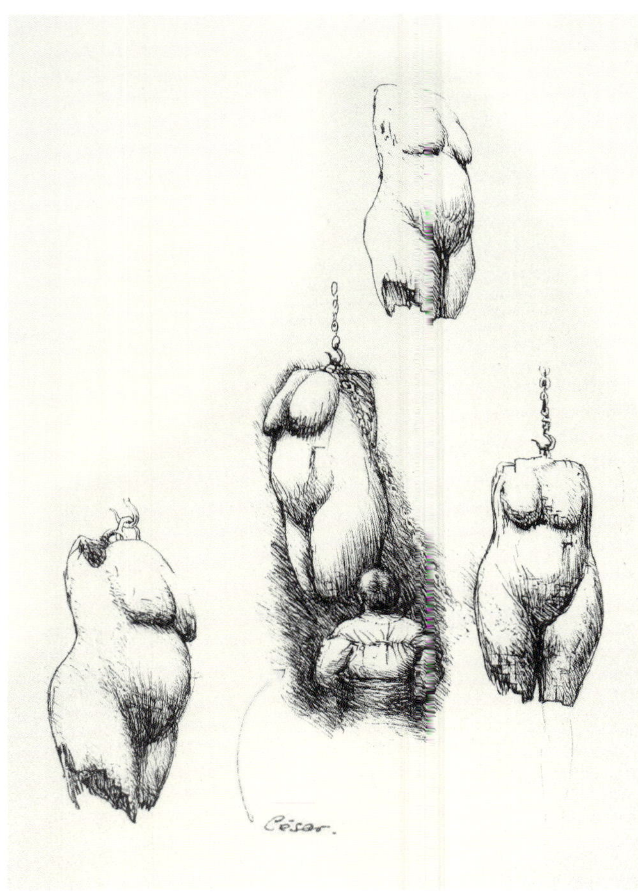

Far left:
César's Studio at Villetaneuse (flat box), 1997.
Pencil and felt pen on paper,
11 ¾ × 8 ¼ in.
(29.7 × 21 cm).

- plaster walls with a patina
- on the walls, drawings, photographs of art pieces, and personal ones I've taken in 1965

Left:
César from the back in the Studio at Villetaneuse, 1990.
Pencil on paper,
11 ¾ × 8 ¼ in.
(29.7 × 21 cm).

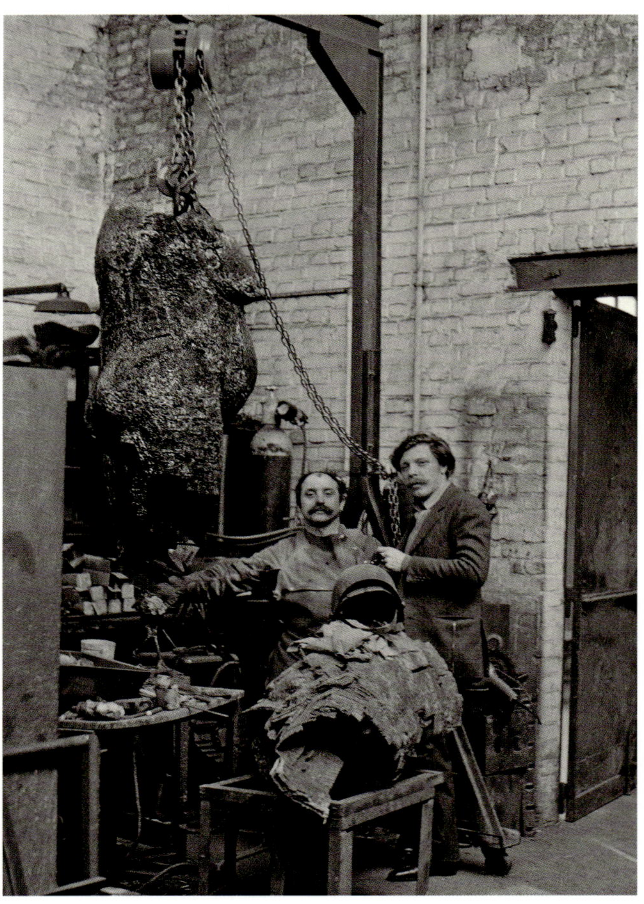

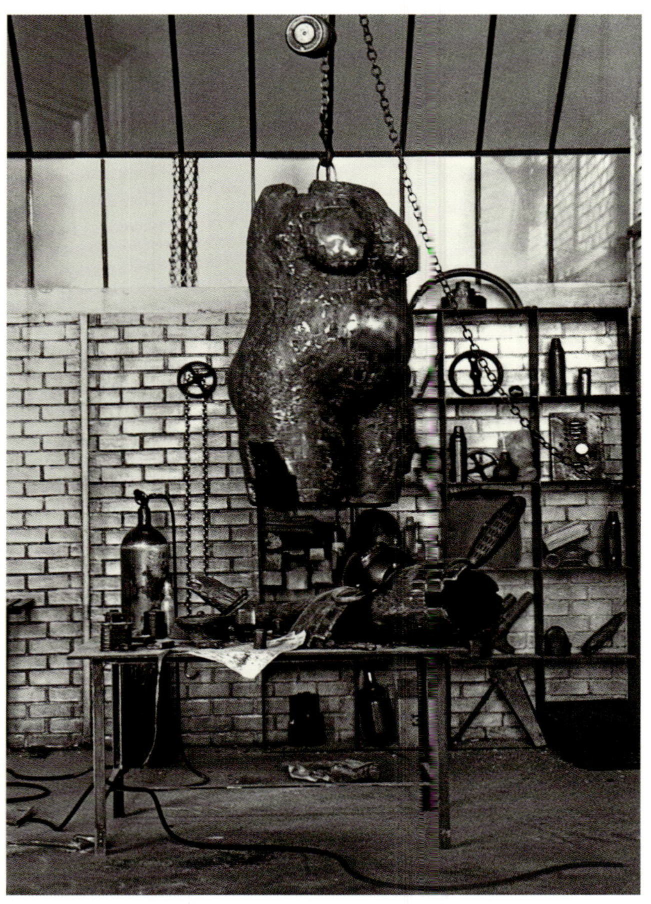

Far left:
Charles and César in the Studio at Villetaneuse, 1965.
Photograph Isabelle Mercanton.

Left:
César's Studio at Villetaneuse III (detail), 2000.

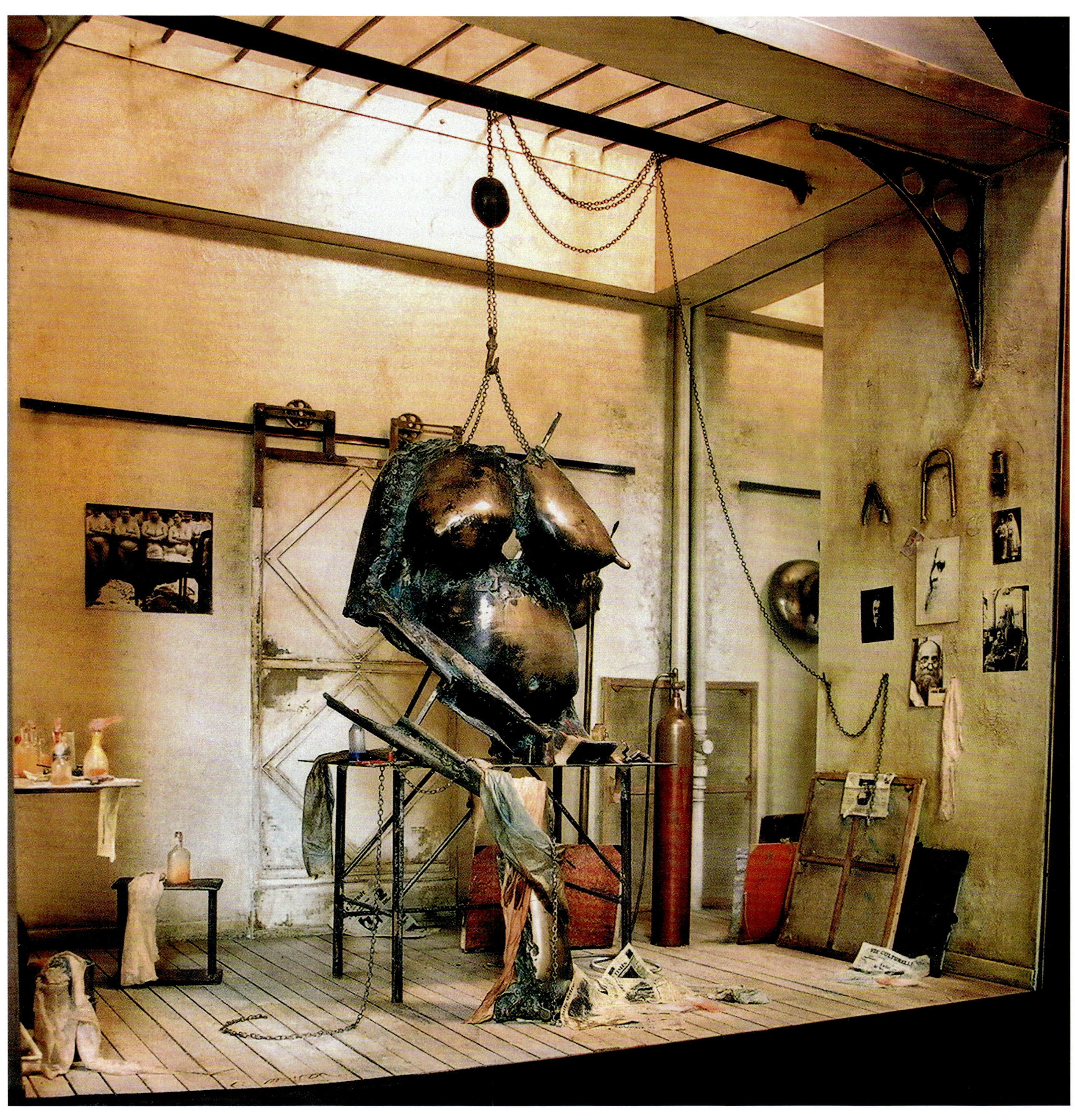

César's Studio at Villetaneuse I, 1999.
Mixed media, 29 ½ × 26 ¾ × 17 ½ in. (75 × 68 × 44.5 cm).

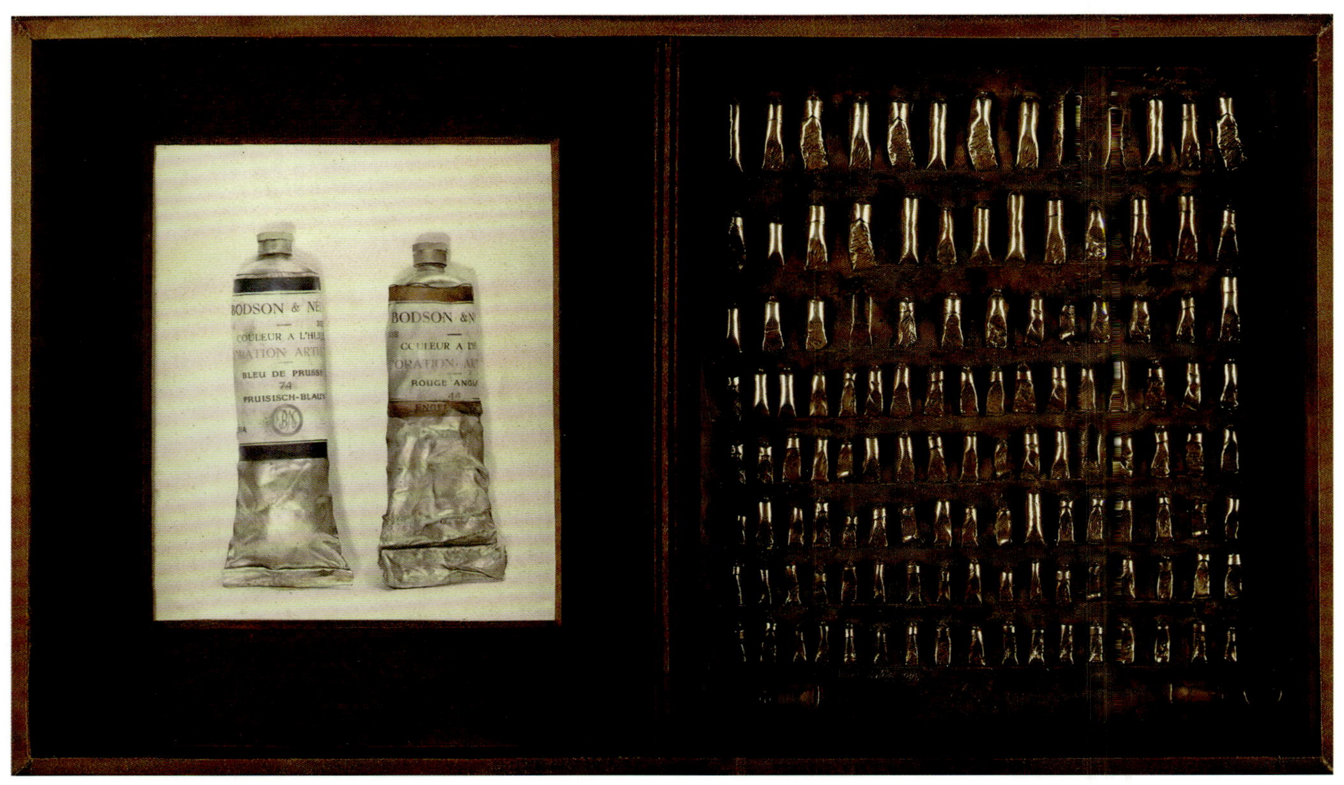

Working Materials (zeugma), 1986. Pencil and gouache on Bristol card, and silver-plated torolith, 12 ¼ × 20 ¾ × 3 in. (31 × 53 × 7.5 cm).

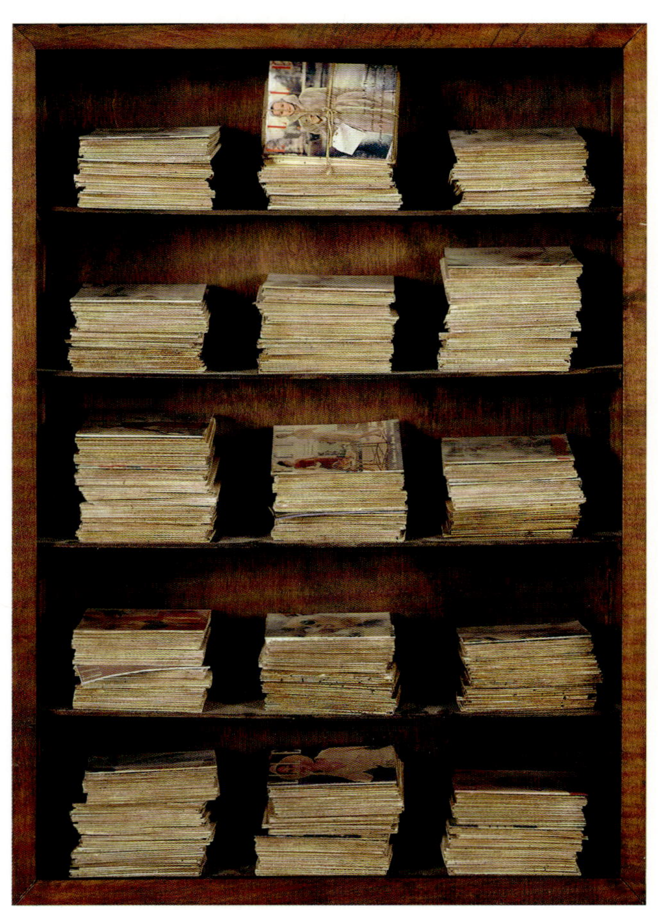

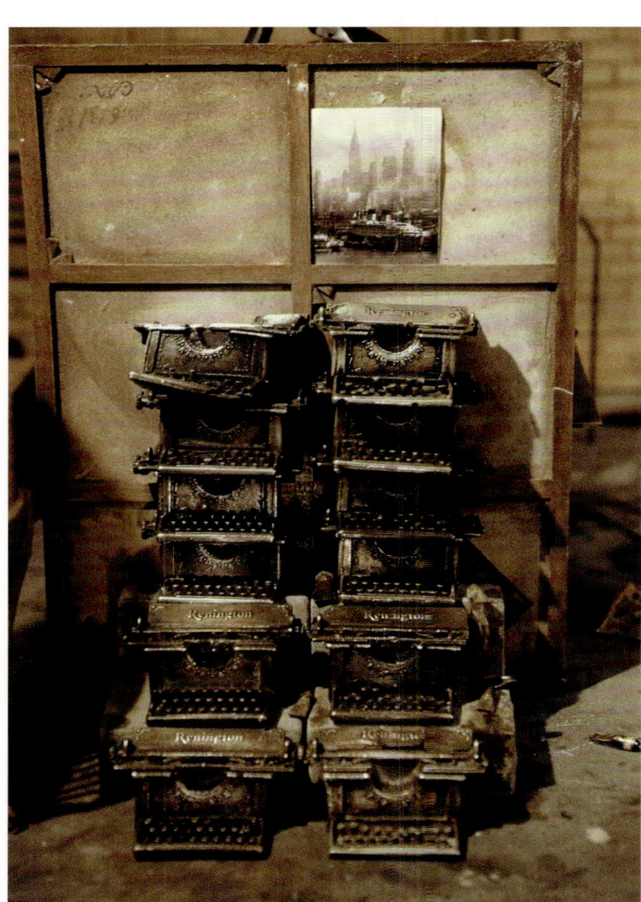

Madame X's Collection of Elle *Magazines*, 1992. Torolith, paper, ink, oil, and wood, 17 ¾ × 15 × 3 ¼ in. (45 × 38 × 8.5 cm).

Accumulation of Remington Typewriters [in The Large Loft, New York], 1988. Photograph.

Arman's Studio,
2001.
Mixed media,
24 ½ × 28 × 33 in.
(62 × 71 × 84 cm).

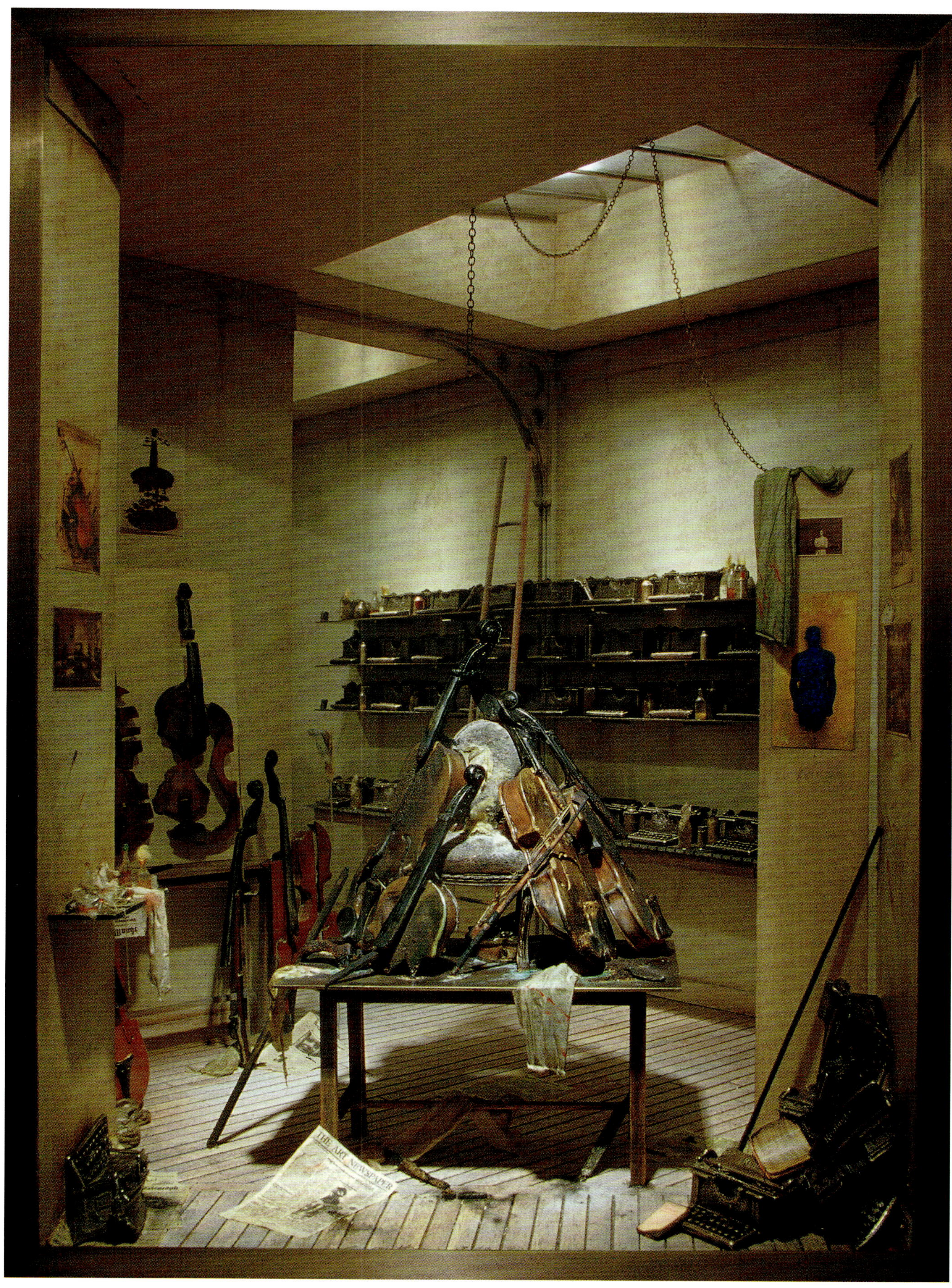

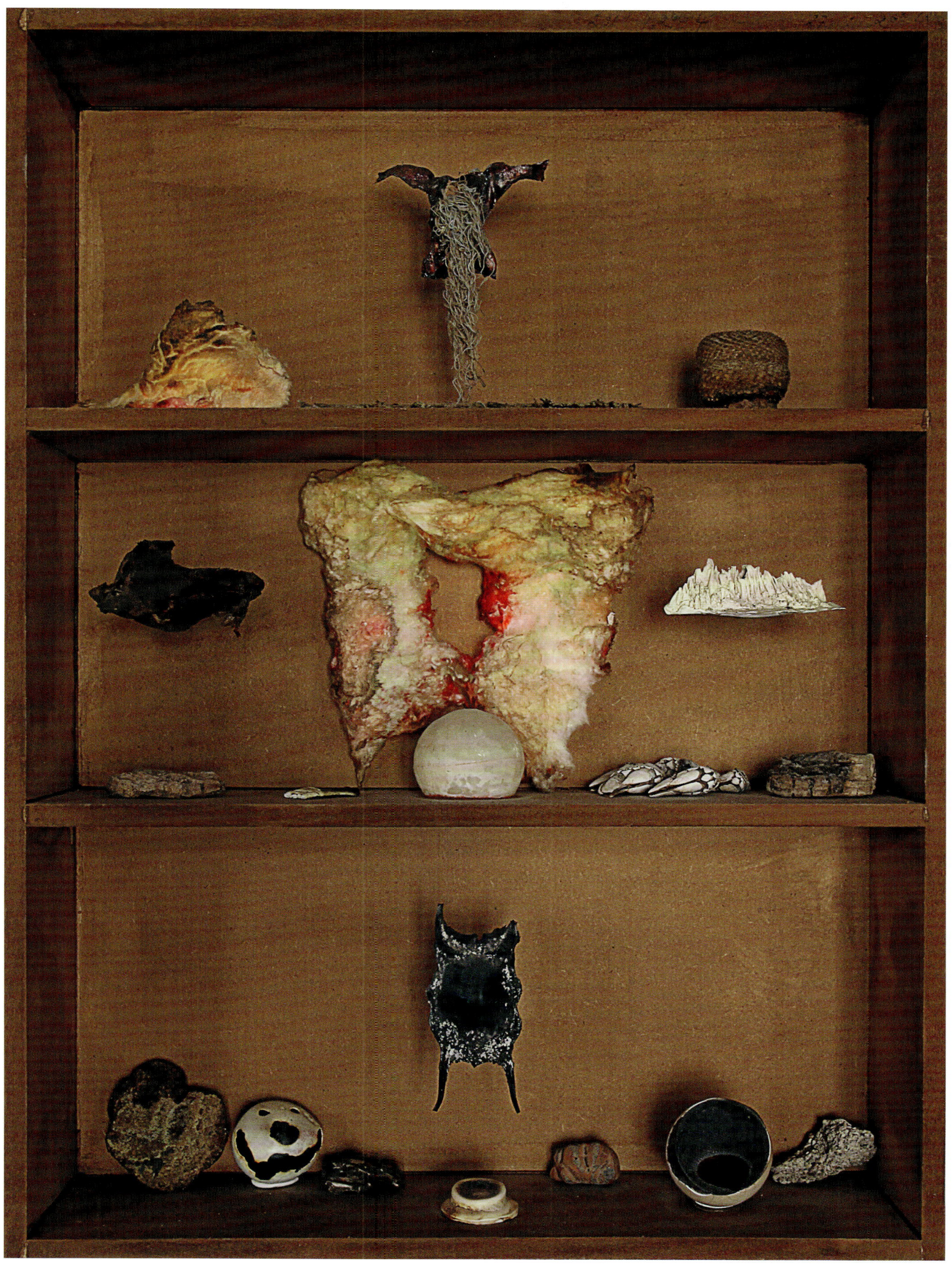

The Wall of a Collector of Odds and Ends, 1998–2008. Mixed media, 19 ½ × 14 ½ × 3 ¾ in. (49.5 × 36.7 × 9.5 cm).

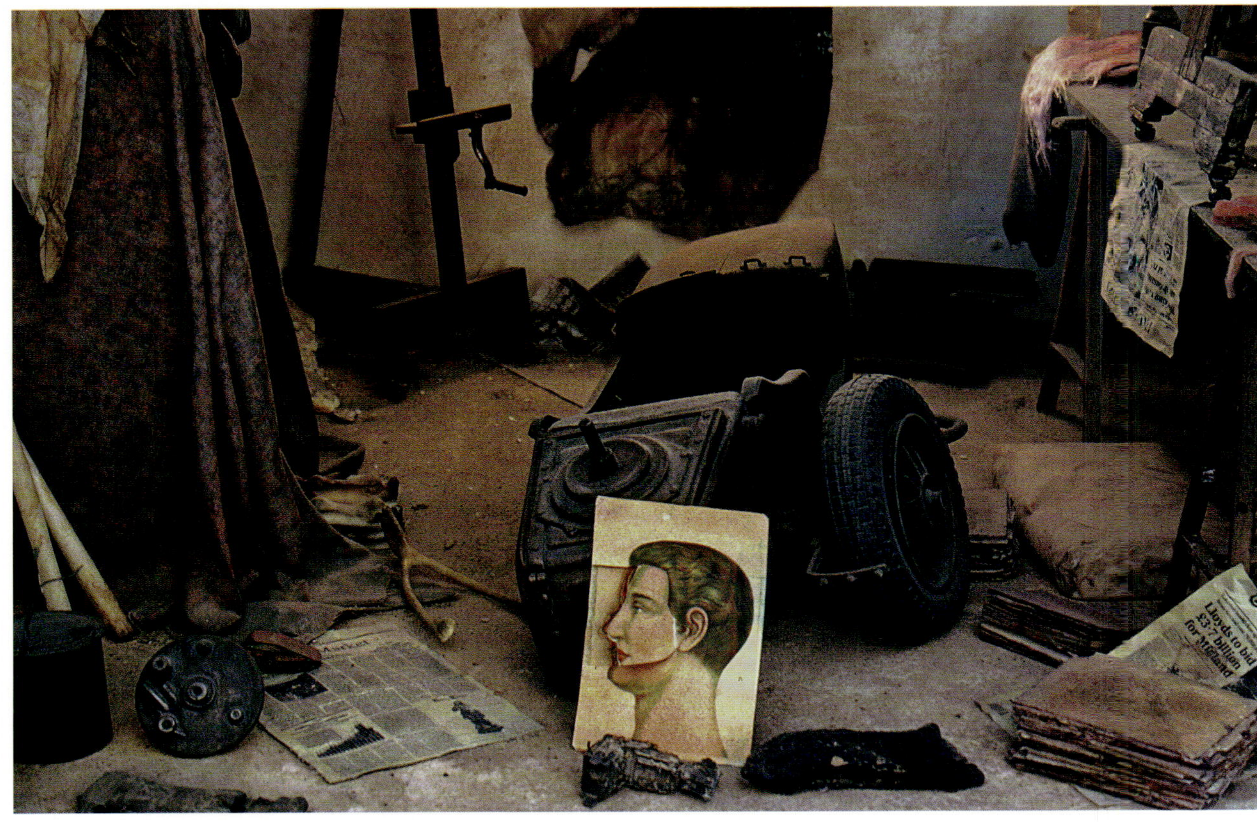

The Storage Room (detail 1), 2008.

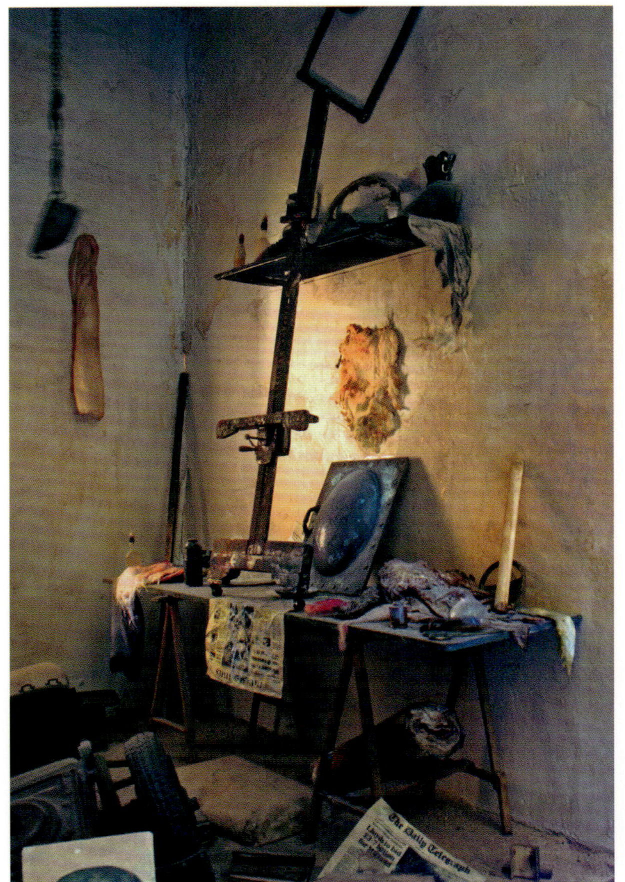

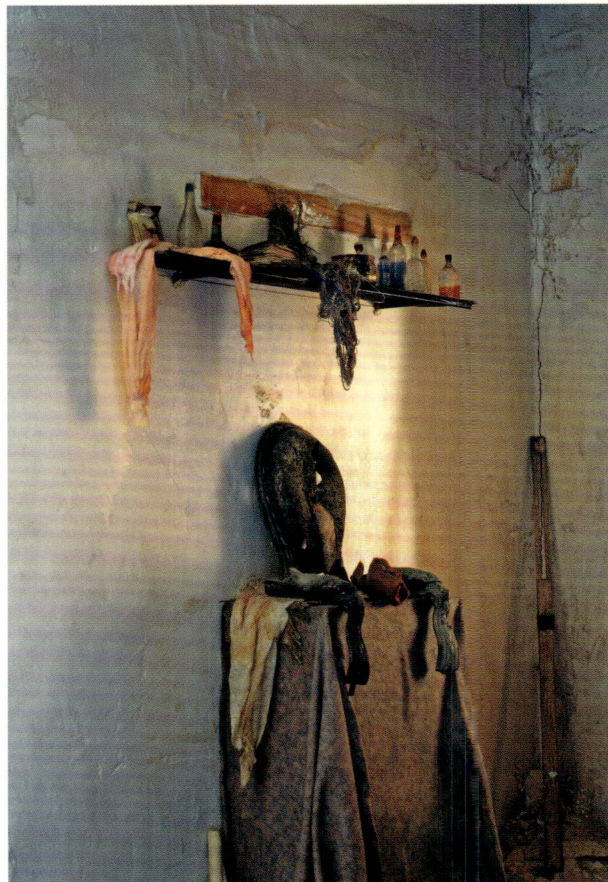

The Storage Room (detail 2), 2008.

The Storage Room (detail 3), 2008.

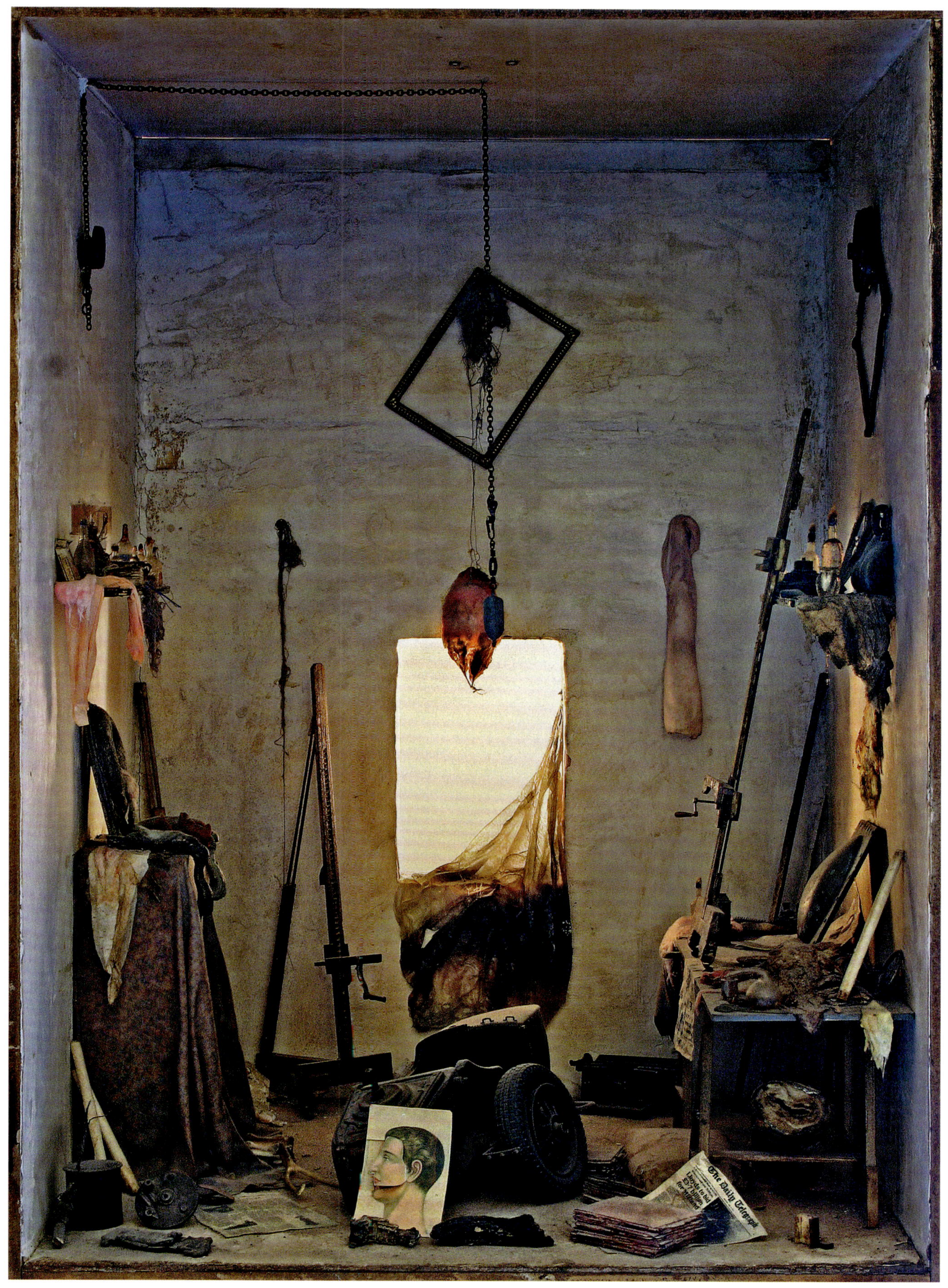

The Storage Room, 2008.
Mixed media,
23 ½ × 17 × 22 in.
(59.5 × 43 × 56 cm).

Photographs
Léonard Matton.

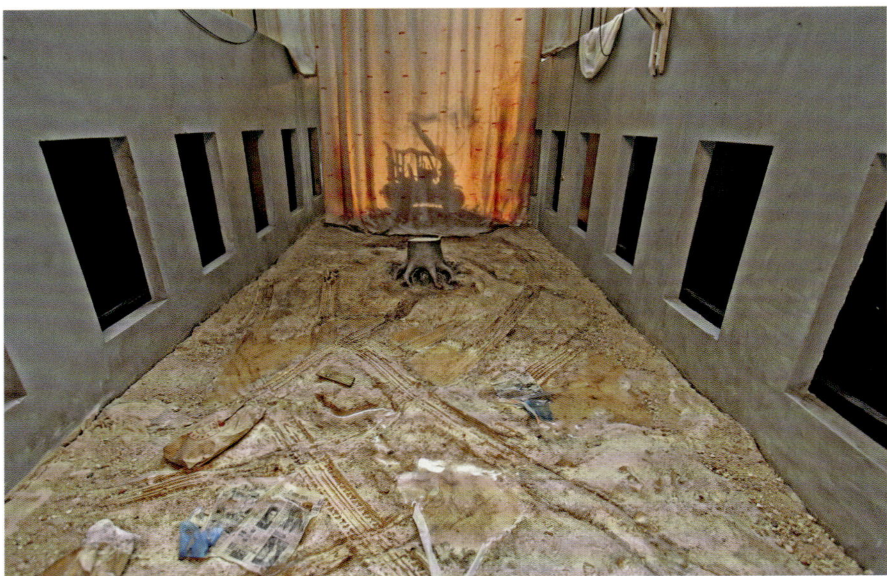

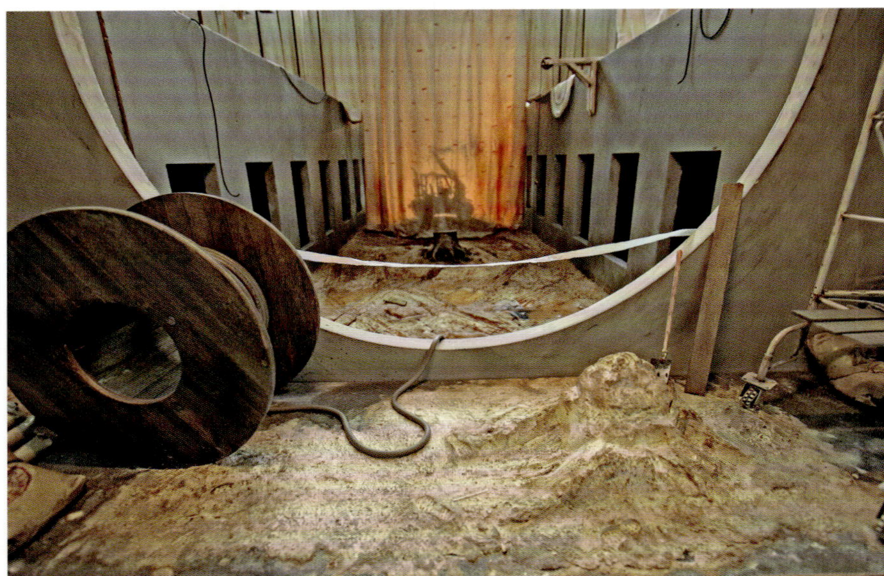

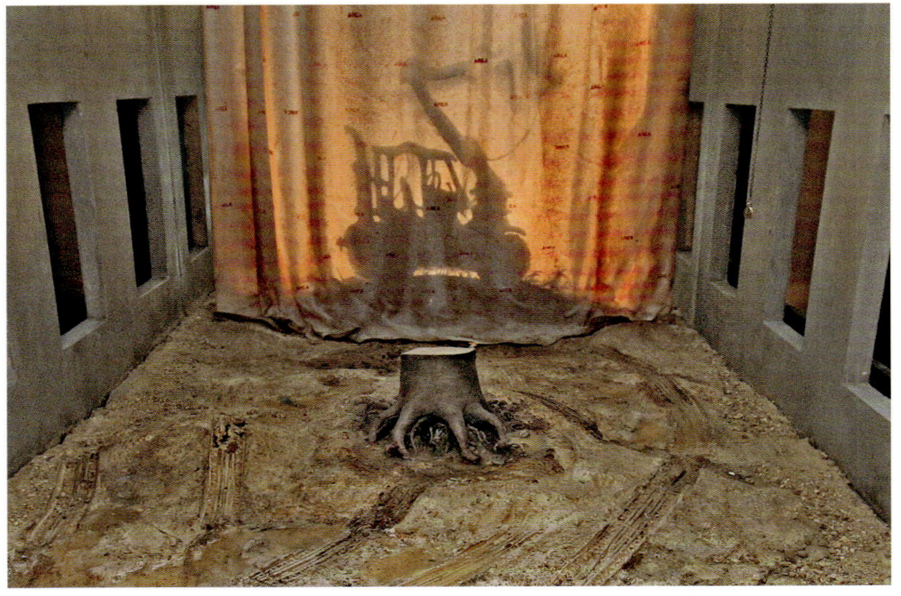

Diptych: 1 Building Site, 1995.
Mixed media, 32 ¼ × 38 ½ × 67 ¼ in.
(82 × 98 × 171 cm).

Building Site, (detail 1).

Building Site (detail 2).

In 1995, the architect Alain Sarfati asked Charles Matton whether he might like to take over a space in the Jules Verne High School in Limours (at that time, under construction), for two works: *The Building Site*, prior to the conclusion of the construction, and *A Miniaturized Tragedy*,–in anticipation of its (improbable and prophylactic) destruction. S.M.

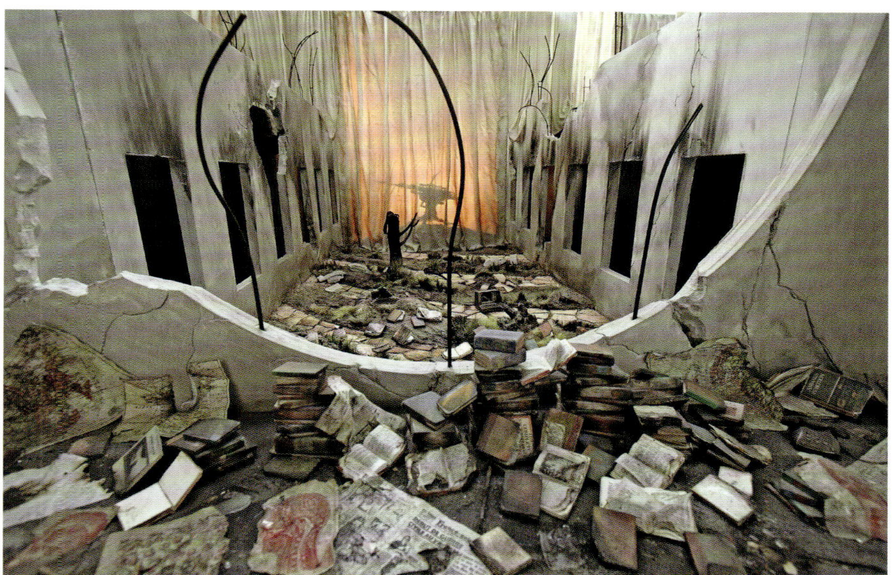

Diptych 2: Miniaturized Tragedy III (detail 1).

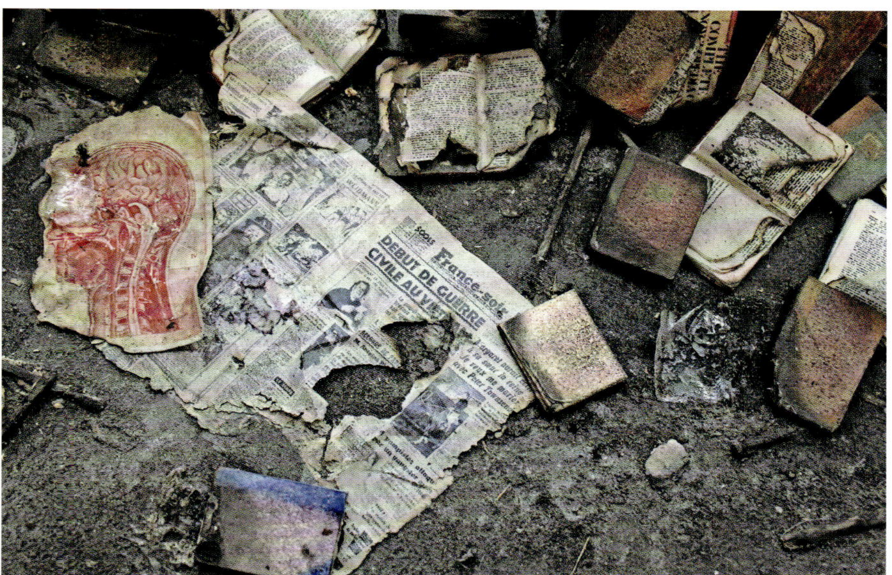

Miniaturized Tragedy III (detail 2).

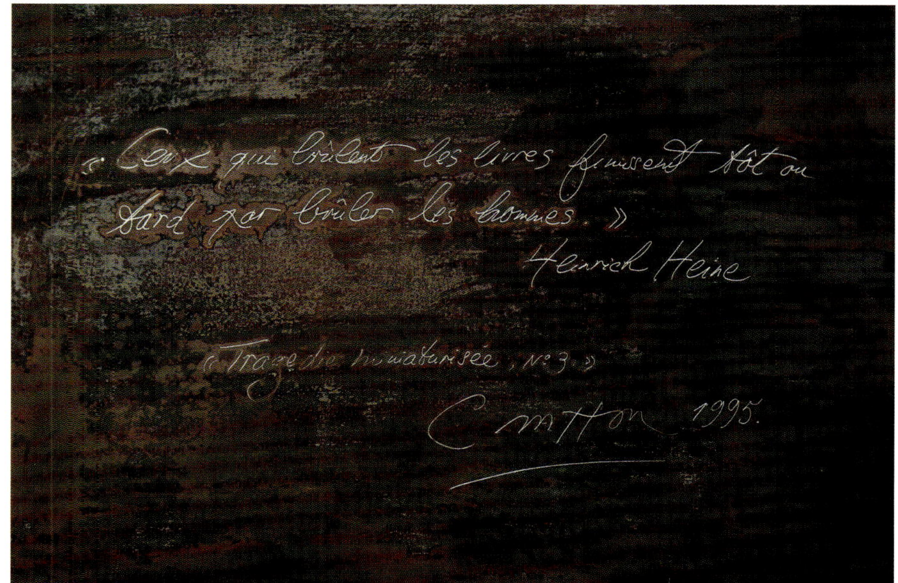

Miniaturized Tragedy III (epigraph on brass plaque outside, "Those who burn books end up sooner or later by burning men. Heinrich Heine.")

Photographs Léonard Matton.

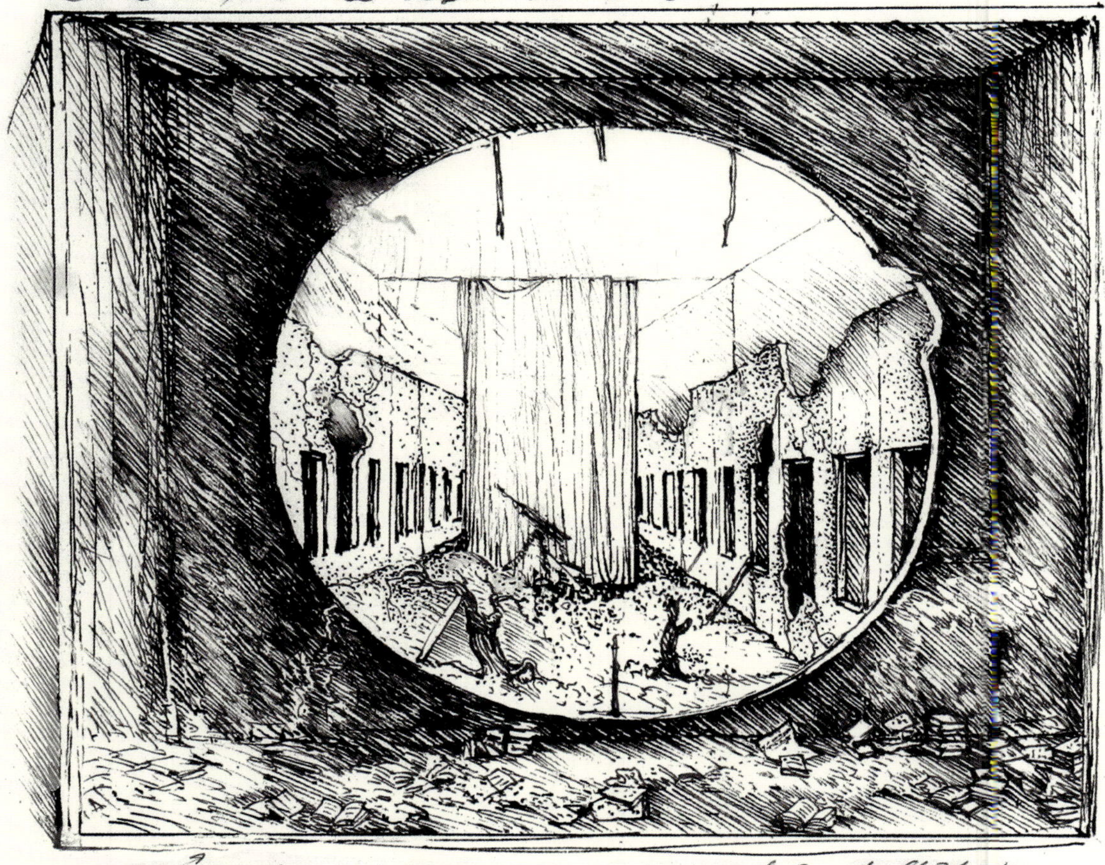

Miniaturized Tragedy III, 1994.
Pencil and felt pen on paper, 7 × 8 ¼ in. (18 × 21 cm).

Sarfati's High School
Burnt books, newspapers, and other objects related to studying.
-Telephone, computer, a small gun, notebooks, many newspapers, essays written by students, letters, books with images, a tiny globe.
On the canvas, the shadow of a machine gun pointing to the sky.

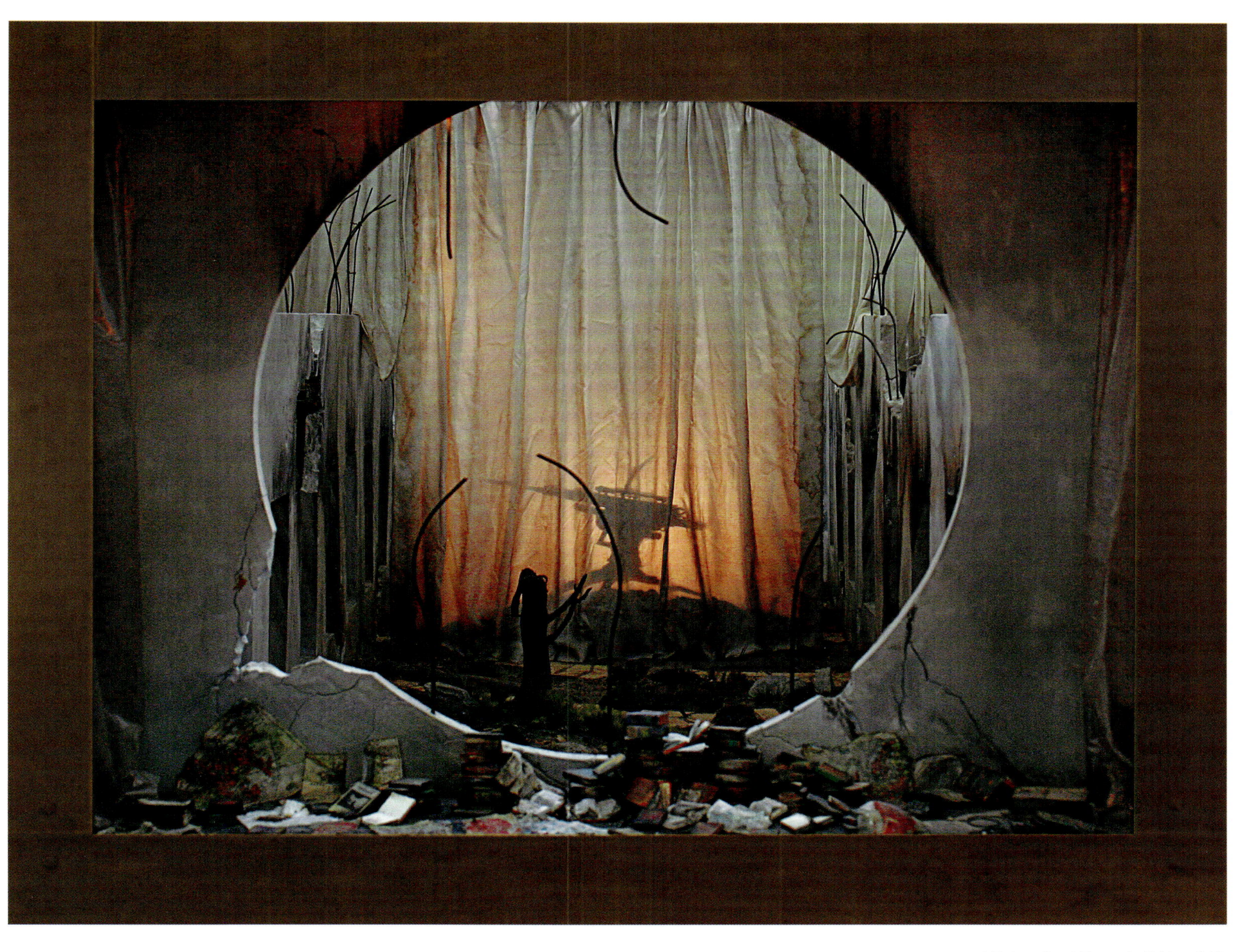

Miniaturized Tragedy III (detail 3).

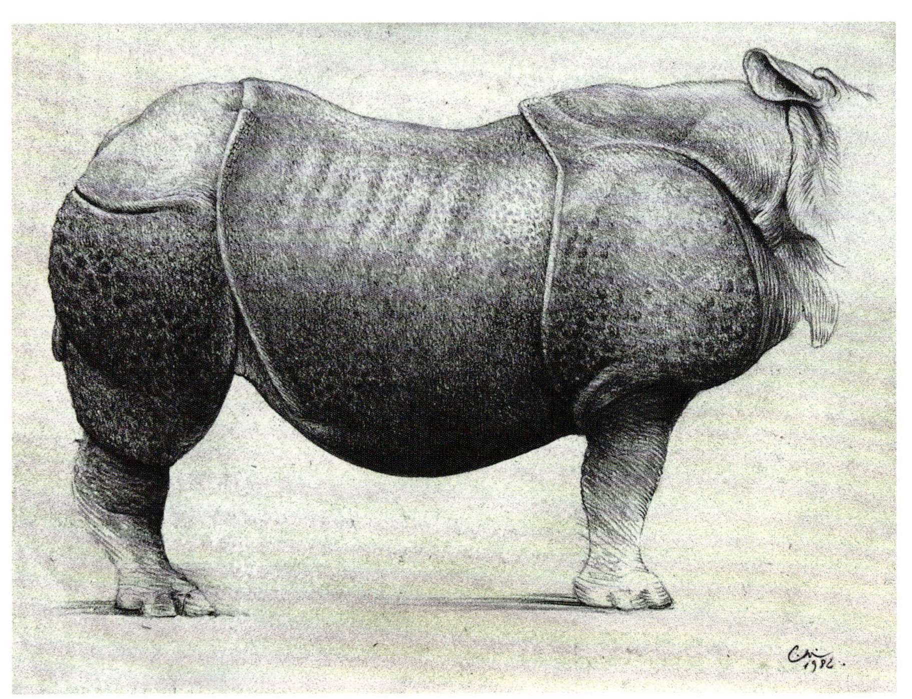

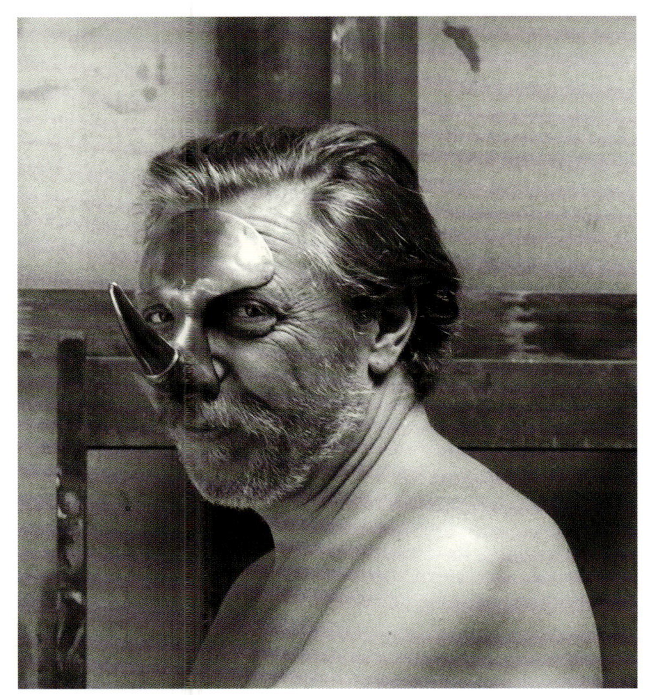

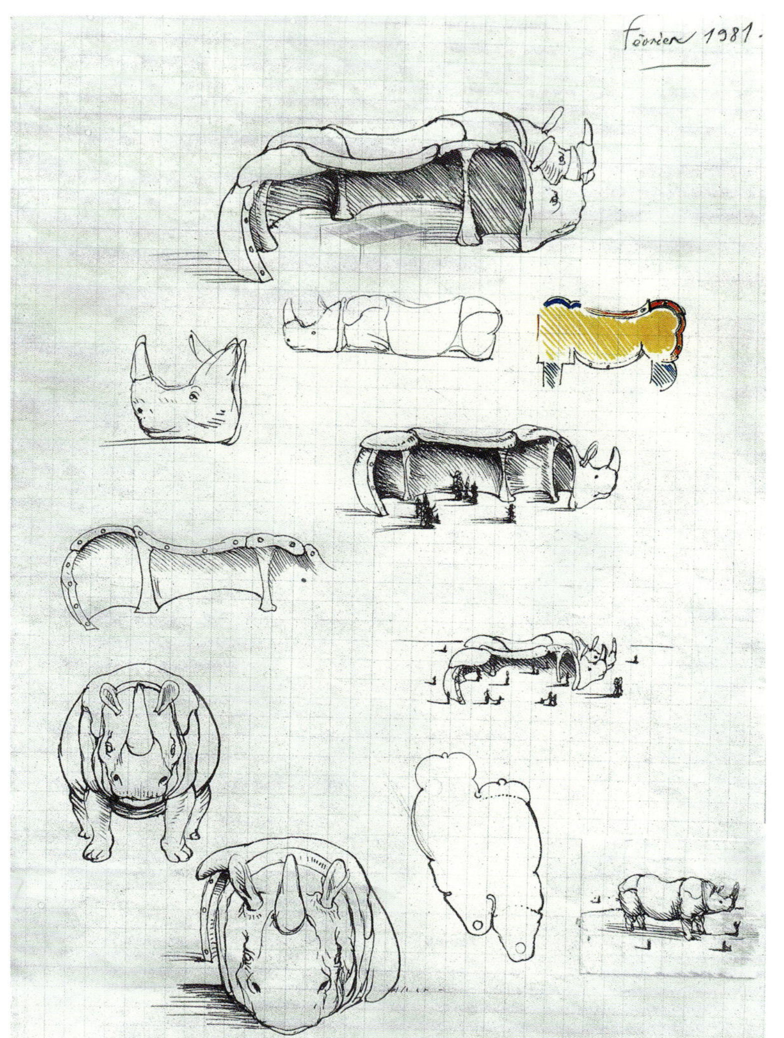

nocériros

Rhynocéros

Rhinocéros

Rinophéros

Rino-féroce

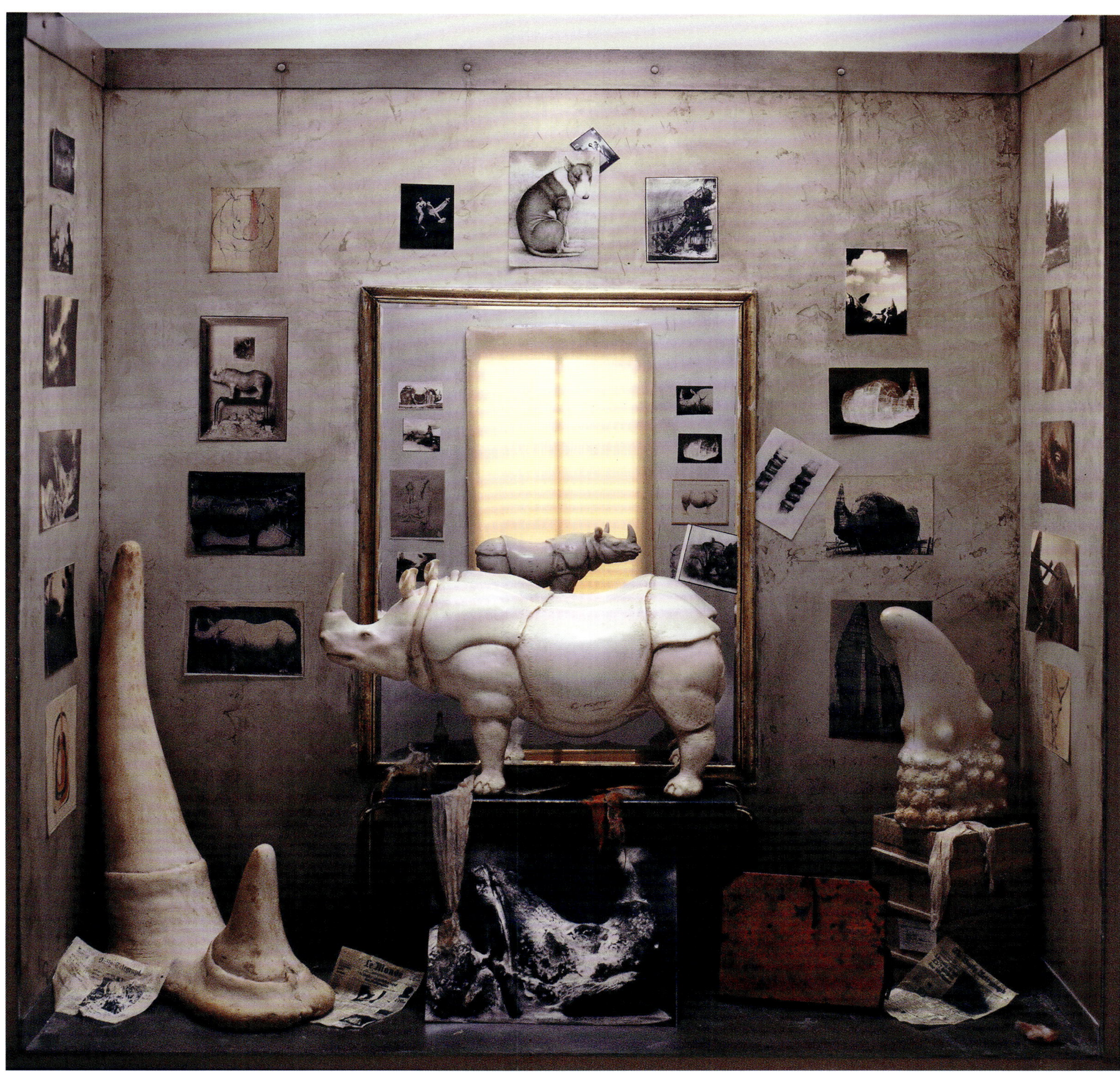

Facing page:
The Rhinoceros, 1980.
Pencil on paper, 9 ½ × 12 ½ in.
(24.5 × 32 cm).

Monumental Rhinoceros (studies), 1981.
Pencil, felt pen, and gouache on paper,
11 ¾ × 8 ¼ in (29.7 × 21 cm).

Self-portrait Rhinoceromania, 1982.
Photograph.

Rhinoceros Writings, 2001.
Felt pen on paper, 11 ¾ × 8 ¼ in.
(29.7 × 21 cm).

Studio of a Rhinoceros Sculptor, 2001.
Mixed media, 24 ½ × 26 × 29 ¾ in.
(62 × 66 × 75.5 cm).

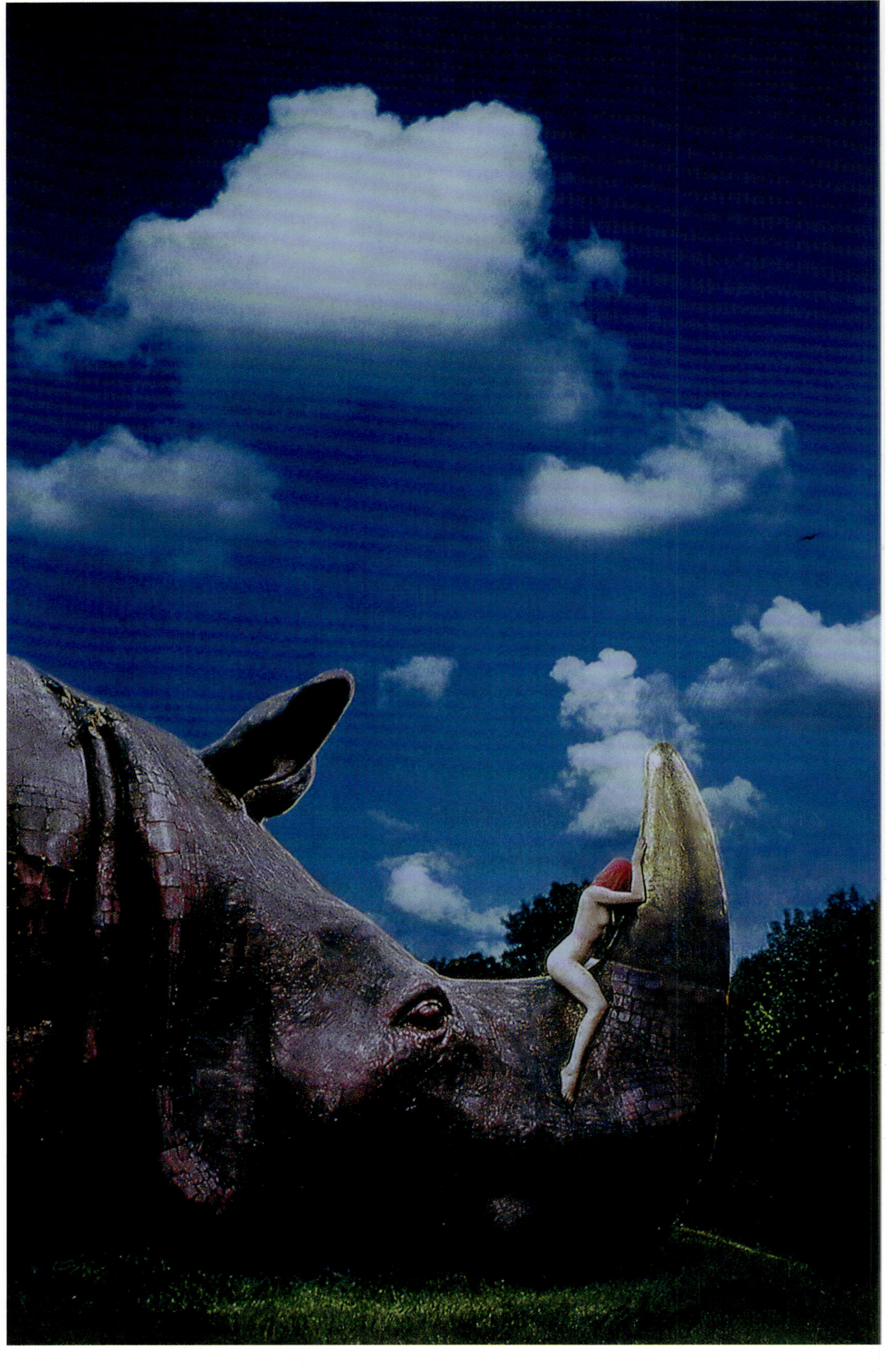

Sylvie on the Rhinoceros at Le Coudray-Montceaux, 1979. Photograph.

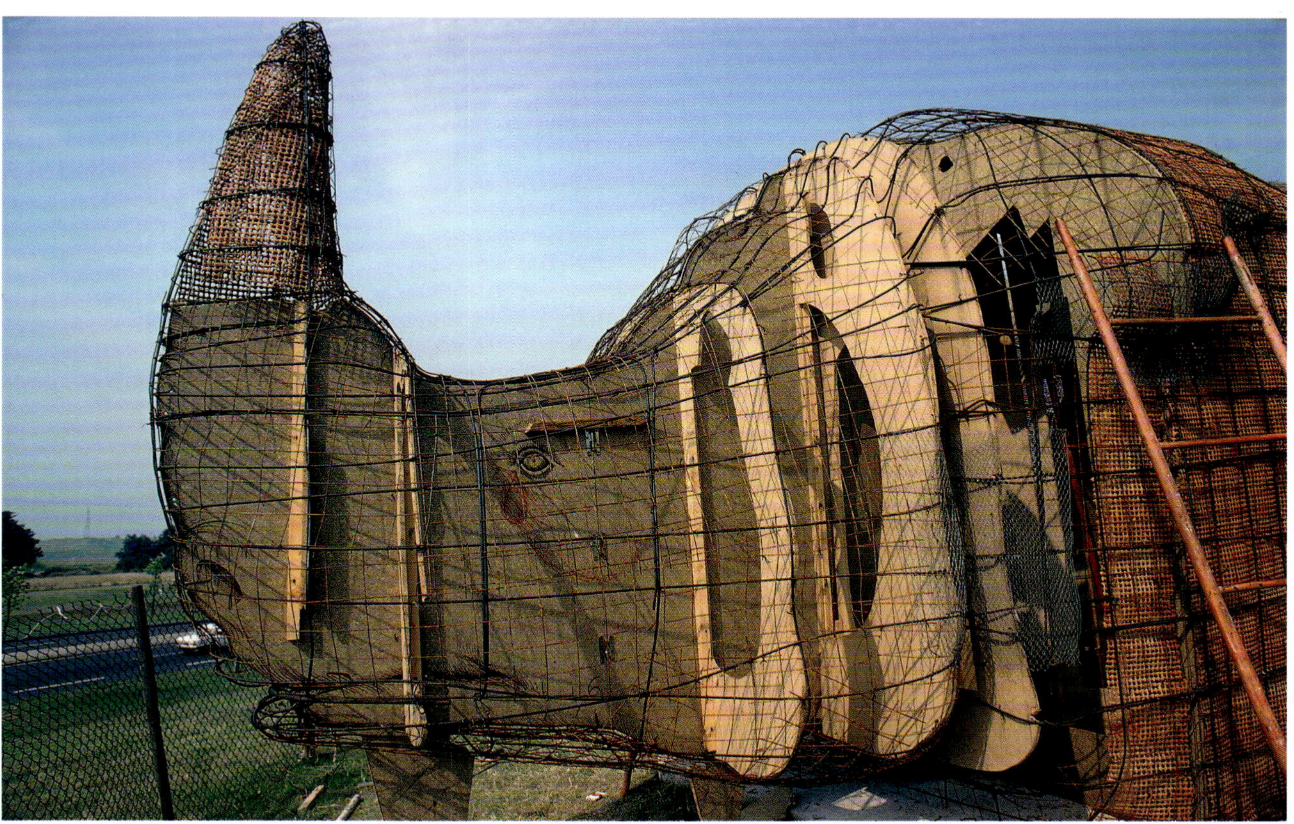

Wooden Armature and Soldered Reinforcement for the Rhinoceros at Évry, 1982.
297 × 590 ½ × 196 ¾ in.
(450 × 1 500 × 500 cm).

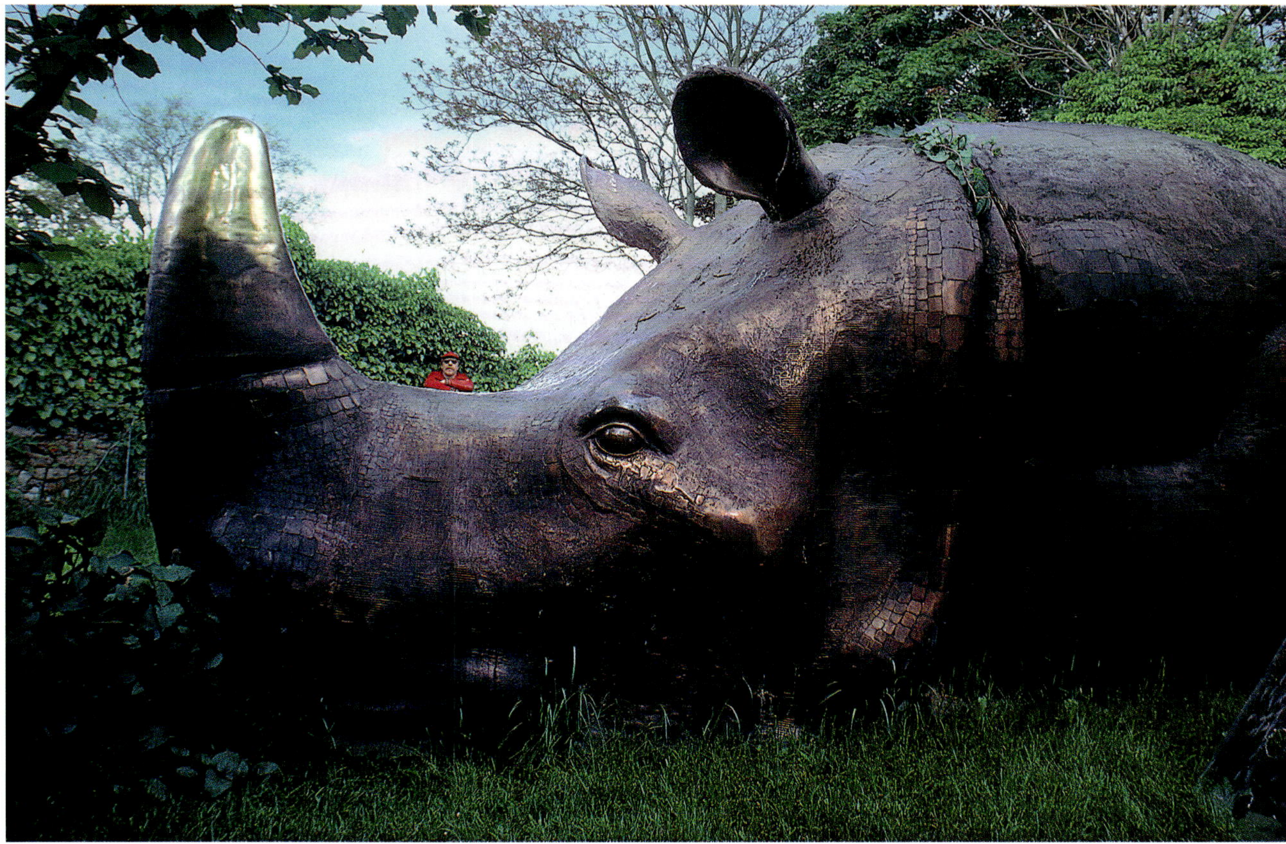

Charles behind the Rhinoceros at Le Coudray-Montceaux, 1981.
Photograph Yann Matton.

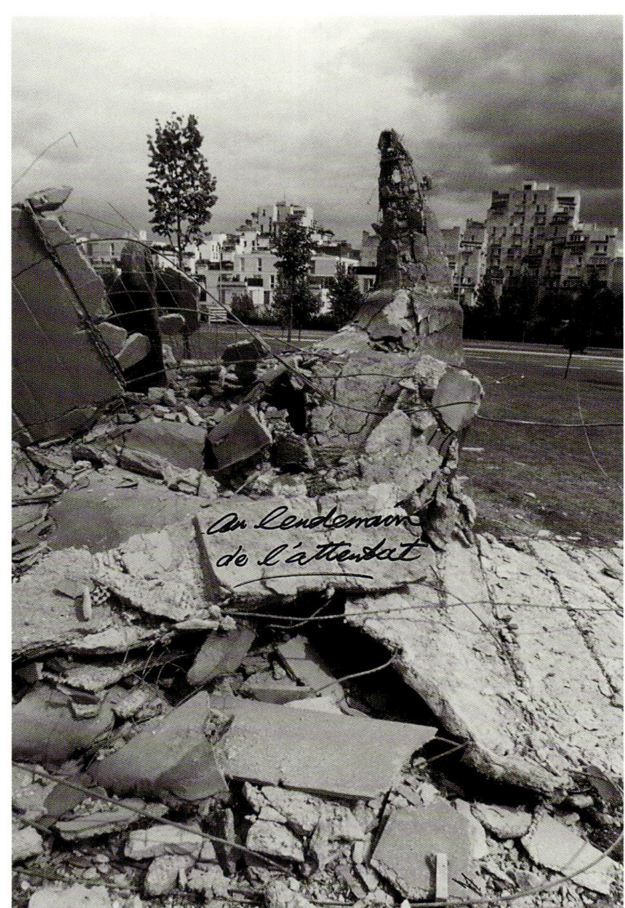

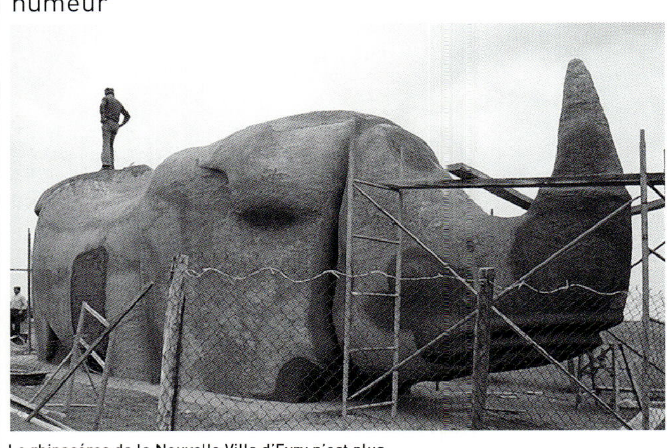
Parispoche

humeur

Le rhinocéros de la Nouvelle Ville d'Evry n'est plus.

In the night of August 23–24 [1982], a huge sculpture (more than 36 feet long, 12 feet wide, and 13 feet tall), created in the hope it might regale the eyes of adults and children alike, was the victim of a bomb attack in the park of Les Loges, in the new town of Évry.

Above all, I'd like to be able to envisage your act as just thoughtless, in that you might have killed or maimed an innocent passerby. I am forced, however, to bow to your professionalism, since a certain degree of competence is required to turn thirteen tons of concrete to rubble. Personally, I like a job well done, and that's what irks me, because we old pros shouldn't muck up each other's work. Because, finally, whoever you are, you know full well that it must have amounted to a lot of work. And, despite everything, you did it, and because you did you must have had your reasons. Is it a hatred of the Asian rhinoceros? Did you disagree with my interpretation of it? Do you harbor an utter loathing of "useless" works of art ... in today's society? Did you want to test some explosives, or were you well paid? In the end, I find it sad and dumb. If only we could know why.

Charles Matton

On the Day after the Attack, August 24, 1982. Felt pen on a silver print.

"An open letter to the person who blew up the rhinoceros," extract from Charles Matton's piece published in *Pariscope,* September 8, 1982

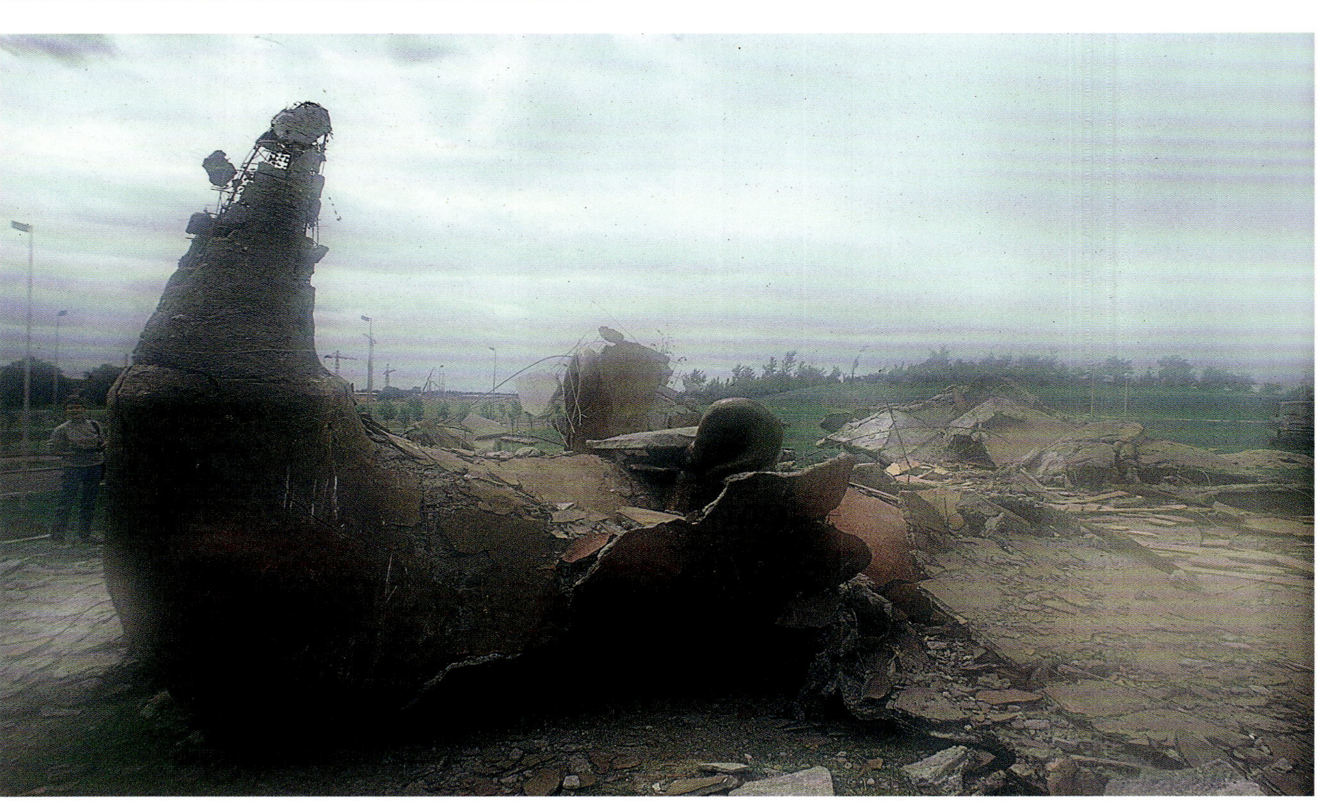

The Évry Rhinoceros destroyed by 15 ½ pounds of TNT, August 24, 1982. Photograph.

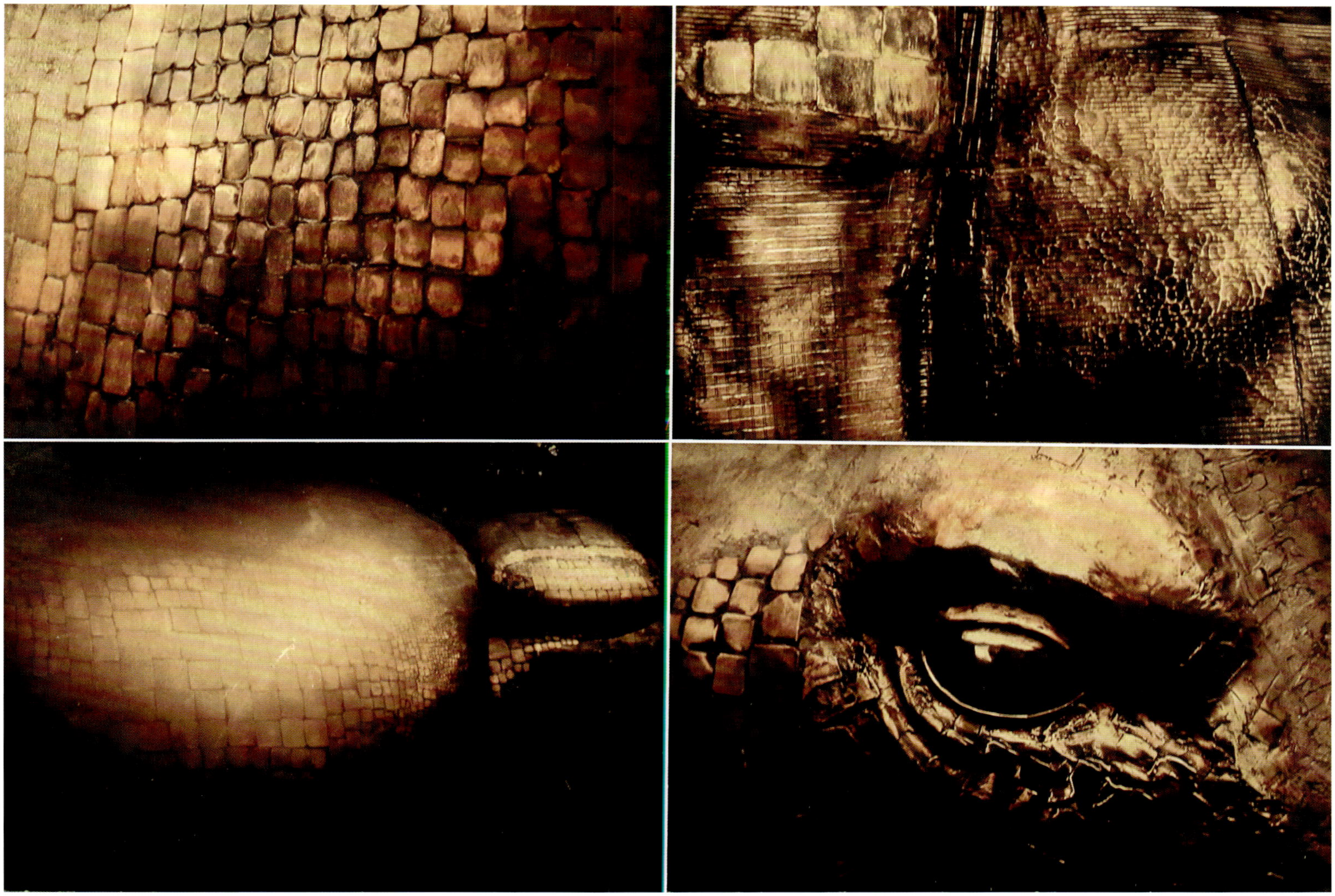

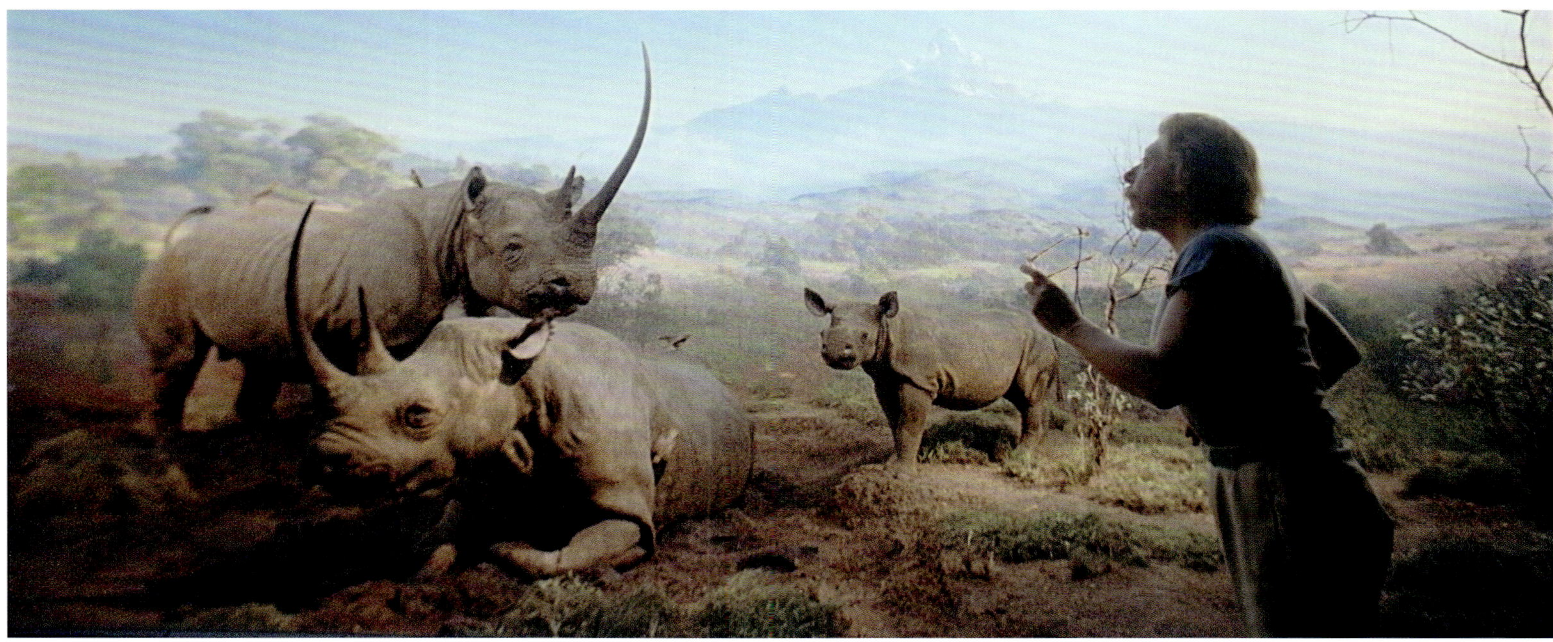

The Rhinoceros at Le Coudray-Montceaux
(four close-ups), 1982.
Bronze and brass.

Charles in front of the Asian rhinoceroses,
Natural History Museum, New York, 1980.
Photograph by Sylvie Matton.

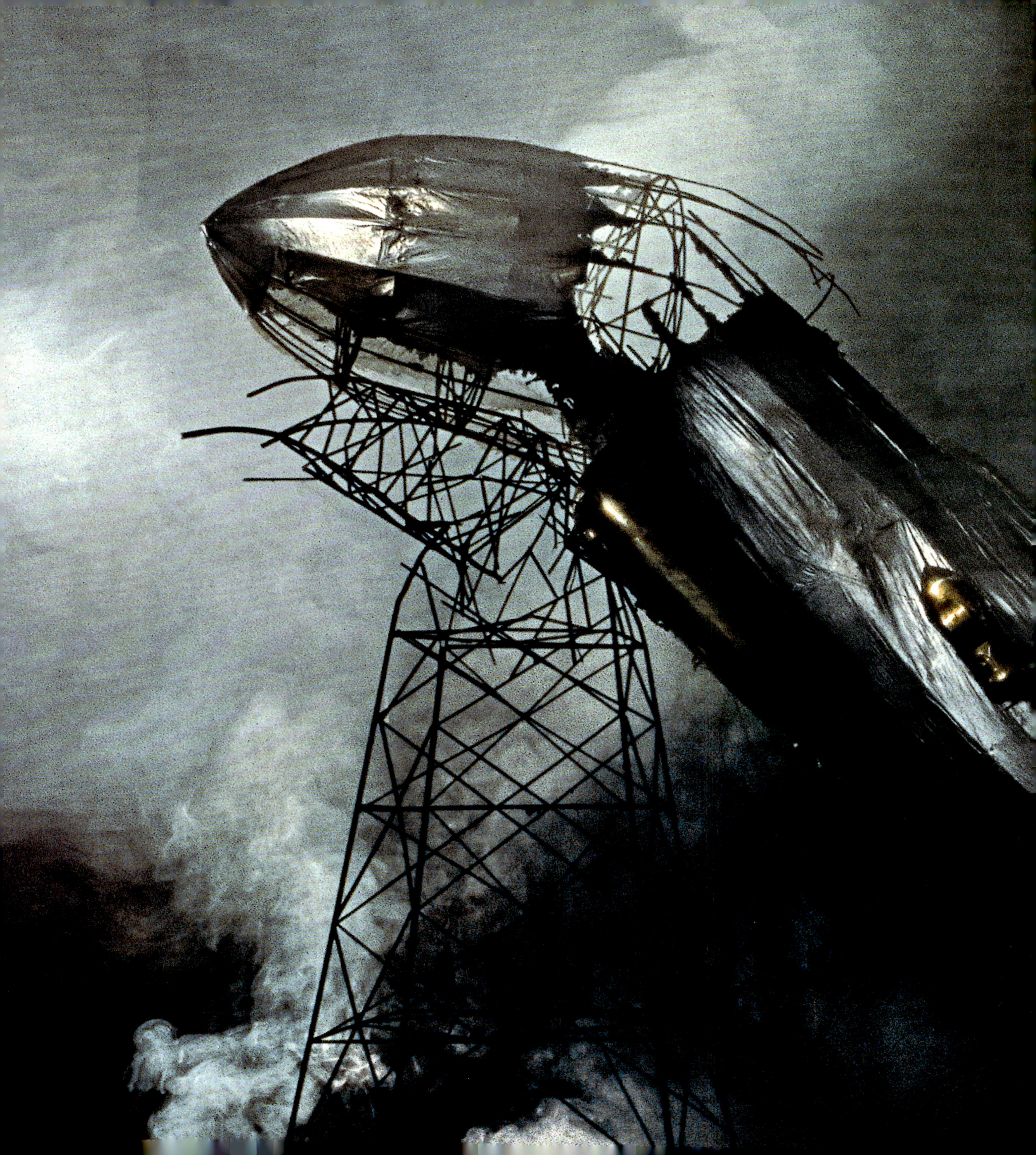

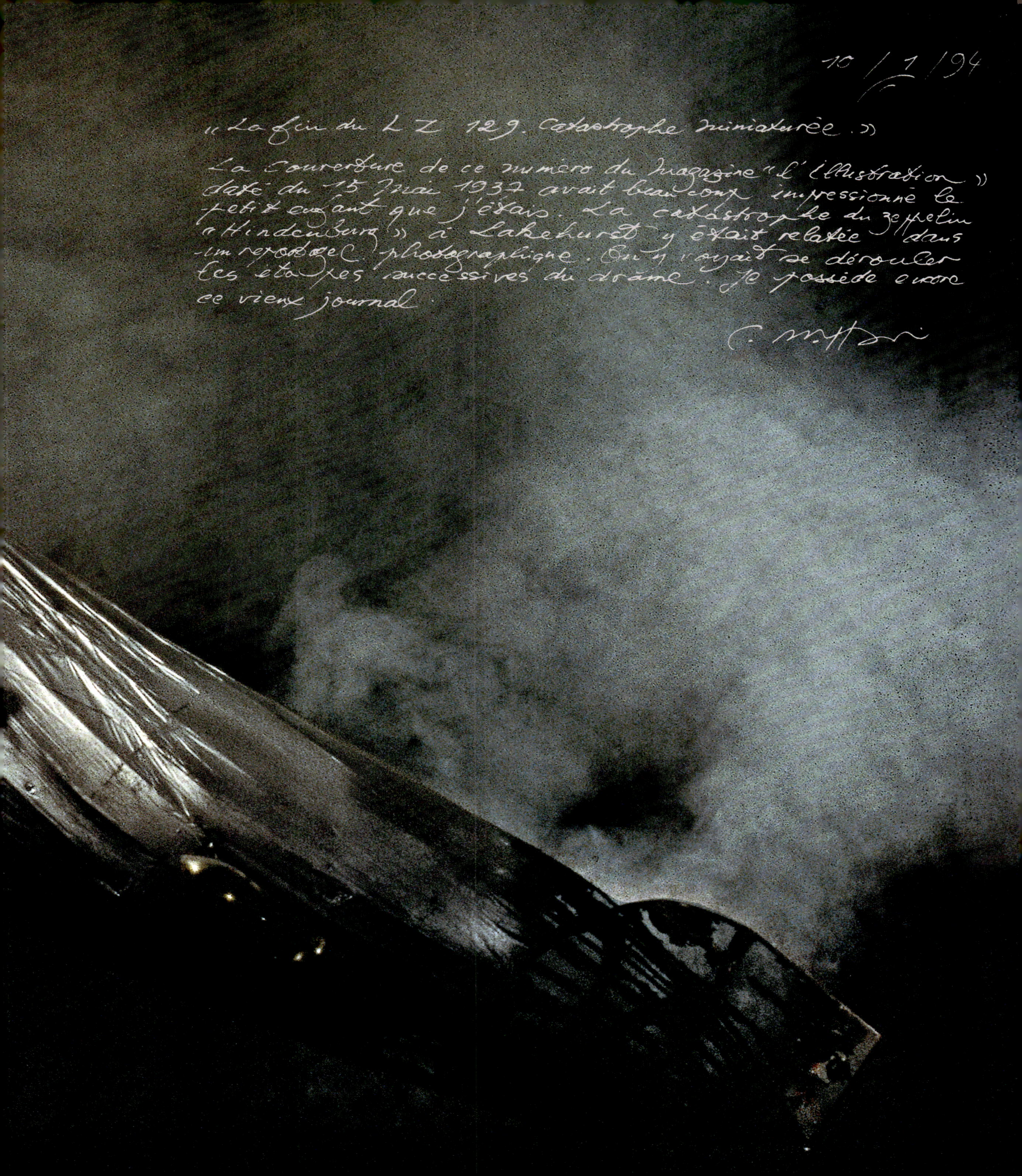

10 / 1 / 94

« La fin du LZ 129. Catastrophe miniaturée. »

La couverture de ce numéro du magazine « L'Illustration » daté du 15 mai 1937 avait beaucoup impressionné le petit enfant que j'étais. La catastrophe du zeppelin « Hindenburg » à Lakehurst y était relatée dans un reportage photographique. On y voyait se dérouler les étapes successives du drame. Je possède encore ce vieux journal.

[illegible]

Previous pages:
The Zeppelin Hindenburg, *Miniaturized Tragedy, I*, 1994.
Mixed media, 41 ¼ × 66 × 21 ½ in.
(105 × 168 × 55 cm).

The end of L Z 129. Miniaturized catastrophe. The cover of this number of the magazine L'Illustration, *May 15, 1937 had greatly impressed the little child I then was. The catastrophe of the Hindenburg zeppelin at Lakehurst was covered in an illustrated report. One watched as each stage of the drama unfolded. I still have this old magazine.*
C. Matton

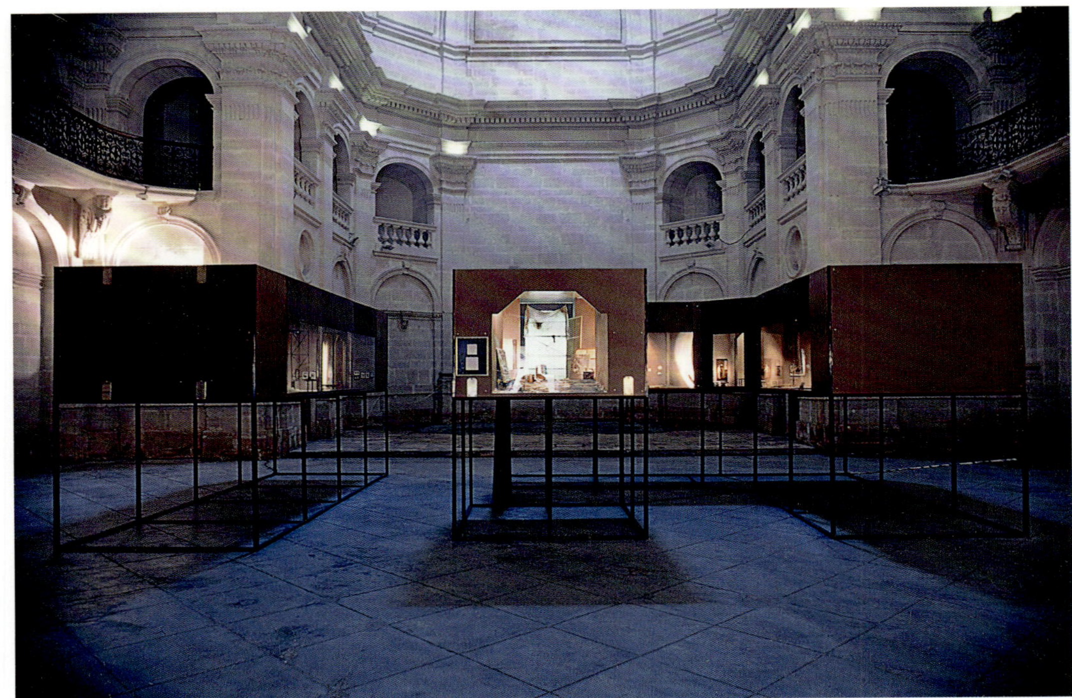

The Scrupulous Reconstitution of an Upcoming Exhibition (shown in 1990 in the Jesuit Chapel at Nîmes), 1989.
Mixed media, 34 ¼ × 322 ¾ × 177 in.
(87 × 820 × 450 cm).

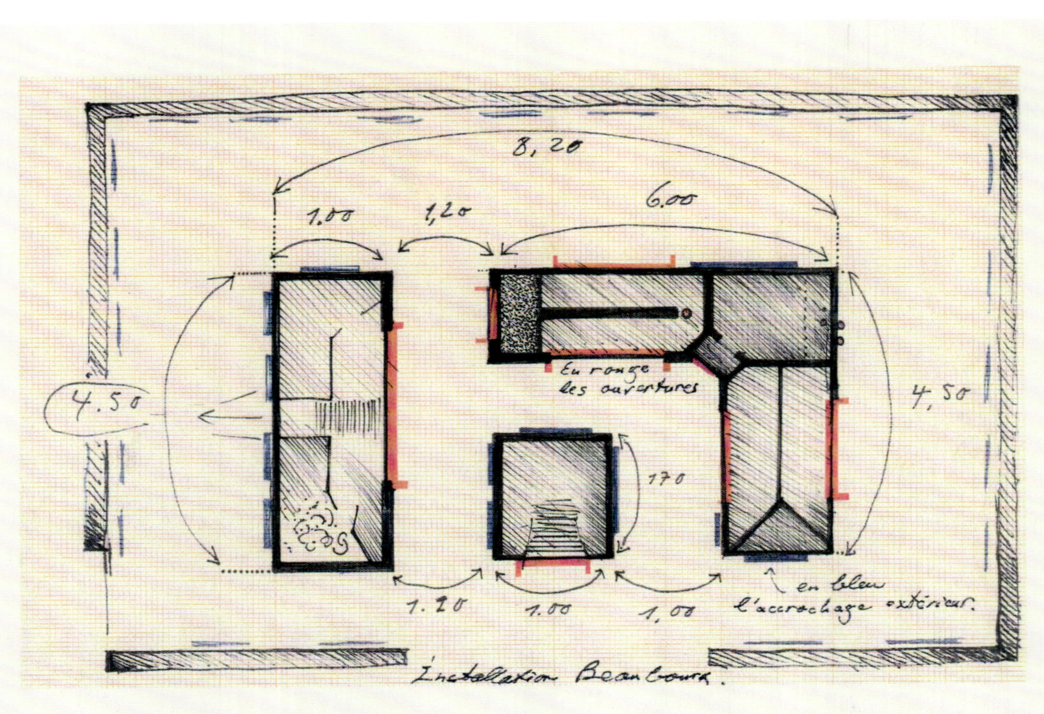

The Scrupulous Reconstitution of an Upcoming Exhibition (plan), 1988.
Felt pen on graph paper,
8 ¼ × 11 ¾ in. (21 × 29.7 cm).

In October 1989, Charles Matton's work occupied the final room in *L'Invention d'un Art* at the Centre Pompidou, in Paris—an exhibition dealing with the historical and artistic links between photography and painting. The conclusion to what was a vast show covering some 27,000 square feet, Charles Matton's large-scale installation took the form of a miniaturized exhibition of his own works. The piece has since been displayed in a number of other venues. S.M.

The Scrupulous Reconstitution of an Upcoming Exhibition (detail 1).

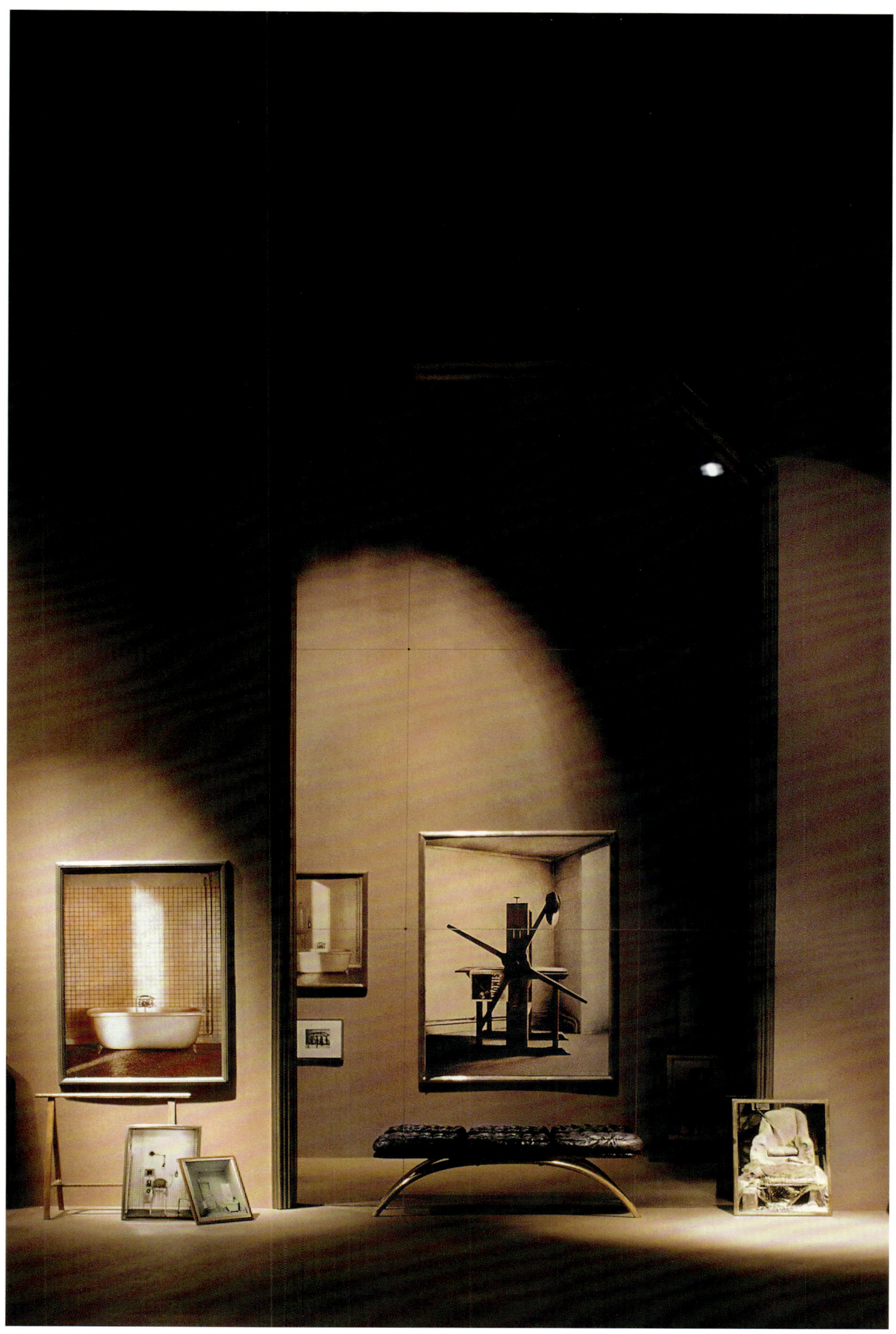

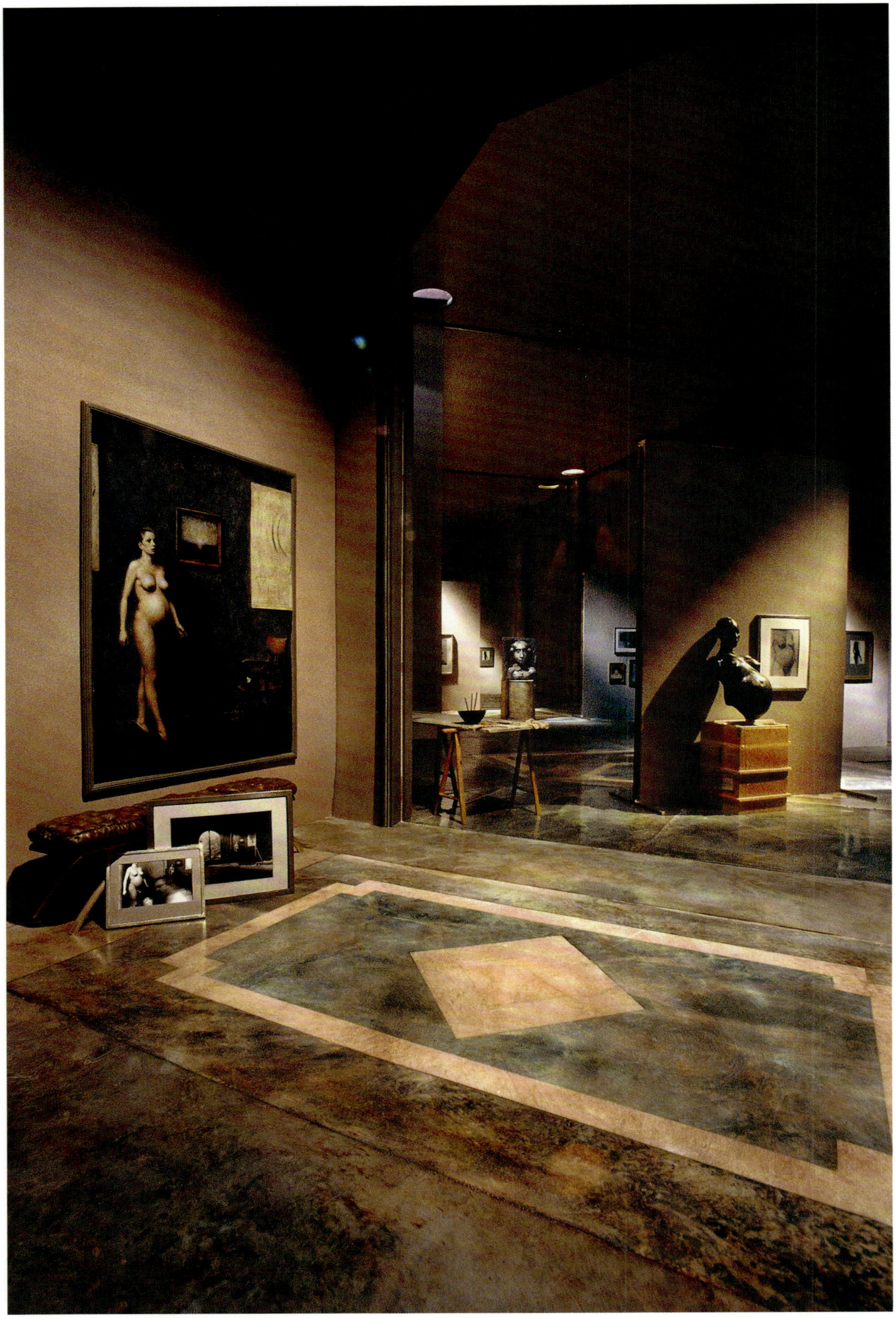

The Scrupulous Reconstitution of an Upcoming Exhibition (corner room, tribute to motherhood).

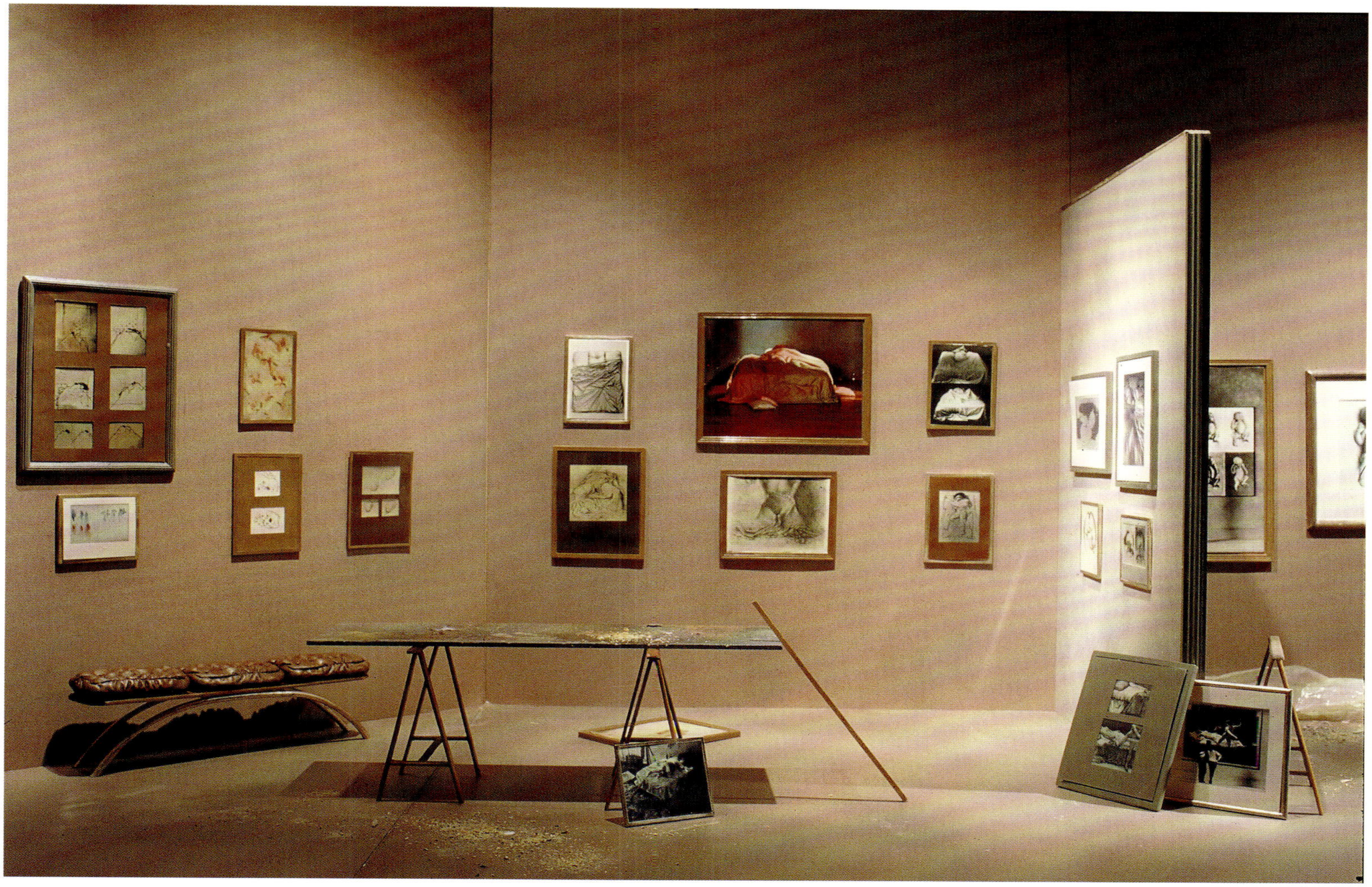

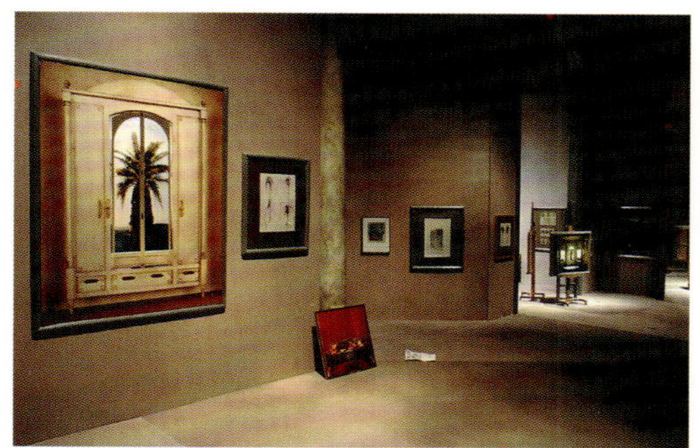

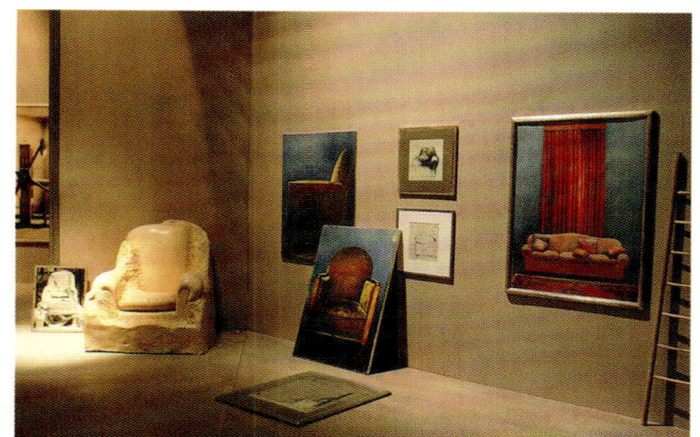

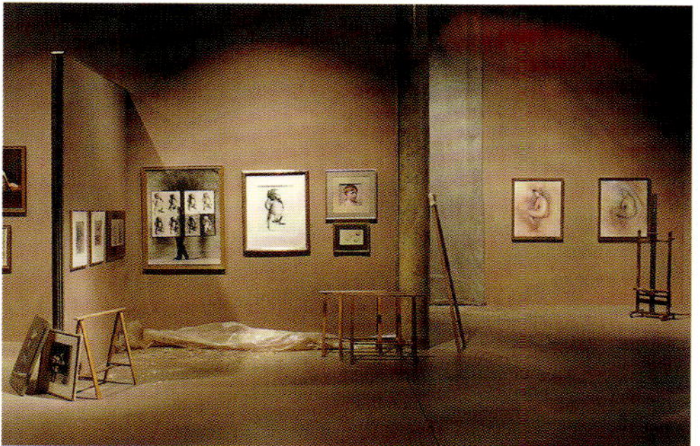

The Scrupulous Reconstitution of an Upcoming Exhibition (details 2, 3, 4, 5).

I think my work is nourished above all by life. If I trace them back to their genesis, my miniaturized spaces have grown from photographs, drawings, paintings, and sculptures, themselves filled with memories of life.

These places each have their story, their dramas, traces of which subsist from the primal image—the visual bolt from the blue—through all the stages of realization, right up to the photographic variations composed in its aftermath that are metamorphosed by light, and from which, with soundscapes or ambient music, one might produce further variants, *ad infinitum*.

What's it all for? What use is art? And, first of all, what is art, anyway? What role does life play in it? What are its consequences for men? (Isn't this the essential question?)

Personal note, November 19, 1997

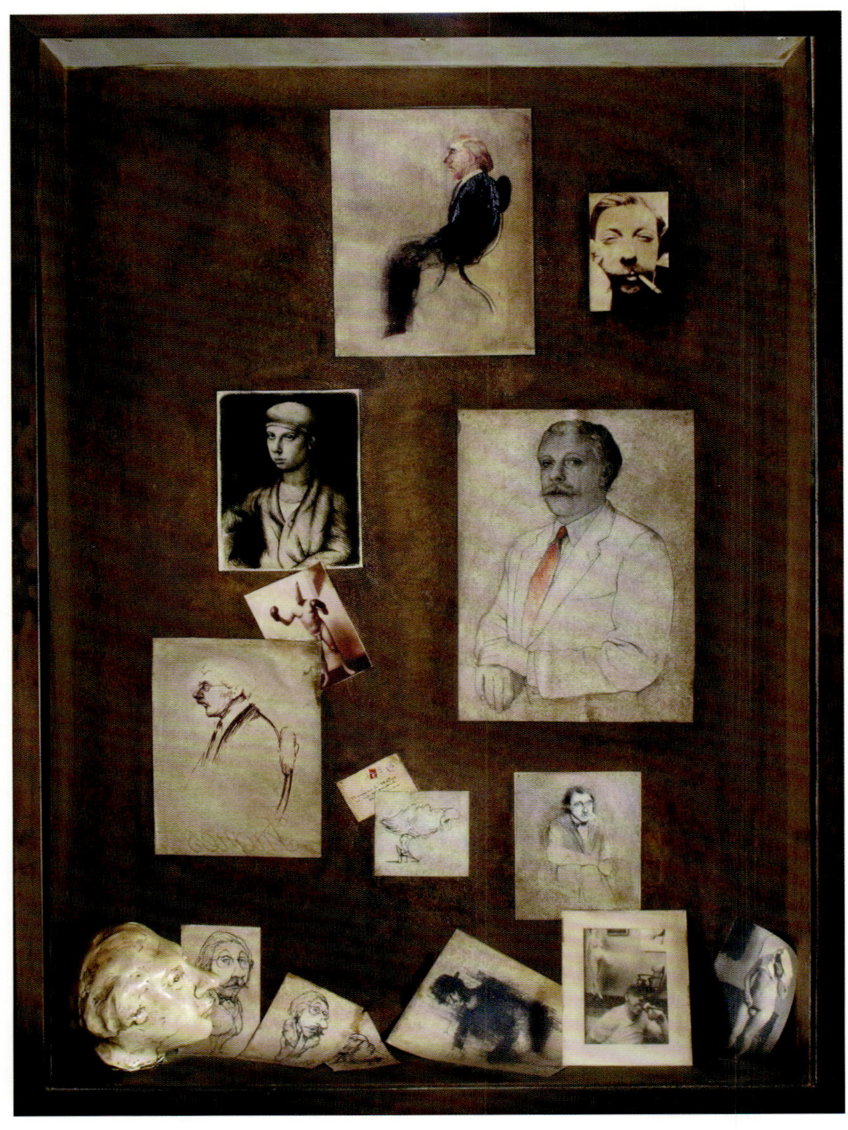

Self-portrait, 1999.
Drawings and watercolors, sculpture, photographs, and wood,
24 ¼ × 25 ¼ × 3 in. (61.5 × 64 × 8 cm).

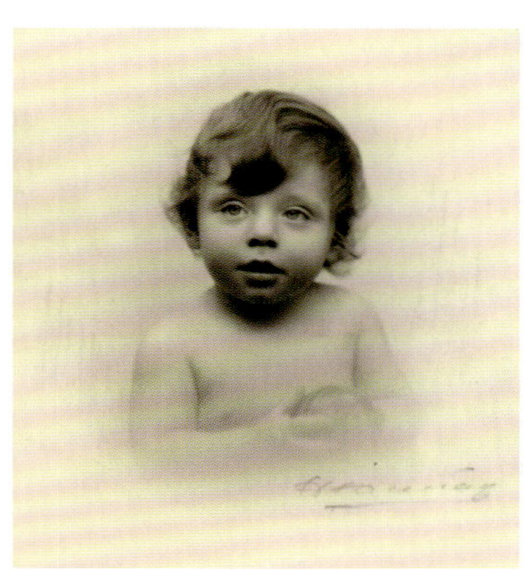

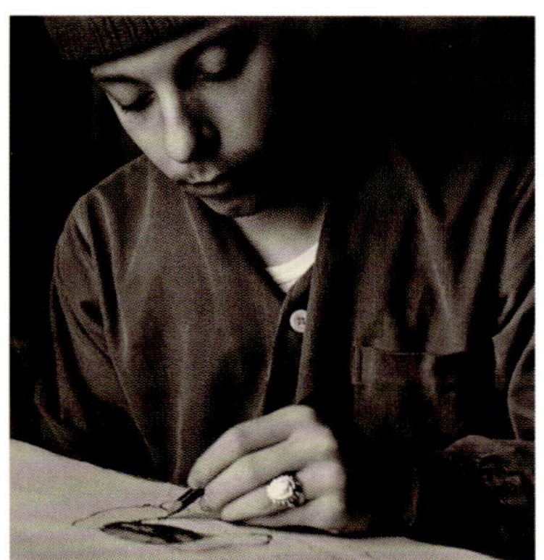

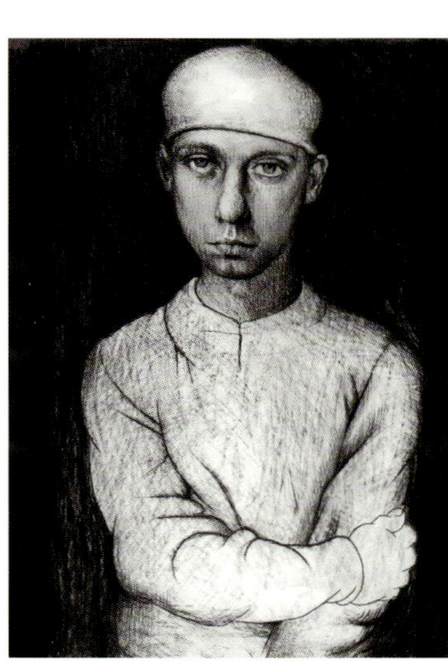

CHRONOLOGY

September 13, 1931–November 19, 2008
Born, lived, worked, and died in Paris.

SELECTED EXHIBITIONS

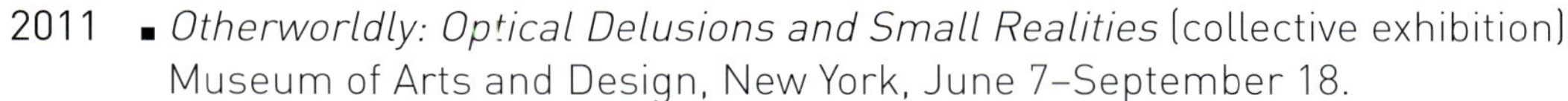

2011
- *Otherworldly: Optical Delusions and Small Realities* (collective exhibition), Museum of Arts and Design, New York, June 7–September 18.
- *Charles Matton*, All Visual Arts, London, September 8–October 5.
- *Charles Matton*, Galerie Agathe Gaillard, Paris, November–December.

2010
- *Charles Matton: Retrospective*. Städtische Museen, Iena, Germany, December 12, 2009–February 21, 2010.
- Permanent installation of *The Library Homage to Perec IV*, at the Bibliothèque Nationale de France, Paris, September 10.
- *Vanitas: The Transience of Earthly Pleasures* (collective exhibition), All Visual Arts, London, October 12–17.

2009
- *Qui a peur des artistes?*, selection of works from the François Pinault Foundation, Palais des Arts, Dinard, France, June 14–September 13.
- *Great Way Prevails-Masterpieces of Modern Art* (collective exhibition), CAFA Art Museum, Beijing, China, May 16–June 17.
- *Found Classics* (collective exhibition), Found Museum, Beijing, China, July 5–August 2.

2008
- *Charles Matton: Selected Works*, Forum Gallery, New York, July 10–September 6.

2007
- *États de lieux*, Maison Européenne de la Photographie, Paris, June 12–September 30.

2006
- Carte Blanche du Ministère de la Culture-Palais-Royal, Paris, March–April.
- Art Paris, March 16–23.
- 21C Museum, Louisville, United States, November 2006–June 2007.
- Permanent installation of a box (*Early Morning at the Café de Flore*) at the Café de Flore, Paris, December 15.

2005 ▪ *Important New Works by Forum Gallery Artists*, Forum Gallery, New York, June 16–August 26.
▪ *Well Done* (collective exhibition), MOCA Taipei, Taiwan, August 6–September 25.

2004 ▪ *Charles Matton, New Works*, Forum Gallery, New York, October 28–December 11.

2003 ▪ *Illusions*, Forum Gallery, Los Angeles, United States, September.
▪ *Art of the Twentieth Century*, Armory Show, New York, November 20–24.
▪ Charles Matton's Universe, Modern Art Gallery, Taichung, Taiwan, September 9– 30.

2002 ▪ *Within These Walls*, Forum Gallery, New York, May 16–June 21.
▪ *Art of the Twentieth Century*, Armory Show, New York, November 20–24.

2000 ▪ FIAC 2000, solo exhibition, Galerie Beaubourg, Pierre and Marianne Nahon, Paris, October.
▪ Galerie Beaubourg, Vence, France, November–December.
▪ *L'Appel de Tanger*, Institut du Monde Arabe, Paris (five Boxes together with manuscripts and photographs), November 9, 1999–January 30, 2000.

1999 ▪ *Matton-Rembrandt*, Maison Européenne de la Photographie, Paris, June 23–September 5.
▪ *Deux ou trois choses que je sais de Rembrandt et de quelques autres*, Galerie Beaubourg, Paris, September–October.

1998 ▪ *Littérature et Bel canto*, Galerie Beaubourg, Paris, September–October.

1994 ▪ *Constat de lieux*, Galerie Beaubourg, Paris, January–February.

1992 ▪ *Rétrospective et Citations*, Centre d'Art Contemporain, Fréjus, France, June–September.

1991 ▪ *Charles Matton*, École Nationale Supérieure des Beaux-Arts, Paris, September 25–November 3.

1990 ▪ *L'Invention d'un Art* (collective exhibition), National Museum of Modern Art of Kyoto and Tokyo (MoMAK), Japan, October.

1989 ▪ Espace Photographique, Paris, March.
▪ *L'Invention d'un Art* (collective exhibition), Centre Pompidou, Paris, October–January.

1987 ▪ *Antipodes*, Palais de Tokyo, Paris, May 6–September 24.

1983 ▪ *Séductions utopiques*, Galerie Robert Delpire, Paris, May.

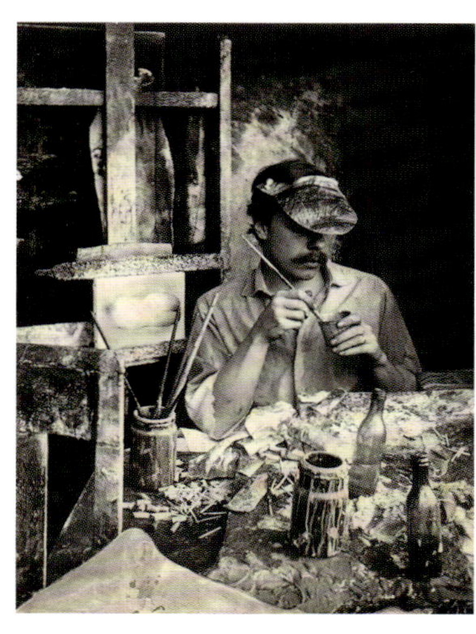

1960–83
Charles Matton stops exhibiting publicly, instead painting for himself and a handful of collectors. Also works for the magazine *Esquire* and publishers Christian Bourgois and Le Club Français du Livre.

1961 ▪ Galerie Raymond Mason and Janine Hao, Paris.

1960 ▪ Cercle Volney (with the sculptor Michel Charpentier), Paris.

STAGE DESIGN

1995 ▪ *The Unexpecting Man*, Yasmina Reza, Théâtre Hébertot, Paris.

1990 ▪ *Mademoiselle Else*, Arthur Schnitzler, Théâtre de la Colline, Paris.

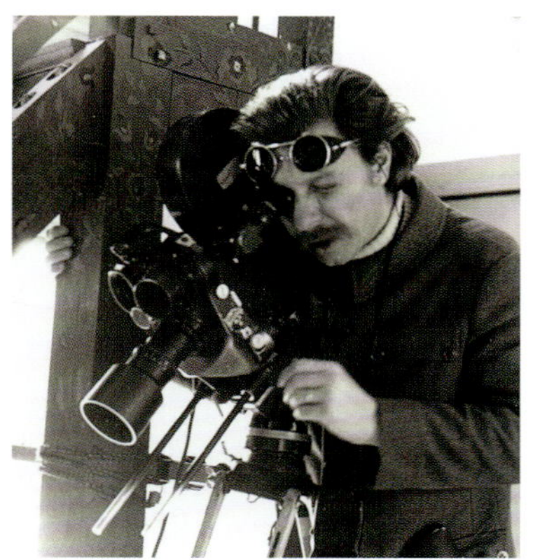

CINEMA (screenwriting and direction)

1998 ▪ *Rembrandt* (114 mins.). Grand Prix 1997 for best script (written with Sylvie Matton).

1994 ▪ *La Lumière des étoiles mortes* (107 mins.).

1976 ▪ *L'Amour est un fleuve en Russie* (110 mins.).

1972 ▪ *L'Italien des Roses* (95 mins.). Premio di Selezione, Venice Film Festival, Critics' Week 1972, Grand Prix Perspectives at the Cannes Film Festival 1973.

1968 ▪ *Mai 68 ou les violences policières* (11 mins.). Selected by Jean-Luc Godard for a screening tour through France.

1966 ▪ *La Pomme ou l'Histoire d'une histoire* (14 mins.). Grand Prix at the Festival of Hyères, Grand Prix at the Paris Biennial.

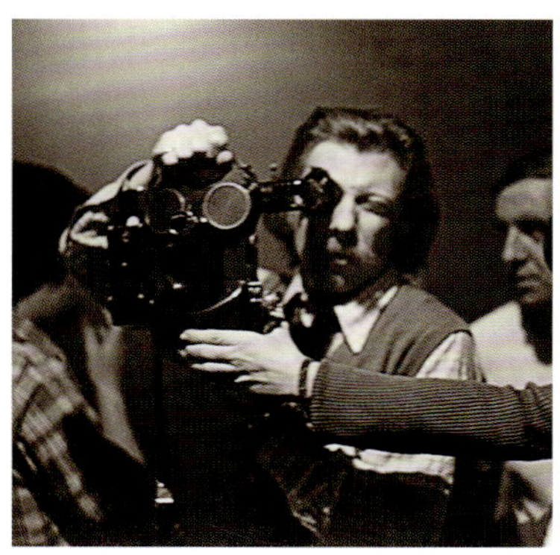

RELATED WORKS

Charles Matton, visiblement. Documentary film, 43 mins. Directed by Sylvie Matton. 2009. Production ARTE-Kuiv.

Douanes. 26 mins. Directed by Sylvie Matton. 1989. Production INA.

SELECTED BIBLIOGRAPHY

BOOKS AND CATALOGS ON CHARLES MATTON

2010 ▪ Robert Fleck, *Charles Matton* (exh. cat.), Städtische Museen, Iena.

2007 ▪ Jean Baudrillard and Charles Matton, *États de lieux* (exh. cat.), Maison Européenne de la Photographie, Paris.

2006 ▪ Françoise Sagan, Jean Baudrillard, and Charles Matton, *Hommage au Café de Flore, Making of* (Publication Carole Chrétiennot).

2002 ▪ Barbara S. Krulik, *Within These Walls* (exh. cat.), Forum Gallery, New York.

1999 ▪ Jean-Luc Monterosso, Sylvie Matton, *Matton-Rembrandt* (exh. cat.), Maison Européenne de la Photographie, Paris.

1992 ▪ Robert Fleck, *Rétrospective et citations* (exh. cat.), Centre d'Art Contemporain, Fréjus.

1991 ▪ Jean Baudrillard, *Charles Matton*, monograph, Paris: Hatier.
▪ Jean Baudrillard (exh. cat.), École Nationale des Beaux-Arts de Paris.

1989 ▪ Françoise Sagan, *Le sacrilège bizarre*, Jean-Luc Monterosso (gen. ed.), (exh. cat.), Espace Photo, Paris.

1987 ▪ Jean Baudrillard, *Antipodes* (exh. cat.), Palais de Tokyo, Paris.

1983 ▪ Jean Baudrillard, *Séductions utopiques* (exh. cat.), Galerie Delpire, Paris.

BOOKS BY CHARLES MATTON

Alain Finkielkraut, Ernest Pignon-Ernest, Charles Matton, *Être artiste aujourd'hui*, Geneva: Éditions du Tricorne, 2002.

Charles Matton, *Rembrandt*, Paris: Éditions J'ai lu, 1998.

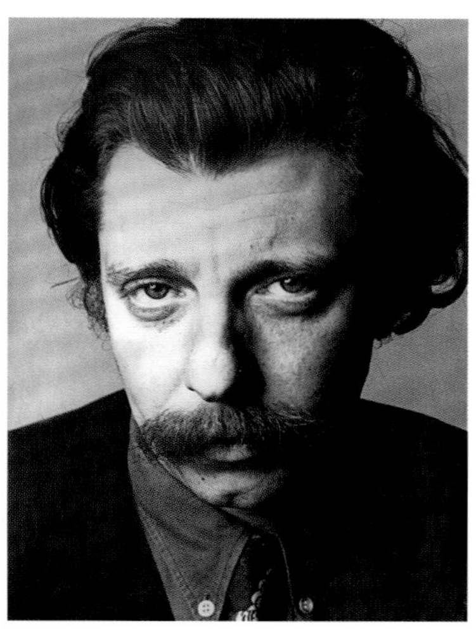

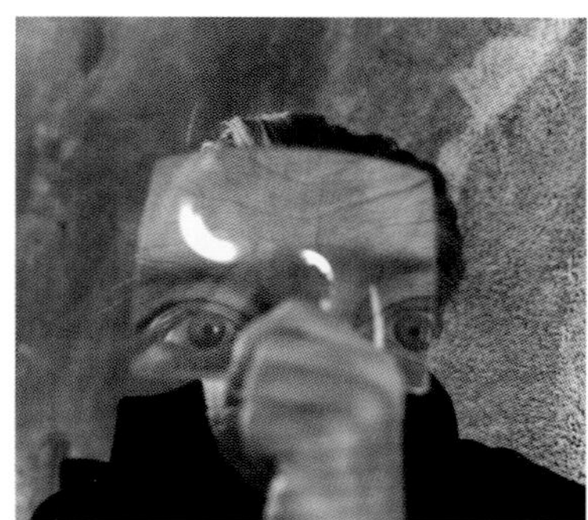

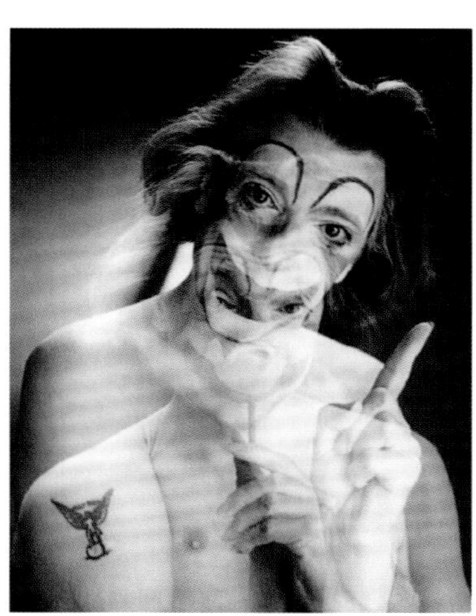

PRESS (selection)

2008 ▪ Laurie Hurtwitz, *Artnews*, July–August.

2006 ▪ Sylvie Matton, *La Revue FMR*, December–January.

2005 ▪ Steven Vincent, *Art in America*, June–July.

2003 ▪ Lily Faust, *New York Art World*, September.
▪ Peter Franck, *LA Weekly*, November.

2002 ▪ Ken Johnson, *New York Times*, 21 June.
▪ Grace Glueck, *New York Times*, 5 July.
▪ Valerie Gadstone, *Art News*, October.
▪ David Frankel, *Artforum*, November.
▪ Edward M. Gomez, *Art and Antiques*, December.
▪ Mathew Guy Nichols, *Art in America*, December.
▪ Sarah Douglas, *Art Newspaper*, December.

1994 ▪ Alain Riou, "Quand un peintre nous offre un grand film," *Le Nouvel Observateur*.
▪ Aurélien Ferenczi, "Matton et ses doubles," *Globe Hebdo*.
▪ Marie-Noëlle Tranchant, "Charles Matton et le mystère des choses proches," *Le Figaro*.

1992 ▪ Jean-Marie Tasset, "Gulliver chez Lilliput," *Le Figaro*.

1991 ▪ Jean-Louis Pinte, "Charles Matton, l'obsession de l'objet," *Le Figaro*.

1989 ▪ Régis Durand, "Présence et silence des formes," *Art Press*.
▪ Lionel Rotcage, "Charles Matton, artiste peintre," *Rolling Stone*.

1987 ▪ Roger Thérond, "Art et réalité," *Photo*.
▪ Françoise Sagan, "Matton, un grand peintre sur une petite planète," *Globe*.
▪ Frédéric Edelman, "Le petit pan de briques," *Le Monde*.
▪ Annie Walther, "Mystification, la seule réalité tangible," *Art Press*.
▪ Véronique Prat, "L'homme qui parlait aux objets," *Le Figaro Magazine*.
▪ Joseph Fitchett, "The Mysterious Aura of Charles Matton," *International Herald Tribune*.

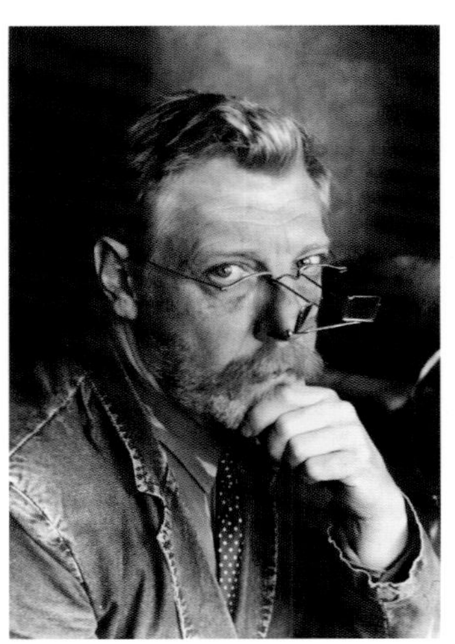

ACKNOWLEDGMENTS

I would like to take this opportunity of thanking all those without whom this book would never have been possible—at least not in its present form—all those who helped in its development with texts or images, as well as all those who contributed to it in ways sometimes unbeknownst to themselves, through their friendship for Charles and/or their support for his work. —S.M.

Charles Matton

Isabelle Blanc, Nicolas Matton,

Jean-François Couvreur, Lisa Chardin, Léonard Matton, Yann Matton,

Joe La Placa, Mark Sanders, All Visual Arts,

Gilles Haeri, Julie Rouart, Sophy Thompson, Jean-Louis Milin, Jean-Luc Monterosso, Maison Européenne de la Photographie,

Alain Regard, Daniel Regard, Camille Giordano, Jean-Marc Henault, Cristina Puerta, David Radzinowicz,

Annie Assouline, Marine and Jean Baudrillard, Nejma and Peter Beard, Carole Chrétiennot, Alain Finkielkraut, Anna Flori, Jean-Jacques Flori, Toby Gilbert, Laurie Hurwitz, Jules Matton, Frédéric Mitterrand, Yasmina Reza, Michel Rotman, Isabelle Sobelman, Frédéric Taddéi, Paul Virilio,

the founding members of the "Cercle des Amis de Charles Matton": Marie-Françoise Audouard, Anne de la Baume, Jérôme Clément, Pierre Donnersberg, Robert Fleck, Jean-Paul Goude, Cécile Guilbert, Jean Lagarrigue, Jean-Philippe Lambert, Elisabeth Quin, Bruno Racine, Julie Rouart, Antoine Sire, Philippe Tesson, Paul Virilio,

and Humbert Balsan, Caroline Bourgeois, Stéphanie Chevrier, Serge and Marina Clément, Raphaël Confino, Robert Delpire, Yves Deschamps, Aliona Ditte, Reno Ditte, Daniel Filipacchi, Cheryl and Robert Fishko, Hélène Guétary, Marianne Lamour, Joël Lécussan, François Léotard, Paul Lepercq, Sarah Moon, Pierre and Marianne Nahon, Véronique Nora-Milin, Régis Pagniez, Jacques Pépion, Jean-Marie Périer, François Pinault, Micheline Renard, Nathalie Rykiel, Matthieu Sombret, Jacques Szulevitch, Astrid and Roger Thérond, Hélène Tibéri, Jo Trublard.

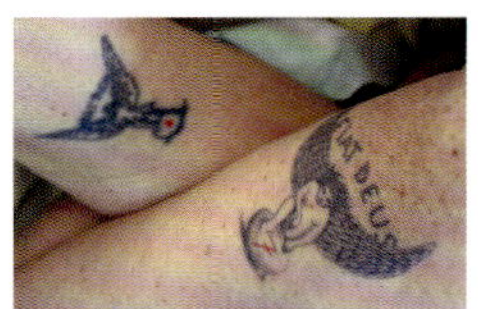